Global Sociology

Global Sociology

ROBIN COHEN

and

PAUL KENNEDY

First published 2000 by
MACMILLAN PRESS LTD
Houndmills, Basingstoke, Hampshire RG21 6XS
and London
Companies and representatives
throughout the world.

ISBN 0–333–65111–1 hardcover
ISBN 0–333–65112–X paperback

A catalogue record for this book is available
from the British Library.

This book is printed on paper suitable for recycling and
made from fully managed and sustained forest sources.

10 9 8 7 6 5 4 3 2
09 08 07 06 05 04 03 02 01 00

Editing and origination by
Aardvark Editorial, Mendham, Suffolk

Printed and bound in Great Britain
by Antony Rowe Ltd, Chippenham, Wiltshire

For Selina and Sue

Contents

List of Illustrations

List of Boxes

List of Tables

Acknowledgements

Many people gave advice to the authors of this rather lengthy book. Robin Cohen would like particularly to thank Richard Higgott, who arranged an affiliation to the Centre for the Study of Globalization and Regionalization, University of Warwick. This gave him precious extra time to write. He would also like to thank Jason Cohen, Selina Cohen, Richard Lampard, Ali Rogers, Shirin Rai, Jill Southam, Steve Vertovec and Anna Winton. Paul Kennedy would like particularly to thank Colin Barker, Tim Dant, Peter Forsland, Angela Hale, Susie Jacobs, Donna Lee, Geraldine Lievesley, Phil Mole, Jonathan Purkis, Peta Turvey, Geoff Walsh and Derek Wynne.

Both of us are grateful to Catherine Gray and her colleagues at Macmillan. Catherine was a just critic and provided a continuous stream of creative comments and searching queries. The anonymous reviewers of the manuscript were meticulous and constructive in their evaluations. Sometimes their advice was contradictory and we found ourselves having to make hard choices between equally useful suggestions. Roy May permitted us to use several photographs from his excellent personal collection. Linda Norris, Maggie Lythgoe and their colleagues at Aardvark Editorial did a sterling job in copy-editing and setting a complex typescript. This book is dedicated to our partners, although that is inadequate thanks for their support over many years.

The author and publisher wish to thank the following for their help in obtaining images and their permission to use these:

AKG London for the pictures of Emile Durkheim and Max Weber on page 5, researched by ISI; Dr Fawaz Aldakheel and the Information Centre, Kingdom of Saudi Arabian Embassy, for Figure 12.2; Ann Ronan at Image Select for Figures 11.1 and 14.1, researched by ISI; Selina Cohen for Figure 15.2 (© Selina Cohen); the Commission for Racial Inequality for Figure 6.1; the Ford Foundation Education Unit for Figure 4.1; Gamma for Figures 2.2 (photo by G. Stuart-Spooner), 9.1 (photo by J. Christensen), 9.2 (© Roger Job), 10.1 (© Alain Buu), 10.2 (© Rolfes/Liaison), 12.3 (photo by Taylor-Fabricius/Liaison), 16.2 (© Noel Quidu), 17.1 (© Anderson/Liaison), 18.1 (photo by A. Ribeiro), 19.1 (© Boyes/Spooner), and the photos of Ted Turner (© Agostini/Liaison) and Rupert Murdoch (© Laurence/Gamma) on page 251, researched by ISI; Professor Steven J. Gold for Figure 13.3 (© Steven J. Gold); Murat Gungor for

Figure 19.2; Image Select for the picture of Karl Marx on page 5, researched by ISI; the Indian Tourist Board for Figure 3.2; the Japan Information and Cultural Centre, Embassy of Japan, for Figure 13.1; Professor Roy May for Figures 4.2 and 15.1 (© Roy May); McDonald's for Figure 13.2; the Nigerian High Commission Library, London, and the National Museum, Lagos, for Figure 3.3; the Oxford University Transnational Communities Research Programme for Figure 1.1; Pablo Petit-Breuille for Figure 2.1 (© Pablo Petit-Breuille); Panos Pictures for Figure 7.2 (© David Dahmen/Panos Pictures) and Figure 8.2 (© Fernando Moleres); the library of the Polish Cultural Institute for Figure 16.1; Patrick Salvadori for Figure 1.2 (© Patrick Salvadori); Still Pictures for Figure 7.1 (photo by J. Maier); the United Nations High Commission for Refugees for Figure 8.1 (photo by A.Hollman).

Every effort has been made to trace all the copyright holders but if any have been inadvertently overlooked the publishers will be pleased to make the necessary arrangements at the first opportunity.

Abbreviations and Acronyms

ACS	automated clearance system
ASEAN	Association of Southeast Asian Nations
BAT	British American Tobacco
BCCI	Bank of Credit and Commerce International
BIP	Border Industrialization Program (Mexico)
CAD	computer-aided design
CAM	computer-aided manufacturing
CAW	Committee for Asian Women
CBN	Central Bank of Nigeria
CEDAW	Convention on the Elimination of all forms of Discrimination Against Women
CFC	chlorofluorocarbon
CLADEM	Latin American Committee for the Defence of Women's Rights
CND	Campaign for Nuclear Disarmament
CPSU	Communist Party of the Soviet Union
DAWN	Development Alternatives with Women for a New Era
DFI	direct foreign investment
DIY	do-it-yourself
ECHR	European Court of Human Rights
EPOS	electronic point of sale
EPZ	export-processing zone
EU	European Union
FAO	Food and Agricultural Organization
G7	Group of Seven (advanced industrial nations – now called the G8)
GATT	General Agreement on Tariffs and Trade (now the WTO)
GDP	Gross Domestic Product
GNP	Gross National Product
GSM	global social movement
HIV	human immunodeficiency virus
ICI	Imperial Chemical Industries
IGO	international governmental organization
ILO	International Labour Organization
IMF	International Monetary Fund
IMR	infant mortality rate
INGO	international non-governmental organization
INS	Immigration and Naturalization Service (USA)
IPCC	Intergovernmental Panel on Climate Change
IQ	intelligence quotient
ISDN	integrated services digital network
ISIS	International Women's Information and Communication Service

IT	information technology		**SSA**	Sub-Saharan Africa
IWMA	International Working Men's Association		**TNC**	transnational corporation
			TVE	town and village enterprise
IWRAW	International Women's Rights Action Watch		**UN**	United Nations
			UNCHR	United Nations Centre for Human Rights
IWTC	International Women's Tribune Centre		**UNEP**	United Nations Environment Programme
LA	Los Angeles		**UNESCO**	United Nations Educational, Scientific and Cultural Organization
M&S	Marks and Spencer		**UNGA**	United Nations General Assembly
MCP	male chauvinist pig (slang)			
MDB	multilateral development bank		**UNHCR**	United Nations High Commission for Refugees
MFA	Multi-Fibre Agreement			
MIT	Massachusetts Institute of Technology		**UNRISD**	United Nations Research Institute for Social Development
NAFTA	North American Free Trade Agreement		**WCED**	World Commission on Environment and Development
NATO	North Atlantic Treaty Organization		**WFS**	Women's Feature Service
NIC	newly industrializing country		**WLUML**	Women Living Under Muslim Laws
NIDL	new international division of labour (theory)		**WMO**	World Meteorological Organization
OECD	Organization for Economic Co-operation and Development		**WTO**	World Tourist Organization (in Chapter 12 'WTO' refers to this organization)
OPEC	Organization of Petroleum-Exporting Countries		**WTO**	World Trade Organization (elsewhere in the book 'WTO' refers to this organization)
PIN	personal identification number			
R&D	research and development		**WWF**	World Wide Fund (for Nature)
RAN	Rainforest Action Network			
SEWA	Self-Employed Asian Women's Association			

part one
Interpretations

1

Introducing Global Sociology

Sociology involves the systematic study of patterns of human interaction. These patterns are often structured by historical events, by beliefs and by social influences acting on an individual, a family or a wider social group. The outcomes are experienced at a number of levels – local, national, regional and global. In trying to explore these processes and levels sociologists sometimes are able to use insights from the other social science disciplines – notably from economics, political science, anthropology and history. However, certain theories and methods are intrinsic to the discipline itself and have evolved over more than 150 years. Many teachers in the discipline insist that students should gain a good grounding by understanding the evolution of the ideas produced by the pioneers of sociology.

We do not dissent from this aspiration, but we will have space to give you only the briefest flavour of the foundations and development of the discipline. How sociologists have set about doing their job in the past is the subject matter for many other introductory texts. In this book, we are concerned with the way in which the subject of sociology illuminates our present world and will have to respond to the future reshaping of all societies. In common with other disciplines, sociology is required to expand dramatically its geographical and intellectual horizons – recognizing that the natures of local communities and national societies are being challenged by profound changes at the global level. This book is concerned with showing how these global changes can best be understood.

THE FOUNDATIONS OF SOCIOLOGY

The discipline of sociology is much older than many of its students believe. It has its roots in the period after the **French Revolution** when political conflict, rapid urbanization and social turmoil convulsed European societies.

Intellectuals sought to explain both the bewildering chaos and the new possibilities around them. Auguste Comte (1798–1857) was the first to use the word 'sociology' in his six-volume work on *Positive Philosophy* (1896), first published in 1842. Comte's intentions and the ideas of some of the other founders of sociology are summarized in Box 1.1.

Key Moment
French Revolution

This was a series of social upheavals that began in 1789 with peasant revolt, monarchical collapse and moderate middle-class leadership. From 1793 to 1795, the urban poor of Paris and other cities, led by radicals such as Robespierre, pushed the revolution in a more violent and nationalist direction. An increasing involvement in European wars also led to the successful mass mobilization of citizen armies and intensified the need to centralize national administration.

Box 1.1   Foundational ideas in sociology

■ **Auguste Comte** wanted to find regularities, even laws, in social life that resembled Newtonian physics. He showed his deference to the scientific model by adopting the term 'social physics'. His ideas were linked to those of scholars in the other two major social sciences – economics and political science. They dismissed philosophy as too speculative, theology as the rationalization of superstition, and history as too subjective and superficial. These writers saw themselves as champions of a new way of understanding reality. They wanted to establish general laws of human behaviour, to formulate hypotheses that could be tested and to develop strict scientific methods (Wallerstein 1996: 31).

■ In the USA, the first department was founded in 1892 while the *American Journal of Sociology*, still the leading journal in the field, was established three years later. The discipline was often concerned with the adaptation of new immigrants to their new settings, with urban settlement patterns (the 'Chicago School' produced celebrated studies in this field), with industrial relations and with community studies.

■ In France, the great French sociologist **Emile Durkheim** (1858–1917) founded the *Année Sociologique* in 1898. It contained a mix of material on law, customs, religion and social statistics. Durkheim himself concentrated on the elements that bind societies together, an issue close to the heart of a society that had experienced the disintegrating effects of revolution and an invasion (in 1871) by Prussia. Durkheim understood that his discussion of how social order and consensus were to be reached necessarily involved comparison with other groups. He tried to understand the religious practices of the Australian Aborigines and systematically collected statistics from a number of European countries to undertake his famous study of suicide.

■ By contrast **Karl Marx** (1818–83), who worked in Germany, France and Britain, saw the waves of rebellion in 1830 and 1848 as ushering in a new era of social revolution. He was consequently interested in class conflict and the dynamics of large-scale social change. He was inevitably constrained in his outlook by being white, male and European, but sought to be international in his outlook. Marx wrote on India and the USA, and as his socialist ideas caught hold he found himself in dialogue with revolutionaries from Russia to Cuba. His daughter, Eleanor Marx, became a pioneer feminist thinker and agitator.

(cont'd)

■ In Britain, **Herbert Spencer** (1820–1903) was preoccupied with slow, long-term evolutionary change. His work paralleled Charles Darwin's writings on the animal and plant worlds. (Incidentally, it was he, not Darwin, who coined the term 'the survival of the fittest', a notion that resonated well with the unregulated capitalism of the period.) Spencer's preoccupation with evolution was complemented by detailed social surveys on the desperate plight of the poor in Britain's cities. **Charles Booth's** surveys, *Life and Labour of the People of Britain*, published over the period 1891–1903, are often cited as classics in this type of sociological inquiry (see, for example, Booth 1967).

■ In addition to work on his native Germany, **Max Weber** (1864–1920) wrote on Spain, Italy and ancient Rome and was fascinated by the different ways in which religious belief facilitated or inhibited the development of capitalism. He was the first sociologist of comparative religion, having examined Hinduism, Confucianism, Buddhism and Judaism, in addition to his famous studies of Protestantism. He had also sketched out an ambitious study of Islam. In his engagement with Marxism he sought to develop a holistic sociology that added to the issue of class identities, questions of status, political power and values – which together would define the opportunity structure available to people.

Karl Marx

Emile Durkheim

Max Weber

THE CHANGING CONTEXT OF SOCIOLOGY

The relationships between time, place and culture yield different social outcomes and these require different forms of sociological investigation. Even the topics that attract the attention of sociologists change as the context changes. Box 1.1 indicates that sociology developed in somewhat different ways in various countries. Sociologists have been responsive to important historical events while international, regional, national and local settings have influenced the character of the discipline. That context influences content is, by the way, true of other disciplines too, including science, engineering and medicine. However, it is particularly true of sociology, given that the discipline links the observer to the subject of the observation so directly and that sociology has become so important a means of interpreting contemporary social life in an imaginative and critical way.

One important limitation of the discipline of sociology is that despite the universalizing ambitions of a number of the founding figures, it has taken a long while for the discipline to expand beyond its heartland in western industrial societies. The study of non-western societies was left to anthropologists who found it difficult to develop general laws applicable to all humanity. They found difference rather than commonality. Looking back at the period of colonialism, one could make out a strong ethical case for preserving difference. Liberal anthropologists defended the integrity of 'their tribe' against what they considered the corrupting influences of colonial administrators, traders and missionaries. Canadian fur-traders bribing Hurons with whisky, the forcible adoption of Aboriginal children by white Australians or the spreading of fatal venereal disease to the Polynesians are hardly edifying moments in the history of encounters between European and non-European peoples.

However, as our subsequent chapters show, it is now too late to wrap people in cellophane and freeze them in a time warp. Our increasing interconnectedness and interdependency has meant we cannot create tribal iceboxes or human zoos. We live in an interdependent globalizing world, in the wake of the Universal Declaration of Human Rights proclaimed in 1948. There are now insurmountable practical and ethical difficulties in defending the practice of cultural separateness. Neither can the differences between peoples be explained simply by giving each of them a different voice. We may not – we are fairly sure we will not – be able to develop a 'social physics' with immutable laws, as Comte wanted. Yet we need ways of comprehending and comparing societies and peoples that apply from Afghanistan to Zimbabwe, from the Aborigines to the Zulu. We require, in Albrow's (1987) telling phrase, 'a sociology for one world'.

THE REVERSION TO NATIONAL SOCIOLOGY

How are we to reach the goal of a sociology for one world? Can we find anything of value in returning to the history of the discipline? As we have seen, some of the trailblazers of sociology – particularly Karl Marx, Max Weber and Emile Durkheim – were in fact very interested in countries outside their own. But despite this promising beginning, from about 1914 to the end of the Second World War, comparative sociology went into decline in Europe and North America. This probably had something to do with the growth of intense nationalist feelings and the attempt to fabricate exclusive, powerful, modern nation states.

As the First World War approached, imperialist and nationalist sentiments were easily inflamed while inter-European rivalry was raging remorselessly. These big events and large-scale forces can often be tellingly illustrated by small examples. Witness the case of the humble dachshund, the German 'sausage dog'. The British are world renowned for their love of animals – the Royal Society for the Protection of Cruelty to Animals was founded as early as 1824. Yet in 1914, as war approached, dachshunds were stoned in the streets of London as a living symbol of the hated 'Hun'. The British monarch, George V, dropped all his German titles and adopted the appellation 'Windsor', the name of one of his castles. German Knights of the Garter were struck off the roll, while grocers with German names were accused of poisoning the public. In this frantic atmosphere, those espousing international causes were derided. Even the inter-

Xenophobia – hatred and fear of foreigners.

national labour movement found itself at the mercy of **xenophobic** passions. Instead of accepting the Marxist message that 'workers have no country', young men lined up to fight for their emperors, tsars, kings and kaisers. Many perished in the withering shellfire and churning mud of the killing fields in France.

Sociologists were inevitably caught up or caught out by this nationalist fervour. Like other academics in that country, in Russia they became little more than servants of the state. Others, who were dissenters or members of victimized minority groups, left their countries of birth. Prominent Italian, Austrian and German scholars had to flee from Fascism and Nazism to other European countries or to the USA. After the Second World War these scholars were to play an important role in internationalizing the discipline and made major contributions to the intellectual life of their adopted countries.

In the period up to 1945 sociologists in the USA and UK remained intelligent observers and critics of their own societies, but they rarely lifted their heads above the concerns immediately around them. In front of their eyes were the mass unemployment caused by the **Great Depression**, the mobilization of men to the front and the deployment of women in the 'home front'. Discussions of social problems and social realities were focused nearly entirely on local community, urban or national contexts.

Key Moment
Great Depression

The Great Depression (1929–39) was the most severe capitalist downturn ever known. By late 1932, in the USA alone, around 15 million workers were unemployed. The crisis began in October 1929 when company share values on New York's Wall Street stock exchange crashed. A number of stockbrokers and investors jumped to their deaths from their skyscraper offices. A series of escalating bank and currency collapses soon turned the crisis into a global one. German Nazism and Japanese Fascism were partly caused by the world economic collapse.

THE ORIGINS OF GLOBAL SOCIOLOGY

The end of the Second World War heralded a new balance of international forces. Japan was one of the defeated countries, yet it had given the European powers a bloody nose and had brought the USA into the war. Without Uncle Sam and the atomic bombs the US air force dropped on two Japanese cities, it is doubtful that the Japanese armies could have been contained. Like other observers, sociologists asked what accounted for this sudden rise to power. Were there certain elements in Japanese culture that generated forms of work and military discipline that had propelled the country into the first rank of industrial powers? And could these elements be understood by non-Japanese social scientists?

There were two other momentous changes after 1945:

1. The old empires were clearly on the way out. Not without bloodshed and mayhem, the British were persuaded to leave India, which became independent in 1947. This was the prelude to the decolonization of the rest of Asia, Africa, the Middle East and the Caribbean. The Dutch left Indonesia in 1949, although the French and Portuguese slugged it out against the tide of history. Eventually they too were forced to abandon their colonial possessions in Asia and Africa, often retreating in the face of armed rebellion. The French left Algeria in 1962 while former Portuguese Mozambique became independent in 1975.

2. There were new actors on the world stage. People of all colours and backgrounds, not just white people, were 'making history'. It had been arrogant and even absurd for white people to believe that they were the only ones who counted. But given the extent of their empires, the superiority of their arms and the dominance of their technology and manufacturing products,

that is exactly what many Europeans and US citizens did believe. All these fanciful convictions of racial superiority were shaken to the roots after 1945.

As you might expect, some people continued to live in the past. However, far-sighted thinkers and politicians realized that the post-1945 period required a change in public consciousness. One example of the new openness was the foundation in Paris of the United Nations Educational, Scientific and Cultural Organization (UNESCO) in 1946. The preamble to its constitution (cited in Banton 1994: 336) set the tone. This declared that:

> The great and terrible war which has now ended was a war made possible by the denial of the democratic principles of the dignity, equality and mutual respect of men and by the propagation in their place, through ignorance and prejudice, of the doctrine of the inequality of men and races.

In these days we would, of course add 'women' to such a statement, although no doubt the drafters intended to be inclusive. The members of UNESCO's governing committees set themselves the task of studying the basis of racial discrimination and over a period of some 30 years provided a number of authoritative statements which were agreed by panels of eminent geneticists, biologists, anthropologists and sociologists. Article 1 of the General Conference of 1978 proclaimed that 'All human beings belong to a single species and are descended from a common stock. They are born equal in dignity and rights and all form part of humanity' (Banton 1994: 336–7).

Not only was there a shift in mood towards universalism, there was a legion of societies 'out there' whose conditions of life, fates and fortunes were largely unknown to western scholars. Led by the USA, but soon followed by Japan and the European countries, 'area studies' programmes were announced or augmented. Scholars were encouraged to find out anything and everything about the formerly colonized countries as well as about the communist countries behind 'the iron curtain'. Moreover, significant bodies of writers and academics, sociologists included, from outside Europe and North America began to make their mark.

Latin America had been decolonized in the nineteenth century, so it was perhaps not surprising that Chilean, Brazilian and Mexican sociologists had time to develop sophisticated theories explaining why their societies remained economically and culturally dependent, despite being politically autonomous for decades. One important Latin American sociologist addressing this issue was Fernando Henrique Cardoso (see Cardoso and Falleto 1969), who was later elected President of Brazil. Other influential contributions came from the Egyptian political economist Samir Amin (1974), the Martiniquan psychiatrist and political activist Frantz Fanon (1967) and sociologists such as the Pakistani Hamza Alavi (1972) and the Jamaican-born Orlando Patterson (1982), who wrote key works on the evolution of slavery and freedom.

Sociologists working in Europe and North America were equally excited by the fresh possibilities of understanding many societies, not just their own. Their theories were many and diverse and we can share only a little of this new ferment of ideas in a few examples (see Box 1.2).

> **Box 1.2   Western sociologists and the non-western world**
>
> ■ **Barrington Moore** (1967, 1972) thought that a comparative historical sociology was needed to understand why some societies prospered while others languished, why some turned into democracies and others dictatorships.
>
> ■ **Clark Kerr** (1983) maintained that the varying paths taken by different societies were ultimately to be joined by the unifying logic of industrialization. Thus, whatever the political differences between regimes, 'convergence' arose because economic goals provoked certain common responses.
>
> ■ Other US sociologists like **Talcott Parsons** (1971) tended to talk in terms of a wider notion of 'modernization', which involved the 'non-western' world 'catching up' with the achievements of the 'western' world and Japan.
>
> ■ Some European sociologists (discussed in Taylor 1979) returned to Marxist ideas of the successive stages of what Marx called 'modes of production' (slavery, feudalism and capitalism for example). Many of the poor countries, they suggested, were locked in an uneasy middle ground between capitalist and non-capitalist modes of production.
>
> ■ The German scholar **André Gunder Frank** (1967, 1969), who worked in Chile for a number of years, was very influenced by the theories of 'dependency' and 'under-development' current in Latin American circles. He both popularized their work by writing in English and extended it in new directions.
>
> ■ Although the term originated with a French journalist, the English sociologist **Peter Worsley** (1967) also drew from writings by Latin Americans, Asians and Africans to define the distinctive characteristics of the 'Third World', one that was relatively poor, neither capitalist nor communist, western or non-western.

What emerged from the disparate contributions of western sociologists was that the paths of development or underdevelopment of individual countries could not easily be predicted. As Crow (1997: 130–57) argues, in some respects this still holds true. The rich countries usually become richer and some poor countries collapse into stagnation, poverty and disorder. However, what was less predictable was that *the pattern of polarization is unstable and inconsistent*. Within the so-called 'Third World' some countries 'took off' and succeeded in economic terms while others bumped along at the bottom. We can contrast, for example, the case of Ghana (not, by the way, the poorest country in West Africa) with South Korea. Crow (1997: 130) cites data showing that, whereas the two countries shared a similar ***gross national product (GNP)*** per capita in the 1960s (about $230), three decades later South Korea was ten to twelve times more prosperous.

Gross national product – a common measurement used by economists to assess a country's wealth.

Again, there were strong social and cultural contrasts between countries. Some, like Singapore and Japan, appeared seamlessly to adapt the values of western countries in their own settings, or to effect a novel and creative synthesis between local and imported cultures. Others, including some societies in the Middle East, found that the religious convictions of their populations jarred with the largely secular, consumerist culture of the West. Many societies that had historically been characterized by large rural populations and agrarian pursuits now suddenly had bloated urban concentrations. Some suggested that they became 'dual societies' – westernized in urban, industrialized areas, yet retaining a strong local identity in the countryside.

Major Concept
THIRD WORLD

An expression used to distinguish the non-aligned poor countries from the First World (the rich capitalist democracies of the West) and also from the Second World (the communist-led countries of the Soviet bloc). Increased differentiation between the rich and poor countries of Asia, Africa, Latin America and the Middle East, together with the political collapse of nearly all the communist countries have meant that the term is of less and less use. Although countries are still highly unequal in their wealth and power, they do not fit neatly into three groups.

If we take into account the diversity of the societies previously classified under the rubric **THIRD WORLD** and the historical rhythms of fortune and misfortune for all countries, it becomes apparent that classifying countries into different subsections of the globe is a perilous and inexact business. Moreover, as we see later in this book, there is a high level of interpenetration between countries (through travel, migration, financial flows and cultural borrowings, to name a few factors). Sociologists found that it was increasingly difficult to isolate a country and to declare that all people living there comprised a single society. In effect, they could not be sure of the difference between the 'internal' and the 'external'.

Wallerstein (1974: 51) made perhaps the most daring and important response to this problem. In the opening book of a series of works, he advanced the notion of 'the modern world system'. Having considered the difficulties of arranging the world into neat hierarchies and of isolating the nation state as the primary unit of sociological analysis, Wallerstein decided he would:

> abandon the idea altogether of taking either the sovereign state or that vaguer concept, the national society, as the unit of analysis. I decided that neither one was a social system and that one could only speak of social change in social systems. The only social system in this scheme was the world system.

This declaration symbolizes what an increasing number of sociologists have come to realize. We have to try to think globally, recognizing that while social changes may vary considerably in each setting, there are overarching processes and transformations that operate at a global level and impact to one degree or another on everybody.

THEMES OF THIS BOOK

This book is divided into *four parts*, each of which has *five chapters*. The four parts cover:

- the interpretations that have been used to explain our increasingly globalizing world
- the differential impact of global changes which have reinforced inequalities or generated new ones
- the ways in which global changes have generated different experiences
- the challenges to, and dynamics of, the newer globalizing tendencies.

There are a number of ways of understanding changes at a global level. These are discussed in INTERPRETATIONS (Part One of this book) and summarized below.

Globalization and globalism

In Chapter 2, we set off on our intellectual voyage – drawing you into our understanding of two key concepts, *globalization* and *globalism*, necessary direction finders for our long journey. The first concept has now spread into common usage and is often found in magazines and newspapers. It refers to the ways in which the world is being knitted together. Many popular accounts focus on the increasingly free flows of goods and money, or economic globalization. But there are many other aspects of globalization. For example, various parts of the world are being pulled together by the increased density and lower cost of travel and communications. Globalization is therefore also about connectivity. Images, ideas, tourists, migrants, values, fashions and music increasingly flow along global pathways. For example, Table 1.1 shows how six large music companies have come to play key roles in the entertainment industry at large. Although Bertelsmann is based in Germany, EMI in the UK and Sony in Japan (the rest have their headquarters in the USA), all are global in their reach and produce and sell in all major international markets.

Table 1.1   The global record companies

Music company	Bertelsmann Music Group	EMI Records	MCA Records (Universal Music Group)	Polygram Music Group	Sony Music Entertainment Inc.	Warner Music Group
Parent company	Bertelsmann AG	EMI	The Seagram Company Ltd	The Seagram Company Ltd	Sony Corporation	Time Warner Inc.
Other media/ entertainment						
Filmed entertainment			■	■	■	■
Radio	■					
Television programming	■		■	■	■	■
Cable	■		■	■	■	■
Video	■		■	■	■	■
Publishing	■					■
Interactive entertainment					■	

Source: McDonald (2000: 97) citing annual reports

The globalization of such social and cultural activities leads to the elaboration of a second, and less well-rehearsed, concept, the idea of *globalism*. Whereas globalization refers to the objective, external ties that bind us together, globalism alludes to the subjective, personal awareness that many of us share common tastes and interests and we are all likely to share a common fate. Of course, a good number of people, normally but not only those in poor remote areas, continue to live lives constrained by unawareness, indifference or a conscious detachment from the world around them. But such insensibility is increasingly difficult to maintain. Jet planes fly overhead, travellers appear as if from nowhere, roads are cut into the interior, telephone lines are strung out, the world's music pulsates from cheap transistor radios, while friends, neighbours and family share what they have seen on the ubiquitous TV screen.

Modernity and the evolution of world society

A major theme of this book (and an abiding concern of sociology) is how social change arises and becomes diffused. Despite the ubiquity of contemporary means of transport, globalization and globalism have not been dropped from the sky by passing aircraft. They are the outcomes of a long evolutionary process whereby small isolated societies and large civilizations came to relate to one another. In Chapter 3, we situate the moments when humankind became increasingly capable of understanding itself collectively. Contacts arose from long-distance trade, from the spread of the world religions such as Islam, Buddhism and Christianity and from the force of colonialism and imperialism. The idea of a universal humanity was developed particularly by European Enlightenment thinkers who, although they recognized that there were 'backward regions', thought all were capable of reaching the end-state of modernity.

There was an undoubted arrogance in this view, which implied that what obtained in eighteenth-century France and Germany was the preferred destination of all humanity. The power of ideas, the success of the European economies and finally the force of military imperialist expansion propelled many areas of the world into an uneasy association. This juxtaposition also involved the effects of industrialization and capitalism, both key concepts, which we will discuss in this chapter.

The world of work

In Chapter 4, we depict substantive changes in the world of work. Rapid and unprecedented technological change and intensifying international competition have led to economic insecurity and the *internationalization* of work. The more vulnerable position of women has led to the *feminization* of work. The development of flexible labour markets has also led to the *casualization* of work.

For the winners, particularly those with portable skills in growing sectors like the information-related industries, these changes herald 'new times' – offering opportunities for greater individual freedom and self-realization and a more democratic, decentralized, less hierarchical workplace and society. The losers see only 'hard times' – dominated by fragmenting businesses, labour redundancies and by part-time and poorly paid jobs. The rise of subcontracting and homeworking in this emerging economic order will also be discussed.

Nationhood and the nation state

The nation state is a relatively recent political organization, dating in its complete form from the French Revolution. Nation states replaced multinational kingdoms, principalities, religious domains and empires. Nationalists wanted their identity to be protected by exclusive access to a territory. The rulers of nation states often dealt harshly with minorities and indigenous peoples, pressing them to assimilate to the dominant group, or isolating or excluding them from the mainstream of social and political life.

It will not be long before there will be 200 'recognized' nation states. (Not all are recognized by the UN, in international law or by other nation states.) Yet the number of peoples demanding autonomy or statehood is perhaps twenty times as great. The growth of religious, ethnic or other sub-national sentiments in short, threatens the nation state system from below. The increasing pace of globalization also threatens it from above. The changing role of the state in coping with these local and global pressures is considered in Chapter 5, which also introduces debates around citizenship and political power.

Global changes are overlaid on old inequalities between people and serve also to introduce new lines of dominance and subordination. These changes are discussed in DIVISIONS (Part Two of this book) and summarized below.

Global inequalities

Sociologists have always given much thought to the problem of how to conceptualize and explain the forms of inequality found in all societies and the ways in which these vary both between societies and over time. The unequal distribution of power, wealth, income and social status between individuals and groups is not randomly distributed but is patterned or structured.

In general, we can say that structured inequalities operate along the three main axes of gender, race/ethnicity and class (although we should not forget other forms of social division based, for example, on age, religion and disability). Each of these generates its own structure of unequal practices giving rise either to institutionalized sexism, racism or class divisions and conflict, respectively. Gender, race and class also crosscut each other in various complex ways, sometimes reinforcing and at other times weakening the impact of existing inequalities. In Chapter 6 we explore the ways sociologists have grappled with various schemes to understand how these forms of inequality shape our lives both in their own right and as they interact with one another.

Transnational corporations

There are hardly more dominant players in global affairs than the transnational corporations. They profit from the increased level of economic globalization and indeed can be said partially to cause this outcome. These ubiquitous organizations are the Trojan horses, or perhaps the battering rams, of international capital. Such is their power and influence that they are often accused of dictating to rich and powerful states, while completely overwhelming poor states. Is this kind of characterization merely evoking an imagined demon rather than constructing a real social science? What are the origins of these organizations? Have they, in fact, escaped their national origins? What is their economic role in integrating the global economy? What are the social consequences, positive and negative, of the TNCs' activities? Do they exercise power without responsibility? In Chapter 7 we consider these questions.

Uneven development: the victims

How do we account for the extremes of poverty and wealth, power and powerlessness, in today's world? According to some theorists, whose views are examined in Chapter 8, the system is rigged to protect the interests of the leading players.

Those who die from famine or in civil wars are the ultimate global losers, but other groups are also highly vulnerable. As the race gets faster, those at the back – refugees, the unskilled, the unemployed or those who experience discrimination – trail even further behind. In 1966 the richest fifth of the world's population enjoyed an income 30 times as great as the poorest – a vivid enough demonstration of social inequality, you might think. However, by 1997 the average income of the rich was 78 times larger. In Chapter 8 we look at the impoverishment of the rural poor, the growth of a refugee problem, the exploitation of new workers in the towns and the swelling ranks of the urban poor.

Failures of global control

Just as globalization and the deregulation of many national economies have allowed banks and TNCs to profit from open borders, so too have the opportunities for cross-border crime blossomed. Global *social control*, an expression that also gains conceptual explanation, has been very difficult to effect. Open-border crime may involve white-collar computer fraud, tax evasion or smuggling but, as we show in Chapter 8, the cutting edge of global crime is the drugs trade, worth $500 billion a year. Those who profit from the trade are the 'drug barons', the smugglers and the dealers. It is difficult to eliminate the trade when it forms so vital a part of the cash income gained by poor farmers in countries like Nepal and Jamaica and while the demand for recreational and addictive drugs in rich countries seems insatiable.

If growing marijuana or opium poppies links some farmers to the global economy, in other places people can neither produce at globally competitive rates, nor grow enough for subsistence. Excluding South Africa, Africa accounts for only 0.7 per cent of world production. Throughout the area south of the Sahara desert and north of the Zambesi River getting adequate food from the land has proved almost impossible in many famine-prone areas. In developing countries, 60 per cent of deaths of the under-fours are caused by hunger. The poor, elderly and women also suffer disproportionately. There is a persistent belief that 'natural causes' promote famine. As we explain, work by sociologists and others has shown a much more complex set of causes at work.

Asia-Pacific: from miracle to mirage?

Many of the contradictory effects of global changes have been manifested in the Asia Pacific – a region that seems to have been on a roller-coaster ride from economic miracle to what some fear might turn into a meltdown. In Chapter 10 we chart the rise of the 'tiger' and 'dragon' economies, their very designations indicating their extraordinary economic success in over the last 3–4 decades. We consider the complex mix of factors involved in this achievement – a favourable international environment, historical, social and cultural factors and the extraordinary trick of mixing market signals with astute political intervention.

Although some doubt the extent of the long-term damage that will result, during 1997 a series of linked financial crises rocked the Asia-Pacific economies. Because they remained fiercely wedded to the goal of achieving very high growth year after year they had become over-dependent on foreign capital, including inflows of speculative investments. As their currencies weakened they had to call on the International Monetary Fund (IMF) to bail them out. The remedies prescribed (for example, the IMF demanded a rise of 70 per cent in fuel prices in Indonesia) inflamed political dissent. By mid-May 1998 a social and political revolution was underway in Indonesia. Can the Asia Pacific recommence its earlier trajectory?

Certain social processes can no longer be understood by a state-centric approach. For example, population pressures, the flows of tourist, global communications and the development of new forms of urban and cultural life create unsettling EXPERIENCES for people in all *nation states and across national frontiers. Part Three of this book analyses these experiences and they are summarized below.*

Population pressures and migration

To both popular opinion and concerned policy-makers, population growth is one of the most critical problems facing the world. Under intense pressure, politicians have sanctioned or encouraged extreme measures to control population. But we need to distinguish evidence about population growth from prediction, projection and prejudice. In Chapter 11, we provide some basic tools with which to do that job.

Surplus population is absorbed in the growing cities. It is absorbed at such a rate that in many of the developed countries those who live in the countryside and depend on it for their livelihood are a small minority of the population (in Britain about 3 per cent). In other countries, particularly China and India and to a lesser extent Nigeria, Brazil and Mexico, a considerable proportion of the population still lives in rural areas. However, the urbanizing tendency is universal. Most migrants are absorbed in the cities of their own countries, usually with great difficulty. The very much smaller group of international migrants has nonetheless managed to inflame public sentiments in the advanced industrialized countries.

Tourism: social and cultural effects

One of the ways in which the boundaries between nation states are becoming blurred is through the travellers, tourists and leisure-seekers, who wish to gaze at all societies and potentially assimilate all of us into a 'global playground'. As we show in Chapter 12, instead of missionaries, explorers and anthropologists, tourists are now cutting their way into the diminishing

Figure 1.1   Investigating global society: the logo of a research programme on transnational communities, Oxford University

protected spaces of previously isolated societies. Does the differential impact of tourism have something to do with the character of the tourists themselves? Or is the distinction between the 'mass' and the 'alternative' tourist too cut and dried? Many travellers act like cultural warriors for the rich, powerful states; others are like the pilgrims of old. Yet others, like sex tourists, simply exploit weaker, poorer people. Tourists expose nearly everyone to a multicultural world where the boundaries between societies and between insiders and outsiders blur. In particular, international tourism compels both host and guest to rethink their own identities.

Consuming culture

Drink a cup of coffee or tea and you instantly connect to the global marketplace. The list of world goods that arrives in this way is formidable and grows all the time. World goods are products which in whole or part are grown, processed, manufactured, recorded, filmed or staged in a multiplicity of locations often far from the place where we finally purchase and experience them. According to Firat (1995: 115) fortunate consumers in the late twentieth century are 'ready to have Italian for lunch and Chinese for dinner, to wear Levi's 501 blue jeans for the outdoor party in the afternoon and to try the Gucci suit at night'. Firat (p. 114) explains that it is not simply the sheer range of available global products which is remarkable, but the fact that one can 'rent a Toyota, listen to Madonna and Sting tunes, enjoy a croissant for breakfast, and follow one's favourite soap opera on television' even in 'the remotest corners of the world'. In Chapter 13 we show how we have become targets to those who wish to sell us consumer goods. Is there an emerging global culture of consumption, linked together by advertising, envy and emulation?

Media and communications

Girding the globe are lines of communication that snake along the seabed, stretch across the terrain and bounce from satellites to earth. As we look at the ubiquitous television screens our sense of distance from other places and other societies suddenly shrinks into insignificance. We live, in a famous phrase, in a 'global village'. As is made clear in Chapter 14, who controls the media and channels of communications and for what purposes provide important sociological data. We will also discuss how the acceptance of the telephone as a mass consumer good and the arrival of linked computer networks raise new possibilities for the sharing of information for interactive communication and for global democracy. The economic and social effects of enhanced global communication will also be considered.

Urban life

For much of human history, life was rural. In the year 1800, 97 per cent of the world's population lived in rural areas. In the year 2000, 254 cities each contained over one million people. The forms of settlement and the ways people lived in cities became the sites of study by some of the world's most eminent sociologists. Durkheim (1933: 17) described the transition from 'mechanical' to 'organic' forms of solidarity, while Park and Burgess (1967) at the University of Chicago looked at the 'ecological patterning' and spatial distribution of urban groups.

In the current era certain cities, called *global cities*, are becoming more detached from their hinterlands and other national cities as they take on the functions of servicing the global economy. Global cities are not only important phenomena in their own right, they are important because of their relationship to each other. Increasingly, many wealthier people living and working in global cities, or travelling there, find that they share conditions of life, attitudes, behaviour patterns and tastes with equivalent residents of other global cities. They lose their national culture or downgrade it in favour of an international and cosmopolitan culture. As once the local yokel was to the town, so the inhabitants of provincial cities may be to those of the global city. However, not only the wealthy make up the population of the global cities. In this chapter we also look at urban processes of social exclusion and in particular at the sociological debate as to the existence or otherwise of an 'underclass'.

All too often, the literature of globalization assumes that people are mere chaff in the wind, unable to influence the nature and direction of social change. In Part Four, titled DYNAMICS AND CHALLENGES, we question this assumption and show how global social movements have emerged or been re-energized. These movements connect struggles at different levels, attempt to reshape the emerging world order and seek to create democratic and participatory possibilities.

Explaining social movements

Globalization is often depicted as an inanimate force, playing out its logic without human intervention. In fact many social organizations are involved in creating links and networks to advance their particular causes. These bodies are called social movements or, when they operate transnationally, global social movements. In Chapter 16, we show how they mobilize groups of individuals for collective action, galvanizing their followers around a central theme that offers a vision of an alternative and preferable existence. The emancipation and empowerment promised by this new order may refer to a variety of present and future experiences including religious, political, cultural or social ones.

Challenges to a gendered world

One important way of constructing 'globalization from below' is found in the rise of various women's networks that have moved to a global scale of activity. The women's movement has been particularly effective in shifting from small, participatory, consciousness-raising sessions to such events as the international women's conferences in Kenya in 1985 and in Beijing ten years later. There is hardly a country in the world where gender relations have not been profoundly altered. Moreover, the time scale for this transformation has been impressively short; most of the force of the movement having been evident only since the 1950s. In addition to its successful grass-roots organization, it is probable that the reason why this movement spread so fast has been the speed and density of communications. This allowed the global transmission of images that changed the consciousness of both women and men. Seeing women in new roles such as police officers, pilots, astronauts and doctors, or seeing women standing up to men in popular 'soaps', questioned conventional stereotypes and gendered divisions of labour.

The green movement

One of the most influential and visible global social movements is the environmental or green movement, discussed in Chapter 18. The development of an environment movement is a major reversal of the prevailing nineteenth century idea of unquestioned progress and civilization, perhaps best symbolized by a white man hacking his way through the Amazonian jungle to bring commerce and Christianity to the benighted natives. Instead, the central idea of the 'greens' is that the planet earth is a fragile ball floating in space. The movement seeks to bring home the extent of the damage wrought to the planet by human beings, referring, particularly, to the value of biodiversity, the stabilization of population growth and the need to resist the commercialization of agriculture.

Communities and belonging

The creation of strong social bonds is one of the most powerful of human impulses and, as we have seen, an abiding concern for sociologists. Paradoxically, for some, the threat of globalization often reinforces family and kinship and other local attachments, ethnic sentiments and religious beliefs. Premdas (1996) claims that there are some 4000 'ethnocultural' groups worldwide, uneasily enclosed in 185 states. In the same year (1996), there were 100 ongoing sub-national conflicts, about 20 classified as 'high intensity'. In Rwanda, Burundi and Bosnia distressing scenes of ethnic intolerance followed. In March 1999 the leaders of the North Atlantic Treaty Organization (NATO) ordered an intensive and controversial bombing campaign of Serbia in retaliation for Serbian military and police attacks on the civilian population in Kosovo.

The global age has thus produced an unexpected and even perverse outcome. Despite, or perhaps because of, the pressures to come together, fierce struggles have ensued to keep people apart. We call this tendency 'localism' (to encompass movements based on religion, race, ethnicity and sub-national sentiments). By contrast, working with the grain of history are those states, groups, organizations and individuals that recognize diversity and difference and seek to foster creative and positive bonds between peoples of different backgrounds. Some are creating ties between themselves that foretoken the development of a transnational and cosmopolitan consciousness (Figure 1.1).

Globalization: utopia or dystopia?

The expression 'globalony' is an American slang word suggesting that those who talk about globalization are reciting, parrot-like, a fashionable slogan without much content. These sceptics argue that trade was internationalized to a great degree even before the First World War; that the nation state is still a popular, effective and viable political unit; and that regional bodies (for example, the European Union) are more significant than the many global bodies that exist in name, but do not do very much.

Figure 1.2   Marlboro cigarettes sold in a Tunisian soukh

Other writers, usually on the left, do not so much dissent from the proposition that globalization and globalism are powerful forces in the contemporary world. Rather, as we explain in Chapter 20, they see such forces as wholly malign. Like the ancient Greek prophet Cassandra, they warn that if their predications are unheeded, there will be dire consequences. They foresee trade wars, massive unemployment, destructive financial speculation, the collapse of poor countries and the 'gutting' of certain cities in the rich countries by violence, crime, alcoholism and drug abuse.

Are these writers too gloomy? Is the emergence of a global society going to generate a benign or malign outcome? We explore this fundamental question also in our concluding chapter.

REVIEW

Sociology is a well-established but also rapidly evolving discipline. Classical sociologists such as Marx, Weber and Durkheim undertook fundamental and important work in comparing different societies, although they never undertook systematic observations in other countries. Unfortunately, their pioneering work on international issues was displaced over the period 1914–45 when sociologists in Europe and the USA were preoccupied with the problems of their own societies. In the wake of the Second World War a new balance of political forces led to a reawakening of comparative and international themes in sociology. This was aided by the new voices of sociologists from Asia, Africa and Latin America, while to these voices were added the insights of sociologists from the countries where the discipline had been firmly established.

Sociology has to adapt to the changing world even as it seeks to explain it. Global changes demand that we extend our state-centric theories, define new research agendas and develop an agreed comparative method. In short the interdependence of the local, national and global demands a *global sociology*. This book is thus published at a particular moment in time. It is an introductory textbook, yet it is not only that, for it seeks to mark the shift in the moorings of the discipline itself. Of course this is an ambitious claim and we do not want to be seen as unrealistic, pretentious or arrogant. Ultimately, the discipline will be transformed by the work of hundreds of theorists and thousands of those engaged in more factually based studies. Work by other social scientists in related fields will also be essential.

Nonetheless a book of this kind fulfils a useful function. There is a powerful conservatism in introductory works on the discipline. Authors use examples from their own societies and work their way through the conventional categories of the family, community, industrial and urban sociology, social institutions, demography, and the sociologies of law, culture, health, religion, gender, deviance, race and ethnicity, sport and so on. Many of these sub-fields are important and enduring and a number of these sub-fields find an importance place in our account too. However, following in the footsteps of a few innovative sociologists before us, we have sought always to move alongside and beyond a state-centric analysis by showing how some aspects of global social change impact on and are influenced by changes at local, national or regional levels.

Box 1.3   Using this book

■ At the end of other chapters you will find some advice on further reading, some suggestions for class work and some questions to think about. (At the end of *this* chapter we suggest some ways of preparing for this course.)

■ Major concepts in sociology are displayed in the text in **BOLD CAPITALS** and are defined in a box in the margin. A shorter definition appears in the glossary in case you lose your place in the text.

■ Key moments are displayed in the text in **Bold Upper and Lower Case** and are described in a box in the margin. A shorter description appears in the glossary in case you lose your place in the text.

(cont'd)

- Difficult words and ideas, often from disciplines other than sociology, are displayed in **bold italic lower case** in the text and defined briefly in the margins of a page. Remember to look also at the glossary at the end of the book where a longer definition or explanation is given.

- A good student will read more than appears in a single sociology textbook, however bulky it is. Use the end-of-chapter references as a guide to your reading – a full list of all the sources referred to in *Global Sociology* appears at the end of the book.

- Many, although not all, universities and colleges will teach a course through the use of a weekly lecture together with supporting classes or seminars. Group work suggestions are provided to you and your instructors for interesting ways in which to analyse and discuss the material.

- Finally, you may want to try your hand at answering some of the 'questions to think about'. You can use these as a way of structuring your revision, or as essay titles or as a way of preparing for your examinations.

- We trust you will enjoy the course.

If you would like to know more ●

Graham Crow's book *Comparative Sociology and Social Theory* (1997) gives a good account of the way in which the sociologists of development came to understand societies other than their own. Chapters 6 and 7 are particularly helpful.

Leslie Sklair's *Sociology of the Global System* (second edition, 1995) has been a pioneering introductory text. Despite the title, he particularly stresses the economic aspects of globalization.

By contrast Malcolm Waters's book, simply titled *Globalization* (1995), is very strong on cultural aspects. It is a small book and looks an attractive buy in the bookshop – but it is harder than it looks.

David Held and his colleagues have also provided a thorough account in *Global Transformations* (1999), concentrating particularly on the economic and political aspects of global change.

Group work ●

Half the class will prepare a list of organizations and social groups that they consider are, or are likely to be, 'global winners'. The other half will list what they think are, or are likely to be, 'global losers'. Do you agree on those listed? Are there some groups and organizations for which the outcome is not yet clear?

Preparatory work

1. Prepare yourself for this course by: (a) thinking about whether you can afford another book other than this one; (b) examining your library card index or online catalogue to see what books they have, using the key readings listed at the end of each chapter in this book as your guide; and (c) surveying what other resources are available, for example, foreign newspapers, good weeklies (like *The Economist*) or CD-ROMs.

2. Take a guided tour of your library.

3. Arrange with your computer centre to hook you up to the Internet. Normally this involves getting a student ID card, then obtaining your user name and password. Ask someone to show you how to visit a web site, if you do not already know. Because the net is itself an aspect of global change, there are thousands of sites relevant to this course. Start with this web site address: www.stile.lut.ac.uk/global.html. The well-known British sociologist, Anthony Giddens, took 'Globalization' as the theme of the 1999 Reith lectures, a prestigious series broadcast by the BBC. As we write this, the lectures are available at www.news.bbc.co.uk/hi/english/static/events/reith_99 but they are available also in book form. The British Sociological Association has started a useful web-based journal, which carries up-to-date postings on important issues of the day. Called *Sociological Research Online*, it can be accessed at www.soc.surrey.ac.uk/socresonline.

4. Look round carefully at the first small group of students you meet taking this course. There will almost certainly be some from other regions, cities or countries. Try to get to know them. They will be an invaluable resource in your understanding of the different facets of global society and they may also turn out to be friends.

5. Read at least one chapter ahead of each week's scheduled lecture. Start with Chapter 2 now. It is a tough one. If you can crack it, you should not have too many subsequent difficulties.

Thinking Globally

CONTENTS

Sociologists have always studied societies other than their own. The discipline contains a rich comparative tradition clearly traceable through the work of its founders Comte, Marx, Durkheim, Weber and Parsons. Nevertheless these pioneers and many subsequent sociologists often regarded societies as if they were separate entities, each with its own clear boundaries. The focal point was on acquiring an understanding of a society's *internal* dynamics and structures, its distinctive historical and cultural traditions, its unique patterns of inequality and its particular directions of social change. Until recently, this procedure was perfectly valid and generated many useful insights. However, the growing significance of global changes for all societies has rendered this approach and the national traditions it generated less meaningful.

In this chapter, we explore the meaning of 'globalization' and 'globalism' and ask what is distinctive about the processes so described. Sociologists are notorious for coining new words and concepts. Do we require yet further additions to our terminology? Why are they needed now? Are globalization and globalism completely new phenomena in the world, and if so, to what extent and in what senses? We must be careful not to suggest that globalization has acquired a purpose and impulse of its own. On the contrary, human actors and social organizations are intimately involved in shaping the nature of global forces. Never before have there been so many opportunities for a growing number of individual social actors to shape local and global forces. Again, never before has there been a greater need for so many decisions to be made or conflicts to be resolved by organizations set up to advance the cause of humanity.

WHAT IS GLOBALIZATION?

According to Albrow (1990: 9), globalization refers 'to all those processes by which the peoples of the world are incorporated into a single society, global society'. These changes are incomplete. They are long in the making and impact on different locations, countries and individuals in a highly uneven manner. They have nevertheless increased in scope and intensity and recently this has been happening at an accelerating rate. We suggest that globalization is best understood as a set of mutually reinforcing transformations that are occurring more or less simultaneously. No single one of these is necessarily more significant than the others. One way of thinking about this is to imagine a number of threads being woven into a length of multicoloured fabric. Once woven together it would be impossible to assign a special role to each thread – each only has value or significance as part of the whole.

However, *before* our cloth of globalization has been woven we can identify at least six component strands, each of which is explained in greater detail later:

- changing concepts of space and time
- an increasing volume of cultural interactions
- the commonality of problems facing all the world's inhabitants
- growing interconnections and interdependencies
- a network of increasingly powerful transnational actors and organization
- the synchronization of all the dimensions involved in globalization.

Changing concepts of space and time

A leading globalization theorist, Robertson (1992: 8, 27), shows how cultures and societies – along with their members and participants – are being squeezed together and driven towards increased mutual interaction. He describes this as 'the compression of the world'. As shared forces and exchanges powerfully structure our lives so the world is becoming one place and one system. With all this comes a radical shift in our understanding of space and time. Here, Harvey's work (1989: 240–54) is especially relevant and useful. He argues that in pre-modern societies, space was understood in terms of concrete localities. Movement was dangerous and difficult while war, pestilence and famine often made social life unpredictable. For most individuals it was safer to remain in those places where they and their families enjoyed fixed and unchanging rights and obligations. Similarly, the memory of past disasters, the passing of the seasons and the cycle of agricultural work determined understandings of time. However, a number of important changes, including the following, gradually altered how people understood space and time:

1. The beginnings of Arab, Chinese, Pacific Islander and European exploration and navigation of the world.

Key Moment

The Renaissance

The word derives from the French for 'rebirth' and refers to the revival of classical philosophy, literature and art in early modern and modern Europe. Over a period of 800 years, starting in the eighth century, artistic and scientific thinking flowered in Europe. This was accompanied by the rise of intellectual life (including the founding of universities), secular states and rational values.

2. Copernicus's theory, published in 1543, which established that the sun, not the earth, was the centre of our planetary system.

3. The discovery of the rules of perspective in visual art.

4. The rise of humanist, people-centred, ways of thinking about human life in place of a solely religious preoccupation spurred by **Renaissance** thinking.

5. The increasing use of the mechanical printing press.

6. The advent of the mechanical clock.

7. The unfolding revolution in transport technology associated with industrialization.

Let us consider transport technology in more detail. Until the advent and increasingly widespread use of the steamship from the 1850s, the movement of all goods was slow, expensive and unreliable. But by the mid-twentieth century, commercial aircraft and large ocean-going vessels (superfreighters) were rapidly shrinking 'real' distances and vastly accelerating – and cheapening – the movement of people and goods.

Table 2.1   Changes in the speed of transport, 1500–1960s

1500–1840	*1850–1930*	*1950s*	*1960s*
Horse-drawn coaches/sail ships	Steamships and locomotives	Propeller air	Jet air
16 kph	56–104 kph	480–640 kph	800–1120 kph

Source: Dicken (1992: 104)

Step by step, often through quite sudden bursts in technical knowledge linked to economic changes, it became possible to measure, divide and so map the physical and temporal dimensions of the world into universal, standardized and predictable units. For example, without the geographical co-ordinates of longitude and latitude, travel by ship or aeroplane would be considerably more difficult. Harvey (1989: 240) calls the outcome of these ideas and discoveries 'time–space compression'.

What are the implications of this shift? Time and distance have dwindled in significance as forces shaping human actions. Less bound by ties to specific places and events, both space and time have become freely available for us to manipulate and control. We can accomplish far more things in any given unit of time and events crowd in upon us at an ever-greater speed. But with life becoming faster, so distance is conquered. Not just in metaphorical terms but in relation to our experiences, the world not only *appears* to be contracting, but in a sense *really is* shrinking. Increasingly we judge distance in terms of the time required to complete a journey not by the number of kilometres between two points. Also, territory has lost its salience now that increasingly no one people is wholly confined to one place and mass travel enables many to experience other cultures. Another implication of the idea of time–space compression is that our social horizons are indefinitely extended. We are less dependent upon particular people and fixed social relationships. Moreover, since the 1950s, mass television ownership, coupled more recently with satellite communications, 'makes it possible to experience a rush of images from different spaces almost simultaneously, collapsing the world's spaces into a series of images on a television screen' (Harvey 1989: 293).

Thus, time–space compression, facilitated by the electronic media, has put many of the world's inhabitants on the same stage and has brought their lives together for the first time. There is scope, even for people who do not know one another personally, to interact meaningfully. Relative strangers can constitute an environmental movement against polluting companies, share their common leisure enthusiasms, hatch business deals or participate in a world media event via satellite television – and all at the same moment in time and across vast distances.

We must remember that the world's inhabitants do not experience these changes equally. Imagine, for example, people living in two villages located 30 miles apart in a particularly poor region of West Africa. Here, the only telephone does not work, the roads are neglected (perhaps they are even impassable during the rainy season) and no one can afford batteries to keep the few radios working. Such people remain almost as far apart in terms of their ability to interact effectively as they were 100 years ago. In a sense, they are *more* distant from each other than people living in, say, Sydney and Paris.

Increasing cultural interactions

Major Concept
CULTURE

Most sociologists tend to define culture as the repertoire of learned ideas, values, knowledge, aesthetic preferences, rules and customs shared by a particular collectivity of social actors. Drawing on this common stock of meanings enables them to participate in a unique way of life. In this usage, the human world consists of a plurality of equal cultures. Each can only be fully interpreted by its participants. With globalization, however, and the increasing interpenetration of flows of meaning between societies and communities, the idea of cultures as bounded, separate and fixed entities is becoming less tenable (see Chapters 12 and 13).

A second component thread of globalization concerns the increase in cultural flows propelled around the world in unprecedented quantities and with great speed and intensity. The term **CULTURE** has a multiplicity of meanings.

For many sociologists, culture is used very broadly to depict all the modes of thought, behaviour and artefacts that are transmitted from generation to generation by example, education or the public record. In an everyday context, however, it refers to specific intellectual, artistic and aesthetic attainments in music, painting, literature, film and other forms of expression. Culture in this sense is particularly rich in imagery, metaphors, signs and symbols. The magnificent stone sculptures executed by the Neolithic peoples of Easter Island is just one illustration (Figure 2.1). With respect to this second depiction of culture, it is important to note that in western societies, earlier distinctions between 'highbrow' and 'lowbrow' or popular culture – enjoyed by ordinary people – have been challenged during the twentieth century. This is linked especially to the rise of the mass media and the widespread dissemination of consumerist lifestyles.

Closely linked to culture, we also need to consider the growing importance of knowledge pertaining to abstract systems of understanding. Unlike culture as a way of life or as artistic forms – where meanings are rooted in particular societies or social groups – abstract knowledge remains constant and applicable in any context, although new items are always being added. This is because it refers to impersonal, largely autonomous and universal (scientific) truths. The elaboration of the binary codes that drive the language of computers provides another example.

Figure 2.1   Stone figures on Easter Island

Throughout most of human history, culture and knowledge were acquired and reinforced mainly in informal, everyday learning situations associated with close relationships in family, church and community life. Their diffusion to other social contexts took place very slowly and in a fragmentary way – for example, through sea voyages, trade, conquest and religious proselytization. Perhaps the most far-reaching of such voyages was that undertaken by **Christopher Columbus** who, with the support of the King and Queen of Spain, set sail in 1492 across the Atlantic to get to India. Instead he reached the Bahamas, the Caribbean and South America.

The cultural interactions arising from increased contact between peoples have gradually exposed all humans to the growing flows of cultural meanings and knowledge coming from other societies. At the same time there has been an immense expansion in the scope and spread of abstract knowledge linked to science and the growing availability of mass, formal education. Moreover, the humble letter has been augmented by the telephone, the fax and electronic networks, rendering communication ever more swift and telling. The electronic mass media enable even those who lack education to encounter new ideas and experiences. All this has generated several important consequences:

1. It has become increasingly possible to lift cultural meanings out of their original societal contexts and transplant them to other societies.

2. We now have the means to access rapidly far greater quantities of cultural meaning of every kind than ever before and from a multiplicity of sources.

3. We can obtain full pictures of other lifestyles, especially through the power of visual images conveyed in television and film.

4. It is increasingly possible (and necessary to our very survival) to know about other people's cultures. If we do not, we run the risk of being excluded from many potential benefits.

5. The electronic mass media of communication, along with fast transport, have the capacity to affect all those who are exposed to it, and to incorporate them into a single experience. Accordingly, we live in what McLuhan (1962: 102) called a 'global village'.

6. We are made conscious that we live in a pluralist, multicultural world and are invited to participate in its many different possibilities embodied, for example, in cuisine, music, religious practices and marriage customs.

7. This last point notwithstanding, it appears that, certainly at present, western and especially US influences dominate the volume and character of cultural and knowledge flows.

The commonality of problems

Interlaced in the fabric of globalization is the growing commonality of problems facing the nations and peoples of the world. Of course, we are entitled to be sceptical concerning how widely such perceptions are shared – since the lives of many people are still governed by long-held social customs, deep religious beliefs and unquestioned national identities. However, their perception of the world is constantly under assault. The media have long brought the events and crises taking place in near and distant locations into our living rooms on a daily and hourly basis. We can recall, in the final decade of the twentieth century, the invasion of Kuwait in 1990, the terrorist incident at the Olympic Games in Atlanta in the summer of 1996, the fires that raged out of control in Indonesia in 1997, enveloping millions of people in a vast cloud of smoke, the famine in the Sudan in 1998 and the pitiable refugees pouring out of Kosovo in 1999. Such events graphically remind us of our common humanity – our vulnerabilities to accident and misfortune – and the existential truth that we all inhabit the same small planet.

While startling visual images are experienced as collective shocks, there are more material reasons for our sense of empathy with other human beings. In our compressed and integrated globe our choices not only rebound on our own lives, they directly affect the lives of others far away. Often, we are unaware of this and do not intend our actions directly to harm distant strangers. For example, the most prosperous fifth of the world's population living in the advanced economies enjoys 64 per cent of global income (Durning 1992: 27–8). Because its global economic clout is so great, its decisions about what to produce and consume, how to invest money, lifestyle preferences and leisure pursuits may cause unemployment, falling export prices and loss of livelihood for workers and peasants in distant lands.

Another reason for sharing concerns is that certain global problems require global solutions. Acting alone, governments can no longer protect their borders, territories or the lives and well being of their citizens from a number of situations. The 1986 nuclear accident at Chernobyl in Ukraine and the subsequent fallout of radioactive material across wide areas of Europe vividly demonstrated our vulnerability. The threat to national currencies from speculation on the world's

The **biosphere** consists of the atmosphere, the oceans, lakes and rivers, the varied and complex systems of plant life and all other living organisms from bacteria to fish, animals and humans.

financial markets and international drug-trafficking are other examples of relative national impotence. Only collaboration between governments and regulation at the global level can provide genuine solutions. Whether or not this will be forthcoming is open to doubt. We are uncertain how far citizens will exercise pressure on governments and agencies at both national and transnational levels.

The impact of global industrialization on the planet's **_biosphere_** perhaps provides the most obvious and compelling example of the shared, global nature of many problems. According to Yearley (1996a: 28), 'the world's growing environmental problems are connecting the lives of people in very different societies... it is ultimately impossible to hide oneself away from these phenomena altogether'.

It is not solely the materialistic lifestyles of the world's rich minority that are responsible for global environmental devastation. In many developing countries, even the poorest and most marginalized people have been driven to abuse their own environments. This arises from rapid population growth and the pressure on governments – from international financial institutions such as the World Bank – to finance huge debts by extending various forms of cash-crop production. Poor people are then forced to cultivate steep hillsides and semi-desert, while companies and wealthy farmers seize the best rain-fed and valley land for cash crops. The less fortunate are compelled to over-graze pastures already crowded with livestock and to strip dry-land zones of their tree covering for fuel. By contributing unwittingly to soil erosion, rainfall depletion and deforestation the world's poorest people also play a role in global climate change that affects us all.

Interconnections and interdependencies

Fast-expanding interconnections and interdependencies bind localities, countries, companies, social movements, professional and other groups, as well as individual citizens, into an ever more dense network of transnational exchanges and affiliations. So important are these networks thought to be that one eminent sociologist (Castells 1996) has suggested that we live in a 'network society'. These networks have burst across territorial borders, rupturing the cultural and economic self-sufficiency once experienced by nations. What drives these networks and empowers those participating in them is knowledge and information. As Castells suggests the power of knowledge flows 'takes precedence over the flows of power' (p. 469). The overall cumulative impact of these interconnections has meant that societies, and their cities and regions, have tended to spread outwards so as to merge and become coextensive with other societies (see our discussion on global cities in Chapter 15). At the same time, the once clear-cut separation between the sphere of national life and the international sphere has largely broken down.

Until quite recently, most social scientists, especially political theorists, thought about interactions at the world level almost entirely in terms of interstate dealings and exchanges. Thus, nation states were considered to be by far the most dominant, if not the only players, in world affairs.

Burton (1972) used the analogy of a snooker game to describe the interactions between states. The movement of each coloured ball (or state) in the game of international relations was determined by the power enjoyed by each government as it sought to interact with and influence other states. Such interactions might involve trade pacts, arms agreements or the pursuit of diplomatic alliances in the attempt to avert wars by winning allies or isolating countries considered likely to pose a military threat. Yet, even for especially powerful players, the actions, positions and movements of all the other balls in the game necessarily restricted their autonomy.

Burton foresaw a further intensifying set of constraints on the actions of state players. An ever denser network of ties and connections was gradually forming that transcended purely inter-state relations because a swelling number of powerful *non-state actors* were forming relationships and pursuing their own interests. Thus, increasingly, the international system consisted of different layers of interactions and connections. As Waters (1995: 28) observes, Burton's metaphor of a snooker table points to a possible future scenario where 'the entire world is linked together by networks that are as dense as the ones which are available in local contexts'. In this view, 'locality and geography will disappear altogether, the world will genuinely be one place and the nation state will be redundant'.

Transnational actors and organizations

Who or what are these leading transnational agents whose actions have done so much to extend and intensify the interconnections across national borders since the Second World War?

Transnational corporations (TNCs)

In many ways these are the most powerful of such agents. We have a much longer discussion of TNCs in Chapter 7, but here we record their most important features:

● their global power and reach – half the largest economies in the world are TNCs not countries

● their key role in creating an interdependent world economy as each TNC superimposes its own global grid of integrated production lines and investment activities across countries and continents dictated by its own, not national, needs

● their connections to the world financial system, including the instantaneous, computerized markets for foreign currencies where the equivalent of $1.2 trillion (a million, million plus) of stateless money are bought and sold every single day.

International governmental organizations (IGOs)

Like TNCs, IGOs constitute an important case of a wider phenomenon – the rising ability of supra-state actors to shape world affairs. Indeed, it is precisely because states cannot solve global problems alone that they have established a large number of IGOs to function at their bidding. However, sometimes, as you might expect, these organizations take on lives of their own. Such bodies first began to be effective in the nineteenth century with the growing need for rules and procedures in order to standardize cross-border transactions. Probably the best-known IGOs are the League of Nations and United Nations (UN), established in the wake of the First and Second World War respectively. By the early 1980s, according to Scholte (1993: 44), there were 700 IGOs, which together convened approximately 5000 meetings a year. The variety of functions they perform for governments is barely shown by the following examples: the World Meteorological Organization; the United Nations High Commission for Refugees (UNHCR); and the Food and Agricultural Organization (FAO).

International non-governmental organizations (INGOs)

Like their national counterparts, INGOs are autonomous organizations not accountable to governments although they may work with them at times. Particular INGOs have often been powerful forces in world affairs. For example, peace, anti-slavery and labour organizations collaborated extensively across national borders in the nineteenth century. The numbers of INGOs have grown at a remarkable rate, especially since the 1950s. Today, their range of activities is vast, encompassing religious, business, professional, labour, political, green, women's, sport and leisure interests among many others. You have probably heard of some of the most famous INGOs, such as Greenpeace, the Red Cross, Oxfam and Amnesty International. But there are literally thousands of others operating transnationally, and many more that mainly confine their operations within nation states. According to Scholte (1993: 44) there were approximately 17 000 INGOs by the mid-1980s, although not all were equally global in scope.

Most INGOs seek to mobilize world opinion for their collective interest or (more normally) for explicitly moral or political causes. This may involve placing direct pressure on governments or on various UN agencies. INGOs skilfully use the global media to focus wider public attention on their concerns. They hope individual citizens will respond by exerting pressure on governments, corporations and other interests. Perhaps they will undertake consumer boycotts, tax protests, demonstrations, occupations of environmentally endangered sites, or simply petition political leaders. Examples of similar actions include the cross-European campaign led by Greenpeace against Shell dumping a redundant oil rig (the *Brent Spar*) into the North Sea and the global pressure generated in opposition to French nuclear testing in the Pacific, both in 1995.

Global social movements (GSMs)

Major Concept
SOCIAL MOVEMENTS
These are informal organiza- tions working for change but galvanized around a single unifying issue. Exam- ples of global social move- ments include the human rights, peace, environmental and women's movements (see Chapter 16).

Although there is a great deal of overlap between these two descriptions, we can consider that particular INGOs are nested within more general global **SOCIAL MOVEMENTS**.

Because the more activist INGOs mobilize world opinion on political and moral issues, their campaigns sometimes mesh with the activities of GSMs. An example of this convergence was demonstrated at the UN's 'Earth Summit' on the environment held at Rio, Brazil, in the summer of 1992. Then, an estimated 20 000 representatives from environmental and other INGOs held an alternative 'green festival' in alliance with people associated with the world's stateless and Aboriginal peoples. The global media generally found this unofficial festival more compelling than the official forum attended by governments and experts.

Diasporas and stateless people

A number of diasporas (such as the Jewish and Parsi) predate the nation state. However, other diasporas arose because of religious, ethnic or political disputes with governments over the demand for full citizen rights, the recognition of

Major Concept

DIASPORAS

These are formed by the forcible or voluntary dispersion of peoples to a number of countries. They constitute a diaspora if they continue to evince a common concern for their 'homeland' (sometimes an imagined homeland) and come to share a common fate with their own people, wherever they happen to be.

semi-autonomy or the granting of independent national status. Their experience of persecution or neglect compelled some to voluntarily leave or seek asylum in other countries thereby forming global **DIASPORAS** of linked, displaced peoples (Cohen 1997). Among such groups are Africans, Kashmiris, Tamils, Sikhs, Armenians and Palestinians.

Distinct from diasporas as they have not been dispersed internationally, there are said to be around 5000 Aboriginal 'nations' (Robertson 1992: 171; Friburg and Hettne 1988) that lack state structures and demand the return of their tribal homelands and proper recognition of their cultural identities. These Aboriginal groups, stretching across Canada, the USA, Australasia and South America, have recently formed a World Council of Indigenous Peoples. They have worked with the United Nations Centre for Human Rights (UNCHR) in the attempt to establish a universal declaration of rights for non-state peoples worldwide.

Like the INGOs, such groups need no convincing that in today's world the expression of local identities is only viable in a global forum and context. To this end they co-ordinate their struggles at the global level and try to harness media opportunities in order to bring attention to their plight. According to Friburg and Hettne (1988), their political activities and intentions are captured exactly in the catch phrase 'act locally but think globally'.

Box 2.1   Acting locally and thinking globally: the runners of Tarahumara

The Tarahumara Indians live in Chihuahua State, a remote region, high up in the mountains of northern Mexico. Here, they have earned a reputation for extraordinary feats of endurance with their champion runners sometimes racing continuously for two days and nights at very high altitudes. Life for the approximately 60 000 Tarahumara people is arduous. Over time they have been forced to move from their original homelands by the pressures of commercial development dominated by white Mexicans, and have been pushed on to higher lands where cultivation is unrewarding. Temperatures often fall to −20° Centigrade in winter.

In the early 1990s, several years of drought – probably linked to heavy deforestation in the area – meant that their 'normal' condition of hunger turned to famine. Most children suffer from malnutrition to some extent and among the poorest communities infant mortality may exceed 50 per cent. Sadly, these pressures have compelled more and more Tarahumara people to migrate in search of temporary or permanent settlement in Mexico's largest cities.

In a bid to gain the world's attention, the leaders of an organization dedicated to alleviating the Tarahumara's conditions – Wilderness Research Expeditions – encouraged their best runners to visit the USA and participate in important athletic events. Running to win international publicity and to raise money for food aid began in 1993.

In late September 1996, six Tarahumara champions spent a weekend running the equivalent of four 26-mile marathon races through the Angeles national forest in California, much of it above the snow line. In doing so they were not equipped with the high-tech, designer sports gear deemed essential by western athletic personalities. Instead, they wore leather sandals made at home. They are said to be rather bemused by all the fuss westerners make about the rules of competition, timetabling and accurate measurements of fixed racing distances. Moreover, they find the experience of running in major

(cont'd)

US events rather boring since back home their races combine long-distance racing with kicking a ball up and down the mountains. Nevertheless, and with the help of Wilderness Research Expeditions, the willingness of these runners to 'go global' generated the funds to distribute 60 tons of food to the Tarahumara people between 1993 and 1996.

Source: Gunson (1996)

Other transnational actors

Daily, huge numbers of ordinary citizens are engaged in forging transnational connections as they travel, alone or in small informal groups, across national boundaries. At their destinations, they may reside as temporary visitors or seek long-term settlement. Whatever their circumstances and motives, they transport their cultures and lifestyles with them while becoming exposed, to various degrees, to the host societies' cultures. Thus, global cultures are juxtaposed and sometimes merged. Among the many categories of individual or small-group travellers we can identify some definite types:

1. Migrants in search of income opportunities in the growth poles of the world economy, such as the buoyant Middle Eastern oil economies in the 1980s.

2. International tourists whose numbers reached 593 million in 1996 compared with 159 million in 1970 (*The Economist*, 8 February 1997: 145).

3. Professionals such as lawyers, journalists, architects and scientists many of whom, according to Hannerz (1990: 237–51), evince a cosmopolitanism that enables them to feel 'at home' anywhere in the world so that they contribute to the formation of a transnational culture.

4. Media, rock/pop and sports personalities.

5. Corporation personnel, business consultants and private entrepreneurs whose multifarious activities knit together the strands of the global economy.

6. A miscellaneous group including students, airline pilots, drug-dealers, diplomats, au pairs and many more besides.

Synchronization of all dimensions

We can point to a final thread in our garment of globalization. All the dimensions of globalization – economic, technological, political, social and cultural – appear to be coming together at the same time, each reinforcing and magnifying the impact of the others.

In the economic sphere, governments have lost some of their power to regulate their economies as a host of largely autonomous agents like international banks, TNCs and currency markets have flourished in the ever more integrated world economy. Although they are formed through inter-governmental agreement, bodies like the World Trade Organization (WTO) have taken on a life of their own and often compel recalcitrant governments to adopt trade policies they see acting against their particular national interest. Meanwhile, the lure of the free market has drawn many more countries into its orbit. This has allowed money values to penetrate every corner of the globe and most facets of social and cultural life.

In political life, citizens in many countries have become alienated from conventional party politics, a trend seen in the drop in voting participation in recent western elections. This does not mean that people are detached from all forms of politics. Instead, many participate in political and social movements. These social movements may operate on a national level and sometimes coalesce rather suddenly. For example, in Britain in 1997 a 'Countryside Alliance' of farmers, hunters and rural residents organized massive demonstrations in London protesting that successive British governments had ignored their concerns. But, as we have mentioned, social movements also operate at a global level (see also Chapters 16, 17 and 18). Here the old issues of national identity, war and security no longer exclusively dominate the political agenda. Instead, participants in global social movements are concerned with additional questions such as how governments can best co-operate to counter global environmental degradation or deal with the economic insecurities resulting from the volatile global money markets.

There is growing mass participation in the market economy by workers, consumers, tourists, listeners and, above all, viewers. This, together with the revolutions in the electronic media and information technology, has generated the basis for the enormous expansion of cultural flows across the world. Culture in all its forms – as consumer aspirations, pop or rock music, religious, moral and ethical values or the political ideologies of democracy and socialism – has become the most recent and perhaps most potent addition to globalization. Transmission takes place through different means – through visual images in the mass media, abstract knowledge, or the social milieux created by more varied interpersonal relationships. The explosive potential for enfeebling national cultures and affiliations and for providing new foci of identity and collaboration between citizens of distant countries has only begun to work its way through the world order.

GLOBALISM: A NEW PHENOMENON

In Chapter 3 we will be reminded that some of the processes involved in globalization have long historical roots although, as we shall show later in this book, a quantitative acceleration of them has recently become evident. What is distinctive and new in the world today is the emergence of 'globalism'. According to Albrow (1990: 8), globalism concerns those 'values which take the real world of 5 billion people as the object of concern... everyone living as world citizens... with a common interest in collective action to solve global problems'. Similarly, although referring to 'globality' rather than globalism, Robertson (1992: 132) defines this as 'consciousness of the (problem of) the world as a single space'. In short, whereas globalization mainly refers to a series of objective changes in the world that are partly outside us, globalism refers to the subjective realm. How have we internalized the changes associated with globalization so that they are now incorporated into our emotions and our ways of thinking about everyday life? Some of the major aspects of globalism are:

- thinking about ourselves collectively while identifying with all humanity
- the end to one-way flows and the growth of multicultural awareness
- the empowerment of self-aware social actors
- the broadening of identities.

Thinking about ourselves collectively

Humankind, and not just a small coterie of intellectuals, has begun to be capable of thinking about itself collectively as one entity. For some of the time at least, our shared concern with the category 'humanity' is beginning to extend beyond our affiliation solely to people of the same ethnic, national or religious identities as ourselves. Applying this idea, Robertson (1992: 183) argues that while we are still a long way from the world being capable of acting 'for itself', the idea of this is becoming more and more significant and pressing. For example, many people, particularly young and educated people, articulate a strong conviction that everyone has certain rights as a human being. They express moral outrage when it transpires that these rights are being violated and demand that human rights are universally protected and enshrined in international conventions and laws.

This involves a clear break with even the recent past. A poignant illustration of this capacity to empathize across old divides was the successful worldwide campaign to effect the release of Nelson Mandela, who had come to symbolize the fight against the denial of human rights in South Africa. His extraordinary human qualities crossed many barriers of caste, class, ethnicity, nationality and religion (Figure 2.2).

Figure 2.2   Nelson Mandela, April 1990, the year of his release from prison and four years before he was inaugurated as State President of South Africa

Major Concept
MODERNITY

The date of Columbus's voyage to the Americas, 1492, can be taken as a convenient symbolic marker opening the modern era. However, the orientations towards modernity only began to crystallize in the seventeenth century. They involved the growth of a questing spirit, a powerful – leaning towards ration-ality – the search for valid, verifiable knowledge – and a belief in the possibility of transforming the material world in the pursuit of social 'progress'. The project of modernity eventually boosted science and culmi-nated in industrialization and urbanization.

Growth of multicultural and transnational awareness

Perlmutter (1991: 898) argues that previous attempts by imperialistic powers to impose 'civilization' on the rest of humanity were based on what he calls a domi-nance–dependence mode of interrelationship. Here, incorporating other groups and societies normally involved conquest. Similarly, access to the 'benefits' of the victor's civilizing values required a willingness to submit to its 'superior' laws and institutions. Now, however, for the first time in history, 'we have in our possession the technology to support the choice of sharing the governance of our planet rather than fighting with one another to see who will be in charge' (Perl-mutter 1991: 901). In this view, the long era of one-sided cultural and political flows is over. At last, nations and cultures are more willing to recognize and accept cultural diversity. Increasingly, too, they regard co-operation around a set of shared values and structures as possible, necessary and desirable.

Giddens (1990: 51–7) makes a similar point when he observes that, although most of the features we associate with **MODERNITY** originated in the West, these forces have now spread and flourish autonomously across the world. Each country is capable of determining its own version of modernity and of projecting this on to the global order, as Japan has done during the last half century. By dissolving the West's former distinctiveness and ability to monopo-lize modern forms of power, the globalization of modernity is simultaneously bringing the period of western dominance to an end (see Chapter 3).

Reflexive social actors and modernity

Globalism contains a further important subjective component. Several writers (Giddens 1990 and 1991; Beck 1992; Beck *et al.* 1994) have pointed to the growing number of social actors who are empowered to exercise **REFLEXIVITY** in their daily lives.

Reflexive individuals tend to be self-conscious and knowledgeable. They seek to shape their own lives while redefining the world around them. In many contemporary societies, the growing number of such individuals has begun to form a critical mass of those willing and able to activate and seize control of the dough of social life through the yeast generated by their own capacities for crit-ical self-determination.

This widening exercise of reflexivity is partly linked to the development of mass education and the wide dissemination not just of scientific knowledge but of the principle of doubt on which scientific method is built. These have provided such keys to citizen empowerment as access to specialized systems of expertise, professional training and the means to acquire various kinds of lay expertise. Suitably armed, reflexive citizens may challenge the truth claims put forward by governments, corporations and by the scientific community itself. But this tendency to criticize powerful institutions is reinforced by an intense disillusionment with the consequences of modernity and the idea of material progress.

Beck (1992) articulates this idea with particular force. He argues that moder-nity and its consequences – relentless economic growth, the unchecked powers of military, technological and scientific institutions – now seem to threaten the viability of the planetary biosphere. Having been liberated from the risks once endemic to an era of economic scarcity (at least in the rich countries), we are

Major Concept
REFLEXIVITY

All humans reflect on the consequences of their own and others' actions and perhaps alter their behav-iour in response to new information. This quality of self-awareness, self-knowledge and contempla-tion is of great interest to sociologists as it speaks to the motives, understand-ings and intentions of social actors. In contem-porary societies reflexivity is said to intensify as every aspect of social life becomes subject to endless revision in the face of constantly accumulating knowledge.

now surrounded with vast new, all-pervasive and possibly uncontainable risks. These are directly caused by the very institutions of science and industry modernity itself engendered. At the same time, Beck argues, the once powerful identities provided by class, family, patriarchal gender relations, community or church has largely been destroyed. This, he continues, is mainly beneficial, for it has helped to enlarge the scope for exercising individual freedom, especially for women.

However, such gains come with costs. Greater personal freedom to define who we are and how we wish to live also compels us to assume full responsibility for determining our own life paths including any mistakes we may make. Thus, we are on our own; our lives have become more insecure. We have greater freedom and more personal responsibility for managing our own lives. In a sense, Beck is arguing, we have no choice, now, but to engage in harsh reflexive activities involving 'self confrontation' (Beck *et al.* 1994: 5) while engaging in the critical appraisal of established institutions because our survival and that of the planet depends on this. The discipline of sociology itself both contributes to our greater capacity for reflexivity and responds to its outcomes.

However, one does not have to confine such insights to the sociologically trained, as the sphere of the global is no longer remote to most humans; it has become 'in here', rooted in our consciousness (Giddens 1994: 95). Because globalization has brought knowledge of other cultures into the heart of our daily lives it has become yet another major force that fosters increasing reflexivity and individualization. According to Rosenau (1990), the capacity for reflexivity has also increased among the most disadvantaged citizens in many developing countries. As he explains, 'today's persons-in-the-street are no longer as uninvolved, ignorant, and manipulable with respect of world affairs as were their forbears' (Rosenau 1990: 13). They have also widened their emotional loyalties far beyond immediate family and community.

Consequently, ordinary citizens everywhere are challenging state power and forging links with their counterparts in other countries. This is caused in part by our realization that governments are often ineffective in the face of 'currency crises, pollution disasters, terrorist attacks, ozone depletion and a host of other problems that transcend national boundaries' (Rosenau 1990: 337). However, technological change, especially the revolution in microelectronics, has played the greatest role through speeding up the flows of ideas, images and information that crash through national boundaries, reminding us of our growing transnational interdependency.

A burgeoning, transnational power base of non-state organizations and increasingly connected global citizens' networks is taking shape. Many of those involved are also highly critical of the established order. This offers a potential for the formation of effective global alliances from below between various groups who seek what Friburg and Hettne (1988: 346–8) call 'alternative' futures built around the idea of a 'post-materialist', more egalitarian world order.

The broadening of identities

A final subjective component of globalism that is helping to change the way we construct our identities and orient ourselves towards life in the world concerns what Robertson (1992: 29) calls 'relativization' and we will call 'broadening'. Today, no person or institution can avoid contact with, and some knowledge of, other cultures. But our allegiance to the particular, local cultures in which most of us remain rooted at any one point in time are altered by our comparisons with and understandings of other cultures. The local or the particular cease to be sufficient as a resource in enabling us to make decisions about our lives and where we belong.

However, the reverse process also becomes important to us; we need to judge and reach some decision on how we feel about other cultures in the light of our participation in the particular and the local. As Robertson (1992: 100) suggests, there is a steady increase in the interpenetration of the local and the global by each other. We can respond to the reality by selection, adaptation or resistance, as explained in the following:

Glocalization – a process whereby global pressures and demands are made to conform to local conditions.

- *Selection* We may select from the global only that which pleases us and then alter it so that it becomes embedded in and accommodating to local conditions and needs. Borrowing from a marketing term employed by Japanese companies which modify their global products to match and blend with each country's cultural requirements, Robertson (1992: 173–4) describes this process as **glocalization**. Here, the global is modified by its contact with the local. Thus, there is no homogenizing force at work here but rather various possibilities of fusion and creativity.

- *Adaptation* Whether we feel moved to reject or to embrace the global, our growing knowledge of the latter almost certainly heightens our awareness of the local and may serve to intensify rather than weaken our feelings of loyalty to it. Thus, it is perfectly possible to participate in the global and the local simultaneously. The British, for example, need not feel any less so because their country has become deeply immersed in the European Union. Rather, their greater exposure to and increased enjoyment of continental cultures might serve to sharpen and enhance, or even help to define, a sense of Britishness.

- *Resistance* Another possibility is resistance. Thus, some religious or ethnic groups are deeply antipathetic to other cultures and try to resist incorporation in the global sphere. They are partly propelled in this direction by their very knowledge of western and other cultures and their suspicion that these may disrupt local values and customs. Neo-orthodox Islamic movements in countries such as Algeria and Iran represent one example of this phenomenon, although this is by no means the only reason for the current strength of militant Islam (Ahmed 1992; Turner 1994: Chapter 6). However, what we see here is that even rejections of the global are driven largely by knowledge of it. The juxtaposition of the local and global has become an important force in world politics and its impact is likely to increase.

REVIEW

In this chapter we have made a crucial distinction between the process of globalization, comprising a series of objective, external elements that are profoundly changing our world, and globalism as a subjective and reflexive awareness of these changes. We have argued that our six processes of globalization are inseparable and synchronous. In identifying the four aspects relating to globalism we have suggested that the dough of social life can be manipulated when people use the yeast generated by their own capacities for critical self-examination. This emphasis is in marked contrast with much of the literature you will read, where individuals are often represented as helpless chaff, victims of the tornado of globalization. We are much more excited by the possibilities that individuals, groups and movements can use the opportunities provided by these changes in order to advance the common cause of humanity.

Even if the writers we cite are only partly correct in their analyses, it would seem that a challenging future beckons us, albeit a rather dangerous one. Ordinary people everywhere have an unprecedented potential to grasp the levers of change. Moreover, much of this is given added tension by our growing capacity to wonder whether certain physical and social limits may now have been reached in humanity's long scramble for material progress. If so, then the project of modernity centred around the nation state may now need to be drastically rethought and renegotiated. Globalism – as both cause and consequence of such ideas – is at the centre of an alternative vision.

If you would like to know more ●

Roland Robertson is a leading sociologist of globalization who blazed the trail that others now follow. Although his book, *Globalization* (1992), is quite advanced, you should sample some chapters, especially 1, 3, 5, 6 and 12.

David Harvey's *The Condition of Postmodernity* (1989) is very wide ranging and raises many issues we discuss later on. Parts II and III are particularly relevant.

H. V. Perlmutter's 'On the rocky road to the first global civilization', *Human Relations*, **44**(9) 1991, 897–920 is an important article.

Robert Holton's *Globalization and The Nation State* (1998) is accessible and useful, too, for Chapter 5 of this book.

Group work ●

1. Working in small groups and drawing on your own pooled experiences, consider all those ways in which globalization has already affected *your* personal life. Organize this list around some key themes, such as holidays, leisure, preferences in cuisine, changing loyalties to sporting teams and future career prospects.

2. List the key threads that make up the warp and weft of globalization. Do you think that one or more of these have greater significance? If so, why? Have we left out any important components in our account? Prepare a comment on the key components of globalization for your class tutor/instructor.

3. Among your close friends and family who have not studied sociology, how many would (a) readily understand what is meant by globalism if it were explained to them and (b) would feel a close affinity towards its ideas? Can you explain these different propensities in terms of the particular biographies of the individuals involved?

Questions to think about •

1. To what extent does the distinction made between globalization as a set of objective processes and globalism as subjective awareness hold true?

2. What is 'time–space compression'? What implications arise from this concept?

3. Identify the main forms of transnational activity in which non-state organizations, movements and individuals engage and evaluate the different ways they may contribute to globalization and globalism.

4. Why is 'reflexivity' necessary to the appreciation of globalization?

chapter 3

Modernity and the Evolution of World Society

CONTENTS

When did humankind first become capable of understanding itself collectively? All early societies fabricated mythologies to explain their origins and to separate themselves from others. For the Sioux, the creator was the 'Great Spirit', for the Yoruba 'Olodumare', for the Jews 'Yahweh' and for the Polynesians 'Maui'. Their human followers would gain protection by the fervour and constancy of their devotion to these different deities. It was but a short step for scattered peoples to understand themselves as distinct 'humans' protected by their own god(s). Other people with whom they came into contact were thought of as potentially dangerous 'barbarians' or 'subhuman'. Through trade, travel and conquest diverse and separated societies across the globe slowly began to relate to each other – although past fears were often not far from the surface.

From about the seventeenth century, the European powers began to outstrip the rest of the world in the sophistication of their ideas, the devastating force of their military technology, the strength of their navies and the organization of economic production. This astonishing transformation in Europe's fortunes eventually enabled it to spread its new institutions all over the globe and triggered the phenomenon we call 'modernity', the logical precursor to the current era of globalization.

In this chapter we examine four successive phases of modernity and global integration:

- the development of forms of proto-globalization among a number of civilizations before the modern era commenced
- the emergence of capitalist modernity in Europe and the region's rise to global dominance
- the colonial and racial domination effected by European powers in various parts of the world
- the transformations that have taken place in the world economy since the Second World War and especially the rise of the USA.

PROTO-GLOBALIZATION

Proto-globalization – early aspirations to universalism that failed to embrace all of humanity or to attain global reach.

A number of the threads making up the garment of globalization described in Chapter 2 were already manifest in the world long before the rise of modern nation states. As empires evolved and religious domains spread, forms of **proto-globalization** developed. Historians of the pre-modern world (Needham 1969; McNeill 1971; Roberts 1992) show how many ancient societies were connected in important ways and how cultural legacies were bequeathed by declining or conquered civilizations. The ancient civilizations of the Middle East and China, of Greece and Rome, unified large areas. Even from the ninth to the thirteenth century, when Europe consisted of a patchwork of separate, fragile kingdoms and aristocratic fiefdoms, it was held together in relative tranquillity by the over-arching framework of Christianity. Christianity provided the following features:

1. The cultural universalism of shared religious belief and ritual.

2. The use of Latin as a common language of inter-state communication in addition to its use in church liturgy.

3. The power and status of the papacy as a mediator between states and a restraining influence on political rulers at many levels.

4. The organizational structure of the Latin Church itself built around various monastic orders, straddling territorial boundaries, and whose members were often drawn from many countries.

In short, the Church functioned as a powerful and unifying trans-European body for centuries (Wight 1977: 26–9, 130–4). It was assisted by other structures, especially inter-state links based on dynastic marriages, the alliances between Christian royal houses and the system of diplomacy involving rules of mutual recognition concerning emissaries and ambassadors (Bergesen 1990: 67–81).

Europe was also involved in multiple relations with other civilizations during this period. The rise and expansion of the Islamic states of the Middle East in the seventh century eventually extended Muslim influence to North Africa and over much of southern Europe. Muslim rulers were finally expelled from their last stronghold in Granada, southern Spain, in 1492. The long struggle to push back the frontiers of Islam helps account for the earlier emergence of powerful monarchies in Portugal and Spain compared with the rest of

Europe. The formation of the Holy Roman Empire in AD 962 – an alliance between Christian states – was also linked to the desire to protect Christendom from external attack (Smith 1991: 59, 62).

During this period, Islamic authority, especially on southern Europe, was considerable. Islam made important contributions to the arts and sciences, the establishment of centralized forms of government and innovations in agriculture – especially the introduction of irrigation systems. These agricultural reforms later proved highly beneficial to the semi-arid countries of Spain and Portugal. The long saga of Islamic–Christian conflict, including the Crusades – designed to liberate Palestine, the 'Holy Land', from Islamic control – created a legacy of mutual mistrust and misunderstanding of each other's cultures and intentions that still endures.

Europe's economy and trading relations also depended on links with other civilizations. Gold, brought across the Sahara by Arab camel caravans from the mines of West Africa, was Europe's most important source of bullion from Roman times until the sixteenth century. The Spanish conquest of South America opened up silver imports (Hopkins 1973: 46). With European traders tending to run a more or less permanent trade deficit with the Orient, bullion flowed east to pay for such items as Indian textiles of unrivalled quality, silk, indigo and spices. Indeed, this trade provided the principal motivation for the first explorations of the globe by Portugal and Spain starting in the fifteenth century. Colonial conquests followed (Smith 1991: 70).

However, it was by no means clear that Christianized Europe would take the lead. Not only had the Islamicized countries provided important sources of knowledge, for example in mathematics, so too had India and Persia. Indeed, other civilizations had long been far ahead of Europe in many spheres. This is especially true of China from where many inventions, ideas and much technological knowledge flowed to Europe during the fourteenth and fifteenth centuries. According to Jones (1988: 73–84) even before this time the Sung dynasty in China had attained hitherto unsurpassed levels of economic development. China had developed irrigation, terracing and manuring in agriculture; the techniques evolved for manufacturing iron, especially the use of coke in blast furnaces; the harnessing of water power for spinning cloth; the growth of specialized regional markets; and state investment in canals and other public assets. Some of these innovations were not widely adopted in Europe until the early eighteenth century.

Despite the significance of these early exchanges between civilizations and the expansionist ambitions of ancient empires like Rome, there are important differences between such forms of proto-globalization and the contemporary situation. This also holds for the universalizing religions of former times, including Islam and Christianity. These were universalizing in the sense that they *aspired* to reach all people. However, they never *attained* the influence that globalization and globalism have achieved in today's world. There are several reasons for this:

1. The globalizing missions of ancient empires and religions did not incorporate more than a minority of people even within their own limited domains of influence.

2. People everywhere lacked detailed knowledge of other cultures. What knowledge the tiny educated minorities possessed was fragmentary and often distorted by bigotry and reliance on a few travellers' hearsay.

3. Most of these ancient empires and religions viewed the world in terms of a clear division between the 'civilized' and the 'barbarian', between those who had been converted and those who lived without the benefits of a 'true' religion. The ancient Greeks and Romans, Islam and Christianity, the empires of Japan and China and the European expansionists all shared such narrow views.

4. Thus, their mission was to *civilize* non-believers or foreign barbarians and this involved a one-way transmission of 'culture' from the superior to the subordinate group. The possibility of mutual acceptance and interaction on equal terms was inconceivable. Refusal by foreign migrants to accept submission or conversion often meant exclusion from mainstream society and persecution.

CAPITALIST MODERNITY: EUROPEAN FOUNDATIONS

A number of significant changes took place in Western Europe between the sixteenth and eighteenth centuries. This 'nexus of features' is known as 'modernity'. As Albrow (1996: 55) maintains, modernity 'included the combination of rationality, territoriality, expansion, innovation, applied science, the state, citizenship, bureaucratic organization and many other elements'. Here, we want to concentrate on three of these elements:

- the emergence of the nation state
- the development of science
- the rise of a body of universal secular thought – 'the Enlightenment'.

> **Major Concept**
>
> **CAPITALISM**
>
> *In capitalist economies wealth-producing resources are largely privately owned rather than being subject to family, community or customary control. Most producers depend on wage employment for their livelihoods instead of self-provisioning, while the goods they produce are commodities sold in markets. Moreover, production is organized almost entirely for profit. This is earmarked for re-investment and further wealth accumulation.*

Each of these developments was mutually reinforcing. Each helped create an environment hospitable to the eventual emergence of industrial **CAPITALISM** and the process of modernity. Drawing on important contributions to historical sociology by writers such as Tilly (1975) and Skocpol (1979), Giddens (1985) argues that the emergence of the European nation state was probably the single most crucial force accounting for the rise of successful capitalism in Western Europe.

The nation state system

Unlike other world civilizations, Europe consisted of a number of autonomous countries in close proximity to one another, each of more or less equal power. Their survival as independent entities in a climate of nearly continuous war required a long process of internal state-building. This culminated in the rise of a succession of powerful rulers. The state's bureaucratic reach and control over its population was progressively strengthened and deepened through such measures as:

- increasing tax revenues
- improving communications
- partially taming the nobility by making it more dependent on the perks derived from state office

- centralizing the nation by suppressing regional identities
- monopolizing the most efficient means of violence for conducting wars
- encouraging and subsidizing technological and craft development
- investing in naval and army strength
- nurturing local trading classes whose wealth could be taxed or borrowed to help finance state expansion.

Mercantilism – a theory prevalent in the seventeenth to early nineteenth centuries based on the idea that a nation's stock of gold and silver signified its wealth.

Alongside all this, many governments pursued a policy of national economic aggrandizement, called *mercantilism*. European states engaged in naval warfare, amassed gold and silver, gave preference to domestic business and, wherever possible, insisted that goods be carried in nationally owned ships.

The key role of actual and potential inter-state violence and competition in stimulating these changes seems clear. What resulted was a fragile balance of power between the various European states and an elaborate system of alliances. No state was sufficiently ascendant to crush its rivals permanently and to create an empire. Had one giant European empire emerged, similar to the Russian or Ottoman empires, internal reform would probably have been stifled as there would have been little external pressure on rulers to tolerate such things as the growth of a vibrant CIVIL SOCIETY of independent entrepreneurs, craftsmen, scientists and intellectuals. Again, in a large empire, high-ranking officials would have been recruited on the basis of aristocratic privilege rather than merit. Moreover, internal reform undoubtedly contributed to making the process of state- and nation-building more effective, for they generated far more resources of every kind than were generally available in empires.

These much-strengthened states also created the momentum for various forms of nineteenth-century state-led industrialization. Moves towards industrialization were further driven by the rise of populist nationalism based on the notion of equal citizenship (an idea we will return to in Chapter 5) generated by the 1789 French Revolution. Other factors were the rapid emergence of an industrial bourgeoisie in Britain and the onset of the world's first major industrial revolution beginning around 1770. In fact, manifestations of industrialism were discernible prior to the 1770s. However, we can usefully date the increasingly widespread deployment of machinery – driven by non-animal sources of power – and full-time wage workers in permanent factories, from around that time. It took about another 70 years for factory production to spread from cotton textiles to most other industries.

The technological and economic lead the industrial revolution gave offered Britain military opportunities not available to other nations. Not surprisingly, the British example was eventually followed by other imitative, modernizing governments in Europe and the newly independent American states in the following decades.

Major Concept

CIVIL SOCIETY

This consists of the networks of political groups and voluntary associations emerging in the social space between the individual and the state. These bodies are engaged in expressing their members' interests and in trying to shape national political culture – its values, goals and type of decision-making practices. A flourishing civil society is likely to foster compromise, innovation, vigorous public debate and the minimizing of state interference in social life.

Key Moment

The Enlightenment

The Enlightenment was a body of influential ideas that gradually spread across Europe during the eighteenth century. Its optimistic view of the potential for human progress through the power of reason was considerably assisted by advances in science and philosophy. Enlightenment thinkers saw the importance of critical reason, scepticism and doubt, but were certain that self-realization could be attained through practical involvement in, and attempts to transform, the material world.

European Enlightenment thought

We have already referred to the **Enlightenment**. This was a body of influential ideas that gradually spread across Europe during the eighteenth century. Its optimistic view of the potential for human progress through the power of reason was considerably assisted by the scientific discoveries and advances achieved in the previous two centuries by people such as Copernicus (Figure 3.1), Bacon and Newton (Badham 1986: 10–20). Their ideas, in turn, contributed to the continuing development of science while boosting the orientations towards modernity. Enlightenment thinkers included such philosophers and writers as Hume, Diderot, Montesquieu, Condorcet, Voltaire, Kant and Goethe (Box 3.1).

Box 3.1   The central ideas of the Enlightenment

1. The notion that humans are social animals whose cultures and individual capacities for good or evil are not innate or fixed but originate in social relationships and so can be modified and improved.

2. A belief in the importance of critical reason, scepticism and doubt.

3. The human capacity to utilise these resources through observation, empirical testing and the acceptance of the fallibility of all knowledge.

4. A consequent rejection of the intolerant, closed ways of thinking associated with blind religious faith and metaphysical speculation.

5. The notion that all human beings have a right to self-direction and development – best achieved where governments became constitutional or accountable.

6. The possibility of attaining self-realization through practical involvement in, and attempts to transform, the material world.

Source: Seidman (1983: Chapter 1)

Figure 3.1   Copernicus minutely examines the globe

Together, the arguments of Enlightenment thinkers added up to a virtual revolution. The ideal modern person was seen as a unique individual with enormous potential for learning and improvement and deserving of the inalienable right to freedom. Implicit in these ideas was the promise of a tolerant, multicultural and secular society engaged in the pursuit of human progress through scientific endeavour and free from unaccountable government, religious bigotry and superstition.

Those who wrote the US Constitution of 1787 in the wake of the **American Revolution** perhaps best exemplified the practical possibilities of the Enlightenment ideals. The Constitution began with the famous preamble: 'We hold these truths to be self-evident, that all men are created equal and have the right to life, liberty, property and the pursuit of happiness.' At the time, it barely entered the heads of the founders of the US state that these rights should also be granted to women, or to Native and African Americans, as these groups' representatives now often angrily point out. We fully concur in their criticisms, but the argument has to be taken one stage further. That the Constitution was proclaimed in universal terms *at all* meant that representatives of the excluded 'others' could eventually use its provisions in their struggles to join the 'self' and the included. This eventually allowed them to mitigate some of the many injustices perpetrated against them.

> ### Key Moment
> #### American Revolution
> *Following a war with the British starting in 1775, the USA became the first modern country to win independence from colonial rule. Representatives of the individual states finally agreed at the Philadelphia Convention in 1787 to establish a federal government with limited powers enshrined in a written constitution.*

Marx's analysis of capitalism

The Enlightenment provided a powerful intellectual critique of the highly regulated forms of feudal life but, as Marx understood more clearly than did his contemporaries, feudalism was also a spent force in economic terms. Its successor *mode of production*, industrial capitalism, was a highly dynamic and indeed unstoppable force for generating social transformation. Many preceding changes had paved the way for the emergence of capitalism, but especially significant were:

A **mode of production** was used by Marx to describe the characteristic social relations that marked particular ways of organizing production. Slavery, feudalism and capitalism are all modes of production in this sense.

- the creation of a fully commoditized economy in which everything, including land and labour, had a price and so could be bought and sold in a market
- the exercise of, often violent, measures to dislodge self-sufficient peasants and craft producers from their farms and workshops – so forcing them in ever greater numbers to live by selling their labour to capitalist entrepreneurs as wage workers.

This separation of direct producers from their *means* of production (from their land, animals and tools) was a crucial precondition for the rise of industrial capitalism. Once self-sufficient producers were brought under the domination of capital, the way was open for three crucial changes to take place in the productive system, changes that had never been realized before on such a scale:

1. Labourers could be organized more efficiently alongside the plant, tools and machinery, for they had in effect contracted to sell their labour for an agreed price to the entrepreneur concerned. The employer, in turn, was therefore free to decide how both equipment and workers should be utilized, for he (it was nearly always a 'he') and not the employees now owned the means of production.

2. Incorporating producers into the system as dependent wage-workers made them unable to supply their own means of daily subsistence from self-employment. This simultaneously transformed them into consumers who would spend their incomes in the very same markets that were being created by the growing capitalist system.

3. Once in existence, capitalism contained certain internal motors that drove it relentlessly onwards to subjugate the remnants of pre-capitalist craft and peasant production, by out-competing them wherever these were encountered and constantly transforming its own system of business organization and technological capacities.

These built-in mechanisms for restless, perpetual change included the drive for profit and business expansion, competition between individual capitalists and firms and the inevitability of class conflict between wage-labourers and entrepreneurs over working conditions and the distribution of profits. Together, these factors impelled capitalists constantly to find ways to cheapen and improve their products so as to capture new markets or to displace their rivals. As the labour force gained in maturity and organizational strength, employers were compelled to raise the productivity of labour by investing in more advanced plant and machinery and adopting more streamlined systems of business organization and marketing.

An important consequence was the tendency for capitalism to expand the productive forces by developing ever more advanced technology, harnessing the power of science, increasing the scale of production and developing business arrangements to facilitate greater capital pooling. Thus, as Marx observed, nothing under capitalism ever remains static for long. Rather, constant change, not only in the productive process but at all levels of society, is inevitable. Another consequence, again apparent to Marx, was capitalism's drive to expand globally (see Box 3.2).

Box 3.2   Marx and Engels argue that capitalism must expand globally

In the passages that follow, Marx and Engels vividly anticipate most of the globalizing consequences we have since come to associate with capitalism. These are: (a) the western drive to incorporate the non-western world into the global economy through imperialist conquest; (b) the necessity for independent but backward countries to adopt their own local capitalist projects; (c) the potentially universalizing power of materialism and rising consumerist aspirations in fostering the desire for change; and (d) the tendency for capitalism to transform societies in rather similar ways wherever it takes root.

'The need for a constantly expanding market for its products chases the bourgeoisie over the whole surface of the globe. It must nestle everywhere, settle everywhere, establish connections everywhere.

The bourgeoisie has through its exploitation of the world-market given a cosmopolitan character to production and consumption in every country... All old-established industries have been destroyed or are daily being destroyed. They are dislodged by new industries, whose introduction becomes a life and death question for all civilized nations,

(cont'd)

by industries that no longer work up indigenous raw material, but raw material drawn from the remotest zones; industries whose products are consumed, not only at home, but in every quarter of the globe. In place of the old wants, satisfied by the products of the country, we find new wants, requiring for their satisfaction the products of distant lands and climes. In place of the old local and national seclusion and self-sufficiency, we have intercourse in every direction, universal interdependence of nations. And as in material, so also in intellectual production... National one-sidedness and narrow-mindedness become more and more impossible...

The bourgeoisie, by the rapid development of all instruments of production, by the immensely facilitated means of communications, draws all, even the most barbarian, nations into civilization. The cheap prices of its commodities are the heavy artillery with which it batters down all Chinese walls, with which it forces the barbarians' intensely obstinate hatred to foreigners to capitulate. It compels all nations, on pain of extinction, to adopt the bourgeois mode of production; it compels them to introduce what it calls civilization in their midst, that is, to become bourgeois themselves. In one word, it creates a world after its own image.'

Source: Marx and Engels (1967/1848: 83–4)

The growth of rationality

In looking at the spread of modernity, contemporary sociologists lay more emphasis on cultural and intellectual changes than on Marx's economic argument. The belief in progress through rationality was a major factor in transforming societies. This idea lies deep in European cultural and political history but was particularly associated with the gradual extension of literacy, the development of science, the pressures for more democracy and the heritage of the Enlightenment. Also, once established, capitalist rationality and modernity were mutually supportive, each creating scope for the other.

Giddens (1990) sees modernity as consisting of three kinds of mutually reinforcing orientations. Together, their power to underpin and shape our world has slowly grown and spread. He oversimplifies the complexity of 'tradition' in arguing that pre-modern people were mostly rooted in specific and bounded locations – village communities – where they spent their lives working, worshipping, raising families and socializing with the same few people. However, there is no doubt that with vastly improved, cheaper and safer means of travel and communication and the ever more precise measurement of space and time, people were increasingly able to experience time and space as separate from each other and disconnected from concrete places. It became possible for social exchanges to flourish independently of place and time, across vast distances and time zones.

Similarly, there was a diminishing dependence on face-to-face ties to particular people and specific social contexts. These changes, or 'disembedding' processes, meant that social life became more dependent on abstract systems of knowledge and impersonal forms of communication. Critical here was the wide dissemination of education and literacy and a generalized use of symbolic tokens such as money and credit. But also essential was the proliferation of expert systems, or professional services, in which clients could safely place their trust.

As we saw in the last chapter, Giddens (1990: 36–45) also sees self-monitoring or 'reflexivity' as fundamental to modernity. He claims that whereas 'all forms of social life are partly constituted by actors' knowledge of them', what is 'character-istic of modernity is… the presumption of wholesale reflexivity – which of course includes reflection upon the nature of reflection itself' (1990: 38, 39). In modern societies, self-monitoring is applied to all aspects of life, it takes place constantly and is undertaken as much by organizations and governments as by individuals. Indeed, the discipline of sociology itself, in collecting and interpreting knowledge about social action, has become heavily implicated in the process of reflexivity at many societal levels. Not only do governments and other agents draw on socio-logical knowledge to assist them in modifying such things as laws and social poli-cies, but the changes brought about in social life as a result of such actions in turn require sociologists to respond by rethinking their concepts.

Giddens (1990) avers that these three orientations facilitate the reordering or 'stretching' of social relationships across the world and sustain complex interac-tions between people situated far apart. Indeed, he explicitly states that modernity is an 'inherently globalizing' force (pp. 63, 177). Important though this argument is, it implies that globalization is simply modernity (plus capitalism and the nation state) writ large. This seems rather a limited view because, as we show in Chapter 2, globalization can be said to have generated certain unique properties, especially the emergence of a global consciousness we have called globalism. This and other features could not necessarily have been inferred solely from a familiarity with the structures and orientations of modernity. As Robertson (1992: 60) insists, global-ization has acquired a 'general autonomy' and 'logic' of its own.

RACE AND COLONIALISM

European countries were able to spread out of their continent precisely because of their economic, military and intellectual lead, often borrowed from other civi-lizations. The decisive advances were in seafaring and navigational techniques – improvements in the compass, navigational charts, astrolabe and rudder – and the use of gunpowder and firearms, cannons and guns (Smith 1991: 56). The Portuguese, who led the field in navigational exploration, reached the tip of southern Africa in 1489. Vasco da Gama finally entered the Indian Ocean in 1497. Brazen exploits, including the defeat of the Muslim fleet in the Indian Ocean in 1509 and the creation of a whole series of forts and trading stations across Asia, soon followed. Thus began the long period of European trading domination over much of the non-western world and the extension of colonial rule that was even-tually to follow (Smith 1991: 77–8).

The European explorers met small, scattered societies (like the Khoi-khoi and San in South Africa) as well as large empires like China. There the emperor and his court believed that theirs was the 'central kingdom' around which all others were scattered. Strange stories abounded. As late as the Opium War (1839–42), waged by the European powers to control the profitable drugs trade, many Chinese thought that Europeans would die spectacularly of the explosive conse-quences of constipation if deprived of rhubarb (used then as a purgative). English sailors were depicted in drawings with tails behind their legs.

Such depictions were the mirror images of the racial bigotry that was eventu-ally to characterize much of the European colonial expansion. We examine race and racism in more detail in Chapter 6. Here we merely note that the disdainful manifestations of nineteenth-century European power contrasted markedly with earlier European travellers' awed wonder and astonishment at seeing the Taj Mahal (Figure 3.2), the delicacy of the Benin bronzes (Figure 3.3), the palaces of Iztapalapa and the massive pyramids of Egypt. At the time of the encounter with Europe these buildings and artefacts showed that other advanced civilizations had often surpassed any equivalent achievements in Europe.

Figure 3.2   The Taj Mahal

Figure 3.3   Benin bronze, representing an Oba (late 16th century, Nigeria)

This more generous spirit was also shown by the Enlightenment thinkers who regarded humanity as a single species on a gradual path to self-improvement, whatever the dissimilarities and lags between peoples and regions. All were capable of reaching the end-state of 'civilization'. There was an undoubted arrogance in such a view, which implied that what obtained in eighteenth-century France and Germany was the preferred destination of all humanity. However, this **ethnocentrism** did not approximate later racist postures and, even in the midst of this ethnocentrism, there was some recognition that humanity had forfeited as well as gained something through 'civilization'. Milton's famous poem *Paradise Lost* and Rousseau's celebration of the 'noble savage' expressed an idea of an Arcadian innocence where minds, bodies and emotions united with the natural world in a symbiotic and healthy innocence.

> **Ethnocentrism** derives from the Greek word for people, *ethnos*. Ethnocentrists see their community or nation as the model against which all others have to be judged.

Most European imperialists and colonialists of the late nineteenth century were not troubled by such reflections. The 'Lords of Humankind' strutted around, annexing territories in the name of their monarchs, sending out governors in plumed hats and announcing they had assumed 'the white man's burden' in civilizing the rest of earth. At the Berlin Conference in 1885 the European powers drew lines on maps and parcelled out great chunks of the world to each other. Enlightenment and Arcadian notions were swept aside as imperialists realized that there were massive fortunes to be made by subordinating the rest of humanity. Rubber trees were stolen from Brazil, gold and diamonds mined in South Africa, lumber logged from the Equatorial forests and opium extracted from China. Sugar, cocoa, tobacco and sisal plantations were established using cheap or coerced labour and speculative capital. These imperialist adventurers, the plantations they started and the financiers who propped them up were the early precursors of the transnational corporations (TNCs) discussed in Chapter 7.

The cruelty that attached to many colonial occupying forces was legendary. Take the case of South West Africa, now Namibia. After declaring that an immense African landmass now belonged to Germany, in October 1904 the military head of the occupying forces, General van Trotha, issued an extermination order directed at the local population, declaring that:

> Inside German territory every Herero tribesman, armed or unarmed, with or without cattle, will be shot. No women or children will be allowed in the territory: they will be driven back to their people or fired upon... I believe that the Herero must be destroyed as a nation.

Within a year that is virtually what happened. The Herero population dwindled from 60 000–80 000 people to 16 000 – a loss of some 75–80 per cent.

> **Social Darwinism** applied, or more often misapplied, to human situations the role assigned by Darwin to the process of natural selection in the evolution of species.

Although many peoples put up spirited fights for their independence, the superiority of European guns and military tactics usually won through. The very ease of these brutal victories promoted ideas of **Social Darwinism**, which European imperialists supposed lent support to the idea that they were inherently superior to the people they colonized. With the legacy of the Atlantic slave trade and the colonial subjugation of all of sub-Saharan Africa other than Ethiopia, it is difficult, even now, for Africans to escape discrimination and prejudice.

After the Second World War there was a new balance of international forces, which was to threaten notions of racial superiority. Japan had given the British a bloody nose in the Far East. Through the force of mass protest and led by a remarkable leader, Mahatma Gandhi, India persuaded the British to leave, becoming independent in 1947. This was the prelude to the decolonization of the rest of Asia, Africa, the Middle East and the Caribbean. European expansion and colonialism had fulfilled its historic mission. It had drawn far-flung parts of the world into a relationship with the global economy. However, it had done so often with great cruelty and without the consent of the colonized peoples who, after 1945, were ready to enter a new era.

CHANGES AFTER 1945 AND THE DOMINANCE OF THE USA

To decolonization were added a number of other important changes between 1945–73, which we shall discuss in turn. Each served to enlarge and deepen the extent to which a world society was evolving:

- a long period of sustained economic growth
- the establishment of the Bretton Woods financial system
- the rise of US global economic power and political leadership
- the widespread adoption of Keynesian national economic management
- the rise of mass consumption and changes in lifestyles
- the spread of English as an international language.

Economic growth

Although estimates vary, during the long boom from 1950 to 1975, the world's economic output is said to have expanded by an unprecedented two-and-a-quarter times (Harris 1983: 30). Using slightly different dates, Hobsbawm (1994: 288) claimed that the 'golden years' of economic growth and technological development from 1950 to 1973 meant that for '80 per cent of humanity the Middle Ages ended suddenly in the 1950s; or perhaps better still they were felt to end in the 1960s'. Although most remained very poor by western standards, even people living in the colonial and ex-colonial countries were caught up in this economic transformation.

By the mid-1950s Europe and Japan had recovered from the devastation of war and were achieving new levels of prosperity. In 1959 Harold Macmillan was re-elected as the British Prime Minister with the famous slogan attributed to him, 'You've never had it so good'. Even the poor developing countries had a good decade with commodity prices for their agricultural produce and minerals attaining heights never achieved before or since. During the 1960s, Japanese might and the rising power of the newly industrializing countries (NICs) became evident, along with rapid rates of industrialization and urbanization in countries like Brazil and Taiwan.

The Bretton Woods financial system

Bretton Woods is the name of a small town in New Hampshire where 44 countries, mainly allies of the USA, met in July 1944 to formulate policies for global economic co-operation. The conference played a major role in stabilizing the post-war financial situation (Brett 1985: 62–79). Here, it was agreed that western countries would operate a system of semi-fixed exchange rates in managing the

Devaluation – lowering the
value of your currency
against that of your
competitor countries to
cheapen the price of your
exports and make their
imports more expensive.

value of their currencies while minimizing as far as possible their use of trade-inhibiting policies such as currency **devaluation**, tariffs and import controls. Meanwhile, the USA agreed to stabilize the dollar – already by far the world's strongest currency – tying its value to gold reserves and permitting its currency to be used freely as world money.

The Bretton Woods system also involved establishing several key economic international governmental organizations (IGOs). Of these, the most important were:

- the World Bank, designed to help individual countries finance long-term infrastructural projects through providing loans at favourable rates
- the International Monetary Fund (IMF) which provided short-term financial assistance
- the General Agreement on Trade and Tariffs (GATT), a world forum to facilitate regular discussions between member countries on measures to reduce trade barriers and related issues.

US global economic power and political leadership

The USA was very powerful economically at the close of the First World War, but periods of isolation and economic protectionism restricted its global role. After the Second World War its economy emerged undamaged with stronger, re-equipped industries. This time it assumed the burden of managing world capitalism, including its central role in the Bretton Woods system. Generously, it kept its own huge economy open to imports while tolerating some protectionist measures by weaker countries while they recovered from war. It also freely permitted the purchase of its technology. The USA became the world's leading creditor nation, supplying grants to Europe (through the Marshall Aid Plan) and Japan. It supplied loans on favourable terms to other countries, although this was something of a Trojan horse, allowing US-located TNCs to penetrate new markets.

The East–West **Cold War** confrontation dominated global politics from 1947 to 1989. It created a bipolar system with each side managed and ruled by its dominant power – the communist bloc by the Soviet Union and the capitalist democracies by the USA. Each side tried to gain the technical lead in a race to acquire supremacy in nuclear arms and space-age technology. President Truman persuaded the US Congress to pour dollars into the national and world economy via arms expenditure and military aid. There were large deployments of troops in Europe and Asia, while the onset of the Korean War helped to encourage the long post-war boom (Arrighi 1994: 273–98).

Successive US administrations encouraged further decolonization by France, Britain and the Netherlands. There were political and economic motives for doing so. The USA wished to prevent the spread of communist movements and regimes, especially in the war-torn Asian countries (although it failed to do so in North Korea, China and Vietnam). It also wanted to penetrate the previously closed colonial markets. The European powers had used these markets as captive outlets for their home industries and as key sources of raw materials for metropolitan industries. The USA now wanted 'a share of the action'.

Key Moment

The Cold War

Led by the Soviet Union and the USA, the world was split into two antagonistic camps over the period 1947–89. This involved an ideological battle between capitalist democracy versus socialist planning, a massive build-up of arms and the twin races to achieve supremacy in nuclear and space-age technology. Despite several flash points, for example in 1948 and 1962 (see time line in Box 3.3), the superpowers themselves never engaged in head-on aggression. Rather, conflict was deflected into regional or minor wars involving the developing countries – as in the Korean and Vietnam Wars.

Box 3.3   Global peace and war

1945   End of Second World War but the onset of the nuclear age when, in August, the US exploded two atomic bombs in Japan. The UN was established and in December it issued the Universal Declaration of Human Rights.

1947   Cold War 'officially' began with President Truman's declaration that the USA would protect democracies from the threat presented by totalitarian (communist) regimes. In Europe, the Iron Curtain – an expression coined earlier by the British war-time Prime Minister, Winston Churchill – divided the communist Warsaw Pact countries from the western NATO (North Atlantic Treaty Alliance) allies.

1948   From June (until May 1949), the USSR blockaded West Berlin. This triggered extensive air lifts to provide food and fuel to the citizens of West Berlin.

1949   China went communist under the leadership of Mao Zedong and drove the nationalist and pro-capitalist forces into exile in Taiwan. The USSR exploded an atomic bomb.

1950–53 The Korean War began in 1950 when the communist North invaded the South with Chinese support. The USA promised military protection for East Asia.

1957   The USSR launched 'sputnik', the first human-piloted space craft. The space-race began in earnest.

1962   Cuban missile crisis. Soviet nuclear missiles placed in communist Cuba led to a confrontation with the USA. The world was poised for nuclear war but this was narrowly averted when Soviet premier Khrushchev agreed to remove the missiles.

1963–75 American military involvement against North Vietnam's largely peasant army. After years of heavy US bombing and escalating conflict, US forces were pushed into a stalemate and withdrew.

1969   Moon landing by US team; the majesty of planet earth became fully apparent to everyone with media access.

1972   Rapprochement between the USA and China following President Nixon's visit.

1980s   President Reagan initiated his 'Star Wars' nuclear 'defence' programme. The sheer expense involved highlighted Soviet deficiencies, especially in computerization, and declining ability to fund the arms race. But it also shackled the USA with colossal national debts ($3 trillion by the early 1990s).

1989   Soviet premier Gorbachev relinquished further claims to 'defend' Warsaw Pact countries; collapse of Eastern Europe communist regimes as popular revolutions broke out. Cold War ended.

1992   End of communism in Soviet Union and ancient Russian empire began to dissolve into independent republics. Gulf War to reverse Iraqi invasion of Kuwait and 'safeguard' world oil reserves. Sanctioned by UN, but demonstrated US leadership and power was now unrivalled.

Keynesian national economic management

John Maynard Keynes was a major twentieth-century economist. In the 1930s, when unemployment brought on by the Great Depression was causing widespread distress, his theories challenged orthodox views on how best to explain and deal with the booms and slumps characteristic of capitalism. They also had important political and social implications. The uncertainties and diverging expectations of consumers, savers and investors often worked against each other and made rational economic decision-making difficult. He saw that, left to themselves, market forces tended to generate widening inequalities of income and wealth, making it impossible for mass demand to reach levels sufficient to keep consumption, investment and therefore employment at politically acceptable levels. He suggested governments play a more proactive role in spending on public investment and stimulating demand – so creating jobs and investment.

Although far from being a socialist, Keynes thought that governments should use the tax system to redistribute income from rich to poor (this is called 'progressive taxation'). He reasoned that the poor would normally spend (rather than save) any increased income and that this would expand the economy by fuelling demand. At the time, such deliberate 'interference' in the working of free markets was regarded as heresy, but his arguments became widely accepted by western governments in the 1940s. With widespread unemployment in the 1930s and political ferment after the Second World War, it is only a slight exaggeration to say that Keynesian policies gave capitalism a new lease of life. They also strengthened the long boom and so contributed to globalization.

Mass consumption and changes in lifestyles

The long boom after the Second World War was triggered by an increasing demand for goods and services. These were produced with corresponding efficiency – using mass production methods based on those pioneered by Henry Ford in his motorcar assembly plants in Detroit (see Chapter 4 for a full discussion). Prosperity helped fuel important changes in social life, especially in the advanced countries. Life expectancy rose and many people were better educated than ever before, even in the developing countries. The consequences of such changes first became widely evident in the 1950s. However, they almost certainly generated cumulative effects, which by the late 1960s were giving rise to the demand for, and higher expectation of, greater personal freedom of choice in all spheres of life. Meanwhile, globalization meant that such powerful influences could not be contained within the rich countries but spread to the communist and developing world through education, the mass media, tourism and TNCs. Box 3.4 provides a time line of these changes.

Box 3.4   The desire for more personal freedom

Private leisure and consumption

1954	Dawn of the TV age. Thirty per cent of households in the UK had TV. (This rose to 89 per cent by 1963.)
1950s	The invention of the 'teenager'. Youth cultures became ever more evident and generated their own markets, musical and other cultural concerns.

(cont'd)

1956	The new genre of 'rock music' emerged. Elvis Presley achieved international fame with 'Heartbreak Hotel' and the film, *Jailhouse Rock*. Adolescent rebellion became fashionable. Popular culture became big business.
1960s	Age of mass ownership of the motorcar got underway. Suburbanization increased while inner-city zones declined. Spread of supermarket shopping.
1960s	The rapid expansion of systems of higher education across the world.
1960s	International tourist travel takes off.

Action for greater personal freedom and justice

1954	Beginning of Civil Rights Movement in the USA by African Americans. Reached its heyday in the mid-1960s.
Mid-1960s	Anti-war Movement in the US against involvement in Vietnam began and spread to Europe. Coalesced with drug culture and with the 'hippie' revolt against continuing bureaucratic restraints on sexual/personal freedom.
1968	May 'revolution' by workers and students in France against the materialist pressures of capitalism.
Late 1960s	Feminist movement for gender equality took off in the USA and soon spread.
1969	Birth of the Gay Rights Movement in the USA.

The spread of English as an international language

The use of English as a world language (ironically called a *lingua franca*) has fostered the emergence of a world society. Historically, spoken English came to occupy this role when Britain emerged as the world's first industrial nation. It controlled the largest empire until well after the Second World War and, until the First World War, was the leading world supplier of investment capital, banking services and commercial shipping networks. When the USA assumed this leading role after 1945, by an accident of history it also happened to be an English-speaking country. Moreover, the USA continues to dominate the various mass media and advertising, which are so influential in shaping global consumer and lifestyle aspirations. As the world economy has grown, so too has its reliance on English as a world language (Table 3.1).

Table 3.1   English language-speakers, 1990

Number of countries where English is dominant	*75 (out of 170)*
Number who speak English as a first language	377,132,600
Number who speak English as a second language	140,000,000
Total English-speakers in the 75 countries	517,132,600

Source: Crystal (1995: 108–9)

REVIEW

A world society does not drop from the sky like an alien invasion. It has been emerging in a halting way ever since the inhibitions induced by local beliefs and mythology were first questioned by the world religions – particularly through the spread of Buddhism, Islam and Christianity. However, a narrow ethnocentric outlook was challenged more fundamentally by the rise of modernity in Europe.

The formation of powerful, well-armed competing nation states provided a basis and a motivation for capitalist industrialization. Meanwhile, the Enlightenment led to new cultural and scientific outlooks that fed into modernizing impulses. Eventually the momentum for change created by the fusion of capitalism and modernity proved to be uncontainable. Empowered by new wealth and technology and energized by capitalist competition for markets and raw materials as well as by national rivalry, the European powers subjected other peoples to their rule. This served to widen markets and spread European languages and social and political institutions.

During the twentieth century globalization has been given another massive boost by the emergence of the USA as a giant economic engine and then as a superpower. From the end of the Second World War and at least up to the 1970s, its economic, ideological and military leadership of the West went largely unquestioned. Although the Soviet Union occasionally challenged the USA, state communism was weaker than it appeared. By 1989, it was failing and soon collapsed.

In recent decades, other trends have become apparent in the moves towards a world society. Globalizing forces have become largely autonomous and self-sustaining. Less and less does their survival or expansion depend upon the actions of particular nations, even very powerful ones. The ability of nations and states to cope with the problems presented by globalization, for example, worldwide pollution or unaccountable TNCs, is likely to depend upon the active support they receive from a whole gamut of transnational groups, interests and experts.

A paradox has become apparent at the heart of globalization. On the one hand, we see the virtual worldwide spread of certain very powerful universalizing trends. Capitalist modernity generates both similar experiences – for example, in education, health, industry, market exchange, urban life – and common aspirations for greater personal freedom. (Of course, not all of these are beneficial as we will see later in this book.) On the other hand, a more complex, polycentric world of competing industrial economies, each with its own version of modernity and particular cultural legacy on offer, has replaced the bipolar one of the superpowers. We live in a world of many robust players, transnational and national, state and non-state, and each is determined to influence local and global events. We will encounter these two themes many times in the chapters that follow.

If you would like to know more ●

Formations of Modernity, edited by Stuart Hall and Bram Gieben (1992), offers a highly accessible discussion of the nature and causes of modernity. You may find Chapters 1, 2 and 6 especially helpful.

Anthony Giddens's *The Nation State and Violence* (1985) provides a readable account of the rise of the European absolutist states.

K. Marx and F. Engels's short pamphlet, *The Communist Manifesto*, first published in 1848, the year of revolutions across Europe, offers a passionate and clear introduction to their theory of capitalism.

A. E. Brett, *The World Economy Since the War* (1985) contains an excellent analysis of the post-Second World War world economy.

Group work ●

1. List and briefly outline the early historical phases of the emergence of world society that we have discussed. What might be added to this list that we have omitted or neglected, and why?

2. Pair off. Each pair will look up the history of the European occupation of one non-European country (Kenya, India, Nigeria, Senegal, South Africa, for example). How would you characterize the racial attitudes of the occupying force?

3. Draw up a list of all the 'economics words' we have used in the final part of this chapter. Start with 'deflation', 'recession', 'protectionism' and mercantilism'. Can you spot any others in this chapter? Find their meanings in a dictionary and write them down.

Questions to think about ●

1. What were the main historical antecedents to the evolution of a world society and why were they limited in their effects?

2. Which one or more of the historical causes discussed do you think exercised the strongest influence in intensifying the process of globalization? Give your reasons.

3. Outline the main ways in which the USA played a leading role in reshaping the post-war world.

4. Why were there such dramatic changes in people's lifestyles, at least in the rich countries, in the 1950s and 60s?

The Changing World of Work

Almost every day, someone reminds us that we live in an age of rapid and unprecedented technological change and intensifying international competition. Some see this as heralding 'new times', offering opportunities for greater individual freedom and self-realization and a more democratic, decentralized, less hierarchical workplace and society. Others see only 'hard times' – a present and future dominated by fragmenting businesses engaged in downsizing their plant and shrinking their cores of permanent employees. This road, they fear, inevitably means widespread unemployment, the casualization of the workforce and widening social divisions.

How people experience and cope with work is a central and enduring theme in sociology, although much recent work in the discipline has been also concerned with consumerism, leisure and personal lifestyles, popular culture and the media. Despite this new emphasis, for most of us the passport that gives access to the pleasures of contemporary non-work life is the money we earn from paid employment in the production of goods and services. What is the changing nature of work in the global age and in what ways do these transformations impact on us? In this chapter we begin by looking at the structural changes that have impacted on the labour market before going on to discuss the effects of these changes on working people's lives.

ACCUMULATION AND REPRODUCTION: AN OVERVIEW

The issues of capitalist accumulation and reproduction have long preoccupied sociologists and others. You will recall that in Chapter 3 we considered Marx's argument that the rise of industrial capitalism in the West required a preceding period of often-violent 'primitive capital accumulation'. State power was used to separate peasants and craftsmen from their independent sources of livelihood and to create private property. Somewhat later Weber, in his famous book on *The Protestant Ethic and the Spirit of Capitalism* (1977) also speculated about the possible cultural – as well as political – origins of early capitalism, which he saw partly in terms of the unique, cumulative legacy of European tradition. This included the powerful tensions evoked by Protestantism that drove individual converts towards a life of ceaseless work and rational striving in the hope of earning religious salvation.

Not only does capitalism first need to be carved, often brutally, out of traditional cultures, but once set on a course for industrialization it cannot operate alone and unaided. Capitalist economies continue to require various kinds of support. From the state, among other things, domestic capital needs taxation policies that encourage investment, some protection in the early stages of industrialization from overseas competition and a willingness to finance public assets that enhance international competitiveness – especially infrastructure and rising educational attainment. For their part, society's members must be willing, for example, to pay taxes, tolerate a degree of inequality, respond to material incentives and be able to cope with constant changes in technology along with the adjustments these dictate in private lifestyles.

'Regulation' theorists such as Aglietta (1979) and Lipietz (1987) have recently added to our understanding of the issue of capitalist reproduction. They argue that despite its proneness to periodic crises, capitalism often passes through long periods of relatively uninterrupted economic growth. However, these eras of stability require the conjunction of two sets of conditions, a 'regime of accumulation' and a 'mode of regulation':

- *A regime of accumulation* This refers to the way production is actually organized in factories, mines, offices and other workplaces. Employers seek to maximize profits both by paying their employees less than the value of what they have helped to produce and by ensuring the efficient control and disposition of labour and machinery at the workplace. Profits are then 'realized' by selling commodities on the market. Both capitalists and society also need to strike some sort of balance between the proportion of profit invested in expansion and the share which is consumed by individuals (as wages) and by governments (through taxation) on public goods such as health and education.

- *A mode of regulation* A regime of accumulation requires a parallel set of conditions, called a mode of regulation. This involves common acceptance of a cluster of rules (for example, in relation to negotiation procedures), norms, institutions, cultural expectations about 'proper' consumption levels and supportive political policies. By guaranteeing social stability and appropriate government these ensure the reproduction of capitalism over time.

When one or both of these sets of conditions ceases to be effective a period of crisis is likely to erupt. Profits fall, economic growth slows down and signs of social conflict and distress become evident. Radical restructuring of the production process and a new mode of regulation may become necessary before a new era of stable accumulation can emerge. Similarly, an enduring period of capitalist accumulation is probably more likely when a suitable regulatory climate is also in place in the ordering of world as well as national politics. Indeed, this seems to have been the case during the years between roughly 1948 and the early 1970s, as we now show.

THE FORDIST REGIME OF ACCUMULATION

Major Concept
FORDISM

Named after its pioneer, the car maker Henry Ford, this industrial system involved the mass production of standardized goods by huge, integrated companies. Each company was composed of many different, specialized departments each producing components and parts that were eventually channelled towards the moving line for final assembly.

As a regime of accumulation **FORDISM** is said to have slowly increased its domination of the world economy from the end of the nineteenth century until the early 1970s. As we will see for much of this time, but especially from about 1948 to 1970, it appears to have been accompanied by a highly effective mode of regulation both at the national and world levels. Henry Ford developed 'Fordism' in his manufacture of the Model-T car at his Highland Park and Rouge plants in Detroit between 1908 and 1916 (Figure 4.1). He is generally credited with pioneering the mass production techniques imitated in many countries. The idea of a moving assembly line was copied from Chicago meat packers who, in the 1900s, adopted the practice of hanging hog carcasses from a moving overhead rail, a technique now used in many industrial processes (Figure 4.2). You will gain some idea of what it was like to work under Fordist conditions from Box 4.1.

Box 4.1   Work experience in a 1960s' Ford motor plant

Huw Beynon's (1973) classic study of the Ford motor plant at Halewood in Liverpool offers a fascinating account of working life at a fairly typical mass production plant in the late 1960s. Here, we briefly glimpse some of the experiences involved. Ford established its three Halewood plants between 1958 and 1963 although its largest UK investment remained at Dagenham. At Halewood, the moving assembly line – which came to symbolize the essentially disempowering nature of twentieth-century machine-dominated 'Fordist' manufacturing – was situated in the same factory where the car bodies were painted and fitted with their final trimmings (lights, seats and so on). Over 80 per cent of the manual workers employed in a car assembly plant supplied back-up support for those working on the line.

About 16 000 different components had to be 'screwed, stuck or spot-welded' (p. 105) to the moving car bodies as they slipped down the line. Each worker was tied to his station and endlessly repeated the same fixed tasks. On average the line workers were allocated two minutes to complete each job depending on the exact 'timing' management judged was sufficient for its completion. When market demand was expanding, the management might decide to speed up the line or reduce the manning levels. This meant frequent changes to work schedules and a need for intensified output. Six minutes out of the 480-minute working day were allowed for visits to the toilet and other natural functions. Unlike workers making or supplying components, those on the moving assembly line were rarely able to increase their output by a burst of effort in order to create a brief space for smoking or chatting with work mates. Moreover, the noise levels

(cont'd)

made talking virtually impossible (workers resorted to hand signals). Workers could not disrupt the smooth sequence of operations by leaving the line or failing to complete a task in the allocated time and it became very difficult to seek temporary relief from work by socializing with work mates.

The loneliness, mind-blowing tedium and relentless pressures occasioned by working on the line generated considerable frustration. Not surprisingly, the changes to manning levels and speed-ups compounded these problems and were all frequent bones of contention between workers and management. They often generated tensions, disputes and work stoppages. How did the employees, especially those working on the line, cope with their jobs? They blanked-out their minds, thought about the relatively high wages they would spend at the weekends (better money than could be obtained by semi-skilled workers elsewhere in Liverpool), joked with their work mates or played tricks on the foremen. Some dreamt of moving to a more 'worthwhile' job.

Source: Beynon (1973)

Major Concept

ALIENATION

Marx believed that it is mainly through creative, self-directed work in the satisfaction of our own needs that we fully realize our inner selves and potential. However, under capitalism workers become estranged or alienated from their skills and their potential since now they are driven to work for capitalists in order to survive and the product of their labour no longer belongs to them. Sociologists have employed this term more generally to describe the powerlessness and lack of creativity believed to be endemic to many aspects of contemporary life.

Major Concept

TAYLORIZATION

This is the name given to the process accompanying Fordism whereby most work processes were scientifically studied by managers so as to find ways to break them down into highly specialized and efficient tasks while removing most of the skill and responsibility formerly exercised by the workers.

From the perspective of the employees, the Fordist production regime involved a number of difficult and **ALIENATING** experiences. Work was fragmented into many different activities, for example welding a particular bolt onto the corner of a toy or operating a specialized machine for pressing out one of the metal pieces used to assemble a refrigerator door. Each worker carried out one of these highly specialized tasks repeatedly, often remaining on the same job for long periods of time. This made work tedious and unsatisfying, but it simultaneously made for overall speed and efficiency.

A precondition for efficient production was the adoption of the principles of 'scientific management', or **TAYLORIZATION,** a term derived from the American engineer Frederick Taylor. From the 1890s, he played a leading role in encouraging US industrialists to measure work activity precisely while establishing the optimum time required for each task. It has been widely argued that Taylorist techniques were ultimately designed to capture the shop-floor knowledge and skills once possessed by workers and to incorporate these into machinery and management practices. This progressively deskilled the workforce and increased management's ability to control the labour process.

In a major study, Braverman (1974) argued that this progressive deskilling of work into a narrowing set of mindless, routine tasks was increasingly spreading to white-collar, office work and even to some managerial and professional activities. However, the use of information technology in many administrative tasks, along with other technological changes, has recently rendered these arguments less clear cut. At the plant level, a techno-structure of scientists, engineers and others became necessary, supported by a hierarchy of managers striving to co-ordinate the levels of multiple activities. The result was that both the creative design processes involved in production and the actual control of the latter shifted decisively from workbench to laboratory and office. These changes in work organization normally enabled management to obtain much higher and perhaps continuously rising levels of worker productivity for each given level of investment in plant and machinery.

Not surprisingly, Fordist plants required heavy and long-term investment in plant, capital-intensive equipment and research facilities. This meant that large complex corporations became the dominant forms of business enterprise in many industries. Despite its negative features, mass production also led to increased productivity, the possibility of higher wages and gradually improving work conditions. Ford introduced the $5 daily wage and considerably reduced working hours as early as 1914, although this was partly an attempt to reduce the high rates of absenteeism and labour turnover generated by the intensity and speed of work required at his plants. Neither did these gains necessarily mean that unions gained full recognition from Fordist employers. Most of the large US corporations only acceded to worker and public demand for unionization as a result of intense plant struggles and political pressure during the New Deal era in the late 1930s or – in Ford's case – in 1941.

Figure 4.1   Ford's Highland Park plant in 1914: flywheel production

The rise of mass consumption society

Rising wages and the increased flow of cheaper, standardized commodities meant that mass production slowly generated the basis – and the necessity – for the era of mass consumption. This was accompanied by the expansion of the advertising industry, the extension of credit facilities for average income earners and the increased importance of sales and marketing. An expanding public sector and the growth of science and administration also boosted the growth of the services sector in Fordist economies. At the same time a leisure society gradually evolved where workers spent their rising wages and growing non-work hours on enjoying the private pleasures of participation in car ownership, holidays, the new media-culture of radio, film and television and the improvement of their homes. In short, Fordism enabled capitalism to solve one of the recurring problems that had slowed economic growth and generated endless conflicts over low wages and unemployment during much of the nineteenth century; namely, the tendency to under-consumption, or narrow markets.

Figure 4.2   Central American bananas cut and packed on Fordist principles

An effective mode of regulation at global and national levels

In the USA, much of this prosperity generated by Fordism began in the 1920s but was delayed by the Great Depression and the Second World War. Elsewhere, the era of mass consumption only really arrived when the long boom got underway in the 1950s along with the widespread diffusion of US management techniques and the re-equipping of post-war industries. Fordism helped to lay the foundations for post-war prosperity in the factories. But the successful Fordist formula also lay in the highly favourable mode of regulation created by government policies such as Keynesianism in the period after 1945.

In Chapter 3 we outlined the main ways in which global forces boosted prosperity after the Second World War. In stimulating these forces the role of the USA was crucial. In its search for new markets and through its desire to ensure the victory of capitalist democracy over communism, the USA increasingly assumed the role of managing the world for the western nation states. This role had various dimensions including:

1. Supervising the Bretton Woods financial system which stabilized currencies and assisted governments facing financial crises, thereby reducing the need for protectionist measures.

2. Providing the leadership to assist the recovery of war-torn Europe and Japan through providing substantial aid and relatively easy access to US technology and its large home market.

3. Taking over political leadership in the main international forums, speeding up decolonization and shouldering the lion's share of Cold War arms expenditure. This military expenditure also fuelled investment and growth.

At the national level, too, we can identify a cluster of policies that provided a good environment for Fordist expansion. In good part these measures were influenced by the western democracies' fear of communism and the spectres of the Great Depression and fascism. The key plank of these measures was an accommodation between labour and capital, including: full union recognition, accepting skill demarcations demanded by workers, linking wages to productivity gains and improving wages, working conditions and pensions. In some companies jobs were traded in exchange for workers' acceptance of Fordist production methods, while other firms, especially in Germany and Scandinavia, adopted more conciliatory worker–manager consultation schemes.

At the same time issues of social cohesion and social justice were given much more attention. The state sought to establish a consensus with its citizenry similar to that being pursued by employers in the work sphere. State intervention was designed to achieved a social-democratic accord. This implied that everyone had a right to a minimum of lifetime protection and security. In the European countries – less so in Japan and USA – governments improved the welfare state. Keynesian spending policies were widely adopted to stimulate growth through increased investment in publicly owned services and enterprises. Full employment policies became the top priority while some attempt was made to achieve income redistribution through progressive taxation.

EXPLAINING THE DECLINE OF THE 'GOLDEN AGE'

The 'golden age' of high production, high consumption and secure employment slowly began to disintegrate in the late 1960s, a tendency that gathered pace during the 1970s. What are the explanations for this decline?

The crisis of Fordism as a production regime

We begin by examining five contradictions that developed within the Fordist production regime itself:

1. In a sense its very success in helping to create a long period of full-employment and rising prosperity – including its ability to generate the tax

revenues to fund improved public services and welfare – was its own undoing. Thus, union power was enhanced by increased prosperity but, while consumer demand continued to expand, many employers were reluctant to risk losing their market share through prolonged industrial conflict. Accordingly, it was hard for employers to resist wage demands and this contributed to the build-up of inflationary pressures. This meant that some firms became uncompetitive.

2. It became more difficult to achieve continuous increases in worker productivity while keeping ahead of wage rises and maintaining profitability. This was linked to the inherent inflexibility of large plants relying on overspecialized equipment in the face of rising consumer sophistication. Union resistance towards increasing work fragmentation and attempts to intensify the pace and machine-driven nature of work also challenged managerial authority. This resistance was widely signalled in 1968 when across Europe, but especially in France and Italy, workers and students demonstrated their antipathy to the 'Fordist bargain' whereby workers agreed to exchange disempowerment at work for greater material prosperity.

3. Profits began to fall in the late 1960s and economic growth slowed. This was exacerbated by wider factors such as the OPEC price rises of the 1970s and the recessions that followed (see later). The central plank of the Fordist regime – the hitherto successful linking of rising profits, wages and productivity and the unspoken agreement that employers would recognize union power and share rising prosperity with workers in exchange for increased output – had been undermined.

4. Already by the 1950s, a consumer youth culture had emerged with no memory of pre-war poverty. For the next decade or two the main priority of most consumers was simply to acquire the new commodities and the social status bestowed by ownership. They bought their first washing machine or second-hand family car and tried to 'keep up with the Joneses' (Murray 1989). This contrasts markedly with the period from the 1970s, when **POST-MODERN** sensibilities were aroused and consumers became interested in the creation of personal identity and individual lifestyles through the possession of fashion and designer goods (Featherstone 1992). In itself, owning a car became rather boring and indeed, obligatory. What mattered was its 'make' and style. Like many other consumer items it became a kind of personal statement concerning the lifestyle image its owner wished to convey.

5. The growing market pressures for more customized goods – designed to meet the individual's personal requirements – helped to cut a giant swathe through the rather rigid Fordist mass production system. In its place, a more adaptable system gradually emerged based, among other things, on smaller enterprises, a greater ability to cope with rapid changes in demand and more immediate contacts between producers and their market outlets.

Major Concept

POST-MODERN

According to postmodernists, unlike the earlier era of modernity, our lives are now said to be less and less determined by family, class, community and national loyalties or by social expectations linked to such things as gender or race. Instead, these structures, along with the moral and political certainties about the nature of truth, reality and destiny with which they were associated, have largely disintegrated. Accordingly we are free to forge our own identities – although this may also cause us some anxiety. In doing so we choose from an increasingly diverse, pluralistic and sometimes confusing cultural repertoire – one that emanates especially from the allpervasive mass media.

Box 4.2   The collapse of the Fordist mode of regulation

At the national level

The relations between labour and capital deteriorate.

Organized labour was increasingly blamed for inflationary wage demands, resisting technological change and wresting control from capital, thereby hitting profits. Consequently, governments:

1. Reduced or abolished minimum-wage laws and employment protection.

2. Weakened trade unions with restrictive legislation and discouraged national pay bargaining.

3. Reduced or ended universal welfare benefits and attacked public spending.

4. Moved towards indirect taxation levied on consumption and cut income taxes on the rich.

5. Abandoned full employment policies.

The social-democratic consensus ends and Keynesianism is rejected
(especially in USA and UK)

1. The free market agenda became pre-eminent leading to privatization, the de-regulation of markets and the creation of more incentives for private business.

2. Keynesian policies became discredited. Thus, government spending to stimulate the economy was now regarded as inflationary and as obstructing free markets and the efficient allocation of resources. Accordingly, public spending on public utilities and welfare was reduced.

3. Monetarist policies – a shift to the control of interest rates and the money supply – became pre-eminent.

4. The control of inflation became the priority.

5. Transnational controls on money and capital flows were abolished. This accelerated the globalization of money, bank lending and stocks and shares.

At the global level

Bretton Woods collapses in the early 1970s and international finance became more disordered.

1. The USA devalued the dollar in 1971 and exchange rates began to float causing currency uncertainty.

2. Banks were allowed to de-regulate their international operations. These banks gradually forming a privatized global credit system outside governments' control and absorbed surplus dollars around the world. This undermined domestic economic policy.

3. From the mid-1970s the IMF and World Bank relaxed their responsibility for monitoring world borrowing. Thus, the vast funds in the global credit system were lent to developing countries often for wasteful purposes.

4. Inflationary pressures built up in the world economy driven by 1, 2 and 3 plus extravagant western spending policies carried out to win elections. (However Keynesian domestic policies and 'strong' trade unions got most of the blame for global inflation.)

The USA's capacity for world economic leadership declines

1. Growing import penetration began to cause de-industrialization in some of the USA's once vibrant regions ('rust-belts'). Rising military spending aggravated inflation and further worsened the balance of payments deficit.

2. Domestic crises and foreign humiliations (defeat in the Vietnam War) rocked the Presidency (for example, Nixon's impeachment in 1976) and domestic political stability.

3. Reagan's policy in the 1980s of further military expansion required a huge rise in interest rates to encourage more lending to the US government via purchases of treasury bills.

4. This precipitated a severe world recession and caused the 'Third World' debt crisis because raw material prices and earnings fell while the cost of debt servicing soared. The US was also saddled with a crippling debt burden, which President Clinton was still struggling to reduce in the 1990s.

A collapsing mode of national and global regulation

Another set of explanations for the demise of Fordism concern the piece-by-piece disintegration of all the elements sustaining a favourable mode of regulation. While it may have been no more than coincidence, from the early 1970s all of these wider forces supporting the Fordist production system seem to have lost something of their former momentum more or less concurrently. As this happened, the Fordist era gradually waned. Depending on which interpretation is utilized, it changed either towards the new era of greater flexibility or to the disorder and uncertainty characteristic of global capitalism today. In the latter interpretation we seem to be left with a system in need of a viable regulatory regime capable of restoring some semblance of the lost golden years. We alluded to some of these issues in Chapter 3. However, Box 4.2 provides a refinement of that earlier discussion along with some further details.

Fordism was also placed at risk by its very success in contributing to the spread of worldwide industrialization, so intensifying international competition. Thus, by the 1960s the war-torn economies of Europe and Japan had recovered. Soon they began to export to the US economy. These exports enabled them to generate the dollars required to repay US loans and purchase American machinery. During the 1960s US TNCs increasingly tried to capture a share of the growing European markets by engaging in DFI as the economic recovery gathered pace. But, quite soon, this accelerated 'Americanization' of European economic life was also matched by a parallel drive on the part of the Europeans to invest directly in the US market.

Meanwhile, Japan had been pursuing a highly successful policy of export-led growth since the mid-1950s with US approval. By the 1970s, technological advance, its investment in overseas trade networks and its keen responsiveness to changing consumer requirements enabled Japan to make massive inroads into the home markets of all its competitors while keeping its own domestic economy relatively closed. At the same time, growing manufactured exports from the NICs, initially of fairly standard, low-value goods also resulted in rising import penetration into the North American and European markets.

The net effect of this rapid increase in international competition – with major cities everywhere displaying all the offices, sales networks, adverts and neon signs of the leading world TNCs – was to place further pressure on companies to increase the distinctiveness of their own products. Cut-throat competition also underlined the importance of price as a factor in competitiveness and highlighted the problem of rising domestic wage levels relative to those in other countries. Higher wages were no longer seen as a boon but an obstacle to Fordist success.

Japanization and the rise of flexible labour

So successful was foreign, especially Japanese, competition by the 1970s that many European and US companies began to imitate Japanese management practices, a process known as **JAPANIZATION**. We can see why from the following data. In automobile production – a core part of the structure of developed economies – Japanese output rose rapidly, reaching 11 million vehicles in 1980 compared to 8 million in USA in the same year (Dohse *et al.* 1985: 117). Also in

---

Major Concept

JAPANIZATION

This refers to the conscious attempt, especially in the 1980s, to imitate the organizational culture developed by Japan's huge companies, such as Toyota, and especially their highly effective strategies with regard to managing labour relations in factories (see also Box 4.3). Such attempts at transplanting Japan's methods to other countries have not always been completely successful.

1980, Japanese home production accounted for 28 per cent of total world output and captured 25 per cent of the US market.

From the mid-1980s Japanization was helped by the fact that a growing number of Japan's TNCs established branch plants in Europe and North America – especially in vehicles and electrical consumer goods. This created yet more opportunities for direct comparisons with Japanese business techniques while exposing workers to unfamiliar labour relations at first hand. These moves by Japanese companies occurred because they were anxious to escape the possibility that their export success would invite protectionist retaliation. Also, the US persuaded Japan's government to re-value the yen in 1985 (the Plaza Accord) in an attempt to make Japanese goods more expensive and so reduce the US trade deficit.

Box 4.3   Japanese production and the rise of post-Fordism

Some writers, such as Dore (1986), Kenny and Florida (1988) and Womack *et al.* (1990), claim that, although Japan was influenced by Fordist techniques after 1945, certain unique social and cultural arrangements have always been built into its very system of factory, work and business organization. These have helped to make its workers highly productive and capable of absorbing continuous technical improvements while enabling its factories to adapt quickly to market changes. Thus, flexibility – the hallmark of post-Fordism – has always been present. Its roots are said to lie in the following arrangements.

The supporting culture of Japanese production systems

■ For workers employed in the largest companies (perhaps one-third of the workforce) employment is guaranteed over a lifetime and the pay system is based on a mixture of reward according to individual performance and seniority.

■ Labour markets are segmented such that workers in progressively smaller companies – right down to tiny rural enterprises – enjoy fewer and fewer benefits.

■ Specialized support organizations for manufacturers (called *keiretsu*) operate across enterprises and industries. They provide all member firms with guaranteed contracts, access to new knowledge and perhaps credit on preferential terms. The *keiretsu* also create chains of subcontracting arrangements permitting companies to minimize their investments and risks while retaining the advantages of specialization.

■ Workshop organization encourages employees to seek constant technical improvements and to accept job and skill rotation as production needs change. A hands-on managerial approach to production and a willingness to value worker experience boost this flexibility.

What results from all this is **just-in-time** and **lean** production. Close proximity to suppliers minimizes the need for companies to carry vast stocks of materials and components. Meanwhile a highly motivated workforce empowered by the approach to management and favourable terms of employment seek constant improvements.

Mean production? However, other writers (Dohse *et al.* 1985; Williams *et al.* 1992; Elger and Smith 1994), see a very different picture. They explain Japanese production efficiency in terms of mean rather than lean production. This is an intensive kind of Fordism based on unlimited managerial control over a super-exploited workforce made possible by the defeat of Japan's organized workers in the early 1950s.

Major Concept

POST-FORDISM

This condition exists where most workers are employed on a temporary or casual basis, enjoy few, if any, pension or other rights and where labour has limited power to organize in order to resist employer demands. Capitalists therefore enjoy much more direct control over their employees than was possible under Fordism including the ability to maintain a highly flexible and adaptable labour force.

This process of reproducing Japan's way of organizing production is important for a couple of reasons: first, it meant that perhaps for the first time during the era of spreading modernization the flow of ideas and models from the West outwards to the rest of the world had been significantly reversed. Japan had become the teacher not the learner. Second, the Japanization of work and business organization – and not simply the increased competition it generated – has been seen by many scholars as a highly significant factor in the worldwide shift towards **POST-FORDIST** or flexible work conditions.

There are two contending arguments in the literature which attempt to throw light on the nature of post-Fordism and whether the forms of production developed in Japan contributed markedly to the worldwide move towards post-Fordist work methods (Box 4.3).

THE AGE OF 'FLEXIBLE' LABOUR AND ECONOMIC INSECURITY

In the advanced countries until the mid-1970s relatively safe jobs were easily found, while welfare standards were rising. People believed they could look forward to a constantly improving future. Now, hardly a day goes by without someone reminding us that we live in an age of 'hard times', one supposedly dominated by unprecedented technological and economic pressures. Change is said to be rushing across the entire globe and sweeping virtually everyone into its harsh embrace. This is especially threatening for the poor and unskilled, but even educated people with marketable credentials face an insecure future of frequent career changes and unreliable incomes.

While we are probably viewing the supposed sharp contrast between the present and the golden post-war years through rose-tinted spectacles, it does seem certain that a major shift has taken place in the nature of work and production. This era of insecurity has been variously described as the era of 'post-Fordism' (Lipietz 1987), 'disorganized capitalism' (Lash and Urry 1987), 'flexible specialization' (Piore and Sabel 1984), 'flexible accumulation' (Harvey 1989), or simply as the age of flexible labour and casualization. Employing the terms 'post-Fordist' and 'flexible labour', we now explore their implications.

Post-Fordism and business organization

Three pressures are increasingly driving capital. Although none of them is new they have all increased in intensity, thereby creating growing uncertainty:

● Contemporary consumers have become much more demanding, giving rise to the 'globalization of style'.

● The globalization of capitalist production has intensified competition between firms and countries, particularly with respect to consumer goods such as clothing, shoes, electronic products and other consumer goods.

● Rapid technological change, especially the application of computers and other electronic refinements to production and marketing, the increased use of adaptable machinery and the switch in some industries to advanced automation and robotization (replacing workers with robots) have heightened the role of knowledge in production. This has also created new opportunities for small businesses to carve out viable and specialized market niches.

Together, these three pressures have compelled businesses to make drastic changes. The premium is on creating an *adaptable* or *flexible workforce* so that companies can respond quickly to changes in market demand and fashion. Employers want job rotation and multi-skilling to be accepted as a matter of course by their employees. Managements have been encouraged to overcome any worker resistance there may be to technological changes which threaten jobs or to organizational arrangements that reduce employees' sense of personal control at the workplace. Accordingly, businesses are likely to regard strong trade unions and tough laws protecting workers from unemployment as obstacles to market success.

Employers also want to *cheapen labour costs* whenever possible and this has encouraged them to develop the following main strategies:

1. The relocation of the more labour-intensive aspects of business to 'safe-labour havens' with low wages, unorganized workers and repressive governments. This is exactly what many TNCs did from the late 1960s when they either moved plants to relatively non-industrialized 'sunbelt zones' within their own countries – such as Texas in the USA – or invested in export processing zones (EPZs) conveniently set up by the governments of many developing countries. (These practices are discussed in more detail in Chapter 7.)

2. TNCs have also striven to match their varying labour and technical requirements to the skills found in different parts of the world while taking into account different cost levels and the quality of available infrastructure. This process of spatially optimizing a company's activities involves seeking rationally to fragment overall operations on a worldwide basis. The world becomes one vast arena onto which companies superimpose their changing grids of multi-faceted activities regardless of national borders.

3. Lower labour costs can also be achieved by reducing the proportion of the workforce whose members are eligible for regular wage increases by virtue of their long period of service or who are entitled to enjoy other advantages like a pension, sickness and unemployment benefits. As this core of permanent employees shrinks they are replaced by a growing army of casualized workers made up of part-time, temporary, seasonal or homeworkers. In short, labour becomes segmented between a permanent core and the casualized majority. The latter normally enjoy few if any rights and are exposed to the constant risk of unemployment because firms are free to disclaim any responsibility for them when the market contracts.

Businesses also seek to minimize their costs and risks by seeking to unscramble their operations and engage in *downsizing*. Basically, this involves shrinking their operations to a core of activities where they enjoy a special expertise, a technological advantage or an established market niche. Simultaneously they subcontract more and more of their manufacturing processes to a multitude of other specialized firms, often on a worldwide basis. This process may also extend to leasing or out-sourcing certain operations –

including marketing, advertising, design, transportation and so on – to small agencies. Franchising represents yet another such activity as in the case of the big food chains such as McDonald's who, in effect, loan the patent of their product to smaller companies on a profit-sharing basis. Increasingly, too, many companies join networks with other small businesses in order to pool ideas and skills, share design, research and other costs or simply to divide up large contracts.

Finally, the need to gauge *rapid and subtle fluctuations in fashion* has compelled many businesses to do two things. One involves using more adaptable, multi-purpose equipment while arranging plant and work organization so that they can produce a wide range of non-standardized products in small batches. The other is to establish much closer contact either with retailers, designers and advertisers or directly with consumers themselves. Here, instant communication made possible by electronic links has proved to be invaluable. Indeed, increasingly the distinction between the service and manufacturing sectors appears to be breaking down.

WORKERS IN THE POST-FORDIST PERIOD

How have all these changes affected workers? Those who earn sufficiently high wages have probably gained as consumers, providing all these attempts to cut costs and increase efficiency *are* in fact being handed onto us in terms of lower prices – something that is not very easy to establish beyond doubt. Perhaps, too, our cravings for variety and individuality are being satisfied. Hopefully, these advantages also compensate for any losses we may experience as insecure wage earners.

However, for a large and perhaps growing proportion of people, living in the North, the South and the former communist world, and including many who are skilled and educated, these compensations may be much less certain. We now offer a selection of key examples illustrating the range of insecure post-Fordist work experiences found in the global economy – in homeworking, in the deindustrializing areas of the rich countries, in Russia and among those who are unable to find even casual work.

Homeworking

As the name suggests, homeworkers are those who are firmly caught in the net of capitalist wage employment but who contribute to production by working within the confines of their own homes, often in dangerous and unsuitable circumstances. Normally they operate at the extreme end of long complex chains of subcontracting activity and are allocated the most labour-intensive – tedious, repetitive and laborious – parts of the overall production process. Wherever they are located, homeworkers have usually been women. Their extreme isolation and dispersal means that it has proved almost impossible to regulate their working conditions, while most homeworkers earn very low rates of pay. All in all they form a highly vulnerable group.

The proportion of the world's workforce who depend on homeworking to supplement meagre household incomes, has risen sharply during recent years as employers have pruned back their (mostly male) permanent staff and relied, instead, on tiny back-street enterprises and homeworkers. Homeworking is one area where women are paid less for producing similar goods. This gender discrimination has operated irrespective of the economic activity in question: homeworking, part-time or seasonal work or simply full-time employment in factories and services. Because women's experiences of greater insecurity, lower pay and poorer working conditions have been so pronounced, some writers see the worldwide move towards post-Fordist flexibility as virtually synonymous with 'global femininization' (Standing 1989). Not only are lower paid women replacing men in numerous occupations but all employees are facing exposure to the same poor conditions of employment that women have typically always experienced (see Chapters 15 and 17).

De-industrialization and 'rustbelt' zones

Together the globalization of industrial production, the widespread adoption of free market economics and the trend towards post-Fordism have led to the de-industrialization of many once established and prosperous regions in the advanced countries. As we show in Chapters 8 and 9, the prime casualties of these rustbelt zones have been blue-collar manual workers. But massive declines in traditional factory employment have often pulled whole communities into a scenario of poverty, mental illness, rising crime and other problems because of the downward spiral created by a huge diminution in worker spending power on local taxes, leisure facilities and the social fabric.

Where new jobs have emerged to replace the permanent well-paid ones that have been lost, the former normally involve non-contractual, insecure forms of casualized work – part-time, temporary or seasonal – lacking prospects or social benefits. Meanwhile, their greater risk of unemployment along with increased dependence on casualized work has meant that blue-collar workers have enjoyed minimal increases in their real incomes for over twenty years. Moreover, many such workers, especially members of migrant communities, can only support their families by undertaking several casualized jobs at the same time.

The former communist countries

The wholesale adoption of post-Fordist, free market solutions in the wake of the collapse of communism has had variable results in the former Eastern bloc countries, with some economies – notably the Czech Republic, Hungary and Poland – showing considerable advances. However, elsewhere, and particularly in Russia, the experience seems to be wholly deleterious, as least in the short term. One Russian worker in four, more than 20 million people, is not paid regularly and delays can be as long as six or even twelve months. According to 1998 figures, Russia's wage debt amounted to $10 billion. In Moscow 400 enterprises have wage debts. Trade union officials claimed there were strikes at 1283 enterprises and organizations in Russia during the first four months of 1998, most concerning the non-payment of wages (Box 4.4).

Box 4.4   Surviving without wages in Russia

How do people manage to survive for months without receiving any wages? The editors of a trade union-supported newsletter interviewed Larisa Seliverstova in mid-1997 to supply the answer to this question. (She is the chairperson of the trade union committee of School Number 10 in Prokop'evsk, Kemerovo administrative division.)

'My salary is now 620,000 roubles ($108) per month. I work one shift, which amounts to 23 hours a week, although almost everyone in our school works a double shift. I have been paid for October 1996, 60 per cent of my pay for January 1997 and 27 per cent of my pay for the summer vacation. I have not received any child benefit (that would add about 70,000 roubles a month to the family budget) since April 1996. We have one child, a nine-year-old son. My husband works in the special department for preventative main-tenance for the suppression of underground fires. He earns 1.2 million roubles, but he was last paid in September 1996.'

If you hardly ever receive any money from your main job, do you or your husband have any chance to earn something on the side?
'We don't have any additional earnings. Basically we work on our garden plot.'

Why does your husband not go somewhere else, if he has not been paid for so long?
'He still has two and a half years to work to qualify for a special pension. Then, certainly, if it goes on he will look for work with pay.'

How do you survive? Does someone help you?
'Our parents help: my husband has two and I have one. My father gives us all of his pension – he is still working. My husband's mother helps with food. Grandpa and grandma completely support our child. They live in a private house, which has a garden, and they also have an allotment. In July, on the eve of [a] day of action, my husband received his wage for last September. His director has gone on vacation so he cannot expect to get any more money before October.'

Source: Extracts from Newsletter 2 (Sept 1997) of the campaign on the Non-Payment of Wages in Russia – www.icftu.org

Social exclusion and economic marginality

In many countries, somewhere between a quarter and one-third of the popula-tion form a marginalized group dependent on state support – where this is available. They engage in multiple and fluctuating forms of low-paid employ-ment, community or family support and semi-criminal activities. The existence of these excluded social minorities is often most noticeable in urban areas and in the advanced countries where capitalist employment for the majority crystal-lized into a complex occupational structure during an earlier period of indus-trialization. Ethnic and racial minorities, usually of recent migrant backgrounds and those with a history of exposure to discrimination, are often found among these marginal groups. However, a large and increasing proportion, whether of native or immigrant backgrounds, are also people with little or no education and few marketable skills.

REVIEW

The era of high productivity, high consumption and employment security is now over. Instead we have moved to a period of economic globalization, rapid technological change, post-Fordism and the widespread adoption of free market policies. In contrast to the 'golden' post-war years, their combined net effect has been to weaken labour's bargaining power and to expose a growing proportion of employees everywhere to the risk of unemployment or to conditions of work and pay that reduce workplace autonomy and increase lifestyle insecurity. At the same time, a growing proportion of the global population have been sucked into, and become dependent upon, the capitalist, profit-oriented market system for their livelihoods.

Globalization tends to be blamed for these and other problems. But increased globalization also needs to be seen partly as a consequence of the widespread adoption of free market economic policies. These have removed earlier constraints on capital flows and torn down the remaining barriers to the spread of capitalist production. At the same time, the work insecurities we have discussed owe as much to the deliberate shift, since the late 1970s, towards de-regulated markets, greater inequality and policies designed to undermine worker's rights and to reduce public spending, as they do to economic globalization.

Meanwhile, as one commentator complains, many governments have allowed themselves to 'become convinced' that only private markets and those who juggle money between them should be permitted to determine the world's shape and direction; not states, political leaders or, presumably, the citizens that elect them (Hutton 1998: 13). As world capitalism becomes more complex and extensive its dependence on a supportive mode of regulation at global (and national) levels, forged by far-seeing and co-operative governments, would seem to be more relevant now than ever before. Even George Soros (1998), one of the most prominent financial speculators who profited from the de-regulation of the global economy, has complained about the present generation of world leaders. He suggests that they seem to lack the imagination and be unwilling to provide the leadership to challenge orthodox views of how the world's economy might better be organized and managed.

If you would like to know more ●●●●●●●●●●●●●●●●●●●●●●●●●●●●●●●●●

J. Allen's chapter, 'Fordism and modern industry' in J. Allen *et al.* (eds), *Political and Economic Forms of Modernity* (1992) offers an excellent, easily read and wide-ranging introduction to the questions associated with Fordism as a system of manufacturing.

The two readers, by A. Amin (ed.) (1994), *Post-Fordism*, and T. Elger and C. Smith (eds) (1994), *Global Japanization*?, both contain up-to-date summaries of the main debates in these areas. They are really aimed at advanced students and academic specialists but most of the readings are nevertheless reasonably accessible and will amply reward those who persevere.

Written in simple but lively prose, the book edited by A. Ross, *No Sweat* (1997), offers a wide range of recent material concerning the various and recent worldwide experiences of casualized workers and their struggles to bring about change.

Group work ●●

1. The class will divide into two groups. Using the text and Box 4.1, one group will draw up a list showing the advantages and disadvantages of (a) being a worker and (b) a consumer during the Fordist era. The second group will follow the same procedure for the current era of post-Fordism. After hearing the two accounts, each student will briefly give reasons why – if such a choice could be made – they might prefer to live under Fordism rather than post-Fordism or vice versa.

2. Working in small groups, students will study the section 'Explaining the crisis of Fordism'. Now draw up a list of possible explanations for the decline of Fordism in their order of relative importance. Write down the reasons for your prioritization. Once every group has given its report the class as a whole might consider two issues: (a) the degree of consensus, if any, concerning the weighting given to global as against other explanations; and (b) the problems involved in engaging in exercises of this kind.

3. Arrange a class discussion/debate around the following topic; 'The world has become too complex for us ever to return to the post-war golden years. What can or should the world's leading figures and organizations (states, IGOs, companies, political leaders, and so on) do in order to construct a global mode of regulation capable of supporting a more stable and prosperous world capitalism?'

Questions to think about ●●

1. Summarize the main differences between Fordist and post-Fordist production *either* (a) as systems for organizing production and dealing with market demand *or* (b) in terms of their effects on employees' work experiences and styles of life.

2. How did changing *global* factors contribute to the decline of Fordism?

3. Evaluate the contradictions of Fordism as a production regime.

4. How and to what extent did Japanization contribute to the rise of post-Fordist casualization?

chapter 5

Nationhood and the Nation State

Major Concept

THE NATION STATE

The nation state is constituted by a government assuming a legal and moral right to exercise sole jurisdiction, supported by force in the last resort, over a particular territory and its citizens. This involves institutions for managing domestic and foreign affairs. From the late eighteenth century ordinary citizens in most western countries began to feel strong loyalties to their nation states, while local and regional identities were suppressed. Popular nationalism has been more difficult to achieve in some developing countries.

In the nineteenth and early twentieth century modernizing governments were largely successful in persuading individual citizens to submerge their personal passions and identities into those of the **NATION STATE**. Three entities, society–people–country, came to be regarded as virtually co-terminous with, even subordinated to, the idea of the nation. In this chapter we look at sociology's contribution to the study of nationalism, the nation state and the idea of citizenship, and how this has changed.

We also assess the power and role of nation states in a global era. Many observers have suggested that in a globalizing world, the capacity of nation states to shape domestic and world change has already declined and may do so further. This has given rise to such concepts as the 'hollow state' (Hoggart 1996) or the 'borderless world' (Ohmae 1994). Some commentators go much further than this, suggesting that the era of the nation state may be ending. Others submit this conclusion is much too premature and that the functions of the nation state are merely changing. We assess this debate and also argue that despite the global changes undermining the exclusive primacy of the nation state system as a focus for political and social action, securing recognition as a nation state is still an urgent goal for many people.

SOCIOLOGY, NATION STATES AND THE INTERNATIONAL SYSTEM

We argued in Chapter 3 that the nation state, particularly in Europe, pre-dated the rise of modernity and industrial capitalism. It acted as a centralizing agency, steadily acquiring control over traders, aristocrats, towns and religious bodies. Driving this process of state building was military and economic rivalry between a number of European nations.

Both the French and **Industrial Revolutions** gave a new and forceful momentum to the processes of state and nation building in the context of international rivalry. The first of these revolutions proclaimed the universal rights of humanity, further centralized the French state and, by unleashing citizen armies, propelled nationalist fervour across Europe's territories. This galvanized the birth and spread of modern popular nationalism. Britain's Industrial Revolution compelled other countries to recognize the potential military threat to their national security posed by a more technologically advanced economy.

One by one the nineteenth-century nation states – in Europe, America and later, Japan – began to push towards the goal of state-led industrialization. They strengthened the structures of the state and imposed reforms designed to remove any remaining obstacles that might impede the release of enterprise, market incentives or scientific and technological learning. As we will see in Chapter 10, faced with even greater external military threats to national survival after 1945, several South East Asian states responded in similar ways.

In short, the forces most responsible for promoting modernization came not just from social pressures created by civil society, they originated within and among the élite who controlled the nation state itself. Thus, as Albrow (1996: 7) succinctly explains 'the story of modernity was of a project to extend human control over space, time, nature and society. The main agent of the project was the nation state working with and through capitalist and military organization'.

Key Moment
INDUSTRIAL REVOLUTION

Britain's industrial revolution led the way for industrialization across the globe and can be dated to around the 1770s, when machinery and full-time waged workers in permanent factories were increasingly deployed in manufacturing processes. The industrial revolution began with the cotton textile industry, but over about another 70 years spread to most other industries in Britain.

Box 5.1   European nation states in the 1990s: towards the past?

Medieval Europe consisted of an assortment of political units with local identities that were often far stronger than any national loyalties. They were also involved in multiple affiliations to cities, to the Catholic Church based in Rome and to various monastic orders. Today, economic integration among the members states of the European Union (EU) continues to deepen. There are plans to extend membership to more countries in the near future. Meanwhile, the EU states are subject to the same kinds of changes as those affecting nation states everywhere. In view of all this, is Europe returning to its medieval past? Perhaps, yes, if the German situation is any indication.

German politics in the 1990s
In common with many countries – for example, the USA, Australia and India – Germany forms a federation with 16 units of provincial government, called Länder, each enjoying considerable political autonomy from the central government. It appears the Länder are trying to extend their 'independence' even further. Thus:

■ Each Länder has established its own offices at, and relationships with, the EU in Brussels in the attempt to obtain resources.   **(cont'd)**

- The Länder have altered the Federal constitution so that they can resist any further ties developing between the central government and the EU of which they might disapprove.

- Some Länder are trying to establish their own special trading relations with nation states outside the EU such as China.

The wider European picture
The German Länder are not especially unusual. For example:

- Much of the previous list is equally applicable to other EU countries where strong regional loyalties and even antipathy to central governments have long been obvious. Catalonia in Spain is one notable example, but Belgium, Italy and France also have regional governments and deep local identities.

- In 1999, even centralized Britain was in the throes of devolving power to newly elected governments in the 'Celtic' regions of Scotland, Wales and Northern Ireland. Many observers suspect England's own regions may follow suit.

- Across Europe, cities as different as Barcelona, Manchester and Lyon are establishing special ties to the EU and to cities in other European countries (and outside the EU!) to obtain grant aid, attract investment and encourage co-operation in sport and education as well as cultural and other exchanges.

- Universities, schools, town councils, professional associations are also making cross-boundary links, therefore bypassing the national government.

Source: Freedland (1999)

Classical sociology and social change

By the middle decades of the nineteenth century many observers were becoming increasingly alarmed by the multiple consequences brought about by industrial capitalism. Not surprisingly, early European sociologists struggled to understand these changes and their dangers and possibilities. At the core of much of their thinking was the attempt to conceptualize the essential features of *traditional* as compared to *modernizing* societies and, in part, to come to terms with the assault that the latter was having upon the imagined virtues of the former. Here we give just three examples of such thinking:

Major Concept
SECULARIZATION

This refers to the declining hold of religious belief and practice over most people's lives during the industrialization process. Growing exposure to scientific knowledge and new ideas, combined with a more materially secure environment, render most individuals less reliant upon the moral and spiritual certainties provided by religion in pre-industrial societies.

- *The loss of community* The German sociologist, Tönnies (1971/1887), mourned the demise of the warm, all-embracing *Gemeinschaft*-type communities of medieval times based on unquestioned friendship and shared beliefs and their replacement by the impersonality even anonymity found in modern, urban *Gesellschaft* societies. The latter are built primarily around loose, often impermanent, essentially contrived and non-overlapping associations. The relationships they contain are driven primarily by the demand for achievement and legitimized by contract and mutual interests.

- *Declining social cohesion and moral order* Another concern theorized by sociologists was the impact industrialism, urbanism and **SECULARIZATION** were having on societal cohesion and the tendency for individual citizens to experience moral and social isolation. Modern societies seemed to be marked by growing materialism, class conflict, egotism and individualism compared to earlier societies. These changes, combined with the declining hold of Christianity threatened to push individuals either into social isolation – due to changes such as rapid urbanization or economic crises – or moral confusion. The latter might occur because modern economic life raised people's expectations to unrealizable levels while leaving them isolated in the face of the collapsing certainties once guaranteed by community and religious values.

● *The conscience collective* To avoid these problems, Durkheim thought that modern societies must evolve a crucial bulwark alongside the integration produced by the division of labour, namely, the emergence of a much more flexible and abstract value system. This would be based on the *conscience collective*, 'a new set of universally significant moral bonds' (Turner 1994: 135) that championed mutual respect for human rights and the sanctity of the individual. Although still at a national level, this resembles the idea of globalism – whereby humans share an intensifying consciousness of themselves as forming one single collectivity – discussed in Chapter 2.

Universalism and nationalism

Interest in universal themes and the progress of all humanity can be traced back to the 1830s via the social theory of Saint-Simon (Turner 1994: 133–5). Durkheim was very influenced by Saint-Simon, especially on the question of how to find a 'new set of universally significant moral bonds' to replace the religious convictions threatened by secularization while cementing together the much more complex national and world orders created by industrialism. However, Durkheim was also strongly counter-pressured by the force of political events. One especially salient experience for him was France's humiliating defeat in the short war with Prussia in 1871, and the powerful patriotic sentiments this generated.

Durkheim began to think that the heady unifying passions generated by French nationalism might provide a substitute for declining moral certainties and societal incoherence. In short, more universalist themes and concerns were largely, although not entirely displaced from Durkheim's thinking. The urgency with which modern nation states sought to deepen their control over industrial societies in the last decades of the nineteenth century was accentuated by the spectre of socialism. Marx had predicted that capitalist exploitation would ultimately create the conditions for an increasingly organized and militant working class to foster a revolution and introduce socialism. This, coupled with abundant actual evidence of working-class strength and the internationalist aspirations of socialism, 'sent shudders through nation-state society' pushing it 'into overdrive to find an alternative and better theories' (Albrow 1996: 45). Another crucial event that reinforced the national leanings of many intellectuals, at least initially, was the outbreak of the First World War in August 1914. Much to the astonishment and deep regret of many, especially those on the Left, this was met by surges of patriotic sentiment right across Europe.

As with other kinds of experts, sociologists were increasingly drawn into the processes whereby states tried to head off social conflict. They conducted research into poverty and similar problems, often with state funding, established specialized teaching programmes linked to these issues and generally contributed to the formation of policies designed to ameliorate adverse social

<table>
<tr><td>

Major Concept

CITIZENSHIP

This involves membership of and inclusion in a national community. Citizenship confers a set of entitlements – to legal equality and justice, the right to be consulted on political matters and access to a minimum of protection against economic insecurity – but simultaneously requires the fulfilment of certain obligations to state and society.

</td></tr>
</table>

conditions. In all these ways their thinking was also increasingly built around the nation state and its needs.

Many governments also began to create a welfare state. This was designed to offer some degree of economic security for ordinary people from the inherent uncertainties of market economies in the form of unemployment, old age, sickness and other benefits. The extension of the state into everyday life created a new form of social bond, **CITIZENSHIP**, which simultaneously excluded the 'foreigners' and deepened the commitment of the 'natives' to the state.

CITIZENSHIP: ENTITLEMENTS AND OBLIGATIONS

Citizenship is basically a modern, western invention. It is underpinned by two principles. One involves the idea that there should be a bundle of *uniform* rights to which everyone is equally entitled. This would have been unthinkable in premodern societies. The second principle concerns an implicit *bargain* or *contract* where, in return for a set of rights or entitlements, citizens are expected to demonstrate loyalty to the nation state and its objectives, while accepting certain obligations or duties. These include the willingness to accept military conscription, to pay taxes, to seek employment and to obey the law. Thus, historically, rulers were able to bring about widespread change successfully by providing citizens with a stake in nationhood and industrialization. This also meant democratization by providing 'an equality of membership status and [an] ability to participate in a society' (Roche 1992: 19).

T. H. Marshall's ideas (1950) about citizenship influenced a generation of thinkers. He observed that citizenship involved three sets of rights which, he claimed, had emerged in a sequence as a result of events taking place approximately in the eighteenth, nineteenth and twentieth centuries. These rights were as follows:

● *Civil rights* were attained first. They includes the right to own property and arrange contracts, to free assembly, speech and thought and the right to expect justice from an impartial legal system based on laws which apply equally to everyone. Where civil rights do not exist, neither personal freedom nor market enterprise are fully realizable.

● *Political rights* confer the ability to participate in national decision making through voting for the political party of your choice at elections. However, political citizenship also implies the right to establish your own movement or to seek direct access to positions of leadership in party, government or some other power-exercising forum.

● *Social rights* involve access to welfare provision that provides a protective floor below which individual and family incomes are not supposed to fall. Normally, social rights include old age, disability, family and unemployment benefits and the right to decent housing, education and health. Hopefully, such minimum security gives everyone an equal chance to enjoy personal autonomy and the benefits of economic growth. Underlying the idea of social rights is the assumption that without them the inequalities and insecurities inevitably generated by capitalism might push some people to levels of permanent poverty where they are too weak to exercise their civil or political rights.

During the past fifteen years, interest in citizenship has revived strongly but this has been accompanied by a critical reappraisal of Marshall's ideas. Here we mention just a few of these newer arguments. First, Marshall's analysis was based far too closely on Britain's history (Mann 1996). Other countries have often had different experiences. For example, Germany began to establish a rudimentary welfare state somewhat earlier than Britain – during the 1880s – and 30 years before universal voting rights were finally established in 1919. Second, citizenship is based on membership of and inclusion in a particular national community. But this means that it simultaneously raises the possibility of exclusion (Lister 1997: Chapter 2). One example is that in a globalizing world, where disadvantaged migrants increasingly seek work or political asylum in the prosperous countries, many will encounter racism and discrimination from officials or host members and will become 'non or partial citizens' (pp. 42, 45) irrespective of their societal contributions. Internal groups too, especially the disabled, women and children have often faced exclusion. In effect, women were 'banished to the private realm of the household and family' (p. 71) because of employment and welfare policies. Until recently it was assumed that they were predominantly carers who neither required nor deserved financial reward or independence because their needs were being met by their husbands as the main family 'breadwinners'. We say more about women, nationalism and the state later on.

Finally, during the last twenty years right-wing thinkers and politicians have also challenged earlier ideas about citizenship. They argue that citizen rights have been stressed far too much while the corresponding duties of citizens to seek paid employment and to assume proper responsibility for family and community commitments have been neglected. Accordingly, many on the Right have criticized welfare rights. Partly this is because of the increasingly heavy burdens they place on public spending especially at a time of high unemployment and the rising costs of health care and old-age provision. But they have also attacked the 'dependency culture' supposedly generated by the welfare state, which is said to undermine individual autonomy and moral responsibility.

Clearly, the sociology of citizenship is being radically rethought. One of the biggest challenges it now faces is from the idea of *global citizenship* as national economies become increasingly integrated, governments are compelled to co-operate and numerous transnational agents collaborate across national borders.

POLITICAL THEORY AND INTER-STATE RELATIONS

As we have seen, during most of its history, sociology can be said to have prioritized the study of single societies and to have rather taken the nation state for granted. Even Marxist sociologists showed little interest in the emerging relationships and connections forming between societies or states until the 1960s. On the Left, this task was left to revolutionary intellectuals such as Vladimir Lenin (the leader of the communist revolution in Russia in 1917) and Rosa Luxemburg (a German revolutionary murdered in Berlin by army officers

Table 5.1   The age of the nation state system

Date	Number of new internationally recognized states	Cumulative totals	Comments
Before 1800	14	14	Not including the Ottoman, Russian, Chinese and Austro-Hungarian empires
1800–1914	37	51	South American countries gained independence from Spain and Portugal plus UK dominions
1915–39	11	62	For example, Ireland, Poland, Finland
1940–59	22	84	Surge of independence for former colonies especially in Asia and Middle East
1960–89	72	156	Veritable flood of developing countries gaining independence in Africa (41), the Caribbean (11), Asia (14) and elsewhere
1990–93	25	183	Dissolution of USSR and Yugoslavia (22 new states) plus Namibia, Eritrea (following war with Ethiopia) and Yemen

Note: A number of countries are caught in anomalous situations, for example: Taiwan (not recognized because of dispute with China); Palestine (still in the process of achieving formal autonomy from Israel); North and South Korea may eventually unite; many countries and territories are still dependencies of some kind. Some very tiny countries – such as Liechtenstein – hold independent status at the UN. In many other countries, civil wars and disputes (such as the Sudan and Sri Lanka) mean that the founding of new states cannot be discounted.
Source: Kidron and Segal (1995)

during an unsuccessful communist insurrection in 1919). Both wrote extensively on the theory and practice of imperialism.

A more academic perspective on international affairs came from political science, through a sub-discipline called international relations theory. We now discuss this briefly.

The realist perspective explained

For a long time international relations theory relied on a particular model of interstate relations called 'the realist perspective'. Like the everyday meaning of the term, the 'realist' label is employed in order to suggest that abstract or idealist considerations are rarely significant in human affairs and certainly not in the sphere of nation state relations. Rather, naked interests and power seeking are normally paramount. Adherents of the realist perspective argue that international politics has certain inherent characteristics. The 'classic' statement of this position is found in the work of its leading early exponent, Morgenthau (1948) who advanced four main positions:

The **sovereignty** of a state lies in its ability to make and enforce its own policies and laws in its own territory and over the people living within its borders.

1. World society, if such can be said to exist, is largely synonymous with the relationships between states.

2. A world of **sovereign** nation states contains an inherent risk of conflicts erupting. This is (a) because states are driven by their very nature to engage in power-maximizing activity – they seek to enlarge their

autonomy and spheres of interest at the expense of others – and (b) because the nation state system is anarchical – by definition it lacks a recognized supranational authority.

3. Accordingly, relations between states are mostly dominated by questions of military security and the need to pursue appropriate foreign policies designed to safeguard national security and maximize international status.

4. The world polity is characteristically hierarchical. States are not equal in their capacity to shape events. The more militarily powerful tend either to dominate weaker states through various kinds of coercion or to take a lead in managing world affairs by forming alliances and trying to achieve a balance of power.

The realist perspective assessed

Different versions of the realist perspective have remained quite influential among international relations theorists. Nevertheless, this view has been increasingly subject to criticism. The insistence by realist theorists that states are primarily preoccupied with matters pertaining to national security and therefore with military matters and defence is increasingly dubious. State agendas have always been much broader than this. Moreover, they have certainly widened very rapidly in the late twentieth century to include such compelling issues as how to manage information flows through the Internet, the global spread of diseases such as AIDS and tuberculosis and the need to deal with environmental issues.

From the late 1960s, economists and sociologists were struck by the rapid growth of powerful non-state, transnational bodies, especially TNCs. The realist perspective was seen to place too much emphasis on a state-centric view of world politics while neglecting the growing importance of transnational exchanges in the world economy. Indeed, the latter were rapidly calling into question the very meaning of national sovereignty and territorial autonomy. Increased interdependence between states required more co-operation between the leading industrial countries and IGOs such as the World Bank and the IMF in order to manage the global economy more responsibly. Unilateral actions by even the most powerful states were therefore less possible.

PUTTING 'SOCIETY' BACK INTO NATIONAL AND GLOBAL POLITICS

Since the 1960s, sociologists' interest in global matters has begun to flourish. Thus, a considerable number of non-Marxist sociologists have joined scholars such as Wallerstein (1974) in the rediscovery of transnational exchanges and relations. At the same time, sociology has offered a much sharper analysis of the shortcomings of international relations theory. In this section we first explore one such recent critique and then discuss two important sociological approaches – deriving from historical sociology and feminism – to the study of nationalism and global relations.

Major Concept
IMAGINED COMMUNITY
The nation is an 'imagined community' in four senses. It is imagined *because the member of even the smallest nation will never know most of its members. The nation is imagined as* limited *because even the largest of nations has a finite boundary beyond which there are other nations. It is imagined as* sovereign *in that is displaces or undermines the legitimacy of organized religion or the monarchy. Finally, it is imagined as* community *because regardless of actual inequality, the nation is conceived of as a deep, horizontal comradeship (see Anderson 1983: 15–16).*

Society and international relations

Here, Shaw's (1994) work is especially illuminating. He makes several criticisms of international relations theory. First, he suggests, international relations theory has largely ignored the state's embeddedness in the many dense networks of class and other interests and identities that make up society. These aggregates of complex social relationships that constitute 'society' are often locked into conflict over questions of ethnic, regional, religious, gender and class affiliation. Accordingly, the emergence of a strong populist sense of national community and identity – during the nineteenth century in many western countries – was all the more remarkable and requires explanation (Shaw 1994: 89, 92).

Second, during the early modernization process, intellectuals, artists, political leaders and others both created the very idea of nationhood (or national community) and brought it more sharply into focus. To describe this process, Anderson (1983) employed the term **IMAGINED COMMUNITY**. Similar tendencies have appeared more recently in some developing countries. In other words, nationhood does not spring into life of its own accord and it is not purely an extension of state power as realists appear to suggest.

Third, the notion of a civil society – social groups with shared interests operating in the political arena – existing between the individual and the state has been revived and developed. Societies have never been simple appendages of states and nations and cannot be regarded as co-terminous with them. In most western nations, and in many others, society preceded the state and the nation, as did individual loyalties to social groups (Shaw 1994: 94).

Historical sociology

A revived interest in comparative historical studies of modernization has also helped to reground the sociological interest in nation states, international life and global exchanges. For example, writers such as Moore (1967), Gerschenkron (1966), Skocpol (1979) and Mann (1988) have explored the circumstances surrounding the successful transitions to industrialization in countries such as Britain, America, Germany and Japan as compared to the failure or delayed nature of such transitions in Tsarist Russia and China. We have already emphasized how these state-led transitions were motivated at least partly by external threats and nation state rivalries. For example, the Napoleonic invasions of Prussia, Austria and Russia between 1805 and 1812, spurred the élites in these countries to embark on the process of modernization, although they were not all equally successful. Between the mid-1850s and 1870s both Japan and Italy also tried to head off the perceived risk of future external domination by embarking on extensive industrialization programmes.

However, it is important not to ignore the role of several other factors making for change:

● Internal pressures from domestic groups were often significant, too. In addition to intellectuals and artists, these arose from an assortment of educated, middle-class and business groups clamouring for more accountable and predictable systems of administration, greater recognition for merit rather than privilege in the allocation of state resources and measures designed to increase economic opportunity.

● The political ferment and economic transformations generated within one country sometimes spilled over and influenced the middle classes in neighbouring or distant ones, stimulating demands on state élites to hasten similar change at home, for example, during the revolutionary unrest across Europe in 1848.

● The need to catch up with more advanced national rivals often generated a 'late development effect' (Gershenkron 1966). This involved states in mobilizing capital for private entrepreneurs but it also involved learning from the achievements of other more advanced modernizers through cultural exchanges. Thus, government officials, intellectuals, technicians, businessmen and others were sent abroad and instructed to decide which institutional innovations – for example legal codes, mass education systems or forms of business organization – should be imitated by the home country. Here, the Japanese propensity to borrow extensively from western countries during its late nineteenth-century period of rapid modernization has often been noted. However, according to Robertson (1992: 92–6) traditional Japanese religion (Shintoism) had always tolerated and absorbed new and multiple religious identities.

The feminist re-assessment

In Chapter 6 we will examine feminist theory and its considerable importance in compelling all academic disciplines to rethink many of their theories and assumptions regarding gender relations. However, some feminist theory has also been central in contributing to sociologists' concern with nation states and global affairs since the 1960s. We now summarize two examples of such contributions, both of which concern women, society and the nation state:

● *Women and the state* Far from being gender neutral the state not only '*treats* women unequally in relation to men... it [also] *constructs* men and women differently' (Yuval-Davis and Anthias, 1989: 6). State power has been used in order to enforce control over women in many ways. One case might be the policies widely adopted by governments during the two world wars. At first, women were pressed into factories, offices and other forms of war work as men were mobilized for military service. Later, governments conducted campaigns to persuade women to return to domestic life when the men were demobilized for fear of social unrest caused by male unemployment. Welfare policy is also important. One example, here, would be the decision to grant or withhold certain child benefits from single mothers. Thus, governments wishing to discourage such families could decide to make such rights conditional upon women responding to certain compulsory training or work schemes.

● *Women and nationalism* The very way in which women's contribution to nationhood is envisaged and understood – whether by ordinary people, established traditions or by state officials – also reveals the hold of certain deep-rooted assumptions concerning the 'proper' role of women in national life (Halliday 1994: 160–4). Yuval-Davis and Anthias (1989) identify several paths that women have been expected to follow in most countries including their role as mothers and as the carriers of their country's unique cultural heritage. One important role is linked to their biological, childbearing capability, which enables them to produce the next generation of male warriors for future wars. Here, population policies have often been crucial in encouraging women to have more children, as in nineteenth-century France and the Soviet Union after the 1917 Revolution. Alternatively, in some cases certain types of women were discouraged from procreating because they were members of so-called 'undesirable' minority groups or 'impure' immigrants.

DOES GLOBALIZATION MEAN THE DECLINE OF THE NATION STATE?

It is useful to set the scene for this discussion by heeding Shaw's (1997: 497) warning 'that it is erroneous to counterpoise globalization to the state' since this can only lead to a 'sterile debate'. Thus, he suggests that instead of saying states' powers are declining it makes more sense to say they are undergoing a transformation in their structures and processes. Such changes are a pre-condition for further globalization and a consequence of it. Shaw also reminds us that this debate has not been helped by confusion over what exactly we mean by the 'nation state'. Normally, people are referring to its 'classic' nineteenth- and early twentieth-century form. Then, there were far fewer autonomous states than now (see Table 5.1). Moreover, most really did rely upon their own independent military capacity in order to protect their sovereign territories and *monopolized the legal control of the right to use violence over their territories and citizens* – which was how Max Weber defined the modern state.

But does this situation exist any longer? Shaw argues that it does not. Only the USA – and the USSR until its demise in 1992 – have actually enjoyed the 'real' sovereignty possessed by most states before 1945 and this includes the vast majority of the new nations formed since decolonization. Why is this? Since the Second World War the dangers and costs involved in maintaining a nuclear and conventional military capability have meant that 'many even of the strongest nation-states have lost or given up the capacity to mobilize violence independently of their allies' (Shaw 1997: 500). Here, NATO is the obvious example of allies sharing military power across borders. By the same token, although the classic nation state is mostly no more, even the weakest modern states normally possess a high-tech military and policing potential for controlling their internal populations through violent repression far in excess of anything available in the nineteenth century.

Bearing these points in mind, we now consider the case for arguing that the nation state's power has dwindled. We begin by employing Held's (1989) useful distinction between *sovereignty* (a state's ability to make and enforce its own policies and laws) and *autonomy* (a state's capacity to achieve its policy goals). A loss of sovereignty has happened (as we saw earlier) but only to a limited extent. It is most noticeable in those states prepared to recognize international law or those that belong to powerful regional blocs such as the European Union. The latter requires member states to devolve some decision-making upon the Brussels-based European Commission and Council of Ministers and to accept certain common directives and regulations.

What is clearer, however, is the extent to which states have lost a good deal of their former autonomy although the nation state system and capitalism's global character have always limited state autonomy to some degree. Held

(1989) identifies the main areas in which most states have progressively lost some of their national autonomy in recent decades:

1. States have to adhere to the demands of IGOs such as the IMF and World Bank when requiring external financial assistance.

2. States have a declining capacity to determine their own military strategies and foreign policies. This is because security arrangements, weaponry and national defence organizations have become integral to joint alliances and power blocs are controlled by unified command structures such as NATO.

3. Following the disintegration of the former Soviet Union with its vast arsenal of weaponry, it is now relatively easy for terrorists, secessionists and criminals to obtain lethal arms, small explosives, and even certain types of nuclear weaponry. This privatization and democratization of the means of destruction represents a further dimension of declining state control (Hobsbawm 1994: Chapter 19).

4. A growing body of international law is increasingly infringing on state autonomy. In general, compliance rests on the interests and goodwill of the states themselves. However, there are significant exceptions to this including several rulings of the European Court of Human Rights (ECHR) on the questions of equal pay and sexual discrimination in the workplace, which have forced member states to alter their national laws (Held 1989: 199–200).

5. The ability of states to determine effective national economic policies is declining in the face of globalization. We now discuss this aspect in more detail.

Economic autonomy

Excluding the special restrictions on members of regional economic groupings, such as the EU and NAFTA, and the rules governing membership of IGOs such as the IMF and GATT (now the World Trade Organization), there are various other important aspects to a loss of economic autonomy:

1. The key role played by TNCs has made some capital far more mobile, even footloose. TNCs can decide where to deploy their various plants across the globe in the most profitable way, what forms of employment policy they prefer and where to deposit their liquid assets.

2. The value of a country's currency and its government's ability to determine interest rates were once important economic weapons. Now, with deregulation of the banks, the growth of 24-hour currency markets and developments in communications technology, the transnational economy is dominated by often uncontrollable money flows (Drucker 1989). Moreover, their endlessly speculative and uncertain nature has given rise to a kind of 'casino capitalism' (Strange 1986). All of this renders the key tools of government economic management decreasingly effective.

3. Governments confront a 'borderless world' but not only with respect to flows of technology, investment and money. According to Ohmae (1994: 18–19) of 'all the forces eating them [territorial boundaries] away, perhaps

the most persistent is the flow of information'. Once governments could monopolize information 'cooking it up as they saw fit' and this enabled them to 'fool, or control the people'.

However, the flows of ideas, images and information made possible by information technology are not amenable to the traditional controls governments have always exercised over the movements of goods and people. The implications for state autonomy are not purely economic. Thus, local citizens' consumer and lifestyle preferences – and perhaps their rising sense of unsatisfied economic expectations – are increasingly shaped by external influences outside government control. This further undermines government policy-making.

The antipathy to modernity

In addition to losing power to supranational and transnational agents, governments are increasingly being questioned and confronted from below by one or more of the following:

- highly informed reflexive citizen networks
- disgruntled ethnic and regional minorities demanding the devolution of some or most central powers to local levels
- widespread public disillusionment with the rhetoric of conventional party politics.

Camilleri and Falk (1992) believe that this discontentment with the nation state, especially in advanced countries, is linked to a rising antipathy towards modernity. Many citizens regard the once unquestioned belief in scientific and material progress as naive and possibly dangerous. The continued preoccupation of governments with these goals strikes many people as absurd, further undermining state power.

This is complicated by the rise of post-modern sensibilities to which we referred in Chapter 4. Many sociologists claim that the changes associated with post-modernity are transforming all social and cultural experiences in a number of ways:

Major Concept
META-NARRATIVES

These are more than simply 'grand' theories claiming to possess demonstrably valid explanations for all societal evolution and change. Rather, they also offer ultimate, epic stories about the truth of human experience. Socialism, for example, insists that history is dominated by the oppression of different groups – from slaves through to workers – and these groups' perpetual struggles against economic exploitation.

1. Former certainties about what constitutes 'truth' are disappearing along with the downgrading of such **META-NARRATIVES** as liberalism, nationalism and socialism as significant factors in our lives.

2. All boundaries and status hierarchies are breaking down: between social groups, between artistic forms and styles and between the once clearly demarcated spheres of social life especially work and leisure, production and consumption and home life and employment.

3. Every aspect and area of cultural and social life is acquiring a money value.

4. The pursuit of individual self-realization, narcissistic enjoyment of the body and the construction of private and distinctive lifestyles are becoming predominant orientations for most people thus highlighting the key role of consumption in contemporary life.

5. Citizens are being swamped with an ever rising volume of information, images and messages. Their sheer quantity and inherently fragmented nature give life a shallow, unreal quality.

Camilleri and Falk (1992) believe that these post-modern sensibilities have created an interpretative crisis not only in social relations and culture but also in national politics. Thus, they leave us exposed to a confusing multiplicity of values and meanings and more liable to criticize the pretensions and ambitions of modernity. They encourage us to challenge and deconstruct the meta-narratives of nationalism and democracy. These now appear parochial and irrelevant. We may see current forms of democracy, for example, as largely vacuous – incapable of reaching the needs or tapping the energies of contemporary citizens.

Cultural pluralism – intensified by globalization – undermines national politics. This is because the historical building blocks of the nation state are an imagined community, territoriality and sovereignty. But these are threatened by the deconstructionist tendencies implied by post-modernity. Thus, numerous forces in our lives mean that it is becoming more and more difficult to think in terms of the 'anchoring' (p. 250) of particular societies to specific places or territories.

By the same token, and increasingly, we also need to unpackage what we mean when we talk about a 'British', a 'Canadian' or almost any other 'national' identity and culture. The following list includes just a few of such post-modern influences that are causing us to question the meanings of 'nation' and 'nationalism':

- instantaneous, transnational communication flows linking people with similar interests and lifestyle concerns through the Internet

- the exposure of most societies, especially the young, to similar media experiences in world sport, popular music, adverts, films and TV programmes and their strong appeal

- the creation of multicultural societies resulting from migrant settlements whose members establish their own vibrant business, media, religious and other cultural enclaves in host societies

- the growing numbers of people who experience other cultures through international tourism

- the increased dependence on foreign companies, at home or abroad, for jobs or contracts.

THE CONTINUING NEED FOR EFFECTIVE NATION STATES

Can the nation state really be in a situation of terminal decline when its long-standing preoccupation with military security, autonomy and national identity continues to shape world politics? Certainly, recent crises remind us of the continuing saliency of unresolved or new military, nationalist, interstate or ethnic conflicts in many parts of the world and of their capacity to ignite tensions. According to Kidron and Segal (1995: 100–1), more than 50 states were engaged in civil wars or in wars against other countries at some point or other between 1990 and 1994. The ending of the Cold War and the collapse of the Soviet Union have given impetus to the resurgence of national and ethnic demands and rivalries. Here are some of the many examples:

1. The crisis in the Balkans which began after the dissolution of Yugoslavia in 1989 and was followed by the eruption of genocide and civil war in Bosnia until 1995 but which has since been rekindled in Kosovo, leading to NATO's bombing attacks against Serbia beginning in March 1999.

2. The Iraqi invasion of Kuwait in 1990 followed by the Gulf War of 1991.

3. The continuing dispute between China and Taiwan, which briefly escalated into armed conflict in 1995, perhaps a foretaste of future conflicts in the Pacific region.

4. The uncertainties over long-established ethnic, linguistic, religious or regional demands for autonomy in Northern Ireland, Canada, Spain and several African countries.

5. The uncertainties surrounding the UN's interventions, especially that body's ability to undertake effective global peace-keeping responsibilities in the light of its failures in Somalia, Bosnia and Rwanda.

6. The proliferation of chemical and nuclear weaponry as a rising number of countries (India, Pakistan, Israel and South Africa) have acquired the capability to produce their own weaponry or seem likely to do so in the near future (Iraq, Brazil and Argentina).

Some of these conflicts are the legacy of a previous government's failure to provide the conditions for successful economic growth or to correct regional and ethnic imbalances in the distribution of economic gains. Others need to be seen within the wider context of globalizing influences. For example, Held (1995: 94) observes that the globalization of information, 'far from creating a sense of common human purpose... has arguably served to reinforce the sense of the significance of identity and difference'.

This encourages peoples without states to demand their own – giving rise to yet more nation states. Alternatively, globalization may enable disadvantaged groups to know more about democratic or material gains made elsewhere and this fuels their determination to seek redress for their grievances including perhaps a demand for independent statehood. There is also a relationship between globalization and nationalism in respect of arms proliferation. New nations buy arms to acquire the symbols of international prestige and independence while arms-manufacturing countries are reluctant to regulate the arms trade because of its contribution to export earnings.

The conflicts fuelled by new nation formation, ethnic hatred, international terrorism and the arms trade, have created enormous difficulties for the UN. Recalling the circumstances surrounding its foundations in 1945 highlights its current predicament. Then, there were far fewer nation states and reaching international agreement was correspondingly easier. Moreover, the UN's remit and structures as laid down in its charter and institutions (in the wake of two world wars) were primarily designed to prevent future conflicts between nations. This left the UN ill equipped to deal with the disputes and civil wars that have been erupting within states in recent years, and it is these that have often dominated the global agenda.

In other words, and despite the forces undermining the nation state system, becoming a recognized nation state is still a popular goal for political movements. As we have seen, following the demise of colonialism after the Second World War the nation state system was vastly extended and the UN played a pivotal, supervising role in this process (Giddens 1985: 283). Moreover, influential though they are, TNCs still lack that crucial ingredient of nation state power – military capacity and the internationally recognized right to possess and exercise it (pp. 283, 291). In this view state power is not shrinking but is shifting to new arenas of activity – or needs to do so (Hirst and Thompson 1992: 373–5).

Meanwhile, in an attempt to force down wages, politicians across the world use globalization as a pretext to cut welfare expenditure, remove trade union rights and deregulate labour markets. Between 1979 and 1990, the Thatcher government in Britain was largely successful in centralizing the state apparatus. This went against all the supposed trends towards the diminution of state power. Ostensibly, it was carried out to liberate market forces from government interference and to make the British economy more competitive internationally. Political power and strong policy preferences in the hands of determined governments remain highly significant.

Finally, as we have stressed, the role of states in overcoming economic backwardness has historically been paramount everywhere. Thus, during the early stages of industrialization most governments invested in infrastructure and education, fostered local capitalists and protected infant industries from foreign competition. Many Asian states have gone much further than this role, as we will see in Chapter 10. It is difficult to see how the remaining poor countries could escape their current situation without adopting similar state-led strategies.

REVIEW

We have examined sociology's contribution to our understanding of the links between society and the nation state, although we have also tried to explain why its interest in global relations has been limited until recent decades. Then we explored both sides of the debate concerning the supposed decline of the nation state in the face of globalizing tendencies and have suggested the need to exercise caution when considering such arguments. Here, it might be useful to end by drawing upon the recent case put forward by Held and Archibugi (1995). They argue that the world needs something they call 'cosmopolitan democracy'. This would mean ensuring 'citizens, wherever they are located in the world, have a voice, input and political representation in international affairs, in parallel with and independently of their own governments' (p. 13). It also 'requires the creation of authoritative global institutions able to monitor the political regimes of member countries and to influence the domestic affairs of states where necessary' (p. 14). Among the many institutional changes this might require are the following: creating regional parliaments; adopting cross-national referenda on such issues as regional transport; strengthening people's rights partly by increasing the powers and influence enjoyed by international courts and reforming the UN to strengthen its effectiveness and legitimacy, for example, by ensuring all regional interests are more genuinely represented and by reducing the UN's current exposure to US influence (Held 1995: 106–9).

Such ideas and institutions are a very long way from being implemented at the present time. However, the daring, innovative nature of such thinking does make some aspects of the debate about the nation state versus globalization look a bit 'old hat'. Perhaps it is time to move on. Certainly the fast-changing realities of the global political order may have left many of these arguments looking rather simplistic. For example, NATO's intervention against Serbia in 1999 has raised yet again the crucial issue of whether, how and under what circumstances the world community is justified in intervening in the internal affairs of other nations, even where vicious governments are blatantly abusing universal humanitarian principles and/or threatening the security of surrounding areas. Sociologists' increasing concern with global relations and its knowledge of such things as the growth of transnational exchanges and more articulate, critical civil societies will enable it to bring fresh insights to the analysis of such pressing issues.

If you would like to know more ●●●●●●●●●●●●●●●●●●●●●●●●●●●●●●●●●

K. Ohmae's *The Borderless World* (1994) is a provocative yet highly accessible book.

K. Mingst's book, *Essentials of International Relations* (1999), offers a solid introductory text to international relations theory.

R. A. Nisbet's *The Sociological Tradition* (1970) still offers a highly readable account of sociology's early development as a discipline. Try Chapters 3 and 4.

Citizenship Today: The Contemporary Relevance of T. H. Marshall, edited by Martin Bulmer and Anthony M. Rees (1996), comprises a very readable set of public lectures on citizenship.

The chapters on democracy by Lewis (Chapter 1) and citizenship and welfare by Riley (Chapter 4) in *Political and Economic Formations of Modernity*, edited by John Allen, Peter Braham and Paul Lewis (1992), would be useful accompaniments to the first part of this chapter.

Group work ●●●

1. Students will consider how they feel about their own sense of national identity. How strong is it and why? Do globalization or regionalization threaten national identities? Do students have other, stronger, loyalties? Everyone will report to the class. How far do individual positions differ and how can this be explained?

2. Working in small groups, students will collect cuttings from quality newspapers/ magazines over several weeks demonstrating: (a) what is happening at the UN; (b) how globalizing forces – for example, western TV programmes – are undermining some government's domestic policies; (c) the tensions arising between states during this period and why. Groups will compile a brief report on their issue to be presented to the class.

Questions to think about ●●

1. Explain how and why, apart from Marxist scholarship, sociology paid little attention to states and global relations until relatively recently.

2. Critically assess the contribution of the realist perspective to our understanding of the world order.

3. Are Marshall's three kinds of 'rights' adequate to an understanding of contemporary forms of citizenship?

4. 'The nation state is in terminal decline, but there is no alternative structure capable of picking up its former functions.' Discuss.

5. What are the chief difficulties involved in considering the debate about globalization and the nation state?

part two
Divisions

chapter 6

Global Inequalities: Gender, Race and Class

Major Concept

SOCIALIZATION

The processes through which we learn to understand, assimilate and reproduce the rules, values and meanings shared by members of our society and which are constantly enacted and negotiated in everyday life. The child's relationships within the family are normally crucial to this learning process – along with school and peer groups – but socialization continues throughout life as we are continuously exposed to different social experiences, including the media.

Sociologists have always given much thought to the problem of how to conceptualize and explain the forms of inequality found in all societies and the ways in which these vary both between societies and over time. The unequal distribution of power, wealth, income and social status as between individuals and groups is not randomly distributed, but is patterned and structured. Particular social groups find themselves persistently denied the same degree of access to social rewards and resources as other groups. Disadvantaged groups are also exposed to forms of discrimination as well as to ideologies, culturally dominant values and learning roles that induce them to accept their 'proper' social place, a process known as **SOCIALIZATION**. Customary beliefs and organized religion have often played central roles in instilling convictions that a given social order is divinely sanctioned, necessary or just.

In general, we can say that structured inequalities operate along the main axes of gender, race/ethnicity and class. Each of these in turn generates its own structure of unequal practices giving rise to institutionalized sexism, racism or class divisions/conflict. The particular manifestation of these axes has varied quite markedly as between different societies, while other sources of inequality such as age, generation and kinship have been rather important, especially in many African societies. Age will become increasingly important in rich western societies and Japan, as the demographic profile changes (see

Chapter 11). Gender, race and class also crosscut each other in various complex ways, sometimes reinforcing and at other times weakening the impact of existing inequalities.

In this chapter we explore the ways sociologists, past and present, have grappled with various schemes and arguments to understand how the three main forms of inequality shape our lives. In doing so we also take account of the fact that the relative significance of different kinds of inequality can change. We also need to remember that inequality is a global phenomenon not simply in the sense that in its varying forms it is found in virtually all societies, but also because wide and growing inequalities are clearly manifest at the world level as *between* societies. These inequalities, together with their possible causes and consequences, are explored in some detail in Chapters 7, 8 and 10.

FEMINISM: CONFRONTING GENDER INEQUALITY

Throughout most of this century, and especially from the late 1960s, there has been a growing awareness of the multiple sorts of oppression to which women in most societies have been historically subjected. Numerous scholars, often women, have undertaken a fundamental re-evaluation of most existing theories in the humanities and social sciences on the grounds that these mostly ignored, or misunderstood, women's historical and contemporary roles (see Box 6.1). Consequently, and especially in sociology, an influential and distinctive perspective has emerged.

Despite their greater visibility arising from this new interest, women's struggles have a long history. During the nineteenth century mainly middle-class or aristocratic women joined such campaigns as the anti-slavery movement and the demand for prison reform. They also began to organize in favour of the extension of voting rights to women, especially in the USA (Stienstra 1994: 44–9). Indeed, in the twenty years or so before the First World War, the **Suffragette Movement** became a highly significant form of mass collective protest in many advanced countries. The demand for voting rights normally went hand in hand with demands that women should enjoy the same educational and job opportunities as men and the same freedom of access to social and public life.

> **Key Moment**
>
> **Suffragette Movement**
>
> *The Suffragette Movement demanded votes for women as a first principle of equality and liberation. The movement was at is height in the USA and the UK in the late nineteenth and early twentieth century, but it was not until women were used 'on the home front' in factories during the First World War that their cause was won. Even then when the vote was conceded in the UK in 1918, only women over 30 were eligible. In the USA, women's suffrage was granted two years later.*

● *First-wave feminism* This liberal feminist concern for the attainment of what were essentially individual freedoms formed the first wave of the women's movement. It involved what Zalewski (1993: 116) calls the 'add women and stir' variety of feminist thought. This is the idea that first and foremost women's liberation required the extension of the Enlightenment principles of equal dignity, respect and rights for all citizens. Everyone, including men, would benefit from the new energies and abilities unleashed once women – the other half of humanity – were free to seek personal fulfilment. Liberal feminism remains influential today, but it has also continued to be largely the preserve of white, middle-class, western women.

● *Second-wave feminism* However, during the early part of the century there were certain intimations of the more radical appeal typical of the second wave of feminism, which burst onto the world scene from the late 1960s, spreading outwards from the USA. A common idea was that women possessed certain distinctive characteristics such as a greater capacity for nurturing than men and a stronger inclination to seek harmonious relationships. It followed that if women could stamp their own more highly developed moral preferences and priorities onto political and public life through the attainment of political power the world might be more peaceful (Stienstra 1994: 52).

Three central propositions emerged from the post-1960s second wave of feminist thinking. After outlining these we proceed to explore them in more detail:

- male and female roles and characteristics are mostly learned and/or imposed on individuals by social and cultural processes and this results in a process of societal engendering

- women's contributions to social life are invariably regarded as less significant than those of men and therefore less deserving giving rise to a condition of gender inequality

- relationships in virtually all societies have been characterized by a long-held cultural acceptance of gender inequalities.

The engendering of femininity and masculinity

In virtually all societies it has been assumed that maleness and femaleness are natural states that cannot be changed. Men supposedly find it easy to be brave warriors, technical experts and clear-headed, rational thinkers free from cloying emotions. Women, we are told, naturally lean towards caring roles and home-making activities. A clear division of labour in the allocation of economic tasks as between men and women has always been partly justified in terms of these supposedly natural, biological differences.

Second-wave feminists disagreed profoundly with these characterizations. Instead, they argued that unlike those *biological* differences that are anatomical and genetic in character, gender is an acquired identity. As Peterson and Runyan (1993: 5) bluntly put it: 'We *learn*, through culturally specific socialization, how to be masculine and feminine and to assume the identities of men and women'. Thus, it is not biology but differing cultural expectations and social treatment that makes us into 'males' or 'females'. Similarly, it is mostly cultural processes that determine whether a person is allocated childrearing and home-making roles along with economic activities linked to domesticity (cooking, cleaning, caring for others) rather than occupations such as hunting, herding animals, working with machines or exercising political leadership.

The gender hierarchy and female subordination

In most societies gendered identities are not only regarded as completely distinctive, forming opposites in a binary system, but they are also evaluated differently. Masculine characteristics are generally assumed to be more socially 'useful', technically 'difficult' to perform and generally more 'important' than feminine ones. Feminists argue that in most societies this results in a hierarchically structured system where gender relations are highly unequal. Women's contributions are judged as warranting less social standing than those of men. Consequently fewer rewards accrue to them and they enjoy less power to shape social relations.

Among the widespread and more general consequences of female subordination are that women's roles have remained largely unrecognized and invisible while their skills and social activities have been consistently devalued. Even the attainment of civil or political rights alongside men is unlikely to remove all the sources of oppression women face since these rights usually refer to public life, not to the private realms of household and family. There women may remain subject to forms of domination from husbands, sons and male kinsmen that may be legitimized by cultural values and/or underpinned by economic dependency.

Major Concept
PATRIARCHY

Patriarchy involves forms of oppression that elevate men to positions of power and authority. Feminist writers argue that patriarchy is so deeply embedded that it appears in early societies as well as in feudal, capitalist and self-proclaimed socialist societies. Those feminists who are influenced by Marxism stress that sexual divisions of labour are functional and related to the evolving class structure. Other writers have pointed to the role of religion or the structuring and labelling of female and male roles. Whatever the origin of this role differentiation (most feminists discount, but some writers include, the different biological functions of men and women) it has now become culturally and even psychoanalytically inscribed. This makes patriarchy difficult to dislodge.

Patriarchal societies and patriarchal relations

Can female subordination only be fully understood within the context of generalized male domination or **PATRIARCHY**? Discussion among feminists regarding the nature, extent and causes of patriarchy has generated an important debate and not a little disagreement. In Box 6.1 we outline the main divisions within recent feminist thinking with regard to the nature, causes and significance of patriarchal relations for women living mainly in modern or modernizing societies. (In this section we examine other societies.)

Early sociologists such as Maine, Engels and Weber defined patriarchy as a system of social organization where the eldest males in a family exercised more or less unconstrained power both over younger males and women and where production was based almost entirely in the household. They regarded patriarchy as a social form specific to certain historical (pre-industrial) eras and societies. For Weber, the classic form of patriarchy existed several thousand years ago in many Middle Eastern societies where direct personal rule was exercised by the elders, social bonds were defined by blood or kinship links and economic activity was nomadic.

Extensive twentieth-century anthropological research has largely confirmed Weber's observations that rule by the oldest males is the most striking and dominant aspect of social organization in pastoral and stateless societies. Social life is mainly organized around allegiance to extended systems of kinship (or lineage) based on descent from a common blood ancestor. Those belonging to the same lineage share property and owe powerful loyalties and responsibilities to each other.

Women normally bear all of the direct responsibility for childcare and domestic life – including fetching water and fuel. However, their burden of biological and social reproduction also encompasses their playing a key role in food production through agriculture. Such women feed their husbands, children and perhaps some of their extended kin not simply through preparing food but by growing a large part of it themselves. This primary role of women in food production has often been ignored or misunderstood – whether by colonial states, agricultural experts seeking to 'improve' the productivity of traditional farming practices, or by the élite of modernizing governments who have ruled such societies since independence.

Box 6.1   Recent feminist debates on patriarchal relations

Radical feminists

Many feminists argued that patriarchy exercises a totalizing influence over women in modern societies. Thus, Millet (1977: 25) defined patriarchy as the 'institution whereby that half of the populace which is female is controlled by that half which is male'. For radical feminists, male supremacy derives from men's ability to control women's bodies – for example in sexual relations, through women's role in childbirth and in the tendency for modern health practices and technology to be dominated by a predominantly male expertise. The latter has systematically stigmatized and excluded the knowledge accumulated by women herbalists and health practitioners in the pre-industrial era. Male dominance is also reinforced by the prevailing ethos of heterosexuality as the supposedly 'normal' form of sexual relations. It is also made possible by widespread male violence especially in domestic life – a situation that has generally been tolerated or ignored by the state. The need for women to *separate their lives* as much as possible from those of men offered one obvious solution to the destructive effects of patriarchy. Another remedy required nothing less than a concerted programme to empower women so that they can challenge male rules and assumptions concerning how life should be organized wherever they prevail. For all its faults (see later in this box) radical feminism has been enormously influential.

The critique of radical feminism

In addition to the emergence of other streams of feminist thought (see later in this box) these radical interpretations were increasingly contested, especially from the late 1970s, partly on the following grounds:

- Because the roots of male domination appeared to lie primarily in women's sexuality and their childbearing/rearing roles, such conceptualizations of patriarchal relations might compel feminist aspirations to lean on those very assumptions from which they had been trying to escape, namely the conventional view that women's subordination is biologically determined.

- These views of patriarchy are employed indiscriminately and without regard for its distinctive relevance as a total way of life to specific historical periods and cultures (see earlier in this box and Kandiyoti 1997).

- It is not clear what is systematic about patriarchy within and across different societies and why it takes many varying forms; how exactly it is grounded in concrete social relations so as to make possible persistent and totalizing male oppression.

Marxist feminists

They argue that the primary source of women's oppression derives from the logic of capital accumulation and profit. Capitalists need to cheapen the cost of producing each generation of workers. The unpaid family domestic labour and child rearing provided by women enables capital to achieve this aim although helped by the social welfare and educational provisions supplied by the state. In addition capital can exploit the reality of women's domestic responsibilities by using this as an excuse to pay women lower wages. For similar reasons they can also conveniently slot women workers into part-time and temporary employment as and when the market demands without the necessity to pay social benefits or provide job security. However, many Marxist feminists have increasingly recognized that certain aspects of patriarchal relations – for example, the widespread resort to male violence – are not always reducible to the needs of capital. Patriarchy often has its own logic, which interacts with capitalist oppression.

The ethnic/race critique of white feminists

Feminists living in the South have argued that the chief sites of female oppression for them may be quite different from their white, western counterparts. Thus, colonial exploitation (and its legacy of devalued local cultures), the need for male-female unity in the struggle to overcome western imperialism and the repression exercised over women by newly independent states have often been much more significant for southern women than the issues of family life and control over sexuality. Similarly, non-white

(cont'd)

women living in western countries often encounter many forms of discrimination that shape their lives much more dramatically than any tensions that may emanate from 'traditional' cultural family values. Even the labour market problems experienced by women from ethnic/racial minorities may be unique to them. Thus, Afro-Caribbean women in Britain are much more likely than white women to take full economic responsibility for family life (Bruegel 1988). They are much more successful than male Afro-Caribbeans in obtaining educational qualifications. Despite this relative success, poverty compels many to seek full-time jobs but ones that are often low paid. White women, with more secure family lives and husbands who are better paid, are much more likely to see the 'problem' of employment in terms of the difficulty of escaping from part-time work.

Post-modern feminism

Post-modernists emphasize the multiple and ever shifting discourses that permeate social life – so that there can be no 'fixed' structures shaping human behaviour or absolute values. They also celebrate cultural differences and insist on the individual's increasing capacity to construct (or deconstruct) lifestyles and the social personæ. All this means that post-modernists have been highly sceptical of many feminist views. Thus, the argument that we can clearly delineate the social category of 'women' and that all women share a common unity of interests, one which clearly divides them from men, smacks of essentialism (a belief in the innate and irreducible nature of things or social entities). It also projects an overly deterministic view of social life, one that overlooks the increasing number of choices women can make concerning how to present themselves as feminine and organize their lives. From a study of women's magazines, for example, Coward (1978) argued that whereas the magazine *Good Housekeeping* expressed femininity in terms of family and household roles, *Cosmopolitan* encouraged women to seek sexual expression through a concern with glamour and bodily beauty. Its articles also assumed that readers had little interest in conventional ideas of domesticity but desired freedom of sexual choice, economic independence and careers.

By contrast, the peoples living in most parts of Asia and some of the Middle East practised a much more intensive and efficient form of agriculture. This involved permanent settlements, customary land rights and the need for frequent manuring, irrigation and deep ploughing reliant on access to heavy animals such as oxen. These societies were much more hierarchical. According to Boserup (1970), intensive, plough-based agriculture created a sexual division of labour in which men played a much more central role in crop cultivation than their counterparts in pastoral and stateless societies. In particular, men assumed the main responsibility for the heavy physical work associated with harnessing animal power to field management and staple cereal production. Women's agricultural contribution involved undertaking lighter agricultural tasks such as weeding, winnowing grain and taking responsibility for dairy products and the rearing of smaller animals.

Superimposed on this division of labour were religious beliefs and customary arrangements that largely confined women to the home or domestic sphere while assigning them to the responsibility and control of husbands and male kinsmen. One extreme form of this was the demand for **purdah** in Islamic societies – although the degree to which such practices were strictly enforced varied a good deal. For example, they were invariably less evident – and less possible – in poorer households. Thus, wealth and social rank also influenced

Purdah is the practice of secluding women by covering their bodies from the male gaze and virtually excluding them, sometimes behind screens, from all forms of public life.

the position of women in such societies. In the more prosperous families of traders, government officials or peasant landowners of substance it was a mark of social status that their women could more or less withdraw from undertaking all but the least onerous economic tasks while their exclusion from public life might be quite strictly enforced.

Kandiyoti (1997: 91) argued that women living in such societies could negotiate with husbands and male kinsmen over the 'patriarchal bargain – protection (from males) in exchange for submissiveness and propriety'. They could also resist changes introduced by men when these threatened female security. Thus, women in patriarchal societies should not be regarded as passive victims. For example, in many parts of sub-Saharan Africa, the spread of market opportunities has often led men to impose heavier demands for farm labour on their wives or to renege on their customary obligations to supply wives with their own land plots. This is to assist them in the cultivation of more commercial crops. Women often responded to such pressures by deserting their husbands, by demanding the payment of wages in return for labour on commercial farms or by devoting more time to their own trading activities. At times, women have also engaged in open dispute with local males.

From private to public forms of patriarchy

It seems clear from the debate outlined in Box 6.1 that any consensus concerning the nature, causes and direction of change associated with patriarchy that may once have existed among feminists has gradually broken down since the late 1970s. Walby's (1990) work is especially useful in enabling us to sift out the most valid claims and take stock of recent changes. Overall, she believes that a major shift has taken place in the forms of patriarchal domination characteristic of industrial societies from the private to the public sphere. Thus, in 'private patriarchy it is a man in his position as husband or father who is the direct oppressor and beneficiary… of the subordination of women' (p. 178).

Various structures operating outside the household have worked to underpin private patriarchal domination. During the last 150 years or so important changes have opened the public sphere to the entry of women. Yet women are still exploited and remain subject to new patriarchal forms because within public life they continue to face certain disadvantages compared to men and tend to experience segregation. This new gender dynamic is discussed at length by Walby (1990) and summarized as follows:

● *Working but still low paid* Not only are women no longer excluded from formal paid employment but by the late 1980s they made up virtually half of the official labour force in most western countries. However, nearly half are employed part time. Also, despite legislation designed to ensure wage equality they continue to earn roughly three-quarters of male wages for the same work. Moreover, they tend to be segregated within certain female-designated employment enclaves such as the caring professions (in health, social work and education) or in low-paid industries and services including catering, garment manufacturing and clerical work.

● *More choice, but still the child carers* Access to paid employment, the attainment by girls of educational levels similar if not increasingly superior to those obtained by boys, the right to divorce and to birth control, and the assignment of formally equal citizen rights have all helped to give women much greater freedom of personal choice and more control over their bodies. Yet, while they can break free from unhappy marriages and even rear children as single mothers such options leave them dependent upon state welfare and legislation, highly susceptible to a life of poverty – for example after divorce – and still faced with the primary responsibility for child care.

● *Sexually free but still in danger* Women still face the very real possibility of male violence in domestic and public life and are exposed to a double standard of personal morality that tends to label them as 'slags' if they choose multiple sexual partners, even though such freedoms clearly benefit men as well, while not exposing them to the same stigma. At the same time, pornography has now become a vast industry and most of this trade degrades women and exposes them to increased risks of personal exploitation and physical danger.

● *New models, old realities* The representations of women in the media appear to offer new models of femininity – promising society's respect for the goals of independence, freedom and equal opportunity. Yet, scratch beneath the surface generated by the glossy images and the message points in a very different direction. Personal fulfilment is still thought to depend on motherhood, heterosexual love and marriage based on lasting relationships. The divorced woman is usually portrayed as returning to the safe fold of male protection through a 'happier' second marriage. Meanwhile, the need to cultivate sexual attractiveness as the key to winning male approval and permanent support continues to be very strongly emphasized throughout all aspects of popular culture.

RACE AND ETHNICITY

The second axis of inequality we consider is race, and its related phenomenon, ethnicity. The word 'race' is now inextricably associated with the idea and expression of 'racism' – discrimination on the grounds of observable difference. This was not always the case. The expression 'the human race' was meant once as a unifying notion, suggesting more commonality than difference. It laid emphasis on a single species, the implication being that we share more common features – physical, biological and social – than those that divide us. To avoid the confusion of using race in the sense of the total human race, it is probably sensible nowadays to talk of 'humanity' or 'humankind'.

'Race' was also used to refer to a group of persons connected by a common origin and sharing common features because of their supposedly common descent. Often such a depiction also included social and historical features such as the evolution of a shared language, a single place of settlement and the development of a political community, what we would nowadays see as a 'nation'. Before the Second World War it was common for people to talk of 'the French race', 'the German race' or the 'British race' in this way – although such notions now seem either quaint or perhaps somewhat sinister.

In general the expression 'race' continues to be used in two senses – first, in a supposedly scientific sense by some biologists and physical anthropologists and second, as a sociological means of understanding how popular forms of heterophobia (fear of difference) are expressed, diffused and acted on.

Evaluating biological notions of 'race'

The idea of classifying people into racial categories started in the sixteenth century and remained an important concern for biologists and physical anthropologists until the 1950s. As Stephan (1982: 171) argues:

> For more than a hundred years the division of the human species into biological races had seemed of cardinal significance to scientists. Race explained individual character and temperament, the structure of social communities, and the fate of human societies... At times this commitment to race subtly modified the reception and interpretation put upon new biological theories. At the very least, belief in the fixity, reality and hierarchy of human races – in the chain of superior and inferior human types – had shaped the activities of scientists for decades.

The scientific credibility of the idea of a racial hierarchy within humankind was fundamentally questioned in the wake of the Second World War. Nazi racism and anti-Semitism had been defeated on the battlefield and their horrific consequences had been witnessed as the starving remnants of the *Undermenschen* (the word used by the Nazis for 'sub-humans') stumbled from the concentration camps. Although their intentions were not genocidal, the ideologists of the **Apartheid** regime in South Africa also used racial categories for discriminatory social practices suggesting, for example, that only certain races were fit for certain tasks.

Key Moment
Apartheid

Apartheid is the Afrikaans word for the system of legalized discrimination that existed in South Africa between 1948–94. Under the Population Registration Act of 1950 the population was classified into different racial categories with education, residence and marriage only permitted within each category. Although the system technically supported difference rather than hierarchy, in practice the good jobs, the best housing, the vote and other favourable opportunities and resources were reserved for the whites. With the election of Nelson Mandela as President in 1994 the system was legally dismantled, although some apartheid-like practices still continue informally.

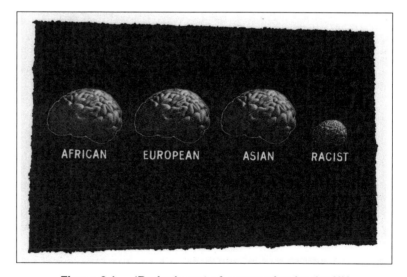

Figure 6.1   'Brains': part of a campaign by the UK Commission for Racial Equality

The association between 'racial science' and political repression all but abolished the word race from polite scientific discourse. However, there remains a small but determined group of biologists and physical anthropologists which insists that it is still important to study sub-species (of the human species) that have developed distinguishing characteristics through segregation or relative isolation. Generally such biologists do not stress *phenotypes* (that is, appearance) but rather more complex and less visible biological characteristics (called *genotypes*). For example, biologists will refer to blood types and their distribution, to particularities of the gene pools and to the chromosomes of different populations.

Box 6.2   Race and intelligence: US experiences

Elementary intelligence quotient (IQ) tests were first applied on Ellis Island, near New York, where 12 million immigrants entering the USA were processed. The fear of allowing simple-minded 'inferior' immigrants from eastern and southern Europe prompted this development. In the First World War, IQ tests were given to army recruits and school pupils. The lower scores of African American and Americans of eastern and southern European descent were held to be attributable to their inferiority, but served only to indicate the cultural and linguistic biases of the tests.

In the 1960s the controversy erupted again around the work of the Harvard educational psychologist, Arthur Jenson (1969), who argued that 80 per cent of variance in IQ performance was attributable to heredity and that African Americans were inherently inferior in certain intellectual abilities. These 'findings' were explosive in that conservative and reactionary politicians used them to block remedial educational and social programmes, such as 'Operation Headstart' – designed to provide early educational support to deprived communities. If, these politicians reasoned, African Americans were incapable through their genetic inheritance of changing their situation, why waste taxpayers' money? There are many problems with this analysis, not least that other groups, unrelated to African Americans, showed a similar gap of 10–15 points in IQ tests, that other African origin groups (like those from the West Indies) did not manifest a gap and that in any case 'to make statements of heritability concerning such a polygenic trait [as intelligence] goes well beyond the scope of modern genetics' (van den Berghe 1994: 151).

Like a bad tune that will not go away but floats back in a slightly different key, Herrnstein and Murray (1994) argued in their 845-page tome, *The Bell Curve*, that inequality is at the heart of the human condition and that difference is in the nature of things. Their racial thinking is only thinly disguised. Instead of 'races', their world is made up of 'clans' (a complete violation of the meaning of this word) each possessing different qualities – all of which, we are told, we should value. Rather than bemoaning the fact that blacks are intellectually inferior to whites (a claim they virtually take for granted), the authors suggest we should celebrate their values of spirituality, movement, dance, rhythm and music. By including a discussion of the low IQ of the white 'underclass' (see later in this chapter and Chapter 15) they hoped to dilute the exclusive concentration on black failures in other, similar literature. Yet these devices are by way of a mask beneath which are still visible the old, discredited claims of biological inferiority and superiority.

Sources: van den Berghe (1994); Malik (1996: 205–9)

If this is science at all, it is a dangerous science. Occasionally, it has to be conceded, it can be used for socially responsible ends – for example in the testing and treatment of a disease such as sickle-cell anaemia, more common in those of African descent. However, discussions of genotype have also been much more dubiously linked to the distribution of intelligence across populations (see Box 6.2). A leading geneticist, Steve Jones (1993), has warned against the tendency to dress up prejudices as science and points out that human beings are the products of about 50000 genes (only about ten of them are concerned with skin colour), which act in complex and unexplored ways. Much of the existing material on heredity and race is simply bad science. The most damaging refutation of biological notions of race lies in the extensive history of the migration and the mixing of peoples – and the breakdown of all reputed 'pure' types.

Sociological notions of race

Sociologists fully accept that race categories are commonly, but normally ignorantly, used in popular discourse and in social and political life. However, they point out that these common categories are imperfectly related to physical attributes like skin, hair or eye colour. For sociologists phenotype (appearance) is important, but only as one social marker – one among many – that serves to generate the categories that regulate the distribution of advantage and disadvantage. The loose use of the expressions 'black', 'Asian' or 'white' provides a good example of how contingent, and temporary, are these popular racial expressions and labels (Box 6.3).

Box 6.3   The strange story of race labels

1. In apartheid South Africa, 'black' meant the totality of non-whites including Indians, Coloured (people of mixed descent), San and Khoi-khoi as well as those of dark-skinned African descent.

2. 'Black' in Australia means of Aboriginal descent. (Incidentally, native Australians have no obvious genetic connection to Africans.)

3. 'Black' in Brazil means somebody who is self-evidently thought to be of African descent. (Many Africans were brought to Brazil as a result of the slave trade.) Indigenous people and those who have mixed ancestry are excluded. According to a popular Brazilian folk wisdom 'Money whitens the skin', so rich black Brazilians are 'white'.

4. In the USA, by contrast, people who are only barely discernibly of African descent will be considered 'black' (often legally so in the Southern states before the 1960s and now socially). They also may well describe themselves as 'black', although this label has been discarded in favour of 'African American'.

5. If we turn to Britain after the 1950s, the category 'black' was used by some of the immigrants from the Caribbean and the Indian sub-continent (together with the radical intelligentsia) to suggest that they were being met with similar hostility or indifference. They saw themselves as forming an underclass or poor section of the working class and being denied access to the most favoured goods and resources.

6. Later, in the UK, those of Indian, Pakistani and Bangladeshi background became more generally known as, and used the self-description, 'Asian'. However, 'Asian' excluded Chinese, Japanese and Malaysian people.

7. These last exclusions are received with particular puzzlement in the USA where the category 'Asian American' definitely includes Chinese and Japanese.

8. Finally, by way of a final absurdity, we might note that in apartheid South Africa, because the Japanese did not fit the local categories and the government was anxious not to offend such a powerful investing and manufacturing nation, the Japanese were regarded as 'honorary whites' by the regime. They were, for example, allowed to stay in 'white' areas and hotels.

One after another, racial labels are found to be to be socially and politically constructed and reconstructed in particular settings. This has led some sociologists to argue that the category 'race' is too insubstantial to consider in a sociological sense. Some, like Miles (1989) would like to abolish 'race' (or always keep it in inverted commas), although they are certain there is a phenomenon called 'racism'. This position is not as bizarre as it may seem. The fact that 'races' are socially constructed does not mean that they are fictional or unimportant. Sociologists often remark that 'what's real in the mind is real in its consequences'. In other words, people think in racial terms – therefore their conduct and behaviour and the wider structure of social action will reflect those beliefs.

Another prominent race relations theorist, John Rex (1986), suggests that we can delineate what he calls 'race relations situations'. If, he argues, inter-group interaction is marked by severe conflict, hostility, oppression and discrimination (all of these going beyond in degree what the competition of a free labour market permits), we have a 'race relations situation'. There are clear practical advantages to this idea. It is both sociological and contextual. It can be used to account for the variety of labels and situations that apply to different groups. For example, the Jews in the context of Nazi Germany were a 'race' while in the context of, say, contemporary USA they are 'only' an ethnic group. Again, because there is often an element of biological determination in the justifications proffered for discrimination, it may be valid to consider that all inter-group hostility of the severity described can be considered a 'race relations situation'.

Ethnicity

As the extent of inter-group conflict has proliferated – in the Lebanon, in Northern Ireland, in the former Soviet Union and Yugoslavia and in Africa, it has become difficult to contain all cases of conflict-ridden interaction between similar-looking groups under the heading 'racial'. This leads to a suggestion that we might distinguish between race and ethnicity in one simple and obvious way. In the case of 'race' social construction is based on physical difference, while the social construction of ethnicity is based on less obvious differences, or social markers, for example those of culture, language and religion.

However, the contemporary use of the notion of ethnicity, or what some writers such as Hall (1992) call 'new ethnicity', goes well beyond a further movement away from biological categorization. Sociologists have sought to find out how 'Otherness' and 'difference' are constructed through discourse, imagery, representation and language, as well as through behaviour. Despite their allusive, metaphorical and literary quality, discussions of Otherness in this mould are inherently more subtle and are often more optimistic than many discussions of racism. They easily admit more liberating possibilities of self-examination and auto-critique while an appeal to conscience, common humanity or self-interest can, Sampson (1993) suggests, be used to reduce perceived difference.

This more open view of identity construction starts from the assumption that, in our post-modern world, identity is more fragmented and that the phenomenon of multiple social identities is much more common than previously had been assumed. Individuals may attach themselves to, or withdraw from, any one identity or category in a more fluid way, depending on the context. This is what is called **SITUATIONAL IDENTITY**.

> **Major Concept**
>
> **SITUATIONAL IDENTITY**
>
> *This arises when an individual constructs and presents any one of a number of possible social identities, depending on the situation. In the most individualistic versions of this phenomenon, an actor deploys an aspect of their identity – a religion, an ethnicity or lifestyle – as the context deems a particular choice desirable or appropriate (see Box 19.1 for a dramatic example of an identity shift).*

There are obvious limits to the manipulative use of situational identity. It is relatively easy to change a religion or one's clothes. It is very difficult to alter one's physical appearance, although the large sales of skin and hair-altering products signify a successful strategy of 'passing', even in such racially divided societies as the USA and South Africa. Despite these limitations, discussions of 'new ethnicities' have been liberating. Diversity and difference can be celebrated, while those who have been traditionally regarded as enduring victims can be more positively seen as evincing but one flexible cultural possibility among many.

CLASS

On 1 April 1999 a surge in the stock market price for his company, Microsoft, meant that Bill Gates was worth $100 billion. His personal fortune is greater than the gross national products of all but the richest 18 nations, and is worth more than twice all the US dollar bills in circulation. If Gates stacked the bills on top of each other, he would have to climb sixteen miles to get to the top (*Daily Telegraph*, 8 April 1999). On that same night, 1 April 1999, there were three million people in the USA sleeping in hostels, shelters or in the streets.

This massive discrepancy of fortune within one country is paralleled by very large discrepancies between countries. Sociologists discuss these and similar differences under the terms social stratification or class. Strictly speaking, class differences are but one form of stratification. Others include:

- *Slavery* In many ancient societies slavery was practised and those with this status were worked to death in mining and constructing the pyramids, religious monuments, irrigation systems and public works. In some settings, like Northern Nigeria, household slaves were treated more benignly, sometimes as favoured servants. But the plantation slaves of the New World were firmly put in their place and until emancipation (1834 in the British Caribbean, 1865 in the USA) were treated as goods and chattels that could be owned, bequeathed or inherited.

- *Caste* Associated principally with Hindu India, a caste system involves an inherited status in which occupations are assigned to one of four theoretically impermeable groups. The priests (Brahmins) claim the highest status, as they are regarded as closest to religious purity. Then follow the warriors, merchants and labourers. The 'untouchables' fall below this ranking and they historically had to undertake the 'unclean' tasks, such as collecting human excrement from cesspools. (Mahatma Gandhi, the great Indian leader, sought to liberate the 'untouchables' by renaming them *Harijan* – people of God – and insisted on them having the full rights of social citizenship.)

Slavery and caste are systems of social closure, although some limited social mobility is sometimes possible. A system of class stratification allows somewhat more, or very much more, movement between classes, although it must always be remembered that movement can be 'downward' as well as 'upward'. There are several ways of understanding how class is defined, how classes are formed and how their power is perpetuated or undermined. Again (as in gender or racial inequality) pre-Enlightenment thinkers tended to assume that class differences were natural or divinely sanctioned. However, sociologists have tended to position themselves around three major perspectives, which overlap to some degree. These are:

- Marxist and neo-Marxist notions of class
- Weberian views of class
- applied definitions of class.

Marxist and neo-Marxist notions of class

Marx's considerable body of writing included intermittent and sometimes inconsistent attention to the issue of class. When he was writing for a popular audience, as he and Engels did in the 1848 *Communist Manifesto*, he tended to simplify his scheme into two 'great' classes, the *bourgeoisie* and the *proletariat*. On other occasions he talked of six different classes in Germany and seven in Britain and wrote also about the peasantry and the *Lumpenproletariat* (the urban poor, without regular employment) in considerable detail. Discussion of the intermediate and adjunct classes surrounding his two 'great' classes were later revived by neo-Marxists.

The basic schema rested on a distinction between 'a class *in* itself' and a 'class *for* itself'. The first was drawn from an observer's (like Marx himself) external and objective description. Marx thought that classes could be defined by the particular relationship they held to the means of production, distribution and exchange. Did they own property, capital or factory premises? Had they inherited money? Did they buy or sell goods or their labour, and at what level? Marx defined the proletariat principally by arguing that they had nothing to sell other than their **labour power** and nothing to lose other than the 'chains' that oppressed them.

Marx was clear that it was a necessary but insufficient definition of class for a common objective situation to be present. Members of a particular class had also to feel subjectively part of that class and seek to defend, advance or maintain their class interests. He described peasants in France as a 'sack of potatoes', artificially bundled together but unable to act on their own behalf. Because of the absence of class consciousness, peasants were not a class.

Marx's model has been criticized on a number of levels. Nowadays, with a family car, a mortgage and a share of capital represented (typically) by a pension, many workers have a lot more to lose than their chains. A significant number of middle-class occupations (clerical, professional, service and information-related) have also developed, which make the idea of a bi-polarized class structure too simple. Managers, small employers and the self-employed also have contradictory class positions which makes them neither workers nor owners of capital. A number of neo-Marxist sociologists such as Wright (1985) have sought to accommodate these changes in revised versions of Marx's class structure. Again, Braverman (1974) has shown how office work – hitherto regarded as an escape from a proletarian blue-collar status – was itself becoming proletarianized by forcing workers in such settings to lose their autonomy.

Weberian views of class

Max Weber thought that Marx's views on stratification were too narrowly structured around economic factors and he insisted that social and political aspects

---

Labour power is the *capacity* to work for a given time, a given rate of pay and at a particular level of skill and effort.

had to be added to round out the picture. Consequently, Weber developed three intersecting aspects of stratification:

1. *class*, which at a descriptive level, is not that dissimilar to Marx's scheme

2. *status groups*, which defined the 'social honour' accorded to a particular group or occupation

3. *political power* (Weber confusingly calls this 'party'), which analysed how people are mobilized to secure their advantage in competitive settings.

Weber's scheme is quite complex but it has generated some important new lines of sociological reflection and enquiry. Following Weber, we need to accept that a multiplicity of class positions arises when his three aspects of stratification – economic class, social status and political power – do not coincide. Thus a ruthless, wealthy capitalist with little sense of etiquette and undiscriminating cultural taste might be denounced as nouveau riche, shunned as a marriage partner by an aristocratic family, excluded from political office and ostracized when trying to join an fashionable club. By contrast a parson, colonial officer, nurse or poet might have little in the way of income, savings or property, yet be a respected and valued member of the community. In effect a stock of **CULTURAL CAPITAL** may offset their meagre financial capital. Finally, a trade union leader or tough mayor of a US city may routinely exercise considerable influence, yet have neither money nor a high status.

Major Concept

CULTURAL CAPITAL

Despite the marked tendencies towards social levelling associated with mass education, affluence, consumerism and highly accessible forms of popular culture, Bourdieu (1984) argues that a dominant 'high' culture continues to flourish. Those whose education or other experiences have enabled them to acquire taste and distinction by investing in various kinds of discerning, detailed, cultural knowledge may be able to gain advantage in the competitive struggle for wealth and power.

Applying class models

The development of schema and typologies of class has proved to be of considerable practical importance in such diverse areas as developing social and employment policy, conducting censuses, marketing goods and services and predicting social and demographic trends. The most commonly applied models of class are based on occupational stratification. It is an immediately compelling argument that the reward system (how much you get paid), the status system (how much you are valued) and the conditions you encounter at work follow occupational lines. Three such models are compared in Table 6.1.

While there is by no means a perfect match between the three schema provided in Table 6.1, there is nonetheless a broad consensus that the class hierarchy matches an occupational scale. This sort of neo-Weberian view of class was virtually unassailable until the early 1990s when it was questioned on a number of grounds. Feminist scholars were concerned that occupational scales tended to favour those in formal employment and miss those in part-time and domestic household work. Women's class position was also rather unproblematically inferred from their husband's or father's occupation. Also, as we have argued in Chapter 4, the nature of work has itself changed and it is more and more likely that individuals will have multiple occupations, at different points of the scale, over their life spans – as well as periods of unemployment. Applied models of the class structure will have to be adjusted to take account of these developments.

Table 6.1   Class schema in the UK

UK Registrar-General's scale	Goldthorpe's scheme (simplified)	Runciman's classes (percentages in 1990)
		Upper class (<1%)
Professional occupations	Professionals/administrators/managers	Upper middle class (<10%)
Intermediate occupations	Non-manual employees/sales personnel	Middle middle class (15%)
	Small proprietors/self-employed artisans	Lower middle class (20%)
	Farmers/small holders	
Skilled occupations	Technicians/supervisors/skilled manual workers	Skilled working class (20%)
Partly skilled occupations	Semi-skilled/unskilled	Unskilled working class (30%)
Unskilled occupations	Agricultural workers	Underclass (5%)

Source and note: Marsh *et al.* (1996: 237–9) citing the work of Runciman (1990) and Goldthorpe *et al.* (1980). The Registrar-General is responsible for the conduct of the decennial census in the UK. Goldthorpe and Runciman are well-known UK sociologists.

GENDER/RACE/CLASS INTERACTIONS

We have seen how difficult it is to move to a consensual view of how each axis of social inequality should be analysed. However, it is also apparent that social reality does not allow the complete separation of these axes. In practice they all work simultaneously and interact with one another. This complexity serves as a useful warning to those who would wish to truncate reality, or order it ideologically. Although we are often enjoined to do this, sociologists cannot in advance of their research decide that the social order is best understood only through one axis – be that gender, race or class.

Many feminists demand that we subordinate class and race categories to the overall determinacy of patriarchy. By contrast, Marxists often dismiss race as an epiphenomenon – a symptom of something else. Sometimes this is presented in a sophisticated way, suggesting that in a complex manner 'race' becomes the mechanism through which class conflicts are refracted and reflected. Sometimes, the notion is more crude. The capitalist class wants to divide worker from worker so they conspire to separate sections of the working class into hostile warring elements. Orthodox Marxists, who think that the key issue about gender equality is to encourage women to join the labour force, also often treat the liberation of women rather narrowly. Just as ideological are those who start from the assumption that everything can be understood through the prism of race. Race is held to be 'primordial', fundamental and logically prior to other forms of inequality.

The attempt to privilege one index of social differentiation can be considered a kind of ideological over-claiming. Although there is no full agreement on this, many sociologists advocate an interactive model. While undoubtedly a massive improvement on the monocausal explanations proffered by each camp, we have also to note some problems in the interactionist model:

1. The answer as to which axis is predominant may be context driven (that is, situational). Alternatively or additionally it may vary over time (that is, be historically driven).

2. We cannot assume an equal salience for each axis and may have to *weight* different forms of social differentiation either through further theoretical argument or through sophisticated statistical analysis. (This is no place to blind you with statistics, but it might be helpful to know that a technique called *multivariate analysis* allows a researcher to hold one factor constant, while varying the others, thus giving a hierarchy of likely causation.)

3. Two or three of the axes may act together, so closely together indeed that it may be difficult to separate them out. Thus someone who is poor, female and black may experience discrimination on all three grounds and in a composite manner. The effects of this composite mode of discrimination are likely to be cumulative and additive and therefore exceptionally difficult to separate, root out or oppose.

REVIEW

By analytically separating three important axes of global inequality – gender, race/ethnicity and class – we have shown how an impressive body of theory and research has developed along each principle. However, the complexity of social reality demands that we pull all these differentiating principles together however difficult this is, theoretically and analytically. Moreover, concentration on the 'holy trinity' of gender, race and class should not blind us to situations where there are other key expressions of inequality. Thus, age, disability, religion, ethnicity, nationality, civil status, health and lifestyles are also very potent axes of organization and identification. These different forms of interest and association appear to be upheld simultaneously, successively or separately to the three main axes and with different degrees of force, conviction and enthusiasm.

We can also note two interesting confluences. First, along each line of differentiation there appears to be a naturalist assumption, followed by a sociological critique. 'Women are the weaker sex', 'Whites are a superior race' and 'The poor will always be with us' are three typical popular (however wrong-headed) beliefs; notions, moreover, that are often supported by pseudo-scientists. Sociologists have been very important in exposing the weak foundations of these naturalist beliefs and have presented coherent social, historical and cultural explanations for the continuation of inequalities.

Second, within each axis, bi-polar models of reality are being discarded in favour of multiply located and expressed forms of identity and organization. Even in the case of the 'opposites' of male and female, the distinction between *sex* (as biologically defined) and *gender* (as socially constructed) has become blurred. This is much reinforced by discussion of gay, lesbian, bisexual and transsexual identities and the development of androgynous musical and dress styles. Ethnicity, particularly the 'new ethnicity' is also about expressing both imagined and self-constructed kinds of identity. Hybridity, cosmopolitanism and transnationalism are now important concepts in debates about race and ethnicity, although this does not mean, of course, that in many places crude racism and nationalism does not still exist (see Chapter 19 for more detail). Finally, contemporary models of the class structure have also embraced fluidity, multi-positioning and contradictory class locations.

If you would like to know more ●

Sylvia Walby's book (1990), *Theorizing Patriarchy*, summarizes the complex debates and evidence on this key aspect of feminist thought in a very readable and clear way.

Kenan Malik's account of *The Meaning of Race* (1996) is lively and interesting while Ellis Cashmore's (1994) *Dictionary of Race* and *Ethnic Relations* should be available in most university libraries and contains excellent short entries by the world's leading scholars.

Class analysis is a little out of favour compared to the 1960s and 1970s when Marxism was an influential political current that sociologists had to consider. A neo-Marxist account of class can be found in Wright's (1985) book, simply titled *Classes*. An influential non-Marxist account on Britain's class structure is Goldthorpe *et al.* (1980).

Group work ●

1. Assigning the work in advance, students will work in small groups to collect material concerning how women are represented in the various media. Different newspapers and magazines could be compared along with an agreed selection of TV programmes and films. How different are these representations and to what extent do they reflect or challenge the main body of feminist theory?

2. Undertake some historical and biographical research on the following figures, all of whom insisted on the importance of 'race': (a) Marcus Garvey; (b) Hendrik F. Verwoerd; and (c) Adolf Hitler. An encyclopaedia will give you a good start on all three, while Cashmore's (1994) *Dictionary of Race and Ethnic Relations* has useful entries on the first two. Present to the group the outline of their ideas and suggest a critique.

3. Examine the class schema listed in this chapter. Group A will put into the rows in any of the three columns the following occupations: computer operator, university professor, nursery school teacher, homeworker sewing garments, an operator in a calling centre, a travel agent, an actor and a self-employed plumber. Provide reasons for your choice and let Group B comment.

Questions to think about ●

1. Compare and contrast the different streams feeding into feminist thought since the 1960s. How far have any divisions been resolved?

2. How useful are theories of patriarchy in depicting the position of women in different societies and eras?

3. What is the difference between ethnicity and race?

4. Is class analysis still important to understanding social inequality?

5. Provide examples about how gender, class and race inequalities (a) reinforce each other and (b) contradict each other.

TNCs: *Their Economic and Social Roles*

CONTENTS

Some writers argue that the globalization of economic life has already proceeded to unprecedented levels and is set to intensify. At the heart of these claims is an assessment of the activities of the transnational corporations (TNCs). These ubiquitous bodies can be seen as the Trojan horses, or perhaps the battering rams, of international capital. Such is their power and influence that they are often accused of dictating to rich and powerful states, while completely overwhelming poor states. Is this kind of characterization demonology rather than social science? What are the origins of these organizations? Have they, in fact, escaped their national origins? What is their economic role in integrating the global economy? What are the social consequences, positive and negative, of TNCs' activities?

It is often assumed that TNCs have a wide sphere of autonomy. This is partly true; certainly this tendency might grow. However, to assess their pros and cons, we need to see their activities in three contexts – when acting alone, when acting in combination with powerful nation states, and when acting in the context of newly industrialized countries (NICs). The advocates and detractors of TNCs can each mount good cases for suggesting that their activities are benign or malign. Table 7.1 summarizes some of the issues we will consider in this chapter.

Table 7.1   TNCs and their social consequences

Process	Positive social consequences	Negative social consequences
TNCs expanding	Providing consumer goods, skills and new technology	Exercising power anonymously and without social responsibility
Forging alliances between powerful nation states and TNCs	States and corporations act jointly to develop research and technology at little cost to taxpayers	Diminution of the state's sovereignty and responsibility to its citizenry
Spread of TNCs to the NICs, especially in the export-processing zones	Provide jobs, raise standards of health and safety and pay taxes	Worker exploitation and too much power placed in the hands of local élites

ORIGINS AND CHARACTERISTICS OF TNCS

Conquest and trade were at the heart of the expansion by the European powers and often provided the crucible within which the TNCs were formed. 'Trade followed the flag', was the slogan adopted by the British imperialists. Often the scale of the operation was, at first, modest. Take the case of the British traders who penetrated the mouth of the Niger River in West Africa. They immediately starting trading with the local chiefs and eventually were successful in persuading the British crown to grant them a charter legitimizing their activities. Thus, the Royal Niger Company was founded. A soap manufacturer in Britain, W.H. Lever, bought the company and then amalgamated it with another trading company, the United Africa Company. The giant Unilever, the biggest UK-based transnational, ranking number 12 in the world, was born. The tropical origins of the company are reflected in the names of some of its products and locations. 'Palmolive' soap referred to the West African palm oil that went into its manufacture, while 'Port Sunlight', close to Liverpool, was where the tropical products were unloaded and processed.

Despite what history books in European schools maintain, overseas expansion was not only a European phenomenon. Less visible, but of profound importance, were the trading networks Chinese, Japanese and Indian merchants established all over East Asia – networks that started on a diminutive scale but often ultimately resulted in very large international enterprises. Let us mention as an illustration one of the big international Chinese trading clans, the long-established Teochiu. In 1939, the clan decided to advance a loan to one of its penniless but ambitious kinsmen arriving in Hong Kong as a refugee. This refugee, Li Ka-shing, has recently bought the sprawling 1986 Expo site in Vancouver for a massive expansion of his international property empire. He is reputedly worth $8000 million, having amassed his fortune from a transnational chain of factories making plastic flowers, buckets, toys and other household items. His economic philosophy is disarmingly simple: 'Plastic flowers are better: you can wash them and they last forever', he said (Seagrave 1995).

As with many of their Chinese and British counterparts, Japanese TNCs had their origins in giant trading companies (*sogo shosha*). National orientations are perhaps more decisive for these TNCs than in the Anglo-American case. Although now enormous integrated commercial, financial and industrial conglomerates, the Japanese corporations' initial and fundamental purpose was trade and the organization of trade.

Characteristics

Many of the world's leading TNCs are engaged in the exploitation of petroleum. Texaco, Shell, BP, Exxon, Gulf and Agip are the most notable and conspicuous. Even if you do not see one of these brand names on the forecourt of a filling station, it may still own the company or supply the petrol from its refineries. TNCs in manufacturing are often involved in producing the ubiquitous motorcar, which despite green protests, is still a healthy money-spinner. About one-third of the 30 biggest TNCs are motor manufacturers. Coming up on the rails, with one or two ahead of the field, are a number of information technology companies. The most prominent is the software giant, Microsoft, but computer and chip manufacturers are also prominent runners. (Chapter 14 contains a full discussion of the importance of information technology.)

An important characteristic of a TNC is that it operates in more than one, sometimes many, countries. Branch plants and subsidiaries, sales, research and development take place on many sites. Why do TNCs wish to locate abroad? Where they are involved in extractive industries or agriculture, the answer is obvious. They have to be where the oil is extracted, the gold is mined or the pineapples grown. However, the principal reasons for decentralization are to secure new markets or to stop their rivals getting there first. The movement of capital away from the USA and Western Europe after the 1970s was also partly to do with the difficulties of securing high profits and subordinating the labour force in the industrialized countries.

Many developing countries had abundant supplies of cheap, unorganized labour. The division of labour into more minute skilled and semi-skilled tasks, which was discussed in Chapter 4, allowed untrained or newly trained workers to attain rapidly the levels of productivity in the countries where industry was long established. The poor countries provided freedom from planning and environmental controls, cheap health and safety standards, tax holidays and other incentives. International transport and communications facilities in the form of containerized shipping, cheap air cargo, computer, telex and fax links had improved dramatically. Especially for low-bulk, high-value goods, it was no longer necessary for the site of production to be near the end market. Moreover, world market factories could be staffed by young women who were likely to remain unorganized (Fröbel *et al.* 1980; Cohen 1987: 220–53).

There are six big *sogo shosha* in Japan, two of which, Mitsubishi and Matsui, are household names in the West. They have massive bargaining power. The six top Japanese TNCs account for 8 per cent of world trade. To communicate between one branch and another, Matsui alone has 500 000 kilometres of communication lines, greater than the distance between the earth and the moon. As long ago as 1986, the daily volume of messages amounted to 110 000 dispatches containing 10 million words (Dicken 1992: 357). The *sogo shosha* provide:

- financial services (credits, loans, guarantees, venture capital)
- information services (up-to-date market profiles, national regulations, technological developments)
- risk-reduction services (insurance, buffers for exchange control regulations)
- organizational and auxiliary services (translations, legal contracts, transport, paperwork and wholesaling).

These services are for their own manufacturing plants as well as for other small companies that otherwise would not be in a position to compete effectively internationally. Although many people are aware of the great strengths of Japan as a manufacturing economy, Japanese TNCs are in fact more prominent in the trade in services (finance, commerce, banking and insurance).

Their number of employees outside the country where their headquarters are located can be used as a gauge of the degree to which all TNCs decentralize their operations. Although many TNCs employ a high proportion of their staff outside the country of origin, the most spectacular examples of this phenomenon are shown in Table 7.2.

Table 7.2   Foreign employees of selected TNCs (%)

TNC	Foreign employees (%)
Nestlé	96
British American Tobacco (BAT)	86
Ford	53
Imperial Chemical Industries (ICI)	52

Source: Dicken (1992)

As each new market is opened up by TNCs, consumer booms can massively fuel their profits. The great new frontier is China, where by the 1990s the biggest consumer boom in world history had begun. By 1995, China was already the third largest economy in the world after the USA and Japan. It is projected to be 'number one' by the year 2010. One seasoned observer of the contemporary Chinese scene (Seagrave 1995: 279) described how for some residents Beijing has thrown off its image as the drab capital of a drab communist country:

> Chinese yuppies were washing their hair in Procter & Gamble shampoo, starting their day with Nescafé instant coffee, driving to work in new Toyotas with electronic pagers clipped to their shirt pockets, then heading for the *karaoke* bars where they can sing along with music videos and mix Hennessey brandy in Coca-Cola. They bought new jeans and pullovers by mail from Land's End catalogues and ordered Tanga panties from Victoria's Secret... As average earnings passed the $1400 a year mark, the majority of people in China for the first time were able to buy such basic consumer items as refrigerators... Given a population of over 1.2 billion, this meant that more human beings were escaping from poverty in one brief period than at any other previous time in history.

As can be inferred from the evocation of famous brands mentioned, the TNCs act as a symbolic and practical demonstration of western affluence and 'freedom', even if that freedom is sometimes individualistic, consumer led and often destructive of other people's opportunities. The former communist regimes found themselves particularly vulnerable to the notion that political freedom equated to consumer choice. On the day after the Berlin Wall came down, East Berlin youth celebrated their release from communist tyranny by swaggering down the main streets, cans of Coca-Cola in hand.

Definition

Having described the origins and some of the characteristics of TNCs, we are now in a position to give a more formal definition. In extending Dicken's argument (1992: 47) we arrive at a fivefold definition: TNCs

- control economic activities in two or more countries

- maximize the comparative advantage between countries, profiting from the differences in factor endowments, wage rates, market conditions and the political and fiscal regimes

- have geographical flexibility, that is an ability to shift resources and operations between different locations on a global scale

- operate with a level of financial, component and operational flows between different segments of the TNC greater than the flows within a particular country

- have significant economic and social effects at a global level.

TNCS AND THE NATION STATE

There are two contrasting views on the capacity of TNCs to challenge the nation state. The first lays emphasis on their *globalizing* capacities, a position we associate particularly with the work of Dicken (1992). The second, a more sceptical view developed by Hirst and Thompson (1996), suggests that while TNCs may have continued and fostered the long-established *international* economy, they have not established a global economy and have not superseded the nation state.

TNCs as globalizing agents

Dicken (1992) argues that the TNC is the single most important force in creating global shifts in economic activity. Ever since the 1950s, world trade – the sum of all the imports and exports bought and sold by all the world's countries – has grown significantly faster than world production. Dicken (1992: 16) sees this as 'a clear indicator of the increased internationalization of economic activities and of the greater interconnectedness which have come to characterize the world economy'.

This, in turn, points to the role TNCs play in binding together national economies. Foreigners own an increasing share of the value of many countries' 'national' assets in part or in whole. By the same token, a growing portion of each country's productive capacity, technological knowledge and skills is an organized extension of the capacities located in other countries. The era of nationally competing and separable capitalisms is now long in the past.

Much of the world's economic system is dominated by TNC decisions about whether or not to invest in particular locations. The resulting flows of raw materials, components and finished products, technological and organizational expertise, as well as skilled personnel constitute the basic building blocks of the global economy.

Figure 7.1   Corporate sale: the 'Avon lady' goes up the Amazon with cosmetics

Figure 7.2   Victims of the Bhopal gas disaster demonstrate against the company in New Delhi, India

TNCs are responsible for an important chunk of world employment, production and trade. This is particularly true of production, where perhaps between one-fifth and one-quarter of all production is in the hands of the TNCs. Measuring trade flows is more elusive statistically, but what is clear is that a high proportion of world trade is intra-firm trade – where one section provides components or expertise to another part of the same TNC. More than 50 per cent of the total trade of the USA and Japan is conducted within TNCs. The Ford motorcar provides a good example. The standard car in its range is appropriately called the 'Mondeo' – or world car. It typically contains parts from 35 countries, most of them produced in the company's own branch plants and subsidiaries. The company skilfully mixes and blends to gain maximum benefit from the costs of labour, technical inventiveness, raw materials and transport. It is therefore able to supply all factories with Indonesian-produced brake pads, or Spanish-produced transmissions. Dual or multiple sourcing of a similar component produces healthy intra-firm competition and is a safeguard against labour protest. If country A's plant is threatened with strike action, country B's similar product can swiftly be brought on-stream.

Another way of understanding the global economic importance of TNCs is to take them as equivalent units to countries. In this measurement, of the 100 most important economic units in the world today, half are nation states and half are TNCs. As there are about 180 recognized states of the United Nations, this means that 130 of these states have economies smaller than the first 50 TNCs. Table 7.3 provides some evidence of the relative economic power of corporations, states and regions.

Table 7.3   Corporate, state and regional economic power

Corporate sales	(US$ billion)	Countries/regions	(GDP US$ billion)
General Motors	132.4	Indonesia	126.4
		Denmark	123.5
Exxon	115.7	Norway	112.9
		South Africa	103.6
Ford	100.1	Turkey	99.7
Royal Dutch Shell	96.6	Poland	83.8
Toyota	81.3	Portugal	79.5
IBM	64.5	Venezuela	61.1
		Malaysia	57.6
Unilever	43.7	Pakistan	41.9
Nestlé	38.4		
Sony	34.4	Egypt	33.5
		Nigeria	19.6
Top five corporations	526.1	Middle East and North Africa	454.5
		South Asia	297.4
		Sub-Saharan Africa	269.9

Source: UNRISD (1995: 154) citing 1992 data

Most of the countries listed in Table 7.3 represent a middle level in terms of their economic power. Yet in their case, let alone those of much weaker countries, powerful TNCs can cause extreme disruption to national economic and social plans. Here are some of the ways in which this might happen:

1. Local capital has difficulty competing. Although TNCs often appear to be benign in employment terms, in order to compete local employers have to lower wage costs and sacrifice quality.

2. TNCs have disproportional marketing power, even for an inferior product. When one of the present authors lived in the Caribbean, local outlets served wonderfully succulent and spicy portions of chicken. They were then undercut by a certain US 'brand leader', which subsidized imported chickens and took losses over a two-year period until it could drive the local firms out of business. Needless to say, the prices for its inferior product soon went up.

3. Local politicians are anxious to encourage inward investment and are often willing to accept corrupt payments in exchange for accepting the company's plans, facilitating its operations and allowing the sending of its profits out of the country without tax. Often these plans conflict with national plans. The poor countries are then often sucked into the cycle of further dependence.

4. TNCs are often in a position to influence tastes and consumption patterns in a negative way. We have already alluded to a fast-food outlet. While not perhaps a pleasant sensation, eating the product is unlikely to be lethal. In at least three other cases, this is precisely the problem:

    a. milk powders for feeding babies are offered through extensive advertising by firms like Nestlé. Not only are they less nutritious than mothers' milk ('breast is best' anti-Nestlé campaigners protested), but they can prove lethal if the formula is mixed with unsafe water

    b. corporations such as BAT use glamorous adverts to promote high-tar cigarettes that are banned in the rich market countries

    c. medicines controlled by doctors, antibiotics, for example, are often freely sold in the street markets of poor countries.

Although the issue of corporate social responsibility is discussed again later, we provide these dramatic examples here to show that in certain situations TNCs have the capacity to subvert and undermine the power of even quite large nation states.

International, but not global agents

Hirst and Thompson (1996: Chapter 4) examined data on more than 500 TNCs from five countries in 1987, and compared these with similar material on more than 5000 TNCs from six countries (France, Japan, the UK, the USA, Germany and the Netherlands) for the period 1992/3. They wished to ascertain whether and to what extent the activities of TNCs deepened integration between national economies while becoming largely independent of both their home and host governments.

They concluded that what stands out most clearly from all dimensions of TNC activity – sales, assets, distribution, profits and number of overseas interests – is the extent to which TNCs 'still rely upon their "home base" as the centre of their economic activities, despite all the speculation about globalization' (Hirst and Thompson 1996: 95). These and other findings lead them to argue that the world economy may have become 'international' but it is certainly not yet a 'globalized economy' (1996: 8–13). They also suggest that the world's economy may indeed be hardly more 'international' than it was before the First World War.

Box 7.1   Case study of a leading TNC, Imperial Chemical Industries (ICI)

ICI's home base is Britain. It was founded in 1926 by merging the four largest UK chemical companies. Some of its nearest world competitors are Du Pont (in the USA) and BASF and Bayer (in Germany). At the beginning of 1999, it employed nearly 59 000 people worldwide and enjoyed a sales turnover of more than £9000 million. In 1989, it was ranked thirty-third in terms of sales turnover in a global list of industrial TNCs. It is the world's largest producer of paint for domestic and industrial (for example, coatings for vehicles) use. It is also a major manufacturer of explosives, industrial chemicals, soaps, textiles, fertilizers and packaging, as well as of materials used by a wide range of other industries such as acrylics and polyurethane. In 1995, more than 4000 of its employees were engaged in various research and development (R&D) activities distributed through regional centres across the world and linked to the specific research needs of different manufacturing plants.

ICI is clearly global in its operations. In all, it directly owns subsidiaries or has entered various partnership arrangements with local firms involving operations in 55 countries. In 18 of these, its activities are confined to setting up branch offices to co-ordinate administrative activity in that country, mostly linked to local sales promotion of its products. However, it has established at least one manufacturing plant in 36 countries and has set up research facilities in 17 different countries. Its achievements in creating a truly global spread of technology, research and production facilities are thus rather impressive. Moreover, this distribution of manufacturing and research capacity is not confined to the leading triad countries, as is often the case with TNCs, although Britain, North America, the EU and (to a much lesser extent) Japan, figure prominently in its investments. This move into Asia and the developing world generally can be seen in the following table, which shows the percentages of ICI's various investments located in different regions or countries in early 1999.

	Manufacturing plants	Research facilities	Sales admin.
UK	14	33	13
North America	32	26	21
European Union and rest of Europe	22	22	26
Australia/New Zealand	2	0	2
Japan	3	6	3
S, SE and E Asia	17	9	23
South America, Africa and the Middle East	10	4	12

Source: ICI Factbook, 1999

On the basis of these and related arguments, Hirst and Thompson (1996) also stress the political limitations to the mobility of capital. Businesses normally prefer to operate where they feel secure and enjoy a comfortable rapport and familiarity with a supportive local culture and market situation. Similarly, the sphere of the economic often consists in large part of relatively immovable plant, equipment and infrastructure as well as employees 'trapped' at any given time in particular locations by community and family responsibilities, job availability, skill and language capacities and the legal restrictions of citizenship. All this presumably means that we can hardly be surprised at the continuing propensity of companies, large and small, to retain strong roots in their home economies. Nor, for the same reasons, is it possible for even the largest TNCs to be completely foot-loose or free from any national control.

Assessment

Despite its obvious relevance and significance, there are two problems with Hirst and Thompson's analysis: one concerns the nature of the empirical evidence and the other involves a theoretical issue.

At the empirical level, there is room for disagreement over how to interpret the available evidence. For example, Dunning (1993b: 291) observes that the largest TNCs, namely those contributing four-fifths of all global activity by TNCs and with annual sales exceeding $1000 million in 1989, together produced approximately one-third of their total output outside their home countries. This estimate is quite close to that of Hirst and Thompson (1996), but whereas they regard it as evidence only for the existence of an international economy, Dunning sees it as an indication of a growing, real integration of a basically global economy. Carnoy *et al.* (1993: Chapter 3) claim that the foreign content of production among the largest TNCs is higher still – between 50 and 90 per cent. Dicken (1992), Dunning (1993a) and Julius (1990) hold that the TNCs' real links with host economies, with respect both to trade and domestic purchases, are often much stronger than Hirst and Thompson's analysis suggests. Moreover, the global strategy of spatial optimization pursued especially by the larger TNCs – reinforcing their parallel attempt to increase inter-market penetration – means that national economies have become closely intertwined with each other. There are also other indications of rising cross-border integration, especially in the European Union and the North American Free Trade Agreement (NAFTA) area.

The second difficulty with Hirst and Thompson's (1996) analysis is theoretical in nature. Adapting an important insight offered by Lash and Urry (1994: 61–2), we argue that it is necessary to distinguish between two rather different aspects of economic life – the cultural, symbolic and knowledge-based component and the more material or physical one. While the first is indeed inherently mobile and capable of rapid learning and transference across and between places and organizations, the second is necessarily rooted in specific locations at any one moment in time. In short, the first is globalizing, the second is necessarily dependent on existing socio-political formations and institutions. It follows that the world economy demonstrates a certain paradoxical and rather skewed character; in some respects it has become highly globalized while in others there are, and may remain, certain finite limits to this process. Accordingly, in one sense the Hirst and Thompson position is perfectly correct, but perhaps rather misleading in another.

Neo-liberalism is an economic doctrine that insists states should never interfere with or constrain free markets, competition or private enterprise. Influential from the eighteenth century, it was side-lined by Keynesianism after 1945 but revived strongly from the mid-1970s.

Hirst and Thompson (1996) mount a powerful case against the notion that economic globalization has reached a stage when TNCs are truly autonomous and governments have been rendered more or less powerless to act in the face of global economic forces. Such a view, they argue, plays into the hands of national politicians and others who, for ideological reasons, may wish to justify various non-interventionist *neo-liberal* policies. It disregards the historical embeddedness of national economies in wider institutions and the supporting role governments until now have always played in furthering national economic development. It also ignores the role only governments can play in initiating modernization in developing countries – perhaps, for example, by taking steps to empower local citizens to tune in more effectively to the growing flows of symbolic knowledge.

The extreme globalization thesis has also been used as a rationale for doubting the possibility or efficacy of joint intergovernmental action – whether led by a hegemonic power, as in the 1950s and 60s, or by a group of leading economies. Can states acting together counter such global problems as rising inequality, joblessness, chronic economic insecurity or the destabilizing effects of floating finance? Hirst and Thompson (1996: Chapter 8) agree that we cannot expect a return to the golden post-war years of US-led, Fordist–Keynesian prosperity, in what was then a much simpler world economy. Nevertheless, they show that successful and concerted attempts by the G7 and OECD countries to regulate the world economy have been evident in recent years. Two examples of international action by states are the co-ordinated interest rate policy to counter falls in global stock markets agreed in 1987 and reducing Japan's huge trade surplus. Much more of the same may be perfectly possible and is certainly desirable. Here, Hirst and Thompson's arguments are refreshing and welcome.

TNCS, NICS AND WOMEN WORKERS

An **export-processing zone** is a free trade enclave where foreign firms producing goods for export are encouraged to locate.

One way in which TNCs have achieved spatial optimization since the 1960s has been through engaging in 'offshore' production located in *export-processing zones* (EPZs), mostly in developing countries. Governments offer special inducements – tax privileges, duty-free imports, the promise of cheap labour, limited or non-existent health, safety and environmental regulations and perhaps free or subsidized plant and infrastructure – to encourage foreign firms to locate their labour-intensive, assembly operations in a given country. Most of the labourers – over 90 per cent in some EPZs – are young women. They are said by some employers to have 'nimble fingers', making them suitable for work on electronic circuit boards. Others point to their industrial discipline. In these characterizations one has to distinguish between convenient stereotypes and the reality facing many female workers in poor countries, namely an adverse labour market and a desperate desire to escape from the powerful forms of patriarchy characteristic of many rural societies.

Industries engaged in making garments, shoes, soft furnishings, toys and other low-value consumer products are the most likely to locate in low-wage regions, including EPZs. So too are those engaged in manufacturing domestic electrical goods and in the assembly stage of the production of semiconductors (when the individual microchips are wired together to form integrated circuits ready to be tested and then incorporated into various final products).

Industrial production in such sites has grown rapidly, as has their export potential. Between 1966 and 1972, US imports of manufactured goods from EPZs located in developing countries increased by an annual average of 60 per cent (Harris 1983: 147). EPZs now flourish widely across the developing world. They have long been prominent in Asia, including China, which established four 'special economic zones', similar to EPZs, as part of its economic reforms in the late 1970s with Shenzhen, adjacent to Hong Kong, being the largest. Caribbean countries have also encouraged offshore development, as have African ones.

One famous EPZ was created by the Border Industrialization Program (BIP) in Mexico where thousands of *maquiladoras* (labour-intensive assembly plants) are located near the US border. This started in 1965 as the result of a deliberate government policy to create local employment in the depressed regions of northern Mexico by exporting low-value manufactured goods to the US market. The US government was also keen to mop up unemployment in the area in the wake of the collapse of an official labour migration scheme to the USA, the *bracero* programme. The US authorities were hopeful that employment in Mexico would reduce the flow of undocumented migrants north of the border. However, this part of the scheme failed because the jobs mainly went to young women (not to males, who were the most numerous migrants), while unemployed people from other depressed regions of Mexico flooded into the area in a desperate attempt to find work. The attempt to create a dam wall to stop the migrants effectively created a 'honey pot' that attracted them (Cohen 1987). Current reports by trade union representatives continue to talk of low wages, long hours and unorganized workers in the *maquiladoras*.

Despite these negative features, the BIP has officially been regarded as a success. In 1994/5, the numbers employed grew by 13 per cent to reach 743 000, while the value of exports rose from $26 300 million to $33 000 million. This represented 39 per cent of the country's total exports. During 1996, the numbers directly employed (there were spin-off jobs in other sectors) rose to 750 689. Unlike the rest of the economy, the BIP factories registered increases in both output and the value of exports, shrugging off the devaluation of 1995 (*Mexican Bulletin of Statistical Information*, July–September 1996: 83). The inducements have now been extended to all export-oriented firms even if they are not located in specific *maquiladoras* zones (Gereffi 1995: 124). Until recently, most Mexican workers employed in these zones were engaged in assembling electrical goods using imported components or in textile and clothing production. Over the last decade, however, serious efforts have been made to upgrade the *maquiladora* manufacturing region by encouraging new industries engaged in more sophisticated and capital-intensive activities such as producing components for cars and computers (Gereffi 1995: 135).

The North American Free Trade Agreement (NAFTA), of which Mexico is a member, should further enhance the export opportunities available to the *maquiladora* plants.

Another EPZ, on the island of Mauritius in the Indian Ocean, has been an unambiguous success. At its inception in 1971, 20 per cent of the population was unemployed. By 1994, unemployment was under 2 per cent and falling. The next year the government informed the International Labour Office that the island hosted 6205 migrant workers, brought in to offset labour shortages.

Although the economic benefits of the EPZ in Mauritius are evident, the provision of employment, again mainly to women in the 16–22 age group, had

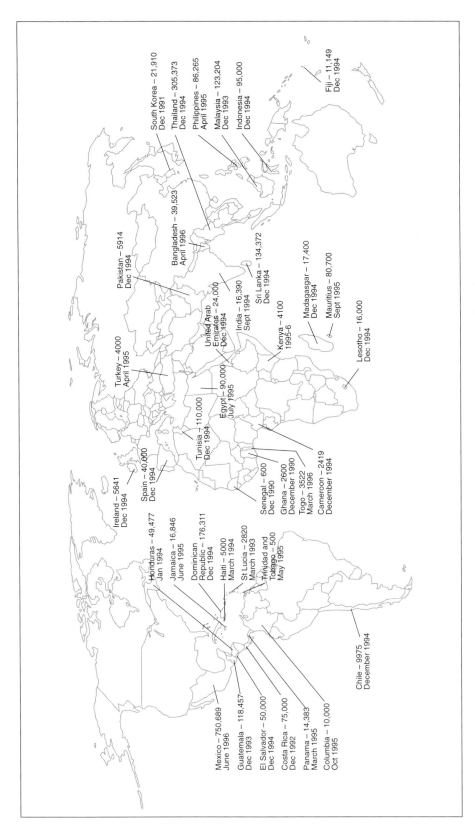

Map 7.1   Distribution of EPZs with number of workers

another benign social consequence. In the 1950s, in the period leading up to independence, British demographers were so alarmed at the rising birth rate in the country that they conjured up images of Mauritians falling off the edge of the island. As we will establish in Chapter 11, increased affluence and more reliable health care generally reduce the need for large families, which has indeed happened in Mauritius. The young women who worked in the EPZ were often grateful for the employment offered and extended their periods of employment, thus reducing the number of years in which they could safely bear children. The result was a massive reduction in the real and projected rise in population.

TNCs: power without responsibility

The primary social criticism of TNCs is that they exercise power without responsibility. In theory, and sometimes in practice, the power of the state is restrained by the due processes of law, by regular elections, and by the capacity of people to organize, demonstrate, advance their views and defend their interests. Although not all states have this degree of democracy, even in the most extreme dictatorships people have managed to bring their rulers to book. Equivalent forms of corporate power rarely have any such constraints on them. The *soga shosha* and other trading companies are often dominated by private, indeed secretive, dynastic families. Other TNCs are supposedly constrained by shareholders, but these are usually large anonymous blocks of shares bought by pension funds, insurance companies and banks with little interest in the company's affairs beyond the central performance indicator – profit.

The international agency UNRISD (1995) argues that the freedoms of TNCs have been significantly enhanced in recent years, especially by generous GATT regimes. For example, they have new rights in international law to enforce patents, trademarks and copyrights, whereas indigenous governments have been unable to enforce demands that local labour be trained or put other conditions on inward investment. UNRISD argues that this corporate power should be accompanied by some social responsibility – to the environment, which is often damaged, to the local community and to the workforce. There are many examples of even respectable, well-known TNCs being blind to their responsibilities in these respects. Let us cite three examples:

1. In 1989, an oil tanker, the *Exxon Valdez*, owned by the then largest petroleum company in the world, struck a reef in Prince William Sound off the Alaskan coast, causing the largest oil spill in history. Nearly 42 million litres of crude oil polluted the beaches, contaminated fishing and destroyed wildlife.

2. Shell in Nigeria and RTZ in Indonesia have continued to exploit natural resources with considerable ruthlessness and indifference to the local communities near which they work and whose land they have appropriated or bought for a song (see Box 7.2).

3. In December 1984, a major industrial disaster took place at Bhopal in central India when poisonous gas leaked from a US plant owned by the Union Carbide Corporation. More than 2800 workers, their families and others in the surrounding community died as a result of the leak. At least 20 000 were injured. Union Carbide has consistently stalled the legal proceedings instituted to gain compensation (Figure 7.2).

Box 7.2   Two cases of corporate blindness in Nigeria and Indonesia

In children's storybooks, the three wise monkeys are said to see no evil, hear no evil and speak no evil. This advice was apparently taken to heart by the oil company, Royal Dutch Shell, and the mining giant, Rio Tinto Zinc Corporation (RTZ). (We also talk about Shell's environmental impact in Box 18.3.)

Nigeria Shell has been pumping oil from the Delta region of Nigeria since 1966. Under the leadership of Ken Saro-Wiwa, an organized opposition group in the Ogoni area sought to get Shell to recognize its social responsibilities. The oil and waste from the plants had been polluting fishing grounds and the villages themselves. Although a few local community projects were supported, the company's principal defence is that it pays its taxes to the federal authorities in Lagos and it is up to them to organize social programmes. Saro-Wiwa was, according to the federal authorities, implicated in the deaths of four Ogoni chiefs who were unfriendly to the anti-Shell movement. Although it was accepted he was not there, he was convicted of conspiracy and executed, despite many calls for clemency from all over the world. On 14 December 1995, against the background of much opposition, Shell announced the continuation of a £2.5 million plant in Nigeria.

Shell claims to have been constrained by the Nigerian government and this cannot be discounted out of hand. However, as political power so often relates to economic muscle, it might be useful to indicate Shell's economic might in relation to that of the Nigerian government (the most powerful government in West Africa) and Ogoniland. In 1992, the company had $96 600 million in total corporate sales, whereas the GDP of Nigeria was less that a third of that, $29 600 million. Limping in at a small fraction of that total was the nominal GDP for Ogoniland at $850 000.

Indonesia RTZ, the world's biggest mining company, thought it would make a financial killing when is invested $1700 million in the Freeport gold mine in Irian Jaya, 2700 miles east of Jakarta, Indonesia. Instead, it has bought into a company that has been accused of killing people. On 5 April 1995, the Australian Council for Overseas Aid issued a report saying that 37 people had been killed or were missing from a village near the Freeport mine. Charges of company involvement in the killings were denied.

As in Nigeria, there is strong evidence of the company polluting the area around the mine. Members of the Free Papua Movement contend that Freeport and the Indonesian government have forced them off their ancestral lands, which they are now polluting. The company owns 2.9 million hectares in the area. The Overseas Private Investment Corporation, a US government agency, provides strong backing for the local people's views. According to it, the mining operations 'have severely degraded the rain forests surrounding the Ajkwa and Minajerwi rivers'. The project 'has created and continues to pose unreasonable or major environmental, health or safety hazards with respect to the rivers that are being impacted by the tailings, the surrounding terrestrial ecosystem and the local inhabitants'.

As in Nigeria, the company insists it is operating within the constraints of the local environmental and security laws. However, it is even more difficult for Freeport and RTZ to distance themselves from the national political context than it is for Shell in Nigeria. Freeport admits that the company provides food, shelter and accommodation to the Indonesian troops guarding the mine. Moreover, the repressive Indonesian regime holds a 9 per cent stake in the mine, which also provides the government with $250 million a year in taxes.

The people of Irian Jaya do not even recognize the Indonesian government's claims to sovereignty, let alone its right to sell their land to TNCs. The Free Papua Movement claims that, to impose its will, the Indonesian government has killed 43 000 natives since 1977. This is water off a duck's back, as far as Jim Bob Moffet, the chief executive officer of Freeport, is concerned. In a classic statement of corporate power without social responsibility he said, 'We are thrusting a spear of economic development into the heartland of Irian Jaya.'

Sources: UNRISD (1995); Moody (1996)

People are, however, capable of opposing corporate social irresponsibility. When, for example, Royal Dutch Shell proposed dismantling an oil rig at sea, which opponents claimed would result in extensive pollution, a mass protest commenced. The company backed down after extensive pressure from consumer and environmental groups in the UK, the Netherlands and Germany – including the commencement of a consumer boycott of Shell petrol.

It is worth noticing that Shell was not opposed by the British or any other government. In the case of the oil rig, social movements such as Greenpeace, which organized transnationally, stopped that particular display of corporate power (see Chapter 18). Equally, in its operations in Ogoniland, Shell was not opposed by the Nigerian government, which was deeply complicit in the company's operations. Instead, a small local protest group was supported by Amnesty International, Greenpeace, PEN (the international writers' lobby) and various other human rights groups. In later chapters, we explicitly deal with the issue of whether global social movements are now counterpoised to global corporations, making the locus of political debate and social contestation a global rather than national matter.

REVIEW

In 1970, there were about 7000 TNCs: in 1992 there were 37 000. Between them, they controlled 200 000 foreign subsidiaries with a combined worldwide sales revenue in 1992 of $5.5 trillion, compared with $2.4 trillion in 1980 (UNRISD 1995: 53). This was the equivalent of almost one-third of total global economic output. Such an amount was considerably greater than the total value of all the goods and services entering world trade through exports by national firms selling directly from their country of origin to a market in another country. TNCs also account for about three-quarters of world trade (Dunning 1993a: 14).

Clearly, economic power of this magnitude will have fundamental effects on the global economy, polity and society. As we have shown, there is a lively debate about whether TNCs have indeed superseded the nation state system both in their political independence and their global economic reach. In their social role, some argue that TNCs do good as well as harm, or do more good than harm. They provide employment, pay taxes that can be used to fund socially beneficial programmes, transfer technology, help industrialize agricultural countries and sell products people want at prices they can afford. Against this rosy view has to be set the evidence that the community, the environment and the company's workers often need protecting from corporate unaccountability and irresponsibility.

If you would like to know more ●

Easily the most accessible book on this topic is Dicken's *Global Shift* (1992) with its useful information on TNCs, changing patterns of world trade and investment and fascinating studies of key industries looked at in a global context.

Hirst and Thompson's *Globalization in Question* (1996), although more difficult, is worth inspection, for it summarizes the main debates in this area and offers a controversial and thought-provoking alternative to the more usual heady views on economic globalization.

Stallings (ed.), *Global Change, Regional Response* (1995), contains interesting recent material on the various regions of the developing world. Chapters 1 and 11 by Stallings and Chapter 4 by Gereffi are especially recommended but all the chapters are useful.

The book published by UNRISD, *States of Disarray* (1995), contains a hard-hitting critique of corporate irresponsibility.

Group work ●

1. For the purposes of debate, one group will adopt the view that TNCs are a force for global economic integration, another that they have not fundamentally moved beyond international trade patterns that have existed for a long time.

2. For the purposes of debate, one group will adopt the view that the TNCs are a force for social good, another that they generate malign social effects.

3. Write to the public affairs office of a large corporation requesting their annual report. (Look at adverts in the *Financial Times* or *The Economist* for addresses.) What defence, if any, does the company give as to its social responsibility? Are you convinced?

4. List all the TNCs you know of in the following categories: oil companies, motorcar companies, pharmaceuticals and chemicals. Compare this list with those of your class mates. Why are these companies familiar to you?

5. Why would you like/not like to work for a TNC?

Questions to think about ●

1. What reasons could be given to support the proposition that the world economy is much more internationalized and integrated than it was before the First World War?

2. Describe the major characteristics of an EPZ. Why did corporations wish to locate there?

3. Evaluate the positive and negative social effects of TNCs in the developing countries.

4. Evaluate Hirst and Thompson's case that economic globalization has not reached a point where TNCs have become truly autonomous agents and governments have not been rendered more or less powerless to act.

5. Examine the origins of the TNCs, noting national differences.

chapter 8

Uneven Development: The Victims

As we have noted before, globalization impacts very differently on different regions of the world. In this chapter we will review how uneven development arises and concentrate on the way in which four particular social groups are disadvantaged. With the collapse of alternative models, market-driven economies are now 'the only show in town'. Yet they seem intrinsically to generate enormous discrepancies in terms of income and opportunity both within and between countries. Many accept this outcome as natural or inevitable. 'The poor will always be with us' is one popular saying. Those who have lost out in the contest for prosperity are seen as lazy, even as biologically inferior. Sometimes the poor and disadvantaged even blame themselves for their condition. A sort of grim humour of capitulation seems to pervade this little British ditty: 'It's the same the whole world over/Ain't it all a blooming shame/It's the rich wot gets the pleasure/It's the poor wot gets the blame.'

Even if many people are socialized to accept a differential outcome fatefully, for sociologists the problem is more taxing and fascinating. Why do some lose and some win? Can the losers ever alter their place in the hierarchy? Is there some relationship between the fact that some win and some lose, that is do some win *because* some lose? Is it therefore in the interests of the rich and powerful to maintain a differential between rich and poor or does that consequence also provide a long-term threat to their continued dominance? Could it be to the ultimate benefit of the powerful that the poor achieve some social mobility and raise their standards of living? Can that social uplift be induced from the top – for example through the actions of benign social democratic politicians? Alternatively, will the only redress come from oppositional social and political movements emanating from the grass-roots level?

In this chapter we will examine two theories of uneven international development – world system theory and the notion that a new international division of labour (NIDL) has emerged. We will then look at whether globalization itself is a force contributing to powerlessness and social marginality. In our case studies we will consider the fate and fortunes of some key deprived social groups – workers in the de-industrializing areas, peasants, refugees and the urban poor.

THEORIES OF UNEVEN DEVELOPMENT

World system theory

Of a number of similar theories, Wallerstein's (1974, 1979) world system theory has been especially influential. His argument is that capitalism and not nation states have created the world order since from its beginning capital has always disregarded national borders and was driven to spill outwards in search of profits. The world system became stabilized into a structured set of relations between three types of country belonging to the dominant *core*, the *semi-periphery* or dependent *periphery* of the overall system. The semi-periphery, characteristically neither as technically advanced or rich as the core countries nor as lacking in autonomy and condemned to dependence as the peripheral countries, serves as a necessary buffer between the other two, dividing the potential opposition to continuing domination by core capital.

The designation of particular countries to a position in this hierarchy is not fixed, so some movement between them is possible – as in the case of Japan's remarkable ability to rise from the periphery in the 1870s to second position in the core bloc by the 1980s. However, movement from periphery to core is normally very difficult since, once their hold over other countries is assured, dominant players can use such control in order to perpetuate various unequal exchanges. Put simply, the latter involves the manipulation of monopoly control over technology and markets in order to underpay countries and producers for their goods and over-charge them for their purchases.

Gradually, and working on a global scale, capitalism has created an increasingly integrated world economy dominated by the logic of profit and the market. By the same token, it has generated excluded, marginal, dispossessed and poor people. This outcome was consequent on an often complex and ever-shifting world division of labour based on two closely related processes. These are:

1. The progressive tying of more and more countries into the global market as specialized buyers and sellers of various commodities (for example minerals, tropical raw produce, manufactured goods or advanced technology).

2. The tendency of capital to maximize whatever kinds of economic advantage was provided in a given country by the prevailing forms of labour process

and class relations. If there were, for example, slaves, serfs, share-croppers, tenant farmers or landless labourers capitalism was able to adapt to or perpetuate these forms of social exploitation (Cohen 1987).

Accordingly, the world capitalist system is dominated by its own logic of accumulation and it works to safeguard and expand the capitalist nature of the overall system at all times and to protect the interests of the leading players in particular. At the economic level it forms one unified system. At the political levels it is pluralistic, while socially it generates the extremes of poverty and prosperity with a variety of intermediate positions.

There have been many criticisms levelled at world system theory – mainly concerning Wallerstein's relative lack of interest in the political dimensions of power, privilege and dispossession and how challenges to the established order are mounted. Bergesen (1990: 70–5), for example, argues that the role of political power was crucial in explaining the origins and spread of capitalism. He argues that it was conquest and the introduction of state structures that enabled the colonial countries to impose various forms of forced labour and unequal trading terms on their dependencies, not their ability to slot already established local market relations into a world division of labour.

Despite this bias towards the economic level, world system theory has several important advantages for those seeking to develop a global sociology, as Wallerstein:

● treats the world holistically and historically

● provides a sense of narrative and development showing how earlier forms of what we have called proto-globalization give way to the age of globalization (see Chapter 2)

● underlines that inequality and unevenness is at the heart of the world system

● but accepts that it is possible, within serious limits, to move up (as well as down) the hierarchy.

Major Concept
NEW INTERNATIONAL DIVISION OF LABOUR

The NIDL divides production into different skills and tasks that are spread across regions and countries rather than within a single company. From the 1970s onwards hitherto agricultural countries, particularly in the Asia-Pacific region, became rapidly drawn into the new international division of labour as key production functions were shifted away from the old industrial zones.

The new international division of labour

Partly in response to the perceived deficiencies of world system theory, a team of German researchers (Fröbel *et al.* 1980) propounded the idea that the **NEW INTERNATIONAL DIVISION OF LABOUR (NIDL)** had emerged. They were reacting particularly to the rapid industrialization of East Asia and the other NICs and to the partial *de-industrialization* of the old heartlands of capitalist production. As we observed in Chapter 7, from the 1960s and 70s there was a growing tendency for some TNCs to locate the more labour-intensive parts of their overall operations in developing countries so creating 'world market factories'.

Advocates of the idea of a NIDL argued that by locating some manufacturing processes in cheap labour havens, little was done to enhance living standards and development prospects in those poor countries affected. By contrast, the export of capital contributed to the growing ranks of the unemployment in the West. The only winners, they argue, are the TNCs. While these theorists suggest that the NIDL has not fundamentally altered the core countries' ability to dominate the world capitalist system, they are alert to the existence of 'global losers' in all countries. Like world system theory theorists, they are sceptical that the periphery will overcome its condition of relative economic backwardness despite its recent, partial shift from dependence on raw material exports to the export of cheap manufactured goods.

Some of the criticisms levelled against world system theory can also be directed at this theory (Cohen 1987: Chapter 7). Certainly it does seem to under-value the capacity of some states in developing countries to use political power in order to create the conditions for a successful transition to at least semi-peripheral status in the world order. The leaders of some successful NICs such as Singapore and Malaysia are very aware of the dangers of being trapped into a cheap labour, low-tech, industrial future. To counter this Malaysia, for example, has founded eleven universities and is planning a 30-mile long and 10-mile deep 'Cybercity' which, it is hoped, will soon supersede Silicon Valley in California (although the turbulence in the east Asian currency markets in late 1997 has temporarily derailed this project).

GLOBALIZATION AND POVERTY

Although both world system theory and theorists of the NIDL have made important contributions to the understanding of global inequalities, some writers argue that the phenomenon of marginality has been greatly deepened by more recent processes of globalization. This view was evident in one of the key conclusions reached at the UN's Copenhagen Summit on Social Development in March 1995 (cited in Townsend 1996: 15–16):

> Globalization had been driven in part by high hopes of shared greater prosperity by the rapid processes of change and adjustment [but it has] been accompanied by more poverty, unemployment and social disintegration, too often residing in isolation, marginalization and violence. The insecurity that many people, especially vulnerable people, face about the future – their own and their children's – is intensifying.

The Summit estimated that more than one billion people in the world live in degrading poverty – disproportionately more women, blacks, children, single parents, unemployed, disabled and elderly people. These data are supplemented by Watkins (1997), a policy analyst working for the charity, Oxfam, who provides a vivid summary of the startling facts of global social inequality. In 1966 the richest fifth of the world's population enjoyed an income 30 times as great as the poorest fifth. By 1997 the average income of the rich was 78 times larger. With 12 per cent of the world's population, Africa has 1 per cent of the world's trade and investment. Yet, as Watkins (p. 17) notes:

> It is not only the citizens of the poorest developing countries who have been marginalized in the Gaderene rush to unleash markets. In some East Asian countries such as China, Vietnam and Thailand massive inequalities have been recorded in the past decade, slowing the rate of poverty reduction. In Latin America, which is set to succeed Asia as the fashionable place to invest, the export boom has not

benefited the poor. There are more poverty-stricken people now than in 1990, while the region's murder rate is six times the global average.

Needless to say, most of the victims of violent crime are poor people.

Is there any way of characterizing 'poverty'? It is an essentially contested concept, partly because in a diverse, dynamic and changing social world, poverty may be perceived differently in different contexts, partly because it is also a political concept, implying and requiring remedial action (Alcock 1997: 6). Sociologists have distinguished between the concepts of absolute poverty, where people live below subsistence level, and relative poverty, which is 'based on a comparison between the standard of living of the poor and the standard of living of other members of society who are not poor' (p. 69). In other words, relative poverty is defined according to social needs rather than basic, material needs; but it can be devastatingly marginalizing in its effects, impacting significantly on people's opportunities in terms of educational achievement, health and employment chances. As a loose description, if not a tight definition, the Copenhagen Summit (UN 1995: 57) proposed that we see poverty as taking the following forms:

> Lack of income and productive resources to ensure sustainable livelihoods; hunger and malnutrition; ill health; limited or lack of access to education and other basic services; increased morbidity and mortality from illness; homelessness and inadequate housing; unsafe environments and social discrimination and exclusion. It [poverty] is also characterized by lack of participation in decision-making and in civil, social and cultural life. It occurs in all countries: as mass poverty in many developing societies, pockets of poverty amid wealth in developed countries, loss of livelihoods as a result of economic recession, sudden poverty as a result of disaster or conflict, the poverty of low-wage workers, and the utter destitution of people who fall outside family support systems, social institutions and safety nets.

Whereas in the Cold War period mass poverty tended to be associated with the so-called 'Third World', some of the tendencies towards marginalization have also appeared in the former 'Second World'. Townsend (1996: 65), one of the world's leading experts on poverty, wrote in some despair of the former Soviet Union:

> I have witnessed the descent of swathes of the population into absolute poverty. Part of that process has been due to the deserved collapse of Communist rule. But part is also due to the implacable policies of the IMF and the World Bank, and the Group of 7, which have insisted, in their conditions for making loans, on measures which are inappropriate either because they are made too soon, are too extreme, or are too little related to the familiar institutions and current needs of large sections of the population. This is a mark of ideologues who care not for consultation and evidence.

The ending of the Cold War has also generated several adverse repercussions for sub-Saharan Africa. The withdrawal of former Soviet support from the communist regimes in Angola, Ethiopia and Mozambique was accompanied by the drying up of western investment – after 1989 much more attracted to the established markets in Asia and the emerging markets in Eastern European countries. The ending of the East–West conflict prevented African countries from exercising their former slender bargaining power by playing off each side in the Cold War contest against the other in the scramble for aid, loans and investment.

Having described the overall character of global poverty, we now need to observe *which* particular social groups in various countries and regions are being notably affected by social fragmentation and marginalization.

WORKERS IN THE DE-INDUSTRIALIZING COUNTRIES

As we have seen in Chapter 4, the global free market has wrought great change in the lives of many people living in the old industrial heartlands of the advanced countries. According to Peet (1987: 21) between 1974–83 approximately eight million relatively highly paid manufacturing jobs, representing a crucial volume of purchasing power, 'disappeared'. These losses were much greater in some countries than others, particularly in Europe, with Britain and Belgium suffering rather more than other countries, such as Germany. By contrast, in southern Europe, Latin America and South East Asia this period saw a rapid creation of new manufacturing employment. In Brazil, for example, jobs in manufacturing grew by 23 per cent, in Turkey by 32 per cent, and in South Korea and Malaysia respectively by a massive 77 per cent and 75 per cent.

By no means all of this manufacturing expansion in the NICs simply replaced lost employment in the advanced countries. Also, some businesses re-located their plants elsewhere *within* the rich countries, for example in the American case to the 'sunbelt' regions of the southern states such as Texas, Florida and Arizona. Nevertheless, perhaps more than in any other decade, the 1970s was a period when a considerable haemorrhaging of manufacturing employment from the 'rustbelt' or 'snowbelt' industrial zones of North America and Europe took place.

The decline of regional or city manufacturing generated a falling local tax base as incomes and retail values collapsed, with a consequent deterioration in public services. The psychological and social effects of falling living standards and unemployment made their impact on the incidence of suicide, murder, mental disorder, domestic violence, divorce and admissions to prisons. Neither did the spread effects of falling earnings stop there. Thus, suppliers and contractors across the USA providing components and other inputs to these industries were also hit. For example, Bluestone and Harrison (1987: 91) describe the case of Michigan where the loss of 5000 jobs in the automobile plants during the 1970s led to further job losses of around 20 000 across the USA. These redundancies occurred not just among component manufacturing suppliers but also in other car-related industries and services such as iron, steel, metal foundries, rubber, transport, car dealers, accountancy and financial services. Many of these jobs had been held by black workers attracted to the industrializing North from the agricultural South a century earlier.

Thus, de-industrialization in certain regions is linked to the rise of new industries in others. Clearly, economic globalization, both as cause and consequence, has been deeply implicated in these changes and so is partly responsible for the accompanying processes of social dislocation, increased economic insecurity and the fragmentation of communities and labour forces. It is important to recognize, however, that globalization has been only one of the factors involved in this long and continuing process of disruptive economic change. For one thing, capitalism has always been highly uneven and unequal in its impact within and between societies and internally driven by perpetual technological and market upheavals. Whole industries, regions and skill structures rise and fall with relentless regularity. Think, for example, about the cotton industry in northwest Britain, which provided the leading edge of the first industrial revolution in the first half of the nineteenth century. Yet, by the 1920s, its worldwide might had waned in the face of growing competition due to the establishment of rival textile industries in America, Europe, Japan, India and Egypt.

By the mid-1980s well over two-thirds of the labour force in the advanced countries had left manufacturing and were classified as service workers while the wages of manual workers in America, and several other countries, have not risen in real terms for over 20 years. The trend towards 'flexible specialization', involving, among other things, increased subcontracting to small firms and pronounced tendencies by all businesses to 'downsize' the permanent labour force and rely increasingly on temporary, casual and part-time labour, also goes some way towards explaining the apparent trend towards 'de-industrialization'. Even where job creation is successful, a large number of citizens in the industrialized countries, especially those of minority origin, are surviving only by relying on two or even three, low-paid part-time jobs.

PEASANTS AND LANDLESS LABOURERS

As capitalist social relations spread unevenly across the globe, one of the most notable 'losers' is the peasantry. In the nineteenth century, social theorists such as Marx assumed the inevitable decline and even disappearance of the peasantry. Modernization and industrialization were thought to signal the end of

Table 8.1   Urban population as percentage of population, 1993 (selected countries)

Country	%	Country	%
USA	75.80	Nigeria	37.66
Russian Federation	75.20	Ghana	35.38
Iraq	73.48	Guyana	35.16
Brazil	70.76	Pakistan	33.62
Dominican Republic	62.92	Indonesia	33.48
Slovak Republic	57.88	Tadjikistan	32.20
Ecuador	56.96	Angola	30.64
Algeria	54.16	Haiti	30.40
Egypt	44.26	Benin	30.38
Cameroon	43.06	China	28.66
Côte d'Ivoire	42.32	India	26.28
Zambia	42.06	Afghanistan	19.28
Senegal	41.30	Bangladesh	17.26
Guatemala	40.66	Ethiopia	12.96

Source: World Bank *Social Indicators of Development* Database at www.ciesin.org/prod/charlotte, consulted December 1997

rural pursuits. There are indeed indications at the end of the twentieth century that urbanization is increasingly the norm (Gugler 1995). Yet the process has been much delayed and is not as fully advanced as had earlier been expected. Table 8.1 shows the extent of urbanization in a number of countries.

As can be readily inferred from Table 8.1, there are large numbers of people still living in the rural areas. Of course, not all of these are 'peasants', an ambiguous term that we have not yet defined. To do so, we need to provide some sense of the nature of rural social differentiation. The class structure of the rural world is every bit as complex as that in the urban areas, although this is often overlooked as sociologists have overwhelmingly concentrated on the latter. An elementary approximation of a rural class structure may look something like Table 8.2.

Table 8.2 A simple rural class structure

Landlords	Live off rented land cultivated by tenants
Rich peasants	Live off own produce and surplus produced by hired hands
Middle peasants	Live off own produce generated mainly by family labour
Poor peasants	Own or rent some land but also have to work for others for their subsistence
Landless labourers	Own no land and have to sell their labour power

Source: Adapted from Bagchi (1982: 149–50)

These class distinctions are overlaid with religious, gender, ethnic and (in India and some other places) caste distinctions, discussed in Chapter 6. For example, scavengers, butchers and leather and night soil workers (collectors of excrement) are at the bottom of the caste hierarchy and, despite the attempt by the government of India to abolish the notion of untouchability, it is difficult for people to escape their occupationally defined and inherited castes.

The disruption of the rural world

What has all this to do with uneven development? The answer is that the rural world has been disrupted in a profound way by the processes of industrialization, urbanization and commercialization. 'The peasantry' has to be understood, therefore, not so much as a residual category (Marx's position) or an unchanging 'traditional' category, but as a differentiated group subjected to and evolving with the new international division of labour. There are now very few peasants who produce entirely for subsistence or even for consumption in the local market. Instead, most rural pursuits are now tied into the global market place.

At the top of the tree are vast agricultural TNCs such as Monsanto (who provide chemical fertilizers, pesticides, herbicides and genetically engineered crops) or Del Monte (whose cans of fruit are available on just about every major supermarket shelf). Such firms are correctly described as being involved in 'agribusiness'. They have bought vast areas of land in many countries, previously held as common land or owned by the middle peasantry, and turned this into a series of 'field factories' – using hired labour to plant, weed, pick and pack the produce. Small and middle farmers have been driven to the wall or can only survive by working part time for the big companies.

Green Revolution – the diffusion of high-yielding varieties of seeds, particularly wheat, maize and rice. (Not to be confused with the green/environmental movement.)

Another important way in which the rural world has been integrated into the global market place is through the **Green Revolution**, which spread high-yielding seeds to the farmers. Governments and research workers saw the Green Revolution as a means of abolishing famine forever. At first, sociologists like Pearse (1980) argued that the unintended consequences of this innovation were highly adverse. Only the richer farmers could afford the pesticides, fertilizer and water to make the seeds most productive. The seeds also worked better on a larger scale so the richer peasantry often bought out smaller farmers. Later social scientists reported a more benign outcome, particularly in Asia. As the cost of the technology fell, often with the help of government subsidies, poor and middle peasants were able to deploy the new seeds.

Elsewhere, the relentless globalization of the market place exposed hitherto protected small producers like the banana growers of the Caribbean to the giant agricultural corporations. The supermarkets of the rich countries demanded a larger, more standardized banana at a price even lower than the Caribbean farmers were able to deliver. The greater bargaining and marketing power of the big international producers were thus able to drive local farmers out of business even in their own local markets. So, for example, it is an everyday sight in a coffee-growing area (say in Latin America) to find on sale a jar of Nescafé containing coffee beans (say from Ghana), processed (say in Britain) and bulk-shipped to the area.

This relentless pressure on the peasantry has driven many of them into penury or landless desperation. They eke out a miserable existence on more and more marginal land or are forced to become landless labourers, drift to the slums around the big urban areas or accept work with such a level of exploitation that it amounts to near-slavery (see Box 8.1).

REFUGEES AND DISPLACED PEOPLE

The ancient Greek writer, Euripides, said in 431 BC that there was no greater sorrow on earth than the loss of one's native land. Yet, little progress has been made in protecting people from this curse. Indeed, the twentieth century can be characterized as a century of the refugee. It is, as we shall see, difficult to get an exact estimate of the scale of the global refugee population. This is partly because the word 'refugee' is used very loosely in the media and in popular conversation but very precisely in international law. 'Those seeking refuge' are, in a common-sense way seen as 'refugees'. 'Refugees' in this loose sense refers to those who have been forced to abandon their homes because of natural disasters, wars or civil wars or are victims of religious or ethnic persecution. In short, the emphasis is on events for which the individual cannot be held responsible.

There is much to be said for the common-sense understanding of the word 'refugee'. It puts our hearts in the right place and doesn't seek to make any fine distinctions between people who are in acute distress. Humanitarian and pro-refugee lobbies typically have a very wide definition of the category and seek to persuade government to offer support to all those in distress.

Box 8.1   'Slavery' in Brazil

A reporter for a Catholic weekly, Pat Marrin, wrote as follows: 'It is difficult to imagine things getting any worse for the millions of landless peasants who inhabit the infamous *favelas*, the squalid slums that ring many of Brazil's big cities. But according to an American-born Brazilian bishop, the same peasants who were forced from their ancestral homesteads into the slums by rich landholders are now being lured by the thousands, with false promises of high wages, to come to Brazil's rugged interior to clear unclaimed land for cattle ranches. Eager volunteers are getting a one-way ticket into slavery, sickness, torture and, sometimes, death.'

She quotes Bishop Herbert Hermes as claiming 'They pile a whole bunch of them into trucks or old rattletrap buses, take them way into the interior, give them a lot of liquor to drink on the way so they don't know where they are going… When they get there, they take away their documents and immediately present them with an outrageously high bill for their transportation, food and drink, and they're already in debt for the rest of their lives. If they try to escape, they're hunted down like animals, tortured, sometimes killed. Those who have escaped and gone to the police have been turned right back to the landholders.'

The bishop continued: 'Complaints to the Brazilian Ministry of Labor and Justice have led to official investigations, but the camps are alerted, even through the police, and by the time the investigators arrive, the workers have been taken two days into the interior, the camps are empty and you can't prove anything… It is hard to find honest people on these commissions, because most of the politicians, congressmen, governors and cabinet ministers are wealthy and many of them are landholders, so they are not too interested in this.'

One major frustration has been just getting so dramatic a human rights story publicized, Hermes argued. He suggested that the media in Brazil are controlled by the government and big money, so his supporters have learned to use the World Wide Web to leap over 'censorship' to reach the outside world. The power of the Internet was brought home to Hermes in April 1997 when he took part in a dramatic confrontation between Brazilian President Fernando Henrique Cardoso and the leaders of a grass-roots protest group that had walked from places all over Brazil.

The two-month-long, 600-mile walk by 2000 peasant farmers from nine regions arrived in the capital on 17 April 1997, attracting national attention and broad support. Hermes and two other Brazilian bishops, along with a dozen other high-profile public figures representing every aspect of Brazilian culture, were invited to witness a meeting between the march leaders and Cardoso. Hermes said the President scolded the marchers for challenging the positive economic data he was receiving from his experts, told them they were either misinformed or in bad faith. Then the President complained about the use of the Internet to 'dirty the image of Brazil', his own image and that of his economic policy. 'I go to Poland to be honored as an intellectual', he said, 'and the first thing they ask about is agrarian reform.'

Source: Extracts from Pat Marrin (1997) 'Brazilian poor used as slaves, bishop charges', *National Catholic Reporter*, 19 September 1997 (www.natcath.com/archives/091997/)

By contrast, the legal definition of a refugee arose as a consequence of a UN Resolution of 1950, which was later incorporated in the 1951 Geneva Convention and the 1967 Bellagio Protocol, both of which were signed by many countries. In paraphrase, protection was to be extended to people outside their country of nationality because of a well-founded fear of persecution by reason of race, religion, nationality and political opinion or membership of a particular social group. This definition sounded – and indeed was – very generous in spirit, but it was made clear that the determination of who was, and who was not, a refugee was very much in the hands of the receiving state. Unfortunately, this gave a virtual *carte blanche* to government officers, who sought ever to narrow the grounds for admission and recognition.

Refugees in the period 1914–89

The global scale of refugee flows in the twentieth century can be indicated in this quick historical overview (cf. Zolberg *et al.* 1989):

1. About 9.5 million refugees arose as a result of the unsettled conditions of the First World War, the revolutionary upsurges in Germany and Russia.

2. The Nazi threat against the Jews and Gypsies generated another wave of refugees. The historical evidence is now convincing that Hitler's initial plan was expulsion, not annihilation. However, as it became clear that most countries were refusing entry to the refugees, Hitler moved to the final solution – annihilation. (This experience provides a potent warning of what might arise in some wealthier countries today if they continue with highly restrictive refugee policies. Are we simply inviting oppressive regimes to commit genocide on their unwanted minorities?)

3. At the end of the Second World War there were eleven million people outside their countries and in need of assistance.

4. State formation often generates large numbers of refugees. The independence of India in 1947 was followed by the creation of Pakistan. Large numbers of Hindus and Muslims crossed to their respective 'sides'. In the same year the formation of the state of Israel created the Palestinian refugee problem. A special agency, the UN Relief and Works Agency for Palestinian Refugees, supervised the creation of camps, especially in Gaza, where the refugees and their descendants (some 2.2. million people) still struggle for their dignity and a decent standard of living.

5. Refugees fleeing from communist regimes during the period of the Cold War were often welcomed in the West, as they provided useful opportunities for scoring propaganda victories. East Germans, Czechs, Hungarians, Russian dissidents and Cubans all fled to the West.

Refugees after the Cold War

Beginning in the late 1970s and early 1980s, but accelerating thereafter, the number of refugees increased dramatically. The total number of 'persons of concern' recorded by the United Nations High Commission for Refugees (UNHCR) rose from about 10 million in the 1970s to 17 million in 1991 and then to a record 27 million in 1995, before falling. The threat to the Kosovars by the Serbian regime in the early months of 1999 will undoubtedly start the upward curve again. At the highest point, one out of every 255 people on this planet was a forced migrant. The expression 'persons of concern' indicates that the definition of 'refugees' cannot be strictly confined to the letter of the Geneva Convention (see Tables 8.3 and 8.4).

Table 8.3   'Persons of concern' to the UNHCR, 1996–97 (by region)

Region	Total of concern 1 Jan 1996	Total of concern 1 Jan 1997
Africa	9 145 400	8 091 000
Asia	7 668 000	7 925 000
Europe	7 689 000	5 749 000
Latin America	211 900	169 000
North America	1 335 400	720 000
Oceania	53 600	75 000
TOTAL	26 103 300	22 729 000

Source: UNHCR Web site www.unhcr.ch/, consulted in Dec 1997

Table 8.4   'Persons of concern' to the UNHCR, at 1 Jan 1997 (by category)

Region	Refugees	Returnees	Internally displaced	Others of concern	Total
Africa	4 341 000	1 693 000	2 058 000	–	8 091 000
Asia	4 809 000	1 241 100	1 719 000	156 000	7 925 000
Europe	3 166 000	308 000	1 066 000	1 209 000	5 749 000
Latin America	88 000	70 000	11 000	–	169 000
North America	720 000	–	–	–	720 000
Oceania	75 000	–	–	–	53 600
TOTAL	13 200 000	3 311 000	4 854 000	1 365 000	22 729 000

Source: UNHCR Web site www.unhcr.ch/, consulted in December 1997

Although there are considerable continuities between forms of refugee migration before and after the Cold War, there were three distinct shifts too:

1. With the collapse of the Berlin Wall a new migratory space opened up. The switch by the former Soviet Union and its allies to a policy of open borders, meant the western countries were confronted with a large number of unwelcome migrants. Where there was a policy of welcoming co-ethnic immigrants – in Israel, Greece and Germany – no great problem arose. Elsewhere, immigration laws designed to keep people out replaced the Berlin Wall, designed to keep people in. With the end of the Cold War, the political refugees of yesteryear are the economic migrants of today.

2. As can be seen in Table 8.4 a considerable number of the refugees and returnees are in Africa and Asia. And within those regions it was the poorer countries that were most affected. War, famine and ethnic conflict commonly

trigger forced migration. But, by the same token, once people have returned to their country of origin they cannot easily be absorbed because of the parlous condition of their countries.

3. The collapse of the Soviet Union also generated Balkanization all over the former eastern bloc, but particularly in the former Yugoslavia. The dreadful practice of 'ethnic cleansing' was all too reminiscent of Nazi Germany. Our TV screens have been filled with images of lines of pathetic people fleeing brutality and civil war in Bosnia, Croatia and Kosovo. In the early months of 1999 over half a million refugees fled from Kosovo to nearby Macedonia and Albania as NATO forces sought to halt the ethnic cleansing carried out by Serbian forces. The NATO intervention may have been morally justified, yet it served also to accelerate the flight from Kosovo.

Internally displaced persons

While the causes of refugee flows have not gone away, the increasing restrictions on entry to stable countries have blocked many possible entry points. The result is the phenomenon of internally displaced peoples (IDPs). This category has been recognized by the UNHCR, but is thought now to be vastly underestimated. One source, based on extensive reports from all affected countries, claims that by the mid-1990s, there were 20–22 million IDPs (Hampton 1998: xv). As one might imagine, most have been displaced by ethnic conflict or civil war – four million in the Sudan, 1.45 million in Afghanistan and 1.2 million in Angola. In Algeria, the violent struggles between the 'Islamicists' (comprising the Islamic Salvation Front, the Islamic Salvation Army, the Armed Islamic Group and Hezbollah) and the secular government have resulted in very large population shifts. A number of other countries exhibit similar problems.

In addition to political conflict, IDPs also arise from environmental changes (for example, the rising sea level), natural disasters and ambitious development projects. The construction of the massive Three Gorges Dam on the Yangtze River in China will displace millions of people. Another important example is India, where the Indian Social Institute numbers those displaced by dam construction at 16.4 million. According to Mishra *et al.* (1998: 145):

> Studies in the northeastern state of Bihar, where millions were displaced by industries, mines and dams, have shown that many displaced families of [so-called] 'tribal' cultivators ended up as casual labourers, with lower standards of living. Uprooted from kin and their forest-based livelihood systems, traditional cultivators lose their identity and means of living.

THE URBAN POOR

The rural areas in many poor countries are incapable of sustaining a self-sufficient life. Dim as the prospects are for obtaining permanent urban employment, the chances of gaining access to some kind of livelihood and to better services are usually greater than in the countryside. The migration that ensues has truly been described as 'of epic, historic proportions' (Harrison 1981: 145). In 1940 the

Figure 8.1   A refugee from Azerbaijan gathers fuel, 1993

towns and cities of the poorer countries housed 185 million. By 1975, the number had swollen to 770 million, over half of the increase being accounted for not by urban increases, but by migration from the rural areas (p. 145).

The newly arrived migrants have a wide variety of occupations and activities. Religious ascetics, the insane, the physically disabled, micro-traders (selling items like matches or nuts), touts for taxis and buses, pickpockets, thieves, prostitutes, handcart or rickshaw-pullers, beggars, those seeking work, apprentices and their 'masters' – all these are part and parcel of the rich social landscape in the cities of the poor countries.

Many of the migrants newly arrived in the urban areas seek to maintain some kind of link to the countryside, for practical and well as emotional reasons. This system is sometimes described as circular migration or a 'dual system' and is succinctly described by Gugler (1995: 544):

> The 'dual-system' strategy is sustained by kinship groups that control rural resources, in particular access to the ancestral lands. The village assures a refuge in a political economy that fails to provide economic security to many of the urban population and that often threatens an uncertain political future. For many urban dwellers, the solidarity of rural kin provides their only social security, meagre but reliable. Often they look forward to coming 'home'.

Despite the resilience of this system in many areas, gradually the ties with the village are cut, the household breaks up and the migrants to the city are on their own. There many have to eke out a miserable existence in the slums. Such temporary settlements go under different names – *favelas and barrios*, cardboard cities and shantytowns. They are characterized by inadequate shelter, poor roads, with no sewerage, electricity or potable piped water. Wider provisions like sports fields, libraries, schools, health centres or parks are undreamed-of luxuries.

Figure 8.2   Garbage pickers in Guatemala

The condition of people living in such settings is so bad that a number of post-Marxist writers conceived the idea that there is a class *below* that of the proletariat. As we saw in Chapter 6, Marx had noticed such a group of people in the dispossessed peasantry who flooded into nineteenth-century Paris. In a pamphlet *The Eighteenth Brumaire of Louis Bonaparte* (1954/1852) he described this group as a '*Lumpenproletariat*', a group that could not cohere because it contained too many diverse elements. He thought it impossible for them to join a revolutionary struggle as 'their conditions of life prepared them more to be 'bribed tools of reactionary intrigue'.

The most famous attack on this view came from Frantz Fanon, the Martiniquan psychiatrist who joined the Algerian anti-colonial struggle. Fanon argued that Marx had failed to anticipate the importance of those who had

> **Box 8.2   The child scavengers of Bangkok**
>
> Child scavengers usually accompany their parents to work in Bangkok, Thailand, often from as young as 5–7 years of age. 'Work' is at one of Bangkok's six dumping sites, where 2200 tons of garbage are placed each day. In the late 1980s researchers observed about 500 scavengers at each site. So dependent are people on what they can find that when new sites are created, the slum dwellers around the site move to the new location.
>
> One site is at Onnood, on the eastern side of the city. The scavengers account for more than 40 per cent of the 473 households in the area. The dumping site is four acres in extent and 15–20 feet high including contaminated wet garbage, gas from decomposed waste, smoke from the slow-burning dry garbage, heat from the sun and the burning site and a noxious smell. Many young scavengers start work early in the morning and finish at 5pm, when they sell their pickings to the merchants. There are also a number of part-time scavengers who work for 3–4 hours after school.
>
> The activity is internally regulated, with particular digging sites being marked out and allocated. Scavenging is said to provide a 'fair source of income to the slum dwellers'.
>
> *Source:* Banpasirichote (1991: 10–11)

moved into the colonial towns and capitals as unemployed and underem-ployed job-seekers. Even using the expression 'workers' for such people was inappropriate, as they were unlikely ever to find work. He uses the same expression as Marx, 'the Lumpenproletariat', but has a more elevated role for them. In Fanon's famous political tract, translated as *The Wretched of the Earth* (1967), they are assigned the role of an 'urban spearhead' to a revolution based in the countryside. In a vivid metaphor Fanon saw this group as a 'horde of rats'. One could kick them away, but they kept coming back – tenaciously gnawing at the roots of the colonial tree.

To signify the political potential of this group other authors have used the expression 'sub-proletariat' or 'peasantariat' to get away from some of the nega-tive connotations of the expression 'Lumpenproletariat'. However, despite hopes by radical writers that they may in some sense take the place of the workers (who were seen as compromised and compliant with the capitalist system), the urban poor do not in general show a revolutionary consciousness. Instead, four forms of social action seem to have emerged:

1. A conservative clinging on to peasant values, even when the conditions for sustaining a connection with the countryside have eroded.

2. A link with populist politicians who, just as Marx surmised, use the urban poor to sustain themselves in power while placating only the most troublesome.

3. A collapse into criminal activity as a way of life and the sole means of livelihood.

4. More hopefully, a reforming self-improving zeal shown by community actions to improve the slum dwellers' environments and standards of living.

This more positive outcome is often helped by the involvement of profes-sionals, students and NGOs who work with the urban poor to obtain basic goods and resources. Their position seems to improve dramatically if there is a strong civil society and some reasonable degree of political democracy. Such improvements arise for an obvious reason – politicians competing for office need votes. If the urban poor can cohere for political action, gradually roads, subsidized building materials, water-borne sewerage and piped drinking water arrive. The level of public services and environmental quality will never be of the sort found in wealthier suburbs, but at least some people will be able to live their lives in relative comfort and safety.

Where civil society and universal democracy are weak, the urban poor are particularly vulnerable. Take the case of China. There the dual system is still alive if not well. A 1997 survey of over 40 000 rural households in China found that 31 per cent obtained at least a proportion of their income from non-farm sources (that is as remittances or wages). But the authorities in the southern Chinese towns are highly alarmed by the numbers of rural workers knocking at their doors. China has a rural labour force of 450 million, including 130 million who are underemployed and 70 million who have migrated outside their home province. An estimated 330 000 migrants arrive in Shanghai *each day* and about 170 000 each day in Beijing. According to newspaper accounts (*New York Times*, 9 January 1998; *South China Morning Post*, 9 January 1998) the authorities have reacted in the following ways:

1. In 1995 the Beijing authorities demolished the shantytown, Zhejiang village, which had housed 100 000 people.

2. Expulsions of migrants by the Public Security Bureau are common.

3. The Shanghai authorities have banned migrants from 23 job sectors, while Beijing has barred them from 20.

4. In the first nine months of 1997 police in fifteen cities returned 190 000 migrants and beggars to their home provinces.

5. The Minister of Public Security, Tao Siju, has said that migrants in urban areas with 'three nos' – no job, no residence permit and no identity card – should be detained and sent home.

6. Internal controls on the movements of workers have been imposed. Between 50–80 per cent of unregistered work-seekers face criminal prosecution.

REVIEW

There have been a number of macroscopic attempts to explain why uneven development, or global inequality, arises. World system theorists, those interested in the new international division of labour and those who write of the social marginality consequent on the process of economic globalization itself, have all provided valuable insights. All three cohere on one central insight – that the spread of capitalist social relations can act like the Grim Reaper – cutting a swathe of death through the agricultural populations and labour forces in many countries, regions and cities. This negative outcome is likely when the adoption of neo-liberal economic practices is disengaged from the nature of society and the form of political governance. This situation is particularly evident in post-communist Russia, where speculative capital and incompetent government have triggered a near-disintegration of society.

In this chapter we have sought to make these general theories 'come alive' by discussing four groups – workers in the de-industrializing countries, peasants, refugees and the urban poor. It may be difficult for those in more favoured situations to comprehend (let alone measure or theorize on) the level of devastation, poverty and human degradation suffered by many in the victim groups. We have already had occasion to quote the ancient Greek thinker Euripides in this chapter when talking of refugees. We cannot resist also mentioning another wise Greek philosopher, Plato, who warned the Athenians that the income of the rich should not exceed the income of the poor by more than five times. Any more would generate economic inefficiency and risk 'the greatest social evil', civil war (cited Watkins 1997). While we might see the wisdom of these remarks, the income inequalities indicated by the data we have quoted earlier in this chapter vastly exceed the maximum ratio suggested by Plato. Indeed, a measure of income disparity may not even be the most salient. The significant differences between the global winners and global losers may turn on such basic issues as the provision of clean water, access to shelter and health care and the chances of surviving infanthood. Certainly, our current phase of global development is a long way from alleviating such deprivations.

If you would like to know more ●

For material on peasants, look at *The Journal of Peasant Studies* – it should be in your library. In addition to some high-quality, although sometimes difficult articles, the journal carries a section called 'Peasants Speak', which reproduces interviews and other material gathered at the grass-roots.

The main organization acting in support of the world's refugees is the United Nations High Commission for Refugees (UNHCR). The UNHCR produces a very helpful biennial volume called *The State of the World's Refugees* and maintains a useful web site at http://www.unhcr.ch/

Alan Gilbert and Josef Gugler's *Cities, Poverty and Development* (1992) provides an excellent overview of urban problems. It is especially good on Latin America and Africa.

The consequences of de-industrialization in the USA, especially for black workers, are considered in Douglas S. Massey and Nancy A. Denton's (1993) book *American Apartheid.*

Group work ●

1. Access the UNHCR's site at http://www.unhcr.ch/. Summarize the main statistical changes to the data on refugees and displacees that have occurred since the data published in this chapter were recorded.

2. Divide into four groups. Each group will advocate the merits of one of the strategies for social action on the part of the urban poor described in this chapter.

3. Various ratios describing the income distribution between poor and rich people have been mentioned in this chapter. There are technical ways of measuring these distributions more precisely. (They are called, just for your information, the

Lorenz curve and the Gini index of inequality.) Discuss how you would set about measuring inequalities from first principles.

4. Divide the group into three. Group A will research the basic facts of poverty in the USA, Group B will research Bangladesh, while Group C will look at post-communist Russia. Each group will report their findings to the class as a whole.

Questions to think about •••

1. Will the poor always be with us, as a popular saying has it?

2. What are the differences between a refugee and an internally displaced person (IDP) and are these differences important?

3. What are the respective merits of world system theory and the theory of the new international division of labour in assessing the nature of global inequality.

4. Assess the extent to which workers in the industrialized countries have been victims of economic globalization.

5. Why does inequality not necessarily result in political turmoil?

9

Failures of Global Control

As we have shown in Chapter 5, the nation state system has experienced serious difficulties in providing suitable and sufficient responses to some of the social, economic, political and security problems that manifest themselves at a global level. Whether it is trying to stop ethnic conflict in Rwanda, Kosovo or Somalia, contain expansionist military leaders like Saddam Hussein or develop a regulatory framework to police flows of capital, bilateral agreements between nations are inadequate. The development of regional blocs, military alliances like NATO and the UN system itself have also not always worked effectively at the global level. While all these issues are of major concern, probably the most important failures of global control that come within our purview as sociologists are crime, drugs and the incapacity to arrest extreme cases of social deprivation, such as famine. This chapter is concerned with these three failures.

Just as globalization and the deregulation of the economy leads to the increased capacity for individual investors, tourists, banks and TNCs to profit from relatively open borders, so too, do opportunities blossom for cross-border crime. In Chapter 12 we record that tourism is the largest *legitimate* sector of the global economy. However, the largest without the qualifying adjective is global crime – bringing in profits of some $500 billion a year. International criminal activity can include anything from people-trafficking (smuggling immigrants), trade in forbidden goods (for example in medicines or artefacts from ancient civilizations), computer fraud, violating patent, licence or copyright agreements, illegal arms-dealing or smuggling cigarettes and stolen cars.

There is some indication that these activities are outpacing illegal drugs as the main sources of income from international crime. For example, one US estimate is that the Chinese triads (criminal gangs) alone make $2.5 billion a year in migrant-trafficking (Martin and Schumann 1997: 208). However, there is little dispute that the profits from the drug trade are also immense and, moreover, highly corrosive in their effects. The turnover in the world heroin market went up more than twentyfold from 1970 to 1990, while the cocaine trade increased more than fiftyfold (Strange 1996: 114). Moreover, fuelling the habits of the many people who are the clients and victims of this trade leads to vastly increased levels of domestic, often violent, crime.

Those who profit from the drug trade are primarily the 'drug barons', the smugglers and the dealers. However, it is difficult to eliminate the trade while it also forms so vital a part of the cash income gained by poor farmers in countries like Bolivia, Nepal and Jamaica and while the demand for recreational and addictive drugs in rich countries seems insatiable. If growing coca, opium poppies or marijuana yokes some farmers to the global economy, in other places people can neither produce enough food for export at globally competitive rates, nor grow enough for subsistence. In developing countries, 60 per cent of deaths of the under-fours are caused by hunger. The poor, the elderly and women also suffer disproportionately. There is a persistent belief that 'natural causes' promote famine. As we explain in this chapter, work by sociologists and others has shown a much more complex set of causes are at work.

Crime, drugs and famine are not the only, but are certainly among the most important, afflictions of global society that have eluded global control and remedy. How do we gauge their extent and effects?

CRIME WATCH

Statistics on crime are notoriously difficult to interpret: indeed the cynical expression 'Lies, damned lies and statistics' seemed almost to have been invented to cover the case of crime. The principal difficulties are threefold:

1. The difference between the incidence of crime and the incidence of *reported* crime (for insurance purposes and other reasons crime might be undeclared).

2. Victim surveys characteristically show a higher incidence of crime than do the police figures. (It may also be in the interests of the police to show they are more effective than they are.)

3. There are difficulties interpreting what 'crime' is, particularly when there are incompatible definitions between different countries.

Property crime and violence

Even bearing such difficulties in mind, it is nonetheless doubtful that statistical anomalies and definitions alone can explain the vast differences in certain recorded crime rates between countries, for example the common crime of car theft – a useful, although insufficient, indicator of the breakdown of law and order (see Table 9.1).

Table 9.1 Reported car crime, 1995 (selected countries)

Country	No of cars (millions)	No of thefts (000s)	Theft per 000 cars
UK	24.8	544.9	22.0
USA (1994)	133.9	1539.3	11.5
France	25.1	287.1	11.4
Italy	30.0	305.4	10.2
Norway	1.7	16.9	10.0
Belgium	4.2	38.2	9.0
Spain	14.2	98.8	7.0
Netherlands	5.6	34.7	6.1
Portugal	2.6	8.3	3.2
Germany	40.5	129.5	3.2
Switzerland	3.2	9.5	2.9
Austria	3.6	5.0	1.4
Total	289.5	3017.7	10.4

Source: The Economist (13 September 1997: 36)

It is tempting to speculate that widening inequalities combined with an increased culture of consumerism in some of the countries listed in Table 9.1 has contributed to their high crime rates. In one account, the authors surmise that the media 'make people more and more cynical as they see that the rich take what they want, and then taunt the rest of society through the media, the movies and advertising with the "good life" of consumerism' (Burbach *et al.* 1997: 22). The same authors quote the conservative US foreign policy adviser, Zbigniew Brzezinski, who argues that a 'permissive cornucopia' has replaced religion and moral values. People are encouraged to want goods but 'much of the world's population, unable to obtain many of these goods, grows frustrated, resentful and rebellious' (p. 23).

Certainly, this explanation for the increases in property and violent crime has some immediate plausibility. As Burbach *et al.* (1997: 22) have it: 'Globalization is spawning its own barbarians who are destroying it from within.' They point to a 'culture of violence' in many of the world's cities and maintain that industrialization and modernization increase criminality – property crimes are four times higher in developed than developing countries. Such comments have to be taken seriously, but they are incomplete. Using 'globalization' as a 'cause' of crime does not always work. Take, for example, the relatively high rate of car theft in France and the very low rate in Germany. In France, the welfare system is still relatively intact and the post-Fordist flexible labour market has barely arrived. Germany, by contrast, offers a more ruthless labour market, with similar rates of unemployment to France, yet a much lower rate of car theft. This contrast suggests that there are more proximate and particular causes of crime in France and Germany. Unfortunately, we cannot explore this phenomenon here.

In the cases of Britain and the USA, however, the general argument does seem to hold up. During the Reagan and Thatcher periods market forces were let rip and, despite the pious claims that a cascade of wealth would 'trickle down', income inequalities widened notably. Although there is some element of fake nostalgia in this, many commentators remarked on the collapse of a community spirit and the diminishing of a sense of a moral obligation to look out for wayward youth or care for the less fortunate. The respectable blue-collar working class was decimated, with massive losses of jobs in the coalmines, the steel mills and the 'rustbelt' areas – where Japanese imports undermined car production, component manufacturing and engineering. In the greater metropolitan area of Chicago there were 616 000 jobs in the manufacturing area in the mid-1950s, three decades later they had shrunk by 63 per cent to 277 000. In Chicago and other US cities such as Los Angeles, New York and Miami the consequent sense of desperation is palpable. 'The violence, fear, alcoholism and drug abuse that grips the underclasses of these cities is directly linked to this despondency and hopelessness' (Burbach *et al.* 1997: 103).

Urban nightmares and racial divisions

Violent crime usually involves poor people attacking other poor people. However, the massive divisions that result from urban social inequalities none the less create a lethal cocktail of fear among those who have money, property and employment combined with resentment among those who are without such goods and resources. A siege mentality results, which has implications both for public and private responses to anticipated and actual crime. In California expenditure on prisons has overtaken the education budget, while in Los Angeles alone there is an average of 35 crimes reported every hour, ten of which are listed as violent crimes such as murder, rape or aggravated assault (Burbach *et al.* 1997: 28–9). US citizens spend twice as much money on private guards as the government does on police (Martin and Schumann 1997: 9). This 'internal measure' of the decay of the nation state is every bit as telling as the argument that nation states are losing the battle to control global capital (see Chapter 5).

Although bad enough, when social inequalities are overlaid with the prism of 'race' the cocktail becomes even more explosive. In post-apartheid South Africa, for example, property crimes involving violence have now reached endemic proportions. Rural–urban migrants who were previously excluded from the cities under the notorious pass law system have now joined immigrants from even poorer countries in the formerly 'white cities'. With little change in white economic power, about 40 per cent black unemployment and the growth of shantytowns, it is hardly surprising that many have turned to crime. The long campaign of armed resistance to apartheid and the civil wars in neighbouring countries have fomented a market in weapons and a gun culture. Wealthier South African citizens, including some blacks who have 'made it', are uneasy about travelling at night and many have turned their homes into fortresses with alarm systems, burglar-proof bars, high walls, guards, dogs and weapons. Armed response units operated by private security firms provide back-up.

A similar scenario unfolds in Brazil, where one property developer has created a 'safe city', called Alphaville, west of São Paulo. He boasts that he is 'creating the conditions for heaven on earth' and knows nothing about the famous French film made by Jean-Luc Godard in the 1960s – also called *Alpha-*

Social control refers to the process whereby rich and powerful actors inhibit, channel and manage the behaviour of the population at large.

ville – that predicted a technological nightmare of total surveillance and *social control* (Box 9.1). Life has truly imitated art. High walls, sensors and spotlights surround the Brazilian Alphaville. Private security officers, often policemen trying to augment their regular salaries, cruise around the periphery. Every visitor must show an identity card and must be authorized by the residents. Nannies, kitchen helps and chauffeurs have their police records checked. Even the residents are rejected if they have criminal records. Some 120 000 people live in Alphaville and there are plans for a dozen more similar cities (Martin and Schumann 1997: 171–2).

Box 9.1   Social control in sociological theory

Social control is necessary to modern societies, in so far as sociologists believe that older forms of customary and communal authority broke down in urbanizing and industrializing societies. At the level of the workplace, the neophyte industrial labourers had to be taught the habits of punctuality, self-discipline, hard work and thrift. In the early factories employers often complained that workers would arrive drunk, take off feast days and often not turn up at all on Monday mornings. 'Punching-in' (to a time clock), penalties for lateness and other forms of surveillance were instituted to overcome these 'bad' habits.

At a more general level, systems of social welfare, prisons, asylums, children's homes as well as mass schooling and even the extension of the franchise have been seen as ways in which those with power, wealth and authority have controlled dissent and potential rebellion on the part of those without these attributes. Of course, one must be careful not to believe that there is some giant conspiracy at work. The 'exigencies of capitalism' can be used to explain too much. The professional and upper classes may be hankering for, and imagining, a nostalgic vision of a peaceful, rural community – which they seek to reproduce for the more general social good not merely their own. And it is important too to remember that the poor, not the rich, are the principal targets of violence and crime. Given their greater exposure, they often favour more extreme measures of social control (like hanging, public executions and beatings).

Since the 1970s sociologists have linked the concept of social control to the study of deviant behaviour in imaginative ways. Social control is now used to refer to more general pressures to induce conformity, pressures that become more insistent from time to time. Stanley Cohen (1972) described these moments as 'moral panics', when the official agents of social control like the police and the courts swing into action against drug-takers or youth gangs. Their interventions are, to some extent, conditioned by the negative labels that are used by the media, who take up the cudgels of middle-class respectability to label negatively groups that have became 'folk devils' in the public imagination. In a complicated feedback loop, some of these groups actually relish their public notoriety – so a process of 'deviancy amplification' develops as each side plays to the gallery.

Michael Foucault made other major conceptual breakthroughs. In his *Discipline and Punish* (1977) he echoes some Marxist views in seeing the 'great incarcerations' of the nineteenth century as part of a common design. Thieves into prisons, workers into factories, lunatics into asylums, conscripts into barracks and children into schools were all corralled in the service of capital. However, Foucault is also interested in more subtle forms of surveillance and discipline. Instead of brutal spectacles like the guillotine, the panopticon designed by Bentham (an all-seeing tower in a prison) engaged in unobtru-

(cont'd)

sive but unremitting surveillance. Discipline was not merely exemplary and demonstrative, but good for you. Psychiatrists, teachers and social workers became the engineers of the deviant mind and the unwitting agents of social control.

In wealthy contemporary societies the capacity for surveillance has been considerably enhanced by technology. Closed-circuit television sets (CCTVs) are placed in many shopping malls and busy streets, while computerized databases and the Internet have generated a new set of 'footprints' that can be followed by a determined investigator. On average adults in the developed world have their details recorded on 300 databases.

Sources: Cohen (1972); Foucault (1977); Mayer (1983: 17–38); Cohen (1985: 25–6)

Still on the horizon, because it is such a recent development, is the likely result of the floating migrant population of 50 million rural Chinese who have been shaken loose from their land and support networks due to the neo-liberal economic reforms. As they increasingly desperately search for employment in the burgeoning cities of south China, they face 'alienation and isolation [and] are likely to resort to crime' (UNRISD 1995: 73).

White-collar crime

White-collar crimes are those perpetrated by more respectable members of society. They often involve fraud.

Globalization greatly enhances the possibilities for *white-collar crime* because of more open borders, computer link-ups and enhanced means of transport and communication. One case in point is the EU where there is no overall authority, yet there are open borders between a number of countries. Where sales tax rates differ, as they do notably in the case of alcohol and cigarettes, smuggling takes place on a massive scale. Although often carried out as a family enterprise by tourists and visitors, cigarette-smuggling is also big business. In 1992, the authorities in Germany confiscated 347 million contraband cigarettes; by 1995 the figure was up to 750 million. (The annual loss of revenue is about 1.5 billion marks.) The cigarettes often arrive from the USA, before being sent to the free ports in Rotterdam and Hamburg (or to the duty-free stores in Switzerland). They are then bought for export by legitimate or illegal companies – the latter registered in Panama, Cyprus or Liechtenstein. The cargo sets off in customs-sealed lorries to cross EU territory for further export, but it never gets there. The traders are often known, but untouchable in that their assets have been safely stored in offshore banks (Martin and Schumann 1997: 208–9).

Smuggling in a more unlikely commodity, chlorofluorocarbons (CFCs), has also become rampant. In 1987, 24 countries signed the Montreal Protocol which was intended to reduce the use of CFCs, which were destroying the fragile ozone layer surrounding the earth, resulting in eye damage and skin cancer. Thought of these consequences did not trouble the smugglers who exported some 20 000 tonnes a year from China and Russia to the USA and Europe for use in many cooling processes, including air-conditioning. CFCs still work better than their safer replacements and they are the ideal product for illegal trade, being colourless and odourless. In Miami, only cocaine had a higher street value than CFCs (*The Economist* 13 September 1998: 78).

Smuggling is often so large in volume that it threatens legitimate trade and can be used to corrupt state officials. Massive 'turf wars' result as criminal gangs carve up exclusive territories the better to suborn bureaucrats, set up extortion rackets and gain access to illegal goods. Between 1992–5, the murder rate in Moscow went up by 50 per cent, much of it explained by the attempts by 3000 organized gangs to drive out their competitors (UNRISD 1995: 72). There is so little distinction between criminal and state activities in Russia that state arsenals of weapons are being plundered for private profits. Sub-machine guns are fed into terrorist organizations while even some of Russia's nuclear arsenal is on the international market. In 1998, the Nobel prize-winning writer, Alexander Solzhenitsyn, excoriated Russia's post-Soviet rulers. He claimed that 'Russia is ruled by a band of selfish people who are indifferent to the fate of the people and do not even care whether they live or die' (*Daily Telegraph* 2 June 1998).

Box 9.2   The Nigerian 'advance fee' scam

At the end of 1997 the Central Bank of Nigeria (CBN) felt compelled to publish a press statement in many of the leading magazines and newspapers worldwide. The CBN recorded that since the early 1990s, it had sought to expose the operations of fraudsters who were operating a hoax, mysteriously known as '419', or the 'advance fee scam'. So far the bank had taken out adverts in 80 newspapers in 12 languages in 36 countries in an apparently vain attempt to expose the gangs. As the CBN officials noted, 'driven by fraudulent tendency, greed and the urge to make quick and easy money at the expense of Nigeria, many of the so-called victims have continued to ignore the [published] warnings'.

How did the fraud operate? Typically it would start with a letter (followed by faxes or telexes) offering to transfer huge sums of money to the recipient's bank account, normally in US dollars. The money, it was hinted, came from certain 'dodgy' transactions, which the authorities were, sooner or later, going to expose. The writer offered to split the money with the addressee. If this letter was answered, it was suggested that in order to release the money certain 'taxes' (that is bribes or fees) had to be paid to key bankers, corporation officials and politicians. The fraudsters lent authenticity to their 419 by sending correspondence on faked letterheads. Sometimes the 'mark' (the target of the fraud) was invited to Nigeria and given red-carpet treatment by phoney bank officers, government officials or others in the scam.

Regrettably, the marks were told, 'registration fees', 'processing fees', unforeseen taxes', 'licence fees', 'signing fees', 'lawyers' fees', 'release fees, 'sales tax' and other inventive fabrications had to be paid upfront before anything could happen. Needless to say once these levies had been paid, the fraudsters took off. It seems barely credible that people could be such fools as to fall for these schemes, but apparently thousands have done so and millions of US dollars are involved.

Three indignant victims (Larry Sorth and Mr and Mrs Tei) sued the CBN in a US court presided over by the appropriately named Hon. Justice Charles A. Sham. Perhaps unsurprisingly Justice Sham concluded that the plaintiffs were not in touch with the CBN, even if they thought they were, and that 'they were, from the outset, aware that the transactions were bogus, fraudulent and too good to be true'.

The CBN described this judgement as a 'landmark case' and once again warned those who received letters like the ones described not to fall victim to 'international criminal syndicates whose nefarious activities have been a source of embarrassment to the CBN and the Nigerian government'.

Source: Central Bank of Nigeria, Press Statement, October 1997

Outright criminal activity has also taken hold in the respectable corridors of Wall Street and the City of London. Just two of the prominent cases were the 'junk bonds' scam – investments sold to an unsuspecting public by Michael Milken – and the 'insider trading' of Ivan Bosky. ('Junk bonds' offered a high yield, but had an even higher rate of default. 'Insider trading' refers to confidential information that is misused to inflate or collapse a share price.) In 1994, in the USA one third of the 100 largest merger deals were preceded by changes in the share price that could only be explained by insider information (Burbach *et al*. 1997: 71).

Corporate crime

As was indicated earlier, it is sometimes quite difficult to decide what is a crime, as various jurisdictions and definitions often confuse the matter. Take the case of the horrific leak of lethal gases from the Union Carbide plant in Bhopal, India, in December 1984. Was this episode the result of crime or merely misfortune?

Pearce and Tombs (1993: 187–211) describe the dire consequences of the event. Over 200 000 local people were exposed to fumes, some 60 000 were seriously affected, more than 20 000 injured, and about 10 000 may have died as a direct result of the leak. Babies with birth defects are still being born. The parent company in the USA denied it had a bad safety record, claimed its Indian subsidiary was to blame and sought to deflect attention by claiming sabotage was involved. The company managed to twist the arm of the Indian government into accepting a very low settlement of $470 million for all victims. This deal was in exchange for a guarantee that Union Carbide would escape prosecution. An attempt to try the case in the USA, where substantial damages would have probably been awarded, was deflected by the company's lawyers. They were able to override the parent company's central role in the design and installation of the plant and 'finger' the Indian government for its poor regulatory apparatus and inadequate inspectorate.

It is perhaps somewhat ambiguous as to whether what we witnessed in Bhopal was 'criminal' rather a gross display of corporate social irresponsibility. No such ambiguity arises in the case of the many banks deeply implicated in 'laundering' the proceeds of crime. It is rare that bank officials are innocent dupes of criminal proceeds. Offshore banking havens are situated at the crossroads of the narcotics trade. Banks in Panama and the Bahamas act to clear the profits from the cocaine trade between Latin America and the USA. Hong Kong is used for the heroin trade between South East Asia and the West while Switzerland, Liechtenstein and Gibraltar shelter the proceeds of the narcotics trade from Turkey and the Middle East. In one of the biggest scandals of recent banking history, the Bank of Credit and Commerce International (BCCI), with a large branch outside the super-respectable Dorchester hotel in London's Park Lane, went 'belly up' in the 1980s. In investigations by the US Senate it was found to be engaged in 'illicit financial services for a very varied group of clients, including Colombian narco-traffickers, Middle East terrorists and Latin American revolutionary groups, as well as tax evaders, corrupt politicians and several multinational companies' (Strange 1996: 118).

DRUGS: DEMAND AND SUPPLY

The trade in drugs crucially depends on a massive demand for illegal substances in Europe and the USA and a pitiful need to continue to grow drugs by farmers in a number of supplier countries. The poorest in the poor countries are linked together with the most desperate in the rich countries. Hargreaves (1992: 3) has summarized the extent of the demand in the USA in the late 1980s and early 1990s:

> Americans consume more cocaine that any other industrialized country. Over 22 million say they have tried the harmless-looking white powder and between two and three million are addicted to it. In 1989, around 2,500 Americans who 'just said Yes' died of cocaine-related causes. In 1990, one in five people arrested for any crime were said to be hooked on cocaine or crack. Americans spend a staggering $110 000 million a year on drugs ($28 000 million on cocaine), more than double the profits of all the Fortune 500 companies put together and the equivalent of America's entire gross agricultural income.

If demand is virtually insatiable, what happens on the supply side of the transaction? Take the case of Bolivia to which, after their reverses in Colombia in 1989, the druglords turned their attention. This poor Latin American country was already the largest producer of raw coca leaf in the world, but between 1989 and 1991 it tripled its production of refined cocaine, placing it in the number two slot worldwide. (Coca is 'refined' by mixing the leaves with sulphuric acid, paraffin and lime, before being dried for export. You are not invited to try this recipe!)

Hargreaves (1992: 34–6) recounts the story of a Bolivian coca farmer, 'Paredes'. He used to farm near to the main Bolivian mining city, Oruro. He raised pigs and sheep, and grew maize. When, in 1983, drought struck, his animals died one by one. His crops failed. The ground was so hard he could not even bury the animals. He left for the coca-growing area where after many misadventures he managed to obtain title to five hectares of land. He worked on another farmer's plot in exchange for a promise of seeds and seedlings, but when the farmer refused to honour his promise, Paredes stole some seeds. Eighteen months later he had his first full harvest. He was in the coca-growing business. Like thousands of other farmers he was attracted to coca-growing, as virtually any other economic activity was fraught with economic insecurity. Between 1980 and 1985, Bolivia's economy had nose-dived. The GNP had dropped by 20 per cent, unemployment had increased from 6 to 20 per cent and inflation had risen to an amazing 24 000 per cent a year. It is perhaps hardly surprising that coca offered such an attractive alternative. Again, Hargreaves (1992: 31) makes the point graphically:

> Imagine there existed a crop that yielded up to four or five harvests a year, for which there was a seemingly limitless demand and which earned the farmer more than any other product. Imagine there existed a crop that needed hardly any pesticides, that flourished in acidic rain-washed soils in which other crops withered and died, and that was highly labour intensive, providing employment and income for hundreds of impoverished *campesinos* [peasants] and foreign exchange for the nation... Such a crop exists... It is called coca.

Box 9.3   'Cherie', the crack-user

A journalist, John Davison (1997), interviewed 'Cherie'. She is a crack-user in her native Handsworth, the area of Birmingham where many black British people live. When interviewed she was in her late thirties or early forties, but had begun her career as an 'exotic dancer' (a euphemism for a stripper) at 16 years of age. At various times she had been a prostitute, a shop lifter and a 'general hustler'. She had four children, each from a different father.

Although irrepressible and still attractive she walked with a pronounced limp, an injury Cherie had sustained in a dispute with a 'Yardie' drug dealer. ('Yardies' are named after the backyard slums of Kingston, Jamaica, which provide breeding grounds for armed criminals and drug-dealers. Yardies often operate in Caribbean expatriate communities – in New York, London and Birmingham.) One of Cherie's friends had borrowed £50 from a Yardie, paid back £30 and claimed that Cherie would be responsible for the remaining £20. When he approached Cherie, she claimed she knew nothing of the debt and 'anyway I don't take shit from nobody'. She was then marched to the third floor of a house, knocked out with a plank and thrown out of a window onto a concrete slab. She broke her hip and elbow.

Cherie was in intensive care and was lucky to survive. 'It nearly killed me psychologically. But at the same time, if my system had not been numb with cocaine I would have died from fright. That's what saved me. That's my excuse for continuing to use it', she joked. She remains a crack-user and an occasional dealer. She sees the drug as evil incarnate, deriving its strength from the psychological dependence it creates. The escape is so complete and so powerful that 'getting back there' is irresistible. 'All you are interested in is getting another stone. You will sell God off the cross in order to get that one pipe. It's Satan himself, that crack stuff. It's Satan himself', she declared.

When the Yardies moved in, crime in the area took a new twist. The 'home boys' had previously rarely resorted to violence, but that had changed. 'Gun warfare is a novelty for the home boys, they are not used to it. Before they were knife men, but you can't fight a gun with a knife. To look big, act big, talk big you have to follow the Yardie way, and that is gun warfare... They are making records about guns, they are not making records about knives', she added.

Why did she still stay in Handsworth, when it was so easy to get shot at, 'knifed up' or run over? 'The concept of life down here is totally different', she quipped. 'It's nice but it's deadly'.

Source: Extracts from an interview by Davison (1997: 10–15)

Given its social and economic importance to a number of countries the drug trade also serves to corrupt the political process. In Russia, Somalia, Jamaica, Afghanistan, Colombia and Indonesia, there is no firm distinction between illegal and legal business activity. There is often a seamless join between crime, politics and business, such that the players can barely tell the difference. Even where there have been determined efforts to crack down on the drug trade, sometime with help of foreign aid, success has been limited. Let us take two examples:

1. In the 1980s the Bush administration provided Colombia with financial aid and military personnel to crack the power of the notorious Medellín drugs cartel, who had effectively acted as a state within a state. After a year on the run, the world's biggest cocaine boss, Pablo Escobar, was finally cornered. Despite his capture, he was still influential enough to dictate the terms of his own imprisonment. He wanted, and got, a ten-acre site, with its own football field and

luxurious furnishings. The authorities had effectively been turned into a free security squad protecting him against his many enemies. Meanwhile, the cartel spread its business to other Latin American countries (Hargreaves 1992: xi).

2. In Italy, the government has at last made determined efforts to crack down on the Mafia. But this has dented rather than fundamentally damaged the organization. Brave magistrates have been assassinated for indicting the Mafia bosses. State seizures of Mafia assets have only amounted to just over one per cent of their estimated wealth (Martin and Schumann 1997: 210). Even when court cases are successful, they often reveal that the Mafia has penetrated into the heart of the political class and even has significant power in the Vatican. The series of *Godfather* movies is, it seems, more 'faction' than fiction.

EXPLAINING FAMINE

As we have shown, some countries like Bolivia and Colombia survive in the global economy by turning a substantial part of their agricultural economy into servicing the demand for narcotics. A similar observation may be made about Nepal, Afghanistan and Jamaica and, to a lesser degree, some other poor countries. However, there are a number of countries, predominantly in Africa, which are even more marginalized from the international economy. Excluding South Africa, Africa accounts for only 0.7 per cent of world production, rather less than Indonesia.

Throughout the area south of the Sahara desert and north of the Zambesi river getting adequate food from the land, then storing and distributing it has proved almost impossible. Bush (1996: 169) says that hunger causes 13–18 million deaths per year worldwide or 35 000 per day. In developing countries, 60 per cent of deaths of the under-fours are caused by hunger. In Africa, he continues, 'the most vulnerable groups are agriculturalists and pastoralists [and] the poor, the elderly and women are the first to suffer'. A 1994 report for the World Bank (cited Bush 1996: 173) depicts an equally bleak picture:

> Over the past twenty-five years agricultural production in Sub-Saharan Africa (SSA) rose by only 2.0 per cent a year, while aggregate population growth averaged about 2.8 per cent per year. Per capita food production has declined in most countries of the continent. Cereal imports increased by 3.9 per cent per year between 1974 and 1980, food aid by seven per cent per year. But the 'food gap' (requirements minus production) is widening. In the early 1980s about 100 million people in SSA were unable to secure sufficient food to ensure an adequate level of nutrition for themselves.

Food insecurity

At a global level there is a surplus of food. Why, then, are so many starving people in the midst of plenty? In the USA and Europe, food is often destroyed or stored to sustain the market price. Each year thousands of tonnes of vegetables are used as landfiller or bulldozed into the sea. The process of hoarding to sustain farm prices has yielded bizarre phrases such as 'butter mountains', 'wine lakes' and 'meat banks'. Why not simply send surplus food to the poor countries? This is not so easy as it might appear. Sending food abroad as aid can sometimes distort and damage local economies. For example, the export of wheat to Nigeria, which started as free aid during the period of that country's civil war (1967–70), altered tastes, undermined local staple crops and ultimately resulted in the displacement of farmers from their land. Nigeria became enmeshed in what Andrae and Beckman (1985) called 'the wheat trap' where precious foreign exchange was used to buy US wheat, which Nigerian consumers now demanded, while attempts to start domestic production failed to provide more than ten per cent of the total needed.

Joining the jigsaw pieces of the world food system together can, in short, result in forcing inefficient farmers to the wall. Many farmers in poor countries not only cannot produce at globally competitive rates, or ward off cheap imports, they have a struggle to keep themselves and their families alive. Is there anything that can be done about this appalling situation? One possible solution would be to create a self-sufficient set of societies, cut off from the rest of the world. Would this provide an answer to the endemic crisis of production? Unfortunately, the precedents for this resolution of the problem are not particularly helpful. The path of self-reliance was one taken by several countries in the wake of decolonization or political revolution.

President Nyerere in Tanzania made a notable attempt to free his country from dependency in the 1960s. He evoked a golden age of African communalism when people had modest resources, but were thought to be happy. Politics was decided by the consensus of the village elders, while guests would be fed for the first night – but handed a hoe to help produce food for the common good thereafter. However, he found these homilies impossible to translate into real policies for the post-independence period. With their expectations aroused by the anti-colonial struggle, Tanzanians demanded the usual clutch of public services – clean water, roads, health care and westernized education – and no amount of local agricultural production was going to pay for this. Instead Tanzania had to rely on the export of its staple crop, sisal, which kept reducing in value as artificial fibres came on-stream. Moreover, the sisal plantations taken into public ownership produced less than those in private hands did. Even more disheartening was that the bureaucrats, concerned to feather their own nests, engaged in what Tanzanian Professor Issa Shivji called 'a silent class struggle' with the government. Eventually, the country was brought to heel, and provided with an IMF package effectively dictating its economic policies. Tanzania was back where it started – a poor country with a subordinate role in the global division of labour.

A much more extreme example of an attempt to create self-sufficiency in food through political means arose when the Khmer Rouge, the Cambodian Communist Party, took control of the country after a civil war commencing in 1975. Under its ideologically fixated leader, Pol Pot, the Khmer Rouge decided that the roots of all evil were the 'non-productive' people in the towns and cities. City dwellers were rounded up at rifle point and frog-marched into the countryside. There they were handed seeds, hoes and shovels and told to farm. Predictably, the results of this hare-brained scheme were disastrous. Those who opposed the plan were ruthlessly killed, agricultural production collapsed and hundreds of thousands of Cambodians perished through starvation and disease.

While neither Tanzania nor Cambodia provides a helpful model, clearly public policy, in both the rich and famine-prone countries, must have something to do with the solution to food insecurity. However, before we can address changes in policy, we need first to understand the fundamental causes of famine. Food insecurity turns into famine for these reasons, each of which we will discuss in turn:

● natural disasters affecting agricultural production
● the lack of entitlements or access to food
● policy failings.

Natural disasters

Natural disasters (for example, droughts, hurricanes, volcanic eruptions and floods) can easily disrupt a precarious agricultural system. In these cases the threat of famine arises from a shortage in the *supply* of food arising from what is called in insurance contracts 'an act of God'. Such is the instinctive and obvious explanation for famine, one that is rarely questioned on the media or in popular discussion. Yet such a view has some real limitations. Why are some societies afflicted with similar disasters able to avoid famine or to recover more rapidly? Have previous agricultural policies and practises contributed to the likelihood of famine arising in the wake of a natural disaster? (For example, deforestation, the burning of wood as fuel and soil erosion through overgrazing might all massively amplify the threat of famine.) Were there sufficient roads and airstrips giving access to the sites of likely famine? Were there adequate storage facilities for grain, edible tubers or rice? Had the pipes and pumping stations for water supplies been planned or installed? Were the civil defence and emergency services organized and trained? Had a failure to promote land reform forced poor people onto marginal land, where they become most vulnerable to sudden climatic or political changes?

Such questions amount to a more sociological explanation for famine – one that critically assesses 'common-sense assumptions' and focuses on the social and political dimensions involved.

Entitlement theory

The most important alternative theory for famine is 'entitlement theory', developed by Sen (1981) (see Figure 9.1) and later extended in his joint work with Dreze (1989). Dreze and Sen (1989: 9), define their concept of entitlement in the following way:

> What we can eat depends on what food we are able to acquire. The mere presence of food in the economy, or in the market, does not *entitle* a person to consume it. In each social structure, given the prevailing legal, political, and economic arrangements, a person can establish command over alternative commodity bundles (any one bundle of which he or she can choose to consume). These bundles could be extensive, or very limited, and what a person can consume will be directly dependent on what these bundles are.

Precisely what these 'commodity bundles' are is a bit cryptic, but it may be helpful to compare them, in the setting of an affluent society, to the contents of a shopping trolley. If you are well-heeled, as you walk down the supermarket aisle you toss things into the wire cage without much thought. The range and cost of the commodities you buy is determined by the cash you carry or, more

Figure 9.1   Amartya Sen, who developed 'entitlement theory'

likely, the credit entitlement you have arranged with your bank. If you are even a little sensitive, however, you will notice that some people, perhaps senior citizens on a modest pension, buy the 'bargains' at the end of the line, carefully look at lists comparing prices, or examine the damaged tins in the 'give-away' rack. In short, a different entitlement is determined by a different purchasing power.

Let us now switch back to the setting of a poor society, like parts of India and most of Africa. Here the issue of entitlement becomes more complex. Either the rural dwellers have very modest cash incomes or they have none at all. In these circumstances other kinds of entitlements intervene. Can the rural dweller go into a local forest and trap or hunt game to supplement a family's diet? Or has that area been deemed a wilderness area, protected by armed rangers hired by the National Parks Commission or World Wide Fund for Nature? Can the poor farmers collect fruit, berries or edible flora and fungi? Or have the big farmers destroyed all these pickings (a last remnant of a hunter-gatherer society) through the private registration of land, the use of herbicides and pesticides, and the production of (often inedible) crops for the world market? Can the peasant call on his landlord for a loan, or will this engender yet another turn of the screw of ***debt peonage***?

> **Debt peonage** – a system whereby loans in cash or kind are made by rich farmers, and paid back by a share of crops or income gained by the debtor or the debtor's descendants.

Can the peasant turn to kin or clan, or are they so far down the road of private capital accumulation that they choose not to help a relative? Can women assert their entitlement to equal treatment, when historically they have been victims of patriarchal family structures?

Suddenly 'entitlement' is not so obvious and the dilemmas faced by the very poor become very acute. Is it better to starve to preserve one's assets, at least letting one's children have the chance to survive? Alternatively, must one throw oneself at the mercy of a local political dignitary, exchanging an oath of permanent fealty and obeisance for immediate relief (and thus, incidentally, rein-venting feudalism)? Can any individual solution be successful or enduring, or does one have to organize to defend collective rights? If that is unsuccessful, finally, is there nothing else to do but to trudge in a pitiful line towards the feeding stations, where earnest white volunteers dole out handouts that have been flown in from all over the world?

Policy failings

Sen's entitlement theory has provided a radical alternative to the 'natural' explanation of famine and has held centre-stage for in-depth discussions of the problem of food insecurity since the early 1980s. Although they do not wish to supersede Sen's theory, other authors – for example Bush (1996) and Keen (1994) – are more insistent on the political factors and failings that trigger famine. It is self-evident that adverse effects on agricultural production can result from civil war as farmers flee the land in fear of their lives. But could some political actors be using famine as a crucial part of their means of prose-cuting a civil war, rather like some retreating armies pursue a 'scorched earth' policy to deny food and matériel to their enemies? This raises the question of whether famine is in the interests of some parties. The beneficiaries of famine might, for example, include:

● merchants, who may be hoarding staples or buying livestock at knock-down prices

● suppliers of grain from other sources

● politicians whose desires for power, territory or hatred of other ethnic groups might incline them either to be phlegmatic about famine in a particular area or do little to help

● a local élite, members of which use the access to global aid flows to feather their own nests, rather than send the supplies to the areas where they are needed.

Keen (1994) takes this logic even further, arguing that in the case of the famines in the Sudan (see Figure 9.2) there was a high level of *intentionality*. According to him, the Islamic Sudanese ruling class used famine as a massive stick to beat the heads of its opponents, particularly the southern Christians. This is a chilling conclusion to reach and although it is developed in relation only to one country, it challenges some of the rival theories used to explain famine. Facing a loss of popularity with its own supporters in the north and an environmental crisis, the regime saw the creation of famine in the south as a way out of its dilemmas. Alluding to Sen's theory, Keen (1994: 13, 14) writes:

Notwithstanding Sen's emphasis on poverty as the root of famine, it was, in a sense, precisely the wealth of victim groups that exposed them to famine. Processes of famine involved the forcible transfer of assets from victim to beneficiary groups in a context of acute political powerlessness on the part of the victims... The 1985–89 famine was the creation of a diverse coalition of interests that were themselves under intense political and economic pressures in the context of a shrinking resource base and significant environmental crisis in the north.

Figure 9.2   Famine in Sudan, 1998

In 1998 when famine in the Sudan loomed again, the country became divided into a religious frontline. Christian charities poured aid into the south, while several Islamic countries supported the government in Khartoum. In short, cruel as this is, famine can be considered as an instrument of politics.

REVIEW

Why do people commit crime? As we have seen, there are likely to be a wide range of proximate causes, otherwise we would find it difficult to explain the wide variety of crime rates across the world. However, there are also some global patterns. Crime increases with prosperity. It increases as rural people are pushed off the land into the shantytowns where there is no work and they have to survive by their wits. Crime also seems to have something to do with social inequality and the perception of that inequality by dispossessed people or those who see themselves as *relatively* deprived.

One debate that has cast more heat than light concerns whether the turn to neo-liberal economic policies has enhanced criminal activity. There are extreme advocates of the free market ideology who would argue that the drug trade (like the trade in weapons or junk bonds) is simply an example of the so-called 'law' of supply and demand. When there is an unfulfilled demand and an excessive supply of a particular commodity, the dealer is simply acting as an interme-diary, with some implication that they act in a morally neutral way, as a provider of services. When dealers and druglords are interviewed they often characterize themselves in such a benign role. In such accounts the market is 'naturalized'. It is 'invisible' and out of the hands of social actors. It is clear that if crime is to be addressed the market has to be managed for the social good although we are no longer certain that many states have the capacity or the willingness to address this issue.

As regards our discussion on famine, the basic problem that remains unresolved at a global level is that there are currently no effective ways of redistributing food surpluses from over-producing to under-producing areas. Attempts to do so through the mechanism of aid often have unintended and negative consequences. No doubt there are many partial solutions involving the extension of credit, the subsidized provision of inputs (like seed, fertilizer, water and pesticides), the training of farmers and developing an effective price-support system. However, in some countries famine has advanced too far to respond to such interventions. Besides, these solutions imply the existence of a benign government. This is hardly the case in Sudan, which might be regarded as a particularly odious and unusual example of the capacity for human wickedness. But 'politics' and famine also seem to have been close companions in Bosnia, Rwanda and Kosovo. Lenin, in his cynical way, suggested that one way of trying to understand a puzzling political situation, is to ask the question 'Who benefits?' It is stretching the argument to say that famine is 'created' by politics in all contexts, but a studious lack of vigour in combating it seems a fairly common finding. This may reflect incompetence or a sense of futility in the face of predestination. However, feeble intervention may also reflect a variation in 'entitlement' between the different victims and, more ominously, the particular political interests of some of the powerful social and political actors.

All three issues discussed here – crime, drugs and famine – seem to testify to the need for a much more radical break with the international, regional and bilateral agreements of the post-1945 period. The control of cross-border crime cannot be left solely to bilateral agreements while reducing the supply of drugs cannot occur until massive transfers of resources and alternative development initiatives are provided for people whose livelihood depends on producing drugs. Finally, interventions for humanitarian purposes, such as in the case of famine, have often shown the limitations of charitable and voluntary effects. When famine is more than 'the hand of God', the only remedy seems to be military muscle supported by a strong human rights agenda. To command widespread support such an agenda has to be legitimized by a transnational agency, perhaps ultimately a world government.

If you would like to know more ●●●●●●●●●●●●●●●●●●●●●●●●●●●●●●●●●●

On global crime, Pearce and Woodiwiss's edited collection (1993) *Global Crime Connections* has useful chapters on corporate crime, fraud in the European Union and US policies to control the drugs trade.

In *Snowfields* the journalist Clare Hargreaves (1992) covers the Bolivian drug trade, while Reuter has a useful book, *Disorganised Crime* (1983), on the markets developed by the Mafia. Reuter has also published a number of studies on the effects of drug interdiction.

Ray Bush's 'The politics of food and starvation', *Review of African Political Economy* **23** (68), 1996, is an excellent article making many good points clearly, while David Keen's *The Benefits of Famine* (1994) develops the idea that famine can arise from deliberate political intent.

Entitlement theory is developed in Amartya Sen's *Poverty and Famine* (1981) and in his book with Dreze, *Hunger and Public Action* (1989). Both are economists not sociologists so it helps to have a little background in economics. Nonetheless, by reading selectively, you will soon get the drift of their argument.

Group work •

1. Study Box 9.2 on the advance fee scam. What does this tell you about (a) the respective regulatory capacities of the governments of Nigeria and the advanced countries and (b) the expectations and prejudices of those falling for the scam?

2. You and a number of your friends have possibly used illegal drugs. Without talking about yourself (you may make yourself liable to criminal prosecution!) recount a story about how 'a friend' was first supplied with an illegal drug. Did your friend know of its origins?

3. Get a large piece of paper (the back of some old wallpaper will do). Half the class will draw a sketch of the habitat of a planned community of 5000 people to be made 'safe' from violent property crime. Indicate the points of entry and exit, the defence and alarm systems and the shared public spaces. The other half of the class will concentrate on showing how the defence systems can be penetrated. Discuss later whether you would like to live in such a safe community.

4. Write to any of the famine relief agencies for their annual report. How do you judge their appreciation of the causes of famine?

Questions to think about •

1. How useful are official statistics to the sociological study of crime?

2. If there is so great a demand and so limitless a supply can the trade in cocaine and heroin be stopped?

3. Show how the patterns of social control have changed in contemporary societies.

4. Why is it possible to argue that different 'entitlements' cause or deepen famines?

5. Have liberal commentators and aid agencies overlooked the extent to which famines have been caused by politicians?

6. Would the chances of famine be reduced if some countries 'dropped out' of the global economy and simply concentrated on feeding their populations from internal resources?

Asia-Pacific: From Miracle to Mirage?

The rapid economic transformations achieved by several East Asian countries since 1945 have occasioned much comment and even bewilderment. How have they become global winners so quickly? Their success is reflected in such epithets as 'tiger' economies, Asian 'dragons' and 'miracle economies'. Is this momentum likely to be sustained into the twenty-first century or does the economic crisis commencing in 1997 signal the beginnings of a meltdown for the region? To answer this question we begin by making a threefold distinction between the different East Asian countries:

1. In addition to Japan, the region's role model and economic dynamo, there are four leading newly industrialized countries (NICs) – South Korea, Taiwan, Hong Kong and Singapore. Their path to rapid industrialization began in the 1950s. We shall refer to them as 'the tigers'.

2. The second tier comprises the founding members of the Association of Southeast Asian Nations (ASEAN) and includes Malaysia, Thailand, Indonesia, the Philippines, Brunei and Singapore. These countries began their industrial ascent in the early 1970s. To borrow a label used by Schlossstein (1991) we shall refer to them as 'the dragons'. (Although officially designated as part of the ASEAN group, Singapore really belongs among the tigers because of its earlier industrialization.)

3. Finally, there is a third, more recent, tier. This includes Vietnam and Cambodia, but particularly China, which now regularly achieves a growth rate of between 8–12 per cent. This turnabout started in the late 1970s after Deng Xiaoping, China's then leader, decided to introduce 'capitalist' reforms and a more open economy.

This chapter says little about South Asia although we refer to India and Pakistan in Table 10.1. By comparison, their economic performance to date has been rather lacklustre. Nevertheless, in 1994, there were 914 million people in India, 126 million in Pakistan and 118 million in Bangladesh. They also have sizeable economies with large industrial sectors. Moreover, India's rate of economic growth has accelerated since 1991, when serious attempts were made to open the economy to more foreign investment and competition, among other reforms. Given its huge population and resources, if recent trends continue India may eventually exercise an enormous impact on the global economy. India is also notable in Asia because, since gaining independence in 1947, it has stood out as a beacon of democracy compared to the repressive regimes characteristic of other developing Asian nations including China, Indonesia until 1998 and South Korea up to the late 1980s.

In this chapter we focus on:

- the overall dimensions of the region's economic achievement so far
- some of the key explanations for East Asia's economic success
- an evaluation of recent problems which have prompted some observers to become more sceptical concerning the region's future prospects.

THE DIMENSIONS OF EAST ASIA'S ECONOMIC ACHIEVEMENT

Their geographical location often means that these societies are referred to as the countries of the Pacific region, or 'Asia-Pacific'. This region's remarkable record of rapid industrialization to date has prompted some observers to argue that the twenty-first century will be the 'Pacific century' – an era when these countries will dominate global technology and world markets. They may also provide the leading cultural and political ideas that will shape our future. According to one measure for calculating GDP, which the World Bank (1996) used in its *Development Report*, four Asian countries were placed in the top ten of the world's economic league, while eight are located in the top 22.

The scale of this achievement is thrown into relief if we remember that before 1750 about three-quarters of the world's manufacturing output came from non-western countries, mostly China and India (Bairoch 1981). Then, 'industrial' activity everywhere was based on handicraft production in tiny units, using simple tools and non-mechanical sources of power. With the onset of the industrial revolution, however, the share of world manufacturing controlled by western countries rose from approximately 20 per cent in 1800 to around 80 per cent at the time of the First World War. By 1914 it was based almost entirely on mechanized technology and modern sources of power. There was no massive decline in handicraft production in India, China and elsewhere. Rather, the change was mostly due to their falling relative share of a vastly expanded modern world production system.

Returning to the present, how can we measure the recent economic surge by the East Asian countries?

Japan and the tigers

According to Johnson (1982: 6), over 'the whole post-war era, 1946–1976, the Japanese economy increased 55-fold'. By the mid-1970s, it 'accounted for about 10 per cent of the world's economic activity, though supporting only about 3 per cent of the world's population'. This constitutes a remarkable transformation given that, as late as 1955, more than two-fifths of the population were still employed on the land (Dore 1984: 3).

Table 10.1   Vital statistics of some Asian economies in a global context, 1994

Selected countries by rank order of GDP. Standard WB $ comparisons	Population (millions)	GDP ($000m) using WB standard comparisons	GNP, $ per capita using WB standard comparisons	GDP ($000m) based on World Bank's PPP calculations and showing new rank order	GNP ($ per capita) calculated by WB on a PPP basis
1. USA	261	6648	25 880	6648 (1)	25 880
2. Japan	125	4591	34 630	2643 (3)	21 140
3. Germany	82	2046	25 580	1587 (4)	19 480
7. Brazil	159	555	2970	859 (9)	5400
9. China	1191	522	530	#2989 (2)	#2510
10. Spain	39	483	13 440	537 (14)	13 740
12. Russian Federation	148	377	2650	682 (11)	4610
13. South Korea	45	377	8260	460 (15)	10 330
14. Australia	18	332	18 000	323 (17)	18 120
16. India	914	294	320	1170 (6)	1280
21. Sweden	9	196	23 530	154 (32)	17 130
22. Indonesia	191	175	880	688 (10)	3600
24. Thailand	58	143	2410	404 (16)	6970
25. Hong Kong	6	132	21 650	–	–
36. Malaysia	20	71	3480	166 (30)	8440
37. Singapore	3	69	22 500	64 (51)	21 900
39. Philippines	67	64	950	96 (43)	2740
42. Pakistan	126	52	430	268 (21)	2130
* Taiwan	20	–	–	264 (22)	13 200

Sources: World Bank Development Report (1996). Figures have been rounded up and down.
* Data on Taiwan are for 1995, *The Economist* 1 March 1997: 23.
# Calculations for China are based on the first World Bank PPP estimate of per capita income (see the following discussion).

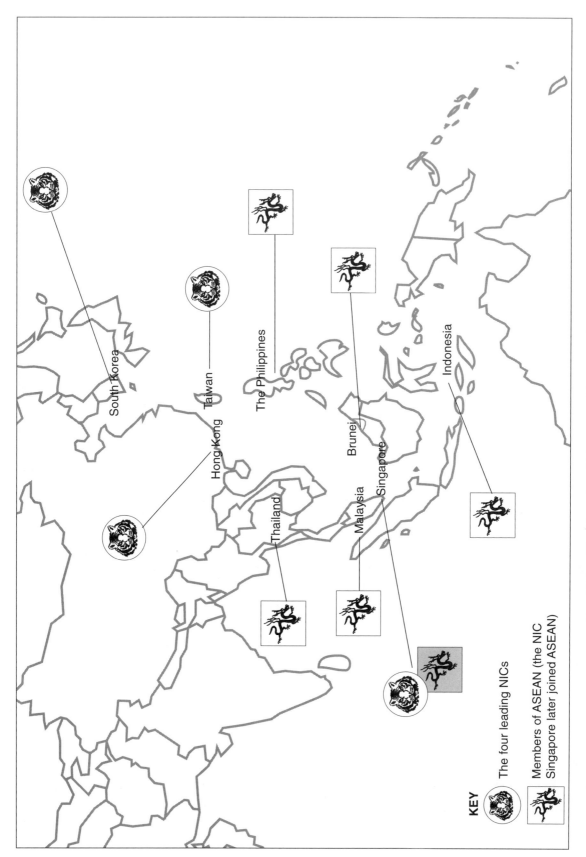

KEY

🐯 The four leading NICs

🐉 Members of ASEAN (the NIC Singapore later joined ASEAN)

South Korea

Taiwan

Hong Kong

The Philippines

Thailand

Brunei

Malaysia

Singapore

Indonesia

Map 10.1   The 'tigers' and 'dragons' of East and South Asia

According to Ozawa (1993), Japan's initial post-war recovery was based on expanding its labour-intensive light industries. By the early 1960s, however, the country had moved into more advanced, heavy industries. Such industries included shipbuilding, steel, chemicals, petrochemicals and machine production. This surge also involved the mass production industries especially in electrical consumer goods and motorcars (Ozawa 1993: 142). Being based on the manufacture and assembly of numerous quality components, such products normally require considerable investments in equipment, incur high R&D costs and rely on a highly skilled workforce. They are also highly profitable because it is such goods that people buy as their incomes rise.

By the early 1980s Japanese industry was entering a further stage of technological upgrading (p. 131). This involved 'computer-aided flexible (or "lean") manufacturing' and a range of knowledge-intensive, energy-saving industrial processes. This record over four decades of purposive restructuring has certainly played a key role in Japan's ability to invade its main rivals' home and export markets. Thus, Japan's share of world manufactured exports had already reached nearly 8 per cent by 1965 and climbed to almost 12 per cent by 1990 (World Bank 1993a: 38).

The industrial progress the tigers achieved in little more than 40 years, from a much lower manufacturing base than Japan's, is equally impressive. In 1962, the World Bank placed South Korea, Taiwan, Hong Kong and Singapore ninety-ninth, eighty-fifth, fortieth and thirty-eighth respectively in its ranking of countries in terms of per capita GNP income levels (cited in Wade 1990: 34). At that time, the Sudan and Zaire – two of the world's poorest countries in the 1990s – were ranked just ahead of South Korea and Taiwan. One way of calculating income levels is in terms of **_purchasing power parity (PPP)_**.

Purchasing power parity adjusts the GNP per capita in accordance with the generally lower costs of living that prevail in many poorer countries.

Official international organizations make wide use of the PPP measure. Some experts regard the country-by-country comparisons it facilitates as more useful than computations based purely on a universal dollar standard. Employing this measure, we find that by 1995 the tiger economies had attained per capita income levels shown in Table 10.2.

Table 10.2   Per capita incomes in selected countries, 1995 ($)

Korea	11 900
Taiwan	13 220
Singapore	22 600
Hong Kong	23 900
All advanced industrial countries (average)	19 400

Source: The Economist 1 March 1997: 23

Along with these huge rises in average incomes, there has been a marked increase in such crucial indices of well being as life expectancy. For example, in South Korea this rose from 53 to 72 years between 1960–1990 (World Bank 1993a: 34).

Like Japan, the tigers have also diversified their industrial capabilities. Between 1963 and the mid-1980s, both South Korea and Taiwan increased their manufacturing output of heavy industrial products – chemicals, plastic, metals, machinery and transport equipment. In South Korea, this proportion rose from 29 to 54 per cent, and in Taiwan from 23 to 60 per cent (Chowdhury and Islam 1993: 91). A similar upgrading took place in Singapore's economy. Moreover, South Korea and Taiwan both now enjoy a substantial share of world production in the manufacture of advanced, high-memory semiconductors and computers. By 1990, Samsung, one of South Korea's largest conglomerates or *chaebol*s, was the world's third largest producer of advanced semiconductors, including 1-Megabit memory chips (Evans 1995: 176).

China and the dragons

Since the 1970s, the dragons have also made considerable strides towards industrialization. Their overall rates of GDP growth have averaged between 7–9 per cent with the higher rates achieved mostly during the 1990s. Growth rates in manufacturing, however, were considerably higher. Indonesia, for example, expanded its industries by 43 per cent in the two years of 1986–7 and then by another 27 per cent in 1987–8 (Schlossstein 1991: 54). Unlike the tigers, Malaysia, Thailand and Indonesia are rich in various mineral and agricultural resources. Thus, their combined share of world manufactured exports from virtually nothing in 1965 to 1.5 per cent by 1990 constitutes a considerable achievement. Malaysia, for example, with perhaps the most spectacular record, increased the contribution of manufacturing towards its GDP from 20 per cent in 1980 to 32 per cent by 1995.

Social indicators were also very positive. According to the World Bank (1993a: 33), the percentage of the population living below each country's officially defined poverty line fell from 50 to 17 per cent in Indonesia between 1972 and 1982, from 37 to 14 per cent in Malaysia between 1973 and 1987 and from 59 to 26 per cent in Thailand from 1962 to 1986.

China's economic record has also been astonishing. After the 1949 revolution and during Mao Zedong's leadership, Chinese development was along full-blooded socialist lines based on central planning, collectivist ownership and a more or less closed economy. The record of economic growth under Mao's variant of socialism was rather impressive especially during the 1950s. Nonetheless, soon after Mao's death, in 1976, various reforms were introduced. These were designed to accelerate growth by permitting market forces, competition and private enterprise to flourish in certain economic sectors and regions. In addition, the government established three 'special economic zones' in southern China – Guangdong province adjacent to Hong Kong, Fujian and the island of Hainan – along with fourteen coastal cities and their local regions.

These huge industrial zones operate an open-door policy with respect to international trade and offer special incentives to foreign capital. They have been spectacularly successful and account for much of China's industrial expansion since 1980. Accordingly, many millions of rural migrants have flocked to special economic zones like Shenzhen, and to cities like Shanghai – probably the largest mass migration in history. These zones and coastal cities have also attracted growing numbers of foreign companies. Much DFI involves joint ventures between overseas companies and the privately owned 'town and village enterprises' (TVEs) (*The Economist* 22 February 1997: 13). Indeed, in recent years, western investors have channelled more DFI towards China than to any other developing country. China's new role in the world economy is revealed by its changed position in the world-exporting league. Whereas in 1978 it ranked thirtieth, in 1992 it was the tenth largest exporter and traded goods to the value of $165 000 million, 2 per cent of world exports (Cable and Ferdinand 1994: 243–5).

Should China's current rates of economic growth continue at their present very high levels, some observers see China as likely to overtake the USA sometime in the next fifteen to twenty years. Certainly, the principle of **exponential growth** suggests that this scenario is possible. Thus, with constant growth rates of around 10 per cent a year China can expect to increase its GNP by a factor of two every seven years. In 1996, new World Bank calculations of China's average per capita income on a PPP basis (*The Economist* 12 October 1996: 79–80) reduced the estimated size of China's GNP to approximately $2 143 000 million placing it third in the world. On this reckoning, it will take China twenty or more years to overtake the USA. Whichever statistical 'guesstimate' proves to be the most accurate, China is clearly in the throes of a gigantic industrialization programme. If this can be sustained it will transform the future parameters of the world economy.

Exponential growth occurs where any increase in a variable such as population, savings or wealth feeds on itself with each new increment contributing to yet further expansion.

Figure 10.1   Hong Kong after the return to China: business as usual?

Figure 10.2   Lee Kuan Yew, engineer of Singapore's success?

EXPLAINING EAST ASIAN ECONOMIC PERFORMANCE

There have been several attempts to explain East Asia's economic success. Most writers point to one or more of the following set of factors which we list, then elaborate on in the following section:

- the construction of an Asian variant of capitalism
- political reasons for urgent economic development
- a willingness to shape market forces and to use imported technology
- Japanese technological leadership which has produced a set of complementary, inter-country, regional linkages
- a benign international environment which favoured the sort of economic development undertaken
- social and cultural factors
- good natural resources in some of the dragons
- the economic role of the Chinese diaspora.

The **developmental state** is an Asian variant of capitalism, bringing together the financial sector, public policy and large companies in a common national effort.

Characteristics of the 'developmental state'

Johnson (1982) and others (for example, White 1984, 1988) have described the governmental system pioneered by Japan from the mid-1920s and later emulated by other East Asian economies as the ***developmental state***.

For a time these developmental states prioritized the achievement of long-term national security above all other concerns. But rapid industrialization was seen as the only certain way to guarantee national security. To this end the state assumed responsibility for setting national growth priorities designed progressively to upgrade industrial capacity. It did this by assigning policy-making to a powerful economic **BUREAUCRACY** that was kept insulated from democratic/parliamentary and other political interests. Co-opting an élite core of technically trained members who also enjoyed considerable public prestige strengthened this economic bureaucracy. At the same time, co-operation and consensus was encouraged between private business, the public sector and other domestic interests.

The principal aim was to construct a technically efficient, expanding domestic economy. To various degrees, Japan, the four tigers from around 1960 and China all embodied the characteristics of the developmental state. In China's case, this has only been since the 'capitalist' reforms were introduced under Deng's leadership in the late 1970s (White 1993). The dragon economies also exhibit similar features. Apart from Indonesia, however, their governments have been rather less authoritarian than those that shaped the tigers' economic ascent before the 1980s. They have also relied rather more on DFI instead of using state policies to empower private, domestic capital (Schlossstein 1991: 19–21). So far, the dragons have also been less systematic about upgrading their populations' educational and technical resources. Nevertheless, they approximate to the developmental state more closely than the model of western economic practice.

Origins of the 'developmental state'

The East Asian tigers were born out of internal political chaos and severe external threats to national survival (Cumings 1987; Castells 1992). This was also partly true of Japan, which narrowly escaped becoming colonized in the mid-nineteenth century. This, coupled with an established western presence in Asia, induced Japanese leaders to regard the reforms required for modernization as essentially defensive strategies (Cumings 1987: 52–3). Following defeat in the Second World War, Japan's subsequent sense of beleaguerment led it to switch from military might to global industrial leadership. Thus, for Japan and the tigers, rapid state-led industrialization was a nationalistic response to a threatening post-war world. The key events in the region were:

1. The Japanese defeat in 1945 followed by nearly a decade of US military occupation. Among the crises which beset Japan until the mid-1950s were massive labour unrest – which eventually led the US administration to impose severe restrictions on trade unions, effectively crushing the working class.

2. The communist invasion of South Korea in 1950, again followed by years of heavy US military involvement in the country's affairs.

3. The communist victory in China in 1949 and its subsequent claims to Taiwan.

4. Following the 1949 communist victory in mainland China, Hong Kong lost its traditional role as the main entrepôt for western trade with China and needed to diversify rapidly into manufacturing exports. It also required continued British military protection. In addition, it benefited from rule by a competent British-staffed civil service determined to avoid the colony's disintegration (Castells 1992: 52, 61).

5. The unrest surrounding the emergence of Singapore between 1959 and 1965 involved class and ideological divisions between strong communist and union groups and capitalist interests. The threat of annexation to Indonesia at independence in 1959 and expulsion from the Malaysian Federation in 1965 also motivated Singapore's bid for growth.

These background events also engendered other consequences. The regional presence of the USA and fear of communist aggression precluded any serious possibility of a socialist route to industrialization. Moreover, the circumstances of national emergency, the emphasis on patriotism and the temporarily weakened nature of civil societies, including labour movements, paved the way for authoritarian government. Lastly, neither Japan nor any of the tigers enjoyed special natural resource endowments. Thus, industrialization and a constant ratcheting-up of technical skills offered them the only path for overcoming threats to national security.

National policies to produce high-speed growth

According to Wade (1990), Amsden (1989) and others the East Asian development states prioritized the following economic strategies:

1. The exploitation of their most abundant resource – cheap labour. Meanwhile, small local firms were encouraged to use 'off-the shelf' technology, easily bought from around the world, in order to replace imported manufactures with local ones.

2. Eventually, the emphasis switched to export-led growth. This reduced the chances of expansion being torpedoed by recurring shortages of foreign exchange. Meanwhile goods with a potential to add value during production gradually replaced low-priced exports.

3. High and sustained investment was encouraged through increased rates of domestic savings and the efficient deployment of foreign loans.

4. Priority was given to the acquisition of advanced technological capacities through constant attempts to raise educational, scientific and infrastructural standards and by empowering domestic firms to assimilate foreign technology.

5. Especially in Japan and South Korea, large diversified companies were provided with the lion's share of national resources. These were companies capable of competing in world markets, achieving scale economies and financing continuous technical learning.

6. Resources such as capital, foreign exchange and government contracts were targeted on certain key advanced industries, leading firms and exporters

---

Box 10.1   Poor connections: the sports shoe saga

During the last twenty years sports shoes have become key items of fashion wear. Their attraction lies partly in their identification with the glamorous world of international sport. The market leaders in this industry – Adidas, Hi-Tech, Puma, Nike and Reebok – have paid considerable sums to world sports stars such as Eric Cantona and John McEnroe in return for their willingness to sponsor or endorse particular products. In 1995 Adidas paid Paul Gascoigne £2 million sterling for wearing the company's boots.

Sports shoe manufacturing requires labour-intensive input making wage levels a significant factor in costs. Thus, from the 1970s most western producers shifted their production sites to the low-wage Asian economies – first to South Korea and Taiwan and later, as wages rose there, to countries such as Indonesia, Thailand and China. These companies operate by subcontracting production to local Asian suppliers while they now concentrate on the more profitable design, advertising and distribution side. How are the rewards distributed? The following data (in US dollars) are based on the example of the costing *per pair* of Nike's 'Air Pegasus' shoe sold in 1994.

Distribution costs plus profits to Nike and retailers (per pair)

Retail price in US shops	$70
Price paid by Nike to subcontractors	$15
Wholesale price at which Nike sold to retailers	$38
Labour costs and social security	$1.66

This means that Nike earned roughly $23 on each pair ($38 minus $15); that is, 33 per cent of the final retail price. However, the share awarded to Asian workers was 2.4 per cent of the final retail price or 11 per cent of the overall factory price. Between two-thirds and 90 per cent of these workers were single women, often from rural areas, between the ages of 18 and 25. Although their working conditions are relatively good compared to other workers, long hours, compulsory overtime, fire and chemical hazards were not unusual. Once they marry or become pregnant, most are liable to be sacked or sent home.

Source: Brooks and Madden (1995)

---

through preferential policies (a policy known as 'picking winners') while their ability to utilize these advantages effectively was carefully monitored by the economic bureaucracy.

These were private enterprise economies. Nevertheless, what underlay all of these controls was a genuine willingness, in Wade's (1990) memorable phrase, to 'govern the market'. Thus, on occasions, the developmental states deliberately ignored market signals and 'got prices wrong' (Amsden 1989) instead of allowing the market to get them 'right'. For example, governments used their control of banks to offer interest rate concessions on certain loans. Several points need to be made about this strategy:

1. Some observers, including the World Bank (1993b), argue that the priority given to market forces and the moves towards trade liberalization supposedly made by the tigers during the 1960s largely explain East Asian success. Such views diverge considerably from those offered by the writers we have discussed.

2. Without considerable bureaucratic competence and discipline, the high degree of interference with market signals and close control over businesses might easily have proved disastrous.

3. Managing the market can only be a successful strategy for a couple of decades. Fairly soon growing economic complexity defies over-regulation, business groups become too powerful and resist such interference and foreign buyers become irritated by the special assistance given to domestic exporters.

Be this as it may, contrary to free market panaceas the East Asian states successfully applied such price-distorting policies until approximately the early 1980s.

Flying geese and tandem development in the region

During the 1930s, a Japanese economist called Kaname Akamatsu used the analogy of geese flying in a V-shaped formation to suggest how Japan could construct a set of complementary relationships between the various economies in East Asia. All might then benefit from an orderly pattern of sequential development. More recently, Ozawa (1993: 141) has described a similar process – which he calls 'tandem development' – based on geographical proximity and Japanese economic leadership. He argues that tandem development since the late 1950s enabled not just Japan but also the tigers and the dragons to move to deeper levels of industrialization simultaneously. The engines of growth in this process were fivefold:

1. From the late 1950s, Japan was willing to spread its investment and technology to the nearby more backward tiger economies by investing in replica branch plants, or by subcontracting. Japan gained both from the cheaper labour available in the satellites and the growing market opportunities in the region as living standards rose.

2. Then, from the mid-1970s, the tigers began to repeat the same process by shifting some of their labour-intensive industries to the dragons as their industries, too, became increasingly technologically sophisticated and domestic labour costs increased.

3. Meanwhile, as first Japan and then the tigers relinquished lower grade activities to the more backward dragon economies, they adjusted their own industries upwards.

4. The success of tandem development also required a commitment on the part of the follower countries to operate an outward-oriented export-led strategy. This helped to push up local wages, create more jobs and enabled fast-growing industries to gain scale economies.

5. Although they initially supplied cheap labour, the follower countries benefited from access to capital, technology, overseas markets and learning opportunities.

The combined effect of all this was to create a 'snowball phenomenon' (Ozawa 1993: 144) with new markets being created as each follower country became an expanding source of world market demand in its own right.

Ozawa's tandem effect became especially evident when a fresh and enormous wave of Japanese investment spilled across East Asia following the 1985 revaluation of the yen. Many of these investments involved the production of standardized, high quality components for re-import to Japan or for export to third countries in the attempt to escape retaliatory measures against Japanese finished goods. So great was this flood of capital that Japanese investment in the four tigers and the ASEAN dragons grew by approximately 50 and 100 per cent respectively *each year* between 1984–89. During 1991, a new Japanese factory opened in Thailand every three days (Fields 1996: 104).

Other writers (for example, Cumings 1987; Bello and Rosenfeld 1990) take a less rosy view of East Asia's regional division of labour arguing that this system merely facilitates Japanese domination. Thus, despite more than forty years of rapid industrialization Taiwan's and South Korea's supposed high-grade industries remain dependent on more sophisticated Japanese technology.

Favourable international circumstances

Various commentators (Johnson 1982; Cumings 1987; Schlossstein 1991) have observed that the post-war decades offered an unprecedentedly favourable climate for growth. This included:

● expanding world markets provided by the long boom until the mid-1970s and growing world trade

● an era of declining import protectionism on the part of the western economies and particularly the openness of the US economy to imports

● the USA's willingness to encourage the transfer of its technology under licence to Japan and the tigers, despite the relatively closed nature of their own economies

● the relatively cheap cost of oil until 1974.

In addition, the spread of the Cold War to the Pacific region brought considerable advantages to Japan, South Korea and Taiwan. Thus, from the US perspective, each assumed the role of frontline bulwark in the struggle to contain the spread of communism. Accordingly, the USA shouldered much of the region's heavy defence burden. Between 1955 and 1978, for example, US military deliveries to Taiwan and South Korea totalled nearly $10 000 million. This excluded the costs of the Korean War, which the USA largely bore (Cumings 1987: 67). Britain took on a similar role with respect to Hong Kong. During the 1950s, five-sixths of South Korea's imports consisted of US aid and grants towards reviving its economy. The USA's war procurement needs during the Korean War boosted Japan's economy because the USA purchased enormous quantities of war materials from Japanese firms. Between 1952–53, these war procurements, together with expenditures by US armed forces stationed in Japan, provided 37 per cent of Japan's foreign earnings (Johnson 1982: 200). Similarly, US military needs during the Vietnam War created a huge demand for industrial exports from Taiwan and South Korea. In the late 1960s, 20 per cent of South Korea's foreign exchange earnings originated from this source (Cumings 1987: 76).

By contrast, the dragon economies and the newly emergent Asian NICs have faced a much tougher economic climate. Schlossstein (1991: Chapter 1) ascribes this to the gradual de-escalation of the Cold War and a reduced US military

Non-tariff trade barriers
involve the attempt to protect
domestic industries by
imposing bureaucratic
regulations about such
things as product 'quality' or
technical standards. The
appearance of free trade is
preserved.

presence in Asia since the 1970s and slower growth in the western economies from around 1974. In addition, years of trade deficits with Japan and the tigers have led the North American and European economies to increase their ***non-tariff trade barriers*** against Asian manufactured exports, or to threaten such retaliation. Meanwhile, the regional trading blocs of the EU and NAFTA in Europe and America may increasingly inhibit inward trade. Finally, the globalization of industry, a process to which these countries are contributing, has intensified world competition.

Religion, society and cultural traditions

Japan and the tigers also derived important advantages from their history and cultural traditions. In order to stimulate modernity it may have been an advantage that the peoples of Japan, South Korea, Taiwan and Hong Kong mostly belong to one broad ethnic group and adhere to one or two ancient religions. Both Japan and South Korea are countries with a long and unique cultural history and have enjoyed centuries of national autonomy. Although Malaysia and Indonesia are officially Muslim societies they also have large cores of indigenous peoples. Moreover, colonialism deepened their ethnic and religious pluralism so that they also contain sizeable Chinese, Christian and Hindu minorities, as well as many smaller distinctive cultural groups. Their unity or otherwise is not, of course, the only way that cultural traditions may constrain, promote or simply influence the emerging character of modern economic life. The interesting debate among sociologists and others on this topic, with particular respect to Confucianism in South East Asia, is briefly outlined in Box 10.2.

Resource endowments

Several factors probably assisted the dragons' drive towards industrialization, compensating them for the dearth of favourable circumstances that boosted Japan and the tigers. One concerns their natural resources including huge mineral, forest and agricultural reserves. Indonesian exports of oil and gas in the late 1980s earned $8000 million each year. The massive fires that broke out in Indonesia in late 1997 have, however, damaged some valuable original forests. Despite its fast growing industries, Thailand continues to export approximately half its agricultural produce including rice, sugar cane and rubber. Malaysia has long been famous for its hardwoods, rubber plantations and exports of tin ore although it has also become a leading exporter of cocoa and oil palm.

Again, tandem development, pivoting on successive waves of Japanese investment followed later by inflows from the tigers, has provided substantial economic buoyancy. Taiwan and Hong Kong were the single largest foreign investors in Thailand and Malaysia respectively in 1990, supplying 51 and 38 per cent of each country's DFI in that year (Ozawa 1993: 130). It has been the absence of a tandem development effect of such dimensions in other world regions, such as sub-Saharan Africa, which partly explains their continuing relative impoverishment.

Box 10.2   Religion, capitalism and the sociological debate on Confucianism

Background

Ever since Weber, sociologists have theorized about the possible links between a society's religion and its propensity to launch into successful capitalist growth. Weber suggested that European Protestantism had encouraged a practical, rational, individualistic, achievement-orientated and accumulative leaning towards everyday economic life – designed to enhance God's glory and win his approval. Widely practised by sect members this had assisted the breakthrough to modern capitalism. By contrast, Weber concluded that Asian religions, including Confucianism, were more likely to inhibit than to foster the emergence of such a capitalist spirit.

Mid-twentieth-century views

After the war, and influenced by Weber, several sociologists came to similar conclusions regarding the wider cultural influence exercised by such Asian religions as Confucianism. Thus, it was seen as a strongly conservative influence:

■ Supposedly it encouraged formalized, ritualistic and static relationships.

■ It was hostile to new wealth from trade, economic change and experimentation.

■ It demanded strict obedience to hierarchical forms of traditional authority.

Reappraising Confucianism

More recently, other writers (for example, Edwards 1992) have argued exactly the opposite. They have credited the Chinese Confucian tradition – which has spread through trade and kinship across much of Asia – with bequeathing a cultural heritage that has benefited the modernization process. This includes:

■ The importance attached to the exercise of moral and political leadership by an élite of educated officials who in a modern situation can claim the right to demand sacrifice and obedience from the population providing they show genuine virtue, skill and patriotism in achieving a prosperity from which all can hope to benefit.

■ The wide respect for learning and discipline which has also been transferred into the modern context via the emphasis on acquiring technical skills and the need successfully to transfer western technology.

■ The belief in collective unity and the pursuit of common purposes now transposed from family and community to factory, office and, indeed, nation.

Evaluation

Presumably, China and the tigers have all gained advantages from this ethos since they share a predominantly Confucian background although the dragon economies also contain important Chinese minorities. However, as Hoogvelt (1997: 209) suggests we may wish to remain rather sceptical of this interpretation given the very different conclusions reached by various scholars and the fact that Asia is a vast region 'noted for its multiple and competing religions'. Perhaps we should conclude by suggesting that while it is hard to see how deep cultural orientations, including religious ones, could fail to leave some kind of imprint on modernizing societies, the extent to which this happens and in which direction is extremely difficult to estimate or predict. Nevertheless, in the age of globalization cultural and religious diversity is a significant economic plus as diasporas can draw in investment, stimulate trade and share skills between their home and host countries.

The role of the Chinese diaspora

Underlying some of these increasing regional investment flows is a 'large, informal Chinese multinational business network extending across East Asia' (Hill 1990: 31) and indeed the rest of the world. This diaspora of some 55 million people, based on common kin, ethnic and religious identities, has been especially beneficial for China. It has generated several important inward capital flows from Thailand, Malaysia, Macao and Taiwan and from Hong Kong into China's 'special economic zones' during the 1990s. Indeed, approximately three-quarters of China's cumulative total inflow of foreign investment in recent years has originated from the overseas Chinese. Capital has also flowed from Taiwan, Hong Kong and Singapore to other parts of East Asia. What these groups carry with them is not only capital and market connections but also entrepreneurial flair and a willingness to assist kin and fellow ethnic members through various capital-pooling arrangements and business sponsorship.

With the growing interdependence of the US economy (particularly its West Coast) and the Chinese Pacific economies of Taiwan, Hong Kong and China, many Chinese are becoming 'hypermobile' migrants who establish a family in one country, start a business in another and are constantly moving between the two. The activities of these 'astronauts' or 'spacemen', as the Chinese call them, have greatly invigorated the turn to the free market in the People's Republic and massively increased its trade with the West (Cohen 1997: 93–4).

THE END OF THE MIRACLE?

Late in 1997, instead of talking about miracles and the unstoppability of East Asian development, many observers began to use such terms as 'crisis' and 'collapse'. What events have prompted this turnabout and how important are East Asia's current economic problems? Although the tigers and dragons flourished until 1997, Japan's economy began to falter in the late 1980s. Whereas Japan's GDP rose by a cumulative total of only 6 per cent between 1992–96, that of the USA increased by 22 per cent (*The Economist* 11 January 1997: 21). In 1998 the economy was in recession. Several factors led up to these events.

1. During the late 1980s, huge stock market and speculative property booms swept through Japan. When these bubbles burst after 1989, stock market and property prices dropped by around 60 per cent and many banks collapsed or were left with a legacy of unpaid loans.

2. Japan was compelled to revalue the yen in 1985. But years of trade surpluses have also made the yen a strong international currency. For both these reasons it appreciated from about 240 in 1985 to approximately 100 yen to the dollar during recent years making Japan's exports much more expensive.

3. As we have indicated Japanese industry responded to this by transferring many plants abroad thereby hollowing out the domestic economy. Consequently unemployment has risen undermining Japan's long-term post-war compact with workers in the largest firms based on the principle of lifetime employment (Cockerill and Sparks 1996).

4. Much of this capital went to Europe and North America but in the twelve months to March 1995, Asia received more Japanese DFI than Europe – an increase of 43 per cent on the previous twelve months. Consequently, manufactured imports from Japanese companies operating in Asia have flooded back to the home market exacerbating unemployment (Fukushima 1996: 65).

5. The close interpenetration of the banks, the corporations, the government and (in some cases) organized crime has meant that it is difficult to contain a collapse in investor confidence once a few bricks of the structure have been dislodged.

During 1997 a series of linked financial crises also rocked the tiger and dragon economies. In part, global factors were responsible. Thus, the sheer size of the capital flows moving around the world during the 1990s was quite remarkable. For example, according to the World Bank (1996), more foreign capital flowed to Asia and Latin America during 1996 than in the whole of the 1980s. Linked to this has been the worldwide deregulation of capital markets since 1980 making transnational fund movements much easier. But in today's world, inflowing capital can just as easily move elsewhere. In addition, because Japan has been so central to tiger and dragon development, the former's problems have hindered them as well. Finally, local problems created largely by government policies also played a part. The East Asian economies have become victims of their own past success in several ways:

1. They remained fiercely wedded to the goal of achieving very high growth year after year and so became over-dependent on foreign capital including inflows of 'hot money' (short-term speculative inflows).

2. In order to restrain inflation and offer safe, attractive havens for foreign capital they tied their currencies to the dollar during the years preceding the 1997 crises while believing that this would not effect the competitiveness of their exports. This led them to believe they could continue to rely on capital inflows.

3. Between July and October 1997, Thailand, Indonesia, Malaysia, the Philippines, South Korea and Hong Kong – in that order – were faced with powerful pressures which drove the prevailing currency and stock market values sharply down. Speculators lost confidence in the ability of these countries to maintain the international value of their currencies while foreign investors tried to move their funds abroad. Share prices tumbled on the local stock markets and 'hot money' withdrew. The Thai baht, for example, lost 40 per cent of its former value between July and November 1997.

4. The East Asian economies were therefore forced to devalue their currencies and raise interest rates creating a severe crisis in national confidence. This is likely to fuel inflation although it will also cheapen their exports in future. This, in turn, has raised alarm bells in the advanced countries at the prospect of a flood of cheap Asian imports threatening future jobs.

5. A dangerously high proportion of the previous inflows of capital seems to have gone into property deals, buying shares in property companies – especially in the case of Hong Kong – investments in wasteful projects linked to

political corruption or, as in South Korea, into various state-directed investments of dubious long-term viability. As property prices plunged with falling share prices and the withdrawal of funds, so banks collapsed across the region or found themselves weighed down with bad debts.

6. The scale of collapsing confidence drove Thailand, Indonesia and South Korea to accept IMF rescue packages involving $17 200 million, $23 000 million and $57 500 million respectively during the summer and autumn of 1997. By 2000 it remained to be seen whether the IMF might need to provide still larger amounts in order to underwrite further capital flights from Asia.

It is obvious that in an economic roller-coaster such as we have described, many investors, property speculators, banks and companies will 'lose their shirts'. But such economic crises always produce many other victims. Thus, press reports in 1997/98 alluded to several potential problems in the region. Some 2–3 million migrant workers, sucked into the booming economies from poorer countries were displaced. Many returned to countries with high unemployment and where families have relied on their remittances. (In Malaysia alone there were 1.2 million registered foreign workers and perhaps 800 000 illegal workers.) Many workers returned to Indonesia, where the regime continued to experience severe political instability in 1998. Indeed, middle-class students, frustrated at the collapse of their prospects, turned on President Suharto. Some lost their lives in forcing an end to his regime. There have been many food riots and looting, particularly in Java. The Chinese minority, who often own small shops in the rural areas, have been targeted by the rioters. All over the region workers have lost their jobs, poor people have lost their savings and those who owe money to banks and moneylenders find themselves being harassed to cover their debts. Many imported goods, including some essential foodstuffs, have increased in price with falling currency values.

During 1998, the crisis also engulfed the western economies. Asian orders for the latter's goods plummeted and their cheapened manufactured imports flooded into Europe and North America. Meanwhile unemployment also rose because some Japanese and South Korean companies have contracted or closed their industrial plants in the West.

Predicting the future is always risky. But there are several reasons for supposing that, ultimately, East Asia will weather this storm. Indeed, by summer 1999, there were strong indications of this for most countries. First, investors need to find profitable outlets. There are few countries that are not beset with one kind of economic problem or another. Thus, it is quite possible that following a period of financial reform funds will eventually flow back. Second, we must remember to distinguish clearly between a country's underlying productive resources – above all its accumulation of technical skills and the ability to reproduce them through education – and the ebb and flow of financial assets. The latter are invariably fickle in today's global economy. On the first count, however, the East Asian economies remain fundamentally strong. Lastly, it is hardly in the interests of the advanced countries to permit a permanent collapse to occur in these economies since such an eventuality might create escalating disorder in the world polity. In any case, the latter have now become too important as markets for the high-tech goods and services upon which the advanced countries increasingly depend for their own livelihoods.

REVIEW

Many countries in the Asia-Pacific region have industrialized rapidly both in relation to the older 'mature' economies of Europe and North America and compared to other developing countries. In addressing many of the possible explanations we have argued that a complex mix of factors was involved. Some parts of the region were historically quite developed and the period of western dominance can be seen as an interregnum. The Cold War led to a favourable set of economic circumstances in the region, including the pumping-in of US aid against the threat or presumed threat of communism. The cultural endowment of many Asian societies was conducive to disciplined work and entrepreneurship – a sort of Asian parallel to Weber's suggestion that there is a complex affinity between Protestantism and capitalism. Above all, there was effective political and economic management. Contrary to the ideas of those in favour of unfettered markets there is little evidence that the successful Asian economies became slaves to the invisible hand of the market. Instead the market was *managed* through targeting key industries, supporting technological innovation through state support and funnelling key national resources to the export effort.

During 1997, for different reasons, the Asian economies faltered badly, but probably not terminally. New growth markets – for example Brazil, Argentina and Mexico – beckoned while the manufacturing sectors in the old industrialized countries revived somewhat, partly by imitating Japanese innovations. In short, there are good reasons to think that the period of continuous massive growth is over. However, the successful Asian economies have invested heavily in education, training and R&D and are likely to be serious players in the emerging information-related global economy.

If you would like to know more ••••••••••••••••••••••••••••••••

The general reader by Simone and Feraru, *The Asian Pacific* (1995) is highly accessible and informative. Slightly more advanced, but including several perceptive chapters, is the book edited by Applebaum and Henderson, *States and Development in the Asian Pacific* (1992).

Several books examine particular countries and more emerge all the time. However, the following remain ground-breaking and sometimes controversial studies: Johnson, *MITI and the Japanese Miracle* (1982); Wade, *Governing the Market* (1990); and Amsden, *Asia's Next Giant* (1989).

For a more sceptical approach to the East Asian situation, see Bello and Rosenfeld's book, *Dragons in Distress* (1990).

Material on China pours out all the time. White's, *Riding the Tiger* (1993) is very thorough and raises important issues.

Group Work ••

1. The class will draw up a balance sheet plotting the gains and losses for the rich western countries due to the rise of Asia now and in the future.

2. Divide the class into teams before the seminar. Using recent material available in newspapers and magazines (such as *The Economist*), and with the assistance of your library's CD ROM collection or the Internet, each group will prepare a 15-minute report on a different East Asian country. Each group's seminar report will focus on the current assessment of their *economic* and *political* situations and the explanations given for their various problems.

3. Using similar resources look at the *social* effects of the East Asian crisis in any two countries of your choice. Each group will provide a 15-minute report to the class.

Questions to think about ●●●

1. Using examples, outline the key characteristics of the developmental state. To what extent do its origins lie in political crises?

2. What are the main sources of difference between the tiger and the dragon economies and how far do these help to explain their varying degrees of economic success?

3. Evaluate the relative importance of Ozawa's 'tandem development' effect in explaining the industrial achievement of the tigers, dragons and China?

4. Have the 'tigers' and 'dragons' now been tamed?

part three
Experiences

Population Pressures and Migration

CONTENTS

The number of people living on earth has increased dramatically. Although estimates vary, in about 8000 BC there were 4.5 million people. In AD 1, there were 170 million. Two thousand years later, at the end of the twentieth century, demographers believe there are about 6000 million. Moreover, despite high infant mortality rates in poor countries, disease, poverty, famine and the spread of HIV, their numbers are rising steeply. In this chapter, we explain how we measure population growth and whether fears of overpopulation are exaggerated. We also investigate what conditions and policies might serve to reduce population growth.

Steep rises in birth rates are normally found in agricultural societies and rural areas. The spectacular growth of urban populations is as much the result of migration to cities as increasing family sizes. High levels of internal migration are often followed by increases in international migration. Although the number of global migrants is small in relation to national migrants, their presence provokes frenzied bursts of xenophobia in receiving countries. What new forms has international migration taken and what have been the reactions to this supposed 'threat'?

THE FEAR OF OVERPOPULATION

Of all global problems, fear of overpopulation is possibly the most prevalent concern of ordinary citizens. The rapid growth in the world's population has been a matter of fierce debate at least since an English Anglican pastor, Thomas Malthus (1973) (see Figure 11.1), published his *Essay on the Principle of Population* anonymously in 1798, when the world's population was then less than one-eighth its current size. The book was highly influential in the nineteenth century – perhaps as important as the writings of the French revolutionaries. It strongly informed the thought of Herbert Spencer (a major early British sociologist) and also influenced Charles Darwin and the Social Darwinists. In the twentieth century, Malthusian ideas ramified through the work of the eugenicists (who wanted to produce a better class of person through selective breeding) and eventually into contemporary discussions of overpopulation in the light of the earth's fragile ecological balance.

Malthus attracted as many enemies as he did friends and followers. Karl Marx bitterly attacked his ideas and mocked him for advocating population restraint while having an indecent number of children himself. According to Nicholls (1995: 324), Marx maliciously misrepresented Malthus while pretending merely to summarize his views. Marx wrote: 'Since [as Malthus argues] population is constantly tending to overtake the means of subsistence, charity is folly, a public encouragement of poverty. The state can therefore do nothing but leave the poor to their fate and, at the most, make death easy for them.'

Nicholls's (1995) view of Malthus is more sympathetic. He does not dispute that Malthus was part of the conservative reaction to the French Revolution and was responding to the threat to family and property that certain revolutionary ideas foretokened. Malthus thought that a breakdown of the old social order would accelerate a natural tendency for population to grow faster than food supply. Malthus's statistical calculations were simple, his basic notion being that food supply would grow arithmetically (as in $1\rightarrow2\rightarrow3\rightarrow4$), whereas population would grow geometrically (as in $1\rightarrow2\rightarrow4\rightarrow8$). He thought the desire for sexual intercourse and the level of human fertility were likely to be constant. (We now know that variations in fertility are possible, for example, through shifts in cultural norms, birth control measures and increased affluence.) But this was a reasonable assumption at the end of the eighteenth century and still probably applies to the majority of the world's population. Because of this constancy, Malthus reasoned that the only way population growth could be halted was through the painful sanction of famine.

Nicholls shows that in several important respects Malthus's contribution was subtler than Marx and his other detractors admitted:

1. In second and subsequent editions of his *Essay*, Malthus accepted that moral restraint (abstinence) and later marriage would impose additional constraints on overpopulation, short of famine.

2. He was not a 'no-growth' theorist and believed it was a religious duty to populate the world. He even lamented 'the present scanty population of the earth'.

Figure 11.1   Thomas Malthus (1766–1834), prophet of doom?

3. He thought emigration could help match population to resources.

4. He was not, as Marx averred, against all forms of state intervention or the enemy of the working class. Indeed, he supported the early socialist Robert Owen in his attempts to promote legislation to limit the use of child labour in the cotton industry.

Despite this corrective by Nicholls, there is no doubt that the expression 'Malthusian', which is now back in fashion, is being used to signify concern about the imbalance between population and resources. This discrepancy can only be resolved, so Malthusians say, by famine or other forms of severe social breakdown. Was Malthus right? In three areas he was not:

1. His crude statistical calculations assumed the doubling of the European population every 25 years. In fact, as historical demographers have pointed out, the population has doubled only after each 50 years (approximately) since 1800.

2. War and disease proved more effective means of birth control than famine. For example, the heavy losses of young men in the First World War seriously slowed down population growth in France and the UK and led to pro-natalist policies in France.

3. The growth in European agriculture has more than kept pace with the growth in population. This is true, too, of much of Asia, including India and China, although yields remain low in both countries.

Despite these major flaws in his analysis, Malthusian ideas have a nasty way of resurfacing, even in the most unlikely settings. Let us take a few examples:

1. A crude version of the Malthusian message provides ammunition to attack particular sections of the population. At various times, there have been accusations that the working classes 'breed like rabbits' or that Africans, Chinese, or other peoples or categories of people are procreating in disproportionate numbers. This form of discriminatory Malthusianism was demonstrated by the eugenics movement – which promoted procreation among a favoured few. A similar logic, in more extreme versions, justified the Aryan-breeding programme of the Nazis and the policies of the apartheid regime: covert sterilization for blacks, pro-natalism for whites.

2. Following a newspaper exposé in 1997, it was revealed that in addition to Nazi Germany, the authorities in Denmark, Norway, Estonia, Finland, Sweden and one of the Swiss cantons had sanctioned the practice of enforced sterilization. Between 1934 and 1976, more than 40 000 Norwegians, 6000 Danes and 60 000 Swedes, mainly women, were sterilized. As late as 1953, and in a country renowned for being socially progressive, the Swedish National Board of Health decided to sterilize a 16-year-old boy, 'Nils', against his wishes on the grounds that he was 'a sexually precocious mixed type'. A 'mixed type' meant that, according to the wall charts supplied by the State Institute of Racial Biology, he was not racially pure (*Guardian* 3 September 1997).

3. The population question is also being coupled with ecological issues. This is an important aspect of global thinking best represented by the idea of 'Spaceship Earth' – a vulnerable ball floating in universal space. The earth is seen as an integrated living system with each living part interacting in a set of interlocking relationships and exchange one with another. However, this is a closed and finite system existing only in the biosphere (a thin skin of earth, water and atmosphere). It has a limited and precarious life. If overpopulation disrupts this system, so it is argued, we will plunge into a self-destructive mode. In this kind of thinking, the sanctity of human life, which is at the heart of so much religious and ethical thought, is subordinated to what is regarded as a greater good.

THE TOOLS OF THE DEMOGRAPHERS' TRADE

From the examples we have seen so far, it is apparent that Malthusian arguments are based on a complex mixture of science (perhaps 'perverted science'), surmise and prejudice. It is difficult to oppose speculation and uninformed opinion without a systematic means of investigating the population issue. To do this, we need to have to hand a few tools of the demographers' trade (demographers deal with the size, composition, distribution of, and changes to, populations).

Although a heavy reliance on statistical methods sometimes alarms those sociology students without quantitative backgrounds, it is important to under-

---

Box 11.1   The demographers' toolkit

1. *Crude birth rate* This measures the number of live births per 1000 members of a population in a given year. The US (1986) figure was 15.3 (down by 11.2 since 1947). The Kenyan rate was 53.8 in the mid-1980s. The sharp drops seen in the USA are even more evident in other advanced countries – for example, in western Europe.

2. The *fertility rate* – the number of live births per woman over her lifetime – is another, more intuitive, way to measure population. It takes a fertility rate of about 2.0/2.1 for a population in a developed country to replace itself. The fertility rate has dropped from 3.8 in 1947 to 1.8 in the mid-1980s in the USA and more dramatically in western Europe. France and Italy (1.2) show very low fertility rates in the 1990s. Singapore, interestingly, was also at 1.2 in the mid-1990s. We will return later to why there are these sharp drops in fertility.

3. Also relevant is the *crude death rate* of the population in any given year. In the USA (1987) it was 8.7 per 1000 of the population. By comparison Chad, a poor country in West Africa, had a death rate of 44.1 per 1000 in the same year.

4. Closely related to the *death rate* is the *infant mortality rate* (IMR) – the number of deaths among infants aged below one year per 1000 of the infant population. Finland, Japan and Sweden have low IMRs (about 6.0), the USA has 10–11; in the worst years of famine in Ethiopia it was 229. The IMR and subsequent child death is particularly significant in determining fertility behaviour. If there is a good chance that your child will die, it is not unreasonable that you will seek to have more children to insure against that contingency.

5. *Longevity* or *life expectancy* is the number of years projected as remaining to an average person of a certain age. Often this measurement is taken from birth, but this can be misleading, especially when the IMR is high. In many developing societies, if you beat the statistical odds to make it (say) to 50, you have a good chance of surviving to 70. Most advanced societies have life expectancies from birth of over 70 for men and over 75 for women. These expectancies are rapidly increasing. Unusually, they have declined by ten years for Russian men since 1989.

---

stand the results, if not all the means, of statistical research. This is because demographers can produce powerful sociological data. The data are not powerful in the sense that they record something dramatic – a civil war, a strike, a prison riot, or a revolt against the poll tax. However, the long-term, drip-feed changes in health, income, social conduct, security, levels of pollution and many other factors are easily missed without a professional, *longitudinal*, statistical analysis. Let us start this analysis by looking at global population projections (Figure 11.2).

A **longitudinal** analysis measures a particular change over a specified period at regular intervals.

Malthus's heirs (called 'neo-Malthusians') often use expressions like the population 'explosion', or population 'time bomb'. Certainly, it would be foolish to deny that there is cause for concern. As Figure 11.2 shows, the world's population is due to grow to 8525 million by the year 2025, with massive increases in China and India. If population growth occurs at that rate it is likely to have severe effects on food supply, urban management, health and social support for the poor.

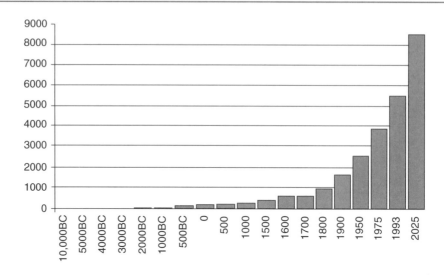

Figure 11.2   Global population growth and projections

In the 1970s, new statistical techniques were developed at the Massachusetts Institute of Technology (MIT). Scholars tried to measure complex interdependencies between different social and economic trends. The Club of Rome (a group of concerned industrialists and civil servants interested in the future) used the MIT team to model different projected scenarios. The team looked at population growth, industrial output, food production, pollution and resource depletion. The standard statistical run (which projected the growth curves in each of these variables based on figures from 1900 to 1970) produced 'overshoot and collapse' (Martell 1994: 25–40).

Given considerable publicity in the 1980s, the Club of Rome's reports led to a widespread belief among policy-makers and the general public that population growth was 'out of control'. This fear was deepened when reliable sociological reports from China indicated that the government's birth control measures were not working.

It is all too easy to forget that projections do not constitute a certainty, but rather act as a credible warning as to what might happen. Present-trend projections are often wrong, sometimes because people change their conduct in response to earlier plausible warnings. The most crucial aggregate change is that the annual growth rate of the world's population has slowed from 2 per cent (1980), to 1.6 per cent (1987) and a projected 1.5 per cent in 2000.

Country studies also provide grounds for optimism that population growth can be slowed. The successful NICs (like Singapore) show a rapidly diminishing birth rate in conformity with those of the wealthy western countries. There also seems no reason to suppose that religion interferes unduly with this pattern, as the cases of Catholic Italy and urban Latin America show. Again, with some exceptions, many countries seem to be following the three stages of the 'demographic transition' that had been observed in earlier decades in Europe, a notion that is explained in Table 11.1.

Table 11.1   The demographic transition

Stage 1	Stable, but high potential growth	High birth rate and high death rate	Population is stable but is 'coiled', ready to spring, therefore potentially high growth	Agricultural society
Stage 2	Transition stage	Continuing high birth rate but falling death rate (for example through better health, sewerage and lower IMR)	This is when population growth really swells	Industrial development takes off
Stage 3	Population stability	Low death rate and low birth rate	Population size remains on a plateau or falls	Prosperous society with developed welfare system

THE WORLD'S POPULATION: CAUSE FOR CONCERN?

There are a number of principal findings by demographers and sociologists in respect of population growth:

1. A consistent result is that economic prosperity is the most powerful predictor of a reduced birth rate in all countries. With better health facilities, the IMR and child deaths decline, so there is less need for 'insurance children'. With adequate benefit systems, pensions and welfare, parents are less dependent on children for support in old age (although this will cause problems, as we shall see) so they do not need to have so many of them.

2. Increased prosperity is usually marked by an increased number of women entering the labour market, often in their childbearing years. If women have careers or hold jobs, the band of years where the greatest fertility arises is reduced.

3. The improvement of women's status and the greater opportunities for women in education also reduce family size.

4. For individuals and families, prosperity rises with fewer children. Acquisitions of clothing, leisure, travel and holidays are enhanced and there is a cultural shift away from children towards consumption.

5. Birth control measures work less efficiently than economic prosperity. Proponents of birth control are often victims of the 'technological fallacy' – the idea that people will use a technology if they are properly informed. This takes little account of the fact that they will ignore the message if they want to do something else. (Extensive birth control clinics and 'shaming techniques' have been available for a generation in East Africa, but with little effect on the birth rate – Figure 11.2.) It also takes little account of human

inventiveness. Procreation and sexual gratification are separated in the minds of all peoples; it is quite possible to have the latter without the pill, condoms, the coil and the rest of the technological package.

6. In developed countries, the main demographic problem is the *low* birth rate, which in the absence of high rates of immigration can have a marked effect on the social pyramid. It moves from its normal shape, through a Christmas tree shape, oak tree shape and finally to an inverted pyramid over the course of about 120 years (see Figure 11.3). Young people predominate at the beginning of the period but gradually elderly people (with their greater health needs and often inadequate pensions) have to be supported by a smaller and smaller number of people of working age.

7. A number of studies in the USA have shown that within a generation, certainly within two, people who migrate from poor to rich countries rapidly conform to the birth rate patterns of their adopted homes.

8. Sex and age composition are crucially important to the issue of how pensions, health and social security benefits will be paid, bearing in mind the changed ratio between the productive and dependent population.

1900	1940	1980	2020

Old people

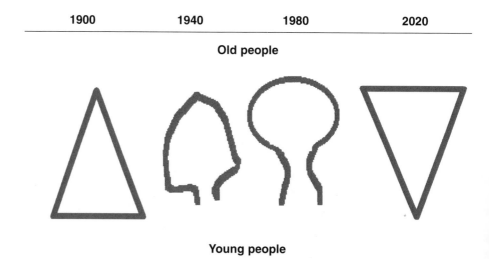

Young people

Figure 11.3   Demographic shapes in developed countries

We have seen how the Club of Rome popularized the argument that unbridled population growth could damage the earth's delicate ecology. But we have to be cautious about two aspects of this proposition. First, there have always been doomsday merchants proclaiming the end of the world. The scientific evidence of ecological fragility has to be separated from the emotional commitment to doomsday thinking by people whose fear and emotions are stronger than their reason. Second, as in many areas where science and politics overlap, there are disturbing signs of the development of a fanatical minority of pro-ecologists. In 1997 in Washington State, USA, loggers were killed with bows and arrows in an attempt to stop them cutting down trees. This sort of conduct is sometimes described as 'ecological fascism'.

There are clear ethical limits to population control measures. Most people would agree that civil war, ethnic cleansing, compulsory sterilization and gas chambers are morally unacceptable. A couple of other practices that have been widely used are at the least morally dubious. Doctors used the first in the 1970s and 1980s in a number of countries (including Sweden, South Africa and the UK). They sought to persuade mothers at the vulnerable moment when they gave birth that sterilization was medically necessary or desirable. The second, used by the government of India in the 1970s, but now abandoned, was to promote sterilization by bribing people with goods (like a radio) or money.

Not only are these practices ethically questionable, there is considerable evidence that they do not work, or work only in a very fragmentary way. Questions of population growth have to be set in the context of environmental degradation, political conflict, land reform and food security (see Chapter 9). Food producers and urban workers need adequate security (Where is my next meal coming from?), political stability (Will my family have a future?) and health care (Are my children likely to survive?). With these elements guaranteed, sometimes at quite low levels of income or service provision, birth rates are likely to decline.

WHERE DO THEY ALL GO? URBANIZATION AND INTERNAL MIGRATION

Despite grounds for consolation that the population problem can be contained, the sheer weight of numbers in some countries creates concern. If there is little or no food for the rural populace to eat, where do they all go? The bulk of population growth is, of course, absorbed by the burgeoning cities in the developing world. Even conservative projections show that by 2010 the majority of the world's population will be urbanized. The speed of this development is unprecedented. Measuring urbanization as 'over 50 per cent of a population living in cities':

● In 1850 no society could be described as urban.
● In 1900 only one could, Great Britain.
● In 1970 nearly all advanced nations were urbanized.
● In the same year there were already 50 cities with over a million inhabitants.

Stage 3 of the demographic transition is often associated with urbanization. Crowded living quarters, finding a job before starting a family and the absence of family pressures to procreate all contribute to the decline in birth rates. This is particularly true of 'successful' cities, where high rates of industrialization and employment obtain.

However, many cities in the developing and underdeveloped countries are far from successful. Tin and cardboard shantytowns (called *favelas* and *barrios* in Latin America) often disfigure these cities. At their worst, these settlements deteriorate into unhealthy, crime-ridden urban slums. Fortunately, some sociologists have observed more positive outcomes of these 'irregular settlements'. Particularly in Latin America, residents have sought to improve their dwellings and have been successful in persuading the municipal authorities to lay on electricity, rubbish collections, schools and health clinics. Others of these new urbanites have continued to effect links – in their population behaviour and other social conduct – with their old villages and the countryside. We therefore witness a dual phenomenon – urbanization without industrialization and urbanization without adequate employment.

As we will explain in Chapter 15, sociologists have been here before. The movement from living off hunting and gathering or herding domesticated animals to sedentary ways of life fundamentally altered the nature of social life. The food surpluses created by the success of agricultural techniques allowed the possibility of developing thriving manufacturing, business and commercial sectors in the towns. But for the bulk of nineteenth-century urbanites life in the cities was dirty, crowded and unsanitary. Piped drinking water was a precious commodity, ash and soot poured from the factory chimneys, while raw sewerage was left at the side of the unpaved streets.

Today we are still wrestling with the social consequences of rapid urbanization. Can the system cope? Can we provide education, health facilities, transport and sanitation on an adequate scale? Will there be an urban explosion with management systems failing? In principle, these issues have been addressed and sometimes spectacularly solved by the advanced industrialized countries. However, the sheer scale and speed of rural–urban migration provides a daunting prospect. Newspaper reports from the mid-1990s claimed that millions of people are moving *each year* from rural to urban areas in China, although a proportion of these are circulatory migrants who periodically return to the countryside (see Chapter 8).

THE CONSTRAINTS ON INTERNATIONAL MIGRATION

It cannot be emphasized too strongly that the bulk of migration is internal. However, some of those who have already made the step from rural to urban areas seek greener pastures in other countries. These international migrants are an important part of the phenomenon of globalization. They take advantage of the increased interdependence of the world's economies and find themselves a place, sometimes a very modest place, in the global labour market (Cohen 1987). They are also active agents of globalization, establishing a dense network of connections between their places of origin and their places of settlement.

Although there are relatively few international migrants compared with internal migrants, in political and sociological terms their movements are highly sensitive. At first sight, the small number involved in international migration is counter-intuitive. After all, as there is virtually free movement of goods, capital, images and ideas, why is there not a similarly free movement of workers? It seems that through inertia, social involvement with a natal community, lack of opportunity, immigration restrictions and xenophobia, the numbers actually crossing international borders for the purposes of settlement are restrained. In western Europe, for example, the percentage of foreigners to locals was 1.3 per cent in 1950. This had more than trebled by 1990, but the last number still represents a very small diminution of the homogeneity of European states compared with the massive inroads of globalization in other areas (Table 11.2).

Table 11.2   Foreign resident population in western Europe, 1950–90

1950		1960		1982		1990	
(000s)	%	(000s)	%	(000s)	%	(000s)	%
5100	1.3	10 200	2.2	15 000	3.1	16 600	4.5

Source: Castells (1996: 308)

One would expect the proportion of foreign-born members of the US population to be much higher given that, like Canada, Australia, New Zealand and
Argentina, it is an immigrant country. And, indeed, this is the case. However,
the peak year was as long ago as 1910, when 15 per cent of the population was
foreign born. With the outbreak of the First World War, the Depression and
immigration controls, numbers were dramatically reduced to about 5 per cent
(1970), a proportion that has only slowly crept up (Figure 11.4).

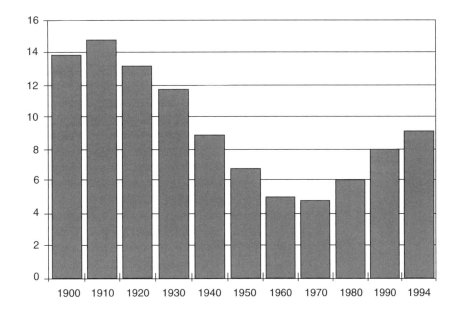

Figure 11.4   Foreign-born population in the USA (%) (Castells, 1996: 232)

NEW DIMENSIONS OF INTERNATIONAL MIGRATION

After the Second World War, labour migration was mainly from the South to the
North – from former colonial territories to their old metropoli, or from adjacent
poorer countries to their richer neighbours. Turks and Yugoslavs went to West
Germany while Mexicans came to the USA in even greater numbers.

In the early 1970s, labour immigration for permanent settlement in the more powerful industrialized countries of Europe and North America virtually stopped. Instead, several new forms of international migration became more evident during the last 25 years. We say 'more evident' because they are not wholly new, but gain additional impetus. Not all these trends are fully visible in all countries. However, given the increased interdependence of the world economy there is little doubt that global patterns of migration will have an impact in the following areas:

- the growth of refugee migration
- the phenomenon of 'immigration shopping'
- the rise in undocumented workers
- the rise in independent female migrants
- the situation of skilled transients
- unskilled contract workers.

Growth of refugee migration

Numbers vary according to the statistical criteria used, but using the word 'refugee' in a general sense to allude to people participating in 'flight migration', most counts put the current number of refugees at somewhere between 18 and 20 million people worldwide. As we saw in Chapter 8, the 1951 Geneva Convention gives a much narrower, legal definition, defining a refugee as someone who is fleeing from a real threat of persecution in their country of origin on the grounds of their background or political opinion. We have seen that this definition is particularly restrictive in practice because the Convention places full responsibility for judging whether a person is, or is not, a refugee in the hands of the admitting state. Given the general fear of migration of all kinds, one can easily imagine many states making very harsh decisions. Again, technically, a refugee can be distinguished from an *asylum-seeker* (one whose claims for refugee status have not yet been recognized) and from an *internally displaced person* (somebody who has been pushed from his or her normal place of residence by war, civil conflict, or an ecological disaster such as a fire, flood, hurricane or volcano).

This last category – the displaced person – has provided a particularly intractable problem for international agencies such as the United Nations High Commission for Refugees (UNHCR), which are concerned with trying to return, settle and integrate such groups. With the end of the war in Kosovo the UNHCR has been charged with the responsibility of resettling about half a million Kosovars. Based on previous experience of the 1980s, if refugees are dispersed far from their homelands only about 25 per cent return. However, given that most of the Kosovars are in camps just across the border, the overwhelming majority are expected to resettle in their native province. At the same time the bulk of the Serb minority in Kosovo is expected to flee to Serbia proper.

Immigration shopping

The next new feature of migration is that no country unreservedly welcomes immigrants of all sorts. There have been formal and informal restrictions on immigration for over a century, often on racial grounds. In 1882, the USA passed an Exclusion Act directed against the Chinese. Asians were, until recently,

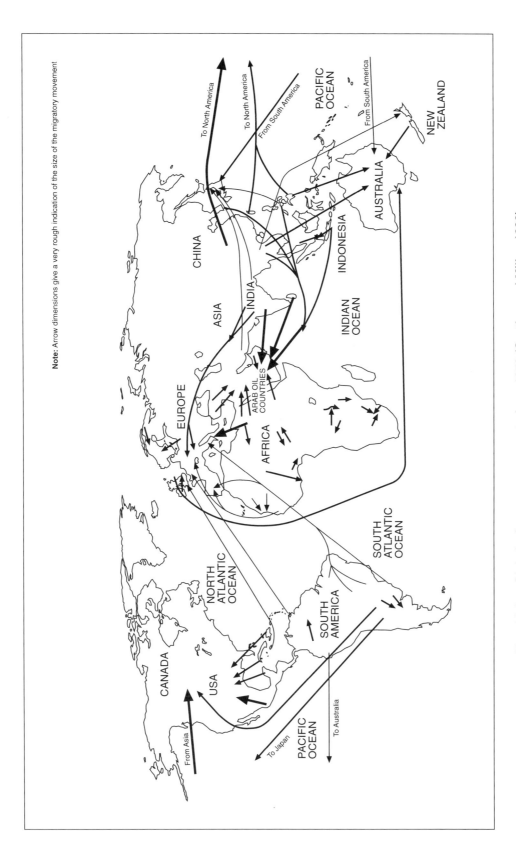

Note: Arrow dimensions give a very rough indication of the size of the migratory movement

Map 11.1   Global migratory movements from 1973 (Castles and Miller, 1998)

regarded as a 'yellow peril' in the USA, Canada and Australia. (In all three places, they are now seen as a 'model minority'.) Europeans were not always welcome either, even in the countries of settlement in which they were dominant. Those going to the USA from the British Isles were the most favoured followed by the Scandinavians and Germans, who were seen as 'worthy peasant stock'. However, Slavs, Eastern European Jews and southern Europeans met a more hostile reception in the USA. So great was the fear of southern Europeans that the eugenicists of the time argued that the so-called 'fecund' and sexually attractive women from southern Europe would induce a state of biological shock in their northern sisters, such that they would not be able to reproduce at all. Southern Europeans would then dominate the USA.

In short, there were always preferences for particular kinds of migrants and always, therefore, some degree of immigration shopping. Nonetheless, the process was not too discriminating. Between 1870 and 1914, 35 million migrants went to the Americas, many to the USA. There was land, there was opportunity, and there were great nations to be built in Argentina, Australia, Brazil, Canada, New Zealand, South Africa and the USA – even if there was considerable disruption, not to say destruction, of the indigenees' way of life.

Now that period is decisively over. No country wants any and all immigrants, but many want small numbers of particular ones. Canada and Australia have perfected a system of selection. They have linked their economic, manpower and immigration departments structurally and are intent on finding special kinds of migrants to fill slots. If dentists are needed in Manitoba, an immigration slot will be created, just as radiographers going to Tasmania are welcomed. (Of course they can't police the system very effectively once migrants have arrived.) Without going into the points systems in detail, what these countries want are skills, youth, good health, education and lack of dependants. Equally welcomed are so-called 'business migrants' who bring wealth and possibly jobs with them.

Undocumented workers

We use the expression 'undocumented' to allude to people often defined as 'illegals'. This is not a matter of being 'politically correct', but technically correct. Since the use of passports became worldwide rather late, only in 1914, illegal residence was a vague concept. In many parts of the world, particularly Africa, it remains so. That some gentlemen sat in a conference room in 1885 drawing lines on a map of Africa does not necessarily make their boundaries a reality in the late twentieth century. Ethnic groups were split and seasonal and pastoral migratory flows continued. This is not unique to Africa. There are similarly permeable boundaries between northern Spain and France and, notably, between Mexico and the USA. States often simply give up the business of trying to police the border – so tolerating undocumented migration.

Undocumented labour is now taking two predominant forms (a) overstaying and (b) deliberate illegal entry (including that organized by intermediaries and agents, known as 'people smugglers'). The first phenomenon reflects the increasingly practical difficulties of managing the turnstiles that turn increasingly fast as more and more people file through. The figure going through the turnstiles in 1994 at London Heathrow – the busiest airport in the world – was 51 million. There is obviously a good deal of leakage through the system as tourists, students and family visitors pass through the gates. Some violate the terms of their entry and work when they are not supposed to (for example, a student who works in a fast-food outlet). Others stay on after their entry visas have expired.

There is increased evidence of organization behind deliberate illegal entrants. Large sums of money change hands, entry certificates and visas are forged and border guards are bribed. Often, travel and shipping agents are involved. An important dimension to illegal immigration is the frequent complicity of employers. The most obvious example here concerns Mexican labour in the USA, particularly before 1986. Up to that point it was illegal to be an undocumented worker, but not illegal to employ one. *Coyotes* (the local name for labour recruiters) commonly supplied gangs of workers on order. Stories of their treatment abound. For example, workers who had finished picking crops were reported to the INS (the Immigration and Naturalization Service) before they could draw their pay. There is often a contradiction between employers (who need cheap or compliant workers, or labour with particular skills and qualities) and the government, which needs to be responsive to public opinion. The unions organizing indigenous workers are also usually on the side of the state.

Women migrants

Feminists in the 1960s declared that women were 'hidden from history'. Generally, this is an accurate observation, but particularly so in the migration field. Many studies of migration dealt with 'the women left behind' in the rural areas. Alternatively, women have been treated as dependent or family members. They are seen essentially as the baggage of male workers. Some of this may have been justified in that males were often the pioneer migrants. However, even historically, we are beginning to turn up evidence that women were more independent actors than previously surmised. Attaching oneself to a settler family often as family servant gave the air of respectability and servility, but it often involved a later escape to some kind of independence.

Immigration law had the same effect. Take the case of Caribbean women coming to the USA or the UK in the post-war period. Much of the legislation during periods of restrictions forbade labour migration but permitted family reunification – on humanitarian grounds or to conform to international law. So women made opportunistic marriages and faked relationships.

Even if we can point to many examples of this sort of activity in the past, it is clear that numerically and sociologically we have entered a new phase of female migration. This is characterized by independent movements in response to a demand for women to enter the global service economy. Some of this is in the sex industry, particularly in Southeast Asia. Hostesses, sex workers and entertainers are required in significant numbers in countries such as Japan – and are generally supplied from China and Thailand. A more respectable version of the trade is in the 'mail order bride' trade – dominated by the Philippines. The Philippines is also the leader in the market for domestic labour, exporting tens of thousands of domestic workers each year to the Middle East and many other countries.

These markets are driven from both ends. On the supply side the Philippine government regards labour exports much like any other export – a foreign currency earner. This is primarily because of the significant remittance income returned by Filipinas abroad. Foreign exchange is also earned on the substantial agency and recruiting fees paid from foreign sources. On the demand side, changes in gender power in western countries have had a significant impact. Young women in the West tend to be less tolerant of 'MCPs' (male chauvinist pigs) and more reluctant to be confined to the kitchen and the home. The indigenous supply of domestic servants in western countries has virtually dried up. As late as the 1920s, hundreds of thousands of British women were in domestic service; now there are hardly any. The gap is filled from abroad.

To brides and domestic workers, add the many waitresses, casual staff in fast food outlets, cleaners, nurses (particularly geriatric ones), secretaries, hotel reception staff and stewardesses supplied from outside the country of work. Campani (1995) argues that women are now the *majority* of international migrants. Although the figures on this are unreliable, it is clear in migration studies that women are moving from being invisible dependants to independent social actors.

Skilled transients

'Hidden from history', in a very different way, are the highly skilled international migrants – professionals, accountants, computer experts, doctors, business managers, construction engineers, consultants and others. Some are freelance, but most work for international companies trying to complete contracts, initiate business deals or develop branch plants in the country of destination. The crucial element here is that migrants are not leaving a place of origin on a one-way ticket. These migrants are variously called 'skilled transients', 'sojourners' or 'denizens' (in the sense of a privileged foreigner). They have no particular civic rights in the new countries in which they work. They do not have the vote, cannot draw on social security and do not have rights of permanent residence. However, they do not really need these facilities and privileges. If they want to vote they can exercise their vote by post. Their companies insure them, often pay for privileged education for their children, provide generous pensions and subsidize family visits. The numbers of such skilled transients, sojourners or denizens are significant. In fact, Findlay (1995) estimates that they constitute the majority of migrants currently leaving the UK.

Unskilled contract workers

Skilled transients, who are in a sense contract workers, are paralleled by unskilled transients who continue to arrive at many destinations. Unskilled foreign contract workers are often exploited ruthlessly and are frequently used as a means to undercut the bargaining power of the characteristically better paid and organized indigenous workers. As in the case of skill transients, the importing states' intention is to avoid permanent settlement. Let us take three examples of contract labour systems, all of which are now showing considerable tensions: the *Gastarbeiter* in Germany, Asian workers in the Middle East and contract labour in South Africa.

The *Gastarbeiter* system in Germany involved the use of temporary labourers mainly from nearby countries like Turkey and Yugoslavia. The idea was to use the workers as and when needed for economic reasons, but not allow the possibility of citizenship on the part of the workers. This would allow them to be deported without difficulty during times of recession. However, the system has virtually broken down. The German state has conceded to demands for family reunification by Turkish workers and many employers now insist on renewing contracts rather than sending valuable workers home and then having to train another cohort. This does not mean that the Turks are having an easy time in Germany. On the contrary, they are subject to increased racism in the wake of German reunification as *Oosies* (former East Germans) demand 'Germans first' programmes and it remains difficult for them to acquire German citizenship.

The Asian supply of unskilled contract workers to the Middle East and Gulf States has not completely broken down, but suffered an enormous shock in the wake of the Gulf War when hundreds of thousands of Asians were repatriated. (Incidentally, this saga of modern migration has not been fully appreciated, particularly the startling role in it of the International Organization of Migration and of Air India. This involved shifting more people in fewer days than at any other period in history, including the Second World War.) This repatriation of Thais, Pakistanis, Indians and Bengalis came at a point when a number of Gulf States were in any case reassessing the system. They were worried about their increasing dependence on foreign labour, which in a number of cases outnumbered the total citizenry. They had vacillated uneasily between insisting on Muslim workers (if workers had to be imported, many mullahs in the region favoured co-religionists), then going the opposite way – namely insisting on non-Muslim labour so as to reduce the chances of demands for permanent settlement.

The South African migrant labour system was probably the largest in the world up to 1989. Temporary migrants supplied the labour for the mines, farms and white households. The high standard of living achieved by many white South Africans was built on the exploitation of many black workers. Like the German *Gastarbeiter* system, the apartheid state sought to deny foreign blacks citizenship. The white government went even further by claiming that black South Africans were citizens of fictive 'independent' states, created by the regime itself. The system is subject to considerable uncertainty in the wake of the collapse of apartheid and the revocation of the notorious 'pass laws' (which restricted movement for the purposes of settlement).

A future wave is likely to see the marrying of the two forms of contract labour – professional and unskilled – in one contract. This is being pioneered and perfected by the Koreans. For example, if a hotel or hospital needs to be built, a tender is placed to include design, materials, construction and labour, skilled and unskilled. Whereas it was common to include architects, civil engineers and foremen, the Korean companies now also include the unskilled labour – often from Korea. A group visa is provided, temporary housing is erected, but the workers are wholly the responsibility of the company. Any who jump ship are met with a penalty to the company, which becomes the privatized immigration service for the purposes of that contract.

REVIEW

To both popular opinion and concerned policy-makers, population growth is one of the most pressing problems facing the world. Since the days of Malthus, commentators and scholars have made grand pronouncements about the world's population. Politicians have sanctioned or encouraged extreme measures to control population – or at least those sections of it they disliked. Precisely because of its controversial nature, it is important to distinguish evidence about population growth from prediction, projection and prejudice. We have provided you with some basic tools with which to do the job. Again, we have summarized some of the most important findings relevant to the population debate, showing, for example, that a demographic transition can be expected for most countries.

Surplus population is absorbed in the growing cities. It is absorbed at such a rate that in many of the developed countries those who live in the countryside and depend on it for their livelihood are a small minority of the population (in Britain about 3 per cent). In other countries, particularly China and India and to a lesser extent Nigeria, Brazil and Mexico, a considerable proportion of the population still lives in rural areas. However, the urbanizing tendency is universal. Migrants are absorbed, usually with great difficulty, in the cities of the developing world. Some – a small but sociologically sensitive group – become international migrants. We have identified and discussed six main areas of forms of contemporary international migration.

If you would like to know more ●

Michael Kidron and Ronald Segal's *The State of the World Atlas* (1995) is visually stunning and provides lots of data in a very accessible form.

D. H. Meadows *et al.* (1992) *Beyond the Limits* reviews the Club of Rome's findings and provides discussion of subsequent debates.

Dorothy Stein's *People who Count* (1995) has useful material on India, China and Tibet and has an unusually strong emphasis on children (see especially Chapter 3).

Dyson's *Population and Food* (1996) is balanced and thoughtful.

Stephen Castles and Mark Miller's *The Age of Migration* (1998) provides an accessible introduction to many of the topics on migration covered in this chapter.

Robin Cohen's edited volume *The Cambridge Survey of World Migration* (1995) provides 95 short articles on various aspects of contemporary migration.

For a migration site with good links, visit www.iom.ch

Group work ●

1. Using a week's supply of a quality newspaper (a broadsheet, not a tabloid) cut out all the articles relating to population and migration. Summarize the principal themes.

2. Talk to your family and friends about 'overpopulation'. How would you characterize their views?

3. List the ethical problems in (a) controlling population and (b) restricting emigration or immigration.

4. Would you like to migrate internationally? (Perhaps you have already done so.) Draw up a list of the reasons why you wish to move and why you wish to stay.

Questions to think about ●●●●●●●●●●●●●●●●●●●●●●●●●●●●●●●●●●●●●

1. Was Malthus essentially right?

2. What reasons would lead you to the view that population growth might stabilize, without famine?

3. Are 'underpopulation' or ageing populations significant problems?

4. Why is international migration so sensitive an issue?

5. What are the most important forms of international migration since the Second World War?

chapter 12

Tourism: Social and Cultural Effects

During the twentieth century leisure has become widely available to ordinary people and forms an increasingly significant part of all our life experiences. In this chapter we concentrate on one major leisure activity, international tourism. First, we consider the ways in which international tourism contributes to *globalization*. Second, we examine how various sociologists have tried to understand the social construction of tourist behaviour. Third, we show that international tourism also contributes to the growth of *globalism* – a more intense feeling of common membership of the human collectivity. It does this by exposing us directly to a multicultural world where the boundaries between societies and between insiders and outsiders (or, if you like, between hosts and guests) are becoming increasingly blurred.

The development of mass tourism often requires cultures, cities, regions or countries to rethink their own unique identities and then package and promote them as products which hopefully will attract people from other cultures. This bringing together of the *local* and the *global* is not without its dangers. Using case studies we will trace the evolving debate among sociologists concerning the supposed harm that contact with global forces may wreak upon the autonomy of traditional cultures. Overlapping with this is a fourth theme. Tourism has compelled us all to become global performers, putting on presentations designed to project our own cultural heritage. This has led to a re-evaluation by some sociologists concerning how we should understand what is meant by 'culture' and 'tradition'.

INTERNATIONAL TOURISM AND GLOBALIZATION

The World Tourist Organization (WTO), based in Madrid, collates statistics on the worldwide flows of people who holiday abroad. It defines 'international tourists' as those who remain in a country for at least twenty-four hours. The WTO includes people who visit in search of leisure and those engaged in business, since these two categories often coincide. It is intrinsic to the definition that both groups are financed from outside the host country. By contrast, workers commuting across local borders from nearby countries and visiting nationals who normally live abroad are not usually counted in the statistics.

Greenwood (1989: 171) suggests that international tourism involves 'the largest scale movement of goods, services and people that humanity has perhaps ever seen', certainly outside wartime. The sheer numbers of overseas holidaymakers have increased at a breathtaking pace since the 1950s. Thus, international tourist arrivals grew by an astonishing 17 times between 1950 and 1990. During 1996 alone international visitors generated global earnings (not including airfares) of $423 billion, a 7.6 per cent increase on 1995 (*The Economist* 8 February 1997: 145). Few alternative industries can match such sustained rates of growth.

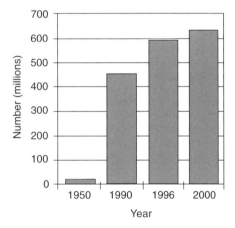

Figure 12.1   International tourist movements (selected years)
(Harrison, 1995: 232; WTO, 1995; *The Economist* 8 February 1997: 145)

There are clearly global implications to movements on the scale indicated in Figure 12.1. However, there are several specific reasons why international tourism and globalization are intimately connected:

1. Tourism is now big business. Until recently it was regarded as the third largest industry in the global economy after oil and vehicle production (Sinclair and Tsegaye 1990), but some observers believe that during the 1990s it has become the world's largest, legal, money-spinner.

2. Like other forms of modernization, international tourism involves assigning a market price to a hitherto free good. 'Culture' is now wrapped and sold to

tourists in the shape of ancient sites, ritual ceremonies and folk customs. Even the everyday life of ordinary people has been turned into a commodity to be sold to tourists.

3.   In any single year the sheer number of international travellers who holiday abroad has become vast and dwarfs all other comparable forms of trans-national mobility, past or present, such as long-term migrants, religious pilgrims, refugees from oppression or seasonal workers. (For example, 'only' 35 million migrants departed from Europe for a new life in the Americas between 1870–1914.)

4.   International tourism has become a worldwide phenomenon, an inescapable 'international fact' (Lanfant *et al.* 1995: 25). It encompasses virtually every country and penetrates most national regions and localities, however remote and inaccessible, while it 'makes itself felt at every level and in all sectors of collective life' (p. 26). In recent decades, even the authorities presiding over the declining, industrial rustbelt zones of North America and Europe, have sought economic revival by turning their run-down mills and furnaces, warehouses, canals and streets into veritable industrial museums.

5.   Unlike the other fast-growing leisure industries (consumerism, the mass media, the arts and sports) international tourism necessarily involves the mass mobility of people who engage in direct social exchanges with hosts and who experience other societies at first hand.

The combined impact of these features is that international tourism has become what Lanfant (1995: 25) called a 'transmission belt' between different ways of life and a vehicle for increased global integration. It is possible to argue that tourism may also exercise a cumulative effect that is considerably greater than any other single agent of globalization. While a similar claim has been made about the TNCs, which have rightly been seen as carriers of technology, capital and the 'culture-ideology of consumerism' (Sklair 1995: 147), the numbers of TNC personnel who move in order to work in foreign countries is quite small. Moreover, their operations normally require or encourage relatively few individuals to engage in direct, face-to-face social interactions across national boundaries.

By contrast, international tourism has an outreach greater than other powerful globalizing forces, even TNCs. As Hannerz (1990: 239) argues, cultural exchanges increasingly involve interactions and social relationships unconfined by territorial boundaries. Wherever cultures are free to coexist and to 'overlap and mingle' through transnational social networks globalization is fostered. Many international tourists contribute to this growth of genuine multicultural understanding and the growing diversity of cultural choice.

The increase in, and distribution of, tourists

There are several explanations for the increase in tourist numbers. As Harrison (1995) argues in the case of Britain, improved standards of living for sections of the working class in the nineteenth century first produced the idea of a 'day out', then the idea of a seaside holiday at the coast. Sea water and sea air were depicted by the doctors as good for you. With increasing affluence and paid leisure time holidays and foreign travel have long ceased to be a luxury confined to aristocratic and commercial élites, as was the case until the late nineteenth century. Instead, the twentieth century has witnessed the emergence of 'the holiday' as a social institution along with the 'democratization of tourism' (Sharpley 1994: 83).

Internationalization has been fostered by the rise of cheaper cruise ships and especially long-haul jet air travel from the 1960s, the advent of the low-cost package holiday and the attempt by ever more governments to promote national tourist industries. A further explanation for the growth of international tourism lies in the post-modern yearning to weave personal lifestyle identities around the signs and symbols associated with different leisure and consumerist activities. Foreign travel is seen as evidence of affluence, sophistication and an adventure-seeking spirit. Foreign landscapes, climates, cuisine and customs offer new arenas and opportunities for people to 'score' sexually or socially, live out their particular fantasies and assume 'diverse social roles in exotic settings' (Turner 1994: 185).

Since 1970, international tourism has itself become increasingly globalized. The rich countries still dominate as destinations for visitors – the USA, Spain, France, Italy and the UK tend to top the list of earning the most through tourism, although their exact ranking varies over time. However, their combined share of world tourist arrivals slipped substantially between 1960 and 1994 (see Table 12.1). Meanwhile, according to Harrison (1992: 8) both tourist arrivals and earnings by the developing countries have risen substantially and reached 21 and 26 per cent respectively by 1989. The developing countries of East Asia and the Asian Pacific have been especially successful in attracting tourist visitors. For example, the numbers of foreign visitors to Indonesia, Thailand, Malaysia, the Philippines, Singapore and Brunei doubled during the 1980s (Hitchcock *et al.* 1993: 1). Together they received over 25 million visitors during 1994 (WTO 1995: 72). In 1996 China experienced the world's fastest increase in tourist earnings, a rise of 20 per cent on 1995. The country was ranked ninth in terms of overall global tourist receipts (*The Economist* 8 February 1997: 145).

Table 12.1 Tourist destinations since 1960 (% shares to selected regions)

Years	1960	1970	1980	1990	1994
North America	20	17	17	13	14
Europe	72	70	66	64	60
Total for North America and Europe	**92**	**87**	**83**	**77**	**74**
East Asia and the Pacific*	–	–	7	11	14

* Includes Japan and Australasia.
Sources: Harrison (1992: 4–5); WTO (1995: 5)

International tourism has also become globalized in that a rising stream of globetrotters now hails from the more prosperous developing countries such as

Taiwan and South Korea. Thus, in 1994 thirteen developing countries were listed by the WTO as among the world's top 30 highest tourist spenders (WTO 1995: 14). Moreover, by no means all of these 'new' tourists are intent on visiting Europe, North America and Japan, although many do. Instead, large numbers are choosing to visit other rapidly developing countries located within their own region.

THE SOCIOLOGY OF TOURISM

Major Concept
THE SACRED AND THE PROFANE

In The Elementary Forms of Religious Life *(1915), Durkheim argued that religious practices and beliefs require a sharp separation between ordinary, mundane activities and objects and those regarded as sacred. The latter are treated with awe and veneration. They bring members of communities together in the pursuit of shared ceremonial activities and group affirmation of deeply held convictions. Whereas the profane is knowable through everyday observable things, the sacred is known only through extraordinary experiences.*

How have sociologists tried to understand tourism? One simple starting point is the idea that holidays and tourism involve 'a leisure activity which presupposes its opposite, namely regulated and organized work' (Urry 1990a: 2). This separation between the routine, work-sphere of everyday life and that of leisure and recreation is not new. It echoes the distinction between the **SACRED** and the **PROFANE** to which Durkheim (1915) drew attention in his study of religious life.

In pre-modern societies the transition from everyday to extraordinary events and experiences was usually linked to important changes in the cycles of religious and social life – saints days, Christmas, birth, marriage and death – as well as the seasons and years (Graburn 1989: 24–5). The risks and expense incurred by travel – for example, pilgrimages to holy places – meant that most poor people enjoyed such religious festivals and social rituals and transitions at home or in their local place of worship. Churches and temples were often built on a much larger scale to the villagers' houses to emphasize that that they were meant to be awe-inspiring. Local celebrations constituted the nearest equivalent to what we now regard as 'the holiday'. (You may have noticed the etymological similarity between 'holiday' and 'holy day'.)

Industrialization and rising mass affluence have enabled the sphere of non-work to become separated from home and identified with travel to distant venues. Yet, some semblance of the excitement and anticipation formally associated with religious concerns and the sacred has survived, although it is mostly de-coupled from its original moorings. Instead, it has become attached to the experiences we now associate with holidays. Accordingly, modern tourism involves what Graburn (1989) calls 'the sacred journey'. This connection between the sacred journey and the prosaic tour is expressed in a slightly different way by Harrison (1995: 240), who argues that:

> 'Modern man' and 'modern women' become tourists in two senses: quite literally they become sightseers but, in addition, they are tourists in a spiritual sense, searching for authenticity and value while beset by continuous change and uncertainty. Through tourism in the latter sense, modernity is provided with its dominating ideology and tourist attractions take on the functional significance previously held by religious symbols. The tourist is thus a modern pilgrim and tourist attractions, be they objects, places or even entire communities or societies are shrines at which authenticity is worshipped albeit in vain: in discovering new sources of authenticity, tourists inevitably pollute that which they seek to preserve.

Just like any other activity the tourist experience is socially constructed. For example, holidaymakers may score more status points in the eyes of their peers if they can afford to take their vacations in an expensive hotel on the French

Riviera – once the exclusive playgrounds of the European aristocracy and wealthy bourgeoisie – rather than in a modern holiday flat on the Costa Del Sol. The year-to-year popularity of different resorts is also a matter of changing fashion. Armies of travel experts, media programmers, theme park organizers and many others cater for all tourist needs.

Figure 12.2   Pilgrims at the Holy Mosque at Mecca

Figure 12.3   'Worshipping' at the shrine of Mickey Mouse

Like prospective parents, the tourists-to-be normally engage in careful preparation and planning long before their anticipated experience. This may involve consultation with friends and family, perusing brochures and travel guides, watching TV holiday programmes and buying all the necessary paraphernalia – such as suntan lotions, florid shirts and camping gear. Moreover, the return to normal life is marked by various social events at which the inescapable souvenirs and photos can be displayed while memories are shared with other pilgrims. Thus, tourism is firmly embedded in social life.

Holiday travel also involves what Urry (1990a) terms 'the tourist gaze'. Urry explains this suggestive phrase by suggesting that while travelling we seek and collect a series of new landscapes. Normally these are 'captured through photographs, postcards, films, models and so on' (p. 3). Meanwhile, national or regional tourist promoters along with tour operators and other professionals construct and perpetuate signs through advertising and other media facilities. Thus, the tourist gaze is 'signposted [by]... markers which identify the things and places worthy of our gaze' (p. 47) while the tourists themselves are trained to decipher these precise meanings. Among others, Urry offers the following examples. 'When tourists see two people kissing in Paris what they capture in the gaze is "timeless romantic Paris". When a small village in England is seen, what they gaze upon is the "real olde England"' (p. 3).

Various attempts have been made to distinguish between the different kinds of tourist. A fundamental contrast is between 'mass charter' tourism and individual or small group holidays (Smith 1989: 12–13). Each basic type has also been identified with one of the two main ingredients of the now secularized and residual sphere of the sacred: (a) the escape to recreation, recuperation and fun; and (b) the rather more 'acceptable' desire for adventure, spiritual renewal or authenticity (see Box 12.1). This dichotomy is significant because mass charter tourists are usually regarded as much more likely to generate a huge economic and social impact on host societies. Mass tourists create a demand for vast resort facilities and services. In addition, this kind of tourist demands as a right that they will enjoy exactly the same standard of western-style amenities as they are used to at home – from modern plumbing to TVs in their rooms, locals who speak their language and home cooking. Smith (pp. 13–14) describes mass tourism in this way:

> Charter tourists arrive *en masse*... and for every 747 planeload, there is a fleet of at least ten big buses waiting to transfer them from the airport to the designated hotel, in the lobby of which is a special Tour Desk to provide itineraries and other group services... Charter tourists wear name tags, are assigned to numbered buses, counted aboard, and continually reminded: 'Be sure to get on the right bus'. Given the requisite organization that makes Charter tourism a high-volume business, to avoid complaints tour operators and hotels have standardized the services to Western (or Japanese) tastes, and there are 'ice machines and soft drinks on every floor'. For Charter tourists, even the destination may be of little importance.

Like other commentators, Smith (1989: 11–12) contrasts these mass tourists with various categories of rarer and presumably more discerning visitors, travelling individually or in small groups. This species may comprise 'explorers' (in search of new experiences and unspoilt terrain) or 'off-beat' tourists (hoping to sample the exotic customs practised by remote societies). Such groups either 'accept fully' or 'adapt well' to local customs, foods, amenities – or the lack of them – without complaint. Indeed, endeavouring to 'fit in' may provide much of the attraction.

Other writers have also commented on the characteristics of these two different types of tourist. For example, most mass tourists have been labelled as 'accidental tourists' (Tyler 1985) who would much rather remain at home with all its reassuring amenities. However, their desire to escape from routine by experiencing fun and recreation – particularly the 'four Ss' of sun, sand, sea and

---

Box 12.1   Tourist development in Ghana: paying homage to a grim legacy

Since the mid-1980s, the West African country of Ghana – once called the Gold Coast because it has supplied gold to Europe and the Middle East for hundreds of years – has developed a new industry. This has involved utilizing the country's bitter legacy, associated with the Atlantic slave trade, as a way of fostering a rather remarkable kind of historical or cultural tourism. Thus, the number of tourist arrivals to Ghana grew from 85 000 in 1985 to 335 000 in 1994. In fact, by the mid-1990s, international tourism had become Ghana's third most important earner of foreign exchange after gold and cocoa exports. Moreover, it is anticipated that the tourist sector will grow in significance as the government gradually improves the standards of the country's hotels, airport and roads and invests in improving its forest-wildlife parks.

At the present time, Ghana's most significant tourist 'attraction' remains the many Atlantic coastal forts built at different times from the end of the fifteenth century by the Dutch, Portuguese, British and French, among others. These forts had a sinister and brutal purpose. Their dungeons were used to hold the captured and branded peoples, brought from the West African interior, while they waited to be shipped – manacled in dark, cramped and unhealthy conditions – as slaves to the plantations of the Americas. In all, it is thought that about ten million Africans were enslaved and transported across the Atlantic to Brazil, the Caribbean and North America from African locations. Beginning in the early sixteenth century, this appalling trade in human life peaked around 1700 but continued until the middle of the nineteenth century.

One of the most famous – or infamous – of Ghana's coastal forts is based at Cape Coast, the administrative centre for British colonial rule until 1877. It is Cape Coast, in particular, that tends to provide a point of focus for many tourists. A considerable and growing proportion of such visitors are African Americans. They come in order to re-discover their homeland and the cultural heritage lost by their enslaved ancestors. But they also arrive as pilgrims mourning the suffering imposed on the original slaves. Many visitors are visibly moved, often to tears, by the haunting memories evoked as the guides conduct them through the dark dungeons.

On a happier note, the Ghana tourist industry also offers many African Americans the opportunity to visit local people, including chiefs, and to participate in ancient ceremonies which re-endow the visitors with their lost African names.

Source: Financial Times (4 August 1995)

---

sex – induces them to travel to distant venues. In a similar vein, Theroux (1986) observed that when on vacation most tourists seek all the familiar comforts of home life but hope to encounter an additional magical ingredient – home-plus-coconut-palm-beaches-by-moonlight. Another example of this phenomenon might be the case of sex tourism (see Box 12.2), which forms a significant part of the holiday industry in countries such as Thailand and the Philippines (Hall 1992; Kruhse-Mount Burton 1995). Here, western men may seek home plus a temporary sexual liaison with local women, sometimes even children, who appear to represent 'the quintessence of the exotic' (Enloe 1989: 28).

Urry's (1990a: 45–6) distinction between the romantic and the collective tourist gaze is also useful. The former is sought by those more discerning travellers who seek to gaze upon areas of supposedly untouched natural beauty or rural idylls where 'traditional' village and farming life is believed to survive unspoiled. The collective gazers generally seek holiday locations such as seaside resorts, theme parks or campsites where there are lots of people. But the presence of large crowds generates congestion and environmental stress – endless car parks, sewerage and piles of rubbish – and attracts a multiplicity of businesses from souvenir shops, restaurants and ice cream stalls to amusement arcades. Nevertheless, the collective gazer enjoys this mélange and only feels comfortable in a thoroughly commercialized milieu.

Box 12.2   Sex tourism in Asia

Tourism does not always bring advantages to local people, particularly in poor countries. Sex tourism is one such case. Since the 1980s this has involved European paedophile rings organizing tour parties of gay men to the Philippines and Sri Lanka seeking sex with young boys. However, sex tourism is mainly associated with the exploitation of women and girls. This has been evident far longer and involves huge numbers of visitors.

In Thailand, tourism is the second highest foreign-exchange earner. But many visitors arrive specifically for the cheap and readily available sex. Once Phuket Island in southern Thailand was a 'paradise beach'. But the image soon turned sour when, in January 1984, a brothel was burned to the ground. The bodies of five young girls aged between nine and fourteen were found in a locked basement. Subsequently it was revealed that brothel-keepers were in the habit of locking up or chaining young girls from the poor northern districts of the country for the delectation of western, Japanese and Chinese tourists. The parents of two of the girls were eventually tracked down. The mother said in a low voice: 'We have ten children and we cannot feed them all. We had to send them to town; there was no other way' (Matsui 1989: 63).

The parents sell their children to 'flesh merchants', who drag them off to 'teahouses' in Chinatown, 'massage parlours' in Patpong Street (Bangkok) or Phuket. A virginal pre-menstrual girl brings a high price around the Chinese New Year when Chinese superstition holds that having sex with a child makes men younger. Thereafter, the young women are on a production line – force-fed birth control pills and typically serving about 1000 customers a year. They are truly described as 'sex workers'.

Helping young women to escape from this fate is not easy. The government and police forces characteristically 'turn a blind eye' and the poor areas of Thailand are dependent on the trade. One Thai sociologist, Chantawipa Apisuk, tried to empower sex workers by giving them education and training. Some of the brothel-keepers reluctantly complied. Ms Apisuk reasoned that with better English their foreign customers would not cheat the women. A prostitute could progress to being a go-go dancer, then to a waitress – the latter a steady job with a regular salary. Some of the sex workers published a newsletter to publicize their plight and a number migrated abroad or moved into salaried employment (Matsui 1989: 66–7).

Manila, in the Philippines, particularly under the Marcos regime, also competed for the title of 'International Sex City'. Here, tour advertisements leave little room for doubt that sex is part of the 'all-inclusive' package. Moreover, the prostitutes are only minor beneficiaries. The industry contains many 'middlemen', each taking their rake-off. One estimate is that the sex worker receives only about ten per cent of the price received.

Sex tourism also shades into the mail order bride business. Potential 'husbands' arrive on package tours to examine 'the goods'. Often these men are fixated by the most reactionary pre-feminist attitudes. Ordering a bride from the Philippines is a statement that they prefer what they believe to be submissive Asian women to their more feisty westernized counterparts. Undoubtedly there are cultural differences between many Asian and western women, but desperation to get out of poverty and to help one's family should not be mistaken for a cultural norm of obedience.

Table 12.2   Types of tourist and their likely impact on host societies

	The mass, traditional or 'bad' tourist	The 'good' or alternative tourist
Tourist flows and numbers involved	Large, steady or continuous flows (often seasonal) and may arrive *en masse*. High-volume capacity.	Small flows and numbers; usually travel individually or in family/ friendship groups.
Primary motivation for the 'sacred journey'	Recreation, recuperation, pleasure, fun. The 'four Ss' plus tropical beaches, unclouded skies, cheap alcohol.	Discovery of the self or of values believed lost in home/industrial society. A search for authenticity, spiritual renewal and contact with nature.
Specific goals and intentions	Seeks public places and crowds; the collective gaze. Home plus the magical 'X' ingredient. Sport activities: swimming, surfing, water-skiing. Sex tourism.	Seeks out the romantic gaze. Yearns to sample exotic cultures, peasant life and ancient sites; the 'Culture', 'Ethnic' or 'Historical' tourist (Graburn 1989). Desires the curative properties of wilderness, remote regions; 'nature' tourism, 'off-beat' (trekking, canoeing). 'Unusual' tourism; for example stays in an Indian village (Smith 1989).
Tourist needs and expectations	Must have full quota of western-type amenities as a 'right'. Desires the familiarities of home living as much as possible.	Needs are relatively few and desires the unfamiliar though may nevertheless hope for basic facilities and something to remind them of home (Cohen 1972). But mostly tolerates rather poor local conditions and may even desire 'primitiveness' as part of the experience.
Main orientation	Passive. Not very sensitive to host society. Social interaction with hosts is mostly confined to tipping the chambermaid or barman or bargaining with the souvenir traders. Relies heavily on the westernized tour guide.	Active, probing, well-prepared. Highly reflexive, knowledgeable and perceptive of host problems. Participates in local culture and society where possible.
Likely impact on host economy and society	Huge economic investment required for numbers and needs of visitors; hotel and beach complexes, airports and so on. Disrupts local cultures because introduces new 'vices' (alcohol, drugs, beach nudity, gambling and so on) and offers western hedonistic role models likely to appeal especially to young people employed in tourist services. Large resorts engender adverse environmental effects.	Tourist facilities needed are more evenly and thinly dispersed across host economy and more low-key. Disposed to interact directly with locals and show interest in traditional culture. Fosters transnational exchange, cultural diversity and understanding. Generally supposed to create few undesirable environmental effects.

Ironically, by discovering untapped tourist venues and then championing these to others the romantic gazers unwittingly blaze the trails that the masses will then follow (Urry 1990b: 32). Thus, the romantic gaze is frequently destroyed and replaced by the collective gaze. Table 12.2 summarizes this discussion. In doing so we have utilized Sharpley's (1994: 84–5) rather tongue-in-cheek formulation of the 'good' and 'bad' tourist with the implication that the latter is synonymous with mass tourism.

Some writers have begun to question these distinctions. One argument is that from the early 1980s a growing minority of tourists began to seek much more challenging holiday experiences, which can be loosely called 'alternative tourism'. Krippendorf (1987: 38, 174–5) argues that this has already 'developed into big business' and will rise from approximately one quarter of all international tourists in 1986 to between one-third and two-fifths by the year 2000.

One form of alternative tourism is what Hall and Weiler (1992: 4–6) describe as 'special interest tourism' – including educational holidays, adventure, health and sport tourism – for example, hang-gliding, rock-climbing or yachting, or vacations built around archaeological digs or the attendance at festivals of fine arts. All such special interest holidays share certain common features especially the desire for self-development and knowledge and a conscious concern to enjoy holidays without inflicting permanent damage on the local culture, society or environment.

Another critique hinges on the rise of what Feifer (1985) deems the 'post-tourist' – someone who has acquired the reflexive capacity we described in Chapter 2. Feifer observes that other places and cultures metaphorically leap out of our TV sets virtually every day. Consequently, we are well-informed concerning the many sites available to us and we realize we can experience these without necessarily visiting them in person. Indeed we revel in choice and wish to experiment with different holiday experiences. This means that post-tourists have become much more self-aware. They are inclined to regard tourism as a game in which they are players who have the advantage of being able to read from a variety of ever changing scripts. In a similar vein, Urry (1990a: 100) observes that tourist enjoyment also involves an element of 'play-fulness', an ironic awareness of being participants in an essentially 'pseudo-event', for example at theme parks and museums (Sharpley 1994: 87). Here, some gazers relish mocking the operators' own pretensions of seriousness.

All this means that the apparent dichotomy between the sacred journey as the pursuit of pure enjoyment by the non-reflexive masses or the quest for self-realization and authenticity by the knowledgeable few has broken down. Most tourists now understand that to different degrees they are simultaneously participants in both experiences.

INTERNATIONAL TOURISM AND 'TRADITIONAL' CULTURAL IDENTITIES

In order to attract visitors and compete in the growing global tourist market, governments and their agents need to give an account of what is special concerning their particular cultures and natural landscapes. Thus, everywhere 'there has been a frantic forging of signs of identity' (Lanfant *et al.* 1995: 32) – the attempt to create and present appealing and easily recognizable images.

Through skilful advertising, brochures and films, paradise regained appears on the beaches of Barbados while a tropical, ancient, exotic wonderland emerges in Malaysia (King 1993: 108).

By the early 1970s this tendency to sell local or national cultures had begun to alarm many observers including some social scientists (Greenwood 1972; Turner and Ash 1975). Their concern was that the business of promoting packaged, local cultures for economic gain, along with the influx of ever growing numbers of foreign tourists, threatened to degrade those very identities which attracted visitors in the first place. We have seen that mass tourism may be especially culpable here.

A further likely consequence might be that shared ancient meanings, religious beliefs and established social relations – which enable people to know who they are and to feel a pride in where they belong – were at risk of disintegrating. Moreover, they were being replaced, allegedly, by a socially divisive, homogenizing western materialist ethos. Some observers argued that all this could be especially alarming in the case of already marginalized and sometimes repressed minorities. Such groups might be pushed by governments or driven by poverty to open their doors reluctantly to foreign guests. But this exposure to alien commercial contamination might be especially damaging given that their traditional cultures provided just about the only resource and protection available to them. In exploring this question we will see how the issues scholars have raised about international tourism have shifted over time.

A case study in the Basque province, Spain

Greenwood's studies (1972; 1989) of an annual public ritual, the Alarde, in Fuenterrabia – a town in the Basque province of northern Spain – demonstrates some of these points. Once a year virtually all the inhabitants come together to perform an elaborate pageant. This commemorates the victory of their ancestors over the French in 1638 when, following a siege lasting 69 days, the invaders were finally overcome. Most social groups and wards in the town contribute either to the elaborate, costumed parades and the march to the town plaza, the mass firing in unison by contingents of armed men with shotguns or simply cheer as onlookers. According to Greenwood the Alarde's ritual significance lies in its ability to re-enact the ancient solidarity of the townspeople which had made victory possible. Originally, the pageant was performed by and for the locals not for outsiders and it provided 'an enactment of the "sacred history" of Fuenterrabia'.

The event takes place in summer and so coincides with the presence of numerous tourists. In 1969, the municipality decided that steps must be taken to ensure the tourist onlookers could also view the pageant and so insisted that the event should be staged twice rather than once as before. When Greenwood returned to the town two years later he discovered that this once 'vital and exciting event had become an obligation to be avoided' (1972: 178). The decision by the municipality to promote this communal ritual as a commercial show for outsiders robbed it of much of its cultural meaning. Greenwood (1989) later reported that the Alarde has survived and has become imbued with political significance, as part of the Basque struggle for greater regional autonomy within Spain. Nevertheless, this example illustrates what may happen when tourism becomes a form of 'cultural exploitation'.

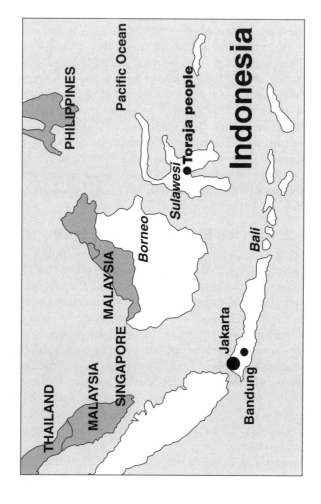

Map 12.1   Indonesia, showing the location of the Toraja people

The revival of Toraja culture, Indonesia

From the late 1970s, however, many observers of international tourism increasingly began to interpret its cultural consequences for host societies in a different light. Instead of destroying local cultural meanings and social relationships, it appeared that in certain situations domestic and international tourism actually helped to preserve them. Thus, for the most part, the tourists who visited remote societies and ancient cultures were not mass charter tourists but were proactive, reflexive, sensitive to local needs and motivated primarily by the search for authentic traditions.

This fascination with exotic customs along with the new spending power brought by visitors to their community encouraged the locals to rediscover a pride in their cultural identity – previously threatened by modernization – and to revive many of their ancient skills. One of the most interesting examples is the case of the Toraja people living in the central highland of the island of Sulawesi, part of Indonesia.

The Toraja people number around 300 000. Over the centuries they have been exposed, like most of the other peoples in Indonesia, to Hindu, Islamic and Christian influences among others (Volkman 1984: 153). Nevertheless, until recently the Toraja retained their ancient religious beliefs based on ancestor worship and the idea that the gods (their dead relatives), nature, living humans and the as yet unborn were linked together in one symbolic system. Simplifying the analysis somewhat, we can say that everyday life was built around four main pillars: the common bonds based on blood (kinship) and marriage ties; the attachment of each kinship group to their colourful, ancestral houses; the enormous importance of elaborate and often lengthy funeral ceremonies, accompanied by singing, processions and dance; and the ritual slaughter of quantities of pigs and buffalo during funerals. Families invited to share the meat had to repay their 'debt' obligation in kind at some future time or risk a loss of social standing (Crystal 1989: 142–3).

The arrival of Dutch missionaries from 1906 onwards meant that many of the funeral rituals continued to be performed but they were increasingly relegated to the status of customs and lost much of their earlier deep, religious content (Volkman 1984: 156–7). Moreover, after Indonesia achieved independence from the Netherlands in 1949, additional changes began to reinforce the effects of Christianity: the spread of schools and education; the determination of the government to modernize Indonesia and create a new sense of national unity; and the migration of many younger people to Indonesia's growth centres in search of employment from the 1970s. Migration rapidly linked the Toraja to the wider world. It also brought new wealth through the earnings brought by returning migrants. Now, even poor, low-status families could engage in funeral ceremonies on a much greater scale than had previously been economically possible or thought socially appropriate (Volkman 1984: 159). This 'ritual renaissance' meant that ceremonial practices were becoming more expensive and elaborate as well as 'more central to Toraja identity' even before the first tourists arrived (Wood 1993: 61).

In 1975 roughly 2500 tourists visited the Toraja region, but by 1985 this had risen to approximately 40 000. In 1986, the Toraja district was second only to Bali as Indonesia's most important tourist development region. By the mid-1980s a small airport had been opened, while bus services, hotels and restaurants mushroomed all across the island and tour operators were ferrying in visitors from across the world and other parts of Indonesia. How has international tourism further altered Toraja society? We can summarize these changes in several ways:

1. Toraja society has been placed firmly on the international tourist and cultural map with growing interest shown in its traditions not only from tourists but also by museums, archaeologists, antique dealers and TV companies around the world.

2. Tourist interest in gazing upon the exotic ceremonies and burial sites and participating in the associated ritual feasting has promoted a 'pride in Toraja's unique and valuable heritage' and a self-conscious attempt to revive ancient religious identity 'as an image though which the outside world can perceive and come to know [the] Toraja' (Volkman 1984: 164).

3. Once declining traditional crafts such as basket-weaving, wood-carving and beadwork have revived bringing yet additional sources of wealth to local people along with the attempt to protect burial sites, to rediscover funeral chants and to develop a historical and archaeological interest in Toraja culture through books and exhibitions.

4. Other groups in Indonesia once derided Toraja culture, but it is now regarded as a vibrant component of national culture. Moreover, neighbouring societies, who once regarded the Toraja as 'savages' (Wood 1993: 62), now treat them with greater respect. Also, although the Christian missionaries continue to attract new adherents they have been forced to recognize the legitimacy of the ancestral religion they once tried to eradicate. Thus, the wealth that has flowed into the Toraja economy has helped to strengthen the wider political influence of this previously neglected region within Indonesia.

5. Tourism has also brought less desirable consequences. Family heirlooms are stolen. Ancient burial sites are desecrated. Also, the less educated, poor residents and religious specialists who continue to participate in traditional life and culture, normally derive few commercial advantages from tourism (Crystal 1989: 166–8).

The Toraja case is far from being untypical. International tourism seems to have stimulated a similar reawakening on the part of many other cultures or ethnic groups, once threatened by the process of modernization, political marginalization, regional neglect or some combination of these. You can read about such cases in the following sources: McKean (1989) and Picard (1995) for the case of Bali; de Vidas's (1995) discussion of the Andean Indians; the Ainu people of northern Japan (Friedman 1990: 319–23); and Rozenberg's (1995) account of the inhabitants of the Spanish island of Ibiza.

WE ARE ALL GLOBAL PERFORMERS NOW

The literature on international tourism and its effects of host societies has led to a re-evaluation by some social scientists of what we mean by 'culture' and 'tradition'. Neither of these categories can be regarded as totally fixed. They are not internalized through childhood socialization, once and for all, neither are they reinforced by unchanging 'external' social pressures that can never be challenged – as some social scientists previously believed. Culture and tradition also do not have clearly defined boundaries.

Instead of invading and then dominating social actors from outside, culture provides 'a "toolkit" of symbols, stories, ritual and world views, which people may use in varying configurations in order to solve different kinds of problems' (Swidler 1986: 273). It provides scope for inventiveness and negotiation by the members of particular societies. It is also constantly evolving and is capable of overlapping with alternative cultures (Clifford 1988). Similarly, the alternative conception of tradition championed by writers such as Hoben and Hefner (1991: 18) suggests that it consists of meanings which are 'renewed, modified and remade in each generation. Far from being self-perpetuating, they require creative effort and investment'. Thus, tradition cannot provide fixed standards against which alternatives or changes can be measured. Accordingly, there can be no such thing as 'authenticity', only ideas which always need to be reinterpreted in the present.

International tourism provides additional reasons for re-thinking what we understand by tradition, authenticity and culture. As we have seen, tourist promotion by governments requires the construction of 'representations' or signs of the local in order to profit by attracting visitors. But international tourism also exposes host societies to the outside world through the tourist gaze. Both aspects begin to alter the nature of host identities (Lanfant *et al.* 1995: 30–40). Partly, this is because the hosts attain greater self-awareness and reflexivity. This is hardly surprising given that they are now in the business – literally – of recasting their identities. In effect, they perform selected aspects of their way of life. In addition, hosts increasingly begin to see a reflection of themselves in the gaze of the onlookers. And what they see is yet another version of the idealized and simplified representation of their culture. This second image partly mirrors that which they have created for commercial reasons. It may also express their visitors' yearnings for spiritual renewal and which might enable them to replace the meanings and traditions they fear have been lost in their own far more commercialized society.

In effect, therefore, these cultural idealizations of traditional culture only exist in the different but linked imaginations of host and guest and they become ever more distorted by the performances and interactions ongoing between tourist and host. Two important consequences follow from all this:

- *The re-invention of tradition* Although tourism enables societies to retain something we might label as 'tradition' and even to regain a once threatened pride in their own identity, the 'traditions' that survive are ones that have been re-invented. They are not the same as the original prototype.

- *The inescapable tourist gaze* At least potentially everyone in the world has become a tourist product. There is no escape for any of us from the gaze of tourist visitors. But, by the same token, this means that everyone is now dependent, in part, on the tourist gaze in order to affirm and perpetuate his or her own identities.

Indeed, the tourist presence both requires and empowers more and more countries to construct a national heritage industry. Not only does this generate employment and valuable foreign exchange earnings it also enables each country to 'guarantee... [its] paternity in the midst of an accelerating process of globalization... securing its present to its past' (Lanfant 1995 *et al.*: 40). Once again, the local and the global have become inextricably bound up with each other.

REVIEW

Tourists are of global significance in terms of the steep rise in their numbers, their economic contribution and their cultural penetration of other societies. Through a series of case studies and summaries of current debates we have presented the 'good' and 'bad' sides of international tourism. Clearly it is diffi-cult to generalize too wildly in this area – around about 600 million tourists of very different dispositions and interests travel each year to about 190 countries. None the less we can ask some suggestive sociological questions.

Does the differential impact of tourism have something to do will the char-acter of the tourists themselves? Or is the distinction between the 'mass' and the 'alternative' tourist too cut and dried? Many travellers act like the cultural battering rams of the rich, powerful states, others are like the pilgrims of old. Yet others, like sex tourists, simply exploit weaker, poorer people. However, some tourists may enhance multi-cultural understanding and awareness. In short, tourism may destroy local cultures or revive them. As tourists and their hosts become aware of these capacities they become actors in the tourist transaction, sometimes turning their own cultures into a pantomime, sometimes recognizing the risible irony in so doing. To parody William Shakespeare: 'All the world's a stage but tourism lets us all come to the performance.'

If you would like to know more ●●●●●●●●●●●●●●●●●●●●●●●●●●●●●●●●

Sharpley's *Tourism, Tourists and Society* (1994) offers a clear and comprehensive survey of the literature. Chapters 3, 5 6 and 7 are especially useful.

Hosts and Guests edited by V. L. Smith (1989), offers fascinating and lively insights into the consequences of tourism for a wide range of societies.

Tourism in South-East Asia, edited by M. Hitchcock *et al.* (1993) includes some very interesting and accessible material concerning the tourist impact on developing countries. Chapters 1, 3, 4, 5 and 11 are particularly useful.

The book edited by Lanfant, Allcock and Bruner, *International Tourism* (1995), contains some difficult material but you will find the introduction and Chapters 1, 2, 3, 4 and 9 challenging and enjoyable.

Group work ••

1. *International tourist promotion*

One class group will investigate special interest tourism and cultural/ethnic/nature holidays while the other will investigate mass charter tourism. Using brochures collected from travel agents and brief interviews with managers each team will report on the following:

(a) How far does the presentation of the two types of holiday differ (in terms of images, styles)?

(b) How far is it apparent that quite different kinds of client are being attracted?

(c) Is there any evidence that the distinction between the two types of holiday is breaking down?

2. *A survey of personal holiday experiences abroad*

Each class member will interview five people who have taken at least two holidays abroad during the last five years and will collate their answers. You should elicit the following information:

(a) Where did they go and why?

(b) What holiday package or arrangements were involved?

(c) Do they think that their foreign holiday preferences have changed over time and why?

(d) Did they think that the locals gained or lost from tourism and in what ways?

(e) What overall conclusions are suggested by these findings?

Questions to think about ••••••••••••••••••••••••••••••••••••••

1. What is the nature of the tourist experience and how may it have changed?

2. Evaluate the different ways in which tourism acts as a globalizing force.

3. How far does tourism destroy host societies?

4. 'We are all objects of a tourist gaze now.' What does this statement tell us about the relation between the local and the global?

chapter

13

Consuming Culture

CONTENTS

Drink a cup of coffee or tea and you instantly connect to the global marketplace. The list of world goods that arrives in this casual way is formidable and grows all the time. World goods are simultaneously produced in a multiplicity of locations while being purchased and experienced by people living in many different societies. According to Firat (1995: 115) fortunate consumers in the late twentieth century are 'ready to have Italian for lunch and Chinese for dinner, to wear Levi's 501 blue jeans for the outdoor party in the afternoon and to try the Gucci suit at night'. But what is really remarkable, observed Firat (p. 114) is not simply the sheer range of available global products but the fact that one can 'rent a Toyota, listen to Madonna and Sting tunes, enjoy a croissant for breakfast, and follow one's favourite soap opera on television' even in 'the remotest corners of the world'.

Our experience of living in the global marketplace is revealed particularly well in the case of food and beverages. Here are just a few examples:

1. By 1993, in the British fast-food sector, fish and chip shops were outnumbered by Indian takeaways (James 1996: 81). Similarly, pizza and pasta have

become 'the most global of global foods' (p. 76) although both have only recently become recognized as *national* foods in Italy and many ingredients in Italian cuisine arrived initially from China (pasta) or from the Americas (tomatoes and peppers).

2. Global cuisine can also be widely found in restaurants located in cities from New York to Manamah in Bahrain, in the Persian Gulf. In the latter, according to Chase (1994: 84), one restaurant offers 'Arabic (Lebanese and Gulf items), Chinese, Indian, pizza and hamburger, and grills' all delivered by Filipino employees to the accompaniment of Greek music.

3. The worldwide popularity of brand-named foods/beverages such as Coca-Cola and the famous McDonald's burger is well-known. For example, in 1996, Coca-Cola sold 13.7 billion unit cases (each of these consists of twenty-four, 8-ounce servings) of their various beverages in 135 countries (Coca-Cola Company 1997: 27).

> **Major Concept**
>
> **IDEOLOGY**
>
> *Refers at a loose level to a reasonably coherent set of assumptions and convictions shared by a particular social group. Pacifists and vegetarians share an ideology in this sense. Where ideologies are totalizing and universal in their claims (for example, communism) they are sometimes referred to as meta-narratives. For some social theorists, ideologies can be contrasted with reason or science, and are used deliberately by ruling groups to obscure real power relations in their own interest.*

In this chapter we explore the globalization of consumption and consider its implications for the way we now experience social and cultural life. Our central theme concerns the impact of what Sklair (1995: Chapter 3) calls 'the culture-ideology of consumerism' evidenced by many in the rich countries, but especially by those living in the developing countries. The adoption of this **IDEOLOGY** has led some observers to fear that continued western and more especially US domination of many industries, along with advertising and the mass media, are giving rise to a new kind of imperialism, one based not on political but on cultural control.

This same process is also said to be creating an increasingly homogeneous world where western lifestyles and brand-goods are in danger of obliterating countless, unique local cultures. In order to examine this theory we first need to explore the multi-dimensional character of consumerism as a universal activity but also its special features under global capitalism. Similarly, we need to consider the very different perspectives – both pessimistic and optimistic – from which sociologists have viewed its contemporary implications.

CONSUMERISM AND EVERYDAY LIFE

As a central part of human experience, consumption has one foot squarely planted in the spheres of politics and economics and another rooted firmly in social life and culture. This has always been the case, but capitalist industrialization and globalization have deepened and accentuated these linkages in several ways:

1. As we saw in Chapter 3, most people's contribution to economic life takes the form of self- or wage employment involving participation in organizations that produce goods or services for sale. This is called 'commodity production'. Meanwhile, buyers satisfy their various needs by using their earnings to purchase things that were produced by vast numbers of people whom they do not know. This is quite different from the self and family provisioning, supplemented by reciprocal sharing arrangements between kin and community members, characteristic of pre-modern societies.

2. The organization of production, transport and distribution through numerous companies and networks of exchange can only function because it is underpinned by certain national and worldwide institutional arrangements. These facilitate financial investment and currency management, guarantee ownership rights and freedom of movement and provide adequate systems of communication. Worldwide production and consumption also create a more interdependent global economy.

3. Our consumption preferences and practices are shaped by social life. We demonstrate our loyalties to others through such things as wearing special uniforms, public displays of hospitality, or generosity through gift giving. Our consumer preferences and styles in everything from clothes and cars to household decorations say important things about who we are or what claims to social status we would like to make.

4. Our possessions also carry various meanings. These are associated with the wider cultural beliefs, values and orientations we share with others. Drawing on this pool of common meanings enables us to communicate, to make sense of the world around us and to express our shared identities and values.

This bridging quality at the societal level is paralleled by the dualistic nature possessed by all goods (Douglas and Isherwood 1978) irrespective of whether we are talking about a pre-modern or capitalist society. On the one hand, goods constitute the 'hardware' of social and cultural life. They possess an intrinsic materiality and utility or what Marx called their 'use-value'; eating rice keeps you alive and clothes protect you from the weather. On the other hand, even the most basic goods simultaneously act as the 'software' of everyday life. They express the meanings with which we have endowed them; they exercise a symbolic significance. Because these meanings are shared our consumer practices can be read and decoded by others. Archaeological evidence indicates that even the most basic utensils used by prehistoric peoples – such as clay water pots – were invariably embellished with decorations. These probably expressed family affiliations, social position or respect for religious deities. They also gave aesthetic pleasure.

In capitalist economies this *universal* duality between function and form acquires a further characteristic because goods become commodities and assume an exchange value in the market. Moreover, as we will see, the cultural meanings that inhere in all goods become highly desirable forms of merchandise in their own right. Finally, because all goods contain symbolic as well as material qualities it is virtually impossible, as some earlier writers suggested, to make a distinction between those that fulfil our 'real' survival *needs* and those that cater merely for our 'inessential' *wants*. No goods are inessential in cultural terms.

THE MEANING OF CONSUMERISM

In pre-modern societies religion and custom provided the chief sources of the meanings 'attached' to goods. Many, such as heirlooms, ceremonial artefacts, houses and tools circulated within families and communities through inheritance and shared ownership. They served as markers of social belonging and of important differences concerning time (the seasons, religious festivals), place, social status and gender. Contemporary advertising companies sometimes imbue goods with seductive meanings borrowed from the global cultural reservoir provided by ancient religions, customs or ethnic identities. Nevertheless, consumption practices today are essentially different from those experienced in the past.

In contemporary successful economies we enjoy a superfluity of goods compared to the past and most are acquired through the market. Normally, private ownership defines our access to these goods. Also, in place of the rather durable non-commercialized meanings which formally adhered to products – derived from an accumulated cultural legacy – the meanings they hold today are often contrived, transitory and placed there for purposes of profit. To understand how and why this happens we need to understand the *semiotic* or symbolic nature of goods. Contemporary sociological discussion of consumption often draws on the study of semiotics as developed by thinkers such as de Saussure (1857–1913) and Barthes (1915–1980). In his own life, de Saussure was a rather obscure professor of linguistics who taught Sanskrit, Gothic and Old High German in France, Germany and Switzerland. But when he died his colleagues and students put together his lecture notes, published in English as *Course in General Linguistics* (1974). This became a classic work in semiotics. De Saussure was mainly interested in *language* – written words or spoken sounds – which carry or signify meanings. We summarize some of his key ideas in Box 13.1.

Semiotics is the study of signs and symbols in language and other means of communication.

Box 13.1   De Saussure's thinking about language and semiotics

1. In studying language, one of his key distinctions was that between:

   a. The *signifier*, the vehicle or form by which meanings are conveyed. In language, signifiers are the actual words we either hear as sounds or read as particular letter combinations and

   b. The *signified*, the mental image or concept which is carried by the signifier.

   c. Together, the signifier and signified form the *sign*. We carry around learned knowledge of signs in our heads and this allows us to de-code them thus

   d. Our ability to read signs enables us to engage in processes of *signification*, that is, to attribute signs with meaning.

2. In language, the relationship between the actual words, or signifiers, and the meanings they convey, the signifieds, is arbitrary. The word for 'bird' could just as easily be 'splift' or 'mnenk'. The image conveyed of a feathery flying creature remains the same whatever 'sound image' (Strinati 1995: 91) we decide to use providing we share it in common. Thus, the meanings of words do not derive from the actual objects to which they refer but from the overall structure of grammatical rules and elaborate systems of word differences that we call language.

3. Contemporary sociologists and semiologists study all forms of representation in order to 'read' or decode their meanings; for example, in art, photographs, sounds, advertisements, logos even the assortment of clothes worn by different sub-cultures – such as teddy boys, hippies, punks and goths (Hebdige 1988; Hall and Jefferson 1993). In doing so, they have adapted de Saussure's basic scheme concerning the sign as made up by the combination of a signifier and signified.

Sources: Thwaites *et al.* (1994); Strinati (1995).

Barthes added to our understanding of signification. You can find excellent analyses of his ideas in Thwaites *et al.* (1994: Chapters 1, 2 and 3) and Strinati (1995: Chapter 3). Barthes argued that in other forms of cultural representation, such as advertisements and clothing, the link between the signifier and the signified is not arbitrary. This is because unlike in language signifiers are manifested through visible cultural items: national flags, a particular style of shoes, a photograph of model X car or a famous TV celebrity.

The messages carried and our ability to read them are not random happenings because those exposed to the same culture have learned the similar codes, social conventions or ideologies. Cultural meanings cluster together and tend to crystallize around certain dominant, clear messages. At the same time they are embedded in particular shared histories and social conditions. In Britain, for example, a bouquet of white carnations usually means 'a wedding' and carries the message of fond congratulations. Other flowers and colours may suggest quite different things. For instance, red roses act as a signifier for an intimate declaration of romantic love. But Barthes also insisted that many signs have been deliberately manufactured and spread by dominant interest groups and social classes – the church, aristocratic élites or the rising capitalist bourgeoisie.

One way or the other, and especially outside language, signs are rarely innocent. Thus, the messages they carry incorporate *value preferences*. We watch a TV news clip that shows the coffin of a US marine draped in the Stars and Stripes being carried from a military plane amidst a sombre scene. The president comforts bereaved relatives, ranks of uniformed dignitaries pay their respects all accompanied by suitably doleful music. The decoded message is: America and its citizens are proud to pay the price of exercising the power and global responsibility necessary to guarantee peace and civilized values in a troubled, disorderly world.

However, such images and the powerful messages they convey work to suppress alternative interpretations. These might lead us to ask why did the US engage in military confrontation in Vietnam, Grenada, Somalia or the Gulf? And who benefited most from these activities? Thus, such signs as the military funeral prompt us to think they depict unavoidable and 'natural' realities but in fact they preclude other possible lines of enquiry and explanation. Where this happens the processes of signification assumes the character of myth-making. Myths acquire the status of timeless truths, but they also inhibit our ability to interpret cultural meanings.

For our purposes, two important questions arise from this discussion:

1. How do we read the meanings which advertisers have attached to the commodities they want us to buy? On the one hand, we may be *cultural dupes* or *dopes* who passively decode these messages or signs exactly as the advertisers hope. On the other hand, we may be *cultural heroes* who are perfectly capable of disregarding such messages altogether or who impose our own meanings irrespective of the advertisers' intentions (Slater 1997: 33–4).

2. What are the effects upon our lives of the relentless volume of swirling messages, images and symbols to which we are subjected? These assail us every time we walk down the street, read a magazine, watch TV, visit the cinema or attend a rock concert or football match where, inevitably, we are also exposed to advertising slogans (Wernick 1991).

A CRITICAL-PESSIMISTIC SCENARIO: CONSUMERS AS DOPES

For purposes of brevity and clarity we now address some of the key arguments about consumption by focusing them around the two opposed viewpoints. In this section we discuss the idea that consumers are innocents in the face of the onslaught of producers, advertisers and market managers. In the next we consider how consumers can strike back and, to some degree at least, assert their autonomy and innovativeness.

Major Concept
COMMODITY FETISHISM

According to Marx, this occurs when an inanimate object is treated as if it required a religious, or even sexual, devotion. In pre-modern societies fetishes were hand-made or rare natural objects thought to embody a spirit that protected the owner from misfortune or disease. Commodity fetishism arises under capitalism because the market system has become much more real and immediate to us than the underlying social relationships (based on inequality and exploitation) which made goods sold in the market possible in the first place.

Commodity fetishism

Employing one of his most powerful concepts – **COMMODITY FETISHISM** – Marx argued that commodity production creates a de-personalized economy. Clusters of unknown, hired workers and machines in different locations produce goods for unknown buyers. The system constructed by capitalism is so complex and impersonal that it is virtually impossible to understand or identify with it. The surface world of commodity exchange thereby conceals the hidden, real world of work and production. At the same time, the opportunity for self-realization available to humankind through creative work and social co-operation is simultaneously denied and compensated for by the attractive possessions on sale in the bazaar and shopping mall. We tend therefore to imbue our purchases with a meaning and significance they cannot possess. We fetishize them – turn them into objects of devotion and magicality when, in fact, a bottle of expensive perfume, for example, is only processed whale blubber with added spots of scent-essence derived from skunks.

Mass consumption

Throughout the twentieth century many writers have been highly critical of the era of mass consumption associated with the rise of Fordist production, a theme we discussed in Chapter 4. Adorno and Horkheimer (1972), for example, argued that expanding Fordist production compelled businesses as never before to feed our desire for more goods while persuading us to abandon still useful products in favour of newer ones. Here, the advertising industry played a major role by producing an endless stream of new meanings – images of exotica, nostalgia, desire, romance, beauty or the good life. These meanings were then embedded in mundane products such as vacuum cleaners, soft drinks and soaps.

When they 'fell for it', consumers were seduced by false needs and impossible hopes since these products were quite incapable of fulfilling their promises. Brand 'Y' shampoos cannot actually improve your love life very much and refitting your living room with fashionable furniture is unlikely to fill a lonely life with friends. Also, the meanings employed in mass consumer culture need to be simple and instantly accessible so that they speed up the turnover of huge volumes of goods. As a result the distinction between 'high' culture (for example, classical music, Renaissance art) and the less sophisticated, but immediately recognizable images offered by popular culture (like comic strips, TV soaps and rock songs) is eroded. The end result, the harshest critics say, is to create a homogenized world of standardized mass products and a bland, stupefying culture, lacking substance.

Figure 13.1   Shoppers on the streets of Tokyo

Signifying culture

In consumer culture the subtle meanings implanted in goods by advertising and seductive packaging – what Baudrillard (1988) called their 'sign-values' – become much more important to us than their material properties. Indeed, the intrinsic use-value of goods may become detached from the advertisers' meanings altogether; the latter becoming free-floating. Either way, increasingly we live in a 'signifying culture'; one that abounds with disconnected messages and it is these, supposedly, rather than the functionality of goods themselves, which we seek. In this scenario what we buy bears less and less relation to our actual needs.

Depthlessness

Another problem is the sheer quantity of signs circulating in our consumer culture. Moreover, signs are inherently volatile. Their meanings often mutate or break free from the object or context they were originally intended to represent. They are also subject to media manipulation. Thus, despite the media and advertisers' emphasis on creating meanings in order to attract our attention, meaning actually eludes us. When it comes down to it, we are unable to find self-realization or ourselves on the supermarket shelves. According to Jameson (1984) all of this destabilizes our lives and gives them a certain depthlessness. We lose our bearings and become disoriented.

Fantasy becomes reality

The media-inspired fantasy world of TV soaps, films and adverts, where messages and symbols flourish, often seem more alive to us than the actual social world we inhabit. The latter shrinks in significance and becomes in a curious way far less real. Indeed, we may seek to imitate and build our lives around one or more **SIMULACRA**. When such fake or fantasy experiences become more real to us than our concrete everyday world Baudrillard (1988) calls this condition 'hyperreality'.

Apart from the followings that grow up around certain films and TV programmes, another excellent example of hyperreality is the enormous popu-

Major Concept
SIMULACRA

Simulacra (singular simulacrum) are entities that have no original or no surviving original in the actual world, but are thought nonetheless to be 'real'. Cult followers – for example of Elvis Presley or of characters in certain TV soaps – seek to emulate their simulacra perhaps by copying their appearance or supposed lifestyles, writing to them for personal advice, or even proposing marriage.

larity of Disney parks in the USA, Japan and France. In 1996, the six Disneyland centres topped the list of theme parks in the world as a whole and together attracted almost one quarter of the 320 million global visitors to such venues (Meikle 1997). Disney parks offer spectacles based on a largely mythical or fairy-tale world of handsome princes and animals, such as Mickey Mouse, imbued with heroic or comical human characteristics. In Disney parks, visitors often mistake living birds and animals for plastic ones; the line between reality and fantasy has been lost. Bryman (1995: 172) speculated that 'the fake worlds of the Disney parks, which represent a non-existent reality, become models for American society, so that a hyperreal America is being constructed which is based on a simulacrum'.

AN OPTIMISTIC SCENARIO: CONSUMERS AS CREATIVE HEROES

The chief difficulty with the negative scenario is that it leaves little space for human agency in the form of consumer autonomy, creativity or reflexivity. It also strongly implies that there is something inherently artificial and trivial about the meanings carried by goods under capitalism precisely because they are produced and sold for profit and obtained through market exchange. This renders them inferior as cultural forms and implicates them deeply in exploitation. There are several counter arguments to this view.

Product differentiation

One of the most striking things about capitalist marketing techniques is the attempt by companies to promote distinctive products. Consumers belong to quite different groups according to their class, education, religion, ethnicity, sexual orientation and type of family responsibilities. Each of these identities may generate marked variations in need and taste. Then there is the question of what stage people have arrived at in their life-course – whether they are adolescents, single people, couples with young children, middle-aged 'empty nesters' or the elderly. Thus, the preferences of different groups not only vary but each person's needs evolve and change over time. Further, people crave difference and distinction and expect the market to provide this. In other words, product differentiation and the cultivation of many taste publics and audiences stand at the heart of capitalist marketing.

Advertising and its limitations

According to Sinclair (1987: 63) those employed in advertising are often highly sceptical about their influence on consumers and 'have learned to doubt the usefulness of advertising'. For one thing, income remains a major constraint on our ability to respond to advertising; 'people (can only) play with the signs that they can afford' (Warde 1992: 27). Our purchases are often determined by habit and time constraints. However appealing the images attached to goods, it seems absurd to suggest that we purchase them *solely* for their sign value. Can-openers, shoes and cars are useful objects and fulfil specific functions. Adverts may attract some people who never buy the goods while others who do have paid little attention to them. Many people adopt a playful attitude towards adverts and enjoy 'sending them up'. In short, there is 'no necessary connection between the symbolic or ideological meaning of advertising and the behavioural responses which people make to it' (Sinclair 1987: 63). Thus, more often than not there is a mismatch of codes; the messages transmitted are not necessarily the same as those that are received by actual consumers.

The social sieve

> ### Major Concept
> #### HABITUS
>
> *In its Latin origins, habitus refers to a typical or habitual condition. For the French social theorist, Bourdieu, it comprises a set of cultural orientations acquired by the members of a given social sub-group. Through their specific life experiences they express and display preferences for a cluster of distinctive tastes in consumption and lifestyles. While the habitus disposes social actors to particular kinds of conduct, it also provides the basis for the generation of new practices (Jenkins 1992: 74–84).*

Based on his influential study of French lifestyles, Bourdieu (1984) argued that every aspect of consumer behaviour – from holidays and choice of wallpaper to foods preferences and clothing styles – say important things about where we belong in society. 'Belonging' in this sense refers especially to our class, education, ethnicity, religion, generation and the place we live (whether city, suburbia, region, small town or village). Shared tastes also provide access to membership of desired groups. Thus, each sub-group expresses its own special **HABITUS**.

Here are three examples of a habitus:

1. Urban factory workers may display art that sentimentalizes family life or romanticizes the rural past.

2. Socially mobile business groups who enjoy first-generation wealth but little education may attend the opera and acquire antiques in an attempt to legitimize their economic gains and rub shoulders with more sophisticated people.

3. Educated professionals are often relatively poor in terms of wealth, income and property but they are able to compensate for this through their acquisition of cultural capital – an acquired body of discerning knowledge and taste, perhaps in jazz, nineteenth-century literature or cubist art.

Clearly, consumption patterns are deeply rooted in the soil of social life. The sign-values attached to goods are not free to shape our needs without the mediation of strong countervailing forces.

Consumption as life enhancing

Many writers have pointed to the rise of a post-modern society and its links to another fairly recent transition – the move towards post-Fordist economies, issues raised earlier in Chapter 4. Post-modern consumers, it is argued, crave distinctiveness, personal service, originality and diversity. In part, this is what has compelled businesses to move towards niche marketing and far more flexible systems of manufacturing. The rise of post-modern sensibilities also means that consumption and leisure play a much more important role in the lives of contemporary citizens than during the era of early industrialization. Then, people were much poorer and work, class consciousness, nationalism and deep loyalties to family and community figured much more largely in people's lives.

Consumer creativity

Returning to the present, Featherstone (1987, 1990), Tomlinson (1990) and others offer a celebratory brand of post-modern thinking. Far from being consumer dopes, they argue that we have become skilled practitioners who have learned how constantly to decode messages and to alter their meanings by imposing our own interpretations. We also negotiate these meanings with others through the social webs in which we are entangled. Increasingly we revel in plurality and difference. In these ways we weave meanings into changing patterns of personal identity. Consumerism has therefore become a vehicle for projecting our particular selves and group affiliations into social space. Certainly, numerous sub-cultural youth groups appear to have done this ever since the 1950s by adopting a ***bricolage*** of clothing styles and a variety of fashions in the perpetually changing pop and rock scene. Thus, we have become the liberated masters not the servants of the consumer society.

Bricolage – an assembly of various apparently unconnected elements.

Such post-modern arguments reassure us that we are not consumer dopes. However, in displacing the earlier one-sided obsession with the compulsions of production and work as the primary source of meaning in people's lives, the post-modernists seem to have substituted another equally skewed scenario in its place. Human creativity in the workplace seems to have been denied or devalued and reassigned almost entirely to the spheres of consumption and leisure. This could be said to play rather conveniently into the hands of capitalist interests and to exclude those without the material means to enjoy consumer culture.

TOWARDS A HOMOGENEOUS, AMERICANIZED GLOBAL CULTURE?

Major Concept
McDONALDIZATION

McDonaldization originally referred to the irresistible dissemination of business systems associated with the US fast-food industry. These aimed to achieve intense control over workers and customers in order to supply cheap, standardized, but quality products in pleasant surroundings. This drive for efficiency and predictability has now spread to many other economic activities and countries so that the McDonald's burger franchising chain is merely the 'paradigm case' (Ritzer 1993: 1) of a much wider formula.

The spectre of world cultural domination through the spread of western consumerism and the rise of increasingly similar materialistic societies worries many observers (see Tomlinson 1990). The fear of Americanization is often even more acute. Sometimes this is described as **McDONALDIZATION**; the delivery of standardized products and their related systems of business control (Ritzer 1993). The McDonald's burger franchising chain is emulated by many other concerns. Certainly, McDonald's own worldwide appeal has been enormous. During 1991 it opened two and a half times more new restaurants abroad than in the USA. In 1992, the first outlet appeared in Beijing, China, with a seating capacity of 700 (pp. 2–3).

Pointing to this widespread fear not simply of US consumerist but also cultural domination, Hannerz (1992: 217) coined a similar term – the 'cocacolonization of the world'. Supposedly, what is at stake here is the destruction of once vibrant and unique religious, ethnic and national identities and not just local dietary customs and small industries. Interestingly, during the immediate post-war years, many Europeans expressed a distinct antipathy to 'Yank culture' and US market domination. The fear of Americanization was particularly strong in France. When, for example, Coca-Cola applied for a licence to begin local bottling in 1948, the French Communist Party won much public support when it implausibly argued that Coke's incursion should be resisted because the company doubled as a US spy network. Others maintained that it represented a threat to French civilization or observed that like earlier Nazi propaganda, Coke advertising exercised an 'intoxicating' effect on the masses (Pendergrast 1993: 241–3).

Figure 13.2   Imperial food: McDonald's restaurant in Moscow

More recently, research has demonstrated how the leading role played by US transnational corporations in expanding post-war markets for consumer products was soon consolidated by similar moves in the 1960s on the part of US advertising agencies and media networks. Accordingly, by the late 1970s, US advertising agencies operating abroad earned 50 per cent of their incomes from these sources (Janus 1986: 127). Indeed, until the early 1980s they virtually controlled the world advertising of consumer goods in most leading markets. Meanwhile, pushed by state initiatives, television ownership grew in many developing countries during the 1960s. The US radio and TV networks were able to sell both the technology required in order to establish communication facilities in developing countries and US programmes (Sinclair 1987: 103).

The net result of all this was to create the channels – either through direct TNC or advertising agency sponsorship of national radio and TV programmes and newspapers – for a vast expansion in consumer demand for US products. Much of this was especially evident in Latin America. For example, Janus (1986: 131) reported that during a single day in 1971, 84 per cent of the adverts transmitted by a popular Mexican radio station involved transnational products. Likewise between 20–50 per cent of advertising space in Latin America's 22 largest newspapers during the mid-1970s was bought by TNCs. Thus, the media 'through commercial audience-maximizing systems built around advertising… encourage… high consumption patterns and the creation of expectations which can only be met by further incorporation into the world economy' (Cruise O'Brien 1979: 129).

In the former communist countries there is little doubt that the arrival of products such as Big Mac burgers were eagerly welcomed in the 1980s (see Figure 13.2). They were seen as powerful symbols which offered access to western freedoms and consumer lifestyles as exemplified in the 'authentic taste of America' (James 1996: 83). Such instances appear to demonstrate a rather simplistic view of western life along with a quite explicit equation of global culture with Americanization or westernization. Are these merely extreme examples of a general stampede towards western culture around the world? Alternatively, are there reasons for thinking that the globalization of consumption will not necessarily lead to a homogeneous, Americanized world? We now discuss the case for taking the latter position.

The experienced consumer

People living in the advanced societies have been exposed longer and more intensively to the attractions of a consumer society than anywhere else. As we have seen, there is a good case to make that the majority has not been turned into a gaggle of consumer dopes. With some possible exceptions, perhaps among children and adolescents, most of us are perfectly able to impose our own interpretations on the goods we buy. Our membership of very different groups also acts as a screening device through which meanings are negotiated and altered. This being so, it is hard to believe that people living in cultures vastly different from our own will not be equally or more capable of demonstrating creative responses. If anything, the potential for a mismatch – the imposition of uncertainty, ambivalence and innovation – between the advertisers' messages and the ways consumers read them is likely to be much greater. As Hannerz argued (1992: 243), the meaning of any external cultural flow is 'in the eye of the beholder'. In addition, involvement in global culture offers ' access to a wider cultural inventory… new resources of technology and symbolic expression to refashion and… integrate with what exists of more locally rooted materials' (p. 241).

The roots of cultural change

Cultural change is not new. The construction of new identities and meanings has often followed in the wake of the religious and other influences that reached societies from outside. Such processes have been going on for thousands of years. Moreover, culture in all its forms is always socially constructed. It consists of a connected body of contrived meanings subject to continuous modifications and additions. Given all this, it is rather paradoxical that many people regard the changing cultural identities of the present era with such fear and distaste simply because they are mediated by the 'forces of a commercial market' (Firat 1995: 121).

Firat suggests that the explanation for this probably lies in the association of markets and money with vulgarity. But this may not be a very convincing reason for such attitudes. Indeed, the 'threat' to cultures from money and commerce may actually be 'less harmful than other forms of invasion because… a commercial invasion allows elements from all cultures to survive as long as they are marketized' (p. 121). In short, the gluing of cultural artefacts and experiences to money incentives and their projection into the world marketplace offers the best guarantee that they will survive. This experience may alter them but, as we have seen, cultural change is inevitable anyway. Also military and other forms of oppression are much more likely to result in the massive destruction of a cultural heritage, as the impact of slavery on African people transported to the Americas amply demonstrates (although even here, and against all the odds, some cultural elements did survive).

Diversity within the homogenizing states

Apart from their native inhabitants, both Canada and the USA were formed out of the cultural ingredients imported from many countries. Indeed, the USA has long been described as the melting-pot society par excellence. The dominant Protestant Anglo-Saxon groups have made determined efforts since the early twentieth century to Americanize (or Anglicize) the masses arriving from Eastern Europe, Italy, Ireland, China, Japan and, more recently, from other parts of Asia, the Middle East and Latin America – especially through the school system. Nevertheless, distinctive ethnic cores survive in many US cities. Most continue to celebrate their linguistic, religious and culinary legacies and to retain connections through marriage and community with those descended from similar migrant backgrounds (Figure 13.3). Visitors to New York, for example, arguably the epicentre of world capitalism, may be struck by its vibrant multicultural ethos. Almost every conceivable cuisine, musical genre, ethnic art, style of dress, language, business form (complete with links into global networks), church and community can be experienced by those who have the desire to do so. Much the same is true for many European countries that are a lot older.

Figure 13.3   Fusion food: Shalom pizza in Los Angeles

The survival of local cultures

American consumer culture from Disney to the TV soap *Dallas* may be strongly present in every culture across the globe but the reverse is equally the case. Several generations of migrant cultural experience have survived prolonged exposure to intensive consumerist and media influences in the wealthiest country. This being so it is not easy to understand why the availability of Kentucky Fried Chicken in the streets of Bombay or the ability to view *Roseanne* in the villages of Egypt are liable to destroy the entire cultural traditions of these or any other developing society. On occasions, some inhabitants of Lagos or Kuala Lumpur may drink Cokes, wear Levi 501 jeans and listen to Madonna records. But that does not mean they are about to abandon their customs, family and religious obligations or national identities wholesale even if they could afford to do so, which most cannot.

Reverse cultural flows

Significant *reverse* cultural flows to the West from Japan and the developing countries located in all world regions are also increasingly evident. Many more are likely in the future especially when and if more non-western countries achieve industrialization. We have already noted some examples such as world cuisine and the Japanese management ethos and more are mentioned later. Another interesting example is the diffusion of traditional Asian medicines, health and fitness practices and approaches to mental health. These have become very popular among a sizeable section of the middle classes in Europe and North America. Among these are yoga, t'ai chi, shiatsu, meditation, chromatherapy, acupuncture and some herbal remedies. A similar process has occurred in the case of the martial arts such as karate, judo, t'ai kwando and kung fu.

SHAPING GLOBAL CULTURE: THE ROLE OF THE LOCAL

Drawing on case studies by empirical sociologists this final section explores three types of response on the part of local cultures to the supposedly homogenizing thrust of global consumerism.

Indigenization

Several studies have explored the ways in which the local captures global influences but in the process transposes them into forms that are compatible with indigenous traditions. The case of Japan is extremely revealing. Clammer (1992) shows how its citizens reveal strong predilections towards acquiring an endless stream of brand-named consumer possessions, which are soon rejected in favour of newer styles. Shopping forms an essential and relished part of leisure, especially among women. Indeed, Clammer argues that the Japanese are quintessentially post-modern in their concern with constructing distinctive styles of dress and other forms of consumption and the need to express subjectivity through creating the right atmosphere at home. However, much of this is rooted in long-established Japanese traditions. These always fostered eclecticism – a delight in selecting new avenues of cultural expression – and prized the acquisition of highly developed aesthetic skills and the ability to juggle with 'semiotically ambiguous' (p. 205) objects. Tradition also values the cultivation of the self in everyday life through appropriate forms of presentation according to social rank, age and gender.

One way in which the preoccupation with aestheticism and presentation is evident concerns the Japanese obsession with wrapping presents. This is done with enormous care and attention to detail so that exactly the right signals are conveyed to recipients. Modern consumerism has also become locked into the ancient Japanese tradition of giving and receiving gifts which continues to provide one of the 'essential ingredients of everyday culture' (p. 206). In addition to family members, gifts are widely given at different times of the year and to a vast array of people from whom favours have been received and to those whose future help may be required. Given the continued flourishing of this ancient gift economy the Japanese have found no difficulty in incorporating the Christian festival of Christmas – despite their adherence to quite different religions – in addition to certain other western inventions such as Mothers' Day and Hallowe'en.

Since the mass media play such an important role in disseminating cultural values – and consumerist expectations – it is worth noting that many developing countries have established their own TV and radio networks, film industries and much else besides. This has certainly been the case in Latin America. Thus, between 1972 and the early 1980s, the previous dependence of Latin American TV networks on US programmes declined. Partly, this became possible through the development and rapid popularity of 'telenovelas' – locally made TV soaps that explored national problems and themes (Rogers and Antola 1985).

The Indian film industry was established in 1912. It offers a particularly interesting case of indigenization with respect to the mass media. Although based in several cities, it is the Bombay production centre, known as 'Bollywood', that has become the most famous. India has the largest film industry in the world and produces over 900 films a year (Kasbekar 1996). Most are exported across South Asia, to Russia, Africa, Latin America and those European cities where migrants have settled. Contemporary concerns with such local themes as the survival of family life in the face of rapid economic change and how 'poor boy' can win 'rich girl' in a society that remains very unequal dominate Indian films. Nevertheless, traditional Hindu and other mythological material also figures prominently – for example, the concern with *dharma* (duty) and kinship obligations. Similarly, the plots and creative forms draw on ancient classical theatre and aesthetic traditions; the love of epic dramas and spectacles, the use of song and the emphasis on romance and a strong emotional content.

Re-invention and rediscovery

In Chapter 12 we explored examples of how tourism has sometimes contributed to the revival of traditional cultures. In the case of consumption, the rediscovery of declining or extinct traditions is especially obvious in the case of cuisine. Visits to most bookshops to examine the cookery section will reveal just how massive and diverse the interest in global foods has become. Similarly, on most days one can watch a TV programme which explores global cuisine. However, the need to compete with the rising popularity of restaurants offering 'authentic' foreign dishes and imported fast-foods has sometimes provoked a new interest in national and local culinary traditions.

Recently, this 'resistance to heterogeneity' (James 1996: 89) has been particularly marked in the UK. Thus, once forgotten or neglected cheeses, sausages, preserves, beers and fruit or vegetable varieties, most highly specific to particular localities, have been found and reinstated in 'traditional' cookbooks. Meanwhile, such delicacies as 'steamed puddings, pies and pastries, bread and butter pudding, tripe, authentic teacakes and muffins' have once again appeared 'on the menus of the more fashionable restaurants' (p. 89).

Chase (1994) offers another example from Istanbul in Turkey. The first hamburgers appeared in Turkish cities in the early 1960s and offered an 'all-enveloping American environment' (p. 75). At that time she feared this would destroy the vibrant local street trade based on Middle Eastern dishes. However, on returning 30 years later she discovered that local foods had not only survived 'the gleaming temples of American fast-food merchandising' (p. 77) but that the variety, popularity and quality of local snacks and dishes had grown. Thus, demand for kebabs, koftes, aubergine with yoghurt, spicy bread appetizers and much else besides from across Turkey had burgeoned in bazaars, shops and cafes. Competition from western foods had played a role in this revival but so, too, had the growth in the city's busy working population, searching for lunchtime sustenance at a time of rising inflation and the impossibility or returning home for midday meals in the face of growing traffic jams.

Creolization

Major Concept
CREOLIZATION

This term describes how cross-fertilization takes place between different cultures when they interact. The locals select particular elements from in-coming cultures, endow these with meanings different from those they possessed in the original culture and then creatively merge these with indigenous traditions to create totally new forms. Although this definition serves most purposes, be warned that 'Creole' is used very inconsistently in different settings.

Unlike indigenization, where the global is used to express essentially local cultural forms, the mixing of ingredients involved in **CREOLIZATION** generates altogether new, fused inventions. We can suppose that such creative blending has always occurred throughout human history. Of course, creolization has encompassed many cultural forms and not just consumerism. For example, in southern Nigeria (and elsewhere in Africa) the absorption of Christianity has led to the fusion of African music and language with standard church liturgy and the incorporation of pre-modern concerns with health and the desire for magical protection against the ill wishes of others into ritual activity. Consequently, many Nigerian churches are very different from their European counterparts.

Here are three contemporary examples of creolization, in food, clothing and music:

● *Food* Key elements from various global cuisine such as soy sauce, Indian curry spices, pesto or Italian sauces are frequently added to traditional stews, grills and pies (James 1996: 91). Combining Coca-Cola with various local alcoholic favourites creates new drinks. Howes (1996: 6) gives the example of Cuba Libre in the Caribbean, made by mixing Coke with rum. James (1996: 77) describes how during a first-class journey by British Rail in the early 1990s she was presented with a 'Dishes of the World' menu. The menu suggested the following: 'Begin with Dim Sum with Hoisin Sauce from China... followed by Duck and Mixed Berry Sauce from south-west France and (end) with Tiramisu from Italy for dessert.'

- *Clothing* This offers another arena for cultural blending. For example, Hendrickson (1996: 117–18) discovered that the rich Guatemalan tradition of weaving as a way of representing social identity, derived from Maya culture, had found its way into various western mail-order catalogues. Here, among other items, she found jackets made from Guatemalan tie-dyed cloth presented in the style of Japanese kimonos and hand-woven, Guatemalan fabrics offered for sale as cowboy blankets, which were supposed to express the earlier frontier ethos of the USA. In any case, the invitation to acquire worldwide ethnic craft products along with contemporary mass produced factory goods speaks volumes concerning the mix-and-match consumer culture now available to us.

- *Music* This is another sphere where creolization has always flourished. Several classical composers borrowed national or regional peasant folk songs drawn from countries such as Russia, Scotland and Czechoslovakia for their symphonies. Much more important in terms of popular music has been the influence of Africa on the immense flowering of musical styles associated with the rise of pop and rock. Thus, not only did early twentieth-century African Americans living in the USA invent jazz in its various forms by drawing on African musical traditions, but the birth of rock in the 1950s grew largely out of the marriage of jazz with country and western music. Such creative combinations have continued until the present and have included further black cultural infusions from West African bands, Caribbean reggae and rap from the USA. But around the world, other cultures, too, have creolized various musical forms. One interesting example is the case of rai, a mix of gypsy flamenco music from Spain, rock and Bedouin folk songs. Rai's foremost exponent, Khaled Hadj Brahmim from Algeria, won a place in the French top 10 singles charts in 1992 and again in 1996 (Myers 1997).

REVIEW

As a preliminary to examining global consumerism, we discussed two contrasting theoretical positions concerning the nature of contemporary consumer culture. We laid particular emphasis on the more positive scenario, arguing that we are often not consumer dopes, but generally interpret and express the meanings implanted in goods by advertising in ways that reflect our personal lifestyle needs and participation in various social groups. (Of course, there are *other* reasons for worrying about consumerism especially its cumulative, environmental impact on the world's biosphere. We examine this issue in Chapter 18).

We also pointed out that although there is some evidence that western or American consumer goods, and the values they carry, are spreading rapidly to the developing world, transnational cultural flows are not one-way. Neither are they totally swamping local cultural forms. Rather, and as in the past, the local normally finds ways to capture, alter and mix external influences with indigenous ones or even to re-invent itself with the aid of new resources brought by the global.

If you would like to know more ••••••••••••••••••••••••••••••

Mysteriously, most writing on consumerism – something we all engage in every day – is not especially easy to understand. However, Slater's book, *Consumer Culture and Modernity* (1997) is more accessible than most and provides a lively introduction to this subject. Try Chapters 1, 2 and 3.

The book edited by D. Howes, *Cross-cultural Consumption* (1996) includes some fascinating material. The introduction and Chapters 2, 4, 6 and 8 are especially useful.

Featherstone is a key writer on post-modern society and consumerism. Try, especially, Chapter 2 in *Consumer Culture and Postmodernism* (1992).

An Introduction to Theories of Popular Culture by Strinati (1995) is clear, comprehensive and very readable.

Group work •••

1. Arrange a visit to two department stores and two supermarkets. By examining the labels and talking to the managers construct a list of all the goods on sale which originate abroad and categorize them by type. In class consider these questions. How many countries are involved? What kinds of goods come from which countries? In which areas do national goods tend to dominate over foreign ones. How can this be explained? What are your overall impressions?

2. Working in groups and pooling your knowledge, construct a rough chronology of rock and pop music since the 1960s. Establish the main types of musical genre and the lines of descent between them. Then consider two questions: Which kinds of young people mainly preferred which genres or fashions? To what extent, when and in what areas have foreign musical influences shaped your own country's tastes?

3. Arrange a class debate in advance on the proposition that: 'the globalization of consumer culture is destroying local traditions everywhere.' After the main speakers have given their prepared talks, each member of the class will give two reasons why they agree or disagree with the proposition.

Questions to think about •••••••••••••••••••••••••••••••••••

1. Are we consumer dopes or consumer heroes?

2. Evaluate the main arguments for the proposition that the spread of consumerism leads to a homogeneous, Americanized global culture?

3. In what ways does the local respond to the arrival of globalizing cultural forces?

4. To what extent have cultural and religious influences from outside Europe and North America affected social life since the 1970s?

CONTENTS

'The medium is the message' was the disarmingly simple motto of the pioneer guru of contemporary media studies, Marshall McLuhan (1962). But what did he mean? Generally systems of communication depend on a sender, a receiver and a means of transmission from the first to the second, and sometimes back again. This third mechanism is the 'medium' or, in the plural sense, the 'media'.

Traditionally, those involved in producing the message saw themselves as all-important. Novelists, film directors, newspaper editors are all still accorded high prestige. Nevertheless, however brilliant and original the message, it only becomes salient if critics, readers and listeners – the audience – recognize the claims of the producers and give them credibility or approval. In the past the nature of the medium was generally disregarded as uninteresting, or seen as inert.

It was McLuhan's great insight to recognize the power of the medium itself to change the message. Hitler and Goebbels showed how the radio, which operated via the centralized transmission of content received in privatized circumstances, could be commandeered as a propaganda device to be monopolized and manipulated for state purposes. The one-way nature of the medium deterred the kind of negative feedback that might be expected by a controversial politician at a public meeting. Since the discovery of printing, the typeface and phonetic alphabet has dominated most written communication. Yet, almost without us being conscious of its supercession, the TV screen took over from the book and newspaper as the most common medium of communication. This had profound consequences. Print favoured systematic exposition and sequential, deductive thinking. TV is best suited, like many conversations, for impressionistic, contradictory or unreasoned discourse (Castells 1996: 331–2). The central role of the medium can be seen in two examples:

1. Academics used to delivering scholarly papers to a respectful audience of colleagues or an attentive class of students usually find themselves at sea in a TV studio, even though both are oral media and the intended message is similar.

2. Listeners to a radio programme (who might be ironing, childminding, cooking or driving while being tuned in) absorb highly selective messages. Sometimes they do this subconsciously, sometimes they choose what they want or need to hear in competition with other sounds, like a baby crying or a dog barking.

We can now begin to understand McLuhan's point. It matters a great deal through what means the message is conveyed, though it is probably best to consider his maxim that the medium *is* the message as a form of poetic licence, making a good point in an exaggerated way in order to convey his meaning more powerfully. However, *that* the medium structures, constrains or influences the message and its reception is now well-established in empirical studies.

The media foster globalization just as they are themselves changed by stepping up to a global scale. In this chapter we will provide a definition and characterization of the media and also examine issues of ownership and content in relation to the growth of the electronic media. We will also discuss how the acceptance of the telephone as a mass consumer good and the arrival of linked computer networks raise new possibilities for the sharing of information for interactive communication and for global democracy. The economic and social effects of enhanced global communication will also be considered.

WHAT ARE 'THE MEDIA'?

The media are agencies and organizations that specialize in the communication of ideas, information and images of our environment, our communities and ourselves. The media also project images about 'others' and their communities. Many journalists and media workers proclaim that all they are doing is collecting and disseminating ideas, information and images. They are, they often protest, not to be blamed for the content of their reports or the consequences that might arise. 'Don't kill the messengers if they bring you bad news', is their refrain, one copied from an ancient Greek saying when a hapless runner brought news of a military defeat.

Such observations would now be regarded as naive. Not only Marshall McLuhan, but many other commentators (and indeed many in the audience) believe that the media are doing all sorts of other things than reporting the news neutrally, whether the wider effects are intentional or unintentional. As John Crace (quoted in Jones and Jones 1999: 94) argues: 'There is no such thing as an impartial news story. Even a story that seems to be politically neutral tells you something about the values of the news organization that produced it by its length and positioning on the page, or its place in the television running order.' Such decision-making forms part of the media's agenda-setting role, whereby they play a significant part in reflecting and shaping public debate. It is also an outcome of the gate-keeping process – the process by which decisions are taken as to which news stories are chosen and which discarded.

In the case of a newspaper, there is formally a nominal difference between the editorial columns (in the broadsheet newspapers they often appear in the centre of the newspaper) and the news pages. However, tabloid newspapers often run political or promotional campaigns on the front pages of their newspapers that elide the difference between advertising, editorial opinion and news. For example, one popular English daily, the *Sun*, made a front-page plea to all its readers to attend a rally at Trafalgar Square to proclaim their anti-European sentiments. The campaign was headed 'Up Yours, Delors' and was a crude personal attack and populist campaign, with virtually no news content, on the former President of the European Union. When the British government urged NATO to bomb Serbia in March 1999, the tabloid's front page was headlined 'Clobba Slobba'.

The UK tabloids have also taken the opportunity to exploit marital discord among members of the British royal family to provide a tonne of unsolicited advice on the future constitutional arrangements of the UK. Many newspapers paid vast sums to 'paparazzi' photographers for intimate pictures of Diana, Princess of Wales, caught in an unguarded moment. Only the mass waves of emotion (again communicated and amplified by the media) surrounding her untimely death, shamed the worst newspaper editors from persisting in their use of intrusive photography. Many seasoned observers of the media reason that this uncharacteristic constraint will be a temporary phenomenon, with commercial considerations soon taking over again.

Information, news, emotions, values and opinions are, in short, intermingled by the media themselves and also interwoven in the minds of the audience. The consequences of this confusion may be seen, at a trivial level, by the fact that actors report that many of their fans are unable to distinguish between a fictional character in a TV serial and the actor who plays the part of that character.

Broadly, the media divide into the print media (books, magazines and news-papers) and the visual/aural media (movies, radio and television). But, as is illustrated in the press coverage of TV serials the media are mutually parasitical, often with a sort of cannibalistic feeding-frenzy taking place. Radio reports the headlines in the press or 'What the papers say'. The newspapers list and review the programmes on the television and radio. Feature movies are adapted from books. The reactionary and eccentric press mogul, William Randolph Hearst (1861–1953), provided the model for the classic movie, *Citizen Kane*. The people in the media select each other as so-called 'celebrities'. 'Famous' journalists and broadcasters appear on quiz games and interview each other on chat shows.

THE POWER OF THE MEDIA

The media's conflation of fact and fiction, or reason and emotion, is important in other ways too. Large media corporations may contrive to use this facility to project images and ideas that work to their own interest rather than the national or international interest. This statement might be thought vastly exaggerated if not for the fact that some corporations have achieved a near monopolistic, complex and overlapping control of newspapers, film archives, television networks, radio stations and satellites. This is true particularly of Rupert Murdoch's News Corporation, but true also of the giants Time Warner/CNN, Disney/CBS and the German-based Bertlesmann/CLT group. The integration of the programming, production, marketing and broadcasting functions in the hands of a small number of media corporations is also increasingly evident.

The combined ownership of different media gives such corporations a global reach that is sometimes seen as threatening democracy, diversity and freedom of expression. The media moguls are able to influence business, international agencies and national governments, which often attend to them as if they were suppliant courtiers presenting themselves for royal approval.

The control of global communications in the hands of a limited number of players began in the nineteenth century and followed the lines of European

---

Box 14.1   The media moguls battle it out

Rupert Murdoch

Ted Turner

Rupert Murdoch
- Personal wealth $6.5 billion
- Heads NewsCorp (valued at $24 billion). Includes:
  - TV – BSkyB, Fox (USA), Star (Asia)
  - Film – 20th Century Fox
  - Newspapers – News International
  - Books – HarperCollins

Ted Turner
- 9 per cent shareholder in Time Warner, which has assets of $26 billion and owns:
  - TV – CNN, TNT, Cartoon Network
  - Film – Warner Brothers, Castle Rock
  - Magazines – *Time*, *Sports Illustrated*, *Fortune*
  - Music – Warner Elektra, Atlantic
  - Books – Warner

Murdoch's newspaper (*The New York Post*) on Turner's wife, Jane Fonda, when she visited Hanoi:

'Just another scatty-brained Hollywood nude-nik.'

A full-page story in the same newspaper was headed 'Is Ted Turner veering towards insanity?'

Turner on Murdoch:

He is a 'slime' and 'a scumbag' who can be compared to the 'late Führer'. 'I don't like him and don't respect him. What's happened in Britain is a tragedy. He came close to having this country [the UK] under his thumb.' 'Rupert's idea of a better world is a world that's better for Rupert.'

Source: Guardian 6 November 1997

expansion, imperialism and colonialism. The old Hollywood movies about the American West frequently illustrate the march of land-based communications technology. The stagecoach operated by such companies as Wells Fargo carried mail as well as passengers and (as shown in the movies) was victim to washed-out roads, broken wheels, lame horses, hold-ups by highwaymen and attacks by Native Americans. The railways and telegraph lines slowly overcame these problems and offered a secure means of communication. However, the capital investment in railways and the reliance on them was so great that whoever owned them was immediately pivotal to the politics and economic life of the time.

A similar logic obtained in the case of the supercession of sailing ships by steam ships. However, perhaps the most important development was cable communications, available from the middle half of the nineteenth century. Cables were stretched along poles, buried underground and laid on the seabed. And news agencies such as Reuters rapidly bought up the smaller companies. Baron von Reuter (1816–99) started his service by initially using pigeons to carry the news between Germany, France and Belgium. European governments soon became alarmed at his near-monopoly of news. Although resident in London, even the British government was so concerned at the thought that Reuter – a German national – could control telegraph lines during times of war that it developed alternative, secret lines of communications.

The dominance of Reuters plus the four other big western news agencies also means that news stories from many parts of the world either are not broadcast, or are trivial, misleading and ethnocentric. In the 1980s, the governments of African, Latin American, Asian and Middle Eastern states sought to use the good offices of the United Nations Educational, Scientific and Cultural Organization (UNESCO) to foster acceptance of stories emanating from their own national agencies. In response, the USA – followed meekly by the UK – walked out of the organization, refusing to pay their contributions. Although the walk-out was complicated by accusation of corruption and mismanagement in UNESCO, it seems that the western media were strongly lobbying for the walk-out and were probably influential in that decision.

The ownership and control of the cables – and later the satellites – is, of course, strategically and diplomatically vital, but it is also commercially and culturally important. Those who own the means of communications can link together vast audiences and potentially feed them with similar and selective messages. Well over three billion viewers watched the opening ceremony of the Olympic Games at Atlanta, while the rites surrounding the death of the Princess of Wales were seen by even more viewers. These major 'events' are, of course, atypical and illustrate only the latent dangers of the control of the airwaves. More gradual and perhaps more insidious are the ways in which television soaps like *Dallas* were thought to convey a narrow, individualistic and materialist message. Fortunately, as we shall see later, audience research on the 'consumption' of *Dallas* does not support such a narrow presumption.

TELECOMMUNICATIONS

The fear of control by governments and owners of large news corporations over the global media is somewhat offset by the capacity of many people (obviously wealth has something to do with *how many* people) to circumvent the media by direct lateral communication. This is particularly true of the telephone system – and more particularly of long-distance telephones. The global telephone network is now very dense, while the cost of calls is rapidly declining. Let us try to demonstrate this growth, by reference to these developments:

- In 1965, 85 per cent of the world's telephone lines were in Europe and North America. There was just one trans-Atlantic telephone cable that could handle 89 calls at a time. A three-minute call from the USA to Europe or Asia typically cost $90.00 at 1965 prices.

- In 1995 the global network comprised more than 600 million telephone lines and over 1.2 billion telephones in 190 countries. The cable and satellite network across the Atlantic handled about a million simultaneous calls between the US and Europe at a typical cost of $3 for a three-minute call, one-thirtieth of the price 30 years earlier.

- Subscribers in New York can telephone London for less than calling Los Angeles.

- Even that reduced price is massively marked up by the telephone companies whose *costs* per one minute call across the Atlantic are a little over one US cent a minute.

Cairncross (1997a) argues that the costs of connectivity will be dramatically driven down by the arrival of wireless systems (bounced off satellites) and the gathering pace of privatization of the telecoms companies. Finland, for example, has 52 companies, while more than 80 new companies have entered the market in the Asia-Pacific region in the 1990s. In the late 1980s, there were 190 companies routing international calls, in the late 1990s there were 5000.

Neither are the benefits of the revolution in telephony totally located in the rich countries. Take the case of mobile telephones. These provide a *supplement* for a well-developed telephone network in countries such as Japan where, in 1996, the share of the population with a mobile telephone doubled from 11.5 per cent to 23 per cent. But mobile telephones are an *alternative* to fixed-line telephone systems in many poorer countries, where the cost of wiring dispersed rural areas may be exorbitant. Clearly, however cheaply mobile telephones can be marketed there will be many unable to take advantage of the new technology themselves. However, indirect connections via low-cost local services, small businesses or NGOs will probably greatly enhance access to a mobile telephone service, even for the very poor. By the year 2001 the International Telecommunication Union estimates that 415 million of the world's 1.4 billion telephones will be mobile (Cairncross 1997a: 22).

Clearly such links have provided a more democratic and less controlled form of communication between friends, families and business and professional associates across the world. The lies and half-truths of politicians can be made to look hollow when comparisons are made by those callers with specialized information. Values and social constructions of reality are also less amenable to manipulation by powerful interest groups.

Figure 14.1   Alexander Graham Bell inaugurates the telephone link between Chicago and New York, 1892. The humble telephone remains at the heart of the modern telecommunications revolution

THE COMPUTER AND THE INTERNET

The arrival of the Internet, which links individual computers through computer networks and modems, also raises democratic possibilities. News groups (sometimes called 'discussion groups') can be set up out of the reach of the media, while opinions, ideas and attitudes can be formulated in dialogue with other people linked to the Internet, often on the other side of the globe. By 1995, the Internet covered no more than 2 per cent of the world's population, but its exponential growth over a very short period suggests that there is plenty of room for further expansion. The media have attempted to get in on the act, with the production of home pages on the World Wide Web, but these have been notably unsuccessful in containing the explosion of information outside of their control.

The democratic possibilities of the Internet are, as yet, unknown and remain controversial. However, the very structure of decentralized control has prevented business and the media from getting too close a control over it. Such is the level of Internet activity that the expression 'informational society' has been used to describe how important are the flows and links that criss-cross the globe. Table

14.1 shows how quickly links to the Internet grew over just three months in 1994. The rate of connection has now accelerated so dramatically that by early 1999

Table 14.1   Internet connections: growth by region over a three-month period, 1994

	1 July 1994	1 October 1994	Growth (%)
North America	2 172 232	2 678 288	23
Latin America/Caribbean	16 619	22 535	36
Western Europe	730 429	850 993	17
Eastern Europe and CIS	27 800	32 951	19
Middle East	8871	10 383	17
Africa	15 595	21 041	35
Asia	111 278	127 569	15
South Pacific and Australia	142 353	154 473	9
Total	3 225 177	3 898 233	21

Source: Spybey (1996: 116) citing Third World Network Features

there were 8.3 million households in the UK connected to the Internet.

The democratic possibilities of the Internet are much enhanced by its decentralization. This is inherent in the system, in that the original design of the Internet was intended to prevent the possibilities of a Russian attack on the Pentagon permanently disabling all military communications. Computer-to-computer connections deliberately bypassed a central switching station, a model that was replicated by the universities and libraries of the world – which rapidly connected to each other through unusual routes. The media moguls, software companies and business interests are now trying to control access to the Net by developing specialized software, searching mechanisms ('browsers') and commercial gateways. They are also buying chunks of sensitive data and information and holding them in electronic stores that can only be accessed by codes, for which a consumer will have to pay. Commercial interests have also made a somewhat desperate attempt to force through international copyright legislation for electronic networks.

Commercial use of the Net has been somewhat inhibited by the difficulties in providing secure controls to prevent the discovery of credit card numbers, bank codes and personal identification numbers (PINs). This is, however, a temporary 'glitch' and has not prevented the use of the Net for small sales and transactions. Ordering books, buying theatre tickets, selecting groceries for delivery and interrogating bank accounts are now routine operations for many customers.

Despite the increased commercialization of the Internet, there is little doubt that lateral links have proliferated faster than business interests predicted and that much of the Internet will escape regulation and commercialization. The anarchist spirit that underlies much of the communication on the Internet has also been heartening to those who have felt oppressed by the global power of the large media corporations.

THE RISE OF INFORMATIONAL SOCIETY

Futurologists extrapolate from existing trends and make more or less sophisticated predictions about the future.

Like some sociologists, *futurologists* and computer buffs are not known for their elegant use of language. Terms such as the 'the informational society', 'information superhighway', 'informatization', IT ('information technology'), 'fourth generation language', ISDN ('integrated services digital network'), 'hypertext' and the like are coined almost as fast as they are discarded for newer and often even more enigmatic vocabularies. Whatever the shifts in vocabulary, a persistent theme is that communication technologies and computer technologies are both developing rapidly in their own right and converging into a set of shared information technologies.

The convergence of communications and computer technologies can be seen in the often bewildering overlap of hitherto separated functions. One can send a fax from a computer via a modem or network. Some fax machines have sophisticated functions like copying, scanning, automatic switching between fax and voice calls, mechanisms for correcting telephone line noise, switching to alternative telephone networks and acting as a printer for a computer. E-mail messages sent over the Internet can contain formatted files from personal computers or networked file stores. Photographic images can be scanned, digitalized, compressed, distorted, stored and transmitted.

Luddites were English artisans who rioted rather than accept mechanical and technical changes.

Simply getting such technologies to work seamlessly and feeling comfortable with them is more than many of us can achieve. Some people have become technophobes or **Luddites** in order to maintain their sense of self-worth in the face of the incomprehensible. Castells (1996: 23; 22–5) goes so far as to argue that even as 'information systems and networks augment human powers of organization and integration, they simultaneously subvert the traditional Western concept of a separate independent subject'. Communications and linked computer systems simulate in important respects a human brain. The 'artificial' in artificial intelligence is rapidly coming to resemble the real thing. It is perhaps not surprising that one patient in psychoanalysis saw in his dream an image of his head behind which was suspended a keyboard. He felt, he said, like a 'programmed head'.

As the machine–human interface begins to naturalize through such emulative technologies as memory chips, virtual reality and artificial intelligence humans will begin to lose the primacy of their own sensory perceptions. In the days of mass production, the notion of **ALIENATION** was used to suggest that the social relations of production were artificial and that human nature was being altered to fit in with the rhythms of machines and assembly lines. Alienation in the informational society is even more profound. Whereas in the industrial age machines mimicked a person's physical characteristics (the clanking robot with arms and legs being emblematic), in the informational age the conscious mind itself is emulated and may eventually be relegated to a marginal status.

Major Concept
ALIENATION

Marx believed that it is mainly through creative, self-directed work in the satisfaction of our own needs that we fully realize our inner selves and potential. However, under capitalism workers become estranged or alienated from their skills and their potential since now they are driven to work for capitalists in order to survive and the product of their labour no longer belongs to them. Sociologists have employed this term more generally to describe the powerlessness and lack of creativity believed to be endemic to many aspects of contemporary life.

INFORMATIONAL SOCIETY: ECONOMIC EFFECTS

The growth of informational society has had profound economic effects. In *The Condition of Post-modernity* (1989) Harvey was particularly interested in the reduction of time it takes for capital to accumulate. The days are long gone when King Midas stacked his gold in his cellar or when medieval bankers wrote letters of credit longhand. Salaries are now normally credited through auto-mated clearance systems (ACSs), while transfers of funds are virtually instanta-neous. Dividends, interest and profit can be remitted relatively freely (although some states still try to prevent this), while investment, loans and credits can flow just as quickly in the opposite direction. The sale and purchase of stocks and shares is also virtually instantaneous.

The very speed (and also volume) of these transactions make them impos-sible for the national authorities to track, police or tax. With the collapse of the Bretton Woods system (see Chapter 3) in the 1970s Germany and the USA stopped trying to control the inflow and outflow of capital. This move was followed by the incoming Thatcher government in Britain in 1979 and, later, by the de-regulation and the freeing of the exchange control mechanisms in many other countries. The financial market became global in character within a few years. This has certainly profited many individuals and companies, but can provoke sudden financial crises in particular countries. These occurred in Europe in 1992–3, Mexico in 1994–5 and in the tiger economies of South East Asia in late 1997 when, for example, the baht (the Thai currency) lost over 30 per cent of its value in three months. Out of 91 Thai finance companies 58 were suspended after the government futilely spent 9 per cent of the country's 1996 GDP trying to keep them afloat (*The Economist* 18–24 October 1997: 131).

As the circulation of money gradually moved outside the control of national governments, new markets in their currencies developed. Perhaps the most notable was the Eurodollar, which trades in Europe outside of the control of the American authorities. Eurodollar deposits were particularly fuelled by 'oil money' after 1973, which sought a home away from the uncertainties of the Middle East. Very large sums were involved – some $50 billion in 1973 rising to $2 trillion in 1987, just fourteen years later. The 1987 figure for Eurodollars was about the same as the total amount of currency circulating in the USA itself at the same time.

As the circulation time of capital is reduced, the effective size of the globe shrinks and it is possible to trade stocks on a 24-hour basis. If London is closed, New York will be open. If that in turn is shut, Tokyo will be open. By linking to the key 'global cities' (see Chapter 15), firms, TNCs and individuals can use these different spaces instantaneously for trade, investment and banking, thus compressing both time and space. The difficulty in immediately spotting the illegal trading activities of the English 'rogue trader' working in Singapore, Nick Leeson, is illustrative of this capacity. In previous decades it would be difficult to imagine that the activities of just one currency trader could have laid low one of the most venerable of British financial institutions.

INFORMATIONAL SOCIETY: SOCIAL EFFECTS

While the sinister power of the media is often denounced, a number of studies in the 1960s showed that it also acts as a force for democratization and 'progres-sive' social change. Lerner (1958) examined a number of remote villages in rural Lebanon. He noticed that rural villagers had developed a passion for owning radios, which allowed them to access stories and information about the world outside. He demonstrated that when connectivity increased, the power of the village patriarchs declined – in other words there was a major shift in power relations. When television arrived, women were able to see western women in roles other than that of filial daughters, modest sisters and devoted mothers. The number wearing a veil dropped and there were other signs of women expressing more personal freedom in their lifestyles.

We must be careful not to display our normative preferences here, but it would perhaps not be going too far to describe the effects of the mass media in Lebanon as 'positive'. The media have also helped to disseminate mass education, provide some encouragement to mass literacy, and provide mass entertainment on a grand scale. The recognition of other peoples' cultures may give rise to sentiments of common humanity or at least to a recognition of cultural diversity.

Despite these positive possibilities and examples, the negative – or presumed negative – effects of the mass media and mass communication worry many observers. Three principal effects are often mentioned, which we list and then discuss:

- the effects of TV on patterns of violence; sexual mores and educational competence
- the creation of a global culture which is becoming increasing homogenized and *Ersatz*, a reduction to the lowest common denominator
- the growth of destructive consumerism.

Negative effects of TV viewing

The first concern – about the effects of TV viewing – has some intuitive support in the upward trend in TV viewing hours. In US homes the television is turned on for an average of seven hours a day. It is estimated that by the age of eighteen the average American child will have witnessed 18 000 simulated murders on TV (Watson 1998: 238). It is only reasonable that many parents, particularly those with young children, are disturbed at the thought of their children arbitrarily drawing images, ideas and behaviour patterns from the screen. However, the connection between lived violence and mediated violence is much debated. Some researchers point out that the most violent period in US history was between 1929–1933 when TV did not exist and that in many poor countries the level of violence experienced is high even where television ownership is low (p. 239). Clearly violence is not *only* caused by television.

However, as Watson (p. 238) avers, the argument cannot be dismissed lightly while 80 research studies affirm the connection between television and actual violence. At the very least 'the more we see of violence, the more we might become insensitive to it, and thus eventually immune to it. Either way it might confirm our view that out there is a dangerous and hostile world.'

Outside the issue of violence, it may be that long hours of television might produce some kind of osmosis effect where people, children in particular, are unable to distinguish fantasy from reality. Some post-modernists of course embrace this elision of a boundary between the imaginary and the real. Fortunately, there seems to be strong evidence that despite the TV being on for so long each day, many people ignore routine programmes. The television becomes something like moving wallpaper – a mildly interesting and changing pattern, rather like coloured heated oil blobs moving up and down in a decorative lamp stand.

The 'dumbing-down' of culture

The second concern – a cultural collapse to the lowest common denominator – has long been the subject of theoretical debate. The Frankfurt School – the name given to a group of intellectuals including Theodor Adorno, Walter Banjamin, Max Horkheimer and Herbert Marcuse, who were associated with the Institute of Social Research at the University of Frankfurt and later in the USA from the 1920s onwards – argued that the products of what they termed the 'cultural industries' were characterized both by cultural homogeneity and predictability, encouraging conformity among audiences and discouraging criticism of contemporary social relations under capitalism. As Marcuse argued: 'the irreversible output of the entertainment and information industry carry with them prescribed attitudes and habits, certain intellectual and emotional reactions which bind the consumers more or less pleasantly to the producers and, through the latter, to the whole. The products indoctrinate and manipulate; they promote a false consciousness which is immune against its falsehood' (Marcuse 1968: 26–7). The media have also been instrumental in spreading what now constitutes only one global language – English, usually American English. Even significant languages, such as French and Spanish, have had to bow to its hegemony. And although more people speak Chinese, they are concentrated in China and the Chinese diaspora. The media have spread English as the global medium of exchange, a situation that applies too to international law, travel, business and diplomacy.

In itself, the use of English does not signify the 'dumbing-down' of culture. However, the rich tapestry of myth, story-telling and literature in other languages may gradually be lost, except to scholars working in arcane fields. Cultures depend on context for their vitality and growth. If children can see little point in learning the language of their parents and grandparents increasingly the complexity and richness of the world will be enfeebled.

Consumerism

We discussed the character of global consumerism in Chapter 13, but it is worth mentioning in this context the way in which consumerism has been effectively diffused by the global media. The goods that are desirable, the music that is hip, the clothes that are fashionable, or the 'look' that is trendy, are all rapidly absorbed through the power of the media. Perhaps surprisingly, this process of consumer imitation and emulation even had profound effects in fuelling the neo-liberal opposition to state communism. The capacity of the media to suggest there is a wonderful cornucopia of goods just waiting on the other side of the hill led many in the former communist countries to confuse the free market with political and social freedom. There is a probably apocryphal, but illustrative story that Fidel Castro and Che Guevara, the famous revolutionary leaders of Cuba, were conscious of this problem. Every day Che would present another glass of fizzy brown liquid to Fidel. Finally Castro shook his head. 'It's no good', he said. 'Until we crack the formula for Coca-Cola the Revolution is doomed.'

The effects of mass media and mass tourism can come together in a negative sense, in that other countries and other cultures become mere objects for consumption. (Some more positive outcomes of mass consumption are also considered in Chapter 13.) The TV provides an endless stream of consumer and food programmes set in 'exotic' destinations. 'Holidays' are prizes given in fatuous competitions and dating programmes. The newspapers are full of travel writing and adverts for low-cost flights. Some companies, notably Disney (Disney World, Euro Disney, and so on) have brought together the consumption of tourism and culture in a single setting. Children can graze on authentic American hamburgers, Cokes, ice cream and popcorn while sitting on a mechanical boat going on a so-called 'Caribbean cruise'. Segments of historical reality are reordered for the purposes of this journey – pirates wave cutlasses, black actors sing 'Ol' Man River' and girls do belly dances in some sort of extra-ordinary pastiche of history, tradition and authenticity.

So, in short, communications do not always lead to multicultural under-standing and mutual respect for other peoples. Instead, the need to annex the media to consumerism leads to an appropriation of other cultures in the greater interest of profits. This double-edged feature of democratic openness, yet commercial closure is also seen in the case of the humble telephones. Although they can be used to foster lateral contacts outside the big media players and help to connect family members, they can also be used to cement shady business deals and used for recreational purposes, not necessarily of a savoury sort. By 1997, international telephone sex chat lines had become a $2 billion business (Cairncross, 1997a: 4).

GENDER AND REPRESENTATION

Through the power of the image the media can also strengthen stereotypes or legitimate long-standing inequalities or class, race and gender. This likely effect has been of particular concern to feminist scholars who have suggested that the media distorts, under-represents or misrepresents women (Van Zoonen 1994; Friedan 1963). Women are normally narrowly portrayed in three ways:

● as wife, mother and housekeeper (thus reinforcing conventionally assigned roles and limiting women's professional horizons)

● as sexual referents who confer their sexual attractiveness onto a prosaic object (thus advertisements show chocolate bars being licked suggestively by conventionally attractive young women)

● as sex objects to be used by men (in some cases in masochistic, perverted and pornographic depictions).

As Van Zoonen (1994: 30) contends, many aspects of women's lives and experiences are not properly reflected in the media: 'Many more women work than the media suggest, very few women resemble the *femmes fatales* of movie and TV series, and women's desires extend far beyond the hearth and home of traditional women's magazines.'

The increasing feminization of the work force and the increased recognition of domestic responsibilities by males have now significantly altered the representation of women in the media. Nonetheless, the bias remains clear. The obverse face of recognizing that images of women are a misrepresentation is the problem that advertisers and the media imply that 'real men' are strong, aggressive and in control. Particularly for working-class males who have less access to economic power or workplace authority 'manhood' is achieved, so the media imply, through a celebration of brawn and the body's potential for strength, force and violence (Katz 1995: 135).

A more complex way of understanding why gender misrepresentation arises in the cinema, television and in advertisements is to argue that the starting point for nearly all visual representation is that of a male. This can be seen at a obvious level in art – where male artists' depictions of the female nude are very common, but where it is virtually impossible to find a female artist's painting of a male nude. In short, 'ways of seeing' are predominantly male. As Berger (1972: 47) wrote: 'Men act and women appear. Men look at women. Women watch themselves being looked at. This determines not only most relations between men and women but also the relation of women to themselves.' The result is that women become trapped in a male gaze. As Gledhill (1992: 193, 4) puts it: 'The subject of [the] mainstream narrative is the patriarchal, bourgeois individual: that unified centred point from which the world is organized and given meaning.' Thus, the spectator is generally masculine while the camera appears to be held by the gaze of a male. The image is designed to flatter or console the male ego.

As we will see also in our next section on social identity, race and the media, a critique of the representation of gender is simultaneously a demand to recognize complexity and diversity. As Van Zoonen (1994: 33) insists: 'Gender should be conceived not as a fixed property of individuals, but as part of an ongoing process by which subjects are constituted, often in paradoxical ways. The identity that emerges is therefore fragmented and dynamic; gender does not determine or exhaust identity.'

THE MEDIA, RACE AND SOCIAL IDENTITY

We have discussed the concentration of media ownership and the integration of the production, marketing and broadcasting functions in the hands of a few corporations. But does this inevitably lead to acceptance of the messages these corporations seek to disseminate? Sociological research warns us against accepting what has been termed the 'hypodermic' model of media effects, whereby audiences are the passive and uncritical recipients of the messages producers choose to convey.

It is not that the effects of the domination of the media are negligible, merely that they are more complex and variable. Take the case of the American TV soap, *Dallas*, which was watched in over 90 countries in the early 1980s and was often indicted – for example by Jack Lang, the French Minister of Culture (quoted in Ang 1985: 2) – as a prime example of US cultural imperialism. Yet different local studies have yielded a catalogue of variable responses to the programme. One of the most significant of these was Ien Ang's study, *Watching Dallas*, published in the Netherlands in 1982 and translated into English in 1985, which found that Dutch women saw the programme 'through the grid of their own feminist agenda' (Morley and Robins 1995: 120). Far from seeing 'JR' as successfully asserting his patriarchal power, respondents to the advertisement Ang placed in a Dutch women's magazine saw the women characters as making ironic jibes at the men's doomed bids for male dominance. Similarly, Fiske (1989: 8) cites the example of Russian Jews watching *Dallas* in Israel and reading it as 'capitalism's self-criticism'. Australian aborigines, American, North African and Japanese audiences have all seen the programme in different ways, through the differently tinted lenses of their own cultures, kinship patterns, religions and norms.

While different audiences are not the victims of an intrusive hypodermic needle, they also cannot be seen as 'semiotic guerrillas', accepting, discarding or refracting the message as they choose (Morley and Robins 1995: 127). The menu from which they have to choose is limited and arguably getting more restrictive despite the increasing number of TV channels and FM broadcasts. On the one hand, the proliferation of channels allowed by new digital technologies allows the development of niche markets (for example, programmes aimed at small ethnic minorities or covering hobbies from paragliding to the restoration of classic cars). On the other hand, commercial pressures, whether driven by the quest for greater advertising or subscription revenue (largely, though not exclusively, achieved through high circulations and audience ratings), have the tendency to make producers opt for the tried and tested formula and to routinize their formats or schedules rather than take creative risks. In capitalist market economies, the audience is treated not as citizens in a given community but as customers in a market and, together, the proliferation of choices and the increasing interactivity of the media allow producers to monitor, segment and target audiences as consumers in increasingly sophisticated ways.

'Complexity' is also at the heart of media consumption in a detailed ethnographic study of young Punjabi people living in Southall, London. Gillespie (1995) shows that the media are having at least five distinct effects on the subjects of her study:

1. Even though the majority of her subjects were Sikhs, nearly all watched Hindi films on the VCR. Some were repelled and perhaps embarrassed by the images of poverty, but many – predominantly the girls – responded to the romantic fantasy provided by the Hindi films. 'When I watch an Indian film, after that I'm in heaven but I don't relate to the real world like I did… they're in rose gardens and the music just springs up from nowhere', commented one girl (p. 85).

2. The Hindu families (and some others) frequently watched the 'devotional soaps' together and young children were encouraged to sit up straight and show their respect to a favourite god, such as Krishna, when he was depicted (p. 89). TV viewing often became a form of worship as the multiple incarnations of the gods were depicted through the latest in audio-visual techniques.

3. While parents often disapproved of their children watching western soaps, many did so, but programmes like *Neighbours* were 'embedded in family life' with aspirations for cultural change being negotiated within a context of shared family values.

4. Young people reacted to the TV news within a framework of being both British and Asian. When the end of Mrs Thatcher's regime was announced, three 16-year-old girls celebrated the end of the poll tax (a then new tax based on the number of people in a household). 'Everyone's really pissed off with the poll tax, five people in my family have to pay it, it's crazy, where do they think we get the money from?' said one (p. 128).

5. By the same token, during the Gulf War when the newspapers became triumphalist in tone, Punjabis in general – but particularly those who were Muslim – were uncomfortably ambivalent. They saw through the obvious western propaganda, yet had to thread their way uneasily through being pro-British (especially in the classroom) and not anti-Muslim (especially at home).

The conclusion one can draw from this rich study is that there is a high level of cultural survival power among many minority groups. The media provide a means of asserting a minority identity. They also provide a means of affiliating to a cosmopolitan culture, and showing loyalty to the country of settlement, but doing so without providing undue offence and provocation to the older generation's values and religious persuasions. The consumption of the media is, in short, a complex and ambiguous matter.

REVIEW

In this chapter we have shown how the media have assumed a relatively independent life, separate from the broadcasters and the audience. Of course, the media cannot exist without social actors, but the message is significantly changed through the medium of communication and this gives a special power to the technology itself and to those to own it, work with it or understand it.

The print media are, perhaps, of lesser concern in this respect, as the process of writing, editing, publishing and reviewing allows a high level of individual judgement on the part of the reader. Shall I buy this book or not? How well has it been reviewed? What do you think of it? Do I like it? These questions can still be asked of much work in the print media. The visual and aural media, however, are more intrusive, more 'thrust' at the audience. It is difficult to look away when passing an offensive advertising hoarding, or not be concerned that the cars and drivers of your favourite sport, motor-racing, are plastered with tobacco sponsors. One can switch off the button on a television set, but only perhaps at the expense of annoying some other member of your household. One can walk out of a movie – but few brave souls do.

These examples can be multiplied, but they all work to a common conclusion. The media have a way of 'getting to you', however reclusive or discriminating you are. This then makes it important that we understand the ownership patterns of the media and appreciate what they are not telling us, as well as what they are. Are they exercising undue influence, which is distorting the democratic political order? Are they acting as the shock troops and missionaries for global capitalism, destroying other ideologies and ways of life other than those amenable to the 'free market' for goods and ideas (Herman and McChesney 1997)? Are they distorting and misrepresenting the lives and aspirations of women and ethnic minorities?

As to the revolution in telecommunications, we have argued that the increased sophistication and use of the telephone and its adjunct technologies, as well as the Internet, have many democratic possibilities that remain to be exploited. At least these developments show that powerful corporate interests cannot monopolize everything. A natural fear of the media moguls and their pretensions also is offset by many detailed studies showing that we do not absorb all we are told by the 'hypodermic needle'. We ignore much, challenge some and most commonly reconstitute the message of the broadcasters according to our own shared values and cultures. Human beings have not (perhaps not *yet*) been forced to bow down to the screen.

If you would like to know more ●

Frances Cairncross, a journalist at *The Economist* has been a very active writer in the field of telecommunications. Her major works are 'The death of distance' (*The Economist* 30 September 1995) and 'Telecommunications' (*The Economist* 13 September 1997a). The first is available at the web site www.economist.com. Her book (1997b), again titled *The Death of Distance*, consolidates her work.

The book edited by Edward S. Herman and Robert W. McChesney, *The Global Media* (1997) argues that the media have become the advance guard of international capital.

Manuel Castells's major work *The Rise of the Network Society* (1996) has a strong prologue and first two chapters that are relevant to this chapter.

As media studies courses have proliferated a number of student-friendly readers (reprints of already published articles) have battled for market share. These include edited books by Briggs and Cobley *The Media* (1997); Boyd-Barrett and Newbold *Approaches to Media* (1995) and Downey *et al. Questioning the Media* (1995). All contain valuable information and argument.

A valuable book on feminist views of the media is Liesbet Van Zoonen's *Feminist Media Studies* (1994)

Group work ●

1. Two groups will watch the main news broadcast tonight. One group will look at the issue of bias 'How is the news slanted'? The other group will speculate 'What has been left out of the news, and why'?

2. Draw up a list of the ten most memorable movies you have seen. Why did they appeal to you?

3. List the soaps you watch. Which characters relate to your personal experience?

4. Clip some advertisements from magazines and newspapers that, in your view, misrepresent gender, class and race. Discuss these with your group.

5. Do some simple research in your library regarding viewing figures for the channels and the number of copies sold of the major newspapers in your region/country. Does this information give you any indication of the political and social views of the majority of people?

Questions to think about ●

1. What are the democratic possibilities of the advances in telecommunications?

2. Why is it important for us to know about the patterns of media ownership?

3. Is culture going to be 'dumbed-down' to the lowest common denominator?

4. Compare and contrast the 'hypodermic needle' with the 'semiotic guerrilla' model.

5. What are the effects of the global media on the social construction and reconstruction of identity?

chapter

15

Urban Life

For much of human history, life was based in the rural world. In the year 1800, 97 per cent of the world's population lived in rural areas of less than 5000 people. Two hundred years later after a period of massive urbanization, in the year 2000, 254 cities had emerged, each containing over one million people. These 254 cites are very different in character, but many fall into certain basic categories:

1. *Ancient* cities such as Baghdad, Cairo, Mexico City, Athens or Rome built on the ruins of settlements that formed the basis of the great urban civilizations of the past. The remains of these great urban cultures are now picked over by tourists trying to capture some of the mysteries and glories of the past.

2. *Colonial* cities, including Caracas, Lagos, São Paulo or Bombay that accompanied or followed colonial expansion. The business districts and wealthy parts of these cities are often like islands surrounded by seas of poverty.

3. *Industrial* cities, for example, Birmingham, Toronto, Frankfurt, Johannesburg, Chicago or Sydney, which became centres of industrial, commercial or financial activity during the period of modernity and the construction of the nation state system. They were also centres of major social change.

4. *Global* cities, such as London, Paris, Tokyo or New York, that were equally important during the modern period, but have now also assumed a particular social character and distinctive role in the processes of global change and integration.

Cities are, by definition, meeting places where new settlers arrive, new market places spring up, new vocations are practised and new sensibilities formed. The culturally diverse cities in the ancient world like Athens gave us the word *cosmopolis*, while it was to Rome that all roads supposedly led. There were cities in the Chinese, Aztec, Ottoman and Holy Roman Empires. There were hundreds of cities before there were nation states. Indeed, for many years there were tensions between European cities and European states. Venice, Antwerp, Genoa and Amsterdam were often economic and political rivals of kingdoms including Portugal, England and France. Eventually some degree of 'mutuality' developed, such that the big cities played important administrative, military and economic roles in the evolution of the nation state system (Taylor 1995: 48–62). Their 'mutuality' was associated only with the period of modernity and essentially depended on the capacity of the state to act to secure its external boundaries, thereby protecting the functions of the major cities located within those boundaries.

Given their importance, urban forms of settlement and the ways people lived in them became the terrains of study by some of the world's most eminent sociologists. Durkheim (1933) for example, described the rural–urban transition as the movement from 'mechanical' to 'organic' forms of solidarity. The first was marked by customary, habitual modes of interaction, the second by social relations based on anonymity, impersonality and contract. Simmel (1950) saw the city as a place where a distinctively modern culture emerged with new forms of 'mental life' and a complex interwoven web of group affiliations. High levels of individualism were not entirely counteracted by these social relations, so conflict and social pathologies were likely to erupt.

The heyday of urban sociology was between the 1910s and the 1930s when it was pivotal to the development of the discipline (Savage and Warde 1993: 7). The central role of urban sociology was reasserted in the 1970s with the recognition of the important global functions of certain cities. In this chapter we will consider the colonial and industrial cities, discussing in the second case the famous Chicago School of sociology, which developed a distinctive method of understanding the 'ecological patterning' and spatial distribution of urban groups. We will then look at the evolution and analysis of global cities.

THE COLONIAL CITY

Perhaps the most obvious observation to make about colonial cities it that they are characterized by extreme and often bizarre juxtapositions. As Roberts (1978: 5) puts it: 'Modern skyscrapers, sumptuous shopping, office and banking facilities coexist with unpaved streets, squatter settlements and open sewage... the elegantly dressed are waylaid by beggars and street vendors; their shoes are shined and their cars are guarded by urchins from an inner-city slum' – or, we would add, a squatter settlement.

Figure 15.1   Urban India: satellite dishes and aerials meet cow dung and sticks

---

Major Concept

INFORMAL SECTOR

That part of urban society characterized by small-scale, labour-intensive, self-generated economic activity. There are minimal capital requirements in joining the informal sector and it relies on unregulated markets and skills acquired outside the formal education system. The sector is rarely controlled by government inspectors, so working conditions, safety checks and environmental standards are minimal. Exploitation and self-exploitation are rife.

In the colonial city there is no necessary association between urbanity and modernity. Unemployment is common, indeed normal, and self-employed forms of economic activity predominant. Although there is some full-time blue-collar employment in factories and white-collar employment in government offices, banks and insurance companies, the bulk of people are located in what is known as the bazaar economy, or the **INFORMAL SECTOR**. Self-employed craftsmen, carpenters, masons, tailors, taxi-drivers, mechanics, 'market mammies' (women traders in cheap commodities) and even farmers raising small livestock are some typical occupations. When one of the current authors lived in Nigeria, a self-proclaimed 'Doctor of Volkswagen' at the side of the road serviced his car. Picking up the car at the end of the day was always a lengthy business as the friendly mechanic took the opportunity of extending his 'test drive' into a prolonged taxi service for the locals.

In short, people survive in the best way they can. While the rich enjoy life-styles similar to the privileged groups in the advanced industrialized countries, the urban poor in colonial cities are often faced by a combination of low incomes, minimal public services and poor housing. Many live in run-down public apartments, crowded tenements and shantytowns made from cardboard, tin and thatch. Giving the difficult life circumstances of the urban poor, sociologists have carefully investigated how far their social and political attitudes provide a threat to the established order.

Research on Latin American cities has generated somewhat surprising evidence of a much more 'conservative' stance on the part of the urban poor than might perhaps be inferred from the extent of their deprivation. Those living in the shantytowns may either work in the formal sector or aspire to find a job there. Their shacks often are improved incrementally as bricks and corrugated iron roofs gradually replace the earlier rough materials. The urban poor also use the cultural and social resources at their disposal to improve their lives in creative ways (Roberts 1978: 141). Religious affiliations might provide emotional support, new ethnicities formed in the slums might be the basis for economic credit and political mobilization, while occasional forays by the conventional political parties in search of votes might provide a route into more conventional politics. Such is the weight of this push to the mainstream that Perlman (1976) has insisted that the 'marginality' of the urban poor is a myth.

THE INDUSTRIAL CITY AND THE CHICAGO SCHOOL

Robert Park, Ernest Burgess and their colleagues and successors at the University of Chicago, starting in the 1920s, undertook the most famous and far-reaching studies of industrial cities. Chicago itself provided the backdrop to their theories and field studies. For Park, writing in 1925 (cited in Kornblum 1988: 548–9):

> The city is more than a set of social conveniences – streets, buildings, electric lights, tramways, and telephones, and so on, something more, also than a mere constellation of... courts, hospitals, schools, police, and civic functionaries of various sorts. The city is, rather, a state of mind, a body of customs and traditions... it is involved in the vital processes of the people who compose it; it is a product of nature and particularly of human nature.

As this quotation indicates, the members of the Chicago School were vitally interested in the *meaning* of the city, or how an urban culture became constituted. Was the city the source of great evil or the fount of human civilization? What moral compromises would be necessary to live there and what conflicts arose between the long-standing residents and newcomers? How were the rival claims of individual achievement and community affiliation to be played out in the new setting? As Castells (1977: 77–8) recalls in a generous tribute to one of the key figures of the Chicago School, Louis Wirth, the chief insights made were that the new forms of social life were structured around the central axes of *dimension*, *density* and *heterogeneity*:

- *Dimension* The bigger the city, the wider is its spectrum of individual variation and social differentiation. This leads to the loosening of community ties, increased social competition, anonymity and a multiplication of interactions, often at low levels of intensity and trust. Direct participation and involvement in social affairs is no longer possible; instead systems of representation have to evolve.

- *Density* reinforces differentiation as, paradoxically, the closer one is physically to one's fellow city dwellers, the more distant are one's social contacts. There is an increasing indifference to anything that does not fulfil individual objectives and this can lead to combative, aggressive attitudes.

- *Heterogeneity* Echoing Durkheim's observations, Wirth suggested that social heterogeneity in ethnic and class terms promotes rapid social mobility.

Membership of groups is unstable as it is linked to the temporary interests of each individual. There is therefore a predominance of *association* (people linking up to further their rational goals) over *community* (a grouping based on descent or long-held status).

In addition to its work on the character of urban culture, the Chicago School is also famous for its notion of the 'ecology' (not what we would nowadays call ecology), or 'zoning' of the city. Essentially, what Park, Burgess and their colleagues sought to do was to show how physical space was related to social space. Their model was based on a set of concentric rings:

- In the centre, large stores, office blocks, theatres and hotels marked the central business district.
- The next ring was the 'zone of transition', with inner-city slums, small industry and areas of urban decay (known in the USA as 'skid row').
- Moving out one ring, we have the zone of the respectable working class, with corner stores, modest but clean dwelling and schools.
- Better family residences and attractive, middle-priced apartment blocks marked the next ring.
- Finally, in a looser, surrounding zone, commuters lived in suburban settings with detached plots, often with big gardens.

The model is not to be read too literally. Not every industrial city has exactly the same profile. For example, urban planners often augment other pressures to counteract inner city decay by encouraging the building of high-income apartments in the central business district, a process known as **GENTRIFICATION**. Nonetheless, with some adaptation, the Chicago school's ecological zone model has continued to provide a useful sociological tool for understanding how big cities work and develop.

> **Major Concept**
>
> **GENTRIFICATION**
>
> *Gentrification is the process whereby run-down inner city areas experience physical and economic regeneration – with a growth of small businesses, theatres, cafes and improved living areas. This may result from the influx of 'trendy' middle-class intellectuals and professionals in the media, the arts or education who then refurbish the old housing stock (see Zukin's study (1981) of loft-living in Greenwich Village, New York). Alternatively the process can arise from the deliberate attempt by landlords, property developers and governments to push new capital investment into entire areas.*

THE NOTION OF A GLOBAL CITY

The most important idea expressing the ways in which power has become spatially redistributed is the notion of a 'global city'. There is no significant distinction between the term 'world city', preferred by some authors and 'global city' preferred by others, although the latter is now more common. John Friedman (1986) first helped to delineate the key characteristics of a world city. He argued that the spatial organization of the new international division of labour required a new way of understanding the role of certain cities. In particular, they embodied a key contradiction between the politics, which still operated on a territorial basis, and economics, which increasing functioned at a global level. Social conflict arose within cities as a consequence of this tug of war. These initial ideas led Friedman to develop what he called a 'world city hypothesis'; an intervention better described as a set of seven propositions:

1. The extent to which a city is integrated into the global economy affects the physical form of the city and the nature of its labour and capital markets.
2. Key cities throughout the world are used as 'basing points' by global capital, the cities themselves being arranged in a 'complex spatial hierarchy'.

3. World cities perform different 'control functions'.
4. World cities are sites for the concentration and accumulation of capital.
5. World cities are destination points for internal and international migrants.
6. Spatial and class polarization is likely in a world city.
7. The social costs generated in world cities exceed the fiscal (tax-raising) capacity of the domestic state.

Box 15.1   African American migration to the North

Cities in the US North, such as Chicago and Detroit, gained their importance at the turn of the twentieth century because of their industrial strengths – Chicago was the centre of the railways, the stockyards and meat-packing industries, while Detroit evolved into the main site of the motorcar and associated industries.

The social heterogeneity of such cities was based on immigration from many European countries and also from the US South. African Americans leaving the South are one of 'the largest and most rapid mass internal movements of people in history – perhaps the greatest not caused by the immediate threat of execution or starvation' (Lemann 1991: 6).

■ 1865–1900 Jim Crow laws promoting segregation were passed after the Civil War in the South. (Jim Crow was a derogatory name for a feeble-minded African American.) The basic mechanism for production (slavery) was destroyed, while embryonic cities in the South were devastated.

■ 1900–1930 Beginning of the boll-weevil infestation, which affected cotton plants. This hit black farmers particularly hard as most were tenants not owners and found it difficult to switch to alternative crops. Most African Americans were driven off their land – to the newly emerging cities of the South, to non-infested areas and finally to the North.

■ 1920–1930 Severe agricultural depression due to overproduction of cotton worldwide. Both blacks and whites were affected.

■ 1930–1950 Precipitous decline of agriculture. Bankruptcy for many farmers and even the big plantation owners. Tenants become part-time hands, or had to migrate North.

■ 1950s to 1970s Displacement of hands through the spread of mechanical cotton-picking.

Fortunately for the departing migrants from the South, during the First World War there was a labour shortage in the industrial North — particularly in the stockyards, the meat-packing industries in Chicago, in transport (where black were employed on the Pullman cars) and in the steelyards. African American songs of this period describe the 'great black migration'. Here are verses from two:

Some are coming on the freight
Some are coming on the passenger
Others will be found walking
For none have time to wait.

I'm tired of this Jim Crow; gonna leave this Jim Crow town
Doggone my black soul, I'm sweet Chicago bound...

Of the 109 000 African Americans in Chicago in 1920, 90 000 had been born in other states, most in the South.

Culturally, this migration led to the most important and influential musical expression since the development of European classical music. Think, for example, of jazz, bop, bebop, Motown (after the 'motor town' of Detroit) and urban blues – including the distinctive sounds of Chicago and Kansas City blues.

Sources: Fligstein (1981); Lemann (1991)

Map 15.1 shows the connections and tiered relationships between world cities as proposed by Friedman.

The world city hypothesis has generated considerable discussion in the literature, notably in Sassen (1991, 1995) and Knox and Taylor (1995). These authors have also considerably extended the notion of a global city in new directions. Their views can be summarized in the following propositions:

1. The corporate headquarters of the major TNCs are based in the global cities. Although as we have seen earlier in this book TNCs are freeing themselves from their territorial origins, there are nonetheless important advantages for a city hosting TNCs' headquarters. The employment they provide is valuable, the TNCs attract important clients for conferences and business meetings and there is a general political pay-off in having another centre of power in a particular city.

2. All the primary cities are based in rich industrial countries. Perhaps the most notable examples are New York, London and Tokyo, which form a West–East axis of tremendous financial power through the strength of their markets.

3. The location of corporate headquarters and stock exchanges is paralleled by the location of the major banks, insurance houses and pension fund managers. A mutually reinforcing economic agglomeration develops in a global city.

4. Within each regional cluster (American, Asian, European) there is a relatively clear relationship between a primary city and its surrounding cluster of small cities. The American cluster comprises the core cities of Los Angles, New York and Chicago. The Asian core is on an axis between Tokyo and Singapore. The European system is London–Paris and the Rhine Valley. Other cities are arranged in a complex hierarchy to these major centres.

5. Global cities are assigned a specialized place in the global international division of labour. This place is sometimes, but not necessarily, coincidental with their administrative centrality. For example, London, Paris, Tokyo, Seoul, Geneva, Stockholm, Copenhagen and Mexico City are global cities and capital cities. However, the global city in Australia is Sydney not Canberra. In South Africa it is Johannesburg not Pretoria; in Canada Toronto and Montreal are global cities, not Ottawa; in Italy Milan qualifies but Rome does not, and so on. These disjunctures are important as they show the capacity of global capital to depart from the old political, religious and administrative logic that informed the choice of the capital city and instead affect an intimate tie with the city with the most appropriate global features.

6. Some cities serve primarily the function of corporate headquarters, some are financial centres, some are political capitals and some are key national centres of economic activity. However, in the long run global cities bring these functions together.

7. Global cities are centres of global transport. A number, for instance Hong Kong, Sydney, Singapore, New York, evolved from their old mercantile functions as natural harbours and ports. But air transport has largely superseded this constraint and there are some cities that have developed themselves as turnpikes for the principal airlines.

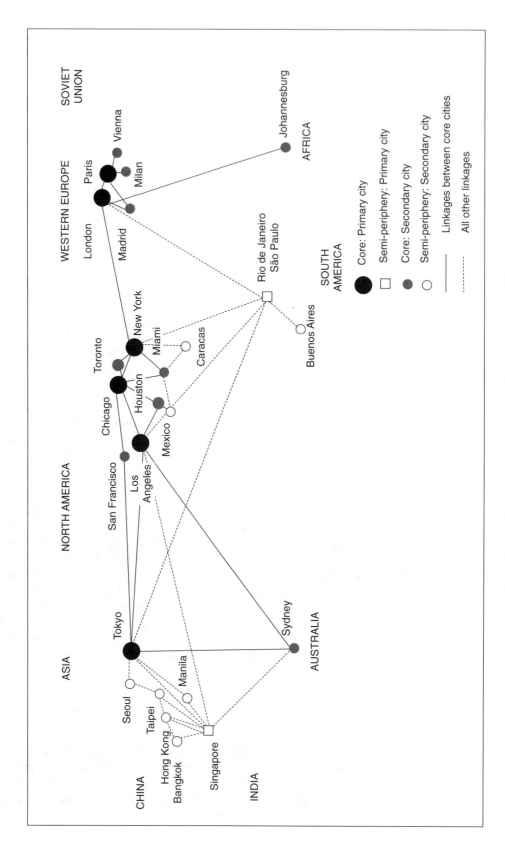

Map 15.1   The hierarchy of world cities (Friedman, 1986)

8. All global cities are densely connected by air to other global cities. The easiest way to comprehend this is to imagine you are in an aircraft and have just opened the airline map lodged in the pocket in front of you. You notice the thin filaments that arc over the globe. Suppose you overlay ten such maps of the leading carriers, you would then have an effective map of the global cities. Of course United Airlines would cluster in Chicago, British Airways in London, Cathay Pacific in Hong Kong – but the collective effect would be to show intense clumping around certain points. Traffic is extraordinarily dense. In the case of London planes leave Heathrow (the biggest of these three airports) every 2–3 minutes while the airport recorded a turnstile figure in 1996 of over 55 million passengers – about a third of these people using Heathrow as the transit and switching point to other destinations.

9. Global cities are centres of communications. Again it is possible to measure this through the density of traffic on the phone, fax, telex and Internet lines, and again the same pattern occurs. Starting in 1985 London's six digits became seven; that will soon increase to eight. A two-digit code (01) moved to two three digit codes (071 and 081) and now to two four-digit codes (0171 and 0181) as the number and density of traffic have increased.

10. Global cities are centre of information, news bureaux and agencies, entertainment and cultural products. TV and recording studios are there, as are many of the major book publishers, magazines and newspapers.

11. As well as being centres for the accumulation of domestic capital the global city becomes the centre for the attraction of foreign, although rarely speculative, capital. Typically, the financial institutions of a global city do not compete too brazenly with the known harbours for 'hot money' (the Cayman Islands, Bermuda or Curaçao) lest they lose their reputation for stability and probity. Rather global cities tend to attract long-term capital investments from all over the world.

The outcome of these further eleven features is, as Friedman had already suggested, that global cities become progressively more integrated to other global cities usually at the expense of their relationship to their hinterland. As transactions and interactions between the global cities intensify they lose their roles as administrative capitals while assuming more global, financial and cultural roles.

The integration of the global cities one with another and the relative lack of connection with their provincial cities and hinterlands was made possible by technological changes as well as by the dwindling importance of the military function of the nation state system. The first factor refers to issues that we discuss elsewhere in this book – the enhancement of electronic communications, the development of cheap travel, the capacity to deskill and internationalize certain jobs through relocation and subcontracting and the consolidation of a global financial market. The second is more nuanced. Of course there are still many powerful cities located within militarily powerful nation states. But the end of the Second World War showed that there was another crucial means of world expansion – through economic might alone. Both Japan and Germany had been forbidden to rearm; yet both have attained a considerable hold on world markets without the threat of force. Austria, Switzerland and Singapore have voluntarily refused to arm. The most powerful TNCs have also accomplished their economic feats without military muscle. These highly visible precedents of economic might without the expense and dangers of a military arsenal have created a pathway for others to follow. And first in line are the global cities who may reaffirm the economic role of the city states of old.

MIGRATION TO GLOBAL CITIES

The broadest change is that global cities become even more international and cosmopolitan than they already were. The languages spoken, the religions practised, the outlooks, consumption patterns, forms of dress and entertainment are drawn more from a multiplicity of cultures than from the national culture alone. Restaurants, music and theatre all are designed to appeal to the transitory visitors and short-term residents that populate the global cities.

International migration of a particular kind develops. 'Denizens' (privileged foreigners) arrive from other countries. Some are professional workers and managers, undertaking contract work for limited periods under the sponsorship of a TNC. Others are entrepreneurs who may be seeking a base for their operations but continue to hold dual (or multiple) citizenships and have residence rights in more than one country. Some of these denizen entrepreneurs have made spectacular inroads into the business élites of their countries of adoption. Egyptian-born Mohamed Al Fayed, whose son dated the late Princess Diana and was killed in a car accident with her, owns the famous store Harrods in London's Knightsbridge. Other notable denizens operating in London are Dickson Poon and David Tang (Box 15.2).

Box 15.2   Messrs Poon and Tang take London by storm

The new Chinese élite in London rather looks down on the people of Chinatown as being of an unsophisticated earlier generation, who sometimes cannot speak English. Their own English was learnt in the posh schools of Hong Kong or the public (that is very private) schools of England where, it is said, there is a quota on the Chinese entrants knocking at the doors.

Thomson (1997) reported that one of the leading Chinese cosmopolitans is **Dickson Poon**, the grandson of a rice farmer, the son of stockbrokers and a graduate of Uppingham public school and the University of California. After borrowing half-a-million pounds from his father he established the exclusive rights to import certain western luxury goods to Hong Kong. In the dog days of Empire the wealthy residents of Hong Kong feared an austere mood from Beijing on the return of the colony. They spent money with wild abandon. Poon, by 1987 the owner of S. T. Dupont, the French manufacturer of gold pens and lighters, profited mightily from this mood.

In 1991 he made his boldest move, buying the upper class, but loss-making British firm, Harvey Nichols. The store has always been a Mecca for Hong Kongers of Poon's background – with its distinctively restrained British style. Turning this 'frayed-at-the-edges' store into 'Europe's most slickly packaged emporium in the middle of the recession is one of the great retail feats of the 1990s. It is also the work of a man who glides effortlessly between two worlds'.

(cont'd)

Poon has also started a chain of restaurants in London named after himself. Conspicu-ously he has avoided Chinatown, preferring instead to set out his wares in Covent Garden and near the City, where he can cater to high spending 'City oafs'.

Someone with an even higher profile is **David Tang**, the grandson of one of Hong Kong's greatest magnates, S. K. Tang. While he was still a student in London in the 1970s he lost his flat gambling in one of London's smart clubs, the Clermont. By 1996 he opened his own club in Beijing catering to the local yuppies. To launch the club in style he flew out 'the cream of London society'. He has more substantial talents too, having taught philosophy at Beijing University and given classical piano recitals for charity.

Tang also managed to create a London fashion in colourful Mao Zedong jackets, made in velvet, which he sells in the Shanghai Tang shop in Hong Kong.

Source and all quotations: Thomson (1997)

However, by no means all immigrants from abroad are highly skilled or priv-ileged. Entertainers, waiters and waitresses, prostitutes, maids, chauffeurs and nurses are also attracted to the global cities. The indigenous labour force has deserted some of these occupations, but employers often prefer foreign workers because they can exploit them more. Students and visitors 'overstay' or ignore the entry conditions on their visas. Illegal entrants and asylum seekers may also be desperate to secure any kind of employment, however demeaning or badly paid. The fear that they may be reported to the immigration authorities gives the employers the whip hand in demanding compliance to their demands. Sometimes illegal migrants work in conditions little better than slavery.

CHANGES IN THE OCCUPATIONAL STRUCTURE

The new international division of labour generates important changes in the occupational structure in all regions, but many of these changes are more visible and more marked in the global cities. In general, we see a strong shift from industrial to service- and information-related employment.

Work is often informalized and subcontracted in increasing conformity to the fluid, flexible work arrangements required by the global economy. By contrast, work in the unionized, high-wage sectors is either gradually or dramatically destroyed. One example of the sudden collapse of an occupational sector is the case of the workers in the newspaper industry in London. In the 1980s, print workers were highly organized, demanded a high level of control over the allo-cation of tasks and were beneficiaries of generous wages and working condi-tions. Nonetheless they were destroyed by Rupert Murdoch's organization, News Corporation. Using a combination of guile and force the company moved most of its titles from Fleet Street to Wapping, adopted new technologies (with the effect of eliminating the role of the compositors and typesetters) and subcon-tracted the distribution of the papers to a non-unionized transport company.

Other changes are seen in the running down of the nationalized or munici-palized industries and public services in favour of consumer led- and insurance-supported services. These include private transport, health care and housing. Even schools and universities are forced to bow to the unyielding impress of the global marketplace. Many schools have to secure business spon-sorship to provide basic facilities like laboratories, while universities have to recruit fee-paying overseas students to maintain their libraries and pay their lecturers. Such is the extent of denationalization that in several countries prison and immigration services are subcontracted. One police force in England persuaded McDonald's to sponsor its patrol vehicles while highly trained and state-certified air traffic controllers in the USA were fired to make way for cheaper, less qualified, colleagues.

The cumulative effect of these occupational changes became particularly visible in the global cities from the 1970s onwards, when substantial losses in manufacturing were accompanied by substantial gains in services (Table 15.1).

Table 15.1   Distribution of employment in New York, London and Tokyo, 1970s and 80s (% of total)

New York	1977	1981	1985
Manufacturing	21.9	18.7	15.4
Services	28.4	31.8	36.3
Wholesale/retail	19.4	20.2	20.2
London	1977	1981	1985
Manufacturing	22.0	19.2	16.0
Services	49.6	40.1	39.8
Wholesale/retail	13.5	19.2	20.5
Tokyo	1975	1980	1985
Manufacturing	25.1	23.5	22.0
Services	20.6	22.7	25.3
Wholesale/retail	27.5	28.5	28.4

Source: Sassen (1991: 109)

THE FEMINIZATION OF EMPLOYMENT

As we have seen the increased entry of women into the labour market is a feature of the global post-Fordist environment, but it is particularly notable in the global cities where fashion, clerical and services occupations are concen-trated. Even though they have gained a stronger foothold in employment, many women workers are paid less than their male equivalents and have highly inse-cure conditions of employment. One important example of the feminization of employment is in the garment and fashion industries, an activity that feeds off an international clientele. It is no coincidence that Hong Kong, Paris, London, New York and Milan are all global cities and the key global fashion centres with the most prestigious catwalks. The glamorous pictures of models reproduced in the women's magazines are supported by a very seamy underside of sweat-shops, low pay, exploitation (normally of women workers) and the hiring of illegal workers to reduce costs. Homeworkers who, Phizacklea (1992: 109) notes, occupy the lowest rung in the clothing industry

> serve as a buffer function for contractors with an erratic flow of work. If there is a rush order or a full book they will receive work, if there is not, they receive nothing. Their rate of pay is exceedingly low... The vast majority of homeworkers are women confined to the home because of domestic responsibilities, particularly the care of pre-school children. Most fail to recognize the hidden costs involved in home-working, which include the purchase or hire of their own machine and running costs. Most homeworking is 'off the book' and a completely precarious occupation.

Homeworkers also address envelopes, perform routine clerical tasks via the Internet or act as remote outposts of 'calling centres'. (Calling centres are linked telephone networks providing directory enquiries and information on timeta-bles, flight prices and products for sale.) Because the 'real' cost of telephone calls (as opposed to what the consumer pays) is now equalizing internationally, calls for big businesses are now often stacked globally with homeworkers' numbers being activated in sequence wherever they happen to be. Bemused customers using their telephone in Milan and wanting to travel on British Airways from Bristol to Newcastle may find their bookings dealt with by a homeworker in New York or Bombay.

Figure 15.2   By August 1999, there were 3000 Internet cafés worldwide providing connectivity to people on the move

The ubiquitous forms of service employment, which are statistically increasingly significant, tend to concentrate employment in the global cities. Low-paid domestic workers – acting as cleaners, hotel and restaurant workers or at checkout counters – are often female. Somewhat better white-collar employment is also available to women as sales personnel in department stores and boutiques, office workers (particularly entering data) and in estate agencies, banks and advertising. Because women historically colonized office work (as typists, telephonists and clerks) with the switch to more information-related employment they are often at an advantage in the labour market. Although their pay and conditions do not often match male workers, in a number of global cities there are now more females than males in paid employment.

REGIONALIZATION AND THE GLOBAL CITY

There is tendency for the *regional* role of certain major cities to be augmented – an enhancement that is often overlooked in the discussion of *global* cities. At least in the medium term, geography is not yet history for many cities. Los Angeles remains the dominant entry point for trans-Pacific migrants, Mexicans and South Americans. New York receives many immigrants from the Caribbean archipelago. Berlin, particularly after the massive redevelopment of the city, will form the hinge between Western and Eastern Europe. Eighty-one per cent of Finnish emigrants head for Sweden, most of them for Stockholm. With its new fixed link, London and Paris are conjoining in a single axial point in Northern Europe, adding a new dimension to their roles as capital cities. Brussels links the Benelux countries. Miami has become the shopping capital and most desirable entry point for migrants from the Caribbean area, especially from the Spanish-speaking Caribbean – Latinos have more than doubled their share of the city's population in the last half century and now form the majority. As Grosfoguel (1995: 164) ironically notes: 'Today Miami is a bilingual city where you can find more stores with signs saying "We speak English" than those saying *"Se habla español"*'.

Just as some cities are regionalizing across frontiers, others are blending their functions and dissolving their boundaries with countries. This is partly because of the accident of geographical proximity, partly because of conscious design. Randstad (the grouping of Amsterdam, Rotterdam, Utrecht and The Hague) is a good example of this development. The addition of Orange, San Bernadino, Riverside and Ventura counties to the core of Los Angeles provides another. Los Angeles now extends over 53,136 square kilometres (Waldinger and Bozorgmehr 1996: 5). The cities of Leeds, Bradford, Sheffield and Manchester in the north of England also form a continuous urban chain linked by motorways.

RACE, THE CITY AND THE US UNDERCLASS

In cities like Los Angeles (see Box 15.3) and Miami, newcomers often edge out or further constrain established minorities such as the African Americans. Some of this last group are often called an 'underclass' – referring to a notion that there is a stratum below that of the proletariat. Many post-Marxist writers have

> **Box 15.3   Los Angeles: the making of a global city**
>
> Los Angeles, 'the City of Angels', is almost twice as large as New York, San Francisco, Chicago and Philadelphia and almost four times the size of Miami. The city has been described as a 'fragmented metropolis' because of its immense sprawl. Tourism, the Hollywood film industry, then a heavy manufacturing base – often depending on Defence contracts – started the flow of immigrants to the city from other parts of the USA, from neighbouring Mexico, but also from across the Pacific. In population terms the result was spectacular. At the turn of the century Los Angeles had 100 000 residents, by 1930 it had added another 2.2 million people. Thirty years on, in 1960 there were 6 million people while at the last census, in 1990 there were 14.5 million people. In population terms, Los Angeles is just behind New York, but if the growth continues its population will soon exceed New York's.
>
> The city partly evolved, and was partly designed, as a chain of low-density suburban settlements linking the valleys that mark the topography of the area. Leading architects were fascinated by this form of urban settlement and praised it for its human scale. However, the logic of a global city soon took over and a 'Downtown' developed – with insurance companies and banks moving in to create new skyscrapers. Much of this investment came from Japanese firms who were riding a massive boom in the 1980s. The old height restrictions of the area were ignored and new high-rise buildings proliferated. One Japanese company, Shuwa, purchased $1 billion's worth of property in a two-and-a-half-month buying spree. The directors of Shuwa 'following the tradition of bringing gifts to new neighbours' made massive donations to the Ronald Reagan Library and to a political campaign run by Major Bradley. He reciprocated by denouncing anyone who objected to the assertion of Japanese economic muscle as a 'racist'. In an allusion to Japan's wartime effort to turn Asian countries they had conquered into a Japanese 'co-prosperity zone', Davis (1991) refers to the Japanese financial involvement in Los Angeles as a 'Pacific co-prosperity zone'.
>
> Although the economic downturn in Japan during the 1990s has mitigated fears of Japanese domination, there is no doubt that Los Angeles provides a key bridge from America across the Pacific to the global cities of Tokyo, Taipei, Hong Kong, Shanghai and Singapore. This is reflected in the changing ethnic composition of the city. For many years the city has been a magnet for migrants from Mexico to whom were added other central Americans tempted by the lure of *el norte.* From the 1980s, however, the city began to attract high-skilled, foreign-born arrivals (we called this group 'denizens'), often from Asia. Waldinger and Bozorgmehr (1996: 16) describe the ethnic mix as follows:
>
> 'Starting from a relatively small base in 1970 the Asian population skyrocketed; as immigrants from China, the Philippines, Korea, Vietnam, and India (in that order) poured into the region. Asians emerged as LA's third largest group, outnumbering the previously established African American population. The newcomers transformed Los Angeles into the capital of contemporary Asian America, pushing it well beyond the other major Asian American centers of New York, San-Francisco-Oakland and Honolulu… [T]he new Asians became a source of extraordinary high-skilled labor, importing school levels that left natives far behind as well as other endowments like capital and entrepreneurial talents that gave them a competitive edge'.
>
> *Sources:* Davis (1991: 134–40); Waldinger and Bozorgmehr (1996: 5–8, 16)

advanced this idea. As we saw in Chapter 8, for example, Fanon (1967), writing about the anti-colonial struggles in Africa, argued that Marx had underestimated the persistence of the peasantry, but more particularly the potential political importance of those who had moved into the colonial towns and capitals as unemployed and underemployed job-seekers. Even using the expression 'workers' for such people was inappropriate, as they were unlikely ever to find work. Fanon uses Marx's expression 'the Lumpenproletariat', but assigned them the role of an 'urban spearhead' to a revolution based in the countryside. Other authors have used the expression 'subproletariat' or 'peasantariat' to get away from some of the negative connotations of the Lumpenproletariat.

Black Power

A lot of this thinking, particularly that of Fanon, was emulated by the Black Power movement in the USA in the 1970s. They saw the black population as in a quasi-colonial state, with the black ghettos being functional equivalents to the European colonies abroad. There, as in the USA, people of African descent were treated as a racially inferior species. There, too, blacks were treated as a labour reservoir that could be drawn on only as and when needed – and otherwise left to rot. The only difference was that the colonies were internal, rather than external. Huey Newton, Malcolm X, Bobby Seale and Angela Davis – leaders of the Black Power and Black Panther movements in the USA – were all influenced by this view to a greater or lesser extent. The movement turned to violence, but this was limited and contained and tended to involve parades in black berets, training in unarmed combat and bellicose posturing with the authorities (and with truculent whites) on the street.

Black Muslims

A different response, but one stemming from a similar view of the issues confronting the urban black population, was seen in the creation of the Black Muslims. Adherents rejected Christianity in general, which was identified with slavery, missionaries and colonialism. However, the Black Muslims objected in particular to the passive ('turn the other cheek') and deferred ('pie in the sky when you die') forms of Christianity. Many blacks changed the names they had inherited from the slave owners to Islamic names. The boxer Cassius Clay, for example, became Mohammed Ali. Mosques were established in most of the black ghettos and highly disciplined congregants and believers collected money for community projects, self-improvement schemes and black enterprises. Those on the political left were very wary of this response to urban deprivation and denounced it as 'black capitalism'. It was nonetheless a powerful means of gaining dignity and self-respect for a small minority of the African American population. The movement probably gained its apogee in the 'Million-Man' march in Washington in October 1995, which was led by Louis Farrakan, the Black Muslim leader.

The current US debate: Auletta's views

The terms of the current US debate about race and urban deprivation have been set by Ken Auletta's book, *The Underclass* (1982) and by William J. Wilson in his influential books, *The Declining Significance of Race* (1978) and *The Truly Disadvantaged* (1987). The common theme to these accounts is that race and racism played a small or at least declining role in the formation of a growing black underclass of unemployed people which, according to most authors, numbers about one-third of the black population.

How is this phenomenon to be explained? Auletta (1982) asserts that deviant and criminal tendencies are common in the urban black underclass, that there is apathy towards training, education and vocational guidance and hostility towards self-improvement and the work ethic. Young women in the black underclass are, he claims, prone to producing large numbers of children at a disproportionately young age. Males and females are generally dependent on welfare or charity. There is something in this argument that resembles earlier arguments by Oscar Lewis (1968) who had intensively studied a poor family's life in San Juan, Puerto Rico – out of which study had been generated the famous, some would say notorious, notion of a 'culture of poverty'.

There are many problems with this line of argument. One is that even if the observations are true, researchers can easily confuse cause with consequence. Culture may be a dependent, not an independent variable (that is it could be an outcome of other non-considered factors). Long-term unemployment may condition attitudes and generate feelings of resignation, acceptance or despair. Racial discrimination may likewise generate such attitudes. The lack of motivation and the work ethic may in fact be relatively healthy responses to an impossible situation of rejection and restricted or non-existent opportunities. If, to turn the argument around, many members of the underclass had optimistic, driving, ambitious, competitive attitudes, they may be expressing a pathology – that is holding an ideology that had no relationship to reality. A culture or sub-culture of poverty may therefore be a healthy and adaptive response to an irremediable situation.

Wilson's views on the underclass

A more influential line of argument has been initiated by William J. Wilson, who was the first systematically to show the extent to which the black community in the USA had become bifurcated along class lines (thus his expression 'the declining significance of race'). He talks, for example of a 'deepening economic schism' in the black community, leading to two outcomes:

1. Talented and educated blacks experience rapid upward mobility comparable to that of whites of similar qualifications. He is not so naive as to suggest that the experience of racism is totally absent for this group. He is also happy to concede that affirmative action (or 'equal opportunities') programmes have helped this top band in their goals. However, he insists that it is *outcome* that is important. Either through their determined efforts to resist discrimination or through the help of affirmative action, the black élite is 'making it'.

2. With regard to the bottom one-third of the black urban population, the underclass, Wilson documents the increasing rates of crime, the increasing number of families headed by low-earning or non-earning females, the rising number on welfare, the large number who lack formal training and skills and the consequent extent of black unemployment.

If we take this list of negative attributes, he continues, the black underclass shows more in common with the white underclass rather than with the rest of the black community. This is the second sense in which there is a 'declining significance of race'. In short, the top band of blacks resembles its white counterparts, just as the bottom band does.

Fainstein's critique of Wilson

Wilson happens himself to be black and was formerly a distinguished member of the sociology department at the University of Chicago. The only significance of his background is that Wilson's views created a storm of counter arguments, particularly among black scholars, who saw him as denying the significance of racial discrimination, denying his own background and indeed painting the situation with 'whitewash'. Nearly all this criticism tended to be misplaced, as it was based on ideological, not sociological, premises. However, Norman Fainstein (1992), who sought to challenge the empirical basis of Wilson's argument, provided a more powerful critique. Using complex statistical data, from the US Census he advances two suggestions:

1. Over the period 1960–83 there is a slow convergence between black and white in educational attainments, although a gap remains. The high achievers are not closing the gap at the rate we would expect from Wilson's thesis, while the low achievers (for example, the percentage with less than four years of high school) are narrowing the gap with their white counterparts.

2. With respect to income, the data lend support to Wilson's thesis. Over the period 1960–83, the poorest African Americans get poorer and the richest get richer, but the trend is very gradual rather than, as Wilson implied, a sharp bifurcation.

Mismatch theory

Is the persistence of a black underclass due to a *mismatch* between the skills black people have and the available opportunities? The theory is that an important proportion of the African American population are in the wrong place with the wrong skills and experience. Kasarda (cited Fainstein 1992: 297–8) is particularly associated with the four-pronged argument that:

1. Jobs with low education requirements are disappearing from the city centre, but blacks in the inner city are particularly dependent on such jobs.

2. They do not have the educational attainments to compete in the knowledge-intensive industries.

3. They cannot get to low-paying suburban jobs as they are dependent on cars and as public transport is poorly developed.

4. They are unwilling to move south or south-west where there are jobs, because they want to retain their benefit dependency in the high-benefit cities of the north-east (where they are partly protected by black politicians).

Fainstein (1992) again questions this argument in fine detail, but more generally suggests that it is not consistent with the actual structure of black employment. In fact blacks are not over-represented in construction, manufacturing and retail trade as the mismatch theorists had argued. They are no more dependent than whites are on manufacturing and are considerably less dependent in respect of construction and retail trade. They are, on the other hand, over-represented in services including hospitals, health care, schools and college. This clearly would expose African Americans to the cuts in public service associated with neo-liberalism.

Despite this dangerous dependence on jobs in the public sector, Fainstein is of the view that the problems of getting employment at all are more important than black under-representation or overrepresentation in any one segment of the labour market. In short, when all is said black under-performance and the continued and even growing underclass have to be explained by racism and racial discrimination. Blacks are not getting jobs because they are black.

REVIEW

While many cities owe their significance to the rise of modernity in Europe, others were developed – warts and all – in the wake of colonial expansion. As people were pushed or walked off the land, the cities of the colonial world swelled, but often failed to provide the employment opportunities associated with mass industrialization. These 'cities of peasants', as well as successful industrial cities like Chicago, have provided the grist to many a sociologist's mill. It may be that the economic, political and technological conditions characteristic of the cities of the global age will provide similarly important sites for sociological analysis.

Global cities are not only important phenomena in their own right, they are where certain distinctive patterns of employment emerge – in particular the move from manufacturing to services. Employment often becomes 'feminized' as old male-dominated skills are discarded and new labour markets formed. New kinds of people, of different ethnic backgrounds and with cosmopolitan outlooks and connections to several countries, enter the global city and often succeed in their quest for social mobility. By contrast, established racial minorities are often marginalized and turned into a so-called 'underclass'.

If you would like to know more ●

Bryan Roberts's *Cities of Peasants* (1978) provides a good account of cities in Latin America.

John Friedman (1986) 'The world city hypothesis', *Development and Change*, 17(1), 69–83 is the classic article with started the debate on global cities.

The most accomplished and extensive work on the theme of global cities is Saskia Sassen's (1991) *The Global City* which has a lot of detail on New York, Tokyo and London. Although lengthy, the book is not difficult and contains excellent data.

One of the US's most eminent sociologists is William J. Wilson, whose books, *The Declining Significance of Race* (1978) and *The Truly Disadvantaged* (1987), are landmarks in the study of deprivation in US cities.

Mike Davis's *City of Quartz* (1991) provides a prophetic left-wing critique of urban development in Los Angeles. A data-rich account of LA is given in Waldinger and Bozorgmehr's edited book, *Ethnic Los Angeles* (1996).

Group work ●●

1. Using the 'ecological' method of the Chicago School and a large photocopy of a map of a nearby city, describe and demarcate its different zones.

2. Split into three groups. Each group will draw up a list of 'global cities' in Europe, Asia or the Americas. Why did you include some and exclude others?

3. Draw of a list of which occupations women (a) dominate or (b) might dominate in the future. Why do you suppose this is the case?

4. What images do you have of Los Angeles? Studying one of the key chapter references on the city (or any recent book you can find in your library) list the ways in which your image differs from the account consulted.

5. Spilt into three groups to engage in the 'black underclass debate'. Group A will look at cultural explanations; Group B will look at the views of William J. Wilson; Group C will advance a 'mismatch theory'.

Questions to think about ●●●●●●●●●●●●●●●●●●●●●●●●●●●●●●●●●●●●●●●

1. What are the main differences between a colonial, industrial and global city (bearing in mind that individual cities might have 'migrated' across these categories)?

2. Why were cities so important to the pre-1945 sociologists?

3. Can global cities detach themselves from the national states in which they find themselves?

4. Why is employment becoming 'feminized' in some cities?

5. What accounts for the continuing under-performance of about one-third of African Americans?

part four

Dynamics and Challenges

chapter 16

Explaining Social Movements

Social movements are agencies of social transformation that emerge in response to certain social changes and conditions. They are also manifestations of popular sentiment and in this they overlap with numerous other kinds of social activity. This means that it is quite difficult to know where a social movement begins and ends. As Wilson (1973: 13) suggested, perhaps it goes too far to include fraternities, youth groups, political parties, sects, nudists, voluntary associations, guerrilla organizations, cool jazz or beat literature under the rubric of 'social movements'. Yet, he continues (p. 5), it is impossible to ignore the influence of such individuals as the Suffragette, the Abolitionist, the Prohibitionist, the Pentecostal, the Black militant or the peace marcher. Even the flying-saucer spotter, the flat-earther, the sabbatarian and the Satanist have managed to attractive sizeable numbers of dedicated followers.

In this chapter we first consider the attempts to theorize the general nature of social movements, especially as they evolved from the 1960s, while discussing concrete examples whenever possible. We then examine why and in what ways some social movements have become increasingly transnational in their orientations. We will call these 'global social movements'. The relationship of global social movements to international non-governmental organizations (INGOs) is complex, as the latter often 'nest' within the former, without being co-terminous with them. We conclude this chapter by arguing that global social movements are vital to our wider understanding of the ways in which global society is being built from below. Our discussion in this chapter will serve to introduce our subsequent two chapters – where the women's and green movements will be considered in detail.

Figure 16.1   A rally of 'Solidarity', the Polish social and labour movement, 1989

DEFINING SOCIAL MOVEMENTS

Given the many aspects of social life covered by the expression 'social movements' you will not be surprised to learn that there is a plethora of definitions and descriptions.

We can start with Wilson's (1973: 8) prosaic definition: 'A social movement is a conscious, collective, organized attempt to bring about or resist large-scale change in the social order by non-institutionalized means.' He prefaces this formal definition with a more imaginative characterization: 'Social movements nurture both heroes and clowns, fanatics and fools... Animated by the injustices, sufferings, and anxieties they see around them, men and women in social movements reach beyond the customary resources of the social order to launch their own crusade against the evils of society. In so doing they reach beyond themselves and become new men and women' (p. 5).

More recent definitions include that of Byrne (1997: 10–11). For him social movements are:

● unpredictable (for example, women's movements do not always arise where women are most oppressed)

- irrational (adherents do not act out of self-interest)
- unreasonable (adherents think they are justified in flouting the law)
- disorganized (some avoid formalizing their organization even when it seems like a good idea to do so).

Finally, we can refer to Zirakzadeh (1997: 4–5) who suggests that a social movement:

- is a group of people who consciously attempt to build a radically new social order
- involves people of a broad range of social backgrounds
- deploys politically confrontational and socially disruptive tactics.

Figure 16.2   The student movement in Indonesia celebrates the removal of President Suharto, 1998

Major Concept

POST-INDUSTRIAL SOCIETY

Refers to societies where the service industries – including the knowledge-, media- and information-based sectors – have become the most important source of wealth and employment. Accompanying this, there-fore, is a relative decline in the contribution of manu-facturing industry to national wealth, a fall in the numbers of manual workers, a huge expansion of university or tertiary education and a growing middle class.

RECENT SOCIAL MOVEMENTS

Many scholars who have written about social movements in the advanced countries argue that they underwent a sea change from the late 1960s onwards. As with all social movements this was apparently linked to certain underlying changes evident in the industrialized countries from around that time. Touraine (1981) tried to capture the outcome of these changes with the term **POST-INDUSTRIAL SOCIETY,** which saw an occupational shift away from manual work to the knowledge and service sector, including information technology, the media, fashion, design and even therapy and counselling services.

A related feature of post-industrial society was a growing middle class of public and private sector employees many working in the rising cultural, media and knowledge industries. Touraine contrasted the 'old' labour and political movements with the 'new' social movements that represented the interests of those working in emerging occupations. The question of whether there was a clear distinction between 'old' and 'new' movements was a lively debate for a while, but we are content with the view that nearly all the changes were more those of degree than of kind. Naturally, social movements respond to new realities and new social demands, but this is a different argument from the idea that they are totally new phenomena. Keeping this important point in mind, we now discuss four ways in which social movements have changed their orientations over recent decades:

- the switch to identity politics
- the rise of 'counter cultures'
- the questioning of authority
- the elevation of grass-roots activities.

The switch to identity politics

According to Giddens (1991: Chapter 7) throughout most of the period of modernization until the mid-twentieth century, social movements were generally concerned with what he calls 'emancipatory politics'. These were struggles against those structures and inequalities that constrained people's freedom to choose their own life experiences. Chief among these compulsions were the heavy weight of tradition (such as religious and customary obligations), material scarcity and poverty and the people's exclusion from access to legal and political rights or the same opportunities to attain wealth enjoyed by ruling groups.

Important examples of emancipatory politics were: the struggles to obtain universal suffrage, freedom of movement, assembly and opinion; the abolition of slavery in the USA and the European colonies; and the rights of workers to engage in free collective bargaining and to curb the worst excesses of exploitation by constructing a welfare state. All of these struggles required social movements to gain some degree of direct control over state power. Thus, workers and socialist movements not only formed trade unions, which could bargain more effectively with capitalists at the workplace, they also established political parties capable of assuming the reigns of government. Armed with such weapons, working classes eventually succeeded in curbing the excesses of capitalism so that it served the interests of the majority a little more fairly than before.

By contrast, contemporary social movements have been less interested in winning direct control over or access to state power. Nevertheless, during the last forty years or so, struggles to extend the full rights and opportunities already won by the majority of citizens to previously disadvantaged or excluded groups have continued to be fought everywhere, but especially in the developing countries. Sometimes, these demands have involved confrontations with the state. In the case of the advanced societies we should include here the social movements associated with the demands of women, religious or ethnic minorities (as in the case of the Civil Rights Movement in the USA during the 1960s), the needs of children and young people, and the struggles of gay and disabled people.

Returning to the main argument, Giddens pointed to a more important difference between earlier and more recent social movements. Thus, he (1991: 214–27) observed that the main focus of social movements has shifted to causes concerning what he calls 'life politics'. These raise the question of how exactly we might prefer to use emancipatory freedoms once they have been won – what kinds of personal and community life we might wish to construct – and what responsibilities individuals must exercise if the guarantee of universal freedom is to continue. Since we all depend on interpersonal relationships and each individual's freedom hinges on exactly how these are arranged, issues of self-realization and questions of personal identity inevitably come to the forefront of our concerns.

This has been particularly evident in the case of the feminist movement, which originated in the USA, swept across the western world in the early 1970s and has now penetrated most societies. As we have seen, feminism challenged patriarchy; the relegation of women to roles defined as culturally inferior. However, it has also gone much further than this by compelling women to confront the question of what kind of life course, values and personal identity they wish to build their lives around. Pressing questions for contemporary feminists include: the nature of sexuality and preferred sexual orientations; the control of biological reproduction (including abortion); who should be entitled to exercise rights over children; the terms on which marriage and other kinds of intimate relationships should be founded; and issues of representation and freedom of expression, such as pornography. Thus, political conflicts and processes have started to dissolve the boundaries between the private and public spheres.

Non-material values and 'counter cultures'

According to Inglehart (1990) and others, growing affluence and material security, associated with economic growth after the Second World War and the welfare reforms implemented by the social democracies at that time, encouraged many people to become much more concerned with the pursuit of non-material values together with more emphasis on issues concerned with their personal fulfilment and identities. This development of a **COUNTER CULTURE** also accounts for the declining appeal of radical, socialist ideas among many workers and others during the same period. Although they may have been in opposition to pro-capitalist parties, they were still seen as 'part of the system'.

Students were particularly associated with the counter cultural movement. A ground swell of student unrest, initially associated with the Civil Rights Movement in the USA, became evident from the early 1960s. This student movement spread to Europe and probably reached its high point during the events of May 1968. These events, in particular, appeared to validate Inglehart's thesis. Then, across Europe, workers, intellectuals and students held strikes and occupied college campuses and factories. They appeared to demonstrate against a society that produced what Marcuse (1968) – a Marxist intellectual living in the USA – called 'one-dimensional man'. In the eyes of many intellectuals this protest involved an attack on two features of industrial society:

1. The dehumanizing consequences of the bureaucratization of industry, government and higher education.

Major Concept

COUNTER CULTURE

Predominantly seen in the richer western countries in the 1960s and 70s, those involved in developing a counter culture opposed the dull, unreflective, self-congratulatory uniformity of conventional political values. They displayed a growing desire for more control over personal development, greater equity and fluidity in social relationships, a heightened respect for nature and promoted the revival of more decentralized, autonomous communities. A turn away from established religion towards eastern philosophies, experimentation with drugs, adventurous popular music and 'way-out' dress codes were also characteristic of the period.

2. The 'bargain' offered by post-war Fordist economies; namely the distorting emphasis placed on economic prosperity and acquisitiveness bought at the cost of relentless disempowerment at the workplace and the decline of community and cultural autonomy.

Box 16.1   Battles in cyberspace: Greenpeace against French nuclear testing

Background events

In June 1995, the French government decided to resume testing nuclear weapons in the South Pacific despite its earlier commitment to respect an international agreement on nuclear non-proliferation. Greenpeace had long campaigned against the French government's adherence to an out-dated view of national security needs fuelled by 'great power' aspirations. For example, Greenpeace had crossed swords with the French government in 1985 culminating in the sinking of the *Rainbow Warrior* ship by the French Navy.

Greenpeace's worldwide campaign: July 1995 to early 1996

During its campaign against the resumption of nuclear testing, Greenpeace operated on many fronts:

■ A petition was signed by more than five million people.

■ Demonstrations were organized around the world including one involving over 15 000 people in Tahiti who blocked roads and demanded that Greenpeace's leading ship be allowed to dock against the wishes of the French government.

■ Networks of supporting groups formed coalitions in many countries to influence world public opinion.

■ Australian public opinion was especially targeted. Here, past admiration for the bravery of Greenpeace warriors and proximity to the nuclear testing zone could be expected to generate strong pressure on the government to use diplomacy in order to oppose French activities.

■ Greenpeace sailed its fleet of five ships into the test area along with its helicopter, divers and several inflatable boats.

Greenpeace also exploited the latest techniques in communications technology

■ Numerous faxes were sent and satellite telephones kept the various campaign messages flowing constantly across the world.

■ Three ships were equipped with the most up-to-date communication systems and so were able to relay powerful images, including colour photos, via satellite.

■ Events were also filmed by helicopter, adding to the dramatic footage that was fed into the global media.

■ Meanwhile, the leading ship sent out messages on the Internet. This enabled individuals, groups and the media to pick up the information relayed by Greenpeace's on-the-spot warriors via its web site, established in 1994.

When the action began, with French commandos boarding *Rainbow Warrior II* and using tear gas against the protesters, the world was left in no doubt concerning the intensity of the South Pacific struggle. A global social movement had beaten one of the world's most powerful nation states, at least at the propaganda war.

Source: Cooper (1997)

Student discontent fed directly into an upsurge of counter cultural movements that soon spread across the western world including the hippy and drug cultures, the anti-Vietnam war movement of the late 1960s and early 1970s and the early stirrings of the green movement. A retreat from the repressive and materialistic lifestyles offered by mainstream consumerist capitalism also involved such things as the establishment of communes and co-operatives, an interest in organic farming and foods and experimenting with eastern philosophy and health practices.

Whether or not all or most students and others who participated in the events following May 1968 perceived it as a struggle against materialist values quite to the same degree as the intellectuals involved is open to debate. Again, in the light of more recent changes, the argument that most people's lives are no longer plagued by endemic economic insecurities now seems distinctly premature.

The questioning of authority

According to writers such as Giddens (1991) and Beck (1992; 1994) the spread of higher education and the developments in communication technology, among other changes, have enabled people in the advanced societies to become more knowledgeable about science, technology and the management of economic life than previously. At the same time, the ever increasing dangers incurred by nuclear energy and weaponry as well as by chemical and biological warfare have spurred many citizens to demand that governments, the military and business corporations relinquish their right to monopolize control over these areas.

The realization that some scientists and technologists had placed their expertise and public prestige at the service of such narrow and unaccountable interests further deepened these demands. The campaigns against the dangers of nuclear energy in North America and Europe, which gathered pace in the 1970s, can be regarded as a concrete expression of such sentiments (Joppke 1993). They also provided a foundation both for the peace movement, which erupted in a new form in the early 1980s in Europe, North America and the Soviet Union (see Box 16.3), and for the wider green movement which we discuss in Chapter 18.

Even the buttoned-up world of markets and business management, once regarded as out-of-bounds to ordinary citizens (except in their limited capacities as individual consumers or shareholders) has become increasingly exposed to detailed public scrutiny and liable to substantial criticism. This has become particularly evident in the case of large companies that decide to market green or ethical products (Kennedy 1996). Making such commercial claims both invites external validation by relevant campaigning groups and requires it. Indeed, such companies may find themselves sucked inexorably into engaging in educational and green-ethical consciousness-raising activities, in order to inform public opinion about their products, that are barely distinguishable from the overt campaigning in which explicitly political groups are engaged all the time.

The upsurge of European public anxiety concerning genetically modified crops and foods in the late 1990s is another case in point although here it remains to be seen whether and how far commercial interests will respond to public concern. Similarly, we are prepared to criticize the economic priorities employed by private companies, governments and IGOs such as the World Bank in their dealings with developing countries. Thus, there has been a demand for the democratization of decision-making in every sphere. Although such demands have not always been met the point is that citizens are no longer prepared to accept that there are legitimate areas of decision-making where they do not have every right to be fully informed and amply consulted.

The elevation of grass-roots activity

The post-1960s social movements have tended to be decentralized and non-hierarchical in mobilizing members for collective action, although there are exceptions to this such as Greenpeace and the African National Congress (ANC) in South Africa. Normally, social movements form loose federations of semi-autonomous groups, rely very much on grass-roots support based on networking activities and usually permit members to arrange their own priorities and strategies of protest. Of course, such practices may also lead to divisiveness within movements, indecision, lack of focus and poorly organized campaigns. Nevertheless, these characteristics allow social movements rapidly to adjust their mode of operations, respond to the constant rush of events, select new targets for mobilization and draw upon a heterogeneous and ever changing mix of supporters. By the same token, each social movement's focus of concern and band of support tends to coalesce and overlap with those of others. For example, many animal rights' supporters are also likely to feel strongly about road-building programmes which threaten wildlife conservation areas and this may simultaneously place them among the various radical green groups. Frequently, one kind of commitment leads quite naturally to another.

Three factors largely explain the emphasis on democratic, decentralized and participatory forms of organization and action:

1. Contemporary social movements are not interested in winning direct control over state power and so they have no need to construct vast, centralized organizations capable of assuming the reins of government.

2. Their aims involve trying to persuade broad sections of the population to adopt new agendas for deep changes in social and cultural life while compelling businesses and other powerful bodies to alter their priorities. Particularly in democratic societies, such goals call for a multiplicity of dispersed and highly diverse grass-roots activities that involve consciousness-raising and exposing the failures of the existing system. Accordingly, the following actions are likely to be effective: demonstrations; petitions, consumer or investment boycotts; land occupations; road actions such as blockades and sit-ins; conferences; high-profile media events; neighbourhood action groups or mass letter-writing to politicians and company directors. Such actions embarrass politicians, undermine their electoral support and threaten the sales, profits, investment sources and reputations of commercial interests.

3. Those who tend to be attracted to social movements are often educated, informed and used to exercising personal autonomy. As such, they would be unlikely to tolerate permanent exclusion from policy-making by impersonal, bureaucratic cliques of largely unaccountable movement leaders. After all, this would fly in the face of the very ethos of self-realization and the need to empower people and civil society, which prompted such individuals to join social movements in the first place.

GLOBALIZATION OF SOCIAL MOVEMENTS: CONSTRAINTS AND OPPORTUNITIES

Transnational co-operation between social movements is not new. Ever since the nineteenth century, peace, anti-slavery, women's, conservationist and workers' movements have sometimes drawn strength from collaboration with similar groups in other countries. Certainly, during the 1960s the civil rights, anti-Vietnam, student movement and the Campaign for Nuclear Disarmament (CND) spread out across national borders.

But we must distinguish between occasional collaboration between largely separate national groups and campaigns specifically designed to be globally orchestrated and which deliberately synchronize national support as a resource in the pursuit of worldwide goals. For example, before the 1980s, green groups in the USA mostly campaigned on domestic environmental issues except in the case of a few attempts to protect international wildlife (Bramble and Porter 1992: 324). By contrast, the peace movement which erupted across Europe, the USA and elsewhere from 1981 was much more self-consciously transnational. It was more globalizing in its scope, effectiveness and thinking about the causes of and the remedies for the risk of nuclear war than any previous anti-war movement (Taylor and Young 1987). Roseneil's work (1997) on the Women's Peace Camp at Greenham Common, in the UK during the 1980s, and which we summarize in Box 16.3, demonstrates this globalizing dimension well.

Until recently, most of the theorizing on social movements by sociologists and others has presumed that the nation state was the natural and obvious location where movements would seek to operate (Princen and Finger 1994: Chapter 3). This is not unrelated to the fact that very real constraints have rendered genuine global activity much more difficult than corresponding actions at the national level. Accordingly, most social movements had to be rooted first and foremost in national struggles dependent on domestic support. However, it can also be argued that social movements possess several features that, in principle, provide them with excellent opportunities as well as motivations for choosing to operate transnationally. Indeed, in certain respects they are much better equipped to do so than states. In Box 16.2 we try to summarize these opportunities and constraints by drawing on the work of Ghils (1992), Fisher (1993), Princen and Finger (1994) and Riddell-Dixon (1995).

You will notice in Box 16.2 that we have included INGOs in the discussion. Estimates of the numbers of INGOs vary from around 17 000 for the mid-1980s (Scholte 1993: 44) to 23 000 in the early 1990s (Ghils 1992: 419). Of course, the number of NGOs operating at the local, grass-roots level is much larger. According to Fisher (1993: xi) there are more than 100 000 such groups in the developing countries (the South) at the present time. These probably serve more than 100 million people. Most are concerned with furthering the immediate economic needs and human rights issues which preoccupy women, the urban poor living in shantytowns or tribal peoples threatened with the loss of livelihood by large development projects such as dams.

Approximately 35 000 associations, which Fisher (1993: viii) calls 'grass-roots support organizations', assist these NGOs. Young professionals, who, either out of a sense of commitment to their fellow citizens or because of

Box 16.2   Social movements and NGOs: possibilities of global mobilization

Opportunities and motivations

Unlike states:

1. They neither exist to protect territories and national interests nor are they tied to diplomatic practices for stabilizing inter-state relations.

2. They can operate without secrecy and are not accountable to electorates.

3. They are not responsible for key problems such as human rights abuses, environmental threats or the poverty which results from development.

4. The concerns they articulate are widely shared by disadvantaged and/or discontented people and so support spills naturally across borders.

5. Accordingly, they can co-operate more easily than states and generate alternative ideas and solutions more readily than states.

Unlike business corporations:

6. They do not represent narrow interests and have no fixed investments to protect. Nor are they engaged in market competition (although they compete for members and media attention).

7. They are relatively unbureaucratic and de-centralized.

In contrast, they share certain unique features:

8. They earn public support by virtue of their altruism, meagre personal gains, openness and willingness to risk their lives.

9. They are adaptable, versatile, in touch with ordinary people and cheap. These qualities have sometimes made them useful to the World Bank, UN and governments who have asked them to administer aid or famine/refugee relief.

10. They mobilize support at many levels.

11. They draw upon a heterogeneous membership, which may be shared with several groups.

12. The diversity of movements and NGOs enables each to draw upon the specialist resources of others.

Constraints on global mobilization

Unlike states and business corporations:

1. They have limited funds, yet the costs of global action are often high – cross-national communication, translations and travel to conferences or to lobby IGOs and governments.

2. Engaging media attention may require stunts which involve access to equipment (for example, Greenpeace ships) and costly operations.

3. Family and work commitments and the costs of long-distance travel inhibit individual participation in transnational actions.

4. Language barriers and problems of inter-cultural communication may undermine co-operation between different national groups despite shared goals.

They often have special needs and problems:

5. Many global social movements and INGOs need technical expertise so they can be taken seriously by scientists, governments and the public while being sufficiently prepared to argue their case. For this they need a core of full-time professionals and reliable databases.

6. Southern groups may only be able to act or collaborate in transnational events if they are subsidized by Northern partners. This can lead to charges of 'paternalism'.

7. Southern NGOs and social movements often have different priorities to those in the North. They are more concerned with human rights issues and the need to overcome poverty among the most deprived groups. Global environmental concerns often take second place. This has given rise to disagreements in the past.

unemployment, have decided to work in a semi-voluntary capacity in these bodies. The primary aim of all these groups is to find alternatives to the top-down, commercially oriented development initiatives pushed by Southern governments, often with the backing of western states, investors and IGOs such as the World Bank. These tend to by-pass the needs and interests of poor people. Many grass-roots support organizations enjoy links to INGOs that provide them with funds, technical expertise, international media coverage and other kinds of external support to assist them in their struggles to secure a fairer deal for local people.

Several writers (including Princen and Finger 1994, Riddell-Dixon 1995 and Fisher 1993) argue that it is useful to regard some, although not all, INGOs as more or less equivalent to social movements. There are various reasons for this:

1. Whatever else they may do – for example, providing famine relief or financing self-help development projects – many INGOs are directly involved in running campaigns. These are designed to influence public opinion and compel governments and IGOs to change their policies.

2. INGOs such as Oxfam, Action Aid, Amnesty International and Friends of the Earth seek to bring about a fairer, more just world. This involves championing the interests of those who are presently disadvantaged by the present one while offering alternative agendas.

3. On occasions, such campaigns involve forms of protest, which are unorthodox, illegal and even dangerous, as in the case of Greenpeace International.

4. The kinds of people who are likely to provide donations to INGOs or who work for them in a voluntary capacity are often similar those who are also directly involved in social movements.

In short, although INGOs are formally designated as organizations and are officially recognized as such, in most other respects and for some of the time, they function in much the same ways as social movements. They also forge close links to the latter and frequently coalesce with them. Moreover, they are often much better placed to operate effectively at the global level than social movements. Here, in effect, they stand in for – and become the mouthpiece of – social movements. Perhaps the easiest way of seeing the relationship is to regard social movements as broad, informal and largely unorganized with relevant NGOs and IGOs 'nesting' under their wings and giving some direction to their campaigns.

GLOBAL SOCIAL MOVEMENTS AND INGOS

We now outline several overlapping changes since the early 1980s that have markedly accentuated the positive reasons for global activity. Similarly, we examine the increasingly concrete opportunities for effective transnational communication, mobilization and collaboration between different sites of potential protest. Meanwhile, the former constraints have diminished. We explore these changes under the following headings:

- the problems of worldwide economic modernization
- shifts in thinking by those who support social movements and INGOs
- changes in communication technology
- the widening repertoire of social movements.

The problems of worldwide economic modernization

Many environmental problems linked to the thrust for economic development both in the North and the South either became clearly evident for the first time or worsened during the 1980s. These included the phenomena of transboundary acid rain, desertification, the dangers of toxic and nuclear waste from factories and power plants, water shortages, urban pollution, declining fish stocks and the damage caused by chemicals seeping into inland waterways and seas. These and other manifestations of damage to the biosphere had clear global causes, their impact was universal and they required global solutions.

The rise of neo-liberal economic thinking in the advanced countries, led by the USA and the UK from the early 1980s, led to the implementation of stringent financial measures designed to reduce public spending and check inflationary pressures. In their dealings with developing countries, the OECD countries, the World Bank and the IMF demanded that the former adopt similar measures. There was also relentless pressure to increase foreign earnings for debt payment by expanding the export of raw materials such as forest products. This further accentuated the extent of environmental deterioration in many developing countries while threatening the livelihoods of tribal, forest and other marginalized groups. According to Korton (1990: 6) these events have provoked a widespread demand for a more autonomous and 'people-centred vision' of economic development among many people living in the South.

As we saw in Chapter 4, neo-liberal economic policies, coupled with the globalization of manufacturing and other changes, also reduced job security especially among manual workers and the less well-educated in the North. Thus the virtual exclusion of huge numbers of people from the benefits of economic growth became a worldwide not just a Southern phenomenon. Indeed, the Indian sociologist Oommen (1997: 51–2) argues that compared to previous upsurges of political action by excluded groups the present one is 'truly transnational in its scale and scope [and] multidimensional in its thrust, because the marginalized are the victims of cumulative dominance and inequality'.

The spread of various forms of collective action and protest to the South, especially the demand for greater economic justice, human rights and more attention to the needs of women, has also been enhanced by the worldwide upsurge of democratization (Lindberg and Sverrisson 1997: 5–11). Partly this was linked to the collapse of communism in the Soviet Union and Eastern Europe between 1989 and 1992. But the abysmal failure of many governments in the South to provide viable development programmes – especially in Africa – forced disadvantaged people, often with the assistance of INGOs, to reassert direct control over their own economic life. This, in turn, helped to strengthen civil society and generate internal pressures for democracy.

The shifting ethos – towards global thinking

According to Hegedus (1989) during the 1980s most supporters of western social movements began to experience a major shift in their understanding and orientation. They realized that their hitherto mostly localized concerns were in fact inextricably tied to much wider global structures and problems. This 'planetization' (p. 19) of understanding encompassed many linked agendas for change; virtually everything needed to be radically rethought. Thus, empowering people in the rich western societies was only meaningful if help was given to enable poor people in the South to assert their rights as well. This is especially relevant with respect to environmental problems. Similarly, from the early 1980s those involved in the peace movement in Europe and North America began to realize that simply pressurizing one's own government to relinquish nuclear arms or curtail military expenditure was not enough (see also Box 16.3). Moreover, the range of actions had to be far wider, for example, compelling arms-exporting countries to curtail their sales to repressive regimes and to divert arms industries into peaceful activities.

Many supporters of social movements also ceased to be concerned only with issues of self-realization and the reconstruction of cultural identities, although these remained important. Rather, they assumed a strong sense of 'personal responsibility for a collective future at a local, national and planetary level' (Hegedus 1989: 22). This links up with our earlier discussion concerning Gidden's notion of life politics where the political has invaded the sphere of domestic/personal lives and relationships. But this can be a two-way process. When the myriad tiny individual or household decisions are aggregated together they may lend their weight to the attainment of much broader, radical changes.

Thus, our very dependence on national and global economic life as consumers, investors, taxpayers or television viewers, coupled to our rights as voting citizens, equips us with ready-to-hand and formidable weapons. We can use these as devices for invading the arena of collective politics and protest if we so wish. Moreover, because so much of our cultural, media and especially our economic life has become so globalized and inter-connected, it is perfectly possible for such individual market and voting preferences to engage with transnational movements and not just local or national ones.

Take the case of ethical and green consumerism. Here, a growing number of people have refused to buy products from companies that engage in activities of which they morally disapprove. The magazine, *Ethical Consumer*, first published in 1989, has built-up a database on the worldwide activities of many large companies. Here are just two examples, selected from its fiftieth edition of December 1997, which demonstrate the power of selective buying by individuals or full-scale consumer boycott campaigns (1997: 29–32):

● *The Body Shop* This store, which is committed to ethical trade, increased its sales for cosmetics and other products by three times between 1990 and 1996. Meanwhile, during roughly the same time period various consumer boycotts led several large cosmetics companies such as Avon, Boots, Max Factor and Yardley, to announce their intention to stop testing their own products on animals.

● *Nestlé* The boycott against Nestlé's products which began in 1977 (the company promoted baby foods where the lack of clean water made it difficult for poor consumers to feed their babies safely) remained active in more than 18 countries during 1997. In the UK alone, the campaign was supported by at least 100 consumer, health or church groups, by 80 student unions and by about 90 businesses.

Box 16.3   Women and the peace movement in the 1980s

Background

A sharp revival of Cold War antagonism became evident from around 1980 bringing new dangers. NATO declared it would soon introduce new ground-launched missiles at its European bases that were capable of achieving a pre-emptive first strike against Soviet military targets. This suggested two things that alarmed old and new peace campaigners alike; NATO had decided it could now win a nuclear war – something not accepted before – and Europe would be the sacrificial lamb should such a programme be implemented.

Personal lives – global forces

A revitalized, anti-nuclear peace movement soon emerged. Partly what drove it was the growing understanding by ordinary people concerning the vast dangers created by the 'globalization of nuclear militarism' (Roseneil 1997: 70) and the perception that each individual's immediate and personal life was inextricably tied to these global forces. But there was also anger that remote and unaccountable élites had assumed the right to speak and act for all of humanity. In the 1980s many simply refused any longer to sit back and allow these élites to go on believing they could exercise such powers unopposed or legitimately.

Women link the personal and the local to the global

Women have a long history of involvement in peace campaigns. However, in the 1980s, a group of women occupied state-owned land and established a Women's Peace Camp directly adjacent to the US military base at Greenham Common in southern Britain. By the end they had occupied it for eleven years. Their aims were:

■ To demonstrate that individuals could and should take personal responsibility for global events.

■ To attract world attention and hopefully rally women in many other countries.

■ Tactically to prevent the military from deploying vehicles – intended to be used for launching the new missiles – from the base.

■ To express the special frustration felt by women everywhere given that the élites who were making decisions of such unprecedented magnitude were not only remote but invariably male.

■ To prove not only that women could act in complete independence of men but that in some situations they could do so highly effectively and without resorting to the tendencies towards violence and hierarchical organization preferred by men.

The women's encampment became a 'global locale' (p. 64) attracting many delegations. Following visits to Greenham, other women's peace camps became established across North America, Europe and Australia. But these interactions meant that Greenham women also learned about the causes and problems faced by women worldwide. They became increasingly aware that issues of peace and arms were closely linked to other questions such as Third World poverty, environmental pollution, the dangers of nuclear power and the plight of miners and their families in the UK and elsewhere.

Source: Roseneil (1997)

According to Hegedus (1989) we have realized that what threatens or concerns one person equally implicates everyone else; solutions are only meaningful if they involve joint struggles. Thus, social movements increasingly involve not only *a new ethic of responsibility* but also *a new practice of self-determination and solidarity* between concrete individuals irrespective of culture or nationality (p. 33, author's emphasis). This was symbolized by the Live Aid rock song, 'We are the world' and the involvement of many rock groups in raising funds for poverty and famine relief in Africa and elsewhere. Hegedus observed that several social movements demonstrated all these qualities in the 1980s including Solidarity in Poland (Figure 16.1), the peace movement across Europe, North America and the Soviet Union and the anti-apartheid movement in and outside South Africa.

In the case of the last, internal struggle by the ANC and its supporters was crucial in bringing about the ultimate collapse of the South African regime in the early 1990s. However, the widespread campaigns across Europe and North America to persuade banks and TNCs to cease lending to or investing in the South African economy and to withdraw their existing assets also played their part. For example, anti-apartheid groups in the USA deployed voter, media and other pressures in order to persuade state and local governments to sell their shares or not to buy products supplied by companies that continued to trade with South Africa. Eventually 164 municipal authorities, including eight of the largest US cities, introduced laws designed to achieve either or both of these goals (Rodman 1998: 29). Similarly, twenty state governments and 72 colleges sold their institutions' shares in companies with South African investments.

Changes in communication technology

The contribution made by communication technology to an emerging sense of common global identity can be traced back to events in the late 1960s. Then, important developments in satellite communications and spreading access to home televisions enabled vast numbers of people across the world to view images of planet earth for the first time. This was associated with the various US voyages to the moon, which culminated in the first actual landing by humans in June 1969. Many people have since argued that these powerful images signalled a fundamental turning point in human experience. We became aware of the beauty of our planet – spinning majestically in deep space – and the need to preserve it at all costs as our only source of mutual sustenance in an otherwise bleak and infinitely vast universe. Similar emotions were activated in the early and mid-1980s when a series of computer-enhanced images taken from space gradually provided a body of clear and incontrovertible evidence concerning the extent to which the **ozone layer** surrounding the planet had become depleted. This had given rise to the 'holes' which are especially noticeable in spring over the Polar regions.

The **ozone layer** is a band of gas encircling the planet between 20 and 50 kilometres above the earth's surface.

In Chapter 14 we explored some of the ways in which recent developments in electronic communications and information technology have generated new opportunities for ordinary individuals and grass-roots organizations to achieve greater autonomy. Personal computers enable small groups to produce and circulate their own literature very cheaply while building up databanks essential for challenging the claims and legitimacy of states and other powerful institutions. The growing use of the Internet facilitates the instantaneous sending of messages and the dissemination of information. However, it also allows groups and individuals separated by vast distances to share their individual insights with ease and feed these into a kind of rapid cumulative learning experience. In Box 16.1 we explored a recent example showing how cyberspace has now become another basic weapon in the global struggles of social movements and INGOs.

The widening repertoire of social movements

All of the preceding changes but especially the recent developments in communication technology have both propelled many social movements and INGOs towards seeking greater global impact since the early 1980s and empowered them to do so. Their techniques for mobilizing support have become more effective in several ways:

1. It has become cheaper and easier to engage in *networking activities* over large distances.

2. This has enhanced the possibilities for *pooling resources*: information; specialist technical knowledge and practical expertise; and, at times, the ability to tap into the particular reservoirs of grass-roots support enjoyed by sister groups. In other words, one of the great strengths of social movements and INGOs, namely their diversity, has also been brought into greater play.

3. While the urgent need to engage in *coalition-building* has intensified, so the opportunities for collaboration have also improved. Indeed, many coalitions not only coalesce across national boundaries and sometimes bridge the deep divisions between North and South (see Box 16.2), they also engender cross-issue alliances facilitated by overlapping allegiances on the part of many individuals. Two examples here are women's and peace groups or indigenous peoples trying to protect the forests, mountain pastures or fishing areas which provide their livelihoods and environmental groups, especially those interested in wildlife conservation (Gooch and Madsen 1997).

4. Social movements and NGOs activate and empower people at *the base of society and connect them directly to the top levels* where power holders determine policy. In doing so they try to bypass conventional channels of influence. Simultaneously, their close contacts with the grass-roots enables them to articulate alternative ideas for change which are then brought into play in the arena of public life and politics.

5. However, when growing horizontal connections between countries augments these vertical links within societies, the stage is set for a multiplier process whereby flows of pressure feed into each other on a cumulative and mutually reinforcing basis.

The ability of social movements and INGOs to shape public opinion and mobilize support for their *lobbying campaigns* has also been considerably enhanced. Clearly, it is far easier and more effective to bring pressure to bear against one government or company if other groups are prepared to pool resources. This might involve synchronizing other kinds of activity linked to related issues at the nation state level and/or mounting parallel campaigns involving additional companies or states. Other tactics may include galvanizing the support of consumers worldwide, combining forces with other groups, capturing media attention and lobbying sympathetic groups at the UN or other IGOs. The case studies outlined in Boxes 18.2 and 18.3 both demonstrate this cocktail of transnational protest activities.

Thus, it is *the multiplicity of levels* through which global social movements and INGOs operate – linking individual and grass-roots activities vertically to the top levels while also establishing horizontal inter-state, state–IGO and cross-issue connections – which explains the much stronger presence of social movement activity in the world today. In effect, their greatly enhanced reach and efficacy mean that social movements have largely overcome the physical constraints of geography on their capacity to mobilize support. Assisted by the media and their close links to INGOs global social movements can short-circuit the cumbersome processes that might otherwise be required in order to mount huge protests by millions of people simultaneously across the world.

REVIEW

Although still resembling earlier models, social movements have undergone several important changes since the late 1960s. In the advanced countries they have developed a potential to incorporate much larger numbers of people. The latter are engaged in an ever widening repertoire of activities designed to challenge established interests and re-construct society by continuously broadening the range of contested issues. Social movements have also become much more widespread and active in the South even though the political climate and available economic resources are considerably less favourable than in the North. Important cross-national, cross-issue and North–South linkages have been established between global social movements since the 1980s, often with the help of INGOs. All of this has coincided with a growing compulsion to recognize the inter-connected and universal nature of the problems we all now confront coupled with enhanced opportunities to engage in more effective strategies for global co-operation.

By understanding the nature and activities of global social movements sociologists have been given a vital tool for examining how global society is emerging from below. In subsequent chapters we will explore this process in relation to particular movements.

If you would like to know more ●

The book by Scott, *Ideology and the New Social Movements* (1990) and the same author's chapter, 'Political culture and social movements' in *Political and Economic Forms of Modernity*, edited by Allen *et al.* (1992) offer readable attempts to synthesize and evaluate the debate concerning social movements.

The Road from Rio by Fisher (1993) bristles with ideas and provides an exciting account of the current situation in the South.

Sasha Roseneil has written extensively on the women's peace movement in the 1980s. The piece from which Box 16.3 is drawn demonstrates very many of the themes discussed in this chapter and is highly recommended.

Social Movements in Development edited by Lindberg and Sverrisson (1997) contains some valuable material. Try especially Chapters 1, 3, 7, 12 and 13.

Group work ●●●

1. Arranged in advance, the students in each of three groups will assume responsibility for contacting and building up a file on either Oxfam, Amnesty International or Friends of the Earth (or similar INGOs). Each group will report on the following: their INGO's current membership, recent objectives and campaigns, affiliated sister groups abroad and forms of transnational collaboration.

2. Students will read this chapter before the class. They will then divide into three groups and each will prepare a brief report concerning this proposition: 'The opportunities for effective transnational action by global social movements and INGOs are outweighed by the obstacles'.

Questions to think about ●●●

1. In what ways did social movements in the advanced societies change from the late 1960s and why?

2. What factors explain the tendency for social movements and NGOs to 'go global' during the last fifteen years or so? Assess their relative significance.

3. Using examples, examine the main strategies for engaging in transnational action which have become increasingly useful to global social movements and INGOs in recent years.

4. Why is the study of global social movements so important for those wanting to elaborate a global sociology?

17

Challenging a Gendered World

CONTENTS

In Chapter 6 we explored the multiple forms of oppression to which women in most societies have been historically subjected. Here, we chart the course of some of the struggles by the women's movement to improve their situation, giving special emphasis to those that have assumed a global dimension. There is a growing literature on the far more numerous local actions by women's groups in ever more countries, including those based in the developing world and you can read about these struggles in books such as those edited by Basu (1995) and Asfah (1996).

As we mentioned in Chapter 6, women became involved in political campaigns during the nineteenth and the first half of the twentieth centuries, including attempts to secure international peace. For the most part this first wave of feminist struggle can be regarded as an attempt to secure for women the same liberal freedoms and opportunities as those already available to men. Second-wave feminism from the late 1960s was much more radical. It led many women to conclude that they had every right to challenge and re-construct the patriarchal world. As Enloe (1989:17) suggests 'the world is something that has been made; therefore, it can be remade'.

HISTORICAL CHALLENGES

The history of non-violent collective action by women remains to be properly explored. However, there is evidence that it was not unknown for women to take the lead in actions such as street demonstrations against high food prices during ancient and medieval times or even to use group singing and dancing as a vehicle for expressing discontent (Carroll 1989). Certainly, from the late eighteenth century onwards, women increasingly made important and sometimes initiating contributions to revolutionary protest – as in the case of the moves against the monarchy during the summer and autumn of 1789 in France. At times they also resisted slavery in the USA, reacted against colonialism and joined or led strikes. Women agitated for better working conditions in factories and textile mills across the world from Lancashire in the UK to the cities of North America and Tsarist Russia (pp. 4–9).

WOMEN IN THE GLOBAL ORDER: AN OVERVIEW

At first sight gender relationships appear to have little intrinsic relevance to the workings of the world order. Yet further analysis soon reveals a different picture. Indeed, according to Enloe (1989: 7) it is gender relations that actually make 'the world go round'. Thus, governments need more than secrecy and intelligence agencies in their conduct of foreign affairs. They also rely on private relationships; they need wives who are willing to provide their diplomatic husbands with social and entertainment services so those men can develop trusting relationships with other diplomatic husbands. The 'comfort women' provided to Japanese soldiers in the Second World War and the toleration of women providing sexual services to US servicemen, also show how manly roles have to be reinforced by the military authorities. In short, governments seek formal recognition of their sovereignty; they also depend on ideas about masculinized dignity and feminized sacrifice to sustain their sense of autonomous nationhood (Enloe 1989: 196–7).

Enloe provides several additional examples concerning the weighty contribution armies of women make to global political and economic life – ones that are obscured by the accepted notions of feminized and masculinized roles:

1. Behind the mainly male officials and leaders who decide national and international affairs lie countless female secretaries, personal assistants, clerks and middle-level personnel who provide everyday continuity and maintain the detailed, routine transactions without which the males would be impotent.

2. As a leading sector in the global economy, the success of tourism often hinges upon huge numbers of badly paid female employees such as hotel chambermaids, waitresses, barmaids, airline hostesses, tour guides, local employees engaged in food preparation and women who provide sexual services for tourists.

3. Women's crucial roles at every link in the commodity chains that bind together the global system of food production and consumption often go unacknowledged. At one end of the food chain are the unpaid wives who

grow subsistence crops to feed their families on local plots while their husbands migrate to work on distant commercial farms for low wages or those women employed as occasional seasonal farm workers on large plantations. Somewhere in the middle are those working on piece rates in food factories perhaps cleaning and packing vegetables or fruit. Yet further along the chain there are the women who work as supermarket checkout assistants selling the final products. Finally, it is the world's housewives who mainly assume the role of consumers.

4. We can add that women also play a central role in social and biological reproduction in childrearing, child care and later preparation of young adults for the marketplace.

CONSTRAINTS ON WOMEN'S MOVEMENTS

In many situations women face more constraints than men when they engage in social movements. Moreover, involvement in social protests often becomes progressively more difficult for women as actions move away from specific localities and contexts. There are several reasons for this dual state of affairs:

1. In many societies women are less likely to have easy access to money and land, they are more likely to live in poverty and tend to be less well educated than men. They are also more likely to be tied down by customary obligations and daily routines that bind them to a host of domestic and productive services of an intrinsically local and fixed kind.

2. Patriarchal social relations reduce women's capacity for autonomy and render them vulnerable and dependent. In some societies they may even be prohibited from participating in any kind of public activity without their husband's permission, including the exercise of voting rights or the ability to pursue outside employment, and may be virtually confined to the domestic compound.

3. All of these eventualities curtail freedom of movement. Unless protests are highly local in orientation and are not perceived as offering some kind of threat to established male rights women's participation may be difficult and dangerous.

4. Especially in the case of women in the South, when they do join protests, these are rarely concerned solely with feminist issues. Rather, their actions are likely to be intertwined either with wider struggles against oppression such as nationalist movements for independence and the demand for democratization (Basu 1995: 9–11) or with environmental threats or peace issues.

5. As the numbers of women engaged in various kinds of protests worldwide rapidly increased, divisions quickly emerged or soon intensified. Of course, these differences can also be viewed as a rich source of diversity offering opportunities for the exchange of ideas and experiences. Yet there is general agreement that they also inhibited progress towards greater world unity particularly in the decade from 1975 to 1985 and probably beyond.

Box 17.1   Power, wealth, work and women: the gender deficits

Inequalities of politics and power

In the mid-1990s women formed half the electorate in all countries but held a global average of only 13 per cent of parliamentary seats and 7 per cent of government posts.

In 1992, the countries with the highest share of parliamentary seats held by women were Finland, with 38 per cent, and Norway, with 37 per cent. In countries such as the USA, France, Russia and Brazil this share was less than 10 per cent. The global average was pulled up by China, with between 20 and 30 per cent.

In stark contrast to these figures, however, a few women have stood out as presidents or prime ministers and were associated with important national policy changes and/or operated successfully in the role of world 'statesmen'. Some highly successful women political leaders were the following:

■ *Indira Gandhi*, Prime Minister of India, 1966–77, and 1980–84.

■ *Margaret Thatcher*, in Britain from 1979 to 1990.

■ *Mary Robinson*, President of Ireland from 1990–97.

■ *Sirimavo R. D. Bandaranaike,* Prime Minister of Sri Lanka 1960–5, 1970–75; re-appointed 1994.

Wealth and production: women's burdens

Based originally on data presented to the UN Committee on the Status of Women in 1981, it has long been demonstrated that across the world women constitute half the population, provide one-third of the paid labour force and provide two-thirds of all the hours spent working. *Yet, they earn only one-tenth of the world's income and own less than 1 per cent of all the world's property.* This situation has probably changed little since 1981 except that since then the proportion of women in the global paid labour force has certainly grown considerably.

Women grow half of all the world's food and rather more than this in many African countries. Yet, strangely, in many regions of the world most agricultural advisers are men. For example in Asia during the mid-1980s, women provided 40 per cent of the agricultural labour force but made up less than 1 per cent of agricultural advisers. Comparable figures for sub-Saharan Africa were 47 and 3 per cent.

Employment injustices

During the 1980s the percentages of top management positions held by women at the UN and the World Bank were 3 and 5 respectively. By contrast, the same figures for women employed in secretarial or clerical capacities at these same institutions were 80 per cent and over 90 per cent. In 1989, less than 20 per cent of the members of the diplomatic missions from all the world's governments based permanently at the UN were women. Only eight women among this 20 per cent held positions of ambassadorial rank.

Women often fare little better in the private sector. In 1992, only 1 per cent of the highest executive positions in leading French companies were held by women while the comparable figure for the 1000 most wealthy companies in the USA in 1989 was lower. Even in the case of much less elevated professional positions, women made up only one-fifth of the lawyers and around 17 per cent of the doctors in 1990 in the USA.

Sources: Tickner (1992); Peterson and Runyan (1993); Kidron and Segal (1995); UN Development Programme (1997)

The main overlapping sources of difference are outlined in Table 17.1. By the mid-1980s, these divisions, especially those defined by racial, historical and North–South differences, were on the way to being overcome. All of the following helped to heal earlier wounds:

- greater personal familiarity through contacts established at conferences and other venues

- more humility by western feminists regarding their assumed right to define the terms of the global struggle against patriarchy

- a realization that global trust and co-operation required a willingness to respect the autonomy of each country's movement.

National differences arise in a number of respects. For example, during the 1970s in countries such as Zimbabwe, Mozambique and Vietnam, many women were caught up in national liberation struggles against colonial or foreign domination. Many Southern women in other countries had shared similar experiences during earlier anti-colonial struggles. In these situations, men experienced oppression just as much as women. The need for unity in struggle persuaded many Southern women to assign gender issues a second-order priority.

Similarly, US and European feminists might have sound reasons for demanding abortion rights for all western women or campaigning against the sexual exploitation of women through media trivialization, beauty shows or pornography. But Southern feminists might have quite different priorities. Here, we might include such problems as repressive forms of state birth control that bear down most heavily against the poorest groups; incidents of rape by police and other state officials committed against those within their jurisdiction; or the widespread death of young wives linked to pressure from in-laws for dowry payments after marriage as in India – the so-called dowry deaths (Kumar 1995).

It would be misleading to suppose that Southern women were not aware of the endemic gender inequalities they faced within their societies or that they were prepared to completely submerge such concerns in the interests of national unity. The desire to tackle such issues was merely postponed. Rather, the way in which women in poor countries differ most from their Northern counterparts lies more in their realization that patriarchy is an aspect of inequality that has to be confronted alongside other injustices: all forms of inequality need to be tackled simultaneously as part of the same struggle. In any case, soon a profusion of Southern groups were finding ways to express their own concerns both at national and regional levels.

By the early 1990s it was evident that these streams feeding into the global flow of women's struggles were becoming stronger and more diverse. Moreover, those contributing to this flow were more and more interested in participating in worldwide as well as purely local feminist debates. What helped to make this easier for Southern women was precisely the fact that they had previously worked to carve out their own areas of independence (Miles 1996: 57–60).

Table 17.1   Diverging goals and interests in women's movements, 1960–90

Main reason for division	Key concerns and goals	Main sources of support	Preferred type of organization
I. Liberal versus more Radical, second-wave feminists (from the late 1960s)	Liberals: pushed for equal citizen rights at state level and tried to raise the status of women at UN and other IGOs. Not trying to change women's wider conditions	Mainly older, educated, middle-class western women. Some were involved in pre-Second World War peace movements and worked for equal recognition for women in the 1948 UN Declaration of Human Rights	Prepared to work within conservative, male-dominated state institutions or IGOs and through global networks of élite women. Sought change through personal influence
	New-wave feminism: wished to remove all forms of male oppression including in domestic life. Celebrated female strengths and values	A younger generation, reflecting the broader class base of educational attainment. Influenced by 1960s' idea that politics is personal	On stream from late 1960s. Sought change through a broad spectrum of activities including own media/ publications, research and independent forums
II. Established mainstreamers working in IGOs versus an emergent more disengaged group (from the early 1970s)	Mainstreamers worked to extend state and UN awareness of women's needs mostly in 'traditional' areas such as health, food and education. Also worked to increase knowledge of gender relations at UN	As above	Lobbied states and key UN agencies via consultative status (right to observe and submit statements at some UN forums and other IGOs). Also worked through the UN Commission on the Status of Women
	Outsiders: more focused on specific issues linked to a wider feminist agenda such as male violence against women, prostitution and the right to choose one's sexual orientation	Mostly western women as above, but beginning to include flows of educated women from the South and/or those previously involved in struggles for national independence	Exercised pressure mainly outside formal institutions especially via networking and own separate groups. Preferred co-operative and non-hierarchical organizations and direct links with grass-roots
III. Rising Southern women's groups versus those with a western membership as in I and II (from the mid-1970s)	Concerned with the limited benefits of economic development for poor women. Carving out own versions of feminism reflecting local not western needs. Some rifts with Northern women over their alleged ignorance of South and racist paternalism	Despite disputes with Northern women, from rather similar backgrounds; privileged, educated, academic, middle class. Not always representative of the interests of poor rural and urban groups though trying to bridge this class gap	Linking to more radical western networks but also forming own regional and global groups; for example, Development Alternatives with Women for a New Era (DAWN), launched in 1984 by Southern activists from Asia, Africa and Latin America. Partly dependent on financial assistance from North

Sources: Bystdzienski (1992); Stienstra (1994); Miles (1996)

GROWTH OF THE WORLDWIDE MOVEMENT

Several significant changes and tendencies boosted the rising volume of effective women's movements from the 1970s and gradually contributed to greater unity and mutual understanding. We outline these changes and then discuss each in more detail:

- the UN and the activities of the older generation of liberal feminists who worked within its institutions helped to create a framework for increased networking

- the women's movement worldwide was invigorated both by the rise of second-wave radical feminism, mainly in the North, and the women's groups emerging in the South

- women worked to create their own autonomous facilities for representing women's views and achieving effective communications.

The UN framework for networking

Despite their conservatism, the work carried out by the older, more privileged generation of liberal feminists and those operating within mainstream governments and IGOs began to bear fruit. Partly because of earlier contributions to the peace process during and after the First World War international women's groups were able to influence global affairs especially through the auspices of the UN from 1945 onwards. Thus, the UN Charter of 1945 specifically referred to the equal eligibility of women to participate in all UN debates and organizations. It also granted consultative status to the representatives of several international women's organizations; the right to attend certain UN sessions and to submit documentation. Further, it set up the Commission on the Status of Women to consider the special needs of women worldwide (Stienstra 1994: 75–86). In addition, the 1948 UN Universal Declaration of Human Rights clearly stated that entitlement to such rights could not be denied on any grounds, including sex.

In the view of many radical feminists these gains did not go nearly far enough towards meeting women's real needs. Nevertheless, they provided a platform from which the influential mainstreamers and liberals could make the case for additional changes while continuing to infiltrate male-dominated institutions. Such pressures along with the rising tide of women's discontent associated with second-wave feminism created a powerful momentum for further change led by the UN. The result was the 1975–85 UN Decade for Women built primarily around three conferences, although others were organized both during and after these years (see Box 17.2).

In some respects the direct results of these three conferences have been meagre. As we have also seen, the first two conferences in 1975 and 1980 exposed certain divisions among women from different world regions and cultural backgrounds although some reconciliation was later achieved. Moreover, many of the more radical feminists preferred to work through their own grass-roots organizations largely outside these official forums until the mid-1980s. Nevertheless, the UN Decade 'was a watershed both for placing women on the international intergovernmental agenda and for facilitating women's co-operation' (Friedman 1995: 23).

Box 17.2   The global women's movement: key events and
            selected achievements

The UN decade of women, 1975–85, key UN-sponsored conferences

■ 1st World Conference on Women, 1975, Mexico City. Attended by 6000 delegates.

■ 2nd World Conference on Women, 1980, Copenhagen. 7000 delegates.

■ 3rd World Conference on Women, 1985, Nairobi. 15 000 delegates from 150 countries. 2000 workshops held.

■ 4th World Conference on Women, 1995, Beijing. Attended by 8000 delegates.

Key consequences of Nairobi conference

■ Far more representatives came from the developing countries and they were much
more inclined to declare their own aims. The animosity between North and South
delegates evident at the previous two conferences was much diminished.

■ Several new regional and international networks were formed in 1985 or soon after.
For example: the Latin American Committee for the Defence of Women's Rights
(CLADEM); the Asia-Pacific Forum on Women, Law and Development (APWD); and
Women Living Under Muslim Laws (WLUML) formed by representatives from eight
Muslim countries. All sought to facilitate exchanges of information on legal matters
pertaining to human and legal rights.

■ Also focused around the issue of women and human rights was the International
Women's Rights Action Watch (IWRAW) launched following Nairobi in 1986. Its
purpose was to lobby governments and international bodies including NGOs on the
issue of human rights and women while promoting and monitoring the progress of the
UN's work.

Other important conferences and events

■ UN General Assembly, 1979. Worldwide pressure from groups demanding change to
protect women from discrimination contributed to the UNGA's decision to support the
Convention on the Elimination of all forms of Discrimination Against Women
(CEDAW). States accepting the convention have to take all steps needed in order to
prevent discrimination. By 1994, CEDAW had been ratified by 133 countries but 40
of these had made 91 reservations, mostly on religious or cultural grounds.

■ Bangkok, 1979. A small group sponsored by the Asian and Pacific Centre for Women
and Development met to try and heal North–South differences on issues relating to
feminist ideology.

■ Bangalore, 1984. A conference to discuss the effects of political crises and large-
scale development programmes on poor women in the South. Led to the formation of
the international organization, DAWN, in 1984, but also to several regional networks
such as Women and Development based in the Caribbean. DAWN became an effective international research organization holding many workshops mostly in the South.

■ Vienna, 1993. The UN Second International Conference on Human Rights. Building
on their earlier dialogues on women and human rights issues, women's groups were
very well-organized and successfully lobbied 160 governments present at the
conference. Also called for an end to gender bias due to religious extremism.

■ Bangkok, 1994. Conference on empowering women in their relations with the media.

■ Cairo, 1994. UN Conference on Population and Development. Women strongly
present.

Sources: Stienstra (1994); Peters and Wolper (1995); Miles (1996)

Second-wave and Southern feminism

Second-wave feminism sought nothing less than a root and branch attack on patriarchy; a rejection of male pretensions to superiority in all spheres and not simply at the level of formal institutions. Thus, the focus of its critique and challenge was much more comprehensive than anything offered by earlier feminist ideas. All of this created a sense of intellectual and moral coherence, which some people might fear but few could ignore. The impetus generated led new-wave feminists to explore many new avenues with energy and confidence. They sought to invade or seek alliances with all previously male-dominated organization including NGOs, trade unions, churches and religious bodies, sports and arts organizations, local and national politics, the professions (especially health, medicine, law) and all knowledge-creating centres such as universities.

Women's groups in the developing countries increasingly joined second-wave feminists. Among the issues included in this widening agenda were the following:

- sex tourism and prostitution across the world

- all forms of public and private violence against women

- the need to persuade governments and the UN to accept that women's rights must be incorporated firmly within the human rights agenda. The issue of women's rights is one of human rights

- the often adverse working conditions experienced by a the growing number of women worldwide employed in export-processing manufacturing industries

- the need to urgently re-think the development aims and priorities promoted both by states in developing countries and powerful IGOs such as the IMF and the World Bank.

Women representing themselves: independent communications

From 1975 onwards women's groups challenged the male-owned and male-oriented world media industries. They knew that how women and their needs are represented – or perhaps misrepresented and trivialized – in the media was critical to any attempt to assert autonomy and counter patriarchy. For example, during the 1970s, less than two per cent of the items included in world news programmes were about women or related to their needs (Byerly 1995: 106).

The first communications network to be established was the International Women's Information and Communication Service (ISIS). In addition to providing a direct channel of international communication between affiliated groups, it also amassed knowledge of interest to women and offered technical training in media skills. Its first task was to publish the proceedings of the International Tribunal on Crimes against Women held in Brussels in 1976. Later, it began to publish various women's journals, among other things. A similar organization, the International Women's Tribune Centre (IWTC), was founded in 1976. It publishes in several languages and aims to be accessible even to poor, semi-literate women (Stienstra 1994: 103–5). In the early 1990s IWTC provided communication and technical services to groups in 160 countries (Miles 1996: 111).

With UNESCO assistance, feminists also set up their own press service in 1978, the Women's Feature Service (WFS). Eventually, various governments, international media organizations and subscribers from eighty countries turned the WFS into a permanent organization based in New Delhi. It supplies programmes and articles on a range of topics relevant to women including the environment, social customs, health and politics. Demand worldwide, but especially in Latin America, has continued to expand (Byerly 1995). Since the 1970s, feminists have also set up study and research centres with educational courses specifically designed to promote an independent perspective. They have also founded women's publishing houses and organized global events in the arts including theatre, music, dance and crafts.

UNIFICATION IN THE FACE OF COMMON PROBLEMS

Increasingly, women have realized that they face common problems. This has encouraged some women's groups to sink their differences and seek various forms of collaboration designed to influence governments, IGOs and other powerful élite institutions. What are these common difficulties?

Environmental degradation

There is growing evidence of global environmental devastation some aspects of which are briefly explored in Chapter 18. Some eco-feminists such as Shiva (1989) have argued that women share a much greater affinity to nature than men and so are more disposed to protect the natural world. They also believe that the burdens of environmentally destructive commercial development projects pushed by governments in the developing countries tend to fall disproportionately on women. Jackson (1993: 405), while expressing caution at the general argument, suggests that:

> [The] impact of environmental degradation is often greater on women because of the over-representation of female headed households among the poor, and because of gender divisions of labour within households which allocate work such as firewood and water collection to women, precisely tasks which become much more difficult with deforestation and falling water tables.

Religious fundamentalism

Another unifying threat during the last decade or more has been the resurgence of various forms of religious fundamentalism and right-wing thinking, the two often being synchronized. These have appeared in countries as different, for example, as the USA, India, some Muslim countries especially in the Middle East, Israel and parts of the former Soviet Union. In the USA, right-wing religious fundamentalism has played a leading role in the movement to reverse the trend whereby many women increasingly seek personal fulfilment and relative autonomy through careers instead of choosing to remain tied predominantly to the home. Opposition, sometimes violent, by 'pro-life' groups in the face of women's desire to control their own bodies through legalized abortion rights has figured prominently in these campaigns. The desire to restore fundamentalist religious values and social practices is associated with the fear that any real increase in women's freedom of choice and action will undermine the foundations of tradition, religion, morality and, it could be argued, male control. Women as the homemakers and childrearers have cemented the main links between respect for a deity and the upholding of religious belief, on the one hand, and the reproduction of society's moral codes from one generation to another, on the other. Because this leads fundamentalists to regard women as both embodying and preserving all that is most sacred and valued in society, they have often insisted on ruthlessly conserving or reinstating women's traditional positions.

India offers an interesting example of the dilemmas faced by women's movements for change. Although there has been a resurgence of Hindu fundamentalism, India is usually and rightly respected as a tolerant country with a cherished regard for the pursuit of democracy and with a long history of social reform and modernization. However, even before the recent rise of religious fundamentalism, governments found it difficult to tolerate or encourage the extension of some constitutional freedoms to women and family life. Thus, the Indian constitution allows governments to intervene in order to prevent discrimination against members of certain lower castes – the latter a legacy of long-established customary practices. However, it does not permit such state interference in customary law where this relates to family life and the domestic position of women (Jaising 1995; Kumar 1995). This state of affairs, in turn, has led women's movements in India to politicize the private realm of husband–wife relations, marriage and family life.

One of the many difficulties that feminists have with fundamentalist religious arguments is that it is not easy to square the contradiction between the supposedly pivotal and elevated position held by women with the frequent evidence of experiences of powerlessness and sometimes abuse at the hands of male kinsmen, husbands and patriarchal institutions. Is the latter *really* so necessary for the preservation of the former and which groups attach such significance to the preservation of tradition at all costs and why? Ultimately, solutions to these dilemmas can only be found by local women's movements struggling to confront them in their own ways and on their own terms. Nevertheless, the spread of right-wing nationalism and religious fundamentalism across many societies has given women yet another reason for seeking global collaboration (Basu 1995: 19).

Accelerating economic globalization

A further recent cause for global concern has been rapid economic globalization. As we saw in earlier chapters, capital has become increasingly foot-loose. TNCs, for example, have become much freer to move plant, technology and goods across the globe while fragmenting production operations between sites located in different countries. In doing so they have remained relatively unencumbered by global or state regulation. At the same time, competition for markets between a growing number of industrializing economies has risen dramatically. Globalization has further highlighted the plight of women worldwide and the need for co-operation by women's groups – including across the North–South divide – in order to construct forces capable of countering the power of mobile capitalism (Basu 1995: 19; Valdiva 1995). We discuss examples of such actions later.

**Figure 17.1   Women delegates assemble for the
world summit at Beijing, 1995**

Neo-liberal ideology and economic policies

Coinciding with economic globalization has gone the rise and spread of neo-liberal economic policies. These have prioritized government spending and tax cuts, the privatization of industry, the de-regulation of markets – including reduced protection for local industries and jobs – and the importance of creating 'flexible' labour markets. Supposedly the latter renders employees more efficient and cheaper even while the same reforms increase the power of capital over labour. Since the mid-1980s, the IMF and the World Bank have imposed neo-liberal 'reforms' on many Southern countries as a condition for help in arranging debt re-scheduling and further loans. Such policies led to higher foods prices with the abolition of subsidies, increased unemployment and widespread cuts in welfare spending on things such as rural clinics as governments were forced to reduce their spending. Much of this has hit the poorer groups hardest and a large proportion of the most disadvantaged consists of single-parent households headed by women.

Box 17.3   **Women, health and globalization**

The sociology of health

Sociologists argue that illness is not determined solely by biological or physical causes. Rather, they link the incidences of different diseases to such factors as occupation, income, gender and nationality. Alternatively, sociologists have explored how patient experiences are socially constructed when doctors, family members (and patients themselves) develop certain expectations concerning the role of the 'invalid'.

(cont'd)

Women and illness

Gender affects distribution, severity and types of illness. The low status of female children and adult women in poor countries often means they are likely to receive less nutritious food and are often less well-educated compared to males. Women are also subject to specific health conditions arising either from motherhood or their exposure to socially imposed conditions including early marriage and male preferences for a large family. Many consequences follow but here are just three:

■ Every year around 500 000 women worldwide die from problems associated with pregnancy or childbirth.

■ The average risk of such deaths among women in many developing poor countries is often about 200 times greater than for women in North America or Europe.

■ Such risks are especially high among adolescent girls under 20 years of age.

Globalization, women's health and the diseases of modernity

■ Communicable diseases, for example through poor water supplies, illnesses caused by infections, parasites or malnutrition are slowly declining throughout most of the developing world.

■ Illness caused by lifestyle changes associated with increased smoking, the higher consumption of sugars, alcohol and drug abuse or greater sexual promiscuity are increasing dramatically.

■ The latter include various cancers, heart diseases, strokes, cirrhosis of the liver and AIDS.

■ Until recently, women in developing countries have been much less likely to smoke than men. But there is growing evidence that like their western counterparts, their cigarette consumption is increasing rapidly. In part, this is linked to advertising campaigns.

■ Future rates of lung cancer and other smoking-related diseases among women are therefore expected to increase dramatically.

Source: Smythe (1993)

PROTECTING HOMEWORKERS

In combination, economic globalization and neo-liberal policies have weakened labour's bargaining power and increased economic insecurity through the creation of an ever larger, casualized labour force – worldwide. Women are certainly not alone in being exposed to these changes. However, they have often taken the brunt of them. In this final section we show how some women have begun networking worldwide in order to counter their situation.

Historically, women have always made a considerable contribution to manufacturing. But much of this has been hidden from view because many women have worked in tiny unregulated enterprises or in homeworking. The 'sweatshop' conditions typical of these activities leave much to be desired. Under homeworking, very low rates of pay, poor, sometimes dangerous, working conditions, the need to meet employer deadlines and the absence of legal rights are all hard for workers to resist because they are dispersed and therefore find it difficult to organize. Work can easily be shifted elsewhere. Moreover, family poverty and the absence of alternative work – especially for women with young children – makes workers dependent upon employers. Employers are also often able to reduce the costs of training the workforce since in industries such as garment production girls often will have already received a basic domestic education in such skills within the family.

The growth of homeworking has been most pronounced in garment making. Here, it has not been confined to the developing world but has spread widely across the cities of the North – often based on the employment of illegal immigrant workers (Ross 1997: 13). Homeworking has also spread to other industries including carpets, shoes, toys, consumer electronics, auto parts and so on (Rowbotham 1993: 9–24). The retailers who sell on such goods increasingly operate as 'hollow companies' (Mitter 1994: 20) because they breakdown production into numerous specialized work tasks and then subcontract these as vast orders to integrated chains of firms across the world. These, in turn, then employ millions of homeworkers. It has been the ability to attain greater producer flexibility and to cheapen costs partly through the increased resort to homeworking that has made it easier for retailers to compete successfully. Their power also enables them to earn very high profits by placing huge mark-ups on the imported price of the final products.

However, it appears that not all the cards are stacked in favour of these powerful retailing companies. Their business strategy carries several risks. Probably the most serious stems from the fact that these goods mostly carry designer labels much prized by consumers, and so they command high prices. But, by the same token this exposes companies to 'potentially embarrassing... human rights violations'. They 'cannot afford to have the names of their designers, endorsers, or merchandising labels publicly sullied [or be] embarrassed by revelations about the exploited labour behind their labels' (Ross 1997: 25). Thus, the public esteem in which a brand-name image is held is worth a great deal of money. Increasingly, the various groups campaigning on behalf of women employed as homeworkers have sought to educate consumers into the principles of ethical or fair trading.

While organizing homeworkers into trade unions at the point of production is very difficult, persuading consumers to join boycotts against companies that condone exploitative work conditions used by their subcontractors can be highly effective. This was shown in the case of the of the partly successful 1995 campaign in the USA against the clothes retailer, GAP. Then, a coalition of university, consumer, trade union, human rights, church and other groups obtained the company's agreement to impose and monitor codes of conduct with respect to the labour conditions prevailing in one of its Central American subcontracting firms (Ross 1997: 26–7; Cavanagh 1997: 40–1). Unfortunately, GAP and other companies depend on such subcontracting relations with many hundreds of similar firms in Central America and elsewhere and the 1995 campaign was unable to change conditions in these.

Feminist groups and some homeworkers themselves are also contributing towards fair trade and other campaigns (Boris and Prugl 1996: 6). Despite the enormous obstacles they face, homeworkers have formed effective organizations in several countries and in some instances these have also engaged in useful international networking activities. For example, the International Labour organization (ILO) is an arm of the UN based in Geneva. Among other roles, it tries to establish worldwide standards for the treatment of workers while monitoring the conditions pertaining in different countries. At a conference held in June 1996 under the auspices of the ILO, an international coalition of feminists, trade unions, homeworkers' associations, NGOs and fair trade organizations were successful in obtaining the adoption of a new ILO Convention for Homebased Workers. Much more work needs to be done in this area. However, in the words of Ela Bhatt, a long-term fighter for homeworkers' rights and general secretary of the Self-Employed Asian Women's Association (SEWA), 'homeworkers are no more invisible' (cited in Shaw 1998: 5).

REVIEW

Women's struggles have made important contributions to the growth of an emergent global society from below – ones that increasingly bind individuals and groups together irrespective of national and cultural identities. The women's movement satisfies the primary criterion of a global social movement, namely 'global reach'. There is hardly a country in the world where gender relations have not been profoundly altered by its impact. Moreover, the time scale for this transformation is impressively short; most of the force of the movement having been evident since the 1970s. The movement was able to spread so fast partly because of its attractive participatory forms of grass-roots organization, and partly because the speed and density of communications allowed the global transmission of positive images of women.

Like other social movements, the women's movement has been partly borne along by its more or less universal appeal. However, in common with other movements its expansion has also been propelled by the compulsion to respond to vast and sometimes threatening forces for change. These appear to be encompassing all the world's inhabitants, especially the less well-off. But perhaps these global changes offer an even greater challenge to women. Partly, this is because the realities of patriarchal oppression and economic disadvantage faced by most women create an almost unprecedented potential for unity of thought and action. However, the resources associated with globalization, especially the communication technologies, faster, easier travel, and with these the ever more rapid dissemination of all kinds of knowledge, also offer women particularly exciting opportunities to benefit from shared experiences and the pooling of acquired knowledge.

If you would like to know more ••••••••••••••••••••••••••••••••

Bananas, Beaches and Bases, by Enloe (1989), is not meant to provide an especially sociological analysis. However, it is witty and accessible and offers a useful way into theorizing about gender.

Miles's Integrative Feminism, Building Global Visions, 1960s–1990s, (1996) provides a clear, overall picture of the evolving face of women's thinking and actions worldwide.

Similarly, many of the readings in Women's Rights, Human Rights, edited by Peters and Wolper (1995), are excellent in disentangling the important subject of women's rights within a legal and cultural context. Try especially the first four chapters along with 13 and 28.

Rowbotham is a central figure in the development of feminist thought. Her 1993 book, *Homeworkers Worldwide*, gives a lively and simple introduction to this topic.

Group work •••

1. Students will read this chapter before the seminar. Working in two groups and drawing on the text, one group will compose a list showing all the feminist directions and priorities pursued by women in the North since the 1960s and the other will conduct a similar exercise for Southern women. After hearing each group's arguments the class will try to explain the differences.

2. Adopt the same procedure as in 1. While one group compiles a list of the women's organizations and networks mentioned – and then tries to categorize them under different headings – the other will assemble a picture of all the different ways various IGOs have played some kind of role in facilitating global feminism since 1945.

3. Four students will agree to prepare a debate around the topic, 'Northern women have more to learn from their sisters in the South than vice versa'. After hearing both sides each class member will give two reasons why they agree or disagree with this proposition.

Questions to think about •••••••••••••••••••••••••••••••••••

1. What have been the constraints on women's actions and to what extent has globalization provided opportunities for overcoming them?

2. Assess the relative significance of the UN and its associated institutions in strengthening the world feminist movement compared to other factors.

3. Drawing on case study material, assess the impact of recent worldwide changes in encouraging women to collaborate transnationally.

chapter 18

Towards a Sustainable Future: The Green Movement

CONTENTS

The **biosphere** consists of the atmosphere, the oceans, lakes and rivers, the varied and complex systems of plant life and all the many other living organisms from bacteria to fish, animals and humans.

Environmentalism is a global social movement that demonstrates a concern to protect nature or the **biosphere**. In this chapter we examine its various claims and goals and ask how valid these are. We also explore the sometimes contradictory modes of protest in which the environmental or green movement is engaged, considering the reasons why its actions have become increasingly transnational. We begin however, with a brief discussion concerning our complex relationship with nature and the role this has played in creating environmental problems.

Until recently the viability of nature, or the biosphere, was not especially at risk from humans. However, our relentless scramble for increased wealth is damaging those very forces that ultimately make material progress and indeed life itself possible. It is hardly surprising therefore that what the green movement seeks to protect the environment from is ourselves 'from the harmful effects of human activities' (Milton 1996: 27). Both human agency and structural forces inter-relate in complex ways in the impact society has on the environment.

A SOCIOLOGY OF NATURE

Sociology tends to view nature both as an objective reality governed by its own physical laws and therefore external to us – although increasingly affected by our actions – and at the same time as an entity subject to the social constructions imposed by human actors. In terms of the first view it is widely accepted that the health of the biosphere is a precondition for the survival of all life. If, by contrast, we think of nature as socially constructed it seems that our actions and feelings with respect to nature are very difficult to make sense of separately from the ways we choose to conceptualize it. Similarly, we tend to imbue nature with different meanings over time and depending upon our interests in varying situations.

Accordingly, nature and its meanings are frequently contested and manipulated. For example, one study of a public inquiry into a planning dispute showed how green groups, opposed to the development of a new landfill site for municipal waste disposal, employed a definition of nature that emphasized its untouched, wilderness qualities and the need to preserve this. The commercial developers, in contrast, argued that the countryside had already been altered by generations of human activity. They were simply proposing to extend this process of 'managing' the land in a caring way (MacNaghten 1993).

How have the deeply rooted conceptualizations of nature present in different kinds of society altered over time and how have these changes shaped the ways we treat nature? Merchant (1990) has identified two crucial historical periods with respect to our attitudes towards nature:

- *Pre-industrial societies* Most pre-industrial societies imagined nature as active, alive and nurturing, akin to a caring mother. She permitted humans to enjoy her bounty but also demanded respect demonstrated through religious ceremonies and sacrifices. Until around 1600, Europeans shared an organic view of the universe where the human and non-human, inanimate and living were all seen as part of the same seamless structure created by God. Similarly, they accepted the idea of ethical restrictions on the exploitation of nature that should be respected. Despite Christianity's insistence on the worship of one transcendental God, most people continued to believe that numerous spirits resided in hills, woods and other wild places – a survival from a pre-Christian era.

- *Nature and modernity* Then, the western view of nature underwent a massive transformation. Scientists, particularly Isaac Newton, saw nature as inert, passive, accessible to human understanding and therefore capable of serving human needs. Meanwhile, other changes such as the spread of Protestantism and the rise of a more commercialized, individualistic ethos in socio-economic relations reinforced the view of nature as something that should be privately owned and that could be controlled and managed for profitable and productive purposes. Nature became tamed. This reconceptualization of nature also became entwined with the prevailing ways of thinking about women and gender relations. Both women and nature were considered to be passive, primitive, emotional forces requiring manipulation and control by the rational, 'higher' masculine forces embodied in science, industry and notions of human progress. Eventually, capitalist modernity – partly a product of this altered perspective – enabled more and more societies to conquer nature and to make human life virtually independent of it.

The contrast between this new western concept of nature and that upheld by people from other cultures was vividly and prophetically portrayed by Chief Seattle of the Sugumish Indians in North America (his name survives in the name of the city). He made the following comment on land grabbing by white settlers in 1855:

> We know that the white man does not understand our ways. He is a stranger who comes in the night and takes from the land whatever he needs. The earth is not his friend but his enemy, and when he has conquered it he moves on. He kidnaps the earth from his children. His appetite will devour the earth and leave behind a desert. If all the beasts were gone, we would die from a great loneliness of the spirit, for whatever happens to the beasts, happens also to us. All things are connected. Whatever befalls the earth befalls the children of the earth (quoted in Kirkby *et al.* 1995: 17).

More recently, observers have suggested that our thinking is undergoing yet another transformation. Now, we are apparently becoming much more ambivalent and uncertain about nature. Thus, we have come to realize how much our past and present pursuit of material development may be harming nature irrevocably. For example, the commercialization of nature for profit through chemical-intensive, high-tech agriculture has led to the extensive 'refashioning' of farming and the 'denaturalization' of foods (Goodman and Redclift 1991). Similarly, our desire to extract pleasure from nature through tourism, outdoor hobbies, theme parks and so on has turned it into little more than a series of consumer products (Strathern 1992). Yet, just as we are becoming increasingly aware of our adverse impact on nature we are developing a powerful yearning to protect it, to rediscover the wild, pristine beauty we imagine it once possessed and to re-unite with it as closely as possible. These yearnings are demonstrated by such things as our growing thirst for organic foods, 'natural', 'healthy' lifestyles and simple, eco-friendly holidays in remote locations.

It seems then, that we demand lifestyles that presuppose the continuing command over and perhaps eventual destruction of nature and yet simultaneously we wish to respect and resuscitate it. Similarly, we are engaged in trying to protect the environment both because we have come to believe in its intrinsic worth and because we have realized that the threat to nature means that our own futures require nothing less. Hopefully, sociology's insights can help us deal more critically and sensitively with these conflicting views and expectations.

THE CHANGING NATURE OF ENVIRONMENTALISM

In Europe, expressions of concern with the human threat to nature have roots in the nineteenth century. Romantic poets such as William Wordsworth eulogized remote regions and country life and depicted them as sources of spiritual values. Indeed, when the earliest environmental organizations began to be established in the mid-nineteenth century, most were focused on conservation issues. Chief among such concerns were the preservation of areas of outstanding natural beauty or the protection of animals and birds – for example, campaigns to discourage people from buying fur coats and hats decorated with feathers. Interestingly, the first effective international conservationist NGO, established in 1922, was concerned with European bird life – the International Committee for Bird Protection (McCormick 1989: 23).

Since the Second World War environmental concerns have undergone three important changes:

1. Although issues relating to wildlife and nature preservation continue to attract huge memberships, as in the case of the World Wide Fund for Nature, environmentalism now encompasses many additional problems. These include the growing threats posed by various kinds of pollution and the fear that diminishing bio-diversity, along with long-term climate change caused by global warming, will harm future generations.

2. There has been a vast growth in the numbers of people joining various environmental NGOs since the late 1960s. Numbers grew especially rapidly during the 1980s. For example, in the USA the twelve leading national organizations enjoyed an estimated combined membership of 11 million by 1990, up from 4 million in 1981. They received overall revenues of $300 million per year (Bramble and Porter 1992: 317). Worldwide, the number of environmental NGOs has also grown rapidly. Thus, Princen and Finger (1994: Chapter 1) suggest that there were around 176 in 1909 but more than 4500 by the late 1980s and most of these were established during the 1980s.

3. Another change is that environmentalism is no longer confined primarily to the North. In many developing countries, the destruction of forests, the displacement of people by dam building or mounting industrial pollution have generated rising alarm.

Table 18.1   The rise of three leading green INGOs

Organization and date founded	Affiliated national groups and worldwide membership in 1997	Examples of campaigns and projects
World Wide Fund for Nature (WWF) 1961	In 31 countries including 12 in the South. 4.7 million	Co-operates with local groups and governments on conservationists' projects in 96 countries, for example elephant and rhino protection in Tanzania and support for an environmental education programme in Pakistan
Greenpeace International, 1971	In 32 countries plus four regional offices. 13 were in the South or in the territories of the former USSR. Had 3 million paid-up members in 158 countries	First achieved media and international acclaim in the early 1970s with campaigns against US and French nuclear testing and in 1975 confronted the Soviet whaling fleet. Contributed to the campaign to turn Antarctica into a world wilderness park in 1991
Friends of the Earth, 1971	Had independent member groups in 56 countries and 23 of these were in the South. Approximately 1 million	One of many campaigns (launched in 1992) was the Mahogany is Murder project to encourage consumers to boycott Brazilian rain-forest timber. By 1994 the six largest DIY chains in the UK had agreed to stop selling mahogany and imports fell by 68 per cent between 1992 and 1996

Source: Authors' data

One striking example of an environmental disaster in the South erupted in September 1997 when thousands of planters and farmers in Indonesia lit fires in order to clear the bush for cash-crop cultivation. This followed the previous mass clearance of forests by international logging companies. At a time of drought, probably linked to global warming, these fires raged out of control over an area of 100 square miles and caused a vast cloud of smoke affecting more than 70 million people in six countries (Harrison 1997).

Other cases of rapid economic change have provoked organized protest. One interesting example is the Kenyan Greenbelt Movement started by Wangari Maathari. By 1990 its members had planted 10 million trees, resisted government building plans in Nairobi and linked up with similar groups in thirty other African countries (Scarce 1990: 152–4). Moreover, environmental concern across the developing world is often linked to wider issues of human rights, women's issues, poverty and extreme inequality. Alternatively, such protest is provoked by the inability of many large-scale, commercial projects to bring employment or improving lifestyles to the poorest people (Kothari 1996).

SPEAKING FOR HUMANITY: THE CLAIMS OF ENVIRONMENTALISM

Environmentalism has increasingly made claims to represent the interests of all humanity. Thus, Milton (1996: 170) states that environmentalism involves a 'transcultural discourse' which is 'not tied to any particular group or location'. Similarly, Yearley (1996a: 151) argues that 'Environmentalism surely counts as one of the best candidates we have for a global ideology and globalizing movement'. He suggests that attempts to unite people irrespective of national affiliations are more likely to be successful in the case of the green movement than similar bids by other social movements. We now consider some of the factors that appear to validate such claims. Then we discuss reasons for regarding them with a degree of scepticism.

The transboundary nature of many environmental problems

Some environmental crises are more or less confined to one location. One shocking instance of this was the release of methylisocynate gas from a plant in Bhopal, India, in 1984 (see Chapter 8). Others occur in one place but have a transnational impact – as in the case of the nuclear explosion at the Chernobyl plant in Ukraine in 1986. This spread radioactive material over much of Europe.

Increasingly, however, we know that many problems are caused not by a single event but by a multiplicity of human activities across the world. Moreover, they do not respect national boundaries but impact on everyone. Thus, acting alone, states can no longer protect their citizens from environmental damage. The main examples of these transnational environmental problems are global warming, ozone depletion, transboundary air pollution – especially *acid rain* – and the declining variety of species able to survive on our planet – the loss of bio-diversity.

Take the case of global warming. Although the evidence is still disputed, especially by the fossil-fuel lobby (Rowell 1996), an increasing number of observers accept that there is growing evidence of climate change. Sometimes

Acid rain is caused by the emission of toxic gases such as sulphur and nitrogen oxides, which are then carried by winds and rain.

this is partly anecdotal; increased storm damage, shrinking glaciers worldwide and a series of severe droughts. But many prestigious scientists, such as those associated with the Intergovernmental Panel on Climate Change (IPCC), argue that the evidence of the build-up of carbon dioxide in the atmosphere or the accumulations of carbon found in ice-core samples from past centuries, compared to recent deposits, strongly suggest that global warming has already begun. The IPCC was established in 1988 to advise governments concerning the evidence for global warming. By 1995, it included nearly 2500 eminent scientists from around forty countries.

Declining bio-diversity is occurring because widespread deforestation and other kinds of commercial development are gradually eliminating the unique habitats in which insect, animal, bird and plant species have evolved. The relentless logging of tropical forests is especially worrying. They cover only seven per cent of the world's land but contain approximately half of its species (Seager 1995: 16). As species diminish, so does the storehouse of possible life forms which we may need in the future for medical or other purposes while our aesthetic delight in the planet's infinite variety is undermined and despoiled.

In part, these problems are becoming global because natural conditions such as the flow of winds, sea currents and tides transport particles, gases, minute amounts of toxic poisons or radioactivity from nuclear power stations. These emanate from numerous locations around the world and are then diffused through the atmosphere and seas. Thus, the pollution-generating and energy-intensive activities to which most people contribute – especially the members of what Durning (1992) calls the 'consuming class' (see Box 18.1) – endlessly push wastes, toxins and gases into rivers, seas, landfill sites and the atmosphere. However, as Beck (1992: 38, 23) has suggested, in this game the perpetrators become the victims through what he calls the 'boomerang effect'. For example, chemical-intensive agriculture eventually leads to declining soil fertility and soil erosion and the disappearance of wild plants and animals. Meanwhile, the lead used in petrol along with numerous other chemical traces may turn up in breast milk consumed by babies in distant cities.

Box 18.1   Consumer desires create a world of waste

The world's 'consuming class' of around 1.1 billion enjoyed per capita incomes of more than $7500 per year in the early 1990s. Most live in the advanced countries but this group also now includes about one-fifth of the wealthier people living in the South. The consuming class eats meat and processed/packaged foods, depends on numerous energy-intensive gadgets, lives in climate-controlled buildings supplied with abundant hot water and travels in private cars and jet aeroplanes. Mostly, it consumes goods that are soon thrown away when fashions change. In sharp contrast, the 1.1 billion *poorest global inhabitants* mostly travel on foot, rely on local resources for shelter and possessions (stone, wood, mud, and so on), mainly eat root crops, beans and lentils and frequently drink unsafe water.

Both of these groups are deeply implicated in global pollution although for very different reasons. Thus, it is poverty and necessity, not greed, which gives the global poor little choice but to increase the pressure on already fragile eco-systems such as semi-deserts and steep hill sides. In between these two groups comes what Durning (1992) calls the *middle income group* of 3.3 billion people. They eat mostly vegetables and

(cont'd)

cereals but are normally well-fed and have access to clean water. They also use bicycles and public transport and their possessions are made to last.

The throwaway economy created by the consuming class generates huge amounts of waste. This includes: the release of toxic poisons from farmlands and factories (linked, partly, to the more than 70 000 synthetic materials created by chemical industries); the emission of greenhouse gases; and the dumping of 'obsolescent' household goods. Thus, in the USA, a total of 3200 kilos of waste is created for every 100 kilos of manufactured products. Disposing of all this waste is expensive and may inflict permanent damage on the environment. Here are some data assembled in the early 1990s.

Packaging
- Packaging created almost half of the municipal waste which industrial countries must process.

- Packaging accounted for 40 per cent of paper consumption in Germany.

- Virtually two-fifths of plastics production in the USA was used for packaging.

- Each US consumer spent $225 on packaging and this included 140 million cubic meters of Styrofoam used for wrapping snacks such as peanuts.

Discarding products
Every year

- Germans reject 5 million domestic appliances.

- US citizens throw away 7.5 million TV sets.

- The Japanese use 30 million disposable cameras.

Advertising
- Advertising plays a big role in fostering consumerism. Total global spending rose from about $39 billion in 1950 to $495 billion by 1990.

- In the early 1990s, fourteen billion mail-order catalogues and 38 billion additional adverts were sent through the US mail system each year.

Sources: Durning (1992); Baird (1997)

The globalization of industrial development

The number of locations across the world that contribute to environmental degradation is increasing fast. Both because of its huge population and rapid economic growth, the case of China is particularly striking. Among many other environmental problems, 300 of China's cities are currently short of water, while four-fifths of China's rivers and lakes are badly polluted. Between 1992 and 1993, 100 000 people were poisoned by pesticides or fertilizers (Smith 1993: 19–21). Moreover, on present rates of growth, China will become the largest emitter of greenhouse gases by the year 2000 and will contribute 40 per cent of global carbon dioxide emissions by 2050 (p. 25). Continued economic development may also mean that most of China's present population of 1.2 billion people will soon join the world's current 1.1 billion 'consuming class'. If so, then, we will see a doubling of the present stress caused by industrialization upon the biosphere.

Meanwhile, growing international trade increases the volume of tankers and ships discharging oil and other substances into the oceans and fills up the skies with air-polluting traffic. Some developing countries – for example in West Africa – have accepted hazardous wastes from rich, environmentally conscious countries although recent international regulations and agreements (in 1989 and 1991) have reduced these practices to some extent. Moreover, the need to generate foreign exchange for debt repayment has encouraged some developing countries to accelerate the rate at which their forests are being cut down. This, in turn, is reducing the planet's capacity to absorb carbon dioxide.

Communications technology and the view from space

Since the mid-1960s, the increased sophistication of communications technology along with space travel have yielded ever more vivid images of planet earth. But satellites also provide much more accurate and compelling evidence concerning the increasingly global rather than purely local extent of environmental destruction (Milton 1996: 177). The effects of relentless logging in the tropics are one obvious example. Another concerns the probable damage inflicted by chemical pollution and ozone depletion on the huge concentrations of minute plant life or sea algae found around many of the world's coasts. The latter also play a major role in absorbing carbon dioxide.

Reasons for scepticism

According to Yearley (1996a: 66) green groups have every interest in claiming that they are working for 'a global mission' on behalf of all humanity. This is because groups that engage in such appeals find this boosts their membership. They may also experience more media attention and greater access to governments and IGOs (pp. 86–92). In effect, adopting a global perspective becomes a path to success. Another reason for doubting the global claims of green activists is that environmental problems do not threaten all human life to the same degree. Islands such as the Maldives or lowland areas in countries such as Bangladesh, for example, may be flooded if the predictions concerning global warming prove correct. However, people living at higher elevations will escape this effect although they may experience other consequences of climate change such as increased droughts. Similarly, wealthy countries will be better equipped than poor countries to cope with such problems as rising sea levels (Yearley 1996a: 78).

Sceptics also point to the deep divisions within the environmental movement. According to Milton (1996: 187), an important minority of radical or 'deep' greens shares 'an anti-globalist perspective'. One example here is the NGO Earth First! which emerged in the USA during the 1980s. It has become famous for its direct action campaigns involving strategies such as disabling bulldozers and spiking trees with iron bars in order to deter building projects and forest logging. Such activists see the relentless worldwide drive for material prosperity and the global linking of national economies together through investment and trade as the main problem. Indeed, what is required is de-globalization – the recovery of lost cultural and local self-sufficiencies – and a return to simpler, more self-reliant, decentralized economies. These groups also reject the theory of sustainable development discussed in the next section.

**Figure 18.1   Looking to the future: the
Earth Summit, Rio de Janeiro, 1992**

Deep divisions are also apparent between governments. Thus, not only are most states reluctant to surrender part of their sovereignty to supra-national regulatory bodies in the pursuit of global solutions but conflicts of interest have arisen on some issues. That between the richer countries and the developing world is probably the most serious. It became particularly obvious during the Earth Summit at Rio in 1992 and it has continued to impede international action ever since, particularly on global warming. The main issues that divide the North and South include the following:

1. The leaders of the South argue that the North's historical culpability for environmental problems is undeniably greater. Currently, the North uses up 70 per cent of the world's energy, three-quarters of its metals, three-fifths of its food and 85 per cent of its wood. Yet it contains barely a quarter of the global population (Athanasiou 1997: 53). For example, with less than 5 per cent of the world's population the USA consumes a quarter of its energy. Partly this is linked to the fact that it has the highest propensity for air travel (Seager 1995: 30) and uses 31 per cent of the world's total vehicles. Not surprisingly, it is also by far the largest single emitting country (19 per cent) of greenhouse gases (Kidron and Segal 1995: 18–23). By contrast, India with over 16 per cent of the world's population currently consumes only 3 per cent of the world's energy (Seager 1995: 72).

2. The South further claims that high living standards in the North are partly a consequence of Southern cheap labour and an unfair international trading

system, which underpays poor countries for their raw materials. The vast transfers of funds in debt repayment since the 1970s to Northern governments and banks has further angered the South.

3. Southern countries therefore expect the North to subsidize the supply of cleaner technologies to poorer countries so that they can industrialize without losing economic momentum or adding massively to global pollution. Similarly, they expect the North to create 'space' in the world economy for Southern development by reducing its own consumption levels. They have also asked for compensation in return for agreeing to slow down the rate of deforestation or taking steps to preserve bio-diversity.

North–South differences surfaced fiercely over the issue of global warming both at Rio in 1992 and Kyoto in 1997 (see Table 18.2). Led by the USA, the advanced countries have argued that future Southern industrialization represents the real danger to the biosphere – especially in the case of countries like China and India with their huge populations and considerable reserves of fossil fuels. Thus, they argue that it make no sense to impose tough environmental limits on the rich countries without insisting that equally sweeping constraints are adopted by the South. Moreover, at the Rio conference the North agreed to find the resources required in order to operationalize Agenda 21 – 'an international programme of action for achieving sustainable development in the 21st Century' (Grubb *et al.* 1995: 97). Here, it was calculated that the South would need to spend $625 billion per year with the hope that the North would provide one-fifth of this sum. So far most Northern countries have not made any such increased contribution towards meeting Southern needs (Dodds 1997: 192).

FRIENDS OF THE GREEN MOVEMENT?

The claims made by environmentalism to represent the interests of all humanity may or may not be entirely valid. But the movement does seem to have achieved a nearly universal appeal and in this sense it evinces a certain global dimension. In this section we consider the support for environmentalism which has come from the top-down actions spearheaded by powerful élite groups, states and international organizations.

State and UN involvement in environmentalism since 1972

As you can see from Table 18.2, governments have sometimes been prepared to act on environmental matters through the auspices of the United Nations General Assembly (UNGA). The United Nations Environment Programme (UNEP) and the World Commission on Environment and Development (WCED) have also become important foci for change.

According to McCormick (1989: 88) the United Nations conference at Stockholm in 1972 'was the first occasion on which the… problems of the global environment were discussed at an intergovernmental forum with a view to actually taking corrective action'. Most of the initiative for instigating the 1972 conference came from the Swedish government. However, it was also strongly supported by several leading scientific and green INGOs. This set a crucial precedent for future world conferences where INGOs later became much more prominent (Willetts 1996: 69). The developing countries also participated despite their suspicions that Northern green concerns might be a ploy to slow down Southern development.

Table 18.2   State and UN involvement in environmentalism: key events

Event/venue and date	Main initiator and representation (if any)	Key outcomes
Stockholm, 1972	Swedish government. Leading politicians from 113 countries and over 250 NGOs	The UNGA voted to establish the UNEP
New York, 1983	The UNGA called for the establishment of the WCED to investigate how economic development and environmental safety could be pursued simultaneously	Gro Harlem (Norway's Prime Minister) was asked to chair the WCED's deliberations. In 1987 the WCED published *Our Common Future*. This offered what became the world's guiding principle of Sustainable Development
New York, 1989	The UNGA called for the convening of the United Nations Conference on Environment and Development (UNCED) at Rio de Janeiro in 1992 (the Earth Summit) to debate the implementation of sustainable development	
Rio de Janeiro, the Earth Summit, 1992	UNGA, UNEP, WCED Attended by government delegations from 178 countries including 120 heads of state, more than 5000 journalists and representatives from 9000 green NGOs and INGOs are said to have attended	Various agreements, but they mostly involved declarations of principle on issues such as climate change and biodiversity rather than binding commitments Agenda 21 offered a set of practical guidelines concerning how countries could implement sustainable development across their economies
Kyoto, Japan, 1997, successor to Rio on slowing global warming	UNEP, UNCED Government leaders and officials from 159 countries plus 10 000 journalists, green activists and industrial lobbyists	An agreement to cut greenhouse gas emissions by an overall 5.5 per cent (on 1990 levels) by 2012 but with varying targets set for different countries. Doubts exist as to its global enforceability or whether the US Congress will agree to its ratification

Sources: McCormick (1989: 101); Princen and Finger (1994); Willetts (1996: 69); Dodds (1997: 4–5)

The 1972 Stockholm conference set in train an important sequence of global activities especially the establishment of the UNEP. Its role was to safeguard the world's environment and co-operate with relevant agencies. Although the UNEP has been underfunded the growing evidence of environmental problems and growing grass-roots influence has boosted its influence. Of course, in between Stockholm 1972 and Kyoto 1997, there have been many other world environmental conferences too numerous to mention. Some have given rise to international agreements such as those reached at Montreal in 1987 and Copenhagen in 1992 on phasing out the production and use of CFCs and other dangerous ozone-destroying chemicals. But the lineage of world events as briefly outlined is probably the most significant.

Sustainable development: a manual for green reform?

The concept of 'sustainable development' offered by the WCED in 1987 provided inspiration as well as a set of clear environmental guidelines. Its central tenet is that the pursuit of economic development is perfectly compatible with greater environmental safety. There are two key reasons for linking these goals together. First, given the South's primary concern with overcoming national poverty it might have been unwilling to co-operate without a parallel commitment to the goal of development. Second, since poverty has been widely recognized as a major cause of global environmental devastation in its own right, reducing it through economic development should simultaneously help the environment. The WCED report argued that three principles must be followed:

1. A commitment to better environmental management must be incorporated into all future economic decision-making procedures whether by states, companies or households. Partly, this means requiring all farms, factories and other businesses to stop using the seas, rivers or the atmosphere as a free dumping ground for their waste. But it also involves giving priority to the development of new technologies that will reduce the amount of energy and materials used in every sphere of economic life.

2. Overcoming worldwide environmental problems requires an inescapable moral pledge to the idea of greater equity. Thus, each generation should desist from squandering the environmental capital it inherits but try to leave the planet in a fit state for their children to use. Similarly, the rich countries should agree to assist the poorer South in its attempts to attain economic development without imperilling the goal of environmental safety.

3. Sustainability also demands that in future we should prioritize issues relating to the quality of life rather than higher material living standards measured solely in money terms. Instead of the obsession with acquiring a second or larger car we would do well to worry more about our ability to breathe city air without contracting asthma or the availability of undamaged scenery along with sufficient leisure time to enjoy it.

Critique of sustainable development

The idea of sustainable development has been widely criticized. According to Lele (1991: 613) the chief difficulty is that it tries to offer 'a 'metafix' that will unite everybody from green activists, conservationists and poor farmers in the South to development-oriented governments and large companies. It therefore fails to provide much of real substance for anyone. For example, as we have seen, the proponents of sustainable development claim that reducing poverty through further economic growth will make an essential contribution to reducing environmental devastation. However, Lele avers (p. 614) that by itself, economic growth has never been sufficient to reduce poverty or inequality. It is difficult to see, therefore, how it can contribute to environmental sustainability in the absence of additional policies aimed at overcoming poverty through redistributing incomes in favour of deprived groups.

Another major critic, Sachs (1993), fears that the concept of sustainability and its related ethos of environmental managerialism have generated a new breed of élite, global 'eco-crats' (p. xvii). This group has hijacked the green agenda from the more radical groups. Unlike many individuals and green activists, the eco-crats do not regard the biosphere as a fragile heritage that needs to be protected for posterity. Rather, they regard it as a 'commercial asset in danger' (p. xvii). The earth's dwindling resources require worldwide management by, and on behalf of, the rich and powerful.

Collaboration with élite institutions: risks and new paths

By and large we should welcome top-down initiatives. Actions by TNCs, IGOs and, above all, by states are usually helpful because they can affect the structural constraints on social behaviour in far-reaching ways. For example, only states can introduce the green taxes, financial incentives and policies required at the national level in order to encourage or compel individuals, corporations and others to adopt more environmentally friendly practices. Moreover, states 'remain the only actors who can legally reach international environmental accords, and... are ultimately held responsible for those agreements' (Clapp 1997: 137).

For this and other reasons, green INGOs and global social movements have often collaborated with élite agents to their mutual advantage. The former have gained because the willingness of UN agencies and states to provide increasing access to important global events has provided green activists with a platform for expressing grass-roots concerns and an opportunity to influence global policy-making. However, states and UN agencies also benefit because green groups enjoy resources that may facilitate the search for environmental solutions. These include technical expertise, a reputation for integrity, an intimate knowledge of local peoples and wide ranging support from the grass-roots, the media, and professionals groups (see also Box 16.2). All of these give green groups considerable bargaining power. In the late 1980s, between 10 and 15 per cent of the development funding provided by the OECD countries to the South was routed through NGOs (Princen and Finger 1994: 34). Another example of collaboration involving the World Bank is discussed in Box 18.2.

However, such collaboration may undermine the autonomy of green groups and their capacity to demand radical change by activating grass-roots pressure. Anything that weakens their capacity to shape global opinion and influence policy-making effectively could jeopardize our future. This is not because green INGOs and global social movements are always right and states or TNCs are invariably wrong – although the public is usually more inclined to trust the former than the latter. Rather, the difficulty is that governments face constraints that may undermine their ability to lead in the environmental arena. In part this is because the primary duty of states is to protect national sovereignty, for example by guaranteeing military security. This makes them reluctant to delegate their powers to supranational regulatory bodies for global environmental purposes.

Even governments with excellent environmental records may, on occasion, find it difficult to operate effectively at the transnational level. Norway's reluctance to sign the international moratorium on commercial whaling in the 1980s is a case in point. At the same time, the absence of a world government and the current reluctance of the USA – the nearest thing we have to a hegemonic power – to do much with respect to green issues means that reaching effective global agreements is fraught with difficulties.

Box 18.2   States, IGOs and transnational alliances: Brazil's rain forests

Struggles in Brazil

In the 1970s an estimated 300 000 Brazilians combined subsistence farming with living sustainably from the Amazonian forests by tapping rubber trees or collecting nuts and other forest products. However, Brazil's government wanted to colonize the region with settlers, loggers and ranchers (the Polonoroeste project) linked to the construction of a massive highway. From 1976, the rubber-tappers resisted these invasions by direct actions such as blocking bulldozers. Led by Chico Mendes, they also demanded the formation of conservation areas farmed by local people for non-timber products ('extractive reserves'). By 1985 they had saved approximately three million forest acres from colonization. In 1986 they joined forces with the native Indians.

Growing transnational support in the 1980s

Alarmed by continuing Amazon deforestation – worsened by Brazil's need to service its huge debts – and the growing threat to wildlife and local peoples, Northern green groups began to oppose further Amazonian development schemes.

■ From 1983, a US coalition of green NGOs pushed the World Bank and other big multilateral development banks (MDBs) to recognize the impact their lending schemes were having upon local people and the environment. The MDBs provide loans for large-scale projects at favourable rates of interest (including Brazil's gigantic Polonoroeste and highway projects).

■ In 1985 many US university groups formed the Rain forest Action Network (RAN). By 1990 there were 150 RAN groups plus another 100 worldwide. RAN supported the coalition to alter MDB lending policies. It also led a consumer boycott of leading restaurant chains such as Burger King because their beef imports came from ranches carved out of South American forests.

■ From 1985, Northern NGOs allied with local Southern groups and with like-minded NGOs in Japan, Canada, Australasia and Europe. These North–South coalitions pooled their ideas concerning environmental and social problems in the Amazon and elsewhere.

■ In 1987, the US Greens invited Chico Mendes to Washington. Helped by worldwide media interest and impressed by his first-hand knowledge about the impact of Brazil's projects on local people and wildlife, the WB/MDBs agreed to change their lending policies. Brazil was required to negotiate an agreement on forest-sharing acceptable to all local groups before its 1987 loan application was accepted. Future loan approvals would incorporate the principle of preserving extractive reserves. The World Bank also agreed to take more account of green issues when deciding future loans.

Postscript to these events

Chico Mendes was assassinated in 1989 and the rubber-tappers were still resisting further encroachments by logging companies and ranchers in 1994. Nevertheless, green INGOs learned much from this episode. It helped to blaze the trail for a number of similar transnational alliances in countries such as Malaysia, Bolivia, India and Indonesia.

Sources: Scarce (1990: Chapter 8); Bramble and Porter (1992: 325–34); *The Ecologist* (1994); *Campaigns* (various issues)

In addition, growing competition to attract foreign investment along with the increasingly foot-loose nature of capital means that governments are less and less willing to take any steps which might deter investment by TNCs (Clapp 1997: 127). Indeed, the unwillingness of states to place too many environmental constraints on TNCs has recently led many green NGOs and global social movements to switch the targets of their campaigning focus to the large global corporations (see Box 18.3). The aim here has been to fill the void in international regulation left by government reluctance to frustrate or annoy business (Newall 1998).

Thus, there are always likely to be situations where states, businesses and other élite interests are reluctant to undertake the environmental policies, which only they can. Green NGOs and global social movements may believe that it is necessary to mobilize pressure from below in order to compel states and others to accept the need for more radical agendas (see the case study in Box 18.2). Yet, the capacity of NGOs and global social movements to act in this way means they must avoid becoming compromised by élite interests. Above all, they must do nothing to lose, indeed they need to expand, their grass-roots support wherever possible. And yet activists need to collaborate with governments, IGOs and business interests wherever possible because the latters' potential role in fostering the conditions for environmental improvement is often paramount. Negotiating a path through this political minefield is difficult and risky.

MOBILIZING BOTTOM-UP SUPPORT FOR LOCAL AND GLOBAL ACTIONS

When it comes to activating grass-roots support green groups may have several aims. One involves the need to mobilize supporters in order to engage in controversial protests and political struggles – perhaps initially little understood or supported. Sometimes, these are directed against clearly identifiable and powerful agents of environmental destruction such as governments intent on implementing massive development projects, oil companies or timber importers. On other occasions, actions are more likely to draw attention to the complicity of ordinary members of the public – for example their preference for obtaining cheap food even where this entails dangerous chemical contamination or cruel methods of factory-farming. We might call this the 'hard' or fighting edge of the green movement.

Environmental groups also need to work consistently at raising the consciousness of ordinary citizens. The reason for this is that to different degrees we all act in ways which contribute towards environmental deterioration, although often unwittingly. As such, we are all potential targets of green criticism. Similarly, not only do we all *need* to contribute to making a greener world but with a little assistance and education most of us, perhaps, are quite *capable* of doing so. More often than not, lifestyle activities such as recycling household rubbish or buying furniture produced from environmentally managed forests demand very little in the way of overt political commitment. Yet when ordinary, everyday lifestyle changes are adopted by large numbers of people they may make a critical contribution to the attainment of green objectives.

Thus, not everything linked to environmentalism requires radical collective action. We might regard such actions as the 'soft' side of environmentalism. Mostly, they have deep roots in individual and domestic life and the need to steadily alter opinion over time. Somewhere in between the two extremes of 'hard' and 'soft' environmental commitment there lies a cluster of supporting actions whereby green groups can count on dedicated minorities to support specific campaigns. These might require joining a mass public protest such as a march or picket. Equally, however, the decision by sympathizers – each mostly working in isolation – to exercise their right to make selective choices as consumers, shareholders, taxpayers or users of various facilities, can sometimes be very effective. Here, the products/services provided by one bank, company or institution are boycotted while those provided by others are favoured.

In Chapter 16 we argued that it is precisely this embeddedness of much social movement activity in life politics and issues of personal identity which enables global social movements and INGOs to transcend purely local protests. Local struggles can then be thrown into the maelstrom of transnational action in the pursuit of global goals. Selective buying campaigns are likely to play a particularly important role because they are relatively easily to activate and co-ordinate across countries simultaneously. Thus, while there are many situation where the most practical policy is to seek global support for solutions to *local* problems – 'act locally but think globally' – increasingly it is both necessary and possible to mobilize local support in order to solve *global* problems.

There are three other factors that have enabled global social movements and INGOs to undertake successful transnational actions:

1. Their skill in focusing worldwide media attention on different environmental crises through various kinds of stunts and the ability to harness the opportunities provided by recent advances in electronic communications.

2. Their bargaining power with respect to élite agents because of their reputation, close ties to sympathetic scientists, their acquisition of technical expertise and their role in educating the public.

3. Their access to many cross-issue and transnational networks, coalitions and alliances in which groups may participate and the growing repertoire of techniques available for political protest.

The ability of green groups to utilize some or all of these resources simultaneously may empower them to lobby élite groups directly. Failing this they may wield the 'implicit threat of embarrassing delinquent governments' (Clapp 1997: 135) or other agents such as TNCs whose environmental record is unacceptable. INGOs are especially effective in activating transnational pressures for change because in addition to political activities as campaigners, they are also organizations run by semi-permanent officials. Consequently, they enjoy continuity, access to regular sources of information and links with other relevant organizations. Many can also fall back on regular financial resources through membership subscriptions. All this gives INGOs considerable flexibility with respect to synchronizing actions across distances and between events and issues. An interesting recent example of how all these processes and resources may work in practice in order to activate green transnational grass-roots support can be seen in Box 18.3.

Box 18.3   Act globally yet think locally: green battles with Shell

Between 1995 and 1997 Shell, one of the world's largest international oil companies, was faced with worldwide criticism and concerted transnational attacks on some of its operations. Two main incidents earned Shell this attention:

■ **Brent Spar** In February 1995 the UK government decided to approve Shell's decision to deal with the de-commissioning of an North Sea oil platform – Brent Spar – by deep-water disposal rather than towing it to land for dismantling.

■ **Nigeria and the Ogoni activists** In November 1995 the Nigerian government allowed the execution of nine activists, including the internationally renowned playwright, Ken Saro-Wiwa. They had long protested about the impact of Shell's oil industry on Ogoni society in eastern Nigeria. For example, between 1982 and 1992 1.6 million gallons of oil were spilled, destroying many fishing and farming communities. When asked by INGOs such as Amnesty International in 1994 to intercede on behalf of the arrested Ogoni activists, Shell said it had no right to interfere in Nigerian state affairs (although earlier it had asked for police and army protection from protesters).

The four-pronged, transnational counter attack

■ Various INGOs **pressurized governments** in the EU and the USA to impose trade and other sanctions on Nigeria with some success (for example, the EU suspended development aid and three US cities stopped buying Nigerian goods). In June 1995, the EU governments urged the UK to insist on a land-based disposal of Brent Spar by Shell.

■ **Direct action** In April 1995, Greenpeace occupied the platform, shadowed by its dinghies and helicopter, invited the press and TV to accompany the occupation and provided video footage of these North Sea events.

■ **Consumer boycotts and demonstrations** In late May, Greenpeace called for European-wide picketing of Shell petrol stations and a boycott of its products. This was especially successful in Germany where sales fell by 70 per cent in some service stations. In mid-June activists attacked some German Shell petrol stations. In November, there were demonstrations and a consumer boycott over the Ogoni executions supported by US groups.

■ **The shareholders revolt** In May 1997, a minority of shareholders, including the WWF, Amnesty International, various churches and other ethical groups, co-operated to introduce a resolution at Shell's Annual General Meeting. They demanded a much stricter corporate policy in future with regard to environmental and human rights issues.

These campaigns seem to have influenced Shell

■ In June 1995, it agreed to a land-based decommissioning of Brent Spar.

■ Financial compensation has been offered for the environmental damage inflicted in Nigeria.

■ Company operations have become more open to public scrutiny and Shell now encourages external auditing of its environmental activities.

■ In May 1998 Shell published its first *Report to Society*. Here, it recognized that: 'Consumers expect us to take a long-term interest in the economic and social well-being of the wider community, including the international community, and reflect this in the sensible development of the world's natural resources.'

Sources: Dickson and McCulloch (1996); Caulkin (1997); Corzine (1997); Rodman (1998); *Ethical Consumer* (1998); www.shell.co.uk.

REVIEW

Environmentalism may have a potentially universal appeal. This is because we all bear some responsibility for green problems and most of us can and perhaps need to contribute to finding solutions through accepting personal lifestyle changes while supporting appropriate public policies. Presumably we also stand to gain from the preservation of a safe, vibrant natural world. In any case, as many countries in the South rush headlong towards industrialization, so environmental distress is becoming globalized.

Because global problems demand global solutions it is hardly surprising that the green movement has increasingly sought to operate transnationally. Partly, what enables green groups to be globally effective is their capacity to construct viable linkages between different countries, groups and issues. But what also empowers them is their growing ability to collaborate with powerful élite interests when that appears useful while activating transnational grass-roots support for more radical agendas whenever the opposition to change displayed by the former makes this necessary.

If you would like to know more ●

Scarce's (1990) book, *Eco-warriors,* offers a lively introduction to green radicalism. Chapter 8 deals with international movements.

Couched in very accessible prose, *How Much is Enough*? by Durning (1992), presents a bold analysis of Northern lifestyles, exposing their contribution to global environmental problems.

Yearley's (1996a) book, *Sociology, Environmentalism, Globalization*, assesses environmentalism's global claims and the debate concerning sustainable development from a thoroughly sociological perspective. Some of these ideas are also explored in Yearley's (1996b), 'The transnational politics of the environment' in Anderson *et al.* (eds), *A Global World?*

John Kirkby and his colleagues (1995) have produced a reader of 39 previously published articles, together with an original introduction to the idea of 'sustainable development', in *The Earthscan Reader in Sustainable Development*.

Group work ●

1. Refer to your library's copy of the journal, *The Ecologist*, published six times each year. Most issues run a feature called *Campaigns*. A group of students could agree in advance to check the back issues of *Campaigns*, listing the various types of green protests discussed and following through how they developed. To what extent did these protests become transnational? What kinds of global connections were established?

2. Arrange a debate on the following proposition; 'The global nature and claims of the environmental movement have been greatly exaggerated'. After the speakers have been heard, each remaining class member will give two reasons why they either agree or disagree.

3. Access Shell's site on the Internet (www.shell.co.uk). Find their latest *Report to Society*. Read this on the Net and respond to the boxes in the section marked 'Tell the Chairman what you think'. Alternatively, you may want to request a copy

of the *Report to Society* from Chris Fay, Chairman and Chief Executive, Shell UK Ltd, Shell-Mex House, Strand, London WC2R 0DX, United Kingdom. Share your impressions of this report with your class.

Questions to think about •

1. Many environmental activists claim that they represent the interests of all humanity. Evaluate the validity of such claims.

2. On balance, who gains most from collaboration, environmental groups or élite interests such as states, IGOs and TNCs? Explain your answer.

3. Examine the obstacles that made it difficult to implement the principle of sustainable development on a realistic basis worldwide?

4. 'We may all be culpable where global environmental problems are concerned but some are much more responsible than others.' Discuss.

CONTENTS

Major Concept

COMMUNITIES

Communities are marked by deep, familiar and co-operative ties between members. In this sense, 'community' is close to Durkheim's idea of social solidarity, which emerges from commitment to a shared set of values. He calls this 'the collective conscience'. A formal definition is given by Nisbet (1970: 47). For him, community 'encompasses all forms of relationship which are characterized by a high degree of personal intimacy, emotional depth, moral commitment, social cohesion and continuity in time'.

A major theme of this book has been that of commonality and difference. In various places we have talked about the ways in which people are pushed apart, treated in unequal ways or socially excluded. In this chapter we are concerned with social *inclusion* – with how social ties are generated and sustained at different levels. One sociologist (Scheff 1990: 4) has proposed that the maintenance of social bonds is 'our most crucial human motive'. The relationship between closeness and distance, he continues, gives rise to a theoretically optimal level of differentiation 'which balances the needs of the individual and the needs of the self. It involves being able to maintain ties with others who are different from self'. These bonds are often formalized in associations, but are usually more loosely expressed in **COMMUNITIES** or other units of belonging.

There are many units of social solidarity – such as the family, organizations including work and voluntary associations, an ethnicity, a religion or a nation. Given the main theme of the book, we are also interested in the possibilities of creating communities at a global level. These different expressions of community can be seen simply as indicating differences in scale, starting from the most immediate and intimate and ending at the most macroscopic and remote. It might be tempting to assume that the ties that bind people most strongly are those that are most immediate and intimate and that those that seem most abstract are the weakest, or virtually nugatory. However, this view is much too simple, as can be seen in the following examples:

- *The nuclear family* Some of the previously most intimate of social bonds, for instance, the nuclear family in industrial societies, are undergoing massive changes. In the USA, for example, over the period 1970–95 the marriage rate fell by 30 per cent, the number of people who had never married doubled, the divorce rate increased by 40 per cent, unmarried-couple households increased by sevenfold and half of all children expected to spend a least part of their childhood in single-parent homes (Tischler 1996: 353–4). Such data partly reflect changing gender expectations, the restructuring of the labour market and more relaxed attitudes to sexual norms, including gay and lesbian partnerships. However, there is no doubt that family life, as conventionally conceived, has radically altered in a significant number of countries in the West.

- *Transnational communities* By contrast, 'time–space compression' has encouraged an increasing volume and intensity of ties (through tourism and migration for example) of people that were previously less intimately linked. Further interconnections and interdependencies have been promoted mainly by the spread of a worldwide economic market and a network of increasingly powerful transnational actors and organizations, such as the TNCs. A sense of global community has also been promoted by common challenges facing all the world's inhabitants – from a threat to the biosphere to poorly policed nuclear arsenals. These planetary problems have generated an awareness of global issues (we have called this 'globalism') and a form of worldwide politics, seen in the growth and support for global social moments like the 'greens' and the feminists.

The bonds felt and experienced by social actors at these different levels are not mutually exclusive. Rather, they are reactive, contradictory and complementary. On the one hand, the scale, pace and intensity of global changes have led to fears of atomization and anonymization. A powerful set of reactions has reasserted the salience and continued viability of local communities and forms of belonging. On the other hand, some intimate characteristics of small, old communities have been transferred to a larger scale. A nation, for example, you will remember from Chapter 5, was memorably described as an 'imagined community'. Again Faist (1998: 221) and others have shown how transnational communities are 'connected by dense and strong social and symbolic ties over time and across space [by] patterns of networks and circuits'. They are 'communities without propinquity, in which community and spatial proximity are decoupled'.

We are thus able loosely to classify 'communities' under the rubrics of *local*, *national* and *transnational*:

1. We call the behaviour of communities that act on a relatively small-scale '*localism*' (a convenient word used to cover all movements based on family, kin, ethnic and sub-national sentiments).

2. A second level, '*nationalism*', seeks to create anew, re-assert or reform the nation state as a continuing focus of loyalty and association.

3. Finally, working, as they see it, *with* the grain of history are those states, groups, organizations and individuals that recognize diversity and difference and seek to foster creative and positive bonds between peoples of different national backgrounds. We will call this tendency 'transnationalism'.

THE RESURGENCE OF LOCALISM

Despite, or perhaps because of all the global forces acting to make people come together, fierce struggles have ensued to continue to keep people apart. Instead of global integration in the wake of the Cold War and increased economic globalization, we have been confronted by many localized ethnic and religious conflicts. As political ideology has receded it has partly been replaced by the politics of identity and community. Premdas (1996) claims that there are some 4000 'ethnocultural' groups worldwide, uneasily enclosed in 185 states. With migration, commerce and travel, nearly all states are now multi-ethnic to some degree: the few exceptions include Somalia, Korea, Botswana and Swaziland. Forty per cent of the world's states have more than five significant ethnic communities. By 1996, there were 100 ongoing sub-national conflicts, about 20 classified as 'high intensity'. To contain these conflicts, some of the peace dividend has had to be spent on 70 000 UN peacekeepers costing $4 billion each year to maintain.

Many observers have been alarmed at the increasingly militant demands for ethnic exclusivity, minority language education, religious separatism, and exclusive territorial entities. The conflicts between Kosovars and Serbs in the Balkans, Hutu and Tutsi in Rwanda, Christians and Muslims in the Lebanon, Jews and Arabs in the Middle East, Tamils and Sinhalese in Sri Lanka, Protestants and Catholics in Northern Ireland – all these examples and many more show the persistence, tenacity or re-emergence of ethnic and religious differences.

This phenomenon presents a paradox to the theorists of globalization. If social, political, cultural and economic changes are all thought to be moving in a global or, macro-direction, how come we see, throughout the world, evidence of the contrary tendency – namely the assertion, or sometimes the re-assertion, of local identities? A partial solution of this paradox may be found in the writings of Stuart Hall. He suggests that globalization at the cultural level has also brought about the fragmentation and multiplication of identities and this may require, paradoxically, a return to the familiar. Hall (1991: 35–6) describes it like this:

> The face-to-face communities that are knowable, that are locatable, one can give them a place. One knows what the voices are. One knows what the faces are. The re-creation, the reconstruction of imaginary, knowable places in the face of the global post-modern which has, as it were, destroyed the identities of specific places, absorbed them into this post-modern flux of diversity. So one understands the moment when people reach for those groundings, as it were, and the reach for those groundings is what we call ethnicity.

In other words, ethnicity is not an irrelevant anachronism to the gathering pace of globalization but a necessary reaction to it. It is true that we are becoming increasingly interdependent in economic and cultural terms, that there is an increased awareness that we are 'one world' facing common ecological, political and security problems. Yet this very process of globalization, the very rapidity of the dissolution of the known world, creates an unexpected effect. People reach out to the habitual, to the communities where they find familiar faces, voices, sounds, smells, tastes and places. Confronted by the pace of globalization they often need ethnicity *more* not less. Confused by the effects of post-modernity, relativism and the deconstruction of their known world, they re-affirm and reify what they believe to be true.

For many people, ethnic ties are a matter of loyalty, of pride, of location, of belonging, of refuge, of identity, trust, acceptance and security. It is the type of attachment that most parents feel for their children and most siblings feel for one another. As Allahar (1994) suggests, such ties imply an unquestioned affinity and devotion purely on the basis of the intimacy of the tie. It is the closest form of association that can be achieved by a collectivity of humans. It expresses their gregariousness and preference for group membership rather than the social rejection of a misfit or the isolation of a hermit. By embracing an ethnic identity, groups of human beings acknowledge that they are part of society and that their survival depends on forces bigger than the individual. The locality into which they were born and which has nurtured them is an object of affection – in that place are others who share their origin and their likely fate.

MARGINALIZING LOCAL IDENTITIES

We have briefly explained why ethnic ties are much more resilient than many observers predicted. Their continuing strength accounts for the simultaneity of globalization and localization. However, we also need to clarify why the force of ethnicity was (relatively speaking) neglected in social theory until the 1980s. There is no doubt that the continuing power of ethnicity, race and religion was overlooked by those who believed that only one global future was possible. In the post-war world ethnicity was also marginalized by the two dominant interpretations of social change, modernization theory and Marxism, which we will discuss in turn.

Modernization theorists

Derived from the eighteenth- and nineteenth-century notions of progress, modernization theorists posited increasing secularization, urbanization, industrialization and rationalization – spread by the emerging state bureaucracies. Ethnicity and nation were things of the past – a receding reality. It had, of course to be conceded that even modern nations, such as Nazi Germany, had experienced massive upsurges of a dangerous nationalist spirit. But this had been defeated and many of the characterizations of the phenomenon used the language of primitivism to describe National Socialism. For example, it was denounced as 'abnormal', 'deviant', or 'atavistic'. The implication was that since Nazism had been vanquished, Germany could be normalized and returned to the modern fold. The academics and educators who were sent into Germany after the war specifically had the task of 'de-Nazifying' the state. Ultimately, rationalism, secularization, constitutionalism and liberal democracy would prevail. This package had, in turn, to be sold to the 'emerging nations'.

Marxists

The second dominant interpretation of social change was Marxism which, like modernization theory, was dismissive of ethnic and national loyalties. As we mentioned in Chapter 6, Marxists argued that ethnicity and nationalism were used cynically by dominant or rising classes for instrumental purposes of their own. Competing élites need masses for raw street power and ethnic appeals worked to arouse the poor and uninformed. Marxists sought to abolish ethnicity as merely an ***epiphenomenon*** or as an instance or false consciousness. For Marxists the only form of true consciousness was class consciousness. But while class may indeed be a powerful form of association, powerful enough sometimes to rival or overdetermine ethnic consciousness, it makes little sense to call the one 'true' and dismiss the other as 'false' consciousness.

> An **epiphenomenon** is something that appears to be of great causal significance, but is really derived from some other primary basis. In overvaluing an epiphenomenon observers mistake a symptom for a reason.

Class consciousness arises, as Marx averred, from an objectively different relationship to the means of production, distribution and exchange shared by those who sell their labour power, own capital or trade in commodities or services. These different positions give them different interests. As is now generally accepted, contemporary capitalism has produced the conditions whereby these interests have become overlapping and thereby diluted. However, a more fundamental critique of the idea of a superordinate class consciousness, is that class awareness is predominantly an awareness of *interest*. And despite the mantras of the Marxists and the free marketeers alike, people live not just by interests alone, but by their emotions. They live by anger, grief, anxiety, jealousy, affection, fear and devotion – precisely those emotions harnessed by localism.

HOW DOES LOCALISM ARISE?

We have argued so far that kinship, ethnicity and religion are much more powerful forces than many of us would, perhaps, like to accept. We have also suggested that localism does not disappear when confronted with the rival claims of class interest, the demands of nation-building, or the impelling force of globalization. The Marxist charge of 'false consciousness' is contradicted by the weight of historical evidence that many more people are prepared to fight and die for their ethnic group, nation and religion than for their class. One barely needs to spell this out. Class war takes the form of strikes, marches and meetings (very rarely are the barricades of class revolution raised). But ethnic, religious and national wars often take the form of mass destruction, ethnic cleansing, saturation bombing, genocide, nuclear attack, defoliation, inquisitions and terrorism.

Even if we accept that ethnicity, race and religion are uncomfortably powerful *subjective* forces, how do we explain how ethnic differences arise? There are four ways, discussed in turn, in which ethnicity can be moulded by structural factors and established patterns of social behaviour:

1. Legal and political restrictions that force differences to remain or create them for the first time.

2. A history of coerced labour that has moulded ethnic work hierarchies.

3. Differences in appearance.

4. The forms of belief that pattern people's responses to difference.

Figure 19.1   Members of the Orange Order, Northern Ireland, commemorate the defeat of the Irish at the Battle of the Boyne in 1690

Legal and political restrictions

In many settings there were legal and political restrictions on which occupations and activities were permitted to subordinated groups. We will give just one, admittedly extreme, example. Until the end of legal apartheid in South Africa in 1989, people designated as 'Bantu', 'white', 'coloured and 'Asian' were legally separated from one another, while the Bantu (black) section of the population was subdivided into ethnicities such as the Zulu, Tswana, Venda and Xhosa. While we can all recognize the artificiality of a number of these distinctions, the argument has to be pressed one stage further. Legalized ethnic distinctions were given force in economic, educational and occupational terms and this deter-mined the limits of opportunity in terms of access to good housing, jobs or health care. Ethnic identities were, in short, not freely selected but *imposed* by law and the threat of state violence.

History of coerced migration

Ethnic, racial and religious differences also arose through various kinds of coerced migration. Colonial and mercantile powers often brought different peoples to new settings for work on their plantations or to further their commercial interests. For example, ten million African slaves were trans-shipped across the Atlantic while 1.4 million Indian indentured workers were sent to the sugar plantations. The governor of Dutch Indonesia even sent warships to capture Chinese on the mainland to help develop his colony. These patterns of involuntary migration led to complex, often three-way, interactions as indigenous people faced outsiders, who faced other outsiders, who all faced representatives of the colonial powers. Alluding to the time and circumstances in which immigrants were brought in, we can see how occupational categories fused with ethnic identities. Thus, we have an evolution of a sort of paired 'ethno-class', a phenomenon evoked by these familiar descriptions such as 'Chinese traders', 'Indian "coolies"', 'Sikh soldiers', 'Irish navvies', 'Lebanese middlemen' or 'Scottish engineers'.

Differences in appearance

A third objective factor which limits the way in way in which ethnicity is subjectively constructed is the one that is both obvious, yet uncomfortable to state openly. Quite often peoples look rather different one to another. In popular language they are white, brown, black or yellow, dark- or light-

---

Box 19.1   Changing identities: Barry Cox becomes Gok Pak-wing

An American journalist, Gregg Zachary (1999), describes how Barry Cox, a 21-year-old man from Liverpool, has pushed at the limits of how far he can change his own social identity. Cox has an English working-class background, eats meat pies and likes cricket. At high school he became fascinated by Chinese popular culture. He experimented with martial arts and enjoyed the soundtracks to the Jackie Chan movies. Hanging around his local fish and chip shops he met many of Liverpool's Chinese community, some of whom run the local 'chippies'.

Frustrated that he could not understand those Chinese who did not speak English, he studied Cantonese and found he could understand and learn it. He worked as a waiter in a Chinese restaurant so that he could practice his language skills and now works in a Chinese grocery store. He has a Chinese name, Gok Pak-wing (meaning 'long life'), and dates a British-born Chinese woman. Gok Pak-wing and his partner's Shanghai-born parents are concerned that she can't speak Chinese.

Although working in a grocery store, Gok's ambition is to be a Chinese pop star. He has already won some local contests, singing such 'Canto-pop' songs in Cantonese as 'Kiss under the moon', 'Kiss once more' and 'Ten words of an angel'. The title of his original song, which his fans love, translates as 'I think I am Chinese. I want to be Chinese'. Despite his obviously English appearance, he seems to have convinced some of his fans. One asked him 'Are you English or Chinese'. Another insisted that his intonation was so good 'his father must be Chinese'.

Cox/Gok's English mother, Valerie, says. 'He lives, breathes and sleeps Chinese. I think he'd actually be Chinese if he could'. Cox/Gok concurs: 'If I didn't mix with Chinese and sing Chinese, what would I be doing now? I'd just be a normal person, nothing special about me. Although I know I'm not Chinese, I'm trying to put myself in a Chinese body.'

Source and all quotes: Zachary (1999)

skinned, Nordic-, Mediterranean-, Latin American- or Asian-looking. Of course these are absurdly unscientific categories, and we recognize that the human species overwhelmingly shares a common set of characteristics and traits. We do not want here to engage in ridiculous exercises in racial typology. Rather we want simply to affirm that *appearance* – technically phenotype – can provide constraints to how far one can imagine oneself into another ethnicity. There are, in other words, bodily limits to the manipulative use of identity changes although many adventurous individuals have managed to push those limits quite far (Box 19.1).

Belief systems

The fourth factor to consider derives from an appreciation of social behaviour. What is the meaning of ethnicity to the actors themselves and how do they respond? The very visibility (or sometimes the fevered imagining) of ethnic differences allow them to be seen as 'primordial' or fundamental, reaching to the very heart of one's social being. This perception may not by shared by an outside observer, but the participants in ethnic interactions and conflicts may firmly believe they are describing reality. Sociologists must start from an acceptance of the gap between the observer's view of reality and the subjective and often irrational meanings, that people use to make sense of their worlds. We need to accept that distinction, because people act out what is in their heads, not in ours. 'What is real in the mind, is real in its consequences' is a tried and tested sociological adage.

Let us illustrate this idea with a simple example in a social setting. If, say, Serbs believe that the Croats are about to bomb their cities, loot their property, rape their women and murder their children, they will seek to defend themselves or will anticipate an attack by initiating one themselves. The Croats respond in kind thus reinforcing the Serb's original perception that Croats are bombers, looters, rapists and murderers. Fiercer attacks are therefore justified. Within a short time historical battles are recalled, vengeance is afoot and further recriminations and atrocities transpire.

Heterophobia – the fear of difference.

The mechanisms involved in these encounters are certainly irrational, but they are not inexplicable. Fear of the unknown and ***heterophobia*** are both marked by a psychological state of unease, extreme anxiety, discomfort and a sense of loss of control (Bauman 1994: 62–82). Competition over jobs, desirable sexual partners, housing, status, or territory compounds psychological *angst*, driving it into a higher gear. Sensing attack, people seek a bond with their friends and a clearer definition of their enemies.

This bonding is sometimes so powerful that some people think it is sacred. The ethnic or racial group, a religious faith – sometimes even a whole nation – become objects of worship, civil religions for which some are prepared to die. Slogans such as 'White is right', 'For king and country', 'Deutschland über alles', 'Christ died for you', 'Black power', 'We must defend ourselves against Muslim fanatics' may seem paltry enough ideas to a 'laid-back' student or an intellectual sophisticate, but they are real enough to the many people who believe in them.

Box 19.2   Islamophobia and how to recognize it

Heterophobia and ethnocentrism are part and parcel of the same phenomenon. Fear of an unknown group leads to anger and misapprehension. Like the pioneer white settlers in the USA featured in Hollywood Westerns the group draws the wagons around itself and prepares to repel all invaders. This 'clannishness' leads to further disparagement, to further defensiveness and so on, in a dispiriting downward spiral. One of the most virulent of all recent hate campaigns is that directed against people of Islamic origin. 'Islamophobia' is a newly coined world and means the dread and horror (from the Greek word *phobia*) of Muslims.

Examples of Islamophobia include those provided by two experienced and, to many readers, respectable English journalists. In the wake of the Oklahoma bombing, in which numerous lives were lost, there was an immediate and unwarranted suspicion in the USA and UK that this was the work of 'Muslim fanatics'. Bernard Levin, a columnist in *The Times* (21 April 1995) wrote: 'Do you realize that in perhaps half a century not more, and perhaps a good deal less there will be wars, in which fanatical Muslims will be winning? As for Oklahoma, it will be called Khartoum-on-the-Mississippi, and woe betide anyone who calls it anything else.' Charles Moore, then editor of the *Spectator* and subsequently editor of the highly respectable *Daily Telegraph*, supplied another doom-laden warning, with social Malthusian overtones (see Chapter 11). Moore opined: 'Because of our obstinate refusal to have enough babies, Western European civilization will start to die at the point when it could have been revived with new blood. Then the hooded hordes will win, and the Koran will be taught, as Gibbon famously imagined, in the schools of Oxford' (*Spectator*, 9 October 1991).

The Runnymede Trust in the UK, set up to promote good race relations and the understanding of cultural diversity established a special commission of academics, writers and religious figures to study the rise of Islamophobia (Stubbs 1997). They argued that unreasonable fear of Islam had seven tell-tale features:

- Muslim cultures are seen as monolithic and unchanging.
- Muslim cultures are regarded as wholly different from other cultures.
- Islam is seen as implacably threatening.
- The Islamic faith is used, it is alleged, mainly for political or military advantage.
- Muslim criticisms of western cultures are rejected out of hand.
- Racist immigration restrictions are associated with Islam.
- Islamophobia is assumed to be natural and unproblematic.

Each one of these supposed 'features' can be challenged by historical and comparative evidence. For example, Islam, as practised in the Middle East, is very different from the religion in Chechenia, Iran and Malaysia. The 'sufis', 'Islamicists', 'modernists' and 'revivalists' all have different interpretations of the Koran. As in the history of Christianity different sects abounded. Moreover Islam civilization has closely interacted with western civilization and made contributions in such diverse areas as architecture, philosophical thought, medicine and the numerals (1, 2, 3, 4, and so on) we all use in our daily life.

This is no place for a detailed refutation of western images of Islam. Rather, as sociologists we need to be critically aware of the structures of power that underpin different discourses and always question 'common-sense' and stereotypical thinking in order to disclose the social structures and processes that inform them.

NATIONALISM AS A REACTION TO GLOBAL CHANGE

Like ethnicity, race and religion, nationalism also seems to be on the increase while globalization runs apace. As we saw in Table 5.1, the number of recognized nation states has proliferated since the foundation of the UN in 1945; from 51 states at the outset, the UN recognized 185 states in 1999. Despite this formal increase in the number of nation states, a number of observers, as we have shown in Chapter 5, suggest that the autonomy of many nation states has weakened. The nation state may become the 'piggy in the middle', rushing from the global to the local level in an attempt to still keep in the game.

The unity of the nation state rests on a myth of a continuous legitimate authority of a single people. But in practice most nation states are diverse, multistranded, rich-layered and plural. Indeed it is part of the achievement of the modern nation state that this complex history has been ideologically suppressed. Mechanisms were developed for dealing with cultural diversity. The religious wars were resolved. Dissidents often emigrated or were expelled. Different languages were reconciled into single *lingua franca*. Flags, anthems, sporting teams, capital cities, grand buildings, icons and symbols reinforced the nation-builders' message. War, trade competition and imperialist rivalries consolidated the processes of national unification. Despite the impress of this history several limitations to the national project remain:

1. The concept of a homogenizing nation means that some features of the national heritage are arbitrarily selected while others are rejected or sidelined.

2. The notion of an essential national character is seriously flawed. Parekh (1995: 141–2) claims that 'the very language of nationality, nationhood and even national identity is deeply suspect. It cannot avoid offering a homogenized, reified and ideologically biased abridgement of a rich complex, and fluid way of life, and drawing false contrasts and setting up impregnable walls between different ways of life'.

3. The nation is sometimes presented as the lowest common denominator. Yet, given its fluidity it is better represented as a series of 'add-on' elements that arrive with each new wave of immigrants.

4. The nation is offered as an object of affection. One is enjoined to love one's country, to revere its institutions, even to fight and die for it in war. In these claims, the nation is a rival form of identification to the sub-national ethnic group. But the nation state is often too large and too amorphous an entity to be the object of *intimate* affection. By contrast, one can marry a spouse of one's own kind and feel the warm embrace of kinship; one can kneel in common prayer with one's co-religionists; one can effect easier friendships with those of a common background; one can eat one's own ethnic cuisine and, in a sense, ingest one's ethnicity. (The reference by African Americans to 'soul food' conveys this idea.)

THE LIMITS OF A MULTICULTURAL NATIONHOOD: THE USA

The inherent difficulty of making something as large as a nation state an object of common affection does not mean that many national political leaders have not tried to pull off that trick. The best known example of an attempt to create a nation from people of diverse cultural backgrounds is the case of the USA. Other nations (such as Australia, Canada, Brazil and post-1994 South Africa) have sought to embrace people of different backgrounds, either because their territories include several groups each claiming a territorial right, or because they were settled by successive waves of immigrants. These 'immigrant countries' comprise some of the most powerful and dynamic nation states in the world. For the nation-builders in these countries the challenge was to create one nation from a multitude of different components. The Latin slogan *Ex pluribus unum* ('from many, one') became the organizing principle. Speaking for the USA at the end of the nineteenth century Theodore Roosevelt put it bluntly: 'There can be no fifty-fifty Americanism in this country... there is room here only for 100 per cent Americanism, only for those who are American and nothing else' (cited in Rumbaut 1997).

This idea of 'Americanism' can be understood both as a state ideology and as something that was diffused from the bottom as well as the top – in night school classes, newspapers, neighbourhood schools and even from church pulpits. Perhaps the most memorable version of this popular message was provided by the American playwright, Israel Zangwill, who in 1908 wrote a Broadway hit called *The Melting Pot*. In his play, one of the characters, a refugee from the pogroms of Eastern Europe, makes this impassioned speech:

> America is God's crucible, the great melting pot where all the races of Europe are melting and reforming! Here you stand, good folk, think I, when we see them at Ellis Island, here you stand in your fifty groups with your fifty languages and histories, and your fifty blood hatreds and rivalries, but you won't be long like that brothers, for these are the fires of God you've come to – these are the fires of God. A fig for your feuds and vendettas! Germans and Frenchmen, Irishmen and Englishmen, Jews and Russians – into the crucible with you all. God is making the American (Glazer and Moynihan 1963: 89–90).

Although he did not invent the phrase, after Zangwill's play the expression 'the melting pot' subsequently became a slogan for all those who believed that civic nationalism, or modernization, or education, or class allegiances, or better communications, would dissolve prior ethnic loyalties. Probably the best known sociological discussion of melting pot theory was Milton Gordon's *Assimilation in American Life* (1964) which, although published over a generation ago, is still widely read. Gordon argued that there was an 'assimilation sequence' whereby people moved from cultural assimilation to structural assimilation and inter-marriage and finally to 'identificational assimilation' (that is, they consciously chose to assimilate).

As Rumbaut (1997) notes it was perhaps difficult for Gordon to imagine what a furore would be caused by his rather innocent use of the idea of assimilation. For many sociologists at the time, as well as many immigrants to the USA, assimilation merely expressed the process of 'learning the ropes' and 'fitting in'.

The bulk of the 35 million immigrants over the period 1870–1914 were European immigrants, who appeared to be only too pleased to be escaping the squalor of the great industrial cities and the depressed agricultural conditions of such countries as Ireland, Italy and Greece. Loud declarations of loyalty to the USA were heard from many of these European immigrants.

Yet doubts soon began to set in. Just before Gordon's book was published his fellow sociologists Glazer and Moynihan (1963) had questioned whether the process of assimilation in the USA had gone as far as was commonly believed. The great exceptions to the assimilation process were the African Americans, who were still trying to assert their basic civil rights, let alone assimilate. The history of coerced (rather than free) migration and slavery had a great deal to do with this outcome, but Native Americans, Asians and others also suffered a high level of discrimination. Even the European groups were highly differentiated in the extent to which they were assimilated – in their private and social lives, certainly, but also in their capacity to compete for public goods they often remained stubbornly unmeltable.

A more fundamental critique of assimilation revolved around the question: 'What are immigrants supposed to assimilate to?' Clearly not all cultures were regarded by the powerful élites as enjoying equal status. Many immigrants found they were being asked to assimilate to an 'Anglo' norm – in terms of language, education, political institutions, religious convictions, social conventions and public expectations. It is now three generations on from the staging of Zangwill's play and we still are waiting for the contents of the pot to melt. If anything, there is an increased conviction and even fear on the part of political commentators that the nation-building project is in serious danger of falling apart (Schlesinger 1992). The ease and cheapness of travel in a global age has reduced the need for taking a 'one-way ticket' to a single American citizenship and way of life.

It seems that the nation state is going to have to adapt to a more complex mosaic of cultures, religions, languages and citizenships. Often an official declaration of 'multiculturalism', 'cultural pluralism' or 'a rainbow nationhood' signals the end of the attempt by policy-makers to assimilate all elements of the population. Canada, Australia and post-apartheid South Africa have probably gone furthest in welcoming this outcome, while the authorities and many commentators in the USA have remained rather wary. However, detailed empirical work by sociologists like Rumbaut (1997) demonstrates that although assimilation is incomplete, this does not necessarily lead to alienation from the core institutions of the USA. Assimilation takes a selective form among the children of recent immigrants. For example, Hispanics may continue to speak Spanish in community settings, are likely to practice Catholicism and will have close links to their home countries. However, they will use the conventional ladders of social mobility and will don their 'straight' Brooks Brothers suits and speak standard American English when interviewing for a job with the American Federal Bank.

TRANSNATIONALISM: CITIES AND DIASPORAS

We have talked of how localism and nationalism have reacted and adapted to global change. But perhaps the most exciting forms of response are the revival and development of forms of transnationalism or cosmopolitanism. Two forms that preceded the nation state and have now revived are *the cosmopolitan city* and the transnational *diaspora*.

The cosmopolitan city

The important role of the city as the reception point to people from many parts of the world can be inferred from the classical Greek roots of the word – *kosmos* (world) and *polis* (city). As we have discussed the functions of global cities at length in Chapter 15, we will briefly remind you of the argument made there. Cities (we argued) pre-dated the nation state system and even during modernity continued as places where diversity rather than ethnic uniformity obtained. It may be that the city state concept will be renewed in the global age (so that places such as Singapore will play equivalent roles to earlier city states such as Venice). But even if the city state form does not take hold universally, 'the global city' within existing nation states will increasingly contain the disparate elements moving from place to place as travel, tourism, business links and the labour market become more organized on a global scale. The social structure of these global cities has indeed already been reshaped to accommodate to their new position in the international division of labour.

Diasporas

While global cities have provided important spatial vessels to contain plurality, the revival of a long-established social organization, a transnational diaspora, has come to symbolize the way in which people are themselves subverting or transcending the nation state system. The word 'diaspora' has particular associations with the Jewish (and later the Armenian and African) peoples living out of their natal lands. These associations particularly evoke the idea of 'victims' – groups that were forcibly dispersed at one moment in history when a cataclysmic event happened. Nowadays the concept is used more widely and imaginatively to include groups which are essentially voluntary migrants (Cohen 1997).

Figure 19.2   The Turkish 'hip-hopper', Murat Güngör, whose music raps about social relations and the everyday life of migrants in Germany

Whatever the impulse for migration, for many people there is no longer the need for 'indentificational assimilation'. Home and away are connected by rapid transport, electronic communications and cultural sharing – part of the process we call globalization. It is now possible to have multiple localities and multiple identities. Nation states can resist these tendencies and seek to stop globalization, but they are increasingly spitting in the wind. They can alternatively go with the flow and seek to adapt to the increasing mobility and complex social identities of their home populations. In practice, a double tendency seems to be emerging. Some cities (the 'global cities') are adjusting to the new pluralist realities, while certain politicians still seek to mobilize or exploit traditional nationalist loyalties, which still carry some conviction with threatened social groups. The cosmopolitanism of Paris and the support given to Le Pen (the leader of France's National Front) in the provincial towns and cities is illustrative of this duality.

As we have seen earlier, among many peoples there is a renewed search for 'roots', what Hall (quoted earlier) called a 'reach for groundings'. Yet this inclination need not imply a narrow localism, a retreat from global realities, an incapacity to respond to the challenges of the ever widening marketplace and to the new ethical and cultural demands stemming from globalization. To meet both needs, for a meaningful identity and a flexible response to burgeoning opportunities, a double-facing type of social organization is highly advantageous. Just such an organization exists in the form of a diaspora. This is not just a contemporary function of diasporas. They have always been in a better position to act as a bridge between the particular with the universal. Among other arenas, this has allowed them to act as interlocutors in commerce and administration.

Many members of diasporic communities are bi- or multi-lingual. They can spot 'what is missing' in the societies they visit or in which they settle. Often they are better able to discern what their own group shares with other groups and when *its* cultural norms and social practices threaten majority groups. Being 'streetwise' may affect the very survival of the group itself. It is perhaps because of this need to be sensitive to the currents around them that, in addition to their achievements in trade and finance, diaspora groups are typically overrepresented in arts, the cinema and the media and entertainment industries. Knowledge and awareness have enlarged to the point of cosmopolitanism or humanism, but at the same time traditional cultural values, which sustain solidarity and have always supported the search for education and enlightenment, have not been threatened.

Diasporas and global business

Cosmopolitanism combined with ethnic collectivism are also important constituents in successful business ventures. Probably the most upbeat analysis along these lines is that provided by Kotkin (1992) in his comparative study of why some peoples seem more successful as entrepreneurs than others. In his quest he provides cases studies of five 'global tribes' – the Jews, the British, the Japanese, the Chinese and the Indians. Gone, for Kotkin, are the traumas of exile, the troubled relationship with the host culture and other negative aspects of the classical diasporic tradition. Instead strong diasporas are the key to determine success in the global economy. As he writes (pp. 255, 258):

Rather than being a relic of a regressive past, the success of global tribes – from the Jews and British over many centuries to the Chinese, Armenians and Palestinians of today – suggests the critical importance of values, emphasis on the acquisition of knowledge and cosmopolitan perspectives in the emerging world economy. In an ever more transnational and highly competitive world economy, highly dependent on the flow and acquisition of knowledge, societies that nurture the presence of such groups seem most likely to flourish... Commercial opportunism overwhelms the narrower economic nationalism of the past as the cosmopolitan global city-state takes precedence and even supplants the nation.

Diasporas score by being able to interrogate the universal with the particular and by being able to use their transnationalism to press the limits of the local.

COSMOPOLITANISM: A CRITIC AND A FAN

As a practice and preference, cosmopolitanism is clearly a massive threat to those who assert that the only way to respond to globalization is to assert a determined loyalty to their ethnic group, nation or religion. Hitler hated the Jews and sought to massacre them precisely because of their multi-faceted international and diasporic identity. To be a critic of cosmopolitanism from such a stable is perhaps to be expected. Far less predictable is a critique mounted by a liberal American historian. In his posthumous collection of essays, Lasch (1995) talks of 'the darker side of cosmopolitanism'. The loosely defined 'privileged classes' or 'élites' are said to be in revolt against the nation state. This is because they no longer identify with it. 'In the borderless global economy, money has lost its links to nationality... The privileged classes in Los Angeles feel more kinship with their counterparts in Japan, Singapore, and Korea than with most of their countrymen' (p. 46). This detachment from the state means they regard themselves as 'world citizens' without any of the normal obligations of national citizenship.

The identification of the élites across frontiers is paralleled by a concern only with their immediate neighbourhood:

The cosmopolitanism of the favoured few... turns out to be a higher form of parochialism. Instead of supporting public services, the new élites put their money into the improvement of their own self-enclosed enclaves. They gladly pay for private health care and suburban private schools, private police and private systems of garbage collection; but they have managed to relieve themselves, to a remarkable extent, of the obligation to contribute to the national treasury. [This is] a striking instance of the revolt of the élites against the constraints of time and place (p. 47).

Lasch's concern is a legitimate one, particularly in the context of the USA. He is very impressed by the virtues of 'small-town democracy' and the traditions of *noblesse oblige* whereby the rich, powerful and fortunate assumed their civic responsibility to look after the less privileged. In a country where (compared with a number of European countries and neighbouring Canada) welfare systems are very underdeveloped, there was a particular reliance on voluntary work with, and charitable support for, the sick, poor and elderly. However, one should not imagine that Lasch's arguments apply purely to the USA. In global cities everywhere, the attachment of the denizens (privileged foreigners) to the state in which they find themselves often can only be described as minimal. This alienation clearly can have dangerous social consequences.

If Lasch sees the danger of cosmopolitanism, Beck (1998: 30) sees its opportunities. Cosmopolitan movements can transcend the appeal to national traditions, values and solidarities in favour of *human* values and traditions in every culture and religion. Such movements can address planetary concerns through new concepts, structures and organizations that can support the need to create transnationalism from below. For Beck the notion of 'world citizenship' is to be embraced not feared. New forms of 'post-national understanding, responsibility, the state, justice, art, science and public understanding' (p. 30) can emerge. This is turn can lead to more advanced forms of democracy, toleration, liberty and mutuality.

REVIEW

In assessing the different levels of community and belonging – localism, nationalism and transnationalism – we have seen that the great hopes of a 'new world order' and of 'a peace dividend' after the end of the Cold War have been sadly disappointed. The world has not witnessed the emergence of a compliant, single culture in which all peoples learn have been forced to love one another. Perlmutter (1991) helpfully depicts the world as being organized vertically by nation states and regions, but horizontally by an overlapping, permeable, multiple system of interaction – communities not of place but of interest, shared opinions and beliefs, tastes, ethnicities and religions. Unlike those who argue that a single homogenized global culture is emerging, Perlmutter more plausibly suggests that multiple cultures are being syncretized in a complex way. The elements of particular cultures can be drawn from a global array, but they will mix and match differently in each setting.

There are many that seek to resist this form of 'hybridization' (see Chapter 20) by creating new certainties, like new states defined on the basis of a single ethno-nationality. The states that emerged from the collapse of the Soviet Union and the disintegration of Yugoslavia provide abundant examples of this inclination. Long-standing residents of many of these 'new nations' were bundled out unceremoniously and told to return to natal lands with which they may not have an association for several generations. At worst this drive for ethnic territorialism leads to 'ethnic cleansing' and even systematic attempts at genocide. Others have resisted hybridization by insisting on a purist parody of their religion or ethnicity. They frequently make demands for job quotas and for first-language teaching in publicly funded schools.

This new insistence on ethnic and religious difference has created many dilemmas for established nation states, which have exhibited a huge variation in the extent to which they are open to newcomers or, by contrast, require cultural and social adjustment on the part of immigrants and residents. A tendency to recognize sub-national claims for devolution or autonomy is evident in the UK, Spain and elsewhere. There is also a big change in attitudes towards immigrants. About half the world's nation states now accept dual citizenship.

Even 'immigrant countries' (for example, the USA), which promoted a singular idea of assimilation on the basis of cultural and social obedience and exclusive citizenship, have been forced to retreat. The world is simply not like that any more; the scope for multiple affiliations and associations has been opened up outside and beyond the nation state. Globalization has meant that there is no longer any stability in the points of origin, no finality in the points of destination and no necessary coincidence between social and national identities (Khan 1995: 93).

Transnationalism has begun to supersede nationalism. We have described how a chain of global cities and an increasing proliferation of sub-national and transnational identities cannot easily be contained in the nation state system. Among the most important of the established transnational identities are diasporas and world religions, the earliest of which preceded the age of globalization by thousands of years. Transnationalism is also evident in key shifts of attitude and behaviour. Many people, not just the people who can be called 'world citizens' or 'cosmopolites' are more willing to recognize and accept cultural and religious diversity. There is an increased knowledge and awareness of other cultures derived from the global media and travel. Knowledge and awareness at least sometimes leads to tolerance and the respect for difference. We remind you of Perlmutter's (1991: 901) remark that now, for the first time in history, 'we have in our possession the technology to support the choice of sharing the governance of our planet rather than fighting with one another to see who will be in charge'. The long era of the naked imperialism is over, along with the one-sided cultural and political flows characteristic of that form of international relations.

If you would like to know more •••••••••••••••••••••••••••••••

There are many readers and textbooks on ethnicity and nationalism. Among the most significant are Anthony D. Smith's *Ethnicity and Nationalism* (1992) and the same author's *Nations and Nationalism in a Global Era* (1995) although it is difficult to choose among this sociologist's many works on the question.

A well-balanced reader titled *The Ethnicity Reader* has been edited by Rex and Guiberrnau (1997).

Michael Ignatieff's *Blood and Belonging* (1994) is a powerful book, based on a television series.

Schlesinger's *The Disuniting of America* (1992) is one of a number of accounts by liberal and conservative American academics and commentators decrying what they see as the excesses of multiculturalism.

Two books on diasporas are Robin Cohen's *Global Diasporas* (1997) and N. Van Hear's *New Diasporas* (1998)

For new developments in the field of transnationalism, consult the web site www.transcomm.ox.ac.uk.

Group work ••

1. Using conventional reference books, plot out the diverse elements and sects within Islam.

2. Prepare a short presentation on Islamophobia, drawing on newspaper articles and your own experience.

3. Divide into two debating teams, the one addressing the proposition that the USA is in the process of 'disuniting', the other that 'assimilation' is still working to integrate that country.

4. What indices would you use to established who is a cosmopolitan? ('Someone who reads a magazine of that name' will be regarded as an inadequate answer!)

5. Divide into two groups. One will address the proposition that global cities can contain transnationalism. The other group will explore the way in which diasporas express transnationalism.

Questions to think about •••••••••••••••••••••••••••••••••••••••

1. In what ways is it erroneous to group ethnicity, race and religion under the category 'localism'?

2. Why does localism arise in the midst of globalization?

3. Why were the force of race and ethnicity so systematically undervalued?

4. To what extent have the immigrant countries failed in their quest to assimilate people of different cultures?

5. Do diasporas 'solve' the problem of bridging local sentiments and global imperatives?

chapter 20

Towards a Global Society: Utopia or Dystopia?

CONTENTS

In Chapter 2 we explored the concepts of globalization (the objective worldwide processes of integration) and globalism (the subjective awareness of living in 'one world'). The extent to which these two processes have advanced remains contentious and besieged by uncertainties. Some anticipate that globalization and globalism will be sufficiently vibrant phenomena to usher in a new global age and to promote the construction of a generally benign global society.

However, this view is strongly contested by other scholars. Those who are overtly hostile to many aspects of globalization on moral grounds are best described as 'critics'. Others, best regarded as 'sceptics', believe that many of the features described are exaggerated or overstated. In this chapter, we will consider four areas of controversy where the critics and sceptics seem to be making useful points – even if we disagree with them either in detail or in terms of the general thrust of their arguments. Then we will turn to the elements we have identified as constituting the building blocks of a global society. We can anticipate the conclusion to this chapter by indicating that while we do not yet see a fully assembled structure of a global society, we already see the lattice-work, the bricks and the mortar that are making that construction happen.

FOUR CONTROVERSIES

In Chapters 5 and 19 we considered one of the major areas of debate relating to globalization, namely the question of whether or not the nation state is declining and, if so, in what sense. We do not need to repeat those arguments here, although you will see that this issue overlaps with several other key questions. The views of critics and sceptics with respect to the remaining areas of contention are best summarized in the form of four propositions, which we state here, before elaborating them and providing a critique:

1. 'Economic globalization is nothing new.'

2. 'A materialist culture will engender uniformity and disempowerment.'

3. 'A clash of civilizations will lead to cultural conflict and violence.'

4. 'Globalization will lead to a dystopian future.'

'Economic globalization is nothing new'

Certainly international trade is not new. As the leading economy for much of the nineteenth century, Britain's imports of raw materials rose by a factor of twenty between 1800–75 (Dunning 1993a: 110). The development of the commercial steamship from approximately 1850 along with the telegraph transformed trade opportunities rapidly in the last decades of the nineteenth century by reducing the previously prohibitive costs and risks involved in the movement of people and bulk goods. Moreover, since competition is intrinsic to capitalism Britain and its emerging industrial rivals – the USA, Germany, France and eventually others – increasingly sought to export finished goods to each other's markets.

These countries also required reliable supplies of foodstuffs, raw materials and fuels for their expanding home markets and growing populations. This need for raw materials led to the scramble for captive colonies, imperial conquest and the division of the world into rival spheres of trading interests, which each country then tried to monopolize. The net result of all this was that by 1914, on the eve of the First World War, a highly internationalized global economy had already emerged. Indeed, Hirst and Thompson's (1996: Chapter 2) boldest claim is that it was hardly less internationalized and open than the current world economy.

A similar case has been made for transnational flows of capital. Thus, direct foreign investment (DFI) by established home companies grew rapidly from about 1870. According to Dunning (1993a: 116), by 1913 it had obtained an importance, proportionately, in the global economy that was not reached again until the mid-1950s. From about 1870, DFI also increasingly supplemented the investment role played by portfolio investment (where finance raised in a home country is used to acquire share-holding interests in a foreign government's or company's own projects rather than directly owned and managed businesses). Moreover, compared to today, where the developing countries receive only about 20 per cent of DFI, before 1913 such flows were much more geographically dispersed – with two-thirds of the total directed to the colonies and dominions, especially Britain's (pp. 117–18).

So, the basic argument made by these critics is that economic globalization is nothing new and nothing special. However, there are several good reasons for doubting whether the world economy *was* as open and integrated before the First World War as during the last four decades. Consider the following:

1. Far fewer countries were involved in international trade and DFI as major actors. For example, as Hirst and Thompson (1996: 22) concede, between them Britain and Germany supplied over half of the world's manufactured exports in 1913.

2. According to Dicken (1992: 27) whereas in the first quarter of this century only eight countries supplied 95 per cent of the world's manufacturing output, by 1986 the number producing this same share had risen to twenty-five.

3. Similarly, before the First World War only a handful of countries were significant overseas investors. One country, Britain, provided the lion's share, with 45 per cent of the world total including both portfolio investment and DFI.

4. By contrast, the TNCs headquartered in many more developed countries are now engaged in DFI (for example, Italy, Canada, Denmark, and Switzerland). Their counterparts in the developing countries (including India, Taiwan, South Korea, Hong Kong, Singapore, Brazil, Argentina and Mexico) have also become significant sources of capital flows.

5. Measured in terms of volume, both international trade (from the 1950s) and overseas investment (from the 1960s) increased dramatically and soon dwarfed the corresponding amounts for any previous era.

6. According to Dicken (p. 51), the average number of subsidiary manufacturing plants established overseas each year between 1965–67 by the largest TNCs was over ten times greater than at any point in the period from 1920–29 and nearly seven times higher than in the years just after the Second World War.

7. The lion's share of the capital outflows through DFI before 1914 (about 75 per cent) was invested in such a way as to facilitate the export of raw materials, especially from the former colonies. Very little, only 15 per cent, was directed towards manufacturing and most of this was located in Europe, America, Russia and Britain's dominions. By contrast, the shared DFI going to raw material procurement by the seven largest capital exporting countries had fallen to 25 per cent by the mid-1970s (17 per cent in 1988) while overall DFI in manufacturing – much of it in technologically sophisticated activities – reached 42 per cent by 1975 (Dunning 1993a: Chapter 5).

8. The share invested in services – especially those relating to business such as banking, insurance and trade distribution networks – has also risen considerably from only 15 per cent in 1914 to 47 per cent by 1988 (Dicken 1992: 59). This huge increase has contributed to furthering the market penetration of manufactured products.

9. The arguments comparing international trade in 1914 to the present period miss the point that each country's trade (imports and exports) and the capital flows it experiences associated with outward and inward DFI are fast becoming indistinguishable (Julius 1990). This is because their integrated, global operations compel TNCs to engage in intra-firm exchanges. A good part of a country's official declared imports and exports actually consist of the cross-border movement of components, semi-finished goods, production-related services and other 'products' between the various subsidiaries of foreign and locally based TNCs.

Assessment of proposition 1

Although we readily accept that there were high levels of international trade in the period just before the First World War we do not believe this significantly dents the argument that we are witnessing a new era of economic globalization. For one thing, prior to 1914 and for several decades after, states were driven by overt and strongly nationalist pressures towards protecting their home economies while seeking to dominate overseas spheres of imperialist influence. But protectionism and imperialism have been declining rather rapidly since the 1950s in most countries. Also, in terms of scale, complexity, the number of actors involved (both state and non-state) and the integration of finance, manufacturing, services and investment, the economic globalization of the last three decades has gone well beyond anything that existed in 1914.

It is sticking our necks out a little also to argue that the national rivalries that preceded the two world wars cannot easily happen again. With many more players, free flows of capital, images and ideas and a more complex and overlapping mesh of transnational networks it is difficult to see how the nation state can haul the weapons of protectionism and nationalism out from their armouries to the extent they once did. Of course, as we have accepted throughout the book, globalization impacts very differently in different parts of the world and there is strong evidence, discussed in our last chapter, that localisms of all sorts are on the move again. However, most of the manifestations of religious and ethnic sentiment are happening at the sub-national level. Where ethno-nationalism has been successful, as in the post-Soviet states, the élites of most of the emerging countries are rushing headlong for global integration, not protectionism. The political and financial crisis in Russia late in 1998 and the political crisis in Serbia will propel a partial reverse to this process. But the former Soviet satellites in the Baltic and Eastern Europe are firmly in the global market economy and it is unlikely that Russia can disengage in any meaningful way.

Although Hirst and Thompson's work (1996) was a welcome reminder of the extent of earlier periods of economic integration, the title of their book, *Globalization in Question*, clearly overstates their case. It may be that they can convince you that *economic* globalization is in question – although we challenge their account on that too – but they understate the crucial point that globalization is about so much else other than economics. Social and cultural factors are ignored. So too are the transmission of shared images through the media, the rise of new 'power containers' (like the global city), and the development of transnational social networks and global politics (like diasporas and social movements). As we hope we have demonstrated, all these and much more are all part of the phenomenon of globalization.

'A materialist culture will engender uniformity and disempowerment'

Another anxiety for those who fear the emergence of a global society, is that everywhere people increasingly experience an ever more bland condition of sameness. Sachs (1992: 102) puts it dramatically when he says 'the homogenization of the world is in full swing. A global monoculture spreads like an oil slick over the entire planet'. Until recently, the overwhelming force for universalization in world affairs was the western-inspired view that progress meant greater humanism and international peace linked to the spread of science, the creation of a unified world market and the pursuit of material improvement for all.

In the days of formal imperialism and colonialism such views enabled the West to legitimize its mission to impose its culture and its political and social institutions on much of the world. The 'trade-off' for the colonized was access to new markets and new commodities. Now the promise of 'one world' achievable through material progress is being replaced by the more disturbing image 'one world or no world' (p. 107) because of impending environmental catastrophe. Such pressures towards universalization are dangerous because they destroy the world's diversity of languages and cultures and undermine people's sense of local identity. If these are lost then the confusion and conflicts this may engender could disempower us in our attempt to solve global problems.

Other writers see the main threat of homogenization coming from the global marketplace led and often controlled by American business. Along with this comes the all-pervasive and seductive imagery peddled worldwide through media influence, also largely monopolized by America. This is the now familiar 'McWorld' of consumer culture and its brand-name icons – Levi 501 jeans, Coca-Cola, Reebok trainers, fast foods including the famous McDonald's burger itself – that are now desired even by the world's poorest inhabitants living in slums and rural backwaters. Sklair (1995: 174, 280) argues that once established, capitalism invariably engenders a powerful and understandable popular appeal among ordinary citizens that is very difficult to counter or replace with a fairer democratic socialist alternative. Other alternatives are thereby precluded. Meanwhile, even those lucky enough to afford to participate in consumerism will ultimately experience dissatisfaction. This is because consumerism cannot cater for people's additional needs for community involvement, personal development and meaningful social relationships. It also brings growing environmental damage (see Box 18.1) to the point where it is difficult to see how the biosphere can remain viable unless limits are placed on the global pursuit of economic goals.

Barber (1995) also fears that the 'McWorld' market system will lead to the standardization of cultures and consumption practices and these, in turn, will bring yet other dangers. For example, the TNCs raise people's expectations through advertising by encouraging consumers to believe that their purchases open new avenues to a better life of opportunity and freedom. Yet most products are quite unable to deliver the kinds of personal self-fulfilment promised in the adverts.

The purchasing power for consumer goods is no substitute for secure employment opportunities, strong community values or the ability of citizens to influence the political process through democratic institutions. Accordingly, the vista of abundant market choice holds out promises it cannot keep. In fact, the TNCs have no interest at all in improving people's real lives or encouraging the strengthening of civil society. Neither do they intend to promote the kind of meaningful transnational solidarity that might empower global citizens to co-operate in overcoming common problems.

Assessment of proposition 2

We share many of the anxieties raised by the writers just cited. Certainly, it would be foolish to deny or ignore the enormous influence exerted by the

Major Concept
HYBRIDITY

Hybridity refers principally to the creation of dynamic mixed cultures. Sociologists and anthropologists who use the expression 'syncretism' to refer to such phenomena have long observed the evolution of commingled cultures from two or more parent cultures. Using the literature and other cultural expressions of colonial peoples, Bhabha (1986) introduced a new twist to the idea. He saw hybridity as a transgressive act challenging the colonizers' authority, values and representations and thereby constituting an act of self-empowerment and defiance.

TNCs over all aspects of our lives. However, although the dangers posed by TNCs and by the spread of capitalism are formidable, the concrete evidence for suggesting that together these produce an irresistible, disempowering and homogeneous culture dominated by American consumerist values is often more apparent than real. Indeed, as has been seen in Chapters 12 and 13 on tourism and consumerism there are powerful grounds for arguing that under capitalism consumers retain far more opportunities for personal creativity and autonomy than these arguments suggest. Moreover, as in the past, the arrival of unfamiliar goods, ideas or artistic forms generally enriches rather than narrows the local repertoire of cultural resources by extending the opportunities to express indigenous 'traditions' and lifestyles. In such situations people exercise selectivity and consciously mix the old with the new to create alternative and **HYBRID** forms.

Increasingly, too, this process of cultural borrowing and mixing works is in reverse since western societies are increasingly absorbing a widening range of cultural experiences from the non-western world. This is readily apparent in a range of activities stretching from culinary, musical and artistic ones to practices and philosophies associated with health, sport and methods of business organization, to name but a few. Neither does the evidence so far bear out the contention that non-western peoples have no defences – and wish to have none – against the onslaught of Americanized material culture. Much depends on specific circumstances such as the degree of support governments provide for local cultures, the details of colonial history or the intrinsic strength of national economies. Sometimes, it is not westernization that poses a threat to cultural survival, but the discriminatory and centralizing polices imposed by dominant religious or ethnic groups on small minority cultures.

'A clash of civilizations will lead to cultural conflict and violence'

We have already discussed Barber's views (1995) on the likelihood of 'McWorldism'. In fact, his arguments on this topic are also relevant to proposition 3 because he observes that many ethnic, religious and national groups around the world are diametrically opposed to the individualistic, materialist hedonism embodied in American consumerism. Indeed, he believes that we are witnessing a growing worldwide resurgence of organizations enflamed with a mission to pursue various kinds of Jihad (the Islamic version of a holy war), sometimes involving the use of terrorist and genocidal violence. In many instances these can be interpreted as direct responses to what such groups perceive as the threat of Americanization and its trivialization of ancient, unique cultures, or the revealed truths originating in divine inspiration. Thus, we appear to be confronted with two scenarios: (a) an unequal but relatively peaceful world where the poor majority are kept in a state of passivity by a promise of the future acquisition of consumer goods; and (b) a dangerous one of contending, fundamentalist warrior causes.

The conservative American writer, Samuel Huntington (1993), appears to go much further than Barber in forecasting a future consisting of cultural and even actual bloody wars between rival civilizations. His argument can be summarized as follows:

1. A 'civilization' consists of the broadest level of cultural identity shared by clusters of ethnic groups, nations or peoples based on common experiences, especially history, religion, language and customs. On this definition there are perhaps seven or eight such civilizations in the world today although each contains important sub-divisions.

2. In the post-Cold War era, neither ideological conflicts, as for example between communism and capitalist democracy, nor the struggles between nation states will continue to shape global politics to the same extent as in the past although the latter remain as very powerful actors. Rather, future conflicts will increasingly develop along the 'fault lines' (p. 29) between civilizations – sometimes exploited by political leaders and groups as a means of enhancing their own interests.

3. Chief among such confrontations may be that between the West, now at the zenith of its global leadership and power, and a coalition of non-western civilizations probably focused around an Islamic–Confucianist axis. The countries drawn together within the Muslim and East Asian civilizations are rapidly increasing their military capability either through imports or by developing their own arms industries linked to industrialization.

4. What binds these and other non-western civilizations together – although much also divides them – is a shared resentment concerning the West's past. They see the West as continuing to impose its version of modernity on the world and to use its current control of international institutions such as the World Bank and the UN to further its own interests. Western concern to prevent the spread of military capability and arms, especially nuclear weapons, to the rest of the world can be readily understood against this background.

5. Several worldwide changes are working to accelerate and intensify this growing sense of 'civilizational consciousness' (p. 25). However, the most powerful of these are probably linked to globalization and modernization, especially the increased interactions between different countries and cultures arising from time–space compression and the yearning gap created in people's lives by the resulting loss of local identities. This gap is increasingly being filled by the revival of various forms of religious and cultural fundamentalism.

Assessment of proposition 3

One of the difficulties with Barber's theory is that not all fundamentalist groups are opposed to consumerism and material prosperity – such values are, for example, embraced by most American revivalist churches. Moreover, many Islamic fundamentalist groups, whether active terrorists or Iran's ruling ayatollahs, are highly ambivalent in their attitudes to modern materialism. They revere the past, but are dependent on advanced technology in order to fight their cause – from faxes, the Internet and television to jet travel and sophisticated armaments along with the market systems that provide them (Hadar 1993).

Moreover, the desire to reject American cultural domination constitutes only part of the explanation for the rise of non-western violent movements operating around the world today. Many recent nationalist and secessionist movements have originated either in the post-Cold War disintegration of the Soviet empire or in situations where minorities have made what some might regard as quite reasonable demands for international recognition as separate nations following long periods of persecution by hostile majority governments. Obvious examples, here, are the Kashmiris, Kosovars, Tamils or Kurds. By the same token, the rise of Islamic fundamentalism in Algeria, Egypt, Iran and elsewhere is linked, among other things, to the inequalities, repression and policy failures that have characterized previous regimes and which western governments sometimes supported or condoned.

In August 1998, President Clinton ordered a missile attack on alleged Islamic terrorist sites located in the Sudan and Afghanistan. This followed the bombing of US embassies in Kenya and Tanzania earlier that month by these same fundamentalist groups. Surely, these – and earlier events of a similar kind – look ominously like a clear foretaste of Huntington's predicted civilizational wars? Certainly, Huntington publicly declared his thesis had been demonstrated. However, there are solid reasons for doubting whether Huntington's analysis is entirely valid. Here, Halliday's trenchant criticisms (1996) are especially telling:

1. The very validity of the notion of civilization can be questioned. Like the idea of nationhood it is based on the assumption that it is possible to identify and represent a set of timeless traditions. In reality, however, it makes much more sense to regard traditions as based on different and conflicting interpretations arising out of cultural creations concocted largely to suit the political interests and purposes of different élites. Thus, the case for an actual or potential confrontation between civilizations is largely a myth because no such clearly demarcated and distinctive entities can be identified.

2. The idea of clearly differentiated civilizations with distinctive cultural boundaries is further thrown into disarray when we remember the extent to which cultures and peoples have always borrowed and mixed each other's technologies, art forms, religious symbolism, and much else besides. Indeed, it seems more likely that with globalization these processes will intensify, not diminish as Huntington's argument implies. If so, then the conflicts he envisages will surely become more not less difficulty to sustain or justify.

3. The fragmentation and conflicts that have occurred within civilizations, based on inter-ethnic or state divisions, have been just as marked as those between them and often much more so. This has certainly been the case in Europe, wracked for centuries by religious, civil and inter-state wars despite the apparent over-arching Christian legacy. Moreover, if we count the recent and continuing bloody conflicts in the Basque region of Spain, Northern Ireland and especially the former Yugoslavia this era did not end in 1945. The Islamic world, too, continues to be deeply divided along national and sectarian lines, among others, notwithstanding the brazen attempts by some westerners to present the alternative image of a 'green peril' – a united Islam bent on destroying its ancient enemy (Hadar 1993).

We will add that if US interventions in Sudan and Afghanistan 'proved' Huntingdon's thesis – which Halliday has, himself, in any case rejected – NATO's attack on Serbia in defence of the Muslim Kosovars completely contradicts the Huntington thesis. Indeed this was noted in March 1999 by a number of editorials in the Pakistan daily newspaper *Dawn* that called on the Muslim world to acknowledge that the leading western powers were *defending* Muslims against Christians.

'Globalization will lead to a dystopian future'

Just as Huntington (and others) present a disturbing vision of the future from the right, so are there prophets of doom from the left. In an original and challenging book Roger Burbach (an American), Oscar Núñez (a Nicaraguan) and Boris Kagarlitsky (a Russian) (Burbach *et al.* 1997) suggest that globalization has triggered a number of counter reactions or anti-systemic movements due to the traumatic shocks and horrors it has engendered in many areas of the world. Their perspective is undoubtedly valuable in that the three authors are representatives of what used to be called 'the First', 'Second' and Third Worlds. They deny that they are opposed to globalization per se. However, they argue that 'the economic forces that currently determine the direction of globalization adversely affect most of humanity and severely limit our [that is, humankind's] ability to create a better world' (p. ix).

Dystopia – an imaginary place where things are as bad as they could possibly be.

Given the dominance of the forces they are opposed to, they can see nothing but a **dystopian** future for all of us. They argue that the form taken by globalization will have the following features:

- *Trade wars* – whereby intense competition between trading blocs leads to instability and speculation between the national currencies. In this respect they see a tension between different sectors of capitalism – with computer firms, biotech companies and TNCs in food-processing favouring free international markets, while steel, farmers and clothing manufacturers will try to defend national markets. Angry French farmers, rebellious peasants in Chiapas (Mexico) and trade union opponents of regional agreements such as NAFTA are all seen as forces resisting the integration of global markets (Burbach *et al.* 1997: 61–3).

- *Global unemployment* – with some 30 per cent of the world's 2.5 billion workers being unemployed. The argument here is that automation and information processing will permanently displace workers from the manufacturing and services sector leaving nowhere for those displaced from the land to go. Beyond the global village, the destitute and outcast will gather (pp. 64–6).

- *Destructive financial speculation* – which will allow unbridled 'robber barons' to indulge in greed and uncontrolled speculation in stocks, bonds, currencies and precious metals. While some fortunes are made in the new computer industries, the bulk of fortunes are made by junk bond scams, insider trading or those playing the markets of casino capitalism. The stability of global accumulation is, Burbach *et al.* suggest, only an illusion: a 'major catastrophe' will arise 'before we get too far into the next century' (p. 73).

- *Collapse of the poor countries* – where the neo-liberal panaceas of the World Bank have resulted in further malnutrition and destitution. Even the proclaimed success of the neo-liberal solutions in places such as Costa Rica and Chile have shown gains only for the wealthy and at the expense of those living in poverty (pp. 85–6).

- *The 'gutting' of the cities in rich countries* – marked by the massive increase of those living on welfare, those permanently unemployed and those scraping by through criminal activities. 'The violence, fear, crime, alcoholism and drug abuse that grip the underclasses of these cities is directly linked to this despondency and hopelessness' (p. 103).

- *The rise of a 'barbaric' bourgeoisie in the post-communist world* – with ineffective and parasitic states, entrepreneurs who lack ethical, intellectual, cultural or professional values, and a 'mafia' comprising old party hacks, state bureaucrats and new 'yuppies'. These groups 'are united by the lack of roots and total disrespect towards any rules and laws as well as by the lack of even minimal moral constraints' (pp. 117–21, 122).

Assessment of proposition 4

One cannot help but admire the concern and passion behind these denunciations of the present form of globalization. Indeed we concur in many of Burbach and his colleagues' observations. The emergence of a new global age is a painful, uncomfortable and often distressing process. Not to recognize this pain, discomfort and distress would be to promote a blinkered perspective, as well as showing a total insensitivity to the many marginalized and excluded people round the world. The angry and desperate Russians in queues outside banks bitterly denouncing their country's flirtation with global capitalism further demonstrate the point.

It is perhaps no coincidence that critics like Burbach and his co-authors draw their indignation from a self-confessed Marxist or socialist background. The Jeremiah-like sense of apocalyptic doom, the inevitable march of historical forces and the fear of fateful technological determinism all draw from that deep well. But it has to be recalled that Marx himself saw the dual nature of capitalism. It was both destructive *and* potentially liberating. Just as capitalism consigned feudalism and slavery to the dustbin of history (just about), so too it can be argued that globalization is undermining nationalism and other impediments to the full realization of capitalism on a worldwide scale.

The argument is *not* the heartless one that 'you can't make an omelette without breaking eggs', but rather that social actors and organizations can do something about the ingredients of that omelette, how it is cooked and served and who gets to eat it. It was very much part of the Marxist tradition to look to social agency to supersede the limitations of the capitalist revolution by instigating another kind of revolution on behalf of humanity at large. The chosen social vehicle for this change, the proletariat, was – according to one's view – either mistakenly identified, or not up to its historical mission. However, there is no need to collapse into an impotent sense of predestination. As another socialist writer argues (Bienefeld 1994: 97), the destructive effects of globalization will arise

> only if we allow it to be so; if we remain deaf to the cries of help from societies presently being destroyed; or to the voices of those who still believe in the possibility of building stable, prosperous societies in which people can live in harmony with nature and with each other, while spending time in less stressful, more interesting jobs and devoting an increasing part of their lives to social and cultural pursuits. Technology has made this dream a possibility; politics must realize it.

AN OPTIMISTIC VISION OF OUR GLOBAL FUTURE

That final observation provides the opening for our more optimistic vision of global future, although we would not consider our position to be utopian. Technological and economic changes *can* allow a positive outcome, but people must try to make that happen. Let us mention some of these more positive changes:

1. A number of observers (for example Reich 1992; Bradley *et al.* 1993; Carnoy *et al.* 1993) argue that a new phase has arrived in the moves towards integration among TNCs. Between 1975 and 1986 there was a 50 per cent rise in the number of scientists and engineers engaged in research and the development of technology. In responding to these changes, some TNCs have downsized and concentrated their technological expertise in core areas of competency. Many others have formed strategic cross-border alliances with overseas companies. Such joint ventures increasingly involve small and medium-sized TNCs and not simply the largest. Both the increasing number of alliances between TNCs and the increase in shared R&D activity strongly suggest that the process of economic integration is deepening quite rapidly and does not always involve greater concentration of capital.

2. The development of niche markets and access to technologies that shrink distance has allowed small specialist companies to survive, sometimes at the level of a family business or a community co-operative. This has revived small-scale, craft and art-based production, often conducted in a humanitarian environment with the minimum of worker exploitation. Artists, potters, cabinet makers, small publishers, alternative health therapists, organic farmers, those making green health products, craft jewellers, small specialist shops, psychoanalysts and poets can all thrive in our global economy and many do. Fair-trading organizations and ethical firms like the Body Shop have linked small peasant producers to a global market on a non-exploitative basis.

3. Even in more conventional settings, work experience is said to be undergoing rapid change. Information technology and electronic communications provide several advantages to employers: firms can co-ordinate their operations more cheaply and easily across considerable distances; customers and producers are linked directly and instantly; many functions such as product design, accountancy and engineering can be easily subcontracted to specialist outside firms, more in touch with rapidly changing markets and production methods; and the design, experimentation and testing of manufactured and other products all benefit from a growing number of computer applications (Bradley *et al.* 1993: 16).

4. At the same time, innovations in manufacturing technologies mean that machines are becoming programmable, multi-functional, smaller and less energy intensive than they once were. The advanced economies are undergoing a steady process of reducing the bulk of the raw material used in production, a process accelerated by using microelectronics so as to miniaturize many products. Apparently, although the GDP in the USA has risen twenty times in real value over the last 100 years its weight, measured in tonnes, has increased little (*The Economist*, 28 September 1996: 43). Contrary

to the prediction of the doom and gloom merchants (and the old Yorkshire saying that 'Where there's muck there's money') economic prosperity *does not* have to produce mountains of waste.

5. There has been a marked rise in the number of viable small firms across the western world since the 1980s or so as the economic and technological barriers to entry have been lowered. Meanwhile, the old hierarchical, pyramid-shaped structure once so noticeable in many large companies is becoming flatter as the emphasis on problem-solving, the need to respond quickly to specific customer requirements and so on combine to place much more emphasis on team work, self-reliance, multi-skilling and close collaboration between employees. Reich (1992) describes these changes in terms of what he calls the increased importance of 'enterprise webs'. Enterprise webs undermine managerial authority, they render business bureaucracy redundant, they disperse control widely within organizations and they therefore empower many employees.

If we think about all these changes while situating them within the context of growing globalization we end up with a much more enticing vision of contemporary business organization. Even very large, global corporations are apparently breaking down internally into overlapping networks of partly self-reliant enterprise webs operating on a more human scale. Meanwhile their external boundaries with domestic suppliers and foreign TNCs at home and abroad are effectively dissolving as these same webs coalesce across companies and countries.

Finally, according to Reich (1992: Chapter 4) wealth creation in more and more sectors increasingly depends on the contribution played by the 'symbolic analysts'. He claims that such people now constitute about 20 per cent of the workforce in the advanced countries. They enjoy specialist, problem-identifying and problem-solving skills. These are critically linked to their grasp of different kinds of symbolic knowledge in creative design including the arts and media, scientific research, oral and visual communications, the ability to engage in strategic thinking and so on. Their centrality to all kinds of economic and creative activity means they command high rewards, are frequently wooed by rival companies and so are increasingly mobile, taking their knowledge, connections and skills with them as they move between organizations and countries. Although Reich's symbolic analysts may be the new 'movers and shakers' of the contemporary world economy, others outside this charmed circle can also benefit. Between 40 per cent and 50 per cent of all jobs in the rich countries are linked to knowledge-creation and information-processing in both manufacturing and services (Carnoy *et al.* 1993: Chapter 2) and it is in this area where four-fifths of all new jobs are being created. Knowledge-based industries now generate more than half of total GDP in the advanced economies.

A nation's wealth creation and its ability to compete increasingly thus depends much more on the skills and creative resources possessed by its citizens, and their capacity to understand, transfer and improve technology, than on the actual ownership of different kinds of tangible assets (Reich 1992: Chapter 12). The most important role any government can now play is to concentrate on raising the knowledge-acquiring capacities of its inhabitants at all levels. We can anticipate, in turn, that this shift will help to generate a more educated, adaptable and reflexive citizenry, more willing and able to question authority, demand autonomy and act as key agents in shaping policy agendas.

Of course, this rosy picture has to be balanced by our knowledge of the many 'global victims' (see Chapters 4, 8 and 9) who have so far been left far behind in the race to knowledge. Again, reflexive citizens using their skills for benign purposes are not the only beneficiaries of globalization – drug-dealers, arms merchants and media moguls are also 'global winners'. Nonetheless it is important to emphasize that the economic and technical changes we have identified and the rise of the symbolic economy can *potentially* generate a more democratic and participatory future global society. Work can be more empowering and even enjoyable, governments can become more accountable, while through the interdependence of the world economy wars can be avoided.

THE MAKING OF GLOBAL SOCIETY

We have considered the possible gains to be made from changes in economic management and technology. There are several other major gains at a social level to be realized from globalization and globalism:

1. An extension of democratic, civil and human rights.
2. The spread of education and literacy.
3. Information and access to communications for all the world's inhabitants.
4. The grown of multicultural understanding and awareness.
5. The empowering of women and other historically disadvantaged groups.
6. The promotion of environment-friendly production systems.
7. The growth of leisure, creativity and freedom from want.

Can any of these dreams be realized? There are those who still pin their hopes on a 'positive nationalism'. Bienefeld (1994: 122), for example, while recognizing the malign as well as the benign aspects of nationalism, nonetheless says that we have little alternative but to rely on a reformed nation state. In what other form, he asks

> can we realistically hope, at the end of the twentieth century to redefine and reconstruct political entities that would allow us to manage the increasingly destructive forces of global competition while providing individuals with the capacity to define themselves as social beings and while containing the risk of political conflict between such political entities?

The question is a good one, but we feel that those who wish to reform the nation state do not adequately recognize how far disillusionment has already set in. In some 'hollowed-out' or 'broken-backed' states, for example in Liberia, Sierra Leone, Myanmar or Somalia, the state has imploded – leaving its former citizens to the mercies of gangs and warlords. But even in the industrialized states, the belief in nationhood and formal democracy has eroded. The former appears increasingly as parochial and irrelevant while democracy seems to offer little more than a hollow administrative system for reaching decisions that do not begin to reach the needs or tap the energies of citizens living in the rapidly changing world. Besides, as we argued in Chapter 5, the cultural pluralism characteristic of the global age undermines the idea of territoriality and sovereignty, the historical building blocks of the nation state.

There clearly is still a need for developing more active national democracies with flourishing civil societies. However, in addition to, and in some respects superseding the nation state are other sites of political encounter and engagement. Let us just mention again some of these sites, which were discussed at greater length elsewhere in this book:

1. At the international level courts, particularly those dealing with human rights and genocide have begun to make effective judgements that transcend domestic legislation.

2. The International Governmental Organizations, such as the UN and its agencies, have made some advances in acting on behalf of a global community – although the UN is still crucially dependent on the members of the Security Council and especially the USA.

3. A proliferation of regional bodies has developed, admittedly with highly variable levels of power and authority.

4. TNCs have generated immense resources and power and are effectively out of the control of the nation state. In Chapter 7 we show how some accept their social responsibilities on a global scale.

5. Transnational communities have developed through enhanced travel and communications.

6. Global cities have evolved to service the needs of the world economy and its cosmopolitan citizens, a development discussed in Chapter 15.

7. Global diasporas and religions have resurfaced to bridge the gap between universalism and the need for linking to one's past (Chapter 19).

8. Global social movements have arisen to help build the global society of the future (Chapters 16, 17 and 18).

We need to say just a little more about global social movements. In sociology there has always been a creative tension between 'structure' and 'agency' – what happens to one and what one makes happen. Social movements are the key agents for progressive and humanitarian social change. Even if they only achieve a small part of the tasks they have set for themselves, their struggles will have been worthwhile. The environment and women's movements have merited our special attention as they both seem to have some transformatory potential but other social movements are also potentially significant in the slow construction of a relatively benign and functioning global society.

REVIEW AND FINAL REMARKS

In this concluding chapter we have partly concurred with those who argue that not everything connected with the making of a global society brings advantages and gains to the human condition. A more integrated world is not necessarily a more harmonious or a more equal one. We are faced with greater risks as well as opportunities. As we have seen throughout the book much transnational activity is atavistic and potentially damaging to others – as in the case of neo-Nazi cells, crime gangs or drug syndicates who operate on an international basis. Some transnational movements and groups may evoke a common universal purpose, yet are divided and made ineffective by internal squabbles.

There are also plausible concerns about the ways in which global homogenization could eventually dilute the local and national particularities, about environmental problems, demographic expansion, joblessness and poverty, the emergence of terrorism, drug-trafficking, and the spread of epidemics throughout the world. Globalization has so far done little to diminish the blight of poverty and wretchedness in which about half of the world's inhabitants is forced to live. Social movements have still not proved effective in mobilizing efforts to reduce global inequalities. Thus, we are not dealing with a unilinear process that will inevitably take us to a better world.

Despite these concessions to the sceptics and critics, we nonetheless argue that globalization has become irreversible and is taking on new forms not previously encountered. Moreover, although the direction in which it may evolve is unclear and certainly not fixed, some global changes are very positive. They provide a greater potential than ever before for the world's inhabitants to forge new understandings, alliances and structures – both from below and in alliance with élite institutions – in the pursuit of more harmonious, environmentally sustainable and humanitarian solutions to local and global problems. The world of work has been transformed and for many lucky citizens the possibilities for a creative engagement with global changes are much enhanced. In itself globalization will lead to neither a dystopia nor a utopia. The future directions of global society depend on us as ordinary world citizens, on what moral positions we choose and what battles we are prepared to fight.

A 'global ecumene', 'a universal humanism', a 'shared planet', a 'cosmopolitan democracy' – these idealistic notions are not realities, but possibilities and aspirations. The world remains lop-sided. Many powerful and wealthy actors profit disproportionately from global changes. Throughout this book we have shown how 'global winners' use their privileged access to power, wealth and opportunity to feather their own nests. The TNCs, crime syndicates, rich tourists, skilled migrants and others are all major beneficiaries of the opportunities for transnational activity. But it behoves us to remind you, in a final word, of the many 'global losers' – the refugees, poor peasants, the underclasses of the collapsing cities – who still peer through the bars at the gilded cages of the rich and powerful.

The key social challenge of the twenty-first century is to prise open the bars for these disadvantaged people so that they can discover the transformatory possibilities globalization has generated. A vibrant civil society and active global social movements provide far-off glimpses of that benign future. However distant, we hope we have encouraged you to see some of the many possibilities for social engagement, co-operation and positive change.

If you would like to know more ●●●●●●●●●●●●●●●●●●●●●●●●●●●●●●●

An articulate and coherent critique of globalization from a Marxist point of view is provided in Roger Burbach *et al.* (1997) *Globalization and its Discontents*.

Robert Reich's book, *The Work of Nations* (1992) should be read together with the contrasting account by Jeremy Rifkin (1995) titled *The End of Work*.

Benjamin Barber's *Jihad vs. McWorld* (1995) speaks of the gloomy visions of a clash of civilizations or a homogenized global consumer culture.

Finally, Richard Falk's *Explorations at the Edge of Time* (1992) is the work of a plausible futurologist.

Group work ●●

1. Divide the class into several smaller groups. Each will examine one of the four propositions from both sides for about thirty minutes and prepare a brief report to be presented to the class. On balance do the various groups agree or disagree with their propositions and why?

2. Working in groups of three or four, students will agree in advance to collect material on particular world political/military/economic crises (perhaps assigned on a regional basis). Before their class presentations each team will summarize (a) the nature of the events/problems and so on within their area and (b) discuss what light their data throws on any one or more of the propositions. How far do the team assessments agree or differ?

3. Some critics of globalization express anxiety concerning the disquieting sense of lost local or national identity that many individuals may feel as a result. Drawing on their own personal experiences, what are the perceptions of the class members themselves on this question and how can they account for them? Are there any apparent overall social indicators that explain whatever individual differences or similarities may emerge?

Questions to think about ●●●●●●●●●●●●●●●●●●●●●●●●●●●●●●●●●●●●●

1. The degree to which the world economy has become integrated is no greater than it was before the First World War. Discuss.

2. Examine and assess the fears expressed in the theories of Barber and Huntington.

3. Discuss the view that a global monoculture will destroy diversity and difference.

4. Using the material in this chapter and any other sources you like, construct: (a) an optimistic scenario for an emergent global society; followed by (b) a critique that traces the possible parallel dangers and difficulties.

Glossary

Acid rain is caused by the emission of acidic gases such as sulphur and nitrogen oxides, mainly from power stations, factories and vehicles. These are carried by winds and rain and may fall on forests, lakes and buildings in distant countries, killing fish or endangering trees, among other things.

Alienation Marx believed that it is mainly through creative, self-directed work in the satisfaction of our own needs that we fully realize our inner selves and potential. However, under capitalism workers become estranged or alienated from their skills and their potential since now they are driven to work for capitalists in order to survive and the product of their labour no longer belongs to them. Sociologists have employed this term more generally to describe the powerlessness and lack of creativity believed to be endemic to many aspects of contemporary life.

American Revolution Following a war with the British starting in 1775, the USA became the first modern country to win independence from colonial rule. Representatives of the individual states finally agreed at the Philadelphia Convention in 1787 to establish a federal government with limited powers enshrined in a written constitution.

Apartheid is the Afrikaans word for the system of systematic, legalized discrimination that existed in South Africa between 1948–94. Under the Population Registration Act of 1950 the population was classified in different racial categories with education, residence and marriage only permitted within each category. Although the system technically supported difference rather than hierarchy, in practice the good jobs, the best housing, the vote and other favourable opportunities and resources were reserved for the whites. With the election of Nelson Mandela as President in 1994 the system was legally dismantled, although some apartheid-like practices still continue informally.

The **biosphere** consists of the atmosphere, the oceans, lakes and rivers, the varied and complex systems of plant life and all the many other living organisms from bacteria to fish, animals and humans. Growing intervention by humans now seems to be placing an intolerable burden on the biosphere so that it is no longer capable of renewing itself or dealing with the wastes created by industrial societies. The increasing emission of gases by factories, power stations and vehicles, for example, is causing more of the sun's heat to remain trapped in the atmosphere, giving rise to global warming. This may affect all life adversely. Transatlantic jets alone burn 30 tons of oxygen per flight and subject passengers and crews to high levels of radiation.

Bricolage An assembly of various apparently unconnected elements. The expression 'brico-lage' is closely associated with Claude Levi-Strauss (1908–), the Brussels-born anthropologist who studied the codes of expression in different societies. There is a lot of pretentious theorizing about what he meant, but the idea is perhaps best conveyed by entering a chain of French 'do-it-yourself' stores called 'M. Bricolage'. There one can find bolts, nails, screws, wood, plastics, paint and thousands of other items that allow you to fashion an artefact of your choice. Those using the expression 'bricolage' assume one can deploy elements from a variety of cultures, lifestyles and identities to fit one's purposes, personality or social opportunities.

Bureaucracy We owe our understanding of the workings of modern bureaucracies principally to Max Weber, who first enunciated the ways in which such formal organizations worked, or were meant to work. Bureaucracies comprise legally recognized positions with clearly defined responsibilities; these positions being hierarchically ordered into career paths. Ideally, bureaucrats follow laws, rules and precedents, operate impersonally and impartially ('without hatred or passion', says Weber), and are committed to efficiency and rationality (Gerth and Mills 1958).

Capital-intensive agriculture involves the substitution of technology, credit, machinery, irrigation, tractors and commercial seed, for human beings growing crops in the old way. In addition to the social consequences of displacing labour, capital-intensive agriculture can carry some risks, for example in reducing biodiversity.

Capital-intensive manufacturing relies on investment in plant rather than labour. This preference may arise where labour is scarce, unco-operative, expensive or well-organized. However, capital intensity may also arise in high-tech industries by virtue of the nature of the materials and product.

Capitalism In capitalist economies wealth-producing resources are largely privately owned rather than being subject to family, community or customary control. Most producers depend on wage employment for their livelihoods instead of self-provisioning, while the goods they produce are commodities sold in markets. Moreover, production is organized almost entirely for profit. This is earmarked for reinvestment and further wealth accumulation.

Christopher Columbus Columbus 'discovered' the 'New World' in 1492. (Of course those who were 'discovered' already knew they were there.) This opened the way for Portugal and Spain to begin colonizing the ancient Inca and other civilizations of South America. It also gave momentum to the circumnavigation of the world, encouraged other European powers to establish plantation economies based on African slave labour in the Americas and led to the establishment of the USA.

Citizenship Membership of and inclusion in a national community. Citizenship confers a set of entitlements – to legal equality and justice, the right to be consulted on political matters and access to a minimum of protection against economic insecurity – but simultaneously requires the fulfilment of certain obligations to state and society.

Civil society describes the dense network made up of numerous voluntary and non-governmental associations that develops in the social space between the individual and the state. Where civil society flourishes – its diversity and authority aided by informed, educated citizens – it will normally keep much of social life free from state interference and will have a decisive influence on political life. Whereas a strong civil society will compel governments to take account of the needs and concerns of the citizenry, where civil society is weak autocracy or oligarchy are common.

The **Cold War** Led by the Soviet Union and the USA, the world was split into two antagonistic camps over the period 1947–89. This involved an ideological battle between capitalist democracy versus socialist planning, a massive build-up of arms and the twin races to achieve supremacy in nuclear and space-age technology. Despite several flash points, for example in 1948 and 1962 (see time line in Box 3.3) the superpowers themselves never engaged in head-on aggression. Rather, conflict was deflected into regional or minor wars involving the developing countries – as in the Korean and Vietnam Wars.

Commodity chains are economic networks linking firms, countries and industries. They span producers, distributors and consumers of goods, increasingly on a global scale. (For a fuller explanation see Gereffi 1995: 113–20.)

Commodity fetishism occurs, according to Marx, when an inanimate object is treated as if it required a religious, or even sexual, devotion. In pre-modern societies fetishes were hand-made or rare natural objects thought to embody a spirit that protected the owner from misfortune or disease. Commodity fetishism arises under capitalism because the market system has become much more real and immediate to us than the underlying social relationships (based on inequality and exploitation) which made goods sold in the market possible in the first place.

Communities are marked by deep, intimate and co-operative ties between members. In this sense, 'community' is close to Durkheim's idea of social solidarity, which emerges from commitment to a shared set of values He calls this 'the collective conscience'. Nisbet (1970: 47) gives a formal definition. For him, community 'encompasses all forms of relationship which are characterized by a high degree of personal intimacy, emotional depth, moral commitment, social cohesion and continuity in time'.

A **counter culture** was seen mainly in the richer western countries in the 1960s and 70s, when those involved in developing a counter culture opposed the dull, unreflective, self-congratulatory uniformity of conventional political values. They displayed a growing desire for more control over personal development, greater equity and fluidity in social relationships, a heightened respect for nature and promoted the revival of more decentralized, autonomous communities. A turn away from established religion towards eastern philosophies, experimentation with drugs, adventurous popular music and 'way-out' dress codes were also characteristic of the period.

Creolization describes how cross-fertilization takes place between different cultures when they interact. The locals select particular elements from in-coming cultures, endow these with meanings different from those they possessed in the original culture and then creatively merge these with indigenous traditions to create totally new forms. The word is used in so many contexts that it is impossible to be comprehensive. 'Creole cooking' alludes to a mixture of tropical and European cuisine, while a 'Creole language' (and the associated words 'krio' and 'criollo') refers to a European language that has been localized. Often the additions of local or other imported words are so great that, for example, French Creole may be unintelligible to a native French-speaker. In the Caribbean, 'Creoles' may refer to people of part-European descent, or those that have been strongly acculturated to European ways.

Cultural capital Despite the marked tendencies towards social levelling associated with mass education, affluence, consumerism and highly accessible forms of popular culture, Bourdieu (1984) argues that a dominant 'high' culture continues to flourish. Those whose education or other experiences have enabled then to acquire taste and distinction by investing in various kinds of discerning, detailed, cultural knowledge may be able to gain advantage in the competitive struggle for wealth and power.

Culture Most sociologists tend to define culture as the repertoire of learned ideas, values, knowledge, aesthetic preferences, rules and customs shared by a particular collectivity of social actors. Drawing on this common stock of meanings enables them to participate in a unique way of life. In this usage, the human world consists of a plurality of equal cultures. Each can only be fully interpreted by its participants. With globalization, however, and the increasing inter-penetration of flows of meaning between societies and communities, the idea of cultures as bounded, separate and fixed entities is becoming less tenable (see Chapters 12 and 13). This is an abbreviated précis of a complex term about which many major books have been written. One early influential account was by the American sociologist, Ogburn (1922).

Debt peonage A system whereby loans in cash or kind are made by rich farmers or money lenders, and often paid back by the debtor through a share of crops or labour. The system is common in Central and South America and India and often results in a demoralizing impoverishment, with the debt being bequeathed to the next and subsequent generations.

Devaluation Lowering the value of your currency against that of your competitor countries. This has the effect of lowering the cost of your exports and increasing the cost of imports. However, this is a blunt tool of economic management. Your currency abroad is weakened while, if you are protecting fundamentally inefficient home industries, you simply put off the day of reckoning when they finally cannot compete.

The **developmental state** refers particularly to the attempt by certain Asian states to foster an Asian variant of capitalism, bringing together the financial sector, public policy and large companies in a common effort to penetrate overseas markets, raise profitability and enhance the security of the state.

Diasporas are often formed by the forcible or voluntary dispersion of peoples to a number of countries. They constitute a diaspora if they continue to evince a common concern for their 'homeland' (sometimes an imagined community) and come to share a sense of a common purpose with their own people, wherever they happen to be.

Dystopia An imaginary place where things are as bad as they could possibly be. The term was coined by the nineteenth-century political economist, John Stuart Mill, as an antonym to 'Utopia' an imaginary, perfect island conjured up by Sir Thomas More in his book of the same name, published in 1516. Following More's lead, sociologists have found that defining the ideal can be very productive. Sociologists such as Max Weber pioneered the use of 'ideal types' (that is end-of-logic models) to help measure the extent of the deviation from the ideal

of different real situations. This method can be a useful tool for sociological reasoning.

Economies of scale arise when savings can be made in the purchase of a large volume of raw materials, the organization of high-output assembly lines or in mass consumption. Bulk purchases are cheaper for producers while many retail outlets have followed the advice to 'pile them high and sell them cheap' – taking smaller profits on each item in exchange for selling more goods. Mass consumption and mass production are closely related.

The **Enlightenment** was a body of influential ideas that gradually spread across Europe during the eighteenth century. Its optimistic view of the potential for human progress through the power of reason was considerably assisted by advances in science and philosophy. Enlightenment thinkers saw the importance of critical reason, scepticism and doubt, but were certain that self-realization could be attained through practical involvement in, and attempts to transform, the material world (see Chapter 3).

An **epiphenomenon** is something that appears to be of great causal significance, but is really derived from some other primary basis. In overvaluing an epiphenomenon observers are thought to mistake a symptom for a reason.

Ethnocentrism derives from the Greek word for people, *ethnos*. Ethnocentrists see their community or nation as the model against which all others have to be judged. By implication other people's ways of thinking and behaviour are aberrant, strange and inferior (Cashmore 1994: 258).

Exponential growth occurs where any increase in a variable such as population, savings or wealth feeds on itself with each new increment contributing to yet further expansion. This causes a variable to double in size every so many years. The formula for calculating how long this doubling process will take involves dividing 70 by the rate of expansion.

An **export-processing zone** (EPZ) is a free trade enclave where foreign firms producing goods for export are encouraged to locate. Normally the EPZ takes the form of a very large industrial estate, but in other cases a whole region is so designated – for example the seventeen-kilometre strip just south of the Rio Grande in Mexico. In all cases EPZs benefit from tax and financial incentives.

Fordism Named after its pioneer, the car maker Henry Ford, this industrial system involved the mass production of standardized goods by huge, integrated companies. Each company was composed of many different, specialized departments each producing components and parts that were eventually channelled towards the moving line for final assembly (see also **Post-Fordism**).

French Revolution This was a series of social upheavals that began in 1789 with peasant revolt, monarchical collapse and moderate middle-class leadership. From 1793 to 1795, the urban poor of Paris and other cities, led by radicals such as Robespierre, pushed the revolution in a more violent and nationalist direction. An increasing involvement in European wars also led to the successful mass mobilization of citizen armies and intensified the need to centralize national administration.

Futurologists extrapolate from existing trends and make more or less sophisticated predictions about the future. Although they are characteristically Delphic in their pronouncements, leading corporations often take serious cognizance of their views. The sociologist/futurologist Alvin Toffler gained a mass readership with books like *The Third Wave* (1981).

Gentrification is the process whereby run-down inner city areas experience physical and economic regeneration – with a growth of small businesses, theatres, cafés and improved living areas. This may result either from the influx of 'trendy' middle-class intellectuals and professionals in the media, the arts or education who then refurbish the old housing stock (see Zukin's study (1981) of loft-living in Greenwich Village, New York). Alternatively the process can arise from the deliberate attempt by landlords, property developers and governments to push new capital investment into entire areas.

Glocalization A term popularized by Robertson (1992: 173–4) to describe how global pressures and demands are made to conform to local conditions. Whereas powerful companies might 'customize' their product to local markets, glocalization operates in the opposite direction. Local actors select and modify elements from an array of global possibilities, thereby initiating some democratic and creative engagement between the local and the global.

The **Great Depression** (1929–39) was the most severe capitalist downturn ever known. By late 1932, in the USA alone, around 15 million workers were unemployed. The crisis began in October 1929 when company share values on New York's Wall Street stock exchange crashed. A number of stockbrokers and investors jumped to their deaths from their skyscraper offices. A series of escalating bank and currency collapses soon turned the crisis into a global one. German Nazism and Japanese Fascism were partly caused by the world economic collapse.

Green Revolution The diffusion of high-yielding varieties of seeds, particularly wheat, maize and rice. This series of research and technological initiatives drew on earlier developments (for example, a hybrid maize was produced in 1933), but it accelerated dramatically in the 1960s. Institutes funded by governments and involving universities, agricultural companies and IGOs were set up in Mexico and the Philippines, among many other places. This was a high-technology-intensive agriculture initiative and is not to be confused with the green/environmental social and political movement, which opposes many of the interventions associated with the Green Revolution. Pearse (1980) provides a good sociological study of the early impact of the Green Revolution.

Gross national product A common measurement used by economists to assess a country's wealth. GNP includes all production by the country's firms regardless of the firms' location. It does not include production by foreign-owned companies. As complex mixes of foreign and national share hold-

ings develop it will be increasingly outdated to try to calculate measurements of this kind.

Habitus referred in its Latin origins to a typical or habitual condition. For the French social theorist Bourdieu, it comprises a set of cultural orientations acquired by the members of a given social subgroup. Through their specific life experiences they express and display preferences for a cluster of distinctive tastes in consumption and lifestyles. While the habitus disposes social actors to particular kinds of conduct, it also provides the basis for the generation of new practices (Jenkins 1992: 74–84).

Heterophobia The fear of difference. An unusual expression that may serve the purpose of distinguishing between an initial encounter where people, somewhat innocently, draw back from the unfamiliar and 'racism', which is a structured, organized and usually vicious plan of attack to subdue an unpopular group. See also **ethnocentrism** and **xenophobia,** which are closely related expressions.

Hybridity refers principally to the creation of dynamic mixed cultures. Sociologists and anthropologists, who use the expression 'syncretism' to refer to such phenomena, have long observed the evolution of commingled cultures from two or more parent cultures. Using the literature and other cultural expressions of colonial peoples, Bhabha (1986) introduced a new twist to the idea. He saw hybridity as a transgressive act challenging the colonizers' authority, values and representations and thereby constituting an act of self-empowerment and defiance.

Ideology refers at a loose level to a reasonably coherent set of assumptions and convictions shared by a particular social group. Pacifists and vegetarians share an ideology in this sense. Where ideologies are totalizing and universal in their claims (for example, communism) they are sometimes referred to as **meta-narratives** (see glossary entry). For some social theorists ideologies can be contrasted with reason or science and are used deliberately by ruling groups to obscure real power relations in their own interest.

'Imagined community' is the term used by Benedict Anderson (1983: 15-16) to describe a nation. It is *imagined* because the member of even the smallest nation will never know most of their fellow members. The nation is imagined as *limited* because even the largest of nations has a finite boundary beyond which there are other nations. It is imagined as *sovereign* in that is displaces or undermines the legitimacy of organized religion or the monarchy. Finally, it is imagined as *community* because regardless of actual inequality, the nation is conceived of as a deep, horizontal comradeship.

Industrial Revolution Britain's industrial revolution led the way for industrialization across the globe and can be dated to around the 1770s, when machinery and full-time waged workers in permanent factories were increasingly deployed in manufacturing processes. The industrial revolution began with the cotton textile industry, but over about another 70 years spread to most other industries in Britain.

The **informal sector** is that part of urban society characterized by small-scale, labour-intensive, self-generated economic activity. There are minimal capital requirements in joining the informal sector and it relies on unregulated markets and skills acquired outside the formal education system. The sector is rarely controlled by government inspectors, so working conditions, safety checks and environmental standards are minimal. Exploitation and self-exploitation are rife.

Japanization refers to the conscious attempt, especially in the 1980s, to imitate the organizational culture developed by Japan's huge companies, such as Toyota, and especially their highly effective strategies with regard to managing labour relations in factories. Such attempts at transplanting Japan's methods to other countries have not always been completely successful.

Labour power is the capacity to work for a given time, a given rate of pay and at a particular level of skill and effort. The notion is used particularly by orthodox Marxists so as to provide a measure of the extent to which the employer 'exploits' the worker, but the expression has fallen out of use elsewhere.

Longevity refers to how long people, on average, are expected to live. Longevity is influenced by such diverse factors as the infant mortality rate (how many babies die at birth or shortly thereafter), by sanitary arrangements, living standards, lifestyles, the level of personal security, the number of car accidents, pollution and diet.

A **longitudinal** analysis measures a particular change over a specified period at regular intervals. Often social statisticians have difficulty in achieving consistency over the long term as the criteria for data-collection change. Nonetheless some impressive results have appeared using this technique.

Luddites were English artisans who rioted rather than accept mechanical and technical changes. It was not just unemployment they feared, but also the threat of de-skilling and lower wages.

McDonaldization originally referred to the irresistible dissemination of business systems associated with the US fast-food industry. These aimed to achieve intense control over workers and customers in order to supply cheap, standardized, but quality products in pleasant surroundings. This drive for efficiency and predictability has now spread to many other economic activities and countries so that the McDonald's burger franchising chain is merely the 'paradigm case' (Ritzer 1993: 1) of a much wider formula.

Mercantilism describes an economic theory and practice prevalent in the seventeenth to early nineteenth century. The theory was based on the idea that the nation's stock of gold and silver signified its wealth. Those countries that did not have their own mines had to engage in aggressive forms of foreign trade to acquire bullion. A country's currency was guaranteed by the amount of gold in the national vaults.

Meta-narratives are more than simply 'grand' theories claiming to possess demonstrably valid explanations for all societal evolution and change.

Rather, they also offer ultimate, epic stories about the truth of human experience. Socialism, for example, insists that the oppression of different groups – from slaves through to workers – and their perpetual struggles against economic exploitation dominate history.

A **mode of production** was used by Marx to describe the characteristic social relations that marked a particular way of organizing production. Slavery, feudalism and capitalism are all modes of production in this sense.

Modernity can usefully be dated to the fifteenth and sixteenth centuries. Symbolically, the so-called 'discovery' of the 'New World' in 1492 and the circumnavigation of the world can be taken as convenient markers opening the modern era. However, the orientations towards modernity crystallized in the seventeenth century and spread and accelerated in their impact during the eighteenth and nineteenth centuries with the growth of a questing spirit, a strong leaning towards the purposive pursuit of material and social 'progress', rationality, industrialization, urbanization and the triumph of the nation state.

The **nation state** is constituted by a government assuming a legal and moral right to exercise sole jurisdiction, supported by force in the last resort, over a particular territory and its citizens. This involves institutions for managing domestic and foreign affairs. From the late eighteenth century ordinary citizens in most western countries began to feel strong loyalties to their nation states, while local and regional identities were suppressed. Popular nationalism has been more difficult to achieve in some developing countries.

Neo-liberalism is an economic doctrine that lays great emphasis on the free market and unconstrained competition. In the eighteenth century it was associated with the Scottish economist Adam Smith, who advocated the virtues of free trade over **mercantilism** (q.v.). Drawing on the work of the Austrian economist Friedrich A. Hayek (1899–1902), neo-liberalism was revived in the 1980s by politicians such as Margaret Thatcher and Ronald Reagan – who helped to spread this philosophy to many countries.

The **new international division of labour** divides production into different skills and tasks that are spread across regions and countries rather than within a single company. From the 1970s onwards hitherto agricultural countries, particularly in the Asia-Pacific region, became rapidly drawn into the new international division of labour as key production functions were shifted away from the old industrial zones.

Non-tariff trade barriers involve the attempt to protect domestic industries by imposing bureaucratic regulations about such things as product 'quality' or technical standards. This may deter importers. Local producers may also be given hidden subsidies. Through these means the appearance of free trade is preserved.

The **ozone layer** is a band of gas encircling the planet between 20 and 50 kilometres above the earth's surface. It filters out the most intensive effects of the ultra-violet radiation coming from the sun, which would otherwise damage animal and plant life by causing extensive cancers and genetic mutations. These dangers have stimulated international moves to ban the production and use of those chemicals – especially the various chlorofluorocarbons (CFCs) which destroy ozone.

Patriarchy involves forms of oppression that elevate men to positions of power and authority. Feminist writers argue that patriarchy is so deeply embedded that it appears in early societies as well as in feudal, capitalist and self-proclaimed socialist societies. Those feminists who are influenced by Marxism stress sexual divisions of labour are functional and related to the evolving class structure. Other writers have pointed to the role of religion or the structuring and labelling of female and male roles. Whatever the origin of this role differentiation (most feminists discount, but some writers include, the different biological functions of men and women) it has now become culturally and even psychoanalytically inscribed. This makes patriarchy difficult to dislodge.

Post-Fordism exists where most workers are employed on a temporary or casual basis, enjoy few, if any, pension or other rights and where labour has limited power to organize in order to resist employer demands. Capitalists therefore enjoy much more direct control over their employees than was possible under Fordism including the ability to maintain a highly flexible and adaptable labour force.

Post-industrial society refers to societies where the service industries – including the knowledge-, media- and information-based sectors – have become the most important source of wealth and employment. Accompanying this, therefore, is a relative decline in the contribution of manufacturing industry to national wealth, a fall in the numbers of manual workers, a huge expansion of university or tertiary education and a growing middle class.

Post-modern (social life) According to postmodernists, unlike the earlier era of modernity, our lives are now said to be less and less determined by family, class, community and national loyalties or by social expectations linked to such things as gender or race. Instead, these structures, along with the moral and political certainties about the nature of truth, reality and destiny with which they were associated, have largely disintegrated. Accordingly we are free to forge our own identities – although this may also cause us some anxiety. In doing so we choose from an increasingly diverse, pluralistic and sometimes confusing cultural repertoire – one that emanates especially from the all-pervasive mass media.

Proto-globalization Early processes of universalism that failed to embrace all of humanity. The major limitations on proto-globalization were the lack of global awareness ('globalism'), the limited development of scientific rationality and the lack of a centralizing, powerful nation state system. What we have called proto-globalization is akin to what Robertson (1992: 54) called 'miniglobalizations'.

Purchasing power parity Calculations of GNP per capita involve making an adjustment for the generally lower costs of living that prevail in many poorer countries compared with the advanced economies. The amount of goods that can be bought in a given country with the amount of local currency officially designated as equal to $1 on the foreign exchange markets may actually be considerably more than what $1 would purchase in the USA.

Purdah is the practice of secluding women by covering their bodies from the male gaze and virtually excluding them, sometimes behind screens, from all forms of public life. Often considerable economic activity goes on in these private household settings.

A **realist perspective** in this book refers to a view which once dominated thinking about the nature of international politics. Realists argued that if there was such a thing as a world society it was largely synonymous with the relations between sovereign states. Moreover, these relations mostly concerned questions of military security and foreign policy that were designed to maximize national power and protect national autonomy in an unruly, anarchical and war-prone system of competing states.

Reflexivity All humans reflect on the consequences of their own and others' actions and perhaps alter their behaviour in response to new information. This quality of self-awareness, self-knowledge and contemplation is of great interest to sociologists as it speaks to the motives, understandings and intentions of social actors. In contemporary societies reflexivity is said to intensify as every aspect of social life becomes subject to endless revision in the face of constantly accumulating knowledge.

The **Renaissance** The word derives from the French for 'rebirth' and refers to the revival of classical philosophy, literature and art in early modern and modern Europe. Over a period of 800 years, starting in the eighth century, artistic and scientific thinking flowered in Europe. This was accompanied by the rise of intellectual life (including the founding of universities), secular states and rational values.

The **sacred** and the **profane** In *The Elementary Forms of Religious Life* (1915), Durkheim argued that religious practices and beliefs require a sharp separation between ordinary, mundane activities and objects and those regarded as sacred. The latter are treated with awe and veneration. They bring members of communities together in the pursuit of shared ceremonial activities and group affirmation of deeply held convictions. Whereas the profane is knowable through everyday observable things, the sacred is known only through extraordinary experiences.

Secularization refers to the declining hold of religious belief and practice over most people's lives during the industrialization process. Growing exposure to scientific knowledge and new ideas, combined with a more materially secure environment, render most individuals less reliant upon the moral and spiritual certainties provided by religion in pre-industrial societies.

Semiotics is the study of signs and symbols in language and other means of communication. Semiotics links the separate disciplines of sociology and linguistics and in recent years has made a major contribution to the study of the hidden meanings of electronically transmitted images.

Simulacra (singular **simulacrum**) are entities that have no original or no surviving original in the actual world, but are thought nonetheless to be 'real'. Cult followers – for example of Elvis Presley or of characters in certain TV soaps – seek to emulate their simulacra perhaps by copying their appearance or supposed lifestyles, writing to them for personal advice, or even proposing marriage.

Situational identity arises when an individual constructs and presents any one of a number of possible social identities, depending on the situation. In the most individualistic versions of this phenomenon, an actor deploys an aspect of their identity – a religion, an ethnicity or lifestyle – as the context deems a particular choice desirable or appropriate.

Social control refers to the process whereby rich and powerful actors inhibit, channel and manage the behaviour of the population at large. Everything from open punishment (like hanging and flogging), incarceration and surveillance is covered by the expression 'social control'. Since the 1970s sociologists have extended the idea to cover the question of how deviant behaviour is labelled, ideologically suppressed and even sometimes encouraged by attempts at social control.

Social Darwinism drew on the ideas on evolution and natural selection that Darwin applied to plants and animals, even though Darwin himself disavowed the idea that human 'races' could be classified. 'Natural selection' was crudely understood by European imperialists as lending support to the idea that they were inherently superior to the people they colonized. Social Darwinism was also a quasi-rational theory used to support population control, immigration restrictions and racial prejudice.

Social movements are informal organizations working for change but galvanized around a single unifying issue. They are often reactions both against conventional party politics and against the traditional left's belief in the transformatory possibilities of working-class movements. Examples of global social movements include those involved in the movement for human rights, the anti-war and anti-nuclear movements, the greens and the women's movement.

Socialization The processes through which we learn to understand, assimilate and reproduce the rules, values and meanings shared by members of our society and which are constantly enacted and negotiated in everyday life. The child's relationships within the family are normally crucial to this learning process – along with school and peer group – but socialization continues throughout life as we are continuously exposed to different social experiences, including the media.

The **sovereignty** enjoyed by states means that they have the sole right to exercise a monopoly of legal and coercive control both over their territories and the people living within their borders. (A fuller understanding of the state and its powers owes much to the work of the sociologist Max Weber.) Nowadays, states have found it difficult to retain their sovereignty without 'pooling' it with allied, often stronger, states. Therefore, although politicians do not always admit this in practice sovereignty is shared. Britain provides a good example in the period of the Cold War, which had a considerable stock of nuclear weaponry, but could not fire it without the agreement of the US president.

The **Suffragette Movement** demanded votes for women as a first principle of equality and liberation. The movement was at is height in the USA and the UK in the late nineteenth and early twentieth century, but it was not until women were used 'on the home front' in factories during the First World War that the cause was won. Even then when the vote was conceded in the UK in 1918, only women over 30 were eligible. In the US women's suffrage was granted two years later.

Taylorization is the name given to the process accompanying Fordism whereby most work processes were scientifically studied by managers so as to find ways to break them down into highly specialized and efficient tasks while removing most of the skill and responsibility formerly exercised by the workers.

Third World An expression used to distinguish the non-aligned poor countries from the First World (the rich capitalist democracies of the West) and also from the Second World (the communist-led countries of the Soviet bloc). Increased differentiation between the rich and poor countries of Asia, Africa, Latin America and the Middle East, together with the political collapse of nearly all the communist countries have meant that the term is of less and less use. Although countries are still highly unequal in their wealth and power, they do not fit neatly into three groups.

White-collar crimes are those perpetrated by more respectable members of society. They often involve fraud. White-collar crime is sometimes defended as 'victimless', although all this usually means is that the victims are less obvious. For example, false claims on insurance policies mean that the premiums for all policyholders will rise.

Xenophobia is hatred and fear of foreigners. When these feelings are applied to a visible minority the expression 'racism' is often used. It is probably better to see 'racism' as a special case of xenophobia than to use it too extravagantly. If used too often terms of scorn soon lose their strength, no longer wounding or even impressing their targets.

References

Adorno, T. and Horkheimer, M. (1972) *Dialectic of Enlightenment*, New York: Herder.

Aglietta, M. (1979) *A Theory of Capitalist Regulation*, London: New Left Books.

Ahmed, A. S. (1992) *Postmodernism and Islam: Predicament and Promise*, London: Routledge.

Alavi, H. (1972) 'The state in post-colonial societies – Pakistan and Bangladesh', *New Left Review*, **74**, 59–81.

Albrow, M. (1987) 'Sociology for one world', *International Sociology*, **2**, 1–12.

Albrow, M. (1990) 'Globalization, knowledge and society: an introduction', in Albrow, M. and King, E. (eds) *Globalization, Knowledge and Society*, London: Sage, 3–13.

Albrow, M. (1996) *The Global Age*, Cambridge: Polity.

Alcock, P. (1997) *Understanding Poverty*, 2nd edn, Basingstoke: Macmillan.

Allahar, A. (1994) *More than an oxymoron: ethnicity and the social construction of primordial attachment*. Unpublished paper, Department of Sociology, University of Western Ontario, Canada.

Allen, J., Braham, P. and Lewis, P. (eds) (1992) *Political and Economic Forms of Modernity*, Cambridge: Polity.

Allen, J. (1992) 'Fordism and modern industry', in Allen, J., Braham, P. and Lewis, P. (eds) *Political and Economic Forms of Modernity*, Cambridge: Polity, 229–74.

Amin, A. (ed.) (1994) *Post-Fordism: A Reader*, Oxford: Blackwell.

Amin, S. (1974) *Accumulation on a World Scale*, 2 vols, New York: Monthly Review Press.

Amsden, A. (1989) *Asia's Next Giant: South Korea and Late Industrialization*, New York: Oxford University Press.

Anderson, B. (1983) *Imagined Communities: Reflections on the Origins and Spread of Nationalism*, London: Verso.

Anderson, J., Brook, C. and Cochrane, A. (eds) *A Global World? Re-ordering Political Space*, Oxford: Oxford University Press.

Andrae, G. and Beckman, B. (1985) *The Wheat Trap: Bread and Underdevelopment in Nigeria*, London: Zed Books in association with the Scandinavian Institute of African Studies.

Ang, I. (1985) *Watching Dallas: Soap Opera and the Melodramatic Imagination*, London: Methuen.

Applebaum, R. P. and Henderson, J. (eds) (1992) *States and Development in the Asian Pacific*, London: Sage.

Arrighi, G. (1994) *The Long Twentieth Century*, New York: Verso.

Asfah, H. (ed.) (1996) *Women and Politics in the Third World*, London: Routledge.

Athanasiou, T. (1997) *Slow Reckoning: The Ecology of a Divided Planet*, London: Secker & Warburg.

Auletta, K. (1982) *The Underclass*, New York: Random House.

Badham, R. (1986) *Theories of Industrial Society*, London: Croom Helm.

Bagchi, A. K. (1982) *The Political Economy of Underdevelopment*, Cambridge: Cambridge University Press.

Baird, V. (1997) 'Trash: inside the heap', *The New Internationalist*, **295**, October, 7–10.

Bairoch, P. (1981) 'The main trends in national economic disparities since the industrial revolution', in Bairoch, P. and Levy-Leboyer, M. (eds) *Disparities in Economic Development Since the Industrial Revolution*, Basingstoke: Macmillan, 3–17.

Banpasirichote, C. (1991) 'Children of the informal sector: an investigation into their lives and work', *New Asian Vision*, **6**(1), 1–32.

Banton, M. (1994) 'UNESCO', in Ellis Cashmore, E. (ed.) *Dictionary of Race and Ethnic Relations* (3rd edn), London: Routledge, 336–7.

Barber, B. (1995) *Jihad vs McWorld*, New York: Ballantine Books .

Basu, A. (ed.) (1995) *The Challenge of Local Feminisms*, Boulder, CO: Westview Press.

Baudrillard, J. (1988) *Selected Writings*, edited by Poster, M. Cambridge: Polity.

Bauman, Z. (1994) *Modernity and the Holocaust*, Cambridge: Polity.

Beck, U. (1992) *The Risk Society: Towards a New Modernity*, London: Sage.

Beck, U. (1994) 'The Reinvention of Politics', in Beck, U., Giddens, A. and Lash, S. (eds) *Reflexive Modernization: Politics, Tradition and Aesthetics in the Modern Social Order*, Cambridge: Polity, 5–55.

Beck, U. (1998) 'The cosmopolitan manifesto', *New Statesman*, **20**, 28–30.

Belk, R. W. (1988) 'Third world consumer culture', *Research in Marketing*, supplement 4, **4**, 103–27.

Bello, W. and Rosenfeld, S. (1990) *Dragons in Distress: Asia's Miracle Economies in Crisis*, New York: Penguin.

Berger, J. (1972) *Ways of Seeing*, Harmondsworth: Penguin in association with the BBC.

Bergesen, A. (1990) 'Turning world-system theory on its head', in Featherstone, M. (ed.) *Global Culture: Nationalism, Globalization and Modernity*, London: Sage, 67–82.

Beynon, H. (1973) *Working for Ford*, Harmondsworth: Allen Lane.

Bhabha, H. K. (1986) 'Signs taken for wonders: questions of ambivalence and authority under a tree outside Delhi, May 1817', in Gates, H. L. Jr. (ed.) *'Race', Writing and Difference*, Chicago: University of Chicago Press, 173–83.

Bienefeld, M. (1994) 'Capitalism and the nation state in the dog days of the twentieth century', in Miliband, R. and Panitch, L. (eds) *Socialist Register: Between Globalism and Nationalism*, London: Merlin, 94–129.

Bluestone, B. and Harrison, B. (1987) 'The impact of private disinvestment on workers and their communities', in Peet, R. (ed.) *International Capitalism and Industrial Restructuring*, London: Allen & Unwin, 72–104.

Booth, C. (1967) *Life and Labour of the People in London. On the City: Physical Patterns and Social Structure.* (Selected writings of Charles Booth, edited and with an introduction by H. W. Pfautz), Chicago: Chicago University Press.

Boris, E. and Prugl, E. (eds) (1996) *Homeworkers in Global Perspective: Invisible No More*, New York: Routledge.

Boserup, E. (1970) *Women's Role in Economic Development*, London: Allen & Unwin.

Bourdieu, P. (1984) *Distinction: A Social Critique of the Judgement of Taste*, Cambridge, MA: Harvard University Press .

Boyd-Barrett, O. and Newbold, C. (1995) *Approaches to Media: A Reader*, London: Edward Arnold.

Bradley, S. P., Hausman, J. A. and Nolan, R. L. (1993) *Globalization, Technology and Competition: The Fusion of Computers and Telecommunications in the 1990s*, Boston, MA: Harvard Business School Press.

Bramble, B. J. and Porter, G. (1992) 'Non-governmental organizations and the making of US international environmental policy', in Hurrell, A. and Kingsbury, B. (eds) *The International Politics of the Environment*, Oxford: Clarendon Press, 313–53.

Braverman, H. (1974) *Labour and Monopoly Capital*, New York: Monthly Review Press.

Brett, E. A. (1985) *The World Economy Since the War: The Politics of Uneven Development*, Basingstoke: Macmillan.

Briggs, A. and Cobley, P. (1997) *The Media: An Introduction*, Harlow: Longman.

Brooks, B. and Madden, P. (1995) *The Globe-trotting Sports Shoe*, London: Christian Aid.

Bruegel, I. (1988) *Sex and Race in the Labour Market*. Paper given at the Socialist Feminist Forum, London.

Bryman, A. (1995) *Disney and His World*, London: Routledge.

Bulmer, M. and Rees, A. M. (eds) (1996) *Citizenship Today: The Contemporary Relevance of T. H. Marshall*, London: UCL Press.

Burbach, R., Núñez, O. and Kagarlitsky, B. (1997) *Globalization and its Discontents: The Rise of Postmodern Socialisms*, London: Pluto.

Burton, J. (1972) *World Society*, Cambridge: Cambridge University Press.

Bush, R. (1996) 'The politics of food and starvation', *Review of African Political Economy*, **23**(68), 169–95.

Byerly, C. M. (1995) 'News, consciousness and social participation: the role of women's feature service in world news', in Valdivia, A. N. (ed.) *Feminism, Multiculturalism and the Media: Global Diversities*, London: Sage, 105–22.

Byrne, P. (1997) *Social Movements in Britain*, London: Routledge.

Bystdzienski, J. M. (ed.) (1992) *Women Transforming Politics: Worldwide Strategies for Empowerment*, Bloomington: Indiana University Press.

Cable, V. and Ferdinand, P. (1994) 'China as an economic giant: threat or opportunity?' *International Affairs*, **70**(2), 243–61.

Cairncross, F. (1997a) 'Telecommunications', *The Economist*, 13 September.

Cairncross, F. (1997b) *The Death of Distance*, Boston, MA: Harvard Business School Press.

Camilleri, J. and Falk, J. (1992) *The End of Sovereignty? The Politics of a Shrinking and Fragmenting World*, Cheltenham: Edward Elgar.

Campani, G. (1995) 'Women migrants: from marginal subjects to social actors', in Cohen, R. (ed.) *The Cambridge Survey of World Migration*, Cambridge: Cambridge University Press, 536–50.

Cardoso, F. H. and Falleto, E. (1969) *Dependencia y desarrollo en américa latina*, Mexico: Siglo Veintiuno.

Carnoy, M., Castells, M., Cohen, S. S. and Cardoso, F. H. (eds) (1993) *The New Global Economy in the Information Age: Reflections on our Changing World*, University Park, PA: Pennsylvania State University Press.

Carroll, B. A. (1989) '"Women take action!" Women's direct action and social change', *Women's Studies International Forum*, **12**(1), 3–24.

Cashmore, E. (ed.) (1994) *Dictionary of Race and Ethnic Relations* (3rd edn), London: Routledge.

Castells, M. (1977) *The Urban Question: A Marxist Approach*, London: Edward Arnold.

Castells, M. (1992) 'Four Asian tigers with a dragon head: a comparative analysis of the state, economy and society in the Asian Pacific Rim', in Applebaum, R. P. and Henderson, J. (eds) *States and Development in the Asian Pacific Rim*, London: Sage, 33–70.

Castells, M. (1996) *The Rise of the Network Society* (Vol. 1 in his *The Information Age: Economy, Society and Culture*), Oxford: Blackwell.

Castles, S. and Miller, M. (1998) *The Age of Migration: International Population Movements in the Modern World* (2nd edn), Basingstoke: Macmillan.

Caulkin, S. (1997) 'Amnesty and WWF take a crack at Shell', *Observer*, 11 May.

Cavanagh, J. (1997) 'The global resistance to sweatshops', in Ross, A. (ed.), *No Sweat*, London: Verso, 39–50.

Chase, H. (1994) 'The *Meyhane* or the McDonald's? Changes in eating habits and the evolution of fast food in Istanbul', in Zubaida, S. and Tapper, R. (eds) *Culinary Cultures of the Middle East*, London: I.B.Tauris, 73–86.

Chowdhury, A. and Islam, I. (1993) *The Newly Industrialising Economies of East Asia*, London: Routledge.

Clammer, J. (1992) 'Shopping in Japan', in Shields, R. (ed.) *Lifestyle Shopping*, London: Routledge, 195–213.

Clapp, J. (1997) 'Threats to the environment in an era of globalization: an end to state sovereignty?', in Schrecker, T. (ed.) *Surviving Globalism*, Basingstoke: Macmillan, 123–40.

Clifford, J. (1988) *The Predicament of Culture: Twentieth Century Ethnography, Literature and Art*, Cambridge, MA: Harvard University Press.

Coca-Cola Company (1997) *Annual Report*.

Cockerill, S. and Sparks, C. (1996) 'Japan in crisis', *International Socialism*, **72**, 27–56.

Cohen, E. (1972) 'Towards a sociology of international tourism', *Social Research*, **39**, 164–82.

Cohen, R. (1987) *The New Helots: Migrants in the International Division of Labour*, Aldershot: Gower.

Cohen, R. (ed.) (1995) *The Cambridge Survey of World Migration*, Cambridge: Cambridge University Press.

Cohen, R. (1997) *Global Diasporas: An Introduction*, London: UCL Press.

Cohen, S. (1972) *Folk Devils and Moral Panics*, London: MacGibben & Kee.

Cohen, S. (1985) *Visions of Social Control: Crime Punishment and Classification*, Cambridge: Polity.

Comte, A. (1896) *The Positive Philosophy*, trans. Martineau, H., London; George Bell and Sons.

Comte, A. (1971/1842) 'Positive philosophy', extract in Truzzi, M. (ed.) *Sociology: The Classic Statements*, New York: Random House, 131–5.

Cooper, A. F. (1997) 'Snapshots of cyber-diplomacy: Greenpeace against French nuclear testing and the Spain–Canada "fish war"'. Discussion paper no. 36, *Diplomatic Studies Programme*, Leicester University.

Corzine, R. (1997) 'Shell opposes toughening of environmental policies', *Financial Times*, 11 April.

Coward, R. (1978) 'Sexual liberation and the family', *m/f*, **1**, 7–24.

Crow, G. (1997) *Comparative Sociology and Social Theory*, Basingstoke: Macmillan.

Crystal, D. (1995) *The Cambridge Encyclopedia of the English Language* Cambridge: Cambridge University Press.

Crystal, E. (1989) 'Tourism in Toraja (Sulawesi, Indonesia)', in Smith, V. L. (ed.) *Hosts and Guests* (2nd edn), Philadelphia, PA: University of Pennsylvania Press, 139–67.

Cumings, B. (1987) 'Northeast Asian political economy', in Deyo, F. C. (ed.) *Political Economy of the New Asian Industrialization*, Ithaca: Cornell University Press, 44–83.

Davis, M. (1991) *City of Quartz*, London: Verso.

Davison, J. (1997) *Gangsta: The Sinister Spread of Yardie Gun Culture*, London: Satin Publications.

Dicken, P. (1992) *Global Shift: The Internationalization of Economic Activity*, London: Paul Chapman.

Dickson, L. and McCulloch, A. (1996) 'Shell, the Brent Spar and Greenpeace: a doomed tryst?', *Environmental Politics*, **5**(1), 122–9.

Dodds, F. (ed.) (1997) *The Way Forward: Beyond Agenda 21*, London: Earthscan.

Dohse, K., Jurgens, V. and Malsch, T. (1985) 'From Fordism to Toyotism', *Politics and Society*, **14**(2), 115–46.

Dore, R. (1984) *Land Reform in Japan*, London: Athlone.

Dore, R. (1986) *Flexible Rigidities: Industrial Policy and Structural Adjustment in the Japanese Economy, 1970–80*, London: Athlone.

Douglas, M. and Isherwood, B. (1978) *The World of Goods: Towards an Anthroplogy of Consumption*, New York: W. W. Norton.

Downing, J. Mohammadi, A. and Sreberny-Mohammadi, A. (eds) (1995) *Questioning the Media: A Critical Introduction*, London: Sage.

Dreze, J. and Sen, A. (1989) *Hunger and Public Action*, Oxford: Clarendon.

Drucker, P. (1989) *The New Realities*, Oxford: Heinemann, 109–33.

Dunning, J. H. (1993a) *The Globalization of Business*, London: Routledge.

Dunning, J. H. (1993b) *Multinational Enterprises in a Global Economy*, Wokingham, Surrey: Addison-Wesley.

Durkheim, E. (1915) *The Elementary Forms of Religious Life*, New York: Collier Books.

Durkheim, E. (1933) *The Division of Labor in Society* (2nd edn), New York: Free Press.

Durning, A. T. (1992) *How Much is Enough? The Consumer Society and the Future of the Earth*, London: Earthscan.

Dyson, T. M. (1996) *Population and Food: Global Trends and Future Prospects*, London: Routledge.

Edwards, C. (1992) 'Industrialization in South Korea', in Hewitt, T., Johnson, H. and Wield, D. (eds) *Industrialization and Development*, Oxford: Oxford University Press, 97–127.

Elger, T. and Smith, C. (eds) (1994) *Global Japanization? The Transnational Transformation of the Labour Process*, London: Routledge.

Enloe, C. (1989) *Bananas, Beaches and Bases: Making Feminist Sense of International Politics*, Berkeley: University of California Press.

Ethical Consumer (1997/8) **50**, December/January.

Evans, P. (1995) *Embedded Autonomy: State and Industrial Transformation*, Princeton, NJ: University of Princeton Press.

Fainstein, N. (1992) 'The urban underclass and mismatch theory re-examined', in Cross, M. (ed.) *Ethnic Minorities and Industrial Change in Europe and North America*, Cambridge: Cambridge University Press, 276–312.

Faist, T. (1998) 'Transnational social spaces out of international migration: evolution, significance and future prospects', *Archives of European Sociology*, **39**(2), 213–47.

Falk, R. (1992) *Explorations at the Edge of Time: The Prospects for World Order*, Philadelphia, PA: Temple University Press.

Fanon, F. (1967) *The Wretched of the Earth*, Harmondsworth: Penguin.

Featherstone, M. (1987) 'Lifestyle and consumer culture', *Theory, Culture and Society*, **4**, 55–70.

Featherstone, M. (1990) 'Global culture: an introduction', in Featherstone, M. (ed.) *Global Culture: Nationalism, Globalization and Modernity*, London: Sage, 1–14.

Featherstone, M. (1992) *Consumer Culture and Postmodernism*, London: Sage.

Feifer, M. (1985) *Going Places*, Basingstoke: Macmillan.

Fields, K. J. (1996) 'The trend towards economic regionalism and its consequences for Asia', in Balaam, D. N. and Veseth, M. (eds) *Readings in International Political Economy*, Englewood, Cliffs, NJ: Prentice Hall, 97–111.

Findlay, A. M. (1995) 'Skilled transients: the invisible phenomenon?', in Cohen, R. (ed.) *The Cambridge Survey of World Migration*, Cambridge: Cambridge University Press, 515–22.

Firat, A. F. (1995) 'Consumer culture or culture consumed?', in Costa, J. A. and Bamossy, G. J. (eds) *Marketing in a Multicultural World*, London: Sage, 105–25.

Fisher, J. (1993) *The Road from Rio: Sustainable Development and the Non-governmental Movement in the Third World*, Westport, CN: Praeger.

Fiske, J. (1989) *Understanding Popular Culture*, London: Unwin Hyman.

Fligstein, N. (1981) *Going North: Migration of Blacks and Whites from the South, 1900–1950*, New York: Academic Press.

Foucault, M. (1977) *Discipline and Punish: The Birth of the Prison*, London: Allen Lane.

Frank, A. G. (1967) *Capitalism and Underdevelopment in Latin America*, New York: Monthly Review Press.

Frank, A. G. (1969) *Latin America: Undevelopment or Revolution*, New York: Monthly Review Press.

Freedland, J. (1999) 'Shangri-la. It's quite a European place-name, the way it splits in two', *Guardian*, 24 March.

Friburg, M. and Hettne, B. (1988) 'Local mobilization and world system politics', *International Journal of Social Science*, **40**(117), 341–60.

Friedan, B. (1963) *The Feminine Mystique*, London: Gollancz.

Friedman, E. (1995) 'Women's human rights: the emergence of a movement', in Peters, J. and Wolper, A. (eds) *Women's Rights Human Rights: International Feminist Perspectives*, New York: Routledge, 18–35.

Friedman, J. (1986) 'The world city hypothesis', *Development and Change*, **17**(2) January, 69–83.

Friedman, J. (1990) 'Being in the world: globalization and localization', in Featherstone, M. (ed.) *Global Culture: Nationalism, Globalization and Modernity*, London: Sage, 311–28.

Fröbel, F., Heinrichs, J. and Kreye, O. (1980) *The New International Division of Labour*, Cambridge: Cambridge University Press.

Fukushima, K. (1996) 'The revival of "big" politics in Japan', *International Affairs*, **72**(1), 53–72.

Gereffi, G. (1995) 'Global production systems and Third World development', in Stallings, B. (ed.) *Global Change, Regional Response: the New International Context of Development*, Cambridge: Cambridge University Press, 100–42.

Gerschenkron, A. (1966) *Economic Backwardness in Historical Perspective*, Cambridge, MA: Harvard University Press.

Gerth, H. H. and Mills, C. Wright (1958) *From Max Weber: Essays in Sociology*, London: Routledge & Kegan Paul.

Ghils, P. (1992) 'International civil society: international non-governmental organizations in the international system', *International Social Science Journal*, **133**, 417–29.

Giddens, A. (1985) *The Nation State and Violence*, Cambridge: Polity.

Giddens, A. (1990) *The Consequences of Modernity*, Cambridge: Polity.

Giddens, A. (1991) *Modernity and Self-identity*, Cambridge: Polity.

Giddens, A. (1994) 'Living in a post-traditional society', in Beck, U., Giddens, A. and Lash, S. (eds) *Reflexive Modernization: Politics, Tradition and Aesthetics in the Modern Social Order*, Cambridge: Polity, 56–108.

Gilbert, A. and Gugler, J. (1992) *Cities, Poverty and Development: Urbanization in the Third World*, Oxford: Oxford University Press.

Gillespie, M. (1995) *Television, Ethnicity and Cultural Change*, London: Routledge.

Glazer, N. and Moynihan, D. (1963) *Beyond the Melting Pot: The Negroes, Puerto Ricans, Jews, Italians and Irish of New York City*, Cambridge, MA: MIT Press.

Gledhill, C. (1992) 'Pleasurable negotiations', in Bonner, F., Goodman, L., Allen, R., Janes, L. and King, C. (eds) *Imagining Women: Cultural Representations and Gender*, Cambridge: Polity in association with the Open University, 193–209.

Goldthorpe, J. H. in collaboration with Llewellyn, C. and Payne, C. (1980) *Social Mobility and Class Structure in Modern Britain*, Oxford: Clarendon.

Gooch, P. and Madsen, T. (1997) 'Conservation for whom? Van Gujjars and the Rajaji National Park', in Lindberg, S. and Sverrisson, A. (eds) *Social Movements in Development: The Challenges to Globalization and Democratization*, Basingstoke: Macmillan, 234–51.

Goodman, D. and Redclift, M. (1991) *Refashioning Nature: Food, Ecology and Culture*, London: Routledge.

Gordon, M. (1964) *Assimilation in American Life: The Role of Race, Religion and National Life*, New York: Oxford University Press.

Graburn, N. H. H. (1989) 'The sacred journey', in Smith, V. L. (ed.) *Hosts and Guests: The Anthropology of Tourism* (2nd edn), Philadelphia, PA: University of Pennsylvania Press, 21–36.

Greenwood, D. J. (1972) 'Tourism as an agent of change: a Spanish Basque case', *Ethnology*, **11**, 80–91.

Greenwood, D. J. (1989) 'Culture by the pound: an anthropological perspective on tourism as cultural commoditization', in Smith, V. L. (ed.) *Hosts and Guests: The Anthropology of Tourism* (2nd edn), Philadelphia, PA: University of Pennsylvania Press, 171–86.

Grosfoguel, R. (1995) 'Global logics in the Caribbean city system: the case of Miami' in Knox, P. L and Taylor, P. J. (eds) *World Cities in a World System*, Cambridge: Cambridge University Press, 156–170.

Grubb, M., Koch, M., Thomson, K., Munson, A. and Sullivan, F. (1995) *The Earth Summit Agreements: A Guide and Assessment*, London: Earthscan.

Gugler, J. (1995) 'The urbanization of the globe', in Cohen, R. (ed.) *The Cambridge Survey of World Migration*, Cambridge: Cambridge University Press, 541–5.

Gunson, P. (1996) 'Indians run for their lives', *Observer*, 29 September.

Hadar, L. T. (1993) 'What green peril?', *Foreign Affairs*, **72**(2), 27–42.

Hall, C. M. and Weiler, B. (1992) *Special Interest Tourism*, London: Belhaven.

Hall, S. (1991) 'The local and the global: globalization and ethnicity', in King, A. D. (ed.) *Culture, Globalization and the World System: Contemporary Conditions for the Representations of Identity*, Basingstoke: Macmillan.

Hall, S. (1992) 'New ethnicities', in Donals, J. and Rattansi, A. (eds) *Race, Culture and Difference*, London: Sage in association with the Open University Press, 252–9.

Hall, S. and Gieben, B. (eds) (1992) *Formations of Modernity*, Cambridge: Polity in association with the Open University.

Hall, S. and Jefferson, T. (1993) *Resistance Through Rituals: Youth Subcultures in Post-war Britain*, Hammersmith: HarperCollins.

Halliday, F. (1994) *Rethinking International Relations*, Basingstoke: Macmillan.

Halliday, F. (1996) *Islam and the Myth of Confrontation*, London: I.B.Tauris.

Hampton, J. (1998) *Internally Displaced People: A Global Survey*, London: Earthscan in association with the Norwegian Refugee Council.

Hannerz, U. (1990) 'Cosmopolitans and locals in world culture', in Featherstone, M. (ed.) *Global Culture: Nationalism, Globalization and Modernity*, London: Sage, 237–53.

Hannerz, U. (1992) *Cultural Complexity: Studies in the Social Organization of Meaning*, New York: Columbia University Press.

Hargreaves, C. (1992) *Snowfields: The War on Cocaine in the Andes*, London: Zed Books.

Harris, N. (1983) *Of Bread and Guns: The World Economy in Crisis*, Harmondsworth: Penguin.

Harrison, D. (ed.) (1992) *Tourism in the Less Developed Countries*, London: Belhaven.

Harrison, D. (1995) 'Tourism, capitalism and development in less developed countries', in Sklair, L. (ed.) *Capitalism and Development*, London: Routledge, 232–57.

Harrison, D. (1997) 'Asia's heart of darkness', *Observer*, 28 September.

Harrison, P. (1981) *Inside the Third World*, Harmondsworth: Penguin.

Harvey, D. (1989) *The Condition of Postmodernity*, Oxford: Blackwell.

Hebdige, D. (1988) *Subcultures: The Meaning of Style*, London: Routledge.

Hegedus, Z. (1989) 'Social movements and social change in self-creative society: new civil initiatives in the international arena', *International Sociology*, **4**(1), 19–36.

Held, D. (1989) 'The decline of the nation state', in Hall, S. and Jacques, M. (eds) *New Times*, London: Lawrence & Wishart, 191–204.

Held, D. (1995) 'Democracy and the international order', in Held, D. and Archibugi, D. (eds) *Cosmopolitan Democracy: An Agenda for a New World Order*, Cambridge: Polity, 96–118.

Held, D. and Archibugi, D. (eds) (1995) *Cosmopolitan Democracy: An Agenda for a New World Order*, Cambridge: Polity.

Held, D., McGrew, A., Goldblatt, D. and Perraton, J. (1999) *Global Transformations*, Cambridge: Polity.

Hendrickson, C. (1996) 'Selling Guatemala: Maya export products in US mail-order catalogues', in Howes, D. (ed.) *Cross-cultural Consumption: Global Markets, Local Realities*, London: Routledge, 106–24.

Herman, E. S. and McChesney, R. W. (1997) *The Global Media: The New Missionaries of Global Capitalism*, London: Cassell.

Herrnstein, R. J and Murray, C. (1994) *The Bell Curve: Intelligence and Class Structure in American Life*, New York: Free Press.

Hill, H. (1990) 'Foreign investment and East Asian development', *Asian-Pacific Economic Literature*, **4**(2), 21–58.

Hirst, P. and Thompson, G. (1992) 'The problem of globalisation: international economic relations, national economic management and the formation of trading blocs', *Economy and Society*, **21**(4), 357–96.

Hirst, P. and Thompson, G. (1996) *Globalization in Question: The International Economy and the Possibilities of Governance*, Cambridge: Polity.

Hitchcock, M., King, V. T. and Parnwell, M. J. G. (1993) *Tourism in South-East Asia*, London: Routledge.

Hoben, A. and Hefner, R. (1991) 'The integrative revolution revisited', *World Development*, **19**(2), 17–30.

Hobsbawm, E. J. (1994) *Age of Extremes: The Short Twentieth Century, 1914–1991*, London: Michael Joseph.

Hoggart, S. (1996) 'The hollow state', *Guardian*, 26 October.

Holton, R. (1998) *Globalization and the Nation State*, Basingstoke: Macmillan.

Hoogvelt, A. M. (1997) *Globalization and the Post-colonial World: The New Political Economy of Development*, Basingstoke: Macmillan.

Hopkins, A. G. (1973) *An Economic History of West Africa*, London: Longman.

Howes, D. (1996) *Cross-cultural Consumption: Global Market, Local Realities*, London: Routledge.

Huntington, S. P. (1993) 'The clash of civilizations', *Foreign Affairs*, **72**(3), 22–49.

Hutton, W. (1998) 'World must wake up to this disaster', *Observer*, 30 August.

ICI Factbook (1999) London: Westerham Press.

Ignatieff, M. (1994) *Blood and Belonging: Journeys into the New Nationalism*, London: Vintage.

Inglehart, R. (1990) *Culture Shift in Advanced Industrial Society*, Princeton, NJ: Princeton University Press.

Jackson, C. (1993) 'Women/nature or gender/history? A critique of ecofeminist development', *Journal of Peasant Studies*, **20**(3), 389–19.

Jaising, I. (1995) 'Violence against women: the Indian perspective', in Peters, J. and Wolper, A. (eds) *Women's Rights, Human Rights, International Perspectives*, New York: Routledge, 51–6.

James, A. (1996) 'Cooking the books: global or local identities in contemporary food cultures', in Howes, D. (ed.) *Cross-cultural Consumption: Global Markets, Local Realities*, London: Routledge, 77–92.

Jameson, F. (1984) 'Postmodernism or the cultural logic of late capitalism', *New Left Review*, **146**, 53–92.

Janus, N. (1986) 'Transnational advertising: some considerations on the impact of peripheral societies', in Atwood, R. and McAnany, E. G. (eds) *Communications and Latin American Society: Trends in Critical Research 1960–85*, Madison, WI: University of Wisconsin Press, 127–42.

Jenkins, R. (1992) *Pierre Bourdieu*, London: Routledge.

Jenson, A. (1969) 'How much can we boost IQ and scholastic achievement', *Harvard Educational Review*, **39**, 1–123.

Johnson, C. (1982) *MITI and the Japanese Miracle*, Stanford, CA: Stanford University Press.

Jones, E. L. (1988) *Growth Recurring: Economic Change in World History*, Oxford: Clarendon.

Jones, M. and Jones, E. (1999) *Mass Media*, Basingstoke: Macmillan.

Jones, S. (1993) *The Language of the Genes: Biology, History and the Evolutionary Future*, London: HarperCollins.

Joppke, C. (1993) *Mobilizing Against Nuclear Energy*, Berkeley: University of California Press.

Julius, D. (1990) *Global Companies and Public Policy*, London: Pinter.

Kandiyoti, D. (1997) 'Bargaining with patriarchy', in Visvanathan, N., Duggan, L., Nisonoff, L. and Wiegersma, N. (eds) *The Women, Gender and Development Reader*, London: Zed Books, 86–99.

Kasbekar, A. (1996) 'An introduction to Indian cinema', in Nelmes, J. (ed.) *An Introduction to Film Studies*, London: Routledge, 365–92.

Katz, J. (1995) 'Advertising and the construction of violent male masculinity', in Dines, G. and Humez, J. M. (eds) *Gender, Race and Class in Media: A Text-reader*, Thousand Oaks: Sage, 133–41.

Keen, D. (1994) *The Benefits of Famine: A Political Economy of Famine and Relief in South-western Sudan, 1983–89*, Princeton, NJ: Princeton University Press.

Kennedy, P. (1987) *The Rise and Fall of the Great Powers: Economic Change and Military Conflicts from 1500 to 2000*, New York: Random House.

Kennedy, P. (1993) *Preparing for the Twenty-first Century*, London: HarperCollins.

Kennedy, P. (1996) 'Business Enterprises as Agents of Cultural and Political Change: the Case of Green/Ethical Marketing', in Barker, C. and Kennedy, P. (eds) *To Make Another World; Studies in Protest and Collective Action*, Aldershot: Avebury.

Kenny, M. and Florida, R. (1988) 'Beyond mass production: production and the labour process in Japan', *Politics and Society*, **16**(1), 121–58.

Keohane, R. O. (1984) *After Hegemony: Co-operation and Discord in the World Political Economy*, Princeton, NJ: Princeton University Press.

Keohane, R.O. and Nye, J. S. (eds) (1973) *Transnational Relations and World Politics*, Cambridge, MA: Harvard University Press.

Kerr, C. (1983) *The Future of Industrial Societies: Convergence or Continuing Diversity*, Cambridge, MA: Harvard University Press.

Khan, A. (1995) 'Homeland, motherland: authenticity legitimacy and ideologies of place among Muslims in Trinidad', in van der Veer, P. (ed.) *Nation and Migration: The Politics of Space in the South Asian Diaspora*, Philadelphia, PA: University of Pennsylvania Press, 93–131.

Kidron, M. and Segal, R. (1995) *The State of the World Atlas*, London: Penguin.

King, V. T. (1993) 'Tourism and culture in Malaysia', in Hitchcock, M., King, V. T. and Parnwell, M. J. G. (eds) *Tourism in South-East Asia*, London: Routledge, 99–116.

Kirkby, J., O'Keefe, P. and Timberlake, L. (eds) (1995) *The Earthscan Reader in Sustainable Development*, London: Earthscan.

Knox, P. L. and Taylor, P. J. (eds) (1995) *World Cities in a World-system*, Cambridge: Cambridge University Press.

Kornblum, W. (1988) *Sociology in a Changing World*, New York: Holt, Rinehart & Winston.

Korton, D. (1990) *Getting to the 21st Century*, West Hartford, CN: Kumarian Press.

Kothari, S. (1996) 'Social movements, ecology and justice', in Osler Hampson, F. and Reppy, J. (eds) *Earthly Goods: Environmental Change and Social Justice*, Ithaca, NY: Cornell University Press, 154–72.

Kotkin, J. (1992) *Tribes: How Race, Religion and Identity Determine Success in the Global Economy*, New York: Random House.

Krippendorf, J. (1987) *The Holiday Makers*, London: Heinemann.

Kruhse-Mount Burton, S. (1995) 'Sex tourism and traditional Australian male identity', in Lanfant, M-F., Allcock, J. B. and Bruner, E. M. (eds) *International Tourism*, London: Sage, 192–204.

Kumar, R. (1995) 'From Chipko to Sati: the contemporary Indian women's movement', in Basu, A. (ed.) *The Challenge of Local Feminisms*, Boulder, CO: Westview Press, 58–86.

Lanfant, M-F., Allcock, J. B. and Bruner, E. M. (eds) (1995) *International Tourism: Identity and Change*, London: Sage.

Lasch, C. (1995) *The Revolt of the Elites and The Betrayal of Democracy*, New York: W. W. Norton.

Lash, S. and Urry, J. (1987) *The End of Organised Capitalism*, Cambridge: Polity.

Lash, S. and Urry, J. (1994) *Economies of Signs and Space*, London: Sage.

Lele, S. M. (1991) 'Sustainable development: a critical review', *World Development*, **19**(6), 607–21.

Lemann, N. (1991) *The Promised Land: The Great Black Migration and How it Changed America*, New York: Alfred S. Knopf.

Lerner, D. (1958) *The Passing of Traditional Society: Modernising the Middle East*, New York: Free Press.

Lewis, O. (1968) *La Vida: A Puerto Rican Family in the Culture of Poverty – San Juan and New York*, New York: Vintage Books.

Lewis, P. (1992) 'Democracy in modern societies', in Allen, J., Braham, P. and Lewis, P. (eds) *Political and Economic Formations of Modernity*, Cambridge: Polity, 89–96.

Lindberg, S. and Sverrisson, A. (eds) (1997) *Social Movements in Development: The Challenges of Globalization and Democratization*, Basingstoke: Macmillan.

Lipietz, A. (1987) *Mirages and Miracles: The Crisis of Global Fordism* (translated by Macey, D.) London: Verso.

Lister, R. (1997) *Citizenship: Feminist Perspectives*, Basingstoke: Macmillan.

McCormick, J. (1989) *The Global Environmental Movement*, London: Belhaven.

McDonald, P., Stokes, J. and Reading, A. (1999) 'The music industry', in Stokes and Reading (eds) *The Media in Britain*, Basingstoke: Macmillan, 88–107.

McKean, P. F. (1989) 'Towards a theoretical analysis of tourism: economic dualism and cultural involution in Bali', in Smith, V. L. (ed.) *Hosts and Guests* (2nd edn), Philadelphia, PA: University of Pennsylvania Press, 119–38.

McLuhan, M. (1962) *The Gutenberg Galaxy: The Making of Typographical Man*, Toronto: Universty of Toronto Press.

MacNaghten, P. (1993) 'Discourses of nature: argumentation and power', in Burman, E. and Parks, I. (eds) *Discourse Analytical Research*, London: Routledge, 52–71.

McNeill, W. H. (1971) *A World History*, Oxford: Oxford University Press.

Malik, K. (1996) *The Meaning of Race: Race History and Culture in Western Society*, Basingstoke: Macmillan.

Malthus, T. (1973/1798) *Essay on the Principle of Population*, London: Dent.

Mann, M. (1988) *States, War and Capitalism, Studies in Political Sociology*, Oxford: Blackwell.

Mann, M. (1996) 'Ruling class strategies and citizenship', in Bulmer, M. and Rees, A. M. (eds) *Citizenship Today: The Contemporary Relevance of T. H. Marshall*, London: UCL Press, 125–44.

Marcuse, H. (1968) *One Dimensional Man*, London: Sphere.

Marrin, P. (1997) 'Brazilian poor used as slaves, bishop charges', *National Catholic Reporter*, 19 September.

Marsh, I. (1996) *Making Sense of Society: An Introduction to Sociology*, London: Longman.

Marshall, T. H. (1950) *Citizenship and Social Class*, Cambridge: Cambridge University Press.

Martell, L. (1994) *Ecology and Society: An Introduction*, Cambridge: Polity.

Martin, H-P. and Schumann, H. (1997) *The Global Trap: Globalization and the Assault on Democracy and Prosperity*, London: Zed Books.

Marx, K. (1954/1852) *The Eighteenth Brumaire of Louis Bonaparte*, Moscow: Progress Publishers.

Marx, K. and Engels, F. (1967/1848) *The Communist Manifesto*, Harmondsworth: Penguin.

Massey, D. S. and Denton, N. A. (1993) *American Apartheid: Segregation and the Making of the Underclass*, Cambridge, MA: Harvard University Press.

Matsui, Y. (1989) *Women's Asia*, London: Zed Books.

Mayer, J. A. (1983) 'Notes towards a working definition of social control in historical analysis', in Cohen, S. and Scull, A. (eds) *Social Control and the State*, Oxford: Martin Robertson, 17–38.

Meadows, D. H., Meadows, D. L. and Randers, J. (1992) *Beyond The Limits: Global Collapse or a Sustainable Society, Sequel to the Limits to Growth*, London: Earthscan.

Meikle, J. (1997) 'Disney leads in theme parks', *Guardian*, 11 September.

Melucci, A., Keane, J. and Mier, P. (1989) *Nomads of the Present: Social Movements and Individual Needs in Contemporary Society*, London: Hutchinson Radius.

Merchant, C. (1990) *The Death of Nature: Women, Ecology and the Scientific Revolution*, New York: Harper & Row.

Mexican Bulletin of Statistical Information (1996) July–September.

Miles, A. (1996) *Integrative Feminism, Building Global Visions, 1960s–1990s*, New York: Routledge.

Miles, R. (1989) *Racism*, London: Routledge.

Millet, K. (1977) *Sexual Politics*, London: Virago.

Milton, K. (1996) *Environmentalism and Cultural Theory*, London: Routledge.

Mingst, K. (1999) *Essentials of International Relations*, New York: W. W. Norton.

Mishra, O., Unnikrishnan, P. V. and Martin, M. (1998) 'India', in Hampton, J. (ed.) *Internally Displaced People: A Global Survey*, London: Earthscan in assocation with the Norwegian Refugee Council, 142–6.

Mitter, S. (1994) 'On organising women in casualised work: a global overview', in Rowbotham, S. and Mitter, S. (eds) *Dignity and Daily Bread*, London: Routledge, 16–52.

Moody, R. (1996) 'Mining the world: the global reach of Rio Tinto Zinc', *The Ecologist*, **26**(2), 46–52.

Moore, B. (1967) *Social Origins of Dictatorship and Democracy: Lord and Peasant in the Making of the Modern World*, Harmondsworth: Penguin.

Moore, B. (1972) *Reflections on the Causes of Human Misery and upon Certain Proposals to Eliminate Them*, London: Allen Lane.

Morgenthau, H. J. (1948) *Politics Among Nations: The Struggle for Power and Peace*, New York: Alfred S. Knopf.

Morley, D. and Robins, K. (1995) *Spaces of Identity: Global Media, Electronic Landscapes and Cultural Boundaries*, London: Routledge.

Murray, R. (1989) 'Fordism and post-Fordism', in Hall, S. and Jacques, M. (eds) *New Times*, London: Lawrence & Wishart, 38–53.

Myers, P. (1997) 'Mixing it in a mad world', *Guardian*, 16 May.

Needham, J. (1969) *The Grand Titration: Science and Society in East and West*, Toronto: University of Toronto Press.

Newall, P. (1998) *Environmental NGOs, Multinational Corporations and the Question of Governance*. Paper given at the conference on transnational social movements at the Department of Sociology, University of Warwick, March.

Nicholls, D. (1995) 'Population and process: Parson Malthus', *Anglican Theological Review*, **77**(3), 321–34.

Nisbet, R. A. (1970) *The Sociological Tradition*, London: Heinemann Educational Books.

O'Brien, R. Cruise (1979) 'Mass communications: social mechanisms of incorporation and dependence', in Villamil, J. (ed.), *Transnational Capitalism and National Development*, New Jersey: Humanities Press, 129–43.

Ogburn, W. F. (1922) *Social Change with Respect to Culture and Original Nature*. New York: B. W. Huebsch.

Ohmae, K. (1994) *The Borderless World: Power and Strategy in the International Economy*, London: Collins.

Oommen, T. K. (1997) 'Social movements in the Third World', in Lindberg, S. and Sverrisson, A. (eds) *Social Movements in Development: The Challenges to Globalization and Democratization*, Basingstoke: Macmillan, 46–66.

Ozawa, T. (1993) 'Foreign direct investment and structural transformation: Japan as a recycler of market and industry', *Business and the Contemporary World*, **5**(2), 129–50.

Parekh, B. (1995) 'Politics of nationhood', in von Benda-Beckman, K. and Verkuyten, M. (eds) *Nationalism, Ethnicity and Cultural Identity in Europe*, Utrecht: European Research Centre on Migration and Ethnic Relations, 122–43.

Park, R. and Burgess, E. (1967) *The City*, Chicago: University of Chicago Press.

Parsons, T. (1971) *Societies: Evolutionary and Comparative Perspectives*, Englewood Cliffs, NJ: Prentice Hall.

Patterson, O. (1982) *Slavery and Social Death: A Comparative Study*, Cambridge, MA: Harvard University Press.

Pearce, F. and Woodiwiss, M. (eds) (1993) *Global Crime Connections: Dynamics and Control*, Toronto: University of Toronto Press.

Pearce, F. and Tombs, S. (1993) 'US capital vs the Third World: Union Carbide and Bhopal', in Pearce, F. and Woodiwiss, M. (eds) *Global Crime Connections: Dynamics and Control*, Toronto: University of Toronto Press, 187–211.

Pearse, A. (1980) *Seeds of Plenty, Seeds of Want: Social and Economic Implications of the Green Revolution*, Oxford: Clarendon.

Peet, R. (ed.) (1987) *International Capitalism and Industrial Restructuring*, Boston: Allen & Unwin.

Pendergrast, M. (1993) *For God, Country and Coca-Cola*, New York: Charles Scribner & Sons.

Perlman, J. E. (1976) *The Myth of Marginality*, Berkeley: University of California Press.

Perlmutter, H. (1991) 'On the rocky road to the first global civilization', *Human Relations*, **44**(9), 897–920.

Peters, J. and Wolper, A. (eds) (1995) *Women's Rights, Human Rights: International Feminist Perspectives*, New York: Routledge.

Peterson, V. S. and Runyan, A. S. (1993) *Global Gender Issues*, Boulder, CO: Westview Press.

Phizacklea, A. (1992) 'Jobs for the girls: the production of women's outerwear in the UK', in Cross, M. (ed.) *Ethnic Minorities and Industrial Change in Europe and North America*, Cambridge: Cambridge University Press, 94–110.

Picard, M. (1995) 'Cultural heritage and tourist capital: cultural tourism in Bali', in Lanfant, M-F., Allcock, J. B. and Bruner, G. M. (eds) *International Tourism*, London: Sage, 44–66.

Piore, M. and Sabel, C. (1984) *The Second Industrial Divide*, New York: Basic Books.

Premdas, R. (1996) 'Ethnicity and elections in the Caribbean'. Working paper no. 224, Kellogg Institute, University of Notre Dame.

Princen, T. and Finger, M. (eds) (1994) *Environmental NGOs in World Politics*, London: Routledge.

Reich, R. (1992) *The Work of Nations: Preparing Ourselves for the 21st Century*, New York: Vintage Books.

Reuter, P. (1983) *Disorganised Crime: The Economics of the Visible Hand*, Cambridge, MA: MIT Press.

Rex, J. (1986) *Race and Ethnicity*, Milton Keynes: Open University Press .

Rex, J. and Guiberrnau, M. (eds) (1997) *The Ethnicity Reader: Nationalism, Multiculturalism and Migration*, Cambridge: Polity.

Riddell-Dixon, E. (1995) 'Social movements and the United Nations', *International Social Science Journal*, **144**, 289–303.

Rifkin, J. (1995) *The End of Work: The Decline of the Global Labour Force and the Dawn of the Post-market Era*, New York: G. P. Putnam's Sons.

Riley, D. (1992) 'Citizenship and the welfare state', in Allen, J., Braham, P. and Lewis, P. (eds) *Political and Economic Formations of Modernity*, Cambridge: Polity.

Ritzer, G. (1993) *The McDonaldization of Society: An Investigation into the Changing Character of Social Life*, Thousand Oaks, CA: Pine Forge Press.

Roberts, B. (1978) *Cities of Peasants: The Political Economy of Urbanization in the Third World*, London: Edward Arnold.

Roberts, J. M. (1992) *History of the World*, Oxford: Helicon.

Robertson, R. (1992) *Globalization: Social Theory and Global Culture*, London: Sage.

Roche, M. (1992) *Rethinking Citizenship: Welfare, Ideology and Change in Modern Society*, Cambridge: Polity.

Rodman, K. A. (1998) '"Think globally, punish locally": nonstate actors, multinational corporations, and human rights sanctions', *Ethics and International Affairs*, **12**, 19–41.

Rogers, E. M. and Antola, L. (1985) 'Telenovelas in Latin America', *Journal of Communications*, **35**, 24–35.

Rosenau, J. N. (1990) *Turbulence in World Politics: A Theory of Change and Continuity*, Princeton, NJ: Princeton University Press.

Roseneil, S. (1997) 'The global commons: the global, local and personal dynamics of the women's peace movement in the 1980s', in Scott, A. (ed.) *The Limits of Globalization*, London: Routledge, 55–71.

Ross, A. (ed.) (1997) *No Sweat*, London: Verso.

Rowbotham, S. (1993) *Homeworkers Worldwide*, London: Merlin.

Rowell, A. (1996) *Green Backlash: Global Subversion of the Environmental Movement*, London: Routledge.

Rozenberg, D. (1995) 'International tourism and utopia: the Balearic islands', in Lanfant, M-F., Allcock, J. B. and Bruner, E. M. (eds) *International Tourism*, London: Sage, 159–76.

Rumbaut, R. (1997) 'Assimilation and its discontents: between rhetoric and reality', *International Migration Review*, **31**(4), 134–55.

Runciman, W. G. (1990) 'How many classes are there in contemporary society?' *Sociology*, **24**, 377–96.

Sachs, W. (1992) 'One world', in Sachs, W. (ed.) *The Development Dictionary*, London: Zed Books, 102–15.

Sachs, W. (ed.) (1993) *Global Ecology: A New Arena of Global Conflict*, London: Fernwood Books and Zed Books.

Sampson, E. E. (1993) *Celebrating the Other: A Dialogic Account of Human Nature*, Hemel Hempstead: Harvester Wheatsheaf.

Sassen, S. (1991) *The Global City: New York, London, Tokyo*, Princeton, NJ: Princeton University Press.

Sassen, S. (1995) 'The state and the global city: notes towards a conception of place-centred governance', *Competition and Change: The Journal of Global Business and Political Economy*, **1**(1), 1–13.

Sausurre, F. de (1974) *Course in General Linguistics*, London: P. Owen.

Savage, M. and Warde, A. (1993) *Urban Sociology, Capitalism and Modernity*, Basingstoke: Macmillan.

Scarce, R. (1990) *Eco-Warriors: Understanding the Radical Environmental Movement*, Chicago: Noble Press.

Scheff, T. J. (1990) *Microsociology: Discourse, Emotion and Social Structure*, Chicago: University of Chicago Press.

Schlesinger, A. M. (1992) *The Disuniting of America*, New York: W. W. Norton.

Schlossstein, S. (1991) *Asia's New Little Dragons*, Chicago: Contemporary Books.

Scholte, J. A. (1993) *International Relations of Social Change*, Buckingham: Open University Press.

Scott, A. (1990) *Ideology and the New Social Movements*, London: Unwin Hyman.

Scott, A. (1992) 'Political culture and social movements', in Allen, J., Braham, P. and Lewis, P. (eds) *Political and Economic Forms of Modernity*, Cambridge: Polity and Open University, 127–78.

Seager, J. (1995) *The New State of the Earth Atlas*, New York: Simon & Schuster.

Seagrave, S. (1995) *Lords of the Rim: The Invisible Empire of the Overseas Chinese*, New York: G. P. Putnam's Sons.

Seidman, S. (1983) *Liberalism and the Origins of European Social Theory*, Oxford: Blackwell.

Sen, A. (1981) *Poverty and Famine: An Essay on Entitlement and Deprivation*, Oxford: Clarendon.

Sharpley, R. (1994) *Tourism, Tourists and Society*, Ripton, Huntington: Elm Publications.

Shaw, L. (1998) *Labour and the Label*. Paper given at the Conference on Global Social Movements and International Social Institutions at Warwick University, Department of Sociology, March.

Shaw, M. (1994) *Global Society and International Relations: Sociological Concepts and Political Perspective*, Cambridge: Polity.

Shaw, M. (1997) 'The state of globalization: towards a theory of state transformation', *Review of International Political Economy*, **4**(3), 497–513.

Shiva, V. (1989) *Staying Alive: Women, Ecology and Development*, London: Zed Books.

Simmel, G. (1950) *The Sociology of Georg Simmel* (translated and edited by Wolff, K. H.) New York: Free Press.

Simone, V. and Feraru, A. T. (1995) *The Asian Pacific*, New York: Longman.

Sinclair, J. (1987) *Images Incorporated: Advertising as Industry and Ideology*, London: Croom Helm.

Sinclair, M. T. and Tsegaye, A. (1990) 'International tourism and export instability', *Journal of Development Studies*, **26**(3), 487–504.

Sklair, L. (1995) *Sociology of the Global System*, London: Prentice Hall/Harvester Wheatsheaf.

Skocpol, T. (1979) *States and Social Revolutions: A Comparative Analysis of France, Russia and China*, Cambridge: Cambridge University Press.

Slater, D. (1997) *Consumer Culture and Modernity*, Cambridge: Polity.

Smith, A. D. (1991) 'Towards a global culture?', in Featherstone, M. (ed.) *Global Culture: Nationalism, Globalization, Modernity*, London: Sage, 171–92.

Smith, A. D. (1992) *Ethnicity and Nationalism*, Leiden: Brill.

Smith, A. D. (1995) *Nations and Nationalism in a Global Era*, Cambridge: Polity.

Smith, R. (1993) 'Creative destruction: capitalist development and China's environment', *New Left Review*, **222**, 2–42.

Smith, V. L. (ed.) (1989) *Host and Guests: The Anthropology of Tourism* (2nd edn), Philadelphia, PA: University of Pennsylvania Press.

Smythe, P. (1993) *Women and Health*, London: Zed Books.

Soros, G. (1998) *The Crisis of Global Capitalism*, London: Little, Brown.

Spybey, T. (1996) *Globalization and World Society*, Cambridge: Polity.

Stallings, B. (ed.) (1995) *Global Change, Regional Response: The New International Context of Development*, Cambridge: Cambridge University Press.

Standing, G. (1989) 'Global feminization through flexible labour', *World Development*, **17**, 1077–95.

Stein, D. (1995) *People who Count: Population and Politics, Women and Children*, London: Earthscan.

Stephan, N. (1982) *The Idea of Race in Science: Great Britain, 1800-1960*, Basingstoke: Macmillan.

Stienstra, D. (1994) *Women's Movements and International Organizations*, New York: St Martin's Press.

Strange, S. (1986) *Casino Capitalism*, Oxford: Basil Blackwell.

Strange, S. (1996) *The Retreat of the State: The Diffusion of Power in the World Economy*, Cambridge: Cambridge University Press.

Strathern, M. (1992) *After Nature: English Kinship in the Late Twentieth Century*, Cambridge: Cambridge University Press.

Strinati, D. (1995) *An Introduction to Theories of Popular Culture*, London: Routledge.

Stubbs, S. (1997) 'The hooded hordes of prejudice', *New Statesman*, 28 February, 10.

Swidler, A. (1986) 'Culture in action: symbols and strategies', *American Sociological Review*, **51**, 273–86.

Taylor, J. G. (1979) *From Modernisation to Modes of Production: A Critique of the Sociologies of Development and Underdevelopment*, Basingstoke: Macmillan.

Taylor, P. J. (1995) 'World cities and territorial states: the rise and fall of their mutuality', in Knox, P. L. and Taylor, P. J. (eds) *World Cities in a World System*, Cambridge: Cambridge University Press, 48–62.

Taylor, R. and Young, N. (eds) (1987) *Campaign for Peace: British Peace Movements in the Twentieth Century*, Manchester: Manchester University Press.

Theroux, P. (1986) *Sunrise with Seamonsters*, Harmondsworth: Penguin.

Thomson, D. (1997) 'Hong Kong on the Thames', *Telegraph Magazine*, 12 April, 38–42.

Thwaites, T., Davis, L. and Mules, W. (1994) *Tools for Cultural Studies*, Melbourne: Macmillan Education.

Tickner, J. A. (1992) *Gender in International Relations*, New York: Columbia University Press.

Tilly, C. (ed.) (1975) *The Formation of Nation States in Western Europe*, Princeton, NJ: Princeton University Press.

Tischler, H. L. (1996) *Introduction to Sociology* (5th edn), Fort Worth, TX: The Harcourt Press.

Toffler, A. (1981) *The Third Wave*, London: Pan.

Tomlinson, A. (1990) 'Introduction: consumer culture and the aura of the commodity', in Tomlinson, A. (ed.) *Consumption, Identity and Style: Marketing, Meaning and the Packaging of Pleasure*, London: Routledge, 1–38.

Tönnies, F. (1971/1887) *Ferdinand Tönnies on Sociology: Pure, Applied and Empirical*, Selected Writings, Chicago: University of Chicago Press.

Touraine, A. (1981) *The Voice and the Eye: An Analysis of Social Movements*, Cambridge: Cambridge University Press.

Townsend, P. (1996) *A Poor Future: Can We Counter Growing Poverty in Britain and Across The World?*, London: Lemos & Crane in association with the Friendship Group.

Turner, B. (1994) *Orientalism, Postmodernism and Globalism*, London: Routledge.

Turner, L. and Ash, J. (1975) *The Golden Hordes: International Tourism and the Pleasure Periphery*, London: Constable.

Tyler, A. (1985) *The Accidental Tourist*, New York: Alfred S. Knopf.

UN (1995) *The Copenhagen Declaration and Programme of Action: World Summit for Social Development* (6–12 March 1995), New York: United Nations Department of Publications.

UN Development Programme (1997) *Human Development Report 1997*, Oxford: Oxford University Press.

UNRISD (1995) *States of Disarray: The Social Effects of Globalization*, Geneva: United Nations Research Institute for Social Development.

Urry, J. (1990a) *The Tourist Gaze*, London: Sage.

Urry, J. (1990b) 'The "consumption" of tourism', *Sociology*, **24**(1), 23–34.

Valdiva, A. N. (1995) *Feminism, Multiculturalism and the Media: Global Diversities*, London: Sage.

van den Berghe, P. (1994) 'Intelligence and Race', in Cashmore, E. (ed.) *Dictionary of Race and Ethnic Relations* (3rd edn), London: Routledge.

Van Hear, N. (1998) *New Diasporas: The Mass Exodus, Dispersal and Regrouping of Migrant Communities*, London: UCL Press.

Van Zoonen, L. (1994) *Feminist Media Studies*, London: Sage.

Vidas, A. A. de (1995) 'Textiles, memory and the souvenir industry in the Andes', in Lanfant, M-F., Allcock, J. B. and Bruner, E. M. (eds) *International Tourism*, London: Sage, 67–83.

Volkman, T. A. (1984) 'Great performances: Toraja cultural identity in the 1970s', *American Ethnologist*, 152–168.

Wade, R. (1990) *Governing the Market: Economic Theory and the Role of Government in East Asian Industrialization*, Princeton, NJ: Princeton University Press.

Walby, S. (1990) *Theorizing Patriarchy*, Oxford: Blackwell.

Waldinger, R. and Bozorgmehr, M. (eds) (1996) *Ethnic Los Angeles*, New York: Russell Sage Foundation.

Wallerstein, I. (1974) *The Modern World System*, New York: Academic Press.

Wallerstein, I. (1979) 'The rise and future demise of the world capitalist system: concepts for comparative analysis', in Wallerstein, I. (ed.) *The Capitalist World-Economy*, Cambridge: Cambridge University Press, 3–36.

Wallerstein, I. (1996) *Open the Social Sciences: Report of the Gulbenkian Commission on the Restructuring of the Social Sciences*, Stanford: Stanford University Press.

Warde, A. (1992) 'Notes on the relationship between production and consumption', in Burrows, R. and Marsh, C. (eds) *Consumption and Class: Divisions and Change*, London: Macmillan.

Waters, M. (1995) *Globalization*, London: Routledge.

Watkins, J. (1997) *Briefing on Poverty*, Oxford: Oxfam Publications.

Watson, J. (1998) *Media Communication: An Introduction to Theory and Practice*, Basingstoke: Macmillan.

Weber, M. (1950) *General Economic History*, Glencoe, IL: Free Press.

Weber, M. (1977) *The Protestant Ethic and the Spirit of Capitalism*, London: Allen & Unwin.

Wernick, A. (1991) 'Globo promo: the cultural triumph of exchange', *Theory, Culture and Society*, **8**(1), 89–109.

White, G. (1984) 'Developmental states and socialist industrialisation in the Third World', *Journal of Development Studies*, **21**(1), 97–120.

White, G. (1993) *Riding the Tiger: The Politics of Economic Reform in Post-Mao China*, Basingstoke: Macmillan.

White, G. (ed.) (1988) *Developmental States in East Asia*, Basingstoke: Macmillan.

Wight, M. (1977) *Systems of States*, Leicester: Leicester University Press.

Willetts, P. (1996) 'From Stockholm to Rio and beyond: the impact of the environmental movement on arrangements for NGOs', *Review of International Studies*, **22**(1), 57–80.

Williams, K., Haslam, C., Williams, J. and Cutler, T. with Adcroft, A. and Johal, S. (1992) 'Against lean production', *Economy and Society*, **21**(3), 321–54.

Wilson, J. (1973) *Introduction to Social Movements*, New York: Basic Books.

Wilson, W. J. (1978) *The Declining Significance of Race*, Chicago: University of Chicago Press.

Wilson, W. J. (1987) *The Truly Disadvantaged: The Inner City, The Underclass and Public Policy*, Chicago: Chicago University Press.

Womack J. P., Jones, D. T. and Roos, D. (1990) *The Machine that Changed the World*, New York: Rawson Associates.

Wood, R. E. (1993) 'Tourism, culture and the sociology of development', in Hitchcock, M., King, V. T. and Parnwell, M. J. G. (eds) *Tourism in South-East Asia*, London: Routledge, 48–70.

World Bank (1993a) *Policy Research Report*, Washington, DC: World Bank.

World Bank (1993b) *The East Asian Miracle: Economic Growth and Public Policy*, Oxford: Oxford University Press for the World Bank.

World Bank (1996) *Development Report*, Washington, DC: World Bank.

Worsley, P. (1967) *The Third World*, London: Weidenfeld & Nicolson.

Wright, E. O. (1985) *Classes*, London: Verso.

WTO (1995) *Yearbook of Tourism Statistics*, Madrid: World Tourist Organization.

Yearley, S. (1996a) *Sociology, Environmentalism, Globalization: Reinventing the Globe*, London: Sage.

Yearley, S. (1996b) 'The local and the global: the transnational politics of the environment', in Anderson, J., Brook, C. and Cochrane, A. (eds) *A Global World? Re-ordering Political Space*, Oxford: Oxford University Press, 209–67.

Yuval-Davis, N. and Anthias, F. (eds) (1989) *Woman–Nation–State*, Basingstoke: Macmillan.

Zachary, G. P. (1999) 'This singing sensation from Liverpool longs to be in Hong Kong', *Wall Street Journal*, pp. 1, 10.

Zalewski, M. (1993) 'Feminist theory and international relations', in Bowker, M. and Brown, R. (eds) *From Cold War to Collapse: Theory and World Politics in the 1980s*, Cambridge: Cambridge University Press, 115–44.

Zirakzadeh, C. E. (1997) *Social Movements in Politics: A Comparative Study*, London: Longman.

Zolberg, A. R., Suhrke, A. and Aguayo, S. (1989) *Escape from Violence: Conflict and the Refugee Crisis in the Developing World*, New York: Oxford University Press.

Zukin, S. (1981) *Loft Living*, London: Hutchinson/Radius.

Index

SUBJECT INDEX

Page numbers in bold signify the glossary entry

resulting from coerced
  migration, 345
supported by belief systems,
  347
disability, 13, 82, 115
disempowerment, 67, 292, 359,
  361–2
division of labour, 81, 101, 164,
  183, 352
  gender/sexual, 102, 104, 379
  new international, 119, 135,
    136–7, 141, 150, 152, 269,
    271, 275, **378**
dragons, *see* tiger and dragon
  economies (Asia)
drugs/drugs trade, 14, 19, 29, 33,
  50, 57, 153, 161–2, 168–70, 221,
  291–2, 317, 367, 372
  trafficking, 29, 372
dystopia/dystopian, 18, 358–9,
  366–72, **376**

E

Earth Summit, 31, 329, 331
economic performance (Asia), 172,
  178–86
economics, 3, 4, 59, 74, 170, 231,
  269, 361
  economies of scale, **376**
education, 26–7, 36, 49, 56–8, 61,
  75, 80, 82, 87, 93, 100, 104–5,
  107–8, 113, 138, 156, 164,
  179–80, 188–9, 199, 202, 206,
  208, 220, 222, 225, 237–8, 252,
  267, 269, 281–2, 289, 291–3, 310,
  314, 324, 335, 342, 345, 350–1,
  353, 370, 374
English language, 57
Enlightenment, 12, 44–7, 49, 52,
  58, 100, 111, **376**
entrepreneurs, 33, 45, 47–8, 87,
  189, 274, 353, 367
environment/environmental, 18,
  26, 29, 31, 34, 44, 66, 85, 119,
  127, 130–2, 138, 142, 146, 167,
  201, 220–2, 245–6, 249, 267, 276,
  295–6, 298–300, 302, 362, 368,
  370–2, 377, 378
  degradation, 34, 201, 314, 327
  state and UN involvement,
    330–2
  transboundary issues, 298, 325–6
  see also Green Movement
epiphenomenon, 114, 344, 376
ethnic/ethnicity, 12, 13, 18–19, 31,
  34–5, 38, 75, 86, 90–1, 99, 103–4,

106–11, 115–16, 141–2, 145–6,
  153, 167, 184, 186, 201, 206, 221,
  226, 229, 233, 237–9, 242, 246,
  262–3, 268, 279, 283, 290, 340–7,
  349–50, 352–7, 361, 363–5, 380
  ethnic conflict, 91, 145–6, 153
ethnocentrism, 52, 58, 252, 348, **376**
eugenics, 196
Exclusion Act (USA, 1882), 202
explorers, 15, 48, 218
exponential growth, 171, 254, **376**
export-processing zone (EPZ), 72,
  127–30, 133, **376**

F

family/families, 3, 11, 18–19, 24,
  27, 37, 39, 44, 49, 67, 74–5, 82–3,
  87, 99, 102–5, 112–13, 126, 130,
  138, 141, 146, 158, 164, 166,
  185–6, 188, 193–4, 199, 201,
  207–9, 220, 225–6, 231–2, 237–8,
  243–4, 250, 260, 262, 269, 281,
  296, 300, 307, 315–18, 340–1, 380
famine, 13–14, 24, 28, 32, 142, 145,
  153–4, 163–5, 167–70, 193–5,
  197, 211, 296–7, 301
  entitlement theory, 165–7, 169,
    170
  food insecurity, 163–5, 167
  natural disasters, 142, 146, 165
  policy failings, 165, 167
Fascism, 7, 66, 201, 377
fashion, 11, 67, 72–3, 181, 217, 239,
  245, 247, 259, 275–6, 289, 326
fast foods, 208, 245, 362
feminism, 4, 85, 87, 100, 102–3,
  105, 113–14, 116, 207, 220,
  260–1, 264, 291, 309–15, 318–20,
  341, 379
  first-wave, 100, 305
  Marxist feminists, 103, 379
  post-modern feminism, 104
  radical, 103, 311
  second-wave, 57, 100–1, 305,
    310–11, 313
  Southern groups, 103, 307, 309,
    313
  western, 103, 291, 309
  white feminists, 103
feudalism, 9, 47, 102, 167, 367, 378,
  379
film/s, 11, 16, 26–7, 57, 65, 91, 116,
  156, 218, 223, 236, 251, 279, 292
  Indian, 244, 262
finance/financial markets/
  financial system, 10, 14, 29–30,

45, 52–4, 61, 66, 68, 83, 89, 113,
  119–21, 127, 131, 133, 139, 160,
  162, 178, 180, 187–8, 213, 232,
  257, 265, 271, 273, 279, 297–8,
  310, 333, 336–7, 353, 359, 361,
  376
  financial speculation, 19, 76, 366
First World War, 6, 18, 30, 54, 57,
  81, 100, 108, 125, 133, 144, 172,
  195, 203, 270, 311, 359–61, 373,
  380
flexible labour, 12, 69, 71–2, 155,
  316, 379
flexible specialization, 71, 140
flying geese (in Asia-Pacific), 182
food, 14, 32–3, 55, 73, 102, 124,
  131, 143, 154, 163–5, 167,
  169–70, 188, 194, 197–8, 201–2,
  207–8, 210, 218, 230–1, 239–40,
  242, 244–5, 260, 292–3, 300,
  306–8, 310, 316–17, 323, 326,
  329, 335, 349, 359, 362, 366, 378
Fordism, 62, 63, 65–6, 68–71, 76–7,
  376, 379–80
French Revolution, 4, 12, 45, 194,
  376
Friends of the Earth, 297, 304, 324
futurologists, 256, 373, **377**

G

Gay Rights Movement (USA), 57
gender, 13, 17–19, 37, 57, 67, 74,
  86–7, 99–102, 105, 111, 114–16,
  141, 208, 233, 244, 260–1, 264,
  305–6, 308–10, 312, 314, 316–17,
  319, 322, 341, 379
  femininity, 101, 104, 106, 306
  feminization of work, 12, 260,
    276–7
  masculinity, 101, 261, 306, 322
Geneva Convention (1951), 143–4,
  204
genocide, 92, 144, 344, 355, 371
gentrification, 269, **377**
global city/cities, *see* cities, global
global future, 343, 368
global networks, 242, 253, 310
global society, 19, 22, 24, 154, 288,
  303, 319, 351, 361, 370–3
global village, 16, 28, 366
globalism, 10–12, 19, 23, 34, 36–40,
  43, 50, 81, 212, 341, 358, 370, 379
globalization, 10–14, 17–19, 21–3,
  26, 28, 33–4, 36–40, 41–3, 50, 56,
  58–9, 68, 71, 74, 76, 88–9, 91–5,
  117, 125, 127, 132–3, 134–7, 139,